American Saint

American Saint

Francis Asbury and the Methodists

JOHN WIGGER

OXFORD
UNIVERSITY PRESS

OXFORD
UNIVERSITY PRESS

Oxford University Press is a department of the University of Oxford.
It furthers the University's objective of excellence in research, scholarship,
and education by publishing worldwide.

Oxford   New York
Auckland   Cape Town   Dar es Salaam   Hong Kong   Karachi
Kuala Lumpur   Madrid   Melbourne   Mexico City   Nairobi
New Delhi   Shanghai   Taipei   Toronto

With offices in
Argentina   Austria   Brazil   Chile   Czech Republic   France   Greece
Guatemala   Hungary   Italy   Japan   Poland   Portugal   Singapore
South Korea   Switzerland   Thailand   Turkey   Ukraine   Vietnam

Oxford is a registered trade mark of Oxford University Press
in the UK and certain other countries.

Published in the United States of America by
Oxford University Press
198 Madison Avenue, New York, NY 10016

© Oxford University Press 2009

First issued as an Oxford University Press paperback, 2012.

Library of Congress Cataloging-in-Publication Data
Wigger, John H., 1959–
American saint : Francis Asbury and the Methodists / John Wigger.
p.   cm.
Includes bibliographical references (p.) and index.
ISBN 978-0-19-538780-3 (hardcover); 978-0-19-994824-6 (paperback)
1. Asbury, Francis, 1745–1816.
2. Methodist Episcopal Church—Bishops—Biography.
I. Title.
BX8495.A8W46 2009
287'.092—dc22
[B]   2009004852

Printed in the United States of America
on acid-free paper

For George Marsden and Nathan Hatch

Contents

Preface

This book has been a long time in the making. At one point I had to take an eight- or nine-month break from writing. When I returned to the manuscript, I jumped into a chapter that seemed to compose itself, as if I had already written it. In fact I had, as I discovered soon afterward. Fortunately, the two versions pretty much agreed with each other, but at that point I realized that it was time to wrap things up.

Along the way I have been helped by a great many people and organizations. I am grateful to the Research Board and the Research Council of the University of Missouri for several years of summer support and travel funding. I also benefitted from a summer stipend from the National Endowment for the Humanities in 1998 and a Mellon Research Fellowship from the Virginia Historical Society in 2000. A research fellowship from the Pew Evangelical Scholars Program, a program of the Pew Charitable Trusts, allowed me to begin research and writing during 1998 and 1999.

I am also grateful to a great many archivists and librarians who have directed me to collections related to Asbury. These include Chris Anderson, Dale Patterson, Ken Rowe, Mark Shenise, and Charles Yrigoyen at the United Methodist Archives Center and the General Commission on Archives and History at Drew University, Peter Nockles and Gareth Lloyd at the John Rylands Library, Deansgate, University of Manchester, Edwin Schell at the Lovely Lane Museum and Archives, Baltimore, Elaine Caldbeck at the Garrett-Evangelical Theological Seminary library, and the late F. Garner Ranney of the

Episcopal Diocese of Maryland archives. I would also like to thank the staffs at Barratt's Chapel, Frederica, Delaware, the Birmingham Public Library, Birmingham, England, the Special Collections Library at Duke University, the McGraw-Page Library, Randolph-Macon College (particularly Nancy Newins), the Southern Historical Collection at the Wilson Library, University of North Carolina at Chapel Hill, St. George's United Methodist Church, Philadelphia, the Staffordshire Records Office, Stafford, England, the Stockport Central Library, Stockport, England, the Library of Virginia, Richmond, and the Virginia Historical Society.

Portions of several chapters of this book appear in "Francis Asbury and American Methodism" in *The Oxford Handbook of Methodist Studies*, edited by William J. Abraham and James E. Kirby (2009), and are used with Oxford University Press's permission.

I owe a profound debt to a number of people who generously shared their knowledge of matters connected to Asbury's life. My sincere thanks to David Hallam for taking me on a tour of "Asburyland" in the West Midlands in June 2003 and offering helpful comments on drafts of the first two chapters, and to Harry Clarke, curator of the Asbury cottage, who kindly shared his knowledge of the cottage and the Asbury family. I am also grateful to Jane Donovan for generously sharing her knowledge of the Foxall family and to Tom Rightmyer for helping me sort out the Episcopal clergy whom Asbury interacted with. Marilyn James-Kracke, who teaches pharmacology, and Louise Thai, who teaches microbiology and immunology, both at the University of Missouri, helped me evaluate Asbury's medical conditions. Paul Treece drew the maps of Asbury's 1793 and 1811 tours. This would be a much less interesting book without their help.

I am also deeply grateful to friends who have read drafts along the way. George Marsden generously read the first (and much longer) draft, and it is a better book for it. John Vickers reviewed some of the chapters dealing with Thomas Coke and Russ Richey offered helpful advice on the early chapters. T. J. Tomlin, now at the University of Northern Colorado, and Josh McMullen, one of my current graduate students, each read the manuscript twice, offering insightful suggestions both times. T. J. also dug up some Asbury letters for me at the Historical Society of Pennsylvania. Angela Bell, John Deken, Homer Page, Becky Showmaker, and Steve Smith read drafts while graduate students at Mizzou, collectively improving the style and content of the book. My colleague Steve Watts offered good advice on how to frame a big biography. I am also grateful to my editors at Oxford, Cynthia Read, Mariana Templin, and Joellyn Ausanka, for skillfully guiding this project through.

My greatest debt is, as always, to my family. Hannah, Allison, Natalie, and Emma are simply wonderful, the best daughters I could imagine. Having them around during this project gave it so much more meaning. My wife, Melodie, has read successive chapter drafts over the years, offering keen observations along the way. I could not have done this without her. Far more important, she remains my truest friend.

American Saint

Introduction

Francis Asbury was worried about the future of Methodism in America as he rode south into Powhatan County, Virginia, in early May 1780. Since emigrating from England in 1771, he had seen the movement gain a foothold in the colonies, only to be thrown into disarray by the American Revolution. Asbury had spent most of the past two years lying low at a friend's in Delaware, fearing for his life because of his association with John Wesley, the founder of Methodism in England and no friend of the revolution. Meanwhile, southern Methodists had decided to ordain themselves, outside of any episcopal oversight, and begin offering the sacraments of baptism and the Lord's Supper, a clear break from the movement's Wesleyan roots in England. Asbury had one last chance to bring them back into the fold at a conference scheduled to meet in Manakintown, Virginia, that May. Most observers predicted he would fail. Southern Methodists had experienced a sustained revival over the past two years, and most of the young preachers hardly knew Asbury. "At that time there was very little room to hope that they would ever recede from their new plan, in which they were so well established," wrote Jesse Lee, who became a Methodist during this revival. Remarkably, Asbury succeeded, with the southern preachers agreeing to suspend administering the sacraments and acknowledge him as the leader of American Methodism.[1]

This much is familiar to historians of early American Methodism, but what Asbury did next was just as important. Rather than return north, he set out on a grueling five-month tour of Virginia and North

Carolina, crisscrossing the region to meet as many people as possible. One of the people he was determined to win over was John Dickins. Dickins had been a leader of the separatist party, and his ties to the South were strong. In April 1779 he had married Elizabeth Yancey, whose family owned a large plantation in Halifax County, North Carolina, and staunchly supported the revolution. At Manakin-town, Dickins was the "chief speaker" for the southern preachers in opposition to Asbury, according to one of the southern preachers who witnessed the debate. Following the reconciliation between the two sides, Dickins was chosen to write a letter to Wesley seeking his advice on how to handle the issue of ordination and the sacraments. No one believed more firmly in the southern position or enjoyed greater confidence among the southern preachers than Dickins.[2]

Their differences at Manakintown only a few weeks before notwithstanding, when Asbury reached North Carolina in mid-June, he made a point of finding Dickins. Asbury could have been vindictive toward Dickins, but instead he drew him in through the common bonds of their faith. The two preached together to five hundred people near Dickins's home on June 18, 1780, and the next day they discussed the possibility of opening a school modeled after Wesley's Kingswood school. They talked late into the night, and Dickins was never quite the same. "I hope John Dickins will ever after this be a friend to me and Methodism," Asbury wrote in his journal. Dickins came away from their brief time together with the same hope, his opinion of Asbury having completely changed now that he had seen him up close. When Dickins's son was born that July, he named him Asbury Dickins, completing a transition from adversary to namesake in the space of a few weeks. John Dickins remained one of Asbury's staunchest supporters, later writing pamphlets defending Asbury's reputation against critics. Asbury won over most of the southern preachers and thousands of ordinary people who turned out to see him in much the same way. His ability to inspire deep and lasting loyalty in others is not easy to define from a distance. He wasn't a persuasive public speaker. Yet in close conversation and small groups he had the ability to draw others to him, to dispel their fears about his motives and inspire them with his sense of purpose. Here was someone worth following, someone whose integrity and piety were above reproach, someone whose vision seemed truly inspired by God.[3]

Francis Asbury lived one of the most remarkable lives in American history, a life that many have admired but few have envied. The son of an English gardener, he became one of America's leading religious voices and the person most responsible for shaping American Methodism. Through sheer persever-ance and dedication to a single goal, he changed American popular religion—and by extension American culture—as much as anyone ever has. America is one of the most religious nations on earth, and Asbury is an important reason why. Yet his dedication to the ministry cost him dearly, requiring that he set aside more worldly desires and ambitions. During his 45-year career in America (he died in 1816), he never married or owned much more than he could carry on horseback. He led a wanderer's life of voluntary poverty and intense introspection. The church and the nation ultimately disappointed him, but his faith never did. Asbury embodies Methodism's greatest successes and its most wrenching failures.

Contrary to this book's title, some might argue that Asbury was neither an American nor a saint. He was born and raised in a small village outside of Birmingham, England, and didn't come to America until the age of 26. Yet he adapted to the landscape and culture of America with surprising speed. Of John Wesley's licensed missionaries to the colonies, Asbury was the only one who stayed through the American Revolution as a Methodist preacher. He developed a remarkably keen sense of what Americans were looking for and how to reach them with the Methodist message of salvation. He traveled at least 130,000 miles by horse and crossed the Allegheny Mountains some sixty times. For many years he visited nearly every state once a year, and traveled more extensively across the American landscape than probably any other American of his day. He preached more than ten thousand sermons and probably ordained from two thousand to three thousand preachers. He was more widely recognized face to face than any person of his generation, including such national figures as Thomas Jefferson and George Washington. Landlords and tavern keepers knew him on sight in every region, and parents named more than a thousand children after him. People called out his name as he passed by on the road. Asbury wasn't born in America, but he came to understand ordinary Americans as well as anyone of his generation.[4]

Asbury's saintliness also requires some explaining. He never claimed that he was especially holy or pure, though he diligently tried to be. Like any good eighteenth- or early nineteenth-century evangelical, Asbury was never satisfied with his own piety or labors. Yet people saw in him an example of single-minded dedication to the gospel that they themselves had never managed to attain, but to which, on their better days, they aspired. In their eyes he was indeed a saint. Though he spent his life traveling, he insisted on riding inexpensive horses and using cheap saddles and riding gear. He ate sparingly and usually got up at 4 or 5 a.m. to pray for an hour in the stillness before dawn. No one believed that Asbury was perfect, and even his most ardent supporters admitted that he made mistakes in running the church. He jealously guarded his episcopal authority, the one issue on which his critics gained traction. Yet his piety and underlying motivations seemed genuine to almost everyone. This is crucial for understanding not only Asbury, but all of evangelical culture in this period. Though they often fell short of their own expectations, evangelicals admired nothing so much as a heart yearning to be poured out in service to God.[5]

Asbury is seldom remembered as an important American religious leader because he didn't exert influence in ways that we expect. Key figures in American religious history are generally lumped into three camps: charismatic communicators, such as George Whitefield, Charles Finney, or Billy Graham; intellectuals, such as Jonathan Edwards or Reinhold Niebuhr; and domineering autocrats—the way in which Joseph Smith, founder of the Mormons, is often depicted.[6] Asbury was certainly neither of the first two. He was known for preaching disjointed sermons that were almost impossible to follow, and he never published a book or sermon of any note. "It seems strange, that sometimes, after much premeditation and devotion, I cannot express my thoughts with readiness and perspicuity," he wrote early in his career, in 1774. This remained true even as he matured and became famous. Relatively late in his career, when his reputation was well established, he still sometimes had difficulty preaching before large audiences. "This excessive delicacy of feeling, which shuts my mouth so often, may appear strange to those who do not know me," he wrote in August 1806. "There are some houses in which I am not sure that I could speak to my father, were he alive, and I to meet him there." He hated face-to-face conflict and rarely took a public role in debates at the church's major conferences. "I am not fond of hurting the feelings of people," he wrote in January 1807.[7]

Scholars usually portray Asbury as falling into the third category, the rigid autocrat. In his massive study of early Methodism in Britain and America, Edward Drinkhouse, historian of the Methodist Protestant Church, concludes that Asbury followed John Wesley in instituting a rigid form of "ecclesiastical Paternalism," designed to stamp out any hint of real democracy in the Methodist movement. Together they created what Drinkhouse called "the Episcopal anaconda," that "bastard thing." More recently, a number of scholars have puzzled over the supposed paradox of a movement that appealed to democratically minded masses while maintaining a rigidly hierarchical structure. One prominent historian writes that during this period American Methodism was "almost ostentatiously hierarchical," with authority continuing "to flow down from the top, not rise up from the bottom."[8]

But Asbury wasn't a distant autocrat. He remained closely connected to the people he led. His legacy is not in books and sermons, but in the thousands of preachers whose careers he shaped one conversation at a time, and in the tens of thousands of ordinary believers who saw him up close and took him (in however limited a way) as their guide. He was the people's saint, an ordinary person who chose to do extraordinary things.

Asbury communicated his vision for Methodism in four enduring ways that came to define much of evangelical culture in America. The first was through his legendary piety and perseverance, rooted in a classically evangelical conversion experience. Piety isn't a word we use much anymore. It simply refers to devotion to God and serving others, to a desire to "love the Lord thy God with all thy heart, and with all thy soul, and with all thy mind," and "thy neighbour as thyself." Where most Methodists, even most preachers, settled for a serviceable faith, Asbury strove for a life of extraordinary devotion. During his forty-five years in America he essentially lived as a houseguest in thousands of other people's homes across the land. This manner of life "exposed him, continually, to public or private observation and inspection, and subjected him to a constant and critical review; and that from day to day, and from year to year," wrote Ezekiel Cooper, who knew Asbury for more than thirty years. He lived one of the most transparent lives imaginable, with no private life beyond the confines of his mind. It is all the more revealing, then, that the closer people got to him, the more they tended to respect the integrity of his faith.[9]

Asbury's spiritual purity produced a "confidence in the uprightness of his intentions and wisdom of his plans, which gave him such a control over both preachers and people as enabled him to discharge the high trusts confided to him, with so much facility and to such general satisfaction," one contemporary observed. Perseverance counted for much among evangelicals, and on this score Asbury had few equals. He relentlessly pushed himself to the breaking point of his health, seldom asking more of other Methodists than he was willing to do. From 1793 on, he suffered from progressively worsening congestive heart failure, probably brought on by bouts of streptococcal pharyngitis (strep throat) and rheumatic fever that damaged his heart valves. As a result, he suffered from edema in his feet made worse by endless hours on horseback with his feet dangling until they were too swollen to fit in the stirrups. Toward the end of his life, he sometimes had to be carried from his horse to his preaching appointments because he couldn't stand the pain of walking, which must have been an inspiring, if bizarre, sight. It left one observer who saw him preach in this condition in "breathless awe and silent astonishment." Asbury's piety brought him respect, even renown, based on sacrifice rather than accumulation of buildings, money or other trappings of power. "It was almost impossible to approach, and converse with him, without feeling the strong influence of his spirit and presence...There was something, in the remarkable fact, almost inexplicable, and indescribable," Ezekiel Cooper wrote shortly after Asbury's death. Even James O'Kelly, who, in 1792, led the most bitter schism from the Methodist church in Asbury's lifetime, acknowledged his "cogent zeal, and unwearied diligence, in spite of every disappointment."[10]

The second way that Asbury communicated his vision was through his ability to connect with ordinary people. Connection was an important word for early Methodists, and Asbury embodied its meaning better than anyone. As he crisscrossed the nation from year to year, he conversed with countless thousands, demonstrating a gift for building relationships face to face or in small groups. It is remarkable how many of those he met became permanent friends, even after a single conversation. They loved to have him in their homes. Asbury often chided himself for talking too much and too freely, especially late at night. He considered this love of close, often lighthearted, conversation a drain on his piety. In reality it was one of his greatest strengths, allowing him to build deep and lasting relationships and to feel closely the pulse of the church and the nation. Henry Boehm, who traveled some 25,000 miles with Asbury from 1808 to 1813, recalled that "in private circles he would unbend, and relate amusing incidents and laugh most heartily. He said 'if he was as grave as Bishop M'Kendree he should live but a short time.' He would often indulge in a vein of innocent pleasantry." Asbury once remarked to John Wesley Bond, who traveled with him during the last two years of his life, that his spirits always rose when he got "into a retired situation, in a quiet, plain and pious family." In these settings Asbury felt most at home. "His conversational powers were great. He was full of interesting anecdotes, and could entertain people for hours," Boehm remembered. "As a road-companion, no man could be more agreeable; he was cheerful almost to gaiety; his conversation was sprightly, and sufficiently seasoned with wit and anecdote," wrote Nicholas Snethen, who was Asbury's traveling companion for several years beginning in 1800. George Roberts remembered that at times Asbury would simply "break out" in song.[11]

He could also be funny, which enhanced his appeal. Methodists didn't generally consider joking and laughter compatible with religion, so the number of stories relating Asbury's humor, often at his own expense, is surprising. Once, when Asbury was near sixty and had been a bishop for nearly two decades, he and the "venerable, portly" preacher Benjamin Bidlack came to the home of a "respectable Methodist" in the Genesee District of upstate New York. Seeing Asbury riding in front, the man mistook him for an assistant and ordered him to dismount and open the gate for the bishop. Bidlack played along, and as he passed by, Asbury bowed low, offering to see to the bishop's horse and bags. When their host realized his mistake, he was "mortified" until he saw how much Asbury enjoyed the joke.[12]

Many recognized Asbury's ability to connect with people on a personal level, though few found it easy to explain. The dissident Methodist preacher Jeremiah Minter concluded that Asbury must have been a "sorcerer," "in league with the devil," to have "enchanted [and] deceived" so many who "thought him a good man." Asbury's only equal in this regard, Minter believed, was the famous evangelist Lorenzo Dow. "With their *sorcery* and enchantments," Asbury and Dow had "bewitched multitudes, who take them to be, as it were, the great power of God," Minter wrote in 1814, two years before Asbury's death. Few would have agreed with Minter's analysis, but many recognized what it was about Asbury that so annoyed Minter. Even James O'Kelly confessed a "disagreeable jealousy" over Asbury's ability to influence those closest to him. Nicholas Snethen came much closer to understanding Asbury in this regard when he wrote that "he was charitable, almost to excess, of the experience of others." People found Asbury approachable and willing to listen to their concerns more than they found him full of inspiring ideas.[13]

The third conduit of Asbury's vision was the way that he understood and used popular culture. John Wesley and Asbury were alike in their willingness to negotiate between competing religious and cultural worlds. In his biography of Wesley, Henry Rack argues persuasively that Wesley acted as a "cultural middleman" between Methodists on the one hand and clergymen and educated gentlemen in England on the other.[14] If so, then Asbury acted as a mediator between Wesley and common Americans. Wesley and Asbury came from significantly different backgrounds, but they shared a realization that the dominant religious institutions of their day were failing to reach most people. The great question they both addressed was how to make the gospel relevant in their time and place. The audience was never far from their minds. This led Asbury to do things in America that he wouldn't have done in England, some of which Wesley disapproved. Asbury, for example, accepted the emotionalism of southern worship in the 1770s, promoted camp meetings in the early 1800s, and reluctantly acquiesced to southern Methodists holding slaves. This mediating impulse, transmitted from Wesley through Asbury, became a trademark of American Methodism.

All religious movements interact with the prevailing culture of their adherents. Popular religious movements like early American Methodism exist in a tension between religious values and the values of the dominant culture, alternately challenging and embracing the larger culture around them. To either completely accept or reject the larger culture is to cease to be either religious on the one hand, or popular on the other. Leaders like Asbury understand this tension and work within it. At times, they call their movements to reject the dominant culture and society. But this rejection can never be complete. Indeed, in ways that these leaders and their followers may never completely acknowledge or even understand, the success of their movements hinge on maintaining contact with the culture around them.

Asbury didn't accept American culture indiscriminately or without reservation. He was deeply suspicious of much of it, and never simply identified the mission of Methodism with that of America. Yet cultural accommodation exacted a price, the clearest example of which was the presence of slavery in the church, a reality that he tacitly accepted, but which haunted him for the last thirty years of his life. Cultural adaptation is also never static, since both the church and the broader culture are constantly changing. Asbury was remarkably well-informed (the product of his travels and love of conversation) and flexible in keeping up with these changes, but everyone has their limits. Though the American Revolution led to a good deal of persecution of American Methodists, Asbury fretted that its end would produce too much prosperity and thereby dampen Methodist zeal. Later he worried that the availability of cheap land in the West would have the same effect, drawing people's attention from spiritual concerns to the cares of this world. As long as they were poor, most Methodists agreed with Asbury that wealth was a snare. But as Methodists became generally more prosperous, they became less concerned about the dangers of wealth, much to Asbury's dismay. By the end of his career he was largely out of step with the church that he was so instrumental in creating. This, in the end, seemed to him a great tragedy.

The fourth way that Asbury communicated his message was through his organization of the Methodist church. He was a brilliant administrator and a keen judge of human motivations. He had a "superior talent to read men," as Peter Cartwright put it. As Asbury crisscrossed the nation year in and year out, he attended to countless administrative details. Yet he never lost sight of the people involved. "I have always taken a pleasure as far as it was in my power, to bring men of merit & standing forward," he wrote to the preacher Daniel Hitt in 1801. The system Asbury crafted made it possible to keep tabs on thousands of preachers and lay workers. Under his leadership, American Methodists anticipated the development of modern managerial styles. No merchant of the early nineteenth century could match Asbury's nationwide network of class leaders, circuit stewards, book stewards, exhorters, local preachers, circuit riders, and presiding elders, or the movement's system of class meetings, circuit preaching, quarterly meetings, annual conferences, and quadrennial general conferences, all churning out detailed statistical reports to be consolidated and published on a regular basis.[15]

At the center of Asbury's system was the itinerant connection. He learned the itinerant system in England under John Wesley, bringing it to America, where it worked even better than it had in England. Methodist itinerant preachers, or circuit riders, didn't serve a single congregation or parish, but rather ministered to a number of congregations spread out along a circuit they continually traveled. Under Asbury, the typical American itinerant rode a predominantly rural circuit 200 to 500 miles in circumference, typically with twenty-five to thirty preaching appointments per round. He completed the circuit every two to six weeks, with the standard being a four weeks' circuit of 400 miles. This meant that circuit riders had to travel and preach nearly every day, with only a few days for rest each month. Often they were assigned a partner, but even so, they usually started at opposite ends of the circuit instead of traveling together. The itinerant system worked well for reaching post-revolutionary America's rapidly expanding population. In 1795, 95 percent of Americans lived in places with fewer than 2,500 inhabitants; by 1830 this proportion was 91 percent. While Methodism retained a stronghold in the seaports of the middle states, Asbury hammered its organization into one that had a distinctly rural orientation adept at expanding into newly populated areas. "We must draw resources from center to circumference," he wrote in 1797.[16]

Despite its success, keeping the itinerant system intact proved the greatest challenge of Asbury's career. From the beginning he faced opposition from those unhappy with its demands and constraints. Some, like Joseph Pilmore, wanted to focus Methodist resources more on the cities of the Atlantic seaboard, where they believed it was important for Methodism to build a base of influence and social respectability. Others, like James O'Kelly, wanted to make Methodism more congregational, allowing preachers who had built up a local following to remain on the same circuit indefinitely. Asbury believed that all such proposals would ultimately limit the movement's ability to reach the most people with the gospel. He maintained that sending preachers where they would have the most telling impact, rather than leaving them where they were most comfortable, was crucial to the success of the Methodist system. For the most part, he succeeded in defending the itinerant system until the last decade of his life. By then a new generation of Methodists, who were accustomed to a higher social status than their parents had enjoyed, began chipping away at his cherished itinerant connection. For all of its usefulness, the itinerant system was rooted in a particular place and time, something that Asbury couldn't really see.

There was another less obvious, but equally important, component of Asbury's system that went to the heart of what it meant to be a Methodist, to practice a method: the necessity of a culture of discipline. As individuals and communities, believers had to take it upon themselves to regulate their spiritual lives, to maintain their own spiritual focus. Neither Asbury nor his preachers could be everywhere at once. This is why, from his first days in America, he insisted on upholding the requirement that all members attend class meetings and that love feasts be limited to active members, creating an atmosphere of mutual trust and support. He delegated authority to others, recognizing that a voluntary system wouldn't work if it relied on coercion from above. It needed to become a central component of people's world view. Though there were plenty of disagreements along the way, Methodists succeeded where other religious groups failed largely because they were more disciplined. Yet this culture of discipline changed over time, much to Asbury's chagrin, as the church itself became more respectable and less countercultural.[17]

Still, the system worked remarkably well during Asbury's lifetime. The Methodist church grew at an unprecedented rate, rising from a few hundred members in 1771, the year he came to America, to more than two hundred thousand in 1816, the year of his death. Methodism was the largest and most dynamic popular religious movement in America between the Revolution and the Civil War. In 1775, fewer than one out of every eight hundred Americans was a Methodist; by 1812, Methodists numbered one out of every thirty-six Americans. These figures are even more impressive given the movement's wider influence. Many more Americans attended Methodist meetings than actually joined the church, particularly in the movement's early, most volatile years. Methodism's theology, worship style, and system of discipline worked their ways deep into the fabric of American life, influencing nearly all other mass religious movements that would follow, as well as many facets of American life not directly connected to the church.

For all of his focus on a single goal, Asbury remained a complex figure. At the core of his personality was a fear of rejection that at times made him seem aloof or severe in settings he found intimidating. He tended to hold others at arms length until he could be sure of their intentions. John Wesley Bond remembered that Asbury himself believed "that by nature he was suspicious." Henry Boehm recalled that at a distance Asbury often seemed "rough, unfeeling, harsh, and stoical." While rarely mean spirited, he feared being taken for a fool. "I grant he had a rather rough exterior, that he was sometimes stern; but under that roughness and sternness of manner beat a heart as feeling as ever dwelt in human bosom," Boehm asserted. Nicholas Snethen, who often opposed Asbury's policies after 1812 and later left the Methodist Episcopal Church, wasn't as forgiving. Snethen believed that Asbury's "suspicious disposition" stemmed "from his well known irritability, his faculty of obtaining the most secret information, and the quickness and penetration of his genius." Yet even Snethen didn't believe that Asbury's "ambition" flowed from "a criminal nature." Like nearly everyone who knew Asbury well, Snethen acknowledged his ability to assess human motivations, or as he said, to judge "human nature." "In what related to ecclesiastical men, and things, he was all eye, and ear; and what he saw and heard he never forgot. The tenacity of his memory was surprising. His knowledge of human nature was penetrating and extensive," Snethen wrote in 1816. Asbury was a keen observer of the human heart, and it often left him melancholy.[18]

Asbury's inability to speak clearly in front of authority figures led him to work through proxies. He was the quintessential backroom negotiator, perhaps his least admirable trait. "In a judicial or legislative capacity he seemed not to excel, and hence he did not often appear to the best advantage in the chair of conferences," recalled Snethen, who observed Asbury at many conferences from 1794 to 1814. "He knew also the art of governing, and seldom trusted to the naked force of authority. Indeed, the majesty of command, was almost wholly concealed, or superceded by that wonderful faculty, which belongs to this class of human geniuses, and which enables them to inspire their own disposition for action, into the breasts of others," Snethen concluded.[19]

Wesleyan perfectionism—Wesley's belief that it was the duty of all believers to seek perfection in this life—also colored Asbury's personality. It heightened his resolve but also his insecurities. His failings instilled in him a genuine humility. By the end of his life any number of churches had been named for him, but "he did not approve of this, and called it folly," according to Boehm. He didn't expect great rewards in this life because he didn't believe he deserved them.[20]

Yet Wesleyan perfectionism wasn't a theology of despair. With diligence, holiness was attainable in this life, if only for brief periods. Ultimately, believers could be confident of God's grace if they held steady. Guiding the church toward this goal became an all-consuming passion for Asbury. "His patience in bearing disappointments was equal if not superior to that of any man I ever knew," remembered Bond. According to Bond, Asbury rarely allowed himself to "repine" or "brood" over past difficulties; instead he turned them over in his mind, thinking "How shall I mend it:—How can things be made better." In fact, Asbury did brood and fret, but it didn't define him. He could sink deep within himself when concentrating on a problem, but this wasn't the same thing. "At times he appeared unsociable, for his mind was engrossed with his work," recalled Boehm. Or, as Bond put it, Asbury "thrust himself into every part of his charge; lest something might be wrong,—lest some part of the cause of God might suffer." Asbury had a thorough and even subtle mind, but he wasn't a quick study or good on his feet. He could work his way through thorny problems, but it took time. The long hours he spent on horseback gave him the space for reflection, prayer, and meditation that he needed. Those who didn't know him sometimes mistook his preoccupation for severity.[21]

Coupled with Asbury's fear of rejection was a genuine compassion for others, especially the downtrodden. He believed that true religion embraced the suffering of the poor and did all that was possible to alleviate it. Resources should be channeled to those most in need, not squandered on luxuries, he believed. This is why he allowed himself few comforts. His clothes were cheap and plain, though he took some care to appear presentable. He once told Boehm "that the equipment of a Methodist minister consisted of a horse, saddle and bridle, one suit of clothes, a watch, a pocket Bible, and a hymn book. Anything else would be an encumbrance." Indeed, Asbury rarely owned much more than this. At the same time, he gave away nearly all the money that came his way. Both Boehm and Bond kept track of Asbury's funds while traveling with him as assistants. "He would divide his last dollar with a Methodist preacher," Boehm recalled. "He was restless till it was gone, so anxious was he to do good with it." Once, in Ohio, Asbury and Boehm came across a widow whose only cow was about to be sold for debt. Determining that "It must not be," Asbury gave what he had and solicited enough from bystanders to pay the woman's bills. "His charity knew no bounds but the limits of its resources; nor did I ever know him let an object of charity pass without contributing something for their relief," Bond wrote. He recalled that Asbury often gave money to strangers he met on the road whose circumstances seemed dire, especially widows. He had his share of failings, but the love of money wasn't one of them. This won him a great deal of respect from almost everyone who knew him.[22]

Asbury used poverty to keep himself honest. The preacher George Roberts believed that Asbury often "carryed his deadness to the world too far . . . by a kind of negligence all most peculiar to himself." When he traveled, according to Roberts, "he did not in common make any calculation of the probability of his expenses or whether he had soficient to supply his wants." To prove the point, Roberts recounts that in 1805 Asbury set out from New York for Boston with only three dollars in his pocket, refusing to take more. This incident proved to be one of Roberts' strongest memories of Asbury.[23] It also illustrates Asbury's deliberate use of his poverty to influence others. Notice that in the story of the widow's cow, people gave in Asbury's presence when they presumably would not have otherwise. Particularly later in his career, when Methodists were becoming more affluent, he knew that his reputation for charity and asceticism could be used as a shield against all kinds of criticism. If money is power, then Asbury was powerless. But of course money is not the only source of power in a religious movement.

If viewed in isolation, Asbury's adult life appears one-dimensional. Much of what makes human life so interesting—family, sexual romance, creating an intellectual legacy—were largely absent from Asbury's life after his arrival in America as a missionary (in the case of sexual romance, completely absent). Perhaps this is why so little has been written about him. Even John Wesley and

George Whitefield married (both unhappily, which makes for a better story). But Asbury's life wasn't flat, revolving as it did around the relationships he formed with other Methodists. Asbury lived his life in public, and the community of Methodist believers spread across the country became his vast extended family. He must be understood in this context or not at all. Like a rock thrown into a pond, his life sent ripples through the Methodist movement to its most distant reaches. Hence, this book has two parallel threads. The first is the story of Asbury's life in its more immediate setting. The second is more or less a collective biography of those Asbury knew best, mostly the itinerant preachers under his charge. Their lives form the human connections through which Asbury's ideas were shaped and through which he transmitted his vision outward. For this reason I have relied not only on his journal and letters, but also on the journals, letters, and memoirs of dozens of others who knew him or had contact with the early Methodist movement.

Asbury was a transitional figure in the development of American religion, promoting the separation of religious leadership from wealth and formal education. The system of religious economy that Asbury and the Methodists were largely responsible for creating—churches unaided and not coerced by government intervention, operating outside the control of social elites—was far different from what had existed in colonial America. Most religious leaders in colonial America were relatively wealthy college educated elites. Lay people occasionally gained public notoriety (Anne Hutchinson, for example), but they rarely held positions of official leadership for very long. Even George White-field, the famous evangelist of the Great Awakening, was a graduate of Oxford University. Such clearly wasn't the case with Asbury, who grew up in a small cottage and had only a few years of common school to his credit. But most of the leaders of large religious movements who followed Asbury looked more like him than the religious leaders of colonial America.

The religious pattern that Asbury was so instrumental in establishing is still with us today. While Methodists themselves are declining in numbers in the United States, other groups that derive from the Wesleyan heritage, including much of Pentecostalism, are thriving, as is evangelical culture in general, which Methodism did much to create. One of the most significant changes in recent decades has been the growth of non-Christian religions in the United States, yet even many of these have been to some degree "methodized." Asbury wasn't an intellectual, charismatic performer or autocrat, but his understanding of what it meant to be pious, connected, culturally aware, and effectively organized redefined religious leadership in America.

I

The Apprentice

It was hot and dusty as Francis Asbury made his way north through New Jersey headed for New York City in July 1792. He had been this way many times before, but the summer heat still surprised him. How could some place so cold in winter be so hot a few months later? England had never been like this.

He was on his way to Lynn, Massachusetts, where the Methodist Church's New England conference would meet during the first week of August. With time to spare, Asbury decided to remain a week in New York City. He spent his time in familiar activities—reading, preaching, writing in his journal, meeting with small devotional groups—the kinds of pursuits that had made up his life for the 20 odd years he had been in America. But he also did something unusual. He recorded a short autobiographical account in his journal. Though Asbury had kept a journal since 1771, he rarely wrote about his early life. Why he chose to do so now isn't clear. Perhaps it was because he had just finished reading a biography of John Wesley, who died the year before.[1] Perhaps it was the city itself, triggering memories of his first days in America and himself as a younger man. Whatever the reason, Asbury now paused to reflect on his life as leader of the Methodist movement in America.

Francis Asbury was born at the foot of Hamstead Bridge in a cottage in the parish of Handsworth, about four miles outside of Birmingham, England. Birmingham is located about 110 miles northwest of London in the West Midlands. His parents, Joseph and

Elizabeth (Eliza) Rogers Asbury, were married on May 30, 1742, when he was about twenty-nine and she about twenty-seven. Joseph was a farm laborer and gardener employed, according to most accounts, by two wealthy families in the parish, the Wyrley Birch family of Hamstead Hall and the Goughs of Perry Hall. Joseph likely tended the large garden at Hamstead Hall, and the Asburys probably ate fairly well. Eliza's family was Welsh, though little else is known of her background. The Asburys had two children born in the cottage near Hamstead Bridge: Sarah, born on May 3, 1743, and Francis, born on August 20 or 21, 1745, though he was never exactly sure of the date.[2]

For much of Francis's childhood, Joseph and Eliza weren't particularly religious people. Francis, or Frank as the family called him, may never have been baptized. His name doesn't appear in the parish register or the Bishop's Transcript for St. Mary's, the parish church of Handsworth, though Sarah's does. Nor does Francis's name show up in any of the records from nearby parishes. He apparently suspected that there was something irregular about his baptism, or lack thereof. He wrote to his parents in October 1795 that he "should be glad [if] you would take the time of my Baptism from the Church register, that I may know it perfectly." They evidently failed to respond, perhaps because they knew no such record existed.[3]

While Francis was still quite young, the family moved to a cottage in the hamlet of Newton, Great Barr, near Wednesbury and West Bromwich. In all likelihood they rented the cottage, which at the time was attached to a brewery, the Malt House. Joseph Asbury probably worked at the Malt House or the nearby brewery farm, and use of the cottage was likely part of his compensation. It is unlikely that the cottage would have been rented to someone not connected with the brewery. The brewery also ran a public house, the Malt Shovel Inn, serving drovers taking trains of packhorses to Birmingham and town dwellers looking for a break in the country. The brewery was later torn down, but the Asburys' home is still standing. Soundly built, the cottage was lived in until the 1950s. It consists of two bedrooms upstairs, two rooms downstairs and a cellar. Much of the family's life together would have been centered in the kitchen and larger downstairs room, with an inglenook fireplace that dominates one wall. This was a modest but comfortable home for the family of an eighteenth-century laborer. Reflecting on this period, Asbury recalled that his parents "were people in common life; were remarkable for honesty and industry, and had all things needful to enjoy."[4]

But he also adds that "had my father been as saving as laborious, he might have been wealthy." Did Joseph Asbury gamble or drink their money away, as proximity to the brewery might suggest? There is some indication of Joseph's failings in his relationship to his wealthy employers. At some point he lost his

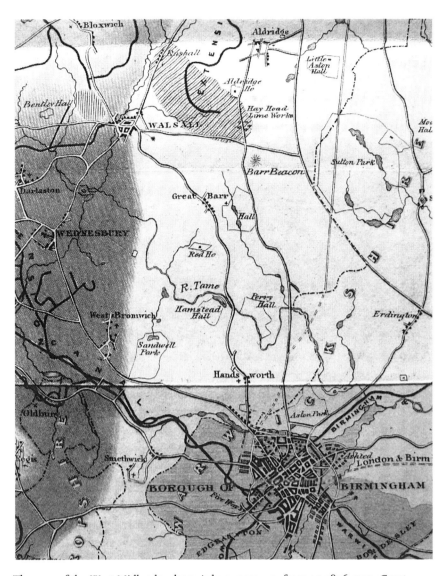

The area of the West Midlands where Asbury grew up, from an 1836 map. Great
Barr is in the top center, four miles north-northwest of Birmingham. Wednesbury is
two and a half miles west of Great Barr, and West Bromwich is two and a half miles
southwest of Great Barr. Hamstead Hall and Perry Hall are south of Great Barr, on
the road to Birmingham. (Detail from map entitled "The Mining and Manufacturing
District of South Staffordshire, Warwickshire, &c." in William Hawkes Smith,
Birmingham and Its Vicinity, As a Manufacturing & Commercial District [London:
Charles Tilt, 1836].)

The Asbury cottage, Great Barr, as it looks today. (Photo by the author.)

position at Hamstead Hall under strained circumstances. In June 1784, Francis wrote to his parents discussing the possibility of them joining him in America. One obstacle was finding work for his father. "I have one Friend, a great man, who would, may be employ my father, in the way he would chuse; but it is too much like Hampstead Hall," Francis wrote. About 1796, two years before Joseph's death, the American preacher Jeremiah Minter asked Asbury: "Mr. Asbury, I have often heard you mention your Mother, but never heard you mention your Father, is he living or is he dead?" When Asbury didn't reply, another preacher answered for him: "it may be that he has no Father." At least not that he cared to discuss.[5]

Relations with the family of Lord Dartmouth, whose estate at Sandwell was located about two miles from the Asburys' cottage, also suggest that the Asburys didn't enjoy a spotless reputation. Dartmouth (1731–1801) was known for his deep religious convictions and close ties to the Wesleys, George White-field, and the countess of Huntingdon. Dartmouth served as secretary of state for the North American colonies from 1772 to 1775, but still insisted that the Wednesbury Methodists call him simply "brother Dartmouth." After they became Methodists, Eliza and Frank probably knew Dartmouth and rubbed shoulders with him at local Methodist meetings. When he served as secretary of state, Methodists of humble background, even some who weren't from the

West Midlands, wrote to him describing their experiences in America. But Asbury never did. Moreover, Asbury's friends and associates in America never mentioned him in their letters to Dartmouth. Why? Perhaps it had something to do with Asbury's father. Francis never felt comfortable around people of wealth and political power, and it is tempting to see this as a product of his family's experience with the local landed gentry of his youth.[6]

Their questionable reputation and limited resources notwithstanding, Asbury's parents were determined that their son would do better, beginning with a decent education. By age five his mother had taught him to read the Bible, and he remained "remarkably fond of reading" during his youth. He later recalled that "my father having but one son, greatly desired to keep me at school, he cared not how long." They sent Frank to the only school in the area at Sneal's Green, a free school about a quarter of a mile from the family cottage. Little is known of the school's master, Arthur Taylor, so it is difficult to tell what his qualifications for teaching school were or what his lessons consisted of. Other Birmingham schoolmasters of this period claimed to offer a wide range of subjects—reading, writing, arithmetic, English, French, Latin, Greek, the use of globes and maps, geography, algebra, geometry, bookkeeping, history, drawing, and natural and moral philosophy—in response to a growing thirst for education among middling families.[7]

Asbury was a diligent, if not gifted, student. Unfortunately, Taylor was "a great churl, and used to beat me cruelly," as Asbury later remembered. His severity "filled me with such horrible dread, that with me anything was preferable to going to school." So, at about age thirteen, he left school and became a servant "in one of the wealthiest and most ungodly families we had in the parish." While living in this home, he "became vain, but not openly wicked." He left this position after a few months to learn a trade, following a common pattern in which children became servants at the age of thirteen or fourteen and young men entered apprenticeships at fourteeen.[8]

As limited as Asbury's schooling was, it wasn't inconsequential and served him well once he turned to preaching. By the standards of the day he had more education than the average workman or apprentice, only about half of whom attended school before beginning a life of work (less than one-third of the girls went to school). Few children remained in school past the age of ten or eleven. The kind of classical education, beginning with the ability to read Latin and Greek, required to attend a university was clearly beyond Asbury's reach, yet he was significantly ahead of the nearly 50 percent of English adult males who were illiterate in the 1750s. As an adult, Asbury was a voracious reader, eventually learning to read some Greek, Latin, and Hebrew. Once in America, he would write thousands of letters and keep a journal for more than forty years.[9]

Asbury left few hints as to how he spent his free time growing up. He does say that as a boy, "my foible was the ordinary foible of children—fondness for play," and that "many" of his Sabbaths were "idly spent, which might have been better improved." He also "abhorred fighting and quarrelling: when anything of this sort happened, I always went home displeased." Perhaps he was one of those boys who habitually spent Sundays playing football in the streets, like his future friend George Shadford, who became a Methodist at about the same time as Asbury. One Sunday the minister of Shadford's Lincolnshire parish chased him and his friends "near a quarter of a mile" when he spied them playing football. It did no good. "I was fond of wrestling, running, leaping, football, dancing, and such like sports; and I gloried in them," Shadford later recalled. The lack of conviction with which Asbury and Shadford condemned their childhood fun suggests that these were mostly pleasant memories. Only after their conversions did they, like many of their generation, come to see play as a waste of time.[10]

Early accounts agree that Asbury was apprenticed to a local metalworker, either John Griffin or Thomas Foxall. Joseph Reeves, who wrote a local history of West Bromwich in the 1830s, believed that Asbury was "bound an apprentice to John Griffin," whose "trade was chape filing." A chape is a metal loop that is used to attach a buckle to a belt or two pieces of metal together. Griffin's shop was only about 40 yards from the Asburys' cottage. Most other sources claim that Asbury was apprenticed to Thomas Foxall, a Methodist who had recently returned to the West Midlands from Monmouthshire in South Wales. If his apprenticeship was under Foxall, Asbury may have learned to slit iron or make "buckle chapes" and "tongues." Slitting involved taking bars of iron, rolling them into sheets and then slitting the sheets into rods that could be used to make nails or other items. Old Forge Mill, where Foxall was a foreman, was located about two miles from the Asburys' cottage on the Earl of Dartmouth's Sandwell estate.[11] The evidence for Griffin is stronger, but Asbury may have worked for several masters, including Griffin and Foxall. In a journal entry from July 1774, Asbury wrote that at age sixteen he was living in "an ungodly family." In another entry he wrote that during his apprenticeship, "I enjoyed great liberty, and in the family was treated more like a son or an equal than an apprentice," which suggests a different setting.[12]

In any event, as a young man Asbury was caught up in the social and economic changes sweeping through the West Midlands. As an apprentice, he entered a world of small artisans, a workshop culture that required flexibility and innovation for success, a society on the cusp of rapid expansion and sweeping change. It was exactly the kind of environment that the Church of England had lost touch with and in which Methodism flourished. The goods that Asbury helped to produce were aimed at an expanding consumer market. West Midlands manufacturers had a keen eye for what would sell. Asbury would later apply this same market sense to the American religious landscape. Having seen a consumer revolution in material goods, he was better prepared to appreciate a consumer revolution in spiritual ideas, exactly what he would encounter in America. The years he spent as an apprentice left an indelible mark on him. In a sense, he never really left the workshop culture of the mid-eighteenth-century Black Country.

Birmingham shops produced a dizzying variety of goods made by bashing metal into seemingly endless shapes. Buttons, buckles, coins, jewelry, nails and so on were made using variations on the same processes: stamping, pressing, grinding, and slitting. Some jobs were highly specialized, requiring years to master. Others were more rudimentary, allowing for skills in one process to be transferred to another. By the eighteenth century, Birmingham was fast becoming the iron working center of England, and its growth was at the heart of the early Industrial Revolution. Historians have long debated the impact and meaning of the Industrial Revolution. While not a single, discrete event, it nonetheless represented a "great discontinuity." Its pace varied across eighteenth-century Britain, with change clustering unevenly across time and space. Partly as a result, the population of England grew rapidly after about 1750, acquiring a more youthful age structure. In 1700 the English population stood at about five million. It was still only about 5.7 million in 1750, but grew to more than 8.5 million by 1800. There was much continuity to English life, but it was also clear to those who lived through this period that England was changing in profound ways before their eyes.[13]

The West Midlands was central to this transformation. The handmade nail trade of the area went back to medieval times, and nail-making remained an industrial mainstay of the Black Country until the nineteenth century. Nail-making was technically simple and relatively easy to learn. Many nail smiths were farmers who made nails part-time to supplement their income. As consumer demand increased, the metalworking industry of the area expanded to include a great number of specialty products. Buttons and buckles (used mostly for shoes) were two of the most important of these consumer products. In 1746, West Bromwich was described as "a large and extensive Parish, and exceeding populous, by reason of the Iron Manufacture which flourishes greatly there, owing to the vast coal mines in the parishes contiguous thereto." As the district's trade grew, it expanded to include London, America, and Europe in a global network. Home markets accounted for the bulk of this expansion, but exports also ballooned. Ships left almost weekly from Bristol, the region's main port, for the American market carrying nails, buckles, and other metal wares produced in the West Midlands.[14]

The work in these new industries could be hard, but it was also surprisingly varied. The vast majority of the West Midland's manufacturing was done on what by later nineteenth-century standards would seem like a very small scale. It wasn't characterized by the "dark satanic mills" of the nineteenth-century cotton textile industry. If anything, the industrialization of this period led to splintering rather than monopoly. Dozens of small manufacturers vied with one another for competitive advantage in an environment that required flexibility and a willingness to adapt. Writing in 1776, Adam Smith noted that Birmingham dealt chiefly in "manufactures for which the demand arises altogether from fashion and fancy."[15] Much the same could be said for nearby villages, including Wolverhampton, Willenhall, Walsall, and West Bromwich. Though the items they produced might fall out of fashion suddenly, producing them generally brought comparatively higher wages. Not surprisingly, the quality of such goods varied enormously. London producers often complained that Birmingham goods were inferior in quality, and many viewed Birmingham's rapid development and freewheeling manufacturing style with distaste. A ballad from this period describes "Old Jemmy":

> Old Jemmy is the top
>> And chief among the princes;
> No mobile gay fop
>> With Birmingham pretences.

Nonetheless, Birmingham area producers gained a reputation for innovation and creativity, leading Edmund Burke to describe Birmingham in 1777 as "the Great Toy Shop of Europe."[16]

Most biographies describe Asbury as a blacksmith's apprentice during his youth, rather than a metalworker caught up in the Birmingham region's rapidly evolving economy. This makes him seem more rustic, and more like the small-scale artisans so common in rural America at the time. But it is also largely inaccurate and unnecessary. Post-revolutionary America had few industrial centers like Birmingham, but it was hardly stagnant. Booming population growth and rapid geographic expansion led to dynamic social change in America, if on a smaller local scale. Where England's expansion was more concentrated and intensive, America's was more diffuse and extensive. Having seen the one, Asbury was psychologically prepared for the other.

From his family's home in Great Barr, Asbury could see both the past and the future. Pack trains regularly passed by the brewery and the Asburys' cottage from the iron and coal fields of Wednesbury, Darlaston and Walsall on their way to Birmingham and the mills along the Tame River. A single train could be forty horses long. The coal they carried sold locally for two shillings a ton but brought ten shillings in Birmingham. Canals were just being built when Asbury left Great Barr, with the first connecting Wednesbury and Birmingham in 1769. These would make the pack horse trains obsolete, isolating Great Barr and dramatically changing life there (another reason why biographers who visited the area in the nineteenth century might have misunderstood the nature of Asbury's apprenticeship). Gone would be the rowdy teamsters and their money. But during Asbury's early years no one could see this coming. What they could see was that the region was expanding dramatically, relentlessly sweeping away older patterns of living.[17]

As a metalworker's apprentice and the son of a common laborer, Asbury understood the lives of working people. Once in America, he established a close bond with American Methodists, the vast majority of whom came from the lower and middling ranks of society. This was particularly true of the preachers, almost all of whom had been farmers, schoolteachers, blacksmiths, shoemakers, carpenters, and artisans of other kinds before turning to preaching. They were accustomed to frequent moves and shifting employment opportunities. Almost none attended college or came from families of more than moderate wealth. The formal education of most was limited to a few years of common school.[18] Small wonder that they accepted Asbury. He was one of them. He understood their outlook on life, their financial worries, their ability to deal with physical hardship and shifting markets, the hopes that drove them forward, the fears that held them back. Once in America, Asbury never owned a home, sleeping for more than forty years in the homes of Methodist believers. He felt at peace in their small cottages, and they knew it.

There was another side to growing up in Great Barr. Despite its semi-rural setting, it was a rough neighborhood. In 1802, Asbury remembered Great Barr as "that dark place of my nativity." The quality of life varied considerably in the newly industrializing areas of England, and the West Midlands was no exception. The new economy brought new opportunities, but also substantial risks. Wages were often inadequate, housing poor, and child labor common.[19] Traveling through Great Barr in 1741 on his way from Walsall to Birmingham, William Hutton passed by a number of metalworking shops in which he saw "one, or more females, stript of their upper garments, and not overcharged with their lower, wielding the hammer with all the grace of the sex." Taken aback, Hutton asked if these women "with smutty faces, thundering at the anvil" shod horses, but was told that they were all "nailers." Asbury would have seen all this (he may have made nails himself), and the constant traffic of drovers passing by his home, or stopping at the Malt Shovel pub for drinks, gambling, and gaming. Wednesbury and the surrounding villages were nationally known for cockfighting and other cruel sports. There was much that

Asbury could take from his upbringing, but there was much that he could leave behind.[20]

Conversion

The roots of Asbury's religious beliefs go back to the death of his sister. Sarah's death in May 1749 at the age of six was a severe blow to Eliza Asbury. Sarah was her mother's "favourite," Asbury later recalled, "and my dear mother being very affectionate, sunk into deep distress at the loss of a darling child, from which she was not relieved for many years." Eliza descended into "in a very dark, dark, dark day and place," suffering from serious depression for years after Sarah's death. Though he says nothing about his father's reaction, the impact on the family must have been severe. Is this when his father began to drink or run into problems at work? Perhaps Asbury's decision never to marry and have children was rooted in these events. George Roberts, an American Methodist preacher who knew Asbury later in life, believed that he came from a small family, since "I never heard him speak of any but his mother." Though Joseph lived until Francis was fifty-two, Roberts was under the impression that Eliza had been "left a widow" when Francis was "very young." Whatever the effect on Joseph, Sarah's death drove Eliza to search for deeper spiritual meaning in life. "She now began to read almost constantly when leisure presented the oppor-tunity," Asbury recalled. "When a child, I thought it strange my mother should stand by a large window poring over a book for hours together."[21]

Sometime during this period the family almost lost Frank. Joseph Asbury stored gardening tools—"long shears, prooning saws, hoes, rakes"—in a room "attached" to the side of the family's cottage. Immediately above the tools there was a hole in the floor of a second story room. One day when Frank was "very young," he got into the upper room and fell through the hole. Joseph heard him cry and called to Eliza, who rushed to see what had happened. Fortunately, the gardening tools had recently been moved and replaced by "a large boiler nearly filled with ashes," which broke the child's fall. Joseph and Eliza remem-bered this near tragedy for years, passing the story on to Frank, who continued to retell it to the end of his life. He interpreted it as an example of God's providence, but it also helps explain why Eliza held on so tightly, to the point of driving him away later in life. In her mind, Sarah's death and Frank's accident must have seemed connected. After losing Sarah, she had been given a second chance with Frank.[22]

Methodism was at the center of Eliza's spiritual awakening. John and Charles Wesley first preached near Wednesbury (less than three miles from

St. Mary's Church, Handsworth, where Sarah Asbury is buried (Photo by the author.)

the Asburys' cottage) in 1742 and 1743, winning followers and stirring up
opposition. The vicar of Wednesbury, Mr. Eggington, was initially sympathetic
to the Wesleys, but by April 1743 "his former love was turned into bitter
hatred," according to John Wesley. The same was true of Mr. Rann, the curate
of West Bromwich, who while "very drunk" rode his horse through an audience
as Wesley preached. In May and June mobs attacked the homes of Methodists,
throwing bricks and breaking windows. When John Wesley returned in October 1743, a mob showed up at night and dragged him, sometimes "catching me
by the hair," as Wesley put it, from Wednesbury to Walsall and back in a "heavy
rain," yelling, "Knock his brains out." It was five hours before Wesley escaped
unharmed. He believed that he had been protected by his guardian angel, but
his brother Charles more pragmatically concluded that "many blows he escaped" because he was so short.[23]

An event like this would have been the talk of the surrounding villages for
weeks and couldn't have escaped the Asburys' notice. Over the next several
months, dozens of Methodists were beaten, had their windows broken, belong-
ings destroyed or looted, and houses pulled down by rioters. One Methodist

family whose house was destroyed by a mob in 1743 at nearby Aldridge, the Aults, moved to Great Barr, near the Asburys, soon after losing their home. The Aults' son, Thomas, was the same age as Frank, and the two became friends (like his father, Thomas became a shoemaker). All told, Wesley's followers suffered more than £500 in damages, a huge sum considering that skilled West Midlands workers usually earned no more than £30 to £40 a year and agricultural workers about half that. The movement nevertheless continued to attract followers, Eliza Asbury among them.[24]

Eliza soon gained a reputation for seeking out anyone in the area with evangelical inclinations. Asbury recalled that as a boy, he was "much ridiculed, and called *Methodist Parson*, because my mother invited any people who had the appearance of religion to her house." Eliza's spiritual hunger was more intense than Joseph's, and she was more central to Frank's spiritual development. This was a common pattern with evangelical groups of the time. Women often joined first and in larger numbers, later bringing their fathers and brothers, husbands and sons into the faith.

Elizabeth Asbury (c. 1790). (From *The Ladies Repository*, vol. 27 [1867]).

Asbury's religious convictions grew along with his mother's and were reinforced in his home. "I learned from my parents a certain form of words for prayer," he later wrote, "and I well remember my mother strongly urged my father to family reading and prayer; the singing of psalms was much practiced by them both." As a young boy at school he "had serious thoughts, and a particular sense of the being of a God; and greatly feared both an oath and a lie." These religious impressions found little support among his school-mates, whom he remembered as "amongst the vilest of the vile for lying, swearing, fighting, and whatever else boys of their age and evil habits were likely to be guilty of: from such society I very often returned home uneasy and melancholy." At age twelve, "the Spirit of God strove frequently and powerfully with me: but being deprived of proper means and exposed to bad company, no effectual impressions were left on my mind." Soon afterward Asbury left school. Once free of peer pressure, his religious life developed at a quicker pace.[25]

At age thirteen, shortly before he entered his apprenticeship, Asbury recorded that "God sent a pious man, not a Methodist, into our neighborhood." Asbury later told the American preacher John Wesley Bond, his last traveling companion, that this man was "a traveling shoemaker, who called himself a Baptist, and professed to be converted. He held prayer meetings in our neigh-borhood, and my Mother, who was a praying woman, and ready to encourage any one who appeared to wish to do good; invited him to hold a prayer-meeting at My Father's house. At that meeting I was convinced there was some thing more in religion than I had ever been acquainted with." He began "to pray morning and evening" and soon grew dissatisfied with the preaching at St. Margaret's, the parish church of Great Barr. He then went to All Saints, the parish church of West Bromwich, where the vicar, Edward Stillingfleet, had created a Methodist haven with the support of the Earl of Dartmouth. At All Saints Asbury heard a number of Church of England clergymen whose broadly evangelical views supported early Methodism, including John Ryland, John Mansfield, Henry Venn, William Talbot, and Thomas Haweis. Under their influence, he began to read "every good book I could meet with," including the sermons of George Whitefield. He remembered this some forty years later when he passed within sight of Whitefield's tomb in Massachusetts. "His sermons established me in the doctrines of the Gospel more than anything I ever heard or had read at that time; so that I was remarkably prepared to meet reproach and persecution."[26]

As Asbury's spiritual curiosity grew, his mother directed him to a Method-ist meeting at Wednesbury where he heard John Fletcher, the vicar of Madeley parish church (located 20 miles northwest of Wednesbury) and one of Wesley's

All Saints' Church, West Bromwich, where Asbury heard Methodist-style preaching. (Photo by the author.)

closest partners among the Anglican clergy, and Benjamin Ingham, one of the early Oxford Methodists who had accompanied the Wesleys to Georgia in 1735. Like many who joined the early Methodist movement, what struck Asbury most about this meeting wasn't the content of the sermons, but the zeal of the preachers and their listeners. He later recalled that he "did not understand" much of what Fletcher and Ingham preached, but the devotion of the people more than made up for this. "I soon found this was not the Church—but it was better," Asbury remembered. "The people were so devout—men and women kneeling down—saying *Amen*. Now, behold! they were singing hymns—sweet sound! Why, strange to tell! the preacher had no prayer-book, and yet he prayed wonderfully! What was more extraordinary, the man took his text, and had no sermon-book: thought I, this is wonderful indeed! It is certainly a strange way, but the best way. He talked about confidence, assurance, &c.—of which all my flights and hopes fell short."[27]

Asbury wasn't alone in his response to Methodist preaching. George Shadford, whose early career paralleled Asbury's and with whom Asbury formed a close friendship in America, first heard a Methodist sermon in Gainsborough, in the north of England, within a year or two of Asbury's awakening. Shadford and a friend had gone to a meeting not "with a design of getting any good for our souls," but to meet two young women. But the preacher's opening extemporaneous prayer was like nothing Shadford had ever heard, and he was hooked. After prayer, the preacher "took his little Bible out of his pocket, read over his text, and put it into his pocket again. I marvelled at this, and thought within myself, 'Will he preach without a book too?'" Sure enough, the preacher "began immediately to open the Scriptures ... in such a light as I had never heard before." Shadford knew that the preacher didn't have a university education, but "something struck" him nonetheless. "This is the gift of God," he concluded. What most impressed him was that the preacher "spoke very closely" about the kinds of sins that Shadford was most ashamed of in his own life. The sermon had a relevance that he hadn't expected. "If this be Methodist preaching, I will come again," he thought. "For I received more light from that single sermon, than from all that ever I heard in my life before." That night he "thought no more about the girls whom I went to meet."[28]

Like Shadford, Asbury now embarked on an intense search for the assurance of salvation. With a friend, he attended another meeting at Wednesbury at which the preacher's text was "the time will come, when they will not endure sound doctrine." Asbury's companion was "cut to the heart," but Asbury remained "unmoved." "I was exceedingly grieved that I could not weep like him; yet I knew myself to be in a state of unbelief." Soon after, when Asbury was about fifteen, Alexander Mather, then about age twenty-seven, was stationed in Staffordshire, where his preaching brought about a revival. Mather had an "iron constitution," allowing him to travel and preach for forty-three years, one of Wesley's most indefatigable preachers. Asbury was moved by his zeal, but not yet converted. Though "the word of God soon made deep impressions on my heart," he struggled for months over the meaning of salvation. Once, while praying in his father's barn with some friends, he "believed the Lord pardoned my sins and justified my soul; but my companions reasoned me out of this belief, saying 'Mr. Mather said a believer was as happy as if he was in heaven,'" something Asbury couldn't claim. Shortly thereafter, however, he came to believe that Christ had "graciously justified my guilty soul through faith in his precious blood."[29]

In its basic outline, Asbury's conversion was classically evangelical. Three decades later he could still vividly recall this train of events; it became the cornerstone of his life. Perhaps he later exaggerated the wonder of his first contact with the Methodists or the intensity of his search for salvation, but the basic structure of his story would have been recognizable to all early Methodists, who had passed through a similar set of experiences. Had their hearts burned when they first heard zealous prayer and passionate, extemporaneous preaching? So had his. Had they struggled under the weight of their sins? So had he. Had they found forgiveness and assurance in Christ? So had he. This common set of experiences provided a crucial bond between Asbury and other early Methodists, in England and America.[30]

Asbury's spiritual journey didn't end with conversion. In typically Wesleyan fashion it served as a gateway, and in following months he was deeply impressed with "the excellency and necessity of holiness." Methodist theology was Arminian in the sense that John Wesley rejected predestination (that God ordained some for eternal life, and others for eternal damnation) and the concept of a limited atonement (that Christ died only for the elect). But Wesley also maintained that humans are completely incapable of reaching out to God on their own apart from God's enabling, or prevenient, grace, a gift given to each person, enabling them to choose between eternal life and eternal damnation. For Wesley, salvation thus became a cooperative effort with God, a relationship that had to be worked out on a daily basis. Wesley saw conversion as a vocation, not a one-time event. It was possible for believers to go on to greater holiness, or to turn from God and lose their salvation.[31]

This sense of faith as a dynamic process led to Wesley's most original and controversial doctrine, "Christian perfection" or "sanctification." Wesley believed that Christians could grow in holiness to the point that they were "freed from evil thoughts and evil tempers," and hence were "saved in this world from all sin, [and] from all unrighteousness." Believers could move beyond conversion to Christian perfection, by which Wesley meant "the humble, gentle, patient love of God, and our neighbour, ruling our tempers, words, and actions." He recognized, of course, that even Christians could never be completely perfect. They would still make "mistakes," and suffer from "ignorance," "infirmities," and "temptations"; "such perfection belongeth not to this life," Wesley noted. Yet faith that stopped at the point of conversion was no faith at all. Like conversion, Wesley believed that sanctification was based on "a simple act of faith," and therefore could be an instantaneous event occurring at almost any point in a believer's life. It nevertheless usually involved a gradual process in which the believer passed through "stages" of increasing holiness. Practical experience taught Wesley that few, if any, attained true and lasting sanctification until just before death. So why did he continue to preach and insist that sanctification could be instantaneous? Wesley's theology always had a pragmatic slant to it, and "constant experience," had shown him that "the more earnestly they [believers] expect this [instantaneous sanctification], the more swiftly and steadily does the gradual work of God go on in their souls." Without the prospect of instantaneous sanctification, believers might become lazy, no longer striving to become progressively more holy, reasoning that they could achieve all the holiness they needed just before death. In doing so, they might even end up losing their salvation. "They are *saved by hope*; by this hope of a total change," Wesley wrote. "Therefore, whoever would advance the gradual change in believers, should strongly insist upon the instantaneous."[32]

Some months after his conversion Asbury experienced sanctification or something very close to it. He wrote that at "about sixteen I experienced a marvellous display of the grace of God, which some might think was full sanctification, and [I] was indeed very happy." The elliptical nature of this passage ("some might think") reflects the Wesleyan notion that all spiritual accomplishments needed to be treated with caution since they might be lost at some future time. Spiritual pride was a sin, and certainly not compatible with the sanctified life. Indeed, soon after "the Lord showed me, in the heat of youth and youthful blood, the evil of my heart: for a short time I enjoyed, as I thought, the pure and perfect love of God; but this happy frame did not long continue, although at seasons, I was greatly blessed." What exactly the "evil of my heart" amounted to Asbury doesn't say. Such vicissitudes of faith were common, almost expected, among early Methodists. Given the responsibility that each person bore for his or her own salvation, how could it be otherwise? Wesley's Arminian theology gave believers control over their spiritual destinies, but at a price. Self examination could never cease until the moment of death. Too much was at stake to give oneself the benefit of the doubt.[33]

Asbury's involvement in the faith deepened as he internalized Methodist doctrines and attended meetings. He developed the habit of walking to Wednesbury every Sunday morning with Thomas Ault and three or four other young men for the early morning Methodist preaching service. They then walked about two miles to All Saints Church in West Bromwich to attend another morning service and one in the afternoon, returning again to Wednesbury for the evening Methodist meeting.[34]

Why did Asbury become such a zealous follower of Wesley? In many respects he was a typical Methodist, responding for the same reasons that so many others did. As in America, English Methodism grew fastest on the peripheries of society, gaining the most of any religious group from the expansion of the English population and economy between 1750 and 1850. English

Methodism was the most successful where large landowners and resident clergy no longer held sway. It grew rapidly in industrial villages, mining and canal communities, seaports, and market towns, particularly where there was a mobile labor force. In places like the West Midlands, the Anglican Church failed to keep pace with the needs of an expanding population and shifting cultural patterns. Conversely, Anglicanism remained strongest in the agricultural low-lands of southern and eastern England where more traditional village life still predominated. Throughout the late eighteenth century Methodists were over-represented among artisans and skilled workers, and underrepresented among rural laborers and tenant farmers. As in America, English Methodism made little impact on unskilled workers. In short, Methodism attracted adherents primarily from social groups in transition. These were the people who most felt the impact of industrialization and the rapid social change sweeping through English society, and for whom the Church of England often failed to provide direct, meaningful spiritual care.[35]

Asbury was one of these people. He came from an area experiencing sweeping economic change and rapid expansion. While his father was a gardener, Asbury learned a new, industrial trade. His apprenticeship seems to have been a fairly good experience, but he was ambitious to do something more. Methodism offered a way to a better future, in this world and the next. It certainly seemed more attuned to the realities of his life than the Church of England, for which he ultimately retained little loyalty. All of these factors contributed to Asbury's attraction to Methodism, but don't fully explain it. He also became a Methodist for intensely personal reasons, centering around those closest to him, the members of his family. His sister's death and his mother's crisis of faith were pivotal in drawing him into the faith. And then there was the inner voice awakened in his heart, beginning a long conversation with God that would last the rest of his life. In the end, religious motivations are always this way, a complex mixture of influences that are by no means clear at the time and equally difficult to sort out later.

2

The Young Preacher

At about age sixteen Asbury "began to read and pray" in public meetings and a year and a half later to "exhort and preach." "We met for reading and prayer, and had large and good meetings, and were much persecuted, until the persons at whose houses we held them were afraid, and they were discontinued," he writes. "I then held meetings frequently at my father's house, exhorting the people there, as also at Sutton Coalfield, and several souls professed to find peace through my labours" (Sutton Coalfield was about four miles east of Great Barr). Most Methodists weren't the kind of people who could attend university, and Wesley didn't require his preachers to have a formal theological education. Instead, they learned on the job, by speaking in prayer meetings and to crowds gathered outdoors. Most of these meetings took place in the homes of believers, where numbers were limited by the size of the house. The main downstairs room of the Asburys' cottage couldn't have comfortably seated more than about two dozen people.[1]

Asbury also attended a class meeting at West Bromwich and joined a band at Wednesbury. These were small groups designed to foster discipline and communal fellowship. The more exclusive of the two, the bands, were modeled after the Moravian bands, which Wesley encountered during his short (and disappointing) mission to Georgia in the 1730s, and later in London. Over time, class meetings largely displaced the bands, becoming the basic building block of Methodism in England and America. Methodists themselves referred to class meetings as the "soul" or "sinews" of Methodism. Class meetings were patterned after the bands and contemporary religious societies in the Church of England, with a Methodist twist. Wesley was in Bristol in February 1742 where local Methodists were looking for a way to retire the debt incurred to build a new meeting room. To accomplish this, a Captain Foy suggested that each member give a penny a week. When someone objected that some members were too poor for even this, Foy proposed assigning ten or twelve of these who lived close to one another to him. Each week he would collect what they could give, making up the balance himself. Others made the same offer, and Wesley divided the Bristol society under these leaders.[2]

No sooner had this system been put in place than Wesley realized that it could be used for more than just fund-raising. One of the Bristol leaders told Wesley that while making his rounds he found a man quarreling with his wife and another member drunk. "This is the thing, the very thing we have wanted so long," Wesley thought. "The *leaders* are the persons who may not only receive the contributions, but also watch over the souls of their brethren." Soon leaders began meeting with their charges as a group each week. The class meeting provided the close nurturing that itinerant preaching couldn't. Wesley introduced the Bristol system in London and thereafter wherever Methodism spread. "It can scarce be conceived what advantages have been reaped from this little prudential regulation," Wesley exulted. "Many now happily experienced that Christian fellowship of which they had not so much as an idea before. They began to 'bear one another's burdens,' and 'naturally' to 'care for each other.'"[3]

The bands were intended for those seeking a higher level of commitment. While all Methodists were required to attend a class meeting, joining a band was voluntary. The only qualification for joining a class meeting on probation (which usually lasted three to six months) was a desire to seek salvation. To remain in a class, one only had to profess a continued desire for holiness. Bands demanded something more. They assumed that members were already converted (justified) and were seeking sanctification. Band members ideally held nothing back, drawing together "as close as possible, that we should cut to the quick, and search" one another's hearts "to the bottom." Bands were segregated according to age, sex, and marital status, with five to ten members in each. Classes were divided more pragmatically. They were originally supposed to include about twelve members each, a size Wesley thought best to promote "intimate acquaintance," though almost from the beginning they exceeded this size. Classes were sometimes segregated by sex where there were enough members to do so, but often they weren't. Over time, the distinction between the two meetings became imprecise and classes largely replaced bands. But in the 1760s both were still in operation.[4]

Methodists realized that only by replacing one community with another could they bring about lasting change. They couldn't simply demand that believers give up popular recreations and pastimes. Bands and class meetings replaced the alehouse (like the one Asbury grew up next to) while public preaching and eventually (in America) camp meetings took the place of fairs and dances.

Some of the "diversions" Methodists opposed seemed innocent enough, including playing cards, quoits, or the game pitch and toss at the pub, or ninepins and smock races for women at parish feasts. But these were often mixed with more brutal sports—boxing, cudgeling (fighting with sticks in which the object was to "fetch blood" from an opponent's head), dogfighting, cockfighting, and bull and badger baiting (in which the animal was tied to a short stake and attacked by dogs)—all accompanied by drinking and gambling on the outcome. At feasts and dances sexual proprieties were also relaxed, and ordinary people were tempted to spend more than they could afford on fashionable clothes. To make matters worse, much of this was done on the Sabbath. "All such diversions as these are the noblest instruments the devil has to fill you with earthly, sensual, devilish passions; to make you of a light and trifling spirit, and, in a word, lovers of pleasure more than lovers of God," Wesley proclaimed in a sermon on "Public Diversions." These kinds of activities made men in particular "throw away, for an idle sport abroad, what your wife and family want at home." As late as 1784 the annual conference of Methodist preachers advised that "none of our brethren make any wake or feast, neither go to any on Sunday; but bear a public testimony against them." Methodist opposition to brutal sports, particularly in manufacturing districts, helps explain some of the violence they in turn faced. Popular recreations were under attack from a variety of reformers in the second half of the eighteenth century, but since Methodists themselves were primarily working people their involvement must have been particularly galling. It is one thing to be criticized by outsiders, quite another to feel betrayed from within one's own community.[5]

Joining a band and a class deepened Asbury's involvement in the culture of the movement. Several early accounts indicate that he was the leader of the class at West Bromwich.[6] If so, what would his duties have involved? Of all the official positions in Methodism, class leaders had the most sustained contact with members. They nurtured and monitored the faith of those under their care primarily through the weekly meeting, which usually began about 8 p.m. with only members and perhaps a few invited guests. Meetings began with a hymn and an extemporaneous prayer focusing on the concerns of those present. After prayer the group would sit (early Methodists always knelt to pray), and the leader would offer a confession of his or her own spiritual condition, of how he or she had fared during the week. According to one early account, the leader would then "inquire into the state of every soul present; saying, 'Well sister, or well brother, how do you find the state of *your* soul this evening?'" Each member would then proceed "without rising, to unbosom his or her mind to the leader; not, as has often been said, by particular confession, but by a general recapitulation of what has passed in the mind during the week." Since all Methodists attended a class meeting, leaders had to be prepared to deal with a range of commitment and experience, offering counsel or encouragement as might seem appropriate. Class meetings were pivotal to the success of the Methodist system, and Asbury's commitment to them never wavered in England or America.[7]

Besides conducting the weekly meeting, class leaders kept attendance records, collected and recorded contributions, visited sick and delinquent members, and kept the circuit preachers informed about the character and status of each member. It was no accident that financial offerings continued to be collected at class meetings. This was thoroughly consistent with Wesleyan theology, which rooted all spirituality in a community context. Methodists gave in front of those who knew them best, and their money went to pay the circuit preacher's allowance and for other local needs, like the Bristol meeting room.[8]

Wesley was always suspicious of the consumer revolution taking shape in the eighteenth century, and his economic teaching was hardly a model for acquisitive capitalism. He never ceased to warn Methodists against the evil of stockpiling wealth. They were to work diligently within the bounds of the law, regarding their labor as a divine calling. The object of their financial ambitions ought to be charity, not luxury. They should provide for their families "plain, cheap, wholesome food, which most promotes health both of body and mind" and whatever else is "needful for life and godliness," and then "fix [their] purpose to 'gain no more.'" Laying up treasures on earth "our Lord as flatly forbids as murder and adultery."[9]

Wesley mostly practiced what he preached, but a growing number of his followers didn't. Methodist discipline gave them the tools they needed to gain a measure of financial success, but they proved reluctant to give it away. As early as 1765, Wesley was complaining that "many Methodists" had grown "*rich*, and thereby *lovers* of the present *world*." In a 1784 sermon, he lamented that "of all temptations none so struck at the whole work of God as 'the deceitfulness of riches.'" Too many were "indulging 'the pride of life,'" and "seeking the honour that cometh of men." "They *gain all they can*, honestly and conscientiously. They *save all they can*, by cutting off all needless expense, by adding frugality to diligence. And so far all is right. This is the duty of everyone that fears God. But they do not *give all they can*; without which they must needs grow more and more earthly-minded." In short, because of their unwillingness to detach themselves from the world around them, many lost their spiritual edge. Even the traveling preachers usually only remained in the itinerancy for a few years before returning to their former trades.[10]

Not Asbury. While others wavered from the full implications of Wesley's economic teachings, Asbury never did. He stuck to the patterns he learned early in his preaching career for the remainder of his life. Any attempt to understand Asbury's later lifestyle must begin with an appreciation for his lasting commitment to Wesleyan standards of piety and discipline. To a greater extent than even Wesley himself, Asbury gave away almost all that he acquired. Throughout his career, he held to Wesley's ideas about the value of hard work, frugality, and sacrificial giving. Once in America, Asbury had little difficulty accepting the ideology of hard work that was so much a part of post-revolutionary America, though, like Wesley, he railed against the evils of accumulating wealth.

While still working as an apprentice Asbury also became a local preacher. Only regularly appointed itinerant preachers were paid for their services, but since their circuits were large, they usually only visited each appointment a few times a month. In their absence the Methodist system leaned heavily on unpaid local preachers. Even thirty years later, this was the moment in his career that Asbury was most proud of, the point at which he found his life's calling. The life of a Methodist preacher was exciting in a way that his apprenticeship wasn't. It combined high purpose (the eternal fate of souls) with the chance to travel and lead. "Behold me now a local preacher!—the humble and willing servant of any and of every preacher that called on me by night or by day; being ready, with hasty steps, to go far and wide to do good, visiting Derbyshire, Staffordshire, Warwickshire, Worcestershire, and indeed almost every place within my reach, for the sake of precious souls." So as not to neglect his duties at the forge, he asked his mother to wake him at 4 a.m. "that I might finish my days work time enough to attend my meetings, which were some times from three to five miles distant." Some of these meetings kept him out until midnight, but he still got up early the next morning. "This I would do four or five nights in the week, besides holding meetings at three or four different places on the sabbath days." He walked to each meeting since he had no horse.[11]

Asbury remained a local preacher for about three years before, in 1766, at age twenty, he took the place of the traveling preacher assigned to the Staffordshire circuit. He had served six and a half years of his metalworking apprenticeship, apparently satisfying his obligations to his master. Like all new itinerant preachers, Asbury had to learn how to manage his new responsibilities. On the ground, Methodism was remarkably decentralized and flexible.

Every Methodist preacher was familiar with Wesley's injunction that "it is not your business to preach so many times, and to take care of this or that Society: but...to bring as many sinners as you possibly can to Repentance, and...to build them up in that Holiness, without which they cannot see the Lord." Methodist culture demanded individual initiative. Though itinerants were expected to stay within the bounds of their circuits and keep appointments made by their superiors, they seldom made exactly the same circuit twice, exercising a good deal of freedom in choosing where they would preach, omitting places where they met with an indifferent reception and adding others that seemed more promising. This system made the most of the energies of young preachers, but it inevitably invited a fair share of rash decisions and misunderstandings.[12]

Even as a twenty-year-old interim itinerant, Asbury internalized this dimension of Methodism. He had been on his first circuit only a matter of weeks before he got crossways with William Orp, Wesley's assistant (or supervising preacher) on the Staffordshire circuit. In May 1766, Orp directed Asbury to keep two preaching appointments, but Asbury decided this could best be done by another preacher, leaving him free to preach elsewhere. "Dear Frank," an exasperated Orp wrote on May 23:

> After haveing so firmly engag'd you to supply Hampton and Billbrook at the end of the Week; I cou'd not but be surpriz'd to hear you are turn'd Dictator. Certainly you must either *think* I was not *able* to see the Places properly supply'd or else that I am fickle and inconstant, and therefore you expect to hear my *new* Mind. I take this Opportunity of informing you, that I shall not be at those Places, and shall expect you to see them supply'd in due time. It is true another Preacher is come, but he goes immediately into the low Round...You have lost enough already by *gazing all around*, for Gods sake do so no more.

Yet it was better to have preachers who erred on the side of initiative than ones who were timid. Orp's letter ends on a conciliatory note: "I Wish I coud see you on your return from Hampton on Sunday Evening. I shall be at Wednesbury if it please God. I have a little concern to mention. I hope you'll call."[13] In the end Orp was satisfied enough with Asbury's performance as a substitute on the Staffordshire circuit to recommend him for a regular appointment the following year.

In August 1767, Asbury joined Wesley's traveling connection on trial (a probationary period for new preachers), becoming one of 104 itinerant preachers serving twenty-six thousand members on forty-one circuits in England, Scotland and Ireland. He was assigned to the Bedfordshire circuit, located about a day's ride north of London and about 70 miles from his parents' home. Bedfordshire was a sprawling, rural circuit where Methodists had faced violent opposition, encompassing about a thousand square miles spread across Bedfordshire and five adjacent counties. Completing a round of the circuit probably took six weeks and included stops at a number of small societies with diverse origins. The society at Bedford had Moravian roots, while the one at Northampton 20 miles to the northwest, was started by a Calvinistic Methodist. There were also societies at Whittlebury and Towcester, 20 miles west of Bedford, at Luton, 20 miles south on the road to London, and at a number of other small villages. While the Moravians attracted the gentry, professionals, farmers, and tradesmen, the Methodists were mostly artisans and laborers, the majority young people and women.[14]

If Asbury had any doubts about preaching, the Bedfordshire circuit provided him with ample reasons to quit. Encouraged by local landowners, mobs at times assailed Methodist preachers on the circuit. At Luton, a preacher was "hit on the head with a dead cat." At Bedford, where meetings were held "in a room above a pig sty" (an unfortunate choice to begin with), the nephew of one of the members took to feeding the pigs during preaching in hopes that the squealing and grunting would drive the people out, according to Jonathan Rodell. Perhaps of greatest concern to Asbury, the spiritual energy of the circuit was ebbing, having reached its height some years before. During Asbury's year on the circuit, membership fell from 208 to 170. When John Wesley toured the circuit in November 1766 and October 1767 (he makes no mention of Asbury) he found some "lively" societies, but the people at Bedford appeared "drowsy" and "heavy." It couldn't have been an encouraging beginning, but Asbury persevered with a resiliency that would characterize his entire career. He was determined to be a Methodist preacher.[15]

Method

To understand Asbury one must understand Wesley's expectations for his preachers. For the remainder of his life, Asbury held firmly to the core of Wesley's instructions concerning the disciplined life of devotion, study, and service. It was a system, a method, that he never abandoned.

Much was required of Methodist preachers. First, they were expected to cultivate an inner spiritual life of intense devotion and discipline. "Be diligent," advised Wesley. "Never be unemployed a moment. Never be triflingly employed. Never while away time: neither spend any more time at any place than is strictly necessary." This was the first rule given to preachers and one that Wesley often repeated. Lest their status go to their heads, Wesley also warned his preachers not to "affect the gentleman. You have no more to do with this character, than with that of a dancing-master. A preacher of the Gospel, is the servant of all." They were to rise at four a.m. on days they preached at five a.m., and by five a.m. on all other days. In the morning and again in the evening they were to spend an hour in prayer, meditation, and reading the Bible and other books. They were also encouraged to fast on Fridays, and to avoid listening to or spreading gossip, or indeed talking too much on any topic. Lest they fall into sexual sin, Wesley advised his preachers to "converse sparingly and cautiously with women: particularly with young women in private." He also urged them to "take no step toward marriage, without first acquainting us with your design."[16]

As part of a disciplined life, Wesley directed his preachers not to use snuff or tobacco, drink "drams," or fall into debt. He also cautioned them to be temperate in their diet. "Do you take no more food than is necessary at each meal?" asked Wesley. "You may know if you do, by a load at your stomach: by drowsiness, or heaviness: and, in a while, by weak or bad nerves."[17]

After seeing to their spiritual balance, Wesley expected his preachers to become progressively better educated. Beyond the minimum amount of reading that could be squeezed into the morning and evening hour of prayer, meditation, and study, Wesley urged preachers to spend "at least five hours" a day reading "the *most useful* books." Along with the Bible, these included Wesley's own works, beginning with his published sermons and notes on the New Testament, and devotional classics such as Wesley's abridgement of Thomas a Kempis's *The Imitation of Christ*. To those who complained "I have *no taste* for reading," Wesley replied, "contract a taste for it by use, or return to your trade."[18] Of course, few Methodist preachers could match Wesley's educational background or his intellectual abilities, but many nevertheless took his advice to heart, spending much of what little spare time they had reading. Many dramatically improved their literacy after becoming traveling preachers, allowing them to record their experiences in letters, journals, and autobiographies, and inspiring them to open schools designed to pass on Wesley's educational legacy. Among these was Asbury.

A third area of responsibility was public ministry. Above all else preachers were to preach the gospel and save souls. "You have nothing to do, but to save souls. Therefore spend and be spent in this work," Wesley declared. This command even took precedence over his advice about reading. "Gaining knowledge is a good thing, but saving souls is a better," Wesley counseled. "If you can do but one, either follow your studies or instruct the ignorant; let your studies alone. I would throw by all the libraries in the world, rather than be guilty of the perdition of one soul." Lest this give an excuse to the lazy, Wesley was quick to add that a preacher's normal duties would leave "abundant time" for study, especially in the early morning hours. "Only sleep not more than you need; talk not more than you need. And never be idle, or triflingly employed."[19]

Time and again Wesley admonished his preachers to do more field preaching (preaching outdoors in public places), and not to neglect preaching at 5 a.m. when they could get at least twenty listeners. Preachers were to be "punctual," never disappointing a congregation by not showing up. They were to guard against formality by preaching Christ-centered sermons that were "close, convincing, searching." But Wesley was also convinced that preaching alone would never make most Methodists holy. He therefore urged preachers to regularly visit members in their homes. "We must instruct them *from house to house*; till this is done, and that in good earnest, the Methodists will be little better than other people." Ideally, these visits would include individual counseling sessions with all the members of the family, including the children. "The sum is; Go into *every house* in course, and teach *every one* therein, young and old; if they belong to us, to be Christians, inwardly and outwardly." As if all of this wasn't enough, preachers had to travel from one appointment to another, meet the classes and bands at each stop, appoint stewards and class leaders, visit the sick, mediate disputes, handle disciplinary cases, and so on and so on.[20]

Wesley clearly required much of his preachers. The regimen of devotion, study, and service he demanded wasn't for the faint of heart. Doubtless, many Methodist preachers failed to live up to Wesley's expectations; the fact that he frequently felt it necessary to restate these rules at the annual conferences (and print them in the conference minutes) indicates as much. But Asbury seems to have made every effort to abide by Wesley's design. Methodist discipline gave Asbury an arena in which he could excel. He could never be well-educated, rich, or politically powerful, but he could be zealously pious and disciplined.

Full Connection

In August 1768, Asbury was admitted into full connection, or conference membership, and assigned to the Colchester circuit on the east coast of England, more than 100 miles from his home. He didn't stay long. On October 26, 1768, he wrote to his parents that he had been transferred to Wiltshire, nearly 100 miles south of Birmingham. Elizabeth Asbury wasn't happy having her son so far from home, but Asbury reminded her that it was her duty to accept God's will. "I hope My Dear Mother You are more Easy[.] why will you morn in Such a manner[?] If you have given Me to the Lord Let it be a free will offering, and dont grieve for me." He often felt the need to repeat this admonition to his mother, who had a hard time letting go of her only surviving child. Perhaps it was in part her overprotectiveness that drove him ever farther from home.[21]

If it was her duty to let go, then it was his to take up his calling in spite of his own limitations. "I have Cause to be thankfull that Such a poor Ignorant foolish Unfaithfull unfruitfull Creature Should be [called to] the work, Chosen of man and [I] hope and trust of god[,] tho I have Don Enough to boath to Cast Me oof for Ever," Asbury wrote in the same letter. "I wonder Some times how anyone will Sit to hear me[,] but the Lord Covers my weakness with his power." This kind of humility was typical, almost expected, of early Methodists, but there was probably a measure of truth in it nonetheless. Even later in life he was never a compelling public speaker.[22]

Asbury's October 1768 letter continues with notes to several people who lived near his parents. The first was Nancy Brookes. He had learned that Brookes was upset with him for not stopping to see her on a recent trip home and tried to explain himself. His time had been short, and he had stopped at her house, but she hadn't been home. "I could [have] been as glad of your Company as any one at barr[,] and wanted it but could not have it[,] but my Dear heart[,] I Shall think no more off it if you Dont[,] tho it gave me Some Little paine," Asbury wrote. Perhaps there was a romantic connection between the two that later fell through. According to one account, it was Asbury's mother who intervened to break off the relationship between Brookes and her son. It may have been Brookes that Asbury had in mind when, in 1784, he wrote to his parents that one reason he had never married was "what once befell me in England." "My dear heart" certainly sounds romantic, but given the sentimental language of the day it is a stretch to connect the two as lovers. Something (someone) "befell" Asbury while a young man in England, but whether or not it was Nancy Brookes is unclear.[23]

Following his note to Brookes, Asbury adds one to his father. "Have you Victory Over Sin and that wich has in time past most Easley bes[e]t you[?]" he asks. Here again is the suggestion that Joseph Asbury was subject to some kind of habitual failing, perhaps drinking (the most common vice of the day).[24]

In August 1769, Asbury was sent back to the Bedfordshire circuit, though he seems to have spent more of the year in Northamptonshire than Bedfordshire, possibly based in Towcester. That same year, Wesley sent Richard Boardman and Joseph Pilmore (also spelled Pilmoor) as his first official missionaries to America. The year on the Bedfordshire circuit wasn't easy for Asbury. His mother was still upset that he was so far from home. He tried to ease some of her fears in November 1769, writing that he was "Sorry that you Should be So troubled on my account Seeing I am in health, and in the Lords work." As the year wore on, things became more difficult. "I dispare almost of holding out to the end, when I think of the difficulties I have to wade thro," Asbury wrote to his parents in July 1770. "I can say with Job, I would not Live alway. or, oh that thou wouldst hide me in the Grave. or with Jonah, tis better for me to die than to Live. oh the peaceable dead are set free. the bliss that I covet, they have." In part this passage reflects the dramatic language of eighteenth-century Methodism. All of life was a struggle to overcome; for the righteous, death was a welcome release from conflict. But it also reveals a deeper level of frustration. "At this time I am in trying circumstances about the people and places; but some times I please myself that I shall go hence and leave these parts," Asbury added. Whatever his problems were, the solution wasn't to return home, but to press farther afield, which was a thoroughly Methodist response.[25]

At the August 1770 conference, Asbury was appointed to the Wiltshire circuit, where he had briefly been stationed two years earlier. Two preachers were usually assigned to each circuit, and in this case Asbury's senior partner was John Catermole, who was "much addicted to melancholy," according to a history of the circuit written in 1826. "After going twice round the circuit [he] retired from the itinerant work," leaving Asbury alone. Conflicts on the circuit, particularly in the Portsmouth society, probably had much to do with Catermole's decision. After his departure, Asbury's "firmness to the rules of Methodism and presence of mind in apparent internal broils were put to the test." Part of the problem was William Norman, the steward at Portsmouth, who was so heavy-handed in his administration of the society that "neither preacher nor people could bear" it. At the same time, local Methodists were faced with violence at the hands of "the lower orders of the people." Asbury managed to replace Norman with another steward, restoring a measure of peace to the society, but not before a good deal of wrangling.[26]

These were the kinds of problems that drove many young circuit riders from the ministry. Imagine a young man of twenty-five (Asbury's age at the time), far from home and alone on a new circuit, having to take on a local leader like Norman, while at the same time being liable to have dead cats and rotten produce hurled at him during preaching. And Portsmouth was only one of the circuit's appointments. In all likelihood there were similar problems at other places. After a while it was all simply too much for most young preachers. The majority left the itinerancy after a few years, usually to marry and return to their trade. Asbury was part of a minority who seemed to thrive on the challenges of the itinerant life, always pushing on in search of a deeper spiritual experience.

So it was that he arrived at the yearly conference in Bristol in August 1771, the only English annual conference he ever attended. One of the matters taken up at this conference was the growing need for preachers in America. American

Methodism had been expanding for several years, with societies established in Maryland by Robert Strawbridge, who had preached in Ireland before emigrating to America about 1760, and in New York by Barbara Heck and her cousin Philip Embury, a carpenter and sometime schoolmaster who had immigrated with a band of fellow Methodists from Ireland, also about 1760. Embury didn't start preaching in New York until the fall of 1766, when, according to tradition, Heck roused his conscience after discovering some of her fellow immigrants playing cards. After sweeping the cards into her apron and throwing them into the fire, she went to Embury's home and implored him to begin preaching. Once he did, a Methodist community quickly took shape. In April 1768, Thomas Taylor, who had come to New York from England the year before, wrote to Wesley informing him that New York Methodists had formed a society under the preaching of Embury and Captain Thomas Webb (a retired British officer who sometimes preached in his uniform), recently agreeing to buy a town lot for £600 to build a chapel. By 1770, Wesley had appointed four preachers to America: Joseph Pilmore, Richard Boardman, Robert Williams and John King. The colonies clearly held tremendous potential for expansion, and American Methodists were anxious for more preachers. Wesley responded by calling for volunteers at the 1771 Bristol meeting who were "willing to go over and help them." He chose two of the five volunteers: Francis Asbury and Richard Wright. Both were young; Wright had only joined the itinerancy the year before.[27]

Sending Asbury made sense. Most of the available preachers were young, and America, though a promising field, was still on the periphery of the English and Methodist worlds. Asbury was both dependable and expendable. He had proven that he had the toughness and resourcefulness needed to deal with difficult circumstances, but wasn't important enough to warrant keeping in England. Asbury's reasons for volunteering are also understandable. He had just finished a difficult year on the Wiltshire circuit with little reason to suppose that his next assignment in England would be any easier. None of them had been so far. Returning home could hardly have seemed like much of a choice, since it would have meant abandoning his call to preach and subjecting himself to an overly protective mother and an embarrassing father. And if there had ever really been anything with Nancy Brookes it was over. A stint in America might be just the thing to hone his spiritual life and give direction to his preaching. Certainly it didn't seem frivolous. The need for gospel preaching in America appeared genuine and substantial.

With this in mind, Asbury found himself bound for the colonies in August 1771 at the age of twenty-six. He first returned home to say a difficult goodbye to his parents and to make a farewell preaching tour. At their final parting, his father, whom Asbury had seldom, "if ever," seen weep, was "overwhelmed with tears," crying out, "I shall never see him again," even though Asbury only expected to be gone a few years. Parting from his mother was even worse. At the last moment he thrust on her his only valuable possession, a silver watch. True to his father's prophecy, he never saw either of his parents again.[28]

They weren't the only ones skeptical of his going to America. "We can scarce believe he is so mad," wrote four Methodist women from nearby Whitchurch to Elizabeth as soon as they heard that her son had left. Were you "willing to part with him, and he willing to part from you?" the women asked. "We think it must be an Instance of much Trouble to both, for indeed we was very much Grieved when we heard Mr. Asbury was going there [to America]." Elizabeth's anxiety was evident to everyone who knew her. "I have often thought of you since the Conference, on account of Frankey's going to America, which must have been an heavy Trial to you, as you have no other Child," wrote a friend from London in 1772.[29]

After saying his goodbyes Asbury arrived in the port city of Bristol without "one penny of money." Local Methodists supplied him with clothes and £10 to see him through the crossing and his first days in America. Together with Richard Wright, he sailed from the small port of Pill, near Bristol, for Philadelphia on September 4, 1771. For the first three days he was "very ill with the seasickness; and no sickness I ever knew was equal to it."[30]

Once accustomed to life at sea, Asbury sat down with his journal to evaluate the mission he had embarked on. His own motivations seemed pure. Was he going "to gain honour?" "No, if I know my own heart. To get money? No: I am going to live to God, and to bring others so to do." Like any good Methodist, Asbury acknowledged that he might fail; if so, "I will soon return to England. I know my views are upright now; may they never be otherwise." This was more a guard against pride than a sign of wavering. Confident of his own motivations, Asbury was also confident that America needed Methodism. He believed that the Friends (Quakers) and Presbyterians had carried on the "work of God" there in the past, but their spirituality had since "declined." Not so the Methodists: "the doctrine they preach, and the discipline they enforce, are, I believe, the purest of any people now in the world."[31] This was, of course, a drastic oversimplification of the situation, but it was also typically Methodist. Wesley's emphasis on human agency and responsibility created a culture in which ordinary Methodists saw themselves as actors in a cosmic drama. Though the son of a gardener and a metalworker's apprentice with little formal education, Asbury believed that he could play an important role in the spiritual destiny of America, if he only remained faithful. As it turns out, he was right.

3

The Promise of Discipline

Philadelphia was bustling when Asbury arrived on October 27, 1771, after a voyage of seven and a half weeks. He was part of a large migration to the colonies following the end, in 1763, of the Seven Years' War (called the French and Indian War in America). The population of the mainland colonies had been growing rapidly for most of the eighteenth century, rising from 1.2 million in 1750 to 2.2 million in 1770 and spreading to the foothills of the Appalachian Mountains. Life expectancy in the seventeenth-century South had been shockingly low, with most immigrants failing to reach the age of forty. This changed in the eighteenth century as life expectancy and family size in the South increased to levels comparable to the North. The end of the war saw a new wave of immigration, with more than 125,000 English, Scottish, and Irish immigrants arriving between 1763 and 1775, the greatest influx from the British Isles during any twelve-year period of the colonial era. Added to this mix were another 84,500 slaves and 12,000 German-speaking immigrants. In all, more than 220,000 Europeans and Africans landed in America between 1760 and 1775, according to Bernard Bailyn. The majority of these immigrants were, like Asbury, single young men.[1]

Alongside this growth, America was experiencing an extension of the consumer revolution Asbury had witnessed in England. Rising prosperity led to generally improved living standards for most Americans. As a result of improved diet, American men were two to three inches taller than their English counterparts on average, and

Americans increasingly built larger houses and produced better furniture and other goods. They also imported more. England's exports to North America increased eightfold from 1700 to 1773, rising 43 percent in the five years from 1768 to 1772 alone. This "empire of goods" fueled the rise of a new consumer culture in America. Common people yearned for an increasing array of new products while the wealthy began to develop genteel sensibilities largely absent in the colonies before.[2] The mid-eighteenth century also saw a "price-revolution" in which the cost of food, energy, and just about everything else increased substantially on a global scale, creating both instability and opportunity.[3] The America that greeted Asbury in 1771 was a noisy, growing society, exactly the kind of environment in which Methodism had done well in England. America was new to Asbury, but not shockingly so.

Asbury faced two immediate challenges. The first was how to deal with a lack of discipline in Philadelphia and New York, Methodism's centers in the North. The second was how to connect with an indigenous form of Methodism in the South, under the leadership of part-time Irish and English preachers and a group of young Americans. Both issues went to the heart of Methodist identity.

First came Philadelphia and New York. After spending about a week in Philadelphia where he preached at St. George's, the most impressive Methodist church in America at the time, Asbury made his way to New York City.[4] There he discovered that Joseph Pilmore and Richard Boardman, John Wesley's first official missionaries to America, had largely confined their ministries to Philadelphia and New York City rather than following Wesley's principle of itinerancy. "I remain in New York, though unsatisfied with our being both in town together," Asbury wrote in his journal on November 19, 1771, shortly after joining Boardman. "I have not yet the thing which I seek—a circulation of preachers, to avoid partiality and popularity. However, I am fixed to the Methodist plan." The question of "partiality and popularity" primarily concerned Pilmore, who had cultivated a following of leading Methodists and non-Methodists in both cities. Two days later the same issue still dominated Asbury's thoughts. "My brethren seem unwilling to leave the cities, but I think I shall show them the way. I am in trouble, and more trouble is at hand, for I am determined to make a stand against all partiality."[5]

Pilmore and Boardman had had little contact with the Methodists in the South, who were largely under the leadership of Robert Strawbridge, Robert Williams, and John King, none of whom were recognized in the conference minutes for 1771. Though the three traveled and preached extensively, technically they acted only as local preachers, meaning that they received no regular salary and were supposed to preach only under the direction of the itinerant preachers. But since Pilmore and Boardman knew almost nothing about Methodism south of the Pennsylvania border, they could give little real direction to Methodists there. The movement in America was in danger of fragmenting almost before it began. "I find that the preachers have their friends in the cities, and care not to leave them," Asbury complained.[6]

The problem with Pilmore and Boardman's approach, as Asbury quickly realized, was that most Americans lived on farms or in small villages scattered across what by English standards was a vast landscape. The largest American city, Philadelphia, had a population of only 28,000 when Asbury landed there, and the largest town in the South, Charleston, South Carolina, had a population of only 12,800 in 1776, which still made it America's fourth largest city. If Methodism was to reach large numbers of Americans, it had to move out into the countryside.

Since Pilmore and Boardman were his superiors, there was little that Asbury could do to force them to see things his way. His answer was to set an example, to throw himself into "the work." From November 1771 to March 1772, he preached in the countryside surrounding New York City, mostly in private homes (Methodists had very few meetinghouses as yet), but on occasion in other settings. On November 23, he preached in the courthouse in Westchester, New York. Two weeks later he returned to preach in the courthouse again, "but the noise of the children, and the ill-behaviour of the unhappy, drunken keeper, caused much confusion." Not to be denied, later that day Asbury preached in the upper room of a tavern. A week later he was in New Rochelle, where he delivered sermons in the Anglican church, and in private homes. During the winter of 1771–1772, he visited more than a dozen small settlements in the countryside surrounding New York City.[7]

As he took stock of his new surroundings, Asbury realized that Pilmore had also compromised the basics of Methodist discipline. Pilmore's journal reveals that prior to Asbury's arrival he seldom met the class meetings and apparently didn't require prospective members to join a class, in part to appear more ecumenical. After attending "an excellent Gospel Sermon at the Moravian Chapel" in New York in January 1771, Pilmore noted in his journal that "Sects and Parties are nothing to me, as I heartily love all the lovers of Jesus." Following Wesley's plan, Pilmore attended services at Anglican churches in New York and Philadelphia, but he went further, frequenting Presbyterian, Quaker, and Baptist meetings. He had "a special regard for the Quakers": "my heart is greatly united with many of that Society." In New York, Pilmore attended a Jewish synagogue and in Philadelphia a Roman Catholic chapel. Later, after meeting with "two Catholick Ladies," he wrote, "I find when the word of God really touches the heart, it soon destroys all distinctions of *Parties*, and brings down the loftiness of man to the dust."[8] In these early days, Asbury also regularly attended Anglican services and at times met with Quakers, Presbyterians, and Baptists, sometimes preaching in their buildings. But his ecumenism stopped short of Pilmore's. He wasn't willing to set aside Methodist discipline in the interests of interdenominational harmony or to further his own social connections.

Like most English Methodists, Pilmore came from a humble background. Though few people knew it, he was an illegitimate child. He was born in the village of Fadmoor, Yorkshire, in 1743 to Sarah Pilmore, a Quaker "servant girl." His father was a steward for a neighboring landowner. He initially denied paternity and sued Sarah for defamation and slander, but lost the case. Sarah eventually married another man, but not until Joseph was around eleven. Growing up, Pilmore worked as a farm laborer. He was converted when he was about sixteen by Wesley, and then attended Wesley's Kingswood School near Bristol for three or four years before joining the English connection on trial in 1765 as an itinerant preacher. Pilmore was clearly sensitive to issues of social rank, the product of his own scandalous birth. The decidedly less hierarchical nature of American society allowed him to satisfy his thirst for improvement to a degree that he had never before imagined. He was constantly aware of the social rank of those around him and delighted in recording meals and other meetings with "gentlemen" and "gentlewomen" in his journal. "I love much to converse with people of good sense and pleasing address," he wrote. Preaching in the countryside around Philadelphia in April 1771 hadn't given him as much "satisfaction" as preaching "in the City," he noted in his journal. "My province seems to be where there are many to hear, as I have always the most liberty in great congregations, and among sensible people."[9]

As he tasted the fruits of life among people of "superior rank," Pilmore decided that he and Boardman were too busy to "go much into the country," or even to alternate between New York and Philadelphia. Either appointment would have suited Pilmore; it was the periodic disruption of moving that grated on him. In December 1771, while in Philadelphia, he complained about swapping appointments with Boardman and "wondered much that he [Boardman] should wish to change in the very depth of Winter!" "I find constant changes are upon the whole hurtful in this City, as well as N. York," Pilmore wrote. "At present I have a most delightful prospect of doing good . . . the Churches of Episcopalians, Lutherans, Sweeds, and Presbyterians, are open to me, and vast multitudes attend the word and seem to embrace it. Yet I must go and leave them: Mr. Boardman wants to be here, and I am obliged to submit. This is rather trying." During the trip to New York, Pilmore groused that "several of my select friends," in Philadelphia "were a good deal dissatisfied at the manner in which I was hurried away."[10]

This isn't to say that Pilmore was lazy or insincere. Far from it. He preached several times a week wherever he was, including maintaining the 5:00 a.m. service when weather permitted. He met frequently with members in their homes and took a special interest in meeting with a group of young men in New York. He also met with prisoners in jail, once accompanying a condemned man to the gallows when no other minister would. Pilmore was largely responsible for working out the deeds to St. George's in Philadelphia and Wesley Chapel in New York so that they wouldn't become independent congregations.[11] Still, Pilmore's and Boardman's ideas about itinerancy and discipline were clearly becoming less distinctively Methodist over time, as Asbury immediately realized.

So it is surprising that to some degree Asbury convinced them to change their approach. On April 2, 1772, he went to Philadelphia to meet Boardman, who told Asbury that he planned to make an exploratory tour through New England, while Pilmore headed south through Virginia. Richard Wright was to stay in New York, while Asbury remained in Philadelphia. "With this I was well pleased," Asbury noted.[12]

Little is known of Boardman's northern tour, but Pilmore continued to keep his journal as he ventured south on a truly remarkable year-long journey from Philadelphia to Georgia and back. Most of the time he traveled alone in a small chaise on poor roads, not always knowing what lay ahead. He eventually reached Savannah, Georgia, in February 1773, his farthest point south.[13]

Yet for all the distance he traveled, Pilmore's thinking remained the same. He still took pleasure in being favored by the local gentry wherever he stopped, and reached out to Anglicans and Baptists (the most influential religious groups, along with the Presbyterians, in the South) with little regard for Methodist discipline. Even where his preaching was well received, he made little effort to organize class meetings or societies. "All the Ladies, and almost every Order of People here, are become Proselytes to Methodism; the Church is quite deserted. I dare say there were near three Thousand People to hear Mr. Pilmore on Sunday in the Fields . . . The Women call him *The dear divine Man*," noted a letter from Norfolk published in the *Virginia Gazette* on July 30, 1772. Nevertheless, Pilmore wasn't instrumental in establishing a society in Norfolk.[14]

In Charleston, South Carolina, Pilmore became friends with the pastor of the Particular (or Calvinist) Baptist congregation, Oliver Hart, whom Pilmore described as "not only *sencible*, but truely evangelical, and very devout." He frequently preached in Hart's church. Following one of these sermons, Pilmore wrote that "the Lord gave me wisdom and power to preach the gospel without controversy or medling with particular opinions." His southern tour also didn't really change his attitude toward itinerating. Before leaving the

Portsmouth and Norfolk region on the outward-bound leg of his journey in November 1772, Pilmore wrote that "the longer I stay in these parts, the more I am desired to preach, and have, by far, the greatest success. Frequent changes amongst gospel preachers, may keep up the spirits of some kinds of people, but is never likely to promote the spirit of the Gospel nor increase true religion."[15]

Pilmore's attitude toward African Americans and slavery during his southern tour is also worth considering, both for what it tells us about his conception of the Methodist mission and for what it reveals about how southern Methodists dealt with the question of race and slavery at this early juncture in their history. While in New York and Philadelphia, Pilmore often took note of African Americans at Methodist meetings, expressing concern for their spiritual condition and their condition as slaves. On several occasions he met with the influential abolitionist Daniel Roberdeau, and he must have gotten an earful from his many Quaker friends on the evils of slavery. "How many of these poor Slaves will rise up in judgment against their Masters, and, perhaps, enter into life, while they are shut out," asked Pilmore after preaching a sermon near Aberdeen, Maryland, at the start of his southern tour. Nevertheless, as he made his way south, his concern for the plight of slaves waned. When men were appointed "to stand at the doors to keep all the Negroes out till the white people were got in" before he preached in Norfolk, Virginia, Pilmore didn't object.[16] Whatever his qualms about slavery, once he went south Pilmore gave up commenting on the evils of the system and even used it to his advantage. Like many Methodists who came after him, he concluded that it was impossible to attract white hearers across much of the South (especially the kind of genteel audiences he coveted) while publically challenging the institution of slavery.

With Pilmore away in the South, Asbury continued to expand the scope of his ministry around Philadelphia and New York, eventually reaching into Maryland. In town he preached almost every day, including at 5:00 a.m., often the morning after an evening meeting. Even on days that he didn't preach in the morning, Asbury was usually up by 5:00 a.m. to spend an hour in prayer. He also kept up Pilmore's practice of meeting with condemned prisoners in jail. In April 1772, Asbury met with four men who were sentenced to die in Chester, Pennsylvania. Two weeks later he and John King returned to the jail, where they found the men "penitent; and two of the four obtained peace with God, and seemed very thankful." Asbury "preached with liberty to a great number of people under the jail wall," and, after accompanying the men to the gallows, King preached to "a vast multitude." When the time of execution came, the sheriff used a trick sometimes employed by colonial officials to shock condemned criminals into better behavior without actually killing them. "The executioner pretended to tie them all up, but only tied one, and let the rest fall," Asbury records. Nevertheless, a few months later when Asbury returned to the jail in Chester, he once again found the three men who had earlier escaped execution, this time charged with another crime.[17]

By far the biggest challenge that Asbury faced during this year was enforcing disciplinary standards. Having grown accustomed to the way things were done under Pilmore and Boardman, New York and Philadelphia Methodists resisted Asbury's attempts to tighten standards. On Saturday, April 25, 1772, he preached "with some sharpness" in Philadelphia and that evening "kept the door" (in other words, excluded all but members) before meeting with the society. A few days later he "heard that many were offended at my shutting them out of society meeting, as they had been greatly indulged before. But this does not trouble me. While I stay, the rules must be attended to; and I cannot suffer myself to be guided by half-hearted Methodists."[18] Only by upholding disciplinary standards could Methodists maintain the community cohesion necessary to nurture the radical spirituality that Wesley and Asbury were looking for. This was far different from Pilmore's more generally ecumenical goal, as both sides knew.

After a preaching tour through eastern Pennsylvania and New Jersey, Asbury returned to Philadelphia in June. There, he preached and met the society, "but felt great dryness, and was grieved to see so much conformity to the world, in the article of dress, among our people." A few weeks later he noted that "our congregations here [in Philadelphia] are small. They cannot bear the discipline and doctrine; but this does not move me." It may not have moved Asbury, but it dismayed Pilmore. "O what a change," he wrote in June 1772 while visiting Philadelphia after the start of Asbury's disciplinary campaign. "When I was here before, the great Church [St. George's] would hardly hold the congregation; now it is not near full! Such is the fatal consequence of contending about *opinions* and the minute [details] of *Discipline*—It grieves me to the heart to see the people scattered that we have taken such pains to gather." But Philadelphia was only a small part of Asbury's vision. The conflict only made him "more desirous to leave the city" and venture out into the countryside.[19]

If things were difficult in Philadelphia, they were worse in New York. When Asbury arrived in the city in August 1772 to replace Richard Wright, he discovered that Wright had "been pretty strict in the society," but then before leaving had "ended all with a general love feast; which I think is undoing all he has done."[20] By "general love feast," Asbury meant a love feast open to all who wished to attend, without regard to their standing as members, exactly the sort of thing he hoped to eliminate. Like class meetings, love feasts originated in

England under Wesley and were patterned after a similar Moravian practice. Only those who had passed an examination by the circuit preacher were supposed to attend. Preachers sometimes gave out admission tickets to identify those who had been duly examined. Love feasts included prayer, singing, a collection for the poor, and the eating and drinking of a little bread and water, an imitation of the fellowship of the early saints rather than the sacrament of communion. But the main focus of the gathering was unrehearsed testimonies from those present (men and women) of struggles and triumphs in the faith, of the wondrous work of God in their lives. Love feasts were intended to be the most intimate of Methodist gatherings, where members could unburden themselves without fear of ridicule or embarrassment. There was little chance of this happening, Asbury believed, if the merely curious were allowed to attend. As he delved further into the condition of the society, he "found broken classes, and a disordered society, so that my heart was sunk within me."[21]

Asbury's view of cities in general ran exactly contrary to Pilmore's. Knowing that he could never master the proper social graces, he felt ill at ease among genteel people. Their lifestyle seemed overly self-indulgent, their reserved manners mitigated against openly expressed spiritual fervor. "'Tis one great disadvantage to me I am not polite enough for the people," Asbury wrote to his parents in October 1772 while still in New York. "They deem me fit for the country, but not for the cities; and it is my greater misfortune I cannot, or will not, learn, and they cannot teach me. But as my father and mother were never very polite people, it is not so strange. And as I was not born so, nor educated after this sort, I cannot help it."[22] Asbury's bias against city life had far-reaching consequences for the Methodist movement in America, constantly pushing it into the expanding countryside where most ordinary Americans lived.

But for now Asbury had to deal with circumstances in New York. His answer was to call a meeting of the entire society on Saturday, September 5. On several points Asbury won agreement, including the institution of weekly collections in class meetings and quarterly collections at love feasts. This helped improve the financial condition of the society, which at the time was £1,100 in debt, much of it incurred to build the John Street church (originally called Wesley Chapel).[23] William Lupton and Henry Newton, the society's two trustees, also agreed to meet with Asbury once a week. Unlike most Methodists, both were wealthy. Lupton initially loaned the New York society £30 to build the John Street church; eventually the society owed him £350. Both were also friends of Pilmore's who opposed Asbury's disciplinary measures. Lupton had been the society's treasurer and was physically imposing, "a man of great size," according to one early account. By agreeing to meet weekly with Asbury, the two at least tacitly acknowledged his authority over them, at least for now.

But on other proposals the people voted Asbury down. They rejected his proposal to add a third steward, whom he would have appointed. When he asked, "Ought we not to be more strict with disorderly persons?" Asbury reports that "very little was said in answer to this." When he asked, "Shall we meet the society on Sunday nights?" he records that "this was opposed by some. But I insisted upon its being the best time; and at last it was agreed to for a season." But when he asked "Who will stand at the door?" to keep out nonmembers during these meetings, no one volunteered.[24]

Two things are clear from this episode. The first is the clarity of Asbury's vision. He knew what he wanted to accomplish and saw himself as capable of providing definition and direction to a movement that had drifted from its course. Methodism had given him a sense of himself that went beyond his upbringing as a gardener's son and metalworker's apprentice. His life was testimony to Methodism's transforming power, to its ability to instill a profound sense of significance in the lives of believers. In England he had been known as Frank. In America he went by Francis, which is how he now signed his name.

The John Street Church, New York City, which opened in 1768. (From Abel Stevens, *History of the Methodist Episcopal Church in the United States of America*, vol. 1 [New York: Carlton & Porter, 1867].)

The second is the clumsy way that he went about trying to get what he wanted. He hadn't yet developed the leadership style for which he later became famous. At this point he didn't realize that he was rarely at his best in front of large assemblies, particularly if they were hostile. His insecurities seemed to get the best of him in these settings. To compensate, he became more aggressive and dogmatic, which was unappealing even to sympathetic listeners. Later in his career he instinctively avoided these kinds of confrontations, preferring instead to talk with people individually or in small groups, where he could relax and where his powers of persuasion were universally recognized to be almost irresistible. He needed the give-and-take of conversation to figure out what other people were thinking. In its absence, he tended to assume the worst and responded accordingly. But for now, at age twenty-seven, he wasn't self-aware enough to discern this about himself. But, then, how many twenty-seven-year-olds are?

Opposition to Asbury's new policies understandably continued. On October 6, he confronted Henry Newton for "frequently avoiding to speak to me—absenting himself from the meeting of the leaders—the appearance of dissimulation—opposing our rules—and consulting persons who were not members of our society." The leaders' meetings that Asbury insisted on must have been a trial for all concerned. William Lupton used the October 9 meeting to tell Asbury that he "had already preached the people away," such that "the whole work would be destroyed." Indeed, Asbury's preaching did deteriorate under the pressure. "Losing some of my ideas in preaching, I was ashamed of myself, and pained to see the people waiting to hear what the blunderer had to say," he recorded after preaching in New York soon after this.[25]

Fortunately for Asbury, Wesley had kept up with the situation in America and took his side. On October 10, the day after his confrontation with Lupton, Asbury received two letters that lifted his spirits. The first was from Wesley, "in which he required a strict attention to discipline," and appointed Asbury to succeed Boardman as assistant, or supervisor, of the preachers in America. The second was from Robert Williams, noting that Asbury had been appointed (probably by Boardman before the arrival of Wesley's letter) to spend the winter in Maryland.[26] Asbury had already heard about the revivals taking shape in Virginia and Maryland, and was anxious to see for himself.

Methodism's Other Half

The first 150 miles from New York City were mostly uninspiring. They were also expensive, costing Asbury £3 of his £24 annual salary, since the New York and Philadelphia societies had neglected (refused, really) to give him an allowance for travel expenses. But the farther south he got, the better he liked what he saw. Maryland and Virginia would prove to be the model for Methodist expansion in the years to come. Though Pilmore and Boardman had spent almost all of their time in the North, southern Methodism was already as large as its New York and Philadelphia counterparts. Most of the movement's growth during the 1770s and 1780s would occur in the South. Here there were few friendly connections between the Anglican Church and Methodists. It was also more rural and depended to a greater extent on the efforts of local preachers, exhorters, class leaders, and other lay volunteers. In general, the level of commitment to spiritual discipline was more in line with what Asbury was looking for.[27]

As he crossed the Susquehanna River in northeast Maryland, he entered a region of Methodist influence created largely through the efforts of local preachers and lay leaders that included Robert Strawbridge, Robert Williams, and John King. The most influential of these was Strawbridge, now about age forty, who had been born in County Leitrim, Ireland, to a farm family of modest means. Following his conversion to Methodism, he preached extensively in Ireland before emigrating to America with his wife in about 1760. From his 50-acre farm on Sam's Creek in Frederick County, Maryland, Strawbridge traveled and preached across much of northern Maryland and into Virginia. He established a class meeting and society in his home, building a meetinghouse nearby. Fiery and independent, Strawbridge began baptizing children as early as 1762, though he wasn't ordained. He planted Methodism in dozens of places across the region, including Baltimore and Harford counties and the eastern shore of Maryland, all without a regular salary. When he neglected his crops to preach, sympathetic neighbors pitched in to tend his fields.[28]

A number of early preachers got their start under Strawbridge, including Freeborn Garrettson, who was from an old Maryland family rooted in the Church of England. After Garrettson heard Strawbridge speak, the two spent an evening talking together. Garrettson "left the house with this sentiment— 'I place this among the most agreeable evenings of my life.'" Another of Strawbridge's early converts was Samuel Merryman, a "bigoted high-churchman" of some wealth who heard Strawbridge preach at Pipe Creek. Merryman was astonished at the "wonderful preacher, that could pray and preach without a book" (in other words, pray without a prayer book and preach without reading his sermon). Following his conversion, Merryman invited Strawbridge to preach in his home. Asbury preached at Merryman's shortly after crossing into Maryland and on several subsequent occasions. Indeed, across much of the upper South Asbury was following in Strawbridge's footsteps.[29]

Like Strawbridge, Asbury reacted with indignation to Anglican opposition in the South. In Kent County, Maryland, he was confronted by Robert Reade, an

Anglican priest who had a B.A. from William and Mary College and was ordained a deacon in 1758 in England (there was no Anglican bishop in the colonies to perform ordinations). Reade's parish, St. Paul's in Kent County, had an annual income of £169 in 1767, a sizeable living well beyond the reach of most farmers and artisans.[30] When Reade discovered that Asbury was a Methodist and not an ordained clergyman, "he spoke great, swelling words, and told me he had authority over the people," threatening Asbury with legal action. Asbury refused to back down, asking Reade if he "had authority to bind the consciences of the people." When Reade responded that Asbury only intended to draw people away from the Anglican church and keep them from their work, Asbury asked "if fairs and horse races didn't hinder them" more. Infuriated that Asbury wouldn't recognize his superior status, Reade followed him into the house where he was about to preach "in a great rage." Following Asbury's sermon, Reade went outside and told the people they "did wrong in coming to hear" Asbury, because he "spoke against learning."[31] Here in a nutshell was the conflict between Methodist preachers and Anglican priests in the South. From ministers' points of view, Methodists were unlearned charlatans seeking to break down the basic foundations of church and society. They took people away from their work and challenged the authority of the clergy, which was based largely on their superior education. From the Methodist perspective, Anglican priests were mostly lazy hirelings, too much addicted to the pleasures of this world and too little concerned with the salvation of souls.

Southern preaching was also loud and dramatic in a way that alarmed many, including Pilmore and even John Wesley, but not Asbury. The most vociferous of the British-born preachers was John King. Dust flew as he pounded the pulpit while preaching at St. Paul's Church in Baltimore. "Scream no more, at the peril of your soul," John Wesley wrote to King in July 1775. "Speak as earnestly as you can, but do not scream. Speak with your heart, but with a moderate voice." Pilmore shared Wesley's misgivings about King. When King arrived in Philadelphia in August 1770, Pilmore wrote that "altho he is by no means fit for the City, he is well qualified to do good in the Country." Pilmore also had his reservations about Robert Williams. When the two first met in November 1769, Pilmore noted that Williams's "gifts are but small, yet he may be useful to the Country people." When Williams tried to preach in Norfolk in November 1772, Pilmore claimed that "the people disliked him so that they made a most horrible noise, so that I was obliged to go and sit among them to keep them in order; when they saw me, they were ashamed, and behaved very well the rest of the time." But Williams evidently believed that Pilmore was quenching the spirit, later refusing to preach when Pilmore was present.[32]

Asbury was much more comfortable with the southern Methodist style than Pilmore, even though he wasn't a fiery preacher himself. He didn't seem to think the shouting and crying of southern Methodists excessive. The closest he came to criticizing the preaching style of Strawbridge, Williams, or King was in 1775, when he wrote "John King preached a good and profitable sermon, but long and loud enough."[33] Asbury didn't see southern exuberance as a threat to the vital piety of Methodism. Quite the opposite. Where the disciplinary problems in New York and Philadelphia seemed to threaten the unity and sap the vitality of Methodism, the vociferous preaching of southern Methodists and the emotional energy of their meetings appeared to enhance both. In the end, this was what mattered most.

Conniving at Some Things

Asbury spent much of the next several months shoring up the organizational structure of Maryland Methodism. As he preached his way across the state, he met and "regulated" class meetings wherever he could, examining them to insure that they maintained disciplinary standards. Whenever he could, he formed new classes and bands. As he did so, he learned of a serious problem connected with Robert Strawbridge.

In December 1772, Asbury conducted his first quarterly meeting in the South, on the western shore of Maryland. Quarterly meetings, which met every three months as the name implies, were first introduced in England in 1748 and became a prominent part of the Methodist system by the 1760s. Quarterly meetings gathered the preachers and people from across a circuit for two purposes. The first was to handle the administrative needs of the circuit, including distributing the money collected at class meetings, licensing new exhorters and preachers, and handling difficult disciplinary cases. The second was to provide an opportunity for Methodists from across the circuit to gather together for worship and fellowship. Over time this second, more public aspect became more prominent. Later, quarterly meetings were extended from one to two days to allow for more preaching, singing, and socializing, eventually evolving into the practice in the early 1800s of incorporating camp meetings into the quarterly schedule.[34]

At the Maryland quarterly meeting, Asbury appointed the six preachers present to circuits in eastern and western Maryland, assigning himself to Baltimore. But the central issue before the conference had to do with the sacraments, which Asbury learned that Strawbridge was administering, even though, like all of the other Methodist preachers in America, he wasn't ordained.[35] Strawbridge left no written justification of his actions, but it isn't hard to see why he did it. Unlike in Philadelphia and New York City, Maryland

Methodists often didn't have easy access to the sacraments through the Church of England. To begin with, Anglican ministers in the South usually weren't friendly toward Methodism, as Asbury himself had already learned. Even if they had been, the Anglican Church's presence in the rural South was very thin.

The Anglican Church was strongest in Maryland and Virginia, where there were few vacancies, salaries were substantial, and the prospects for marrying well were good. Salaries averaged £184 in 1767 in Maryland and £100 to £150 in the late 1760s and early 1770s in Virginia. Anglican clergy in the Chesapeake could expect to live like gentlemen. "The clergyman's income permitted most ministers to buy land, livestock, and slaves, to educate their children well, purchase wheels, collect libraries, and silver, mahogany, musical instruments, and other luxuries suggesting a life of comfort," writes one historian of the Maryland and Virginia clergy. But, as another historian of the Anglican clergy in Maryland writes, "if the Church is considered as a body of men charged with responsibility for ministering to the spiritual needs of the laity, rather than a closed organization with personal slots to be filled, it was much less successful." As the population grew, parish sizes increased significantly. In 1712 there had been 1,829 parishioners per Anglican minister in Maryland; by 1775 there were 4,400 parishioners per clergyman. Ministering to so many across the vast distances that parishes typically encompassed would have taxed the endurance of truly zealous ministers, which the gentlemen clergy of the Chesapeake generally were not.[36]

The church's reach was even more limited farther South, especially in North Carolina, where the Anglican establishment was weakest, and where it faced increasing pressure from Presbyterians and Baptists. The irascible and acerbic Charles Woodmason, an Anglican missionary to the Carolina backcountry, complained that, "owing to the Inattention and Indolence of the Clergy," the Church was "being eaten up by Itinerant Teachers, Preachers, and Imposters from New England and Pen[n]sylvania—Baptists, New Lights, Presbyterians, Independents, and an hundred other Sects." These would soon include the Methodists, who agreed with Woodmason's assessment of Anglican weakness, if not with his high church snobbery. While traveling through North Carolina in 1772, Joseph Pilmore, who generally avoided criticizing the Anglican Church, nevertheless described the people as "sheep having no Shepard." The region he traversed on this leg of his journey, Pilmore wrote, "is two hundred miles wide, and is settled near four hundred miles in length from the sea, and the Church established as in England; yet in all this Country there are but eleven Ministers!" Eleven priests for 80,000 square miles is thin indeed. Fewer than a dozen priests remained in North Carolina by 1775, and many vestries ceased functioning. Only five priests stayed during the American Revolution.[37]

Strawbridge saw it as his obligation to provide the sacraments to those who were otherwise cut off from them. While John King remained neutral, Strawbridge "pleaded much" at the quarterly conference for the right to continue doing so, as "did the people, who appeared to be much biased by him," according to Asbury. Asbury tried to hold his ground, telling "them I would not agree to it at that time, and insist[ing] on our abiding by our rules." But his position was undercut by precedents established by Richard Boardman, who "had given them their way at the quarterly meeting held here before." As a result, "I was obliged to connive at some things for the sake of peace," Asbury wrote.[38]

What to do about Strawbridge came up again at the first general conference for all the preachers in America, convened by Thomas Rankin, Wesley's newly arrived head of the American movement, in Philadelphia in July 1773. Under Rankin's direction, the conference called on all Methodists to attend an Anglican Church to receive the sacraments, and urged the preachers "in a particular manner to press the people in Maryland and Virginia to the observance of this minute." Asbury didn't even bother to include this rule in his journal account, realizing that it was only wishful thinking. When the discussion turned to Strawbridge, the minutes stipulated that "every preacher ... is strictly to avoid administering the ordinances of baptism and the Lord's supper." But Asbury added in his journal, "except for Mr. Strawbridge, and he under the particular direction of the assistant."[39]

The following August, Asbury held a quarterly meeting near Baltimore where he read the minutes from the Philadelphia conference "to see if brother Strawbridge would conform." But Strawbridge, who was present, was "inflexible," declaring that he "would not administer the ordinances under our direction at all." As Asbury had guessed, Strawbridge had no intention of relinquishing his authority to a conference that met in Philadelphia, headed by someone (Thomas Rankin) who had never even been to Maryland.[40]

Asbury's loyalty to the Church of England was never as abiding as Wesley's, Pilmore's, or Rankin's, and he had some sympathy for Strawbridge's position. A month before the quarterly conference, Asbury told a Reformed minister that it "did not appear to be my duty to administer the ordinances at *that time*," leaving open the possibility that it might be in the future.[41] Still, at this point Asbury realized that endorsing Strawbridge's practice would fragment the movement and lead to conflict with Wesley. Strawbridge's concerns were local in scope. Asbury saw a bigger picture, but for now Strawbridge's influence over Maryland Methodism was simply too great. Asbury's solution was to compromise enough to keep Strawbridge in the fold, leaving the final outcome for another day.

Discipline

George Shadford and Thomas Rankin had arrived in the spring of 1773, sent by John Wesley to enforce the Methodist system of probationary membership and closed class meetings, love feasts, and society meetings. Wesley wrote to Rankin shortly after his arrival that "there has been good, much good done in America, and would have been abundantly more had Brother Boardman and Pilmoor continued genuine Methodists both in doctrine and discipline. It is your part to supply what was wanting in them. Therefore are you sent." Shadford, who turned thirty-four in 1773, was six years older than Asbury, and the two soon struck up an easy friendship. Both came from artisan backgrounds and had experienced conversion and begun preaching at about the same time. Asbury had joined the itinerancy in 1767, Shadford in 1768. Shadford had a friendly manner and was the most compelling preacher of Wesley's missionaries. "I let you loose, George, on the great continent of America," Wesley wrote to Shadford just before he embarked for the colonies. "Publish your message in the open face of the sun, and do all the good you can."[42]

Rankin proved more difficult, though Asbury was initially glad to turn over leadership of the movement to him, hoping that he would have the clout to deal with recalcitrant leaders in New York and Philadelphia. Rankin, who turned thirty-seven in 1773, was born in Dunbar, Scotland. He was raised in a moderately religious home by a stern father, a brewer by trade, "who was very severe in the government of his children." Rankin later confessed that "my constitutional sin was a proneness to anger when offended." Converted under the preaching of George Whitefield in his late teens, Rankin soon became a devout Methodist. "I now saw the whole economy of Methodism in the most favourable light. The class & band meetings, meeting of the society, body bands, love feasts &c. I saw the great utility of these, and it gave me the utmost pleasure, to conform to every part."[43]

He also came to deeply admire John Wesley, poring over all of Wesley's writings that he could get his hands on. Rankin took his first circuit appointment in 1761, and Wesley soon learned that he could count on him to consistently enforce discipline on preachers and people alike. In 1764 Wesley appointed Rankin to the Cornwall circuit where an "eccentric" preacher named Darney "had preached for years . . . Mr. Wesley, with my brethren, thought I might be able to cure him." Unable to rein Darney in, Rankin dismissed him from the circuit, with Wesley's approval. Discipline was the one thing that Rankin never let slide. Unlike Pilmore, he had few aspirations toward social advancement or ordination in the Church of England and was more at home in the countryside than in Philadelphia or New York. Where Shadford was likeable and easy to get along with, Rankin could be blunt and confrontational. Soon after his arrival in America, Wesley felt it necessary to remind him not to tell the people "continually 'You are dead,' for that will surely make them so." No one ever accused Rankin of excessive charm.[44]

Joseph Pilmore joined Asbury in Philadelphia on June 3, 1773, to welcome Rankin and Shadford to America, though Pilmore had his reservations. These were confirmed the next day as he sat glumly through Shadford's sermon, entitled "True Old Methodism," in which Shadford "seemed to intimate the people had wanted it till now." The weight of Wesley's disapproval had been building on Pilmore for some time, and now it threw him "into such distress, that it presently destroyed my health ... [so] that I was on the very borders of Melancholy, and in the utmost danger of losing my senses."[45]

At the general conference in July 1773, Rankin didn't assign Pilmore and Boardman anywhere, presumably because, as Rankin later wrote, they "were to return to England." Asbury notes that the conference ended with "debates" "relative to the conduct of some who had manifested a desire to abide in the cities, and live like gentleman ... It was also found that money had been

Thomas Rankin (1738–1810). (From Abel Stevens, *History of the Methodist Episcopal Church in the United States of America*, vol. 1 [New York: Carlton & Porter, 1867].)

wasted, improper leaders appointed, and many of our rules broken." The preachers in question could only have been Pilmore and Boardman. They sailed for England in January 1774, where Boardman immediately rejoined the British conference, subsequently preaching in Ireland and London.[46]

Pilmore spent most of the next two years trying to secure ordination in the Church of England. In May 1774, Anglicans and Methodists in Norfolk, Virginia, sent him three documents intended to strengthen his hand with the Bishop of London. These included a petition signed by fifty-seven laymen, some of considerable wealth, urging the bishop to ordain Pilmore and promising to provide him with no less than £70 per year if the bishop did so. Asbury probably knew of this plan as early as March 1774, when he met a Quaker in Maryland who "said it gave him pain to think that Joseph Pilmoor should go home for ordination." But the Virginians' support wasn't enough to win over the bishop. Writing to a friend in Virginia from London in July 1775, Virginian William Lee correctly predicted that "As to Mr. Pilmore, his being reputed a Methodist will be an insuperable bar to his obtaining ordination from the Bishop of London who is a very high Churchman, & very inimical to every sect of Protestants except his own." Pilmore reluctantly returned to the Methodist fold in 1776, accepting an appointment to London.[47]

Pilmore's departure marked a turning point for American Methodism. While not particularly well-suited for evangelizing in cities (as Pilmore correctly perceived), the circuit system established under Asbury and Rankin proved remarkably resilient and flexible, capable of closely following the contours of American territorial expansion. Had Pilmore's vision won out, American Methodism would have drifted toward some form of congregational organization with tighter clerical control, a system that would have favored cities and towns over rural areas. Because the circuit system allowed preachers to spend only a few days a month at any one place, it paradoxically demanded more lay participation. Despite initial opposition from influential lay leaders in New York City and Philadelphia, the sense of direction and definition the movement's rules provided strengthened Methodism's core constituency. The discipline of the class meeting, society, and love feast served to foster the kind of radical spirituality necessary to meet the hardships of building a new religious movement. On this much, Asbury and Rankin agreed. What to do about southern Methodism was another matter.

4

Southern Persuasion

As conflict between the colonies and Great Britain escalated, Asbury increasingly seemed out of place next to Wesley's other licensed itinerants in America. While they continued to see American Methodism as strictly an extension of Wesley's European connection, Asbury accepted that America was culturally different from England, with its own set of needs. Only George Shadford's cultural sensitivity approached Asbury's, particularly in the South. There, Asbury took on the role of mediator between Wesley and American Methodists, relying on an expanding network of personal connections with believers across the region, men and women, some wealthy, most not. They could see that he cared about their concerns and in turn trusted him. This proved crucial in the South, where a uniquely American form of Methodism took shape in the fires of revival. Asbury would spend most of the next ten years in Maryland, Delaware, and Virginia. Along the way he had to contend with sickness, criticism from British colleagues, and continued dissension among northern Methodists. All the while he relentlessly pursued his interior devotional life, without which all else would have been pointless.

After holding a quarterly meeting near Baltimore on August 2, 1773, Asbury continued across northeastern Maryland preaching and checking up on class meetings. Maryland was "the greatest part of the work" in America, he wrote to his parents on September 5, 1773, noting that "we have many Country-Born preachers and Exhorters." Monitoring and licensing these was another of his projects in the

South. Asbury knew that the few full-time preachers in America could never satisfy the need for preaching and nurturing of members. Still, not all of those who wanted to preach or lead were suited for it. A couple of days after licensing two exhorters west of Baltimore, he "was much distressed on account of so few preachers well qualified for the work, and so many who are forward to preach without qualifications." He could only hope that they would improve with time.[1]

Among the many success stories of encouraging gifted young leaders in the South was Philip Gatch. Gatch had grown up in a nominally Anglican home near Baltimore. His parents, "though destitute of experimental religion . . . paid some attention to its restraints and forms," Gatch later remembered. Then, in early 1772, Methodist Nathan Perigo began preaching in Gatch's neighborhood. Gatch had never "witnessed such energy nor heard such expressions in prayer before." He fell under deep conviction, and his "distress became very great." His family feared he "was going beside" himself, and his father forbade him from going to Methodist meetings, declaring "that his house should not hold two religions." Gatch himself had "heard of the Methodists driving some persons mad" and wondered if it was happening to him. As it turned out, he kept his sanity and soon experienced conversion in much the same way that Asbury and countless others had. "I felt the power of God to affect me body and soul. It went through my whole system. I felt like crying aloud. . . . my poor soul was set at liberty. . . . Ere I was aware I was shouting aloud."[2]

Gatch's parents and most of his siblings soon joined the church as well. Feeling an urge to speak in public, Gatch prayed that he would first experience sanctification. This he did in July 1772. Still, "my rebellious heart rose in opposition to the counsels of God," and he resisted the call to preach. Deeply distressed, he became physically sick. While in this "low condition," Gatch "dreamed that I used a certain remedy and recovered." When he awoke, he "told my dream, the remedy was provided, and I at once began to recover."[3]

That fall, Asbury formed a circuit that included Gatch's neighborhood and gave Gatch a copy of Wesley's tract, "Thoughts on Christian Perfection." "I found in Mr. Asbury a friend in whom I could ever after repose the most implicit confidence," Gatch wrote. Under Asbury's and Perigo's encouragement, Gatch began to exhort and then preach. After he preached near Baltimore, a friend asked him to stay and preach again in the afternoon, but Gatch agreed only to exhort since he had already preached the only sermon he knew! At the quarterly meeting near Baltimore in August 1773, Asbury and Rankin sent Gatch to his first circuit appointment in New Jersey. Asbury's encouragement proved crucial in helping Gatch, then only twenty-one, overcome his fear of leaving home for a strange country. "He was well calculated to administer to my condition, for he had left father and mother behind when he came to America," Gatch wrote.[4]

In September 1773, a month after his return to Maryland, Asbury was struck with malaria, a disease that had dogged new immigrants to the Chesapeake region since the early seventeenth century. Asbury had first visited the Chesapeake in the late fall and winter of 1772–1773, when the mosquitoes that carry the malaria-causing parasites are less active, reducing the chance of infection. On this second trip he wasn't so fortunate. Malaria is a reaction of the body to an invasion of parasites transmitted by mosquitoes. By the 1770s malaria was endemic from Georgia as far north as Pennsylvania. It hadn't been common in the Birmingham region of England, and Asbury knew nothing of the disease before traveling to the Chesapeake. Four malaria infections affect humans. Of these, Asbury appears to have had *Plasmodium malariae*, which is characterized by quartan fevers (occurring approximately every seventy-two hours, or every four days, counting the day the fever begins as the first day of each cycle), often accompanied by chills and sweats, anemia, an enlarged spleen, and a relapse in the spring, often several months after the primary attack. The initial rhythmic fever spikes (as high as 106F) usually last for several weeks, as Asbury soon learned. On September 18 he was taken with a fever, and again on the 21st he was "seized with a quartan ague." By the 24th locals had warned him that "this was the day in course for my ague to return," and it did. This was followed by fevers on September 27, October 1, the night of October 3, and October 6, after which Asbury left off keeping his journal for nearly two weeks. Though usually not a killer, malaria is a great debilitator, sapping a person's energy and lowering their ability to resist other diseases. Asbury's experience reflected this. Early in his illness he spent a good deal of time reading and kept up his journal. By the second week of October he couldn't even manage this. On November 4 he could at last report that "my disorder seems to be going off, though I mend but slowly."[5]

During the course of his illness, Asbury took almost no medicines, other than a little hartshorn, or ammonium carbonate, which is used as a source of ammonia in smelling salts and as an expectorant. He had little access to doctors in the South, which is just as good considering what they often did to their patients. For fevers, doctors typically recommended frequent bleeding, purging of the bowels with laxatives such as cream of tartar, and vomiting through the use of emetics such as tartar emetic. Bleeding, purging, and vomiting were thought to relax the tension in the bloodstream, thus restoring its balance with the nervous system. Unfortunately they could also seriously dehydrate an already sick patient. Doctors might also prescribe a blister, applied to a sensitive part of the skin, which was thought to remove poisons or ill humors from the body. In reality, blisters caused a second-degree burn that then became infected; observers mistakenly regarded the resulting discharge of pus as toxins being drawn from the body. The tragedy was that the sicker a patient became, the more aggressively doctors prescribed such treatments. This was the age of heroic medicine, in which it was assumed that a desperate illness called for a desperate remedy. Fortunately, Asbury always had the sense to avoid the most dramatic cures. He did have a blister placed under his ear in early January 1774, but seems to have suffered few other treatments during his illness. Once he reached New York City in June, he began taking emetics.[6]

If he was fortunate to avoid much of the medical treatment available in the South, he was also fortunate to come under the care of Methodist women. As he traveled, Asbury, like all Methodist itinerant preachers, spent most nights in the home of a member or movement sympathizer. These homes were often overseen by widows and women who were more committed to the movement than their husbands, as had been the case with Asbury's own mother. As with nearly all evangelical movements of the eighteenth and nineteenth centuries, women constituted a majority of Methodist adherents, forming the backbone of early Methodism. The journals of the itinerant preachers of this period contain reference after reference to widows and other women who opened their homes to preaching, and afterward provided meals, lodging, and encouragement for the preacher. Many young preachers developed close and long-lasting friendships with older Methodist women. It is difficult to image how the itinerant system could have successfully operated without these sorts of relationships in an era when Methodists owned few meetinghouses and had little money to work with. As late as 1785, the Methodists owned only sixty chapels, while preaching in more than eight hundred places.[7]

Asbury had already formed friendships with a number of women (most older than him) since his arrival in America. Among these was Mary Withey, whom Asbury met in April 1772 during his first journey south to Maryland. A widow, Withey kept the Columbia Hotel in Chester, Pennsylvania, that Asbury claimed "was one of the best houses of entertainment on the continent." (By entertainment Asbury meant good food, comfortable lodging, and wholesome conversation without fiddle playing, dancing, and other more worldly activities.) Over the years, Asbury often stopped in Chester, eventually preaching Mary Withey's funeral sermon in 1810.[8] Other women who figure prominently in his travels from this period include Prudence Gough, Rebecca Ridgely, and the widow Phoebe Bond, at whose home near Fallston, Maryland, Asbury frequently preached during 1772 and 1773. One of Bond's sons, John Wesley Bond, later became Asbury's last traveling companion during the final years of his life. Like nearly all eighteenth-century people, Asbury saw men and women as essentially different from each other. But they could be spiritual equals, which in the Methodist world counted for much. Asbury believed that all believers ought to be actively involved in promoting holiness. No one could sit idly by as the drama of salvation unfolded in the lives of their loved ones and neighbors. Hadn't his mother taken in the preachers who came to her door? Methodism provided a common language and set of experiences that Asbury could share with Methodist women, at least older women with whom there was little sexual tension. With women his own age he was never entirely comfortable.[9]

During the worst of his malaria attack in October 1773, Asbury was fortunate enough to land at the home, near Aberdeen, Maryland, of Josias and Sarah Dallam, who had a reputation for looking after traveling preachers. Sarah, according to another itinerant of this period, was "truly a Moth^r in Israel." For several weeks while Asbury lay sick in bed, Sarah "waited upon me day and night." This care may well have meant the difference between life and death for someone in Asbury's condition, with no family or home of his own, dependent on the hospitality of others. "I shall never forget the kindness, or discharge the obligations I am under, to Mrs. Sarah Dallam," a grateful Asbury wrote in his journal. "God grant, that the same measure which she has meted out to me, may return upon herself and her children." Asbury often visited the Dallams over the years, and after "my once dear" Sarah's death, he visited her grave in 1799 and 1800. Thereafter he only visited the family twice, indicating that it was Sarah he really came to see.[10]

Asbury lay sick in bed for about a third of the final four months of 1773 and continued to suffer from anemia into the spring of 1774, when he apparently suffered the typical spring relapse associated with malaria. Not until April 1774 could he report that "I was able to walk some distance to-day, and believe the Lord is about to restore me to health." During his illness he tried to stay as active as he could, preaching and conducting other business between agues and fevers. When confined to bed, he tried to read or meditate. Disease offered another opportunity to test his spiritual commitment, to measure his willingness to give all in the cause of the gospel. "Lord, ever draw my heart after thee!" he wrote in January 1774. "May I see no beauty in any other object, nor desire anything but thee! My heart longs to be more extensively useful, but is, at the same time, filled with perfect resignation to God in all my affliction."[11]

In May 1774, Asbury packed his saddle bags and set out for Philadelphia, where the second American conference opened on the 25th. The preachers gathered there had much to feel good about. Membership had increased from 1,160 to 2,073 during the year, with most of the gains in the South. The number of full-time preachers assigned to circuits was also up from ten in 1773 to seventeen in 1774. Most of these were southerners who knew Asbury better than Rankin.

Much of the growth in the South occurred despite the opposition of Anglican clergymen like Robert Reade, who had earlier challenged Asbury. Young as they were, Methodist preachers rarely backed down from these encounters. A case in point is William Watters, the first native-born American preacher, who turned twenty-two in October 1773. At one of Watters's appointments the next month on the Kent circuit in Maryland, Samuel Keene, the Anglican rector of St. Luke's Parish in Queen Anne County on Maryland's Eastern Shore, unexpectedly showed up, threatening to sue the owner of the house because it wasn't licensed for preaching. Keene, about forty years old at the time, had been ordained in London in 1760. Undaunted, Watters moved the congregation outdoors and preached there, where the law couldn't prevent him. Watters's text for this occasion was "Seek ye the Lord, while he may be found, call ye upon him while he is near" (Isaiah 55:6). Like all Methodist preachers, Watters preached extemporaneously, without notes. But on this occasion he recorded a synopsis of his message in his journal, one of the few examples we have of what an early Methodist preacher actually said. Speaking with "feeling and liberty," Watters began by "shewing that my text presupposed the greatest loss—The favor and image of God." He then declared "that this loss might now be remedied, and to this end was the exhortation given in the text—Seek ye the Lord while he may be found." "Hear it, O! my friends with inexpressible joy!" Watters exclaimed. "You may all find in the second, what you lost in the first Adam. Call ye upon him while he is near. Gracious encouragement—you need not go far to find the inestimable blessing—the Lord is near—he is at your doors—at your hearts. Call on him and open your hearts by faith, and the Lord will come in this day—this hour—this moment." Here was the essence of the Methodist message: that God was near at hand, that anyone—everyone—might know the joy of salvation this moment.[12]

But such an opportunity also implied responsibility. Watters next "observed the dreadful consequences of neglecting to seek the Lord while he was to be found." He warned his audience that God's "spirit would not always strive with man—that the day of grace would not always last. Call on him therefore while he is near. Before he removes from you his Gospel. . . . Before he gives you up to your own hard hearts, and suffers your consciences to become seared as with an hot iron. Before he swears in his wrath you shall never enter into his rest. Before he gives you up to the devil, to suffer the vengeance of eternal fire."[13] God's offer of redemption wasn't to be trifled with. Once rejected, it might never be reclaimed. Death could come quickly and unexpectedly, as it often did in the eighteenth-century South. This was a message that resonated with the people Watters encountered on the Kent circuit. Presented in words that they could understand, in a setting where they felt comfortable, it offered them the opportunity to seize control of their spiritual lives, to know for certain their eternal destiny.

Watters went out of his way not to offend the Anglican minister any more than necessary, but some of his colleagues weren't so careful. One of these was Abraham Whitworth, at the time one of Asbury's young protégés in the South, who was working the Kent circuit with Watters. Immediately following one of Whitworth's sermons, Samuel Keene, the same Anglican minister who had challenged Watters, stood up and took "great exceptions" to Whitworth's "having preached the knowledge of salvation by the remission of sins." In an attempt to assert his social and religious authority, the minister "informed the congregation, that he had been *so* many years in such an academy, *so* many in such a college—and had studied divinity so many—and been preaching the Gospel so many; yet he knew nothing of his sins being forgiven, or of being converted." Keene, who had a bachelor's and a master's degree from the University of Pennsylvania, also objected that Whitworth was "a young man, without a college education, and that such ought not to be allowed to preach at all." Whitworth didn't back down. While he admitted that "*he* could not boast of *his* learning," he maintained that only those who had been converted and called by God were qualified to preach.[14] This was a critical distinction. Since none of the early Methodist preachers could hope to acquire a college education or the social position that went with it, they had to find another way of validating their ministries. They did so not by ridiculing learning, but by declaring that education alone wasn't enough. God's word could only be understood by those who knew him firsthand. Keene's faith only went half way, according to Whitworth, since he had the knowledge but not the experience of God's saving grace.

To demonstrate this, Whitworth suggested a test of his qualifications and Keene's. As the congregation looked on, he proposed that the "parson might choose him a text any w[h]ere in the Bible, and he would preach from it immediately, and then he would choose one for the parson, which he must preach from, and they should judge which was the best qualified to preach the Gospel, the parson by his learning, or he by the grace of God." According to Watters's account, the idea "was popular, and took with the people, more than many arguments would have done," but Keene refused, excusing himself "by saying it was late in the day." The contest Whitworth proposed would have been more of a challenge for Keene, a gentleman used to reading a prepared text without interference from anyone, than it was for a Methodist itinerant who preached extemporaneously almost every day, often interacting with his audience as he spoke. While Whitworth was willing to have the people judge his calling, Keene relied on his education and social standing. The difference between the two was clear. Methodism offered a faith that was immediate and dramatic, a faith that focused on the individual's ability to choose without requiring deference to another's education or social status. These kinds of encounters shaped Methodist opinions about the Anglican (later Episcopal) church in the South and fueled the revolt against dependence on Anglican clergy for the sacraments.[15]

Despite the movement's growth, there was a growing undercurrent of distrust between Rankin and Asbury. At the Philadelphia conference in May 1774, "the overbearing spirit of a certain person had excited my fears," Asbury wrote, referring to Rankin. "My judgment was stubbornly opposed for a while, and at last submitted to." Over the summer the two exchanged a series of letters that brought Asbury "pain." The problem was Asbury's growing influence over the young southern preachers and his identification with their concerns. By September he had determined to "drop all disputes as far as possible," but the problem wouldn't go away.[16]

Asbury and Rankin were alike in some ways, but it was their differences that now became crucial. Both were firm disciplinarians who preferred the "plain" religion of country people to what they found in Philadelphia and New York. "What trouble do I find by the members of the Society here, and at New York; by not having our discipline inforced from the beginning! This has given me pain, and it is likely to cause more," Rankin wrote while in Philadelphia during the winter of 1773–1774. "The people in this City . . . love a Superficial manner of preaching. There is also a very great unwillingness to bow to the Methodist discipline without which I never expect to See a deep and lasting work among this people." The same was true in New York City, where Rankin was "surprised at the extravagance of dress which I beheld, and in particular among the women." He believed that he had been deceived by "the wonderful accounts I had heard in England" about American Methodism. "I was led to think that there must be some thousands awakened, and joined as members of our societies; but I was now convinced of the real truth." Many previously counted as members were "not closely united to us," he now concluded, sounding very much like Asbury.[17]

Yet if Rankin and Asbury agreed on the value of Methodist discipline and the need to reach out to the countryside, they saw America and American Methodists in fundamentally different ways. Rankin was one of Wesley's insiders for whom the center of the Methodist world would always be in England. The farther one got from John Wesley (figuratively and literally) the farther one got from Methodism. Asbury, on the other hand, had begun to see American Methodism as a separate entity, if still under Wesley's guiding hand. Asbury respected Wesley's teaching, but had never spent more than a few hours with the man himself. Soon Rankin and Asbury would be at loggerheads over "the spirit of the Americans."[18]

Returning to New York City at the end of May 1774, Asbury fell back into the same controversies he had left there nearly two years before. One of his most severe critics this time around was John Chave, the society's collector whom Asbury had appointed in 1772. Chave had earlier written an "unkind and abusive letter" directed at Asbury and was "still exerting all his unfriendly force" against him. Asbury stubbornly held his ground, particularly with regard to the necessity of members attending class meetings. At a Sunday night society meeting on June 21, he "spoke plainly of some who neglected their bands and classes; and informed them that we took people into our societies that we might help them to become entire Christians, and if they willfully neglected those meetings, they thereby withdrew themselves from our care and assistance."[19]

The six months that Asbury spent in New York, from May to November 1774, were difficult. Though it was almost a year since he had contracted malaria, he was still weak and vulnerable to fevers and swelling in his legs, feet, and hands. It didn't help matters that he continued to push himself as a way of measuring his devotion. Between September 1773, when his malarial symptoms first appeared, and July 1774, he managed to preach about three hundred times and ride nearly 2,000 miles. But his pace slowed once he reached New York City. Partly because of frequent illnesses that confined him to the city, a place he never really liked, Asbury engaged in more intro-spective self-examination than he had in the South, as on November 18 when he chided himself for "unguarded and trifling conversation." Earlier, in New York, he complained that "a cloud rested on my mind, which was occasioned by talking and jesting." Here again was his suspicion that laughing and talking too much in conversation with others was one of his worst failings. His love of conversation led, he feared, to "the appearance of levity," or "a degree of cheerfulness bordering on levity," and he fretted over "my disposition to trifle in conversation" and "being too free in conversation with my friends." When in good spirits he could control these impulses, directing them to wholesome purposes, but when stressed, as was now the case, his tongue became too free, or so he thought.[20]

At times, even in New York City, Asbury could feel at least satisfied with himself, as on June 14 when he wrote that "some people, if they felt as I feel at present, would perhaps conclude they were saved from all in dwelling sin," another oblique reference to the possibility that he might be sanctified. Such thoughts were always short-lived, no more so than on this occasion. The next day he was once again "under heavy exercises, and much troubled by manifold temptations." In this case, even Asbury could see that too much introspection was dangerous. "I find it hurtful to pore too much on myself," he added in the same journal entry. "True, I should be daily employed in the duty of self-examination, and strictly attend both to my internal and external conduct; but, at the same time, my soul should steadily fix the eye of faith on the blessed Jesus, my Mediator and Advocate at the right hand of the eternal Father."[21]

One solution to the problem of roiling emotions was to rely on the judgment and advice of other Christians. This, of course, was the rationale behind the Methodist system of class and band meetings, where the more experienced could give advice to those struggling to come to terms with life's many problems. As he struggled to work through his own emotional swings, Asbury urged New York Methodists to take seriously their commitment to these institutions. That this was a problem in New York was driven home to him after he attended a class meeting with "little depth." "It is a great folly to take people into society before they know what they are about," Asbury wrote following this meeting. "What some people take for religion and spiritual life is nothing but the power of the natural passions." The key was to only admit those who were genuinely seeking "*real holiness*." As he met with the bands, Asbury attempted to show "them the impropriety and danger of keeping their thoughts or fears of each other to themselves: this frustrates the design of bands; produces coolness and jealousies towards each other; and is undoubtedly the policy of Satan."[22]

For all his efforts, Asbury was never more than moderately successful in New York and Philadelphia, which only reinforced his conviction that neither city could serve as a model for Methodism in America. On this much Asbury and Rankin agreed. "I do not know that ever I saw two places, so highly favoured with Gospel Ministers, as Philadelphia and New York are; and I never knew two cities, wherein there was so little good done, after so much faithful preaching," Rankin wrote to the Earl of Dartmouth in December 1774. "Except of few Hundreds, it seems to me that a deadly slumber has got hold of the inhabitants in the above cities." The resistance of city Methodists in the North to more structured discipline forced Asbury to turn south, where Methodism was thriving with its own distinctive character.[23]

In December 1774, Asbury went to Philadelphia to change places with Rankin, who was supposed to replace him in New York City, though he didn't immediately do so. As Rankin lingered in Philadelphia, Asbury asked permission to go to Baltimore, but Rankin refused. To have both of them stay in Philadelphia seemed a waste of energy. "What need can there be for two preachers here to preach three times a week to about sixty people?" Asbury wondered. But Rankin wasn't about to let Asbury have his way. It was now clear that Rankin resented Asbury's influence over the younger preachers in the South and questioned his judgment in appointing some of them to preach. By

this time Abraham Whitworth had fallen into heavy drinking and been expelled from the ministry. Rankin blamed Asbury for sending out someone so
unstable, though Asbury claimed that at the time Whitworth's "heart was right
with God." According to Rankin, when he and Asbury met in Philadelphia in
early December 1774, "we talked over different matters respecting the work,
and also removed some little, and foolish misapprehensions, that had taken
place in his mind." Asbury wasn't so sure who was being foolish here. "The
conduct of Mr. Rankin is such as calls for patience," he complained. Left
unchecked, Rankin's disgust with all things American might do serious
harm. "Mr. Rankin keeps driving away at the people, telling them how bad
they are. . . . It is surprising that the people are not out of patience with him,"
Asbury wrote that January.[24]

Rankin could certainly appear aloof and "exceeding rough," according to
the itinerant William Duke, who rode circuits under Rankin's direction from
1774 to 1777. Nicholas Snethen, who never personally knew Rankin, later
remembered older colleagues say that Rankin "was a pattern of neatness and
preciseness in the minutia of manners, and was equally attentive to the
manners of others. Every day his large white wig was carefully adjusted and
powdered, and every particle of dust and down carefully brushed from his
clothes." At one meeting, according to Snethen's sources, Rankin caught "a
young American preacher, sitting in a lolling position at a table with his chair
leaning back." Dismayed, "Mr. Rankin rose, and in the presence of the company, adjusted the chair and the position of the occupant, adding at the same time
a suitable admonition." Even if the story is apocryphal, it illustrates Rankin's
reputation among the American preachers.[25]

At any rate, Rankin now wanted Asbury in Philadelphia where he could keep
an eye on him. Asbury tried to give at least the appearance of compliance. In
January 1775 he wrote to Edward Dromgoole in Kent County, assuring Dromgoole
that he wasn't "offended" with him, as Dromgoole feared. Rather, Asbury had
"dropt writing" because, "my influence and fellowship among the younger preachers [h]as been much suspected, as stirring them up against those the[y] should be
in subjection to." By curtailing his contacts with southern Methodists, Asbury
hoped to mollify Rankin enough to gain a measure of freedom. At the same time,
Rankin began writing to John Wesley urging him to recall Asbury to England.[26]

While conflict with Rankin simmered, Asbury once again fell sick, this
time with ulcers in his throat. For treatment, he first tried "purges, and a
mixture of nitre and fever powder." When this predictably failed to give relief,
he gargled with a mixture of "sage tea, honey, vinegar, and mustard," followed
by "mallows with a fig cut in pieces," and then more gargling with "sage tea,
alum, rose leaves, and sugar loaf." Sage leaves contain a volatile oil that can

produce sweating and act as an astringent, and alum also acts as an astringent. After about a month Asbury was once again well enough to preach.[27]

No sooner had Rankin left for New York on February 22, than Asbury left for Baltimore on the 27th. Crossing into Maryland, he met with an unlikely ally, Robert Strawbridge. Entering "into a free conversation with him," Asbury noted that Strawbridge's "sentiments relative to Mr. Rankin corresponded with mine." If they could agree on little else, at least they could both be thankful that Rankin's reach didn't extend very far south.[28]

In late March 1775, Asbury met in Baltimore with Robert Williams, who told him about the recent revival in Virginia. Asbury had first heard of this a year before when he had been told (probably by William Watters) that crowds there sometimes numbered two or three thousand at Methodist meetings. Now Williams told him of "five or six hundred souls justified by faith, and five or six circuits formed" in Virginia. Anxious to see for himself, Asbury returned to Philadelphia in May and then sailed for Norfolk, Virginia, at the end of the month.[29]

Virginia Fire

The southern revival of 1773 to 1776 is important for two reasons. First, it created a model of Methodist expansion that Asbury and others followed for nearly forty years. Second, it hastened a transition in Asbury's thinking, defining his willingness to accept a more interactive, American version of Methodism, even if it bordered on enthusiasm. Asbury had little to do with creating this awakening; it was already well under way before he could get there. While some of the leading figures in the early stages of the revival later came to regret what they had set in motion, Asbury never looked back.[30]

One of the early leaders of the revival was the Anglican priest Devereux Jarratt, rector of Bath Parish in Dinwiddie County, located in southern Virginia below Petersburg. Forty years old in 1773, Jarratt claimed to come from a humble, artisan background. In reality, his grandfather owned a 1,200-acre plantation in New Kent County, Virginia, and his parents owned a sizeable "plantation" and slaves. Jarratt's marriage to Catherine Claiborne significantly increased his wealth and social standing. Catherine's mother was a Ravenscroft, one of the leading families of southern Virginia, and her father owned one of the largest plantations in Dinwiddie County.[31]

Jarratt's parents were solidly Anglican, teaching him prayers and reading to him from the Bible and Book of Common Prayer to such an extent that other children called Jarratt "parson." Following the deaths of his parents, Jarratt moved in with one of his brothers, where he left off attending church, and his religious convictions all but disappeared. Then, at age twenty, while teaching school, Jarratt experienced conversion under Presbyterian preaching and soon began to prepare for the ministry. Though he saw little life in the Church of England, largely "on account of the loose lives of the Clergy, and their cold and unedifying manner of preaching," Jarratt decided to seek ordination in the Church of England, an understandable decision given his social background and family connections. Following his ordination in London on January 1, 1763, Jarratt returned to Virginia to become the minister of Bath Parish, a position he held for the next thirty-seven years.[32]

Though he chose to become an Anglican priest, Jarratt didn't forget the role that New- Light Presbyterianism had played in his conversion. He turned his parish into a center of evangelical revivalism, a project that earned him the reproach of many of his fellow clergyman, who, according to Jarratt, refused to let him preach in their churches, calling him "an enthusiast, fanatic, visionary, dissenter, Presbyterian, madman, and what not." Despite opposition, even before the arrival of the Methodists Jarratt had formed his own preaching circuit of some 500 or 600 miles, preaching up to 270 times per year. By 1781, Asbury was "persuaded there have been more souls convinced by his [Jarratt's] ministry, than by that of any other man in Virginia." Given all that they had in common, it is little wonder that Jarratt initially welcomed the Methodists, who seemed to share his two primary passions: evangelical religion and faithful adherence to the Church of England.[33]

According to Jarratt, the Methodists joined the Virginia revival when Robert Williams extended his preaching into Sussex and Brunswick counties, immediately south of Dinwiddie County, in 1773. Williams was typical of early Methodist preachers in his social background, preaching style, and ability to connect with common people. Jarratt described him as "a plain, artless, indefatigable preacher of the gospel: he was greatly blessed in detecting the hypocrite, razing false foundations, and stirring believers up to press after a present salvation from the remains of sin." By 1775, the revival in southern Virginia was, in Jarratt's words, "as great as perhaps was ever known, in country places, in so short a time," spreading to Prince George, Lunenburg, Mecklenburg, and Amelia counties. Methodist membership in the region grew from 291 in 1774 to 955 in 1775 to 4,379 in 1776, including nearby circuits in North Carolina. By 1776 more than 60 percent of all American Methodists lived in southern Virginia and North Carolina.[34]

George Shadford arrived on the Brunswick circuit in 1775, quickly becoming the revival's most effective preacher. Though there was "a gracious work of God" in other parts of Virginia and North Carolina, nothing equaled "that which took place in Brunswick circuit, where George Shadford was travelling at the time," according to Jesse Lee, who witnessed the revival himself. Apart from his eloquent preaching, Shadford did two important things that furthered revival ends, both of which were consistent with Asbury's conception of Methodism. First, he embraced the falling, crying, and shouting of worshipers and those under conviction, such that at his meetings "it was quite common for sinners to be seized with a trembling and shaking, and from that to fall down on the floor as if they were dead," according to Lee. Like Asbury, Shadford didn't see this as an end in itself, but as a legitimate indicator of awakening, conviction, and release from sin. Second, Shadford pushed for the continued development of small groups led by the laity, particularly class meetings. When Shadford arrived on the Brunswick circuit, he found many new converts "joined together . . . in a very confused manner. Many of them did not understand the nature of meeting in class; and many of the classes had no leader." A firm believer in Methodist discipline, Shadford set out to organize classes and build Methodist community identity. The results were astonishing, so much so that Jarratt invited Methodists to form classes and societies in his parish, an invitation he would soon regret. Once Asbury reached the revival, he continued

George Shadford (1739–1816), the most eloquent of the preachers John Wesley sent to America. (From Abel Stevens, *History of the Methodist Episcopal Church in the United States of America*, vol. 1 [New York: Carlton & Porter, 1867].)

Shadford's policies despite growing opposition from Rankin to what he saw as the revival's excesses.[35]

Asbury entered Virginia for the first time on May 29, 1775, arriving in Norfolk on a ship from Philadelphia. His first impression was unfavorable, but then Norfolk and Portsmouth had that effect on people. For several years they had been known as a "dry and barren land" among Methodists, and hadn't participated in much of the current revival, which was centered farther west. William Watters, the first native born American itinerant preacher, had found "little satisfaction" among the Methodists in either city three years earlier, judging their "form of religion" to be "very superficial indeed." When Joseph Pilmore had returned to Portsmouth from South Carolina, the first thing he heard was two "well dressed" men "swearing most horridly" on the ferry. Throwing up his hands, he "exclaimed aloud—'Well! If I had been brought to this place blindfolded I should have known I was near Norfolk.'" Asbury's initial assessment was much the same. Discovering that local Methodists "had no regular class meetings," he set out to organize the members into classes, noting that "without discipline we should soon be as a rope of sand."[36]

As had been the case in New York and Philadelphia, some took offense at the new standards. On August 5, 1775, Asbury had a conversation with one of Norfolk's earliest Methodists, who argued that "the people should be kept in society" even "if they did not meet in class." He also "intimated, that, instead of preaching the Gospel," Asbury was simply "exposing their faults." But Asbury held his ground, convinced, like Shadford and Rankin, that a person's spirituality was directly proportional to their commitment to discipline, beginning in the classes and bands. "Well may the kingdom of heaven be compared to a net, which is cast into the sea, and gathereth all, both good and bad," Asbury noted in his journal after meeting the Portsmouth society in October 1775. The preacher's job was to sort the catch, throwing back what wasn't fit to keep. There were twenty-seven in the society when Asbury first arrived, "but I have been obliged to reduce them to fourteen; and this day I put out a woman for excessive drinking . . . No doubt but Satan will use all his endeavours to thrust in some who are unsound and insincere, so that they, by their ungodly conduct, may help him to bring reproach on the spiritual Church of Christ. And unless the discipline of the church is enforced, what sincere person would ever join a society, amongst whom they saw ungodliness connived at?" The Virginia revival would bear out the effectiveness of these measures.[37]

In late October 1775 Asbury headed south to the Brunswick circuit and the heart of the revival. At the time, Brunswick embraced fourteen counties in southern Virginia and two in North Carolina. "God is at work in this part of the country; and my soul catches the holy fire already," he wrote as he entered this region. More than seven hundred people attended a two-day quarterly meeting led by Asbury and Shadford in early November. Though camp meetings weren't invented for another twenty-five years, multi-day quarterly meetings essentially served the same purpose, bringing together Methodists and the curious from across a circuit. At another meeting Asbury preached to about four hundred people, one of whom "was struck with convulsive shakings." By January 1776, he could write that "Virginia pleases me in preference to all other places where I have been."[38] Taken as a whole, the Virginia revival was exactly what Asbury had been looking for since he arrived in America.

The Virginia revival was the first in a long series of recognizably Methodist revivals that characterized the movement into the early nineteenth century. It contained elements usually present when the movement was most successful in spreading its message and expanding its following: small group gatherings that nurtured intense spiritual devotion and community identity, and large public meetings that featured dramatic, forceful preaching and emotionally charged worship. Exhorters and class leaders often figured prominently in these meetings since there weren't enough preachers to go around. In a letter to Jarratt, the Methodist exhorter Thomas Saunders noted that it was "no strange thing" to hold "a Sunday meeting, although there was no preacher" present, with the result that at times "ten, fifteen, yea near twenty have been converted." "It is common with us for men and women to fall down as dead under an exhortation; but many more under prayer—perhaps twenty at a time," Saunders added in July 1776. Jarratt agreed, noting that impromptu prayer meetings were "singularly useful in promoting the work of God," sometimes lasting "for five or six hours" at a time. At one of these meetings in May 1776, sixty to eighty people "continued in prayer all night, and till two hours after sunrise," according to Jarratt. The result of this meeting and a love feast held the day before was that "in two days thirty of my own parish have been justified, besides others of other parishes."[39]

Nearly everyone who wrote about the Virginia revival noted the centrality of the class meetings. As elsewhere, class meetings became the building blocks for Methodist communal identity and spiritual nurture, the foundation for future expansion. "It is no strange thing for two or three to find the Lord at a class meeting," Thomas Saunders wrote to Jarratt in May 1776. Jarratt himself noted that "sometimes twelve, sometimes fifteen find the Lord at one class meeting." In July, John Dickins, who became a Methodist itinerant preacher the next year, wrote that at one class meeting, "we suffered all that desired it, to stay." Although allowing nonmembers to attend was irregular, given the scarcity of preachers Dickins decided to temporarily bend the rules. He wasn't disappointed. After Dickins questioned each member about their spiritual lives, "the fire of God's love was kindled." As some cried out for mercy, others were converted to "faith in Jesus." "Surely this was one of the days of Heaven!" Dickins wrote. Even the local skeptic, Isham Whitehead, was converted after inadvertently joining the meeting. Whitehead had been leaning against the outside door, watching the meeting through a crack. When someone suddenly opened the door, Whitehead tumbled in. Overwhelmed and "unable to stand," he lay on the "floor quite helpless," listening and watching the proceedings until, "two or three hours" later, "he rose and praised a pardoning God."[40]

Love feasts, held in conjunction with quarterly meetings, served as the culmination of much of the groundwork done in smaller gatherings. At love feasts, "as many as pleased" would stand "one after another" and speak "in few words, of the goodness of God to their souls," Jarratt wrote. At a love feast in Jarratt's parish, "the power of the Lord came down on the assembly like a rushing mighty wind; and it seemed as if the whole house was filled with the presence of God. A flame kindled and ran from heart to heart. Many were deeply convinced of sin; many mourners were filled with consolation; and many believers were so overwhelmed with love, that they could not doubt but God had enabled them to love him with *all* their heart."[41]

But there was a darker side to the revival, at least in the minds of some. Devereux Jarratt, Anglican priest that he was, worried that the revival encouraged too much in the way of religious enthusiasm. He fretted over what he saw as the revival's excesses, almost as much as he relished its accomplishments. On May 7, 1776, Jarratt wrote to Archibald McRobert (or McRoberts), another Virginia Anglican priest sympathetic to the Methodist revival, that while more than forty had been converted in his parish during the past week, "yet there were some circumstances attending" the meetings "which I disliked—such as loud outcries, tremblings, fallings, convulsions." Equally disturbing was "the praying of several at one and the same time. Sometimes five or six, or more, have been praying all at once, in several parts of the room, for distressed persons," while "others were speaking by way of exhortation: so that the assembly appeared to be all in confusion, and must seem to one at a little distance, more like a drunken rabble than the worshipers of God." These were gatherings at which the laity took an active part, at which ordinary Methodists expressed themselves openly. For an Anglican priest, even one so evangelical as Jarratt, this wasn't an altogether comfortable circumstance.[42]

Jarratt soon managed to stamp out much of this exuberance in his neighborhood, but at a price. As the intensity "abated, the work of conviction and conversion usually abated too." He had to admit that such phenomena were an integral and vital part of the revival. "Where the greatest work was—where the greatest number of souls have been convinced and converted to God, there have been the most outcries, tremblings, convulsions, and all sorts of external signs," he wrote in September 1776. Conversely, wherever these things were "publicly opposed," "the effect has always been this: the men of the world have been highly gratified, and the children of God deeply wounded." This was exactly the sort of trade-off that Asbury was unwilling to make as he worked to promote the Virginia revival.[43]

Unlike Asbury, Thomas Rankin shared Jarratt's misgivings about the revival's emotional character. Like Jarratt, Rankin at times felt overwhelmed by the response of Virginia Methodists. While traveling with Shadford, Rankin stopped to hold Sunday meetings at Boisseau's (often written Bushill's) Chapel in Dinwiddie County on June 30, 1776. He preached in the morning, met the society, and then returned to preach again at 4 p.m. Near the end of his sermon "the very house seemed to shake, and all the people were overcome, with the presence of the Lord God of Israel!" Rankin had never seen the like before.

> Numbers were calling out aloud for mercy, and many were mightily praising God their Saviour; while others were in an agony, for full redemption in the blood of Jesus! Soon, very soon, my voice was drowned amidst the pleasing sounds of prayer and praise! Husbands were inviting their wives, to go to heaven with them; and parents calling upon their children, to come to the Lord Jesus: And what was peculiarly affecting, I observed in the gallery (appropriated for the black people) almost every one of them upon their knees; some for themselves, and others for their distressed companions. In short, look where we would, all was wonder & amazement!

This continued for two hours, until "with the greatest difficulty" Rankin and Shadford persuaded the people to go home. Here was a revival, the likes of which Rankin had been praying for since his arrival in America, that exceeded his expectations, but also defied his control.[44]

A week later as he preached at White's chapel in Amelia County, with the house crowded and four hundred or five hundred standing at the windows and doors, Rankin "was obliged to stop again and again, and beg the people to compose themselves. But they could not: some on their knees, and some on their faces, were crying mightily to God all the time I was preaching." The fact that "hundreds of negroes were among them, with the tears streaming down their faces" didn't offended Rankin, a staunch abolitionist, though it may well have disturbed others looking on. Still, after the novelty wore off, Rankin became increasingly hostile to this kind of ecstatic, participatory worship.[45]

When he returned to Boisseau's Chapel a week later on July 14, 1776, he was determined to quiet things down. That morning, according to Jesse Lee,

Rankin "gave us a good discourse . . . and tried to keep the people from making any noise while he was speaking." But as soon as Rankin left to "get his dinner," "the people felt at liberty, and began to sing, pray, and talk to friends, till the heavenly flame kindled in their souls, and sinners were conquered, and twelve to fifteen souls were converted to God." Rankin returned to preach again in the afternoon, though most of the people seem to have wished he hadn't. When he couldn't stop them from crying aloud and shouting out prayers while he spoke, he finally gave up and turned the meeting over to George Shadford, who strode to the front and "cried out in his usual manner, 'Who wants a Saviour? The first that believes shall be justified.'" That did it; the place erupted. Shadford embraced the assembly's emotional energy such that "in a few minutes the house was ringing with the cries of broken hearted sinners, and the shouts of happy believers." Rankin could only look on in dismay.[46]

As Rankin's opposition to southern Methodist worship grew, Asbury stepped forward to defend the revival. He and Rankin had both come to Virginia with high hopes. While Rankin left disturbed that American Methodists were moving beyond English patterns, Asbury, who had always been on better terms with the mostly young southern preachers, embraced the new style. At a subsequent conference of the preachers, Rankin launched into a tirade against "the spirit of the Americans," criticizing southern Methodists for putting up with "noise" and "wild enthusiasm" in their meetings. He urged that "a stop must absolutely be put to the prevailing wild-fire, or it would prove ruinous." Though he "had done all he could to suppress it," Rankin was "ashamed to say that some of his brethren, the preachers, were infected with it." As Rankin railed on, Asbury "became alarmed, and deemed it absolutely necessary that a stop should be put to the debate, and this he thought could be most easily and safely done by a stroke of humour," according to Thomas Ware, who witnessed the event. Jumping up, Asbury pointed across the room and said, "I thought,—I thought,—I thought," to which Rankin asked, "pray . . . what did you thought?" "I thought I saw a mouse!" Asbury replied. This joke, which must have been perfectly timed because otherwise it isn't that funny, "electrified" the preachers, and in the ensuing laughter Rankin realized that he had lost. He had become the butt of a joke, rather than the voice of wisdom. The result was "alike gratifying to the preachers generally, and mortifying to the person concerned," according to Ware. Deeply offended, Rankin nevertheless "deemed it best, for the present, to let it pass." But he didn't soon forget who had made him the object of public laughter.[47]

This episode is revealing in two ways. First, it demonstrates the degree to which Asbury had reconciled himself to southern zeal. While he was no enthusiast—he seems never to have been among the shouters, jumpers, and fainters at these noisy meetings—he didn't share Rankin's fears about southern worship. If this was the way that southerners took to the gospel, then Asbury was willing to make room for it, as all the preachers could now see. "Mr. Asbury always sided with those who deemed it dangerous to" oppose "those gusts of feeling that always did accompany deep and lasting revivals of religion," Ware wrote. "The friends of order, he used to say, may well allow a guilty mortal to tremble at God's word, for to such the Lord will look; and the saints to cry out and shout when the Holy One is in the midst of them."[48]

Second, this exchange helps explain Asbury's quirky (from an eighteenth-century perspective) ability to control small group discussions, something that many contemporaries alluded to, but few attempted to explain. Laughing in public wasn't something early Methodists encouraged, and Asbury often chided himself for excessive "mirth." Salvation was serious business, and the eternal fate of souls was never to be taken lightly. And yet it was Asbury's ability to use humor to redirect potentially explosive discussions that in part made him so effective in these situations. The danger of looking foolish would have been great, but Asbury knew his audience.

American preachers remembered Rankin's opposition to the revival's emotional energy for years to come. At a quarterly meeting in southern Virginia in 1790, Thomas Ware was reminded of the 1776 awakening in the same neighborhood "under the ministry of Mr. Boardman, [John] King and others." But in the earlier case, "Mr. Rankin, Mr. Wesley's general assistant, so violently opposed it that it soon declined." By distancing himself from Rankin, Asbury preserved much of his reputation among American Methodists.[49]

Taking a larger perspective, the revival's success further exposed the chronic shortage of qualified preachers, a problem that would dog Asbury and the movement for decades to come. Part of the problem lay in the fact that the movement was growing faster than new preachers could be trained through service as exhorters, class leaders, and local preachers. More worrisome was the tendency of young preachers to marry and locate (settle down to farm or practice a trade) after only a few years in the ministry, often when they were just beginning to find their voice. The life of an itinerant preacher was hard, requiring him to travel almost constantly in trying conditions. Asbury and his colleagues took it for granted that this was no life for a married man with a family, particularly since the people gave barely enough to support single preachers and showed no inclination to give more to support a preacher's family. Still, the constant attrition troubled Asbury. Whenever he could, he urged young preachers to avoid young women (as opposed to the movement's "mothers in Israel"). "My dear Billy," he wrote to the new itinerant William Duke, "Learn [to] stand at all possible distance from the Female Sex[,] that you be not betrayed by them that will damp the young mind and sink the aspiring soul and blast the prospect of the Future Man." A year later, Duke, who was only sixteen years old when Asbury wrote to him, confessed that "my mind has been strangely engaged in love," which doesn't seem at all strange for someone his age. Despite such temptations, Duke didn't immediately marry, though he eventually left the Methodists.[50]

Many others left more immediately, however. On September 26, 1775, Asbury learned of the death of the venerable Robert Williams. But Williams had already married and settled on a farm near Portsmouth by that time. A few months later Asbury met John King and his new wife, Sallie Seawell, the day after their wedding. King preached for two more years before he too located in North Carolina. In March 1776, Asbury met with the preacher John Wade in an effort to convince him "to decline his thoughts of studying and settling, and return to his circuit." Though Asbury thought he had succeeded, a year later Wade too was gone. And then there was Robert Strawbridge, who had by the summer of 1775 "discovered his independent principles, in objecting to our discipline," according to Asbury, further widening the gap between himself and the rest of the movement's leadership. From this point forward, Asbury spent much of his career in America simply trying to keep enough competent preachers in the field.[51]

These challenges notwithstanding, the South remained the center of Methodist expansion for the next decade. What preachers the Methodists could field gave them the advantage over other religious groups, particularly the Anglicans, who failed to an even greater degree to keep up with the South's geographic expansion. At the annual conference in May 1776, Thomas Rankin noted that "if we had reason to mourn over the decrease of the work, in the Northern Circuits, we had abundant cause to bless the Lord, for the great increase in Maryland, Virginia, and North Carolina." It was here, in the South, that Asbury joined with American Methodists to hammer out a new identity for the movement, but not before a war nearly pulled it all apart.[52]

5

One Revolution

War would soon be upon them. Even Asbury, determinedly apolitical as he was, knew it. In late January 1776, he received a letter from Rankin telling him to return to Philadelphia by the first of March. Asbury delayed his departure for the North until late February, arriving in Philadelphia on March 19, having traveled more than 3,000 miles in the past year. Everywhere he went he heard reports of fighting between British and American forces, or saw preparations for the almost certain conflict to come. For Asbury, all of this was little more than a regrettable distraction, drawing people's minds away from the fate of their eternal souls. "If it is thought expedient to watch and fight in defence of our bodies and property, how much more expedient is it to watch and fight against sin and Satan, in defence of our souls, which are in danger of eternal damnation!" he wrote in September 1775 after learning that British marines had ransacked a printing office in Norfolk. By March 1776, Asbury had heard rumors that a British man-of-war was moving up the Chesapeake Bay toward Baltimore, leaving "the people greatly alarmed" and "the town . . . in commotion." Thereafter, the "congregations were but small, so great has the consternation been."[1]

At the outset, it wasn't obvious that John Wesley would take a strong stand on the war. He had long advised his preachers to avoid meddling in politics. "It is your part to be peace-makers, to be loving and tender to all, but to addict yourselves to no party," he wrote to Thomas Rankin in March 1775. It also wasn't obvious early on that Wesley would oppose the American position. Writing to the Earl of Dartmouth, secretary of state for the colonies, in June 1775, Wesley confessed that he couldn't help but think of Americans as "'an oppressed people" who "asked for nothing more than their legal rights, and that in the most modest and inoffensive manner that the nature of the thing would allow."[2]

All of this changed for Wesley once the disruptive social and economic impact of the revolution became clear, particularly its hostility to the king. Wesley wasn't so much concerned with what the revolution would do to America as with what it might do to England. "If a blow is struck, I give *America* for lost, and perhaps *England* too," he wrote to his brother Charles in June 1775. Thoughts of the English Civil War a century before came quickly to mind. On August 23, 1775, Wesley wrote to the Earl of Dartmouth to counter reports "that trade was as plentiful & flourishing as ever, & the people as well employed & as well satisfied." From Wesley's observations, just the opposite was true. "In every part of England where I have been (& I have been East, West, North & South within these two years) trade in general is exceedingly decayed, & thousands of people are quite unemployed." Food was so scarce that many were reduced to "walking shadows." Wesley found that people mostly blamed the king. "They heartily despise his Majesty, & hate him with a perfect Hatred. They wish to embrue their hands in his blood; they are full of ye Spirit of Murder and Rebellion." This was a dangerous situation, and Wesley now saw it as his duty to speak out.[3]

At about the same time that he wrote to Dartmouth, Wesley came across Samuel Johnson's pamphlet *Taxation No Tyranny*. Borrowing liberally from Johnson (his critics would say plagiarizing), Wesley reduced Johnson's argument in length and complexity, making it more suitable for a broad audience. Published as *A Calm Address to Our American Colonies*, the pamphlet sold for two pence, but did little to calm anyone's feelings. Wesley reminded his readers that England enjoyed more civil and religious liberty than any nation on earth. Why would anyone rebel against such a benevolent government? The answer, Wesley wrote, was that "designing men" in England had duped the Americans into believing that they were oppressed. "Determined enemies to monarchy," these men were willing to risk all to bring down the king and replace him with a republican form of government. "Would a republican government give you more liberty, either religious or civil?" Wesley asked. Far from it. "No governments under heaven are so despotic as the republican; no subjects are governed in so arbitrary a manner as those of a commonwealth.... Republics show no mercy." The only sensible course was to "fear God and honour the King!" Following up a theme from his earlier pamphlet, *Thoughts Upon Slavery*

(1772), Wesley reminded readers that the only real slave in America was "that Negro, fainting under the load, bleeding under the lash!"[4]

Wesley's pamphlet sold a hundred thousand copies in a few months, creating a storm of protest in the process. Though few copies reached America, his views became generally known, and he continued to publish on the topic for several years. In subsequent pamphlets, particularly *A Calm Address to the Inhabitants of England* (1777), Wesley shifted much of the blame for the war from anti-monarchists in England to the Americans themselves, and he continued to call for loyalty to the king. "Do any of you *blaspheme God, or the King?*" Wesley asked his fellow Methodists. "None of you, I trust, who are in connexion with *me*. I would no more continue in fellowship with those, who continue in such a practice, than with whore-mongers, or sabbath-breakers, or thieves, or drunkards, or common swearers."[5]

Other British Methodists, including John Fletcher, joined John Wesley in criticizing the Americans. Charles Wesley wrote hundreds of pages of poetry condemning American patriots, those "fiends from hell," and the conduct of British leaders who had bungled the war effort. Like John, Charles drew a connection between the American Revolution and the English Civil War. The American patriots, according to Charles, were guilty of conducting the war

> By burnings, ravages, and rapes,
> And villainy in a thousand shapes

By comparison, John Wesley seemed a moderate.[6]

British preachers in America, including Thomas Rankin, could easily perceive the direction of the Wesleys' opinions and increasingly spoke out against the American cause. Except for Asbury. The Wesleys' perspective on the conflict no longer made sense to him. After meeting Rankin in Philadelphia in March 1776 and receiving an "affectionate letter" from John Wesley, Asbury declared that he was "truly sorry that the venerable man ever dipped into the politics of America." Had Wesley "been a subject of America, no doubt he would have been as zealous an advocate of the American cause" as he now was of the British. The gulf between Wesley and Asbury in this regard ran deep. Wesley was an Oxford-educated clergyman and gentleman who saw it as his duty to uphold church and king. For Wesley, republicanism undercut the essential social hierarchy that supported the moral order of the universe. Asbury had come to the more American view that the old order was inherently flawed, a human invention, and not a very good one at that. None of this is surprising given that Wesley was a priest of the established church and Asbury wasn't. Asbury had grown up within sight of political power (Dartmouth's estate in particular), but without any expectation that it would ever concern him directly. For Asbury, faith and politics were never connected in the way they were for Wesley. All human governments were corrupt, and none deserved absolute allegiance. Of Wesley's licensed missionaries to America, only Asbury divided Wesley's theology, which he held firmly to, from Wesley's political and social views, which he increasingly distrusted. His position on the conflict was much closer to that of the majority of the American preachers. Most eventually supported the American cause, but initially agreed with the itinerant William Duke, who saw the coming conflict as "nothing but a prospect of ruin & desolation."[7]

Asbury also refused to leave America, even when he had other opportunities and Wesley called him home. In February 1775, Asbury received a letter from Antigua urging him to take over the leadership of Methodism on the Caribbean island. Nathaniel Gilbert, the island's leading Methodist, had died the year before, leaving Antiguan Methodists without a leader.[8] Asbury believed that John Wesley had "given his consent" to the plan, but he nevertheless held back. Meanwhile, Wesley wrote to Rankin on March 1, 1775, advising that Asbury "return to England the first opportunity." While this letter was in transit, Asbury wrote to Wesley apparently seeking advice (the letter doesn't survive). Wesley responded through Rankin on April 21, 1775, acknowledging Asbury's letter and advising him not to go to Antigua, but to return to England immediately. Asbury and Rankin had already butted heads, and Wesley, while remaining sympathetic toward Asbury, essentially took Rankin's side. "I apprehend he will go through his work more cheerfully when he is within a little distance from me," Wesley confided to Rankin on May 19, 1775. "I doubt not but Brother Asbury and you will part friends.... He is quite an upright man." Rankin wasn't so sure, but he communicated Wesley's orders to Asbury, who nevertheless spent the remainder of 1775 in Virginia.[9]

Even after he received an August 7, 1775, letter from Rankin saying that he, Martin Rodda, and James Dempster "had consulted and deliberately concluded it would be best to return to England," Asbury held back. He couldn't bring himself "to leave such a field for gathering souls to Christ, as we have in America. It would be an eternal dishonour to the Methodist, that we should all leave three thousand souls, who desire to commit themselves to our care; neither is it the part of a good shepherd to leave his flock in time of danger: therefore, I am determined, by the grace of God, not to leave them, let the consequences be what it may." Fortunately, by this time Wesley had also changed his mind, forestalling a further showdown with Rankin. Writing to Rankin in August 1775, Wesley allowed that he was "not sorry Brother Asbury stays with you another year. In that time it will be seen what God will do with North America, and you will easily judge whether our preachers are called to remain any longer therein." On that Asbury had already made up his mind.[10]

Taking the Waters

In May 1776, Rankin assigned Asbury to Baltimore, but he lasted less than a month in the city before landing sick and "shattered" at the home of Prudence and Henry Gough. The Goughs were one of a number of prominent Baltimore area Methodists. They had been awakened, to use Methodist parlance, under Asbury's preaching the year before. Henry became an exhorter for a time, but later left the church before rejoining in 1801, again under Asbury's preaching. Prudence never wavered, remaining a lifelong Methodist and part of a network of wealthy Methodist women in the Baltimore area. "Mrs. Gough hath been my faithful daughter; she never offended me at any time," Asbury wrote in August 1800. A successful Baltimore merchant, Henry Gough maintained a 1,100-acre estate, Perry Hall, which included a mansion assessed at $9,000 in 1798 (by comparison, a Methodist circuit preacher earned $64 a year at the time, and most working people made little more). When Thomas Coke visited Perry Hall in December 1784, he wrote that the "new mansion-house" that Gough "has lately built, is the most elegant in this State."[11]

Prominent families becoming Methodists gave the movement an important advantage in the upper South, conveying a degree of legitimacy. Asbury realized this, but they also intimidated him. The only thing that he had in common with families like the Goughs was Methodism. In this regard Asbury and John Wesley were quite different. Though from a family of only modest wealth by gentry standards, Wesley could command the attention of the well-heeled. There was much about his Oxford experience that Wesley later rejected, but he usually included the title "Fellow of Lincoln College" on the title pages of his books. He had great sympathy and even admiration for the working people of England, but it was the sympathy of an outsider. When he traveled, Wesley routinely lodged with wealthy supporters, who were nevertheless not Methodists, rather than stay in the homes of more humble members.[12] Asbury never adopted a similar practice. His early life was more commonplace than Wesley's and he never tried to fashion himself into a gentleman. Apart from the common bond of Methodism, Asbury never felt comfortable around men of wealth and high manners. Once Henry Gough fell away from the faith, Asbury became a less frequent guest at Perry Hall. But that was in the future. In his present distress he needed help.

At the insistence of the Goughs, who frequented Berkeley Springs in northern Virginia (now West Virginia), Asbury decided "to go to the warm springs, and make a trial of them for the recovery of my health." This wasn't an easy decision since the springs were a place of leisure, the pursuit of which was one of the worst sins that might befall a Methodist preacher. Henry Gough and Samuel Merryman accompanied Asbury to Berkeley Springs, also known as Bath, one of the oldest of the mineral springs resorts in the South. These resorts didn't really reach their heyday as vacation centers for the "gay and fashionable" until the nineteenth century, but even in 1776 elites and social climbers met at Berkeley Springs to drink, gamble, socialize, and take the waters. Asbury recounts preaching in a theater and sleeping "under the same roof with the actors," during a subsequent visit in 1785. (Early Methodists never attended the theater, which they dismissed as voyeurism.) The springs, in other words, were a fair approximation of hell on earth from a Methodist perspective.[13]

In his journal entries during his stay at the springs, Asbury goes out of his way to emphasize how busy he was, which of course defeated the whole point of going there. Owing to the summer rush, the house where he found lodging was crowded, even by eighteenth-century standards: "The size of it is twenty feet by sixteen; and there are seven beds and sixteen persons therein, and some *noisy children.*" Despite these distractions, he settled into a routine that included reading about a hundred pages a day, praying five times a day in public, preaching in the open air every other day, and lecturing in prayer meetings every evening. He injured his voice on one occasion by preaching so loudly "that the people who were in their houses might hear." At another meeting "many were affected, and one man fell down," which assured him that "I am in the line of my duty, in attending the springs." If God was working through his preaching, then he couldn't be too far from his proper calling, though most of the other vacationers probably disagreed. Like a politician at a sports event, Asbury's presence only reminded people of what they had come there to escape, if only for a time. There is something comical about his stay at the springs, though he would have failed to see the humor in it. When he left in late August, he concluded that it was "the best and the worst place I ever was in; good for health, but most injurious to religion."[14]

He returned to the springs five more times in subsequent years, but the results were always the same. "I cannot get the people to attend preaching except on the Sabbath," he groused during a month-long hiatus at "this place of wickedness" in the summer of 1786. "I will return to my own studies: if the people are determined to go to hell, I am clear of their blood," he fumed after another disappointing attempt at preaching in the summer of 1787. Berkeley Springs stood for everything Asbury opposed. It was expensive (four dollars per week in 1785), determinedly irreligious, and wholly given over to the pursuit of "vanity." After 1793 he quit going.[15]

A Rumor of War

After returning to Baltimore, Asbury spent all of 1777 in Maryland, preaching mainly in the region around Baltimore and Annapolis. The war had already cut off Norfolk, Virginia, from the list of preaching appointments and would soon do the same for Philadelphia and New York as they fell behind British lines. Membership declined from 6,968 in 1777 to 6,095 in 1778, reflecting the confusion of war.[16]

Regardless of their politics, Asbury and his colleagues couldn't escape the war. Methodist preachers were widely suspected of having loyalist sympathies, which was in fact often the case with the British-born preachers. Most of the American-born preachers weren't loyalists, though their pacifism was easily misunderstood. Caught in the middle were the British-born preachers who supported the American cause, or who, like Asbury, wanted to remain neutral.

Consider the case of John Littlejohn. Born in England in about 1755, Littlejohn arrived in Maryland in 1767 with his new master, storekeeper Thomas Broomfield, on a brig with a crowd that included sixty-five indentured servants and fourteen convicts. After leaving Broomfield, Littlejohn worked as a saddle maker, storekeeper, and shop foreman in Norfolk, Annapolis, and Alexandria. A prophetic dream led to his conversion in 1774 early on in the Virginia revival. In a few short years Littlejohn moved from convert to exhorter to class leader to preacher. Feeling "greatly impressed" with "my duty to preach," he joined William Watters on the Berkeley circuit in 1776. For the next year he threw himself into the heart of the Virginia revival, traveling from circuit to circuit speaking to crowds great and small.[17]

Shortly after he began preaching in 1776, Littlejohn noted that "most of the people suppose the preachers are all Torys," but "they are mistaken if they think I am one." He believed it "lawfull under our oppress^n by Great Britian" to take up arms in defense of his new country. When he heard a Methodist near Baltimore declare that "no Man can be a Christian who goes to War," Littlejohn "advised him not to judge rashly," saying "that those who were will[in]g to defend their rights, enjoyed more of the power of Relig^n." On another occasion, when "one of the Brethren said much ags^t fighting," Littlejohn "told him if he was not at liberty to fight he ought to refrain," but "not judge those . . . who differed from him." Littlejohn's journal contains several accounts of Methodists jailed for refusing to serve, forced to pay for substitutes, or simply "dragg^d to the Camp" against their will.[18]

The position of the Maryland preachers was further complicated by their refusal to take the Maryland oaths of allegiance that the state legislature passed in 1776 and 1777. These acts initially imposed only modest fines for preaching without taking the oath, such as the £5 Asbury was fined for preaching a sermon in June 1776. But in August 1777 General Howe's army landed on the Eastern Shore and began an overland march to Philadelphia, which it captured that fall. With the British so close at hand, the Maryland legislature became more determined to root out loyalist opposition, culminating in the Security Act of 1777. The act required all males older than eighteen to swear an oath in front of a local justice before March 1, 1778, implying that they were willing to take up arms against the British. Those who refused were specifically barred from preaching in the state. Most of those arrested for preaching without taking the oath were Methodists. After Littlejohn refused to sign the oath in March 1778, he was nearly "tarred & feathered by some of the bett^r sort, as they suppose they are."[19]

If all of this wasn't enough to cast doubt on the patriotism of Methodist preachers in general, some preachers openly supported the British cause. Like Wesley, Thomas Rankin's sentiments were clearly with the English government. By August 1775, he had decided to return to England, only to change his mind a few weeks later. Rankin went instead to Philadelphia and New Jersey in November 1776, where he entered into political intrigue with Thomas Webb, a retired British army officer who had fought in some of the pivotal battles of the French and Indian War in America, losing his right eye. Webb had converted to Methodism in 1765, thereafter preaching extensively in New York, New Jersey, and Pennsylvania, sometimes in his uniform. While generally admired, he was loquacious, flamboyant, and always something of an eccentric. "Captain Webb does not wilfully tell lies, but he speaks incautiously; so that we must make large allowance for this whenever he speaks, otherwise we shall be deceived. . . . I fear his wife will have need of patience," John Wesley wrote to Thomas Rankin in December 1773.[20]

Considering Webb's military background, it isn't surprising that he remained an ardent loyalist during the revolution. While living in New Jersey in December 1776, Webb, at considerable risk, crossed the Delaware River into Pennsylvania and learned of Washington's plan to attack Trenton on Christmas Day. Rankin was staying with Webb at the time, and together they informed Colonel Thomas Stirling of the plan on December 21. Fortunately for Washington, the British failed to take Webb's information seriously. But his spying didn't

Thomas Webb (d. 1796), who often preached in his uniform. (From Abel Stevens, *History of the Methodist Episcopal Church in the United States of America*, vol. 1 [New York: Carlton & Porter, 1867].)

escape the notice of American forces, who ordered Webb to leave New Jersey. Asbury saw him in Baltimore in April 1777, but left Webb's name out of his journal, only referring to him as "an old friend." When Webb returned to New Jersey, he was arrested, taken before Congress, and paroled to Bethlehem, Pennsylvania. About a year later he was exchanged for an American captured by the British, subsequently returning to England with his family, where he continued to lobby for support of the British army in America.[21] None of this did the image of Methodism any good with American patriots.

Nor did Rankin's continuing exploits. Rankin was back in Baltimore in September 1777, where he attended a dinner party given by the Goughs at Perry Hall. The guests included Captain Charles and Rebecca Ridgely, Captain John Sterrett and his wife, John Littlejohn (who recorded the events of the evening in his journal) and five others. Like Prudence Gough, Rebecca Ridgely was a devout Methodist and friend of Asbury's. The Ridgely mansion, Hampton, was assessed at $12,000 in 1798. Sterrett, a Presbyterian and an officer in the Maryland militia, got into an argument with Rankin during dinner over the conduct of loyalists near Baltimore, with Rankin supporting them much to Sterrett's consternation. Flying into "a voilent pass[n] [passion]," Sterrett pushed his plate away, saying that he had as much religion as Rankin did. As the two continued to argue, Sterrett pushed back his chair and unbuttoned his waistcoat, calling Rankin a "scoundrel, Villian [and] Tory." After pointing out that Wesley "had employ[d] his Tongue & pen ags[t] [against] the States," Sterrett declared that "every" Methodist preacher was a "tool" of the English government and ought to be stopped from traveling. One of the women present (it isn't clear who) came to Rankin's defense, leading Sterrett to turn on Rankin once again, saying "you coward[,] you are all a parcel of Villians, & I will take care of you, if ever I meet you in Balt[imore]." Then screaming "I can[t] bear it," Sterrett rushed toward Rankin. Littlejohn expected "a battle," but instead Sterrett passed by Rankin and left the room. "All was confusion," Littlejohn reported, and the dinner party ruined.[22]

Later that month Rankin fled to the Chesapeake Bay and joined the English fleet bound for Philadelphia, but not before preaching "in favour of the British cause," according to Littlejohn. After wintering in Philadelphia, he returned to England in March 1778, which Littlejohn concluded was "a bless[g] to those who remain in the work."[23]

Rankin had come to America with high hopes, believing that God had important work for him to accomplish here. "I know & feel that God is with me . . . that my way is made plain before me" he wrote to a friend just before sailing in 1773. But things hadn't worked out as he had hoped, despite initial successes. "For the first 3 years I was in America, the prospect was truely pleasing, with respect to the work of God: Many were awakened, and many converted to Jesus," he wrote in July 1778. Then the war intervened, "these wretched times," and Rankin only barely "escaped from the hands of cruel & Bloody men." He was so happy to be back in London that he could scarcely eat or sleep for eight or ten days. Rankin clearly favored England, "this happy and highly favoured land," and took it as another sign of Asbury's stubbornness and disloyalty to Wesley that he didn't as well. "Brs. Shadford, Rodda, & myself; have got happily among our Brethren once more; and Br. Asbury might have been here also, but he was unwilling to leave a few Books behind," scoffed Rankin.[24]

Asbury, on the other hand, had come to suspect that Rankin's motives had more to do with politics than religion. By urging all the British preachers to return to Britain, Rankin was attempting "to sweep the continent of every preacher that Mr. Wesley sent to it and of every respectable traveling preacher of Europe," Asbury wrote to Joseph Benson in England. To sweeten the deal,

Rankin "told us that if we returned to our native country, we would be esteemed as such obedient, loyal subjects that we would obtain ordination in the grand Episcopal Church of England and come back to America with high respectability after the war ended." On the contrary, Asbury knew that preachers who fled would be hard pressed to win back the trust of the people.[25]

Partly because of the conduct of Rankin and his British colleagues, the remaining preachers found it increasingly difficult to travel and preach. Asbury's chaise was "shot through" as he rode near Annapolis in April 1777, and John Littlejohn quit traveling by the end of 1778. Still, Asbury couldn't bring himself to leave America. Unlike Wesley, he considered "political subjects" to be "out of my province," something that ordinary people had little control over and therefore ought not to meddle in. When he first began to hear news of the war, "a fear rose" in his mind as to what might happen. "But it was soon banished by considering—I must go on and mind my own business, which is enough for me; and leave all those things to the providence of God." All temporal concerns, particularly with regard to politics, were ultimately a distraction from a higher calling. What difference did it make which government people lived under if, in the end, they landed in hell? Surely the greater good was to continue preaching under whichever political faction prevailed. With this in mind he determined to stay in America and weather the storm, if possible.[26]

Hiding Out

The year 1778 began in the midst of a bitterly cold winter. Asbury had been in America for seven years, but he still marveled at the weather. Since he spent much of his time outdoors, riding from one meeting to the next, the weather was a significant part of his life. What amazed him the most was how much the temperature varied from summer to winter, North to South, a much greater range than in England. "People suffer much more in winter by cold, and in summer by heat, here than in England," he noted. The one was just as difficult as the other. Though winter brought "judgment weather," by June he was complaining that he found "the heat of the weather too great for close study; it flags the spirits, and strangely debilitates all the powers of body and mind in a manner that is seldom felt in Europe, unless for one month in the year."[27]

The cold wasn't the only chill that Asbury felt during the winter of 1778. Unable to preach in Maryland because he wouldn't take the oath of allegiance, he moved to Delaware, which didn't require an oath. There he took up residence at the home of Judge Thomas White, who owned a considerable estate near Whiteleysburg. Asbury later remembered White as "my patron, good and respectable Thomas White, who promised me security and secrecy." Fifteen years older than Asbury and an Anglican by upbringing, White was led to Methodism by his nephew, Dr. Edward White. Their homes were within a mile of one another, and Asbury preached in Edward White's barn.

By moving to Delaware, Asbury avoided the Maryland oath, but he couldn't escape the war. In fact, the move brought him closer to the heaviest fighting in the region. By the end of September 1777 General Howe had defeated Washington's continentals at Brandywine Creek, Pennsylvania, and had moved into Philadelphia, forcing Congress to flee the city. Asbury spent most of the next two and a half years in Delaware, but even here he feared that it was too dangerous to travel openly.

Thomas White's cautious approach to politics appealed to Asbury. White was, in the realm of Delaware politics, a moderate conservative, part of a faction that had taken control of the state government from the more radical, independence-minded Whigs the previous year. It was during this period of conservative control that White won his appointment as a chief justice of the Kent County Court of Common Pleas. But as the war intensified during the winter of 1777–1778, Congress and neighboring states (particularly Maryland) pressured Delaware to take a more active role in the revolution, and the political climate changed in favor of the pro-revolutionary Whigs. Coupled with White's conservative (some would say Tory) political views was his support of Methodism. He and Asbury had intended to keep the latter's presence at the Whites' quiet, but this proved impossible as a steady stream of Methodists made their way to Whiteleysburg to see Asbury. Almost immediately after his arrival in February 1778, he held a quarterly meeting in Edward White's barn, with "many people" attending "from different parts." Several of the preachers who visited Asbury at the Whites', including Samuel Spraggs and George Shadford, soon crossed over to the British side. This didn't go unnoticed by local Whigs. After Shadford's departure in March for Philadelphia, then under British control, a gloom fell over Asbury: "three thousand miles from home— my friends have left me—I am considered by some as an enemy of the country—every day liable to be seized by violence, and abused." He may well have had a premonition of what was to come, though it would be Judge White, not Asbury, who would be taken.[28]

Asbury probably also chose the Whites because of Mary White, Thomas's wife. Originally from a prosperous family in Sussex County, Delaware, Mary White was a sometime class leader and "a mother in Israel in very deed," according to the preacher Thomas Ware. On one occasion, years later, Mrs. White took in the itinerant preacher Benjamin Abbott, who, like nearly all of his colleagues, periodically doubted the value of his preaching. Sensing his despair, White took Abbott by the hand, "exhorting me for some time" with "wholesome admonitions." This was just what Abbott needed at the moment, dispelling the doubts that clouded his mind. "Sister White, I believe, was an Israelite indeed, in whom there was no guile," Abbott later wrote. In many respects the Whites' home seemed the perfect refuge. They were sincere Methodists of considerable means, for whom the expense of keeping Asbury wasn't a burden. What he didn't know was that Thomas White's political star was falling, and the war was about to close in on the family.[29]

As the fighting moved south out of New England and New York, the Delmarva Peninsula (which is divided between Delaware, Maryland, and Virginia, hence the name) took on increased strategic importance. The peninsula was a particular concern to Congress because it contained one of the highest concentrations of loyalists anywhere in the states. Maryland politicians and military leaders had the clout to challenge Eastern Shore loyalists, but Delaware patriots faced proportionally stiffer opposition and therefore had to proceed more cautiously in pressing for support from the general population. This meant that Asbury never had to take an oath in Delaware, but it also meant that he lived in the perpetual uncertainty of an active war zone.[30]

On March 26, 1778, Congress, "having great reason to expect an invasion of Delaware," passed a resolution authorizing White's arrest as someone "whose being at large will be dangerous to the independence of" the state. The arrest came a week later. "This night we had a scene of trouble in the family," Asbury recorded on April 2. "My friend Mr. Thomas White was taken away, and his wife and family left in great distress." Four days later Asbury left the Whites, riding "through a lonesome, devious road, like Abraham, not knowing whither I went." "Weary and unwell," he found shelter in an unidentified home (he left out the name to protect his host) late at night. He intended to stay there "till Providence should direct my way," but the following night "a report was spread which inclined me to think it would be most prudent for me to move the next day." That night Asbury "lay in a swamp till about sunset," and then was "taken in by a friend," John Fogwell, who lived near Sudlerville, Maryland, about 15 miles north of the Whites' home. Fogwell had been transformed from a drunkard to a Methodist by blind Mrs. Rogers, a Methodist "missionary" (probably an unlicensed exhorter) in Queen Anne's County. Returning to Maryland involved considerable risk, since Asbury hadn't taken the state's loyalty oath, but then so did staying at the Whites'. He spent about three weeks at Fogwell's, reading and praying, not daring to preach.[31]

Asbury left Fogwell's on April 29, 1778, and returned to the Whites', where he intended "spending these perilous days in retirement, devotion, and study."

After eleven days, he was joined by the recently paroled Judge White, who had successfully challenged his arrest on legal grounds. This was a positive sign, but Asbury's mind remained "strangely twisted and tortured, not knowing what to do." He remained in Whitleysburg for most of the next year, spending much of this time in reading and prayer. If he couldn't ride and preach, he had to find something else to do; idleness was out of the question for a Methodist preacher. Asbury set himself a regimen that included praying several hours a day and reading the Bible, particularly the book of Revelation, which at one point he determined to read at least a chapter from every day. Revelation's vision of God's sovereignty amid tumult and upheaval must have been comforting in these seemingly apocalyptic times. Along with his English Bible, he plodded through Greek and Latin texts of the Bible and read just about anything else he could get his hands on. It wasn't a life he enjoyed. In October 1778, he considered leaving America, writing "I am desirous to do what I can for the salvation of immortal souls which inhabit America; but if Providence should permit men to prevent me, then I am clear, and must labour where the door is open." The strain of confinement began to take a toll on his health. After preaching near the Whites' home in November 1778, he "returned to my temporary home, in a much better state of health then when I went out. Thus is my life at present chequered: I come home, and grow sick, then go out and grow better; and return to meet affliction again."[32]

Staying in America rather than returning to England was perhaps the single greatest gamble of Asbury's career. Then again, none of his options seemed very good. There was little to draw him back to England. He had left there a junior preacher. If he returned, he could expect little more than a single circuit appointment, particularly since he had alienated himself from Rankin, Wesley, and most of the British preachers. Beyond that, leaving the ministry to return to his parents' home and the little village outside Birmingham was unthinkable now that he had tasted the life of travel, preaching, and leadership.[33]

But his present prospects weren't encouraging either, limiting him to a small orbit around the Whites' estate. As he brooded, troubling news of violent attacks and the arrests of fellow preachers stirred a mixture of fear and guilt in Asbury. It begged the question of why he too wasn't out risking jail and violence to preach the gospel. In March 1778, Asbury learned that William Wrenn, who had become a traveling preacher the year before, had been "cast into prison at Annapolis." A few days later he heard that Joseph Hartley, who had joined the traveling connection in 1776, had been "apprehended" in Queen Anne's County, Maryland, for preaching without having taken the state oath. Hartley subsequently spent three months in the Talbot County jail, preaching so effectively through his cell window that his accusers began to worry that "if the preacher was not turned out of jail, he would convert all the town." In all, some twenty Methodists were indicted in 1778 for preaching in Maryland, including John Littlejohn, William Duke, and Henry Gough. Meanwhile, Asbury remained at the Whites'. "Sometimes I have been afraid that I have done wrong in retiring from the work," he confided to his journal in June 1778.[34]

As he brooded at the Whites', Asbury met fairly regularly with preachers who were still traveling full-time. The most active was Freeborn Garrettson, who did more than anyone to hold Delmarva Methodism together from 1778 to 1780. Garrettson began his appointment on the Kent circuit in May 1778 without taking the Maryland oath. A few days after visiting Asbury at the Whites' in June 1778, Garrettson was accosted by a Queen Anne's County judge, who used a stick to knock him off his horse and beat him senseless. Undaunted, Garrettson continued to travel and preach across the peninsula. That September, in Dover, he was mistaken for a follower of Cheney Clow, a "backslidden Methodist" who led an armed band of some three hundred loyalists. Garrettson only narrowly escaped a mob numbering in the "hundreds," crying, "He is one of Clowe's men—hang him—hang him." Two months later in Salisbury, Maryland, a sheriff tried to arrest him, but backed down after Garrettson reminded him that he was "a servant of the Lord Jesus." In June 1779, he was "pursued by a party of men, who way-laid me, and the head of the company, with a gun presented, commanded me to stop." Garrettson was saved on this occasion by the women of his party, who leaped from their horses and seized the man's gun until Garrettson had passed by. Despite all of this, during the preceding fifteen months Garrettson preached in "more than a hundred new places." After spending a few months in Philadelphia and New Jersey, he returned to Dorchester County, Maryland, in February 1780. There he was arrested and thrown into the county jail at Cambridge, where he "had a dirty floor for my bed, my saddle-bags for my pillow, and two large windows open with a cold East wind blowing upon me." It took several weeks for friends to secure his release, during which time Asbury "heard of the severity used to brother Garrettson in Cambridge jail."[35]

Asbury couldn't have missed the contradiction between his own conduct and what he asked others to do. One of those Asbury kept at his post was John Littlejohn. Littlejohn had been considering marrying and locating (in other words leaving the ranks of the traveling preachers to settle down and take up a trade) since the summer of 1777. Over the next year he sought the advice of a number of Methodists, including George Shadford and Thomas Rankin, as to what he should do. They all urged him to continue preaching. In response to a letter from Littlejohn, Shadford wrote back that "he does not approve of my locating." About the only person who didn't want Littlejohn to continue itinerating

A young Freeborn Garrettson. (From Ezra S. Tipple, *Freeborn Garrettson* [New York: Eaton & Mains; Cincinnati: Jennings & Graham, 1910].)

was his mother, who wasn't a Methodist and who threatened to disinherit him if he continued. By June 1778, Littlejohn, then stationed on the Kent circuit in Maryland, had reached a crisis point. With "the rage of the people ags^t [against] us," the Maryland preachers "were all confined to a few places; & no prospect of our in largement." Littlejohn wanted to believe that this was reason enough to quit, but he could "not leave my appoint[ment] wth propriety without" Asbury's "consent." So, risking arrest as a Tory spy, Littlejohn made the dangerous journey to see Asbury in Delaware and open his heart to him. Whatever else he said, Asbury sent Littlejohn back to preach on the Baltimore circuit, taking the place of the recently departed Shadford.[36]

How could Asbury ask Freeborn Garrettson, John Littlejohn (a fellow English immigrant), and others to take risks that he himself wouldn't? To some extent Asbury probably was more vulnerable than the other preachers. As the last of Wesley's official English missionaries and a leader of the Methodist movement in America, Asbury attracted greater suspicion than the

American-born or less well-known preachers. But only marginally so. A certain defensiveness later crept into Asbury's reflections on his stay at the Whites'. In August 1804, he reacted to an account of American Methodism's early days by Charles Atmore, an English preacher, by claiming that Atmore's picture of his relative inactivity while hiding at the Whites' "is a mistake." Taking exception to Atmore, Asbury claimed that while at the Whites', "I went where I thought fit in every part of the state, frequently lodged in the houses of very reputable people of the world and we had a great work. I think near 1800 were added in that state during my stay, about 20 months." True, but Garrettson could claim more of these converts than Asbury. Similarly, in response to Jesse Lee's *A Short History of the Methodists*, published in 1810, Asbury wrote to "correct" Lee in only "one fact." Contrary to Lee's mild assertion, that Asbury "shut himself up" at the Whites' home, Asbury argued that his Delaware "seclusion" had been "in no wise a season of inactivity; on the contrary, except about two months of retirement, from the direst necessity, it was the most active, the most useful, and most afflictive part of my life." If he didn't preach on a few Sabbaths, "if I did not, for a short time, steal after dark, or through the gloom of the woods, as was my wont, from house to house to enforce that truth I (an only child) had left father and mother, and crossed the ocean to proclaim,—I shall not be blamed, I hope, when it is known that my patron, good and respectable Thomas White . . . was himself taken into custody by the light-horse patrol: if such things happened to him, what might I expect, a fugitive, and an Englishman?"[37]

Asbury had a point. During 1778-his least active year-he still preached at least ninety-five times, plus attending numerous prayer meetings and other informal gatherings at which he spoke. Among those converted under Asbury's preaching at the Whites' was Joseph Everett, who fell under conviction after hearing Asbury preach in March 1778. In 1780, Everett began preaching on the Dorset circuit and soon became one of the most powerful Methodist voices on the peninsula. Another of Asbury's converts during this period was Richard Bassett, who later served as governor of Delaware. In 1778, Bassett stopped to spend the night at the Whites' while on his way to Maryland. When he noticed a group of dark-cloaked men also in the house, he asked Mary White who they were. She told him that they were Methodist preachers, "some of the best men in the world." Alarmed for his reputation, Bassett prepared to leave immediately. But White convinced him to stay for supper, where his opinion of Methodism changed after "considerable conversation" with Asbury. Asbury visited Bassett's home the next year, where the two talked late into the night, initiating a friendship that lasted more than thirty years.[38]

Still, memory made these activities seem more important to Asbury than they appeared at the time. While at the Whites' from 1778 to 1780, he was wracked by doubts and guilt. Should he risk doing more? As an English commoner, Asbury had less faith in the law's ability to protect him than many of his American counterparts. As a young man, he had heard stories of how mobs in Wednesbury, near his home, had harassed Wesley and his followers, destroying their property with impunity. Fear of authority figures was part of his core personality, perhaps a product of his family's shaky reputation growing up. His courage wasn't in facing down a mob, but in enduring a relentless schedule of travel, preaching, and meetings that, except for the difficult months of 1778 and 1779, consumed his life. Each required courage, but of a different kind.[39]

The Life of the Mind

As the war limited his opportunities to travel and preach, Asbury spent more time reading and praying. In December 1776, after returning to Baltimore from Berke-ley Springs, he set a goal of spending three hours a day in prayer. By March 1777 he was praying seven times a day, and soon as many as ten or twelve times. His reading began, naturally enough, with the Bible, including some reading in a Greek New Testament and a Hebrew Old Testament. Other books included: Thomas Newton's *Dissertations on the Prophecies, which have been remarkably fulfilled, and are at this time fulfilling in the world* (1754), the third time he had read Newton; Wesley's *Notes on the New Testament* (1755); Isaac Watts's *Death and Heaven; Or the Last Enemy Conquer'd, and Separate Spirits Made Perfect* (1722); Richard Baxter's *Call to the Unconverted* (1658), *Gildas Salvianus, the Reformed Pastor* (1656), and Baxter's devotional classic, *The Saints Everlasting Rest* (1650); the first sixteen volumes of the sixty-five-volume *An Universal History from the Earliest Account of Time* (1747–68), a collection of sermons by Samuel Walker published in 1763; and William Law's *Serious Call to a Devout and Holy Life* (1729).[40]

This was a surprisingly eclectic mix. The books Asbury read were the sort of thing that any well-read American might pick up if they had an interest in religion. Most were bestsellers of the period, available in several editions. Some were published in America, but most were printed in Britain. As much as he could, he tried to breathe in the intellectual winds that happened to blow his way.[41]

During his period of greatest inactivity, between January 1778 and April 1779, Asbury continued to read everything he could get his hands on, leading to one of the few extended theological reflections in any of his writings. He began that January with *The Genuine Works of Flavius Josephus, the Jewish Historian*, by William Whiston (1667–1752), which remained the standard

English translation of Josephus into the twentieth century.[42] After finishing Josephus, Asbury came across an edition of Martin Luther's *Commentary Upon the Epistle to the Galatians*, which he read during the last week of January. In February he read the "works" of John Flavell (1630–1691), a Presbyterian minister and prolific writer who had attended Oxford as a servitor. Asbury evidently had a copy of Flavell's collected works, first published in London in 1701 in two volumes. At the same time he read Flavell, Asbury read "Hartley," possibly Thomas Hartley (1708–1784), who published a collection of sermons in 1754, or perhaps David Hartley (1705–1757), author of *Observations on Man: His Frame, His Duty, and His Expectations*.[43]

After spending March and the first week in April reading the Bible, sometimes in Greek and Latin, Asbury picked up a copy of *Christian Letters* by Joseph Alleine (1634–1668), which, he noted, Alleine "wrote in prison." Alleine's most famous book, *Alarm to the Unconverted*, initially sold twenty thousand copies when it was posthumously published in 1671 and is still in print today.[44] Next Asbury read the book of Revelation, accompanied by John Wesley's *Notes on the New Testament*. He then read Philip Doddridge's *The Rise and Progress of Religion in the Soul* in two days, nearly three hundred pages in most editions. A popular devotional manual, *Rise and Progress* had been translated into Dutch, French, and German. Asbury found himself "pleased, instructed, and affected" by the book, concluding that "an abridgment of this book would be of great service to our societies."[45]

During the last week in April, he read John Bunyan's *The Holy War*, while also rereading the book of Revelation, "with Mr. Wesley's Notes upon it." Bunyan (1628–1688) was most famous as the author of *The Pilgrim's Progress*, but *Holy War* was also readily available in America. By the end of May, Asbury had begun Robert Barclay's *An Apology for the True Christian Divinity: Being an Explanation and Vindication of the Principles and Doctrines of a People Called Quakers*, while also working his way through the book of Job.[46]

For much of the summer and fall of 1778 Asbury left off recording what he read. In November he noted that he had begun reading through Doddridge's paraphrase of the New Testament in six volumes, plowing through volume four by mid-December. Later that month he read a biography of Doddridge by one of his students, Job Orton, that "quickened" his "soul." In his last journal entry for the year he tried to fill in some of the gaps. "I have generally read of late about a hundred pages a day, in Hervey's Dialogues, the Lives of Gilbert, Harper, Langston, Brainerd, &c." Hervey's *Theron and Aspasio: Or a Series of Dialogues and Letters, Upon the Most Important and Interesting Subjects* proved particularly interesting to Asbury. An Anglican priest, Hervey (1714–1758) had joined the Oxford Methodists under Wesley in 1733 while a student. *Theron and*

Aspasio tells the story of the conversion of Theron, "a Gentleman of fine Taste," to evangelical faith under the guidance of his friend, Aspasio. In a series of seventeen conversations and twelve letters, Aspasio describes for Theron "the *authentic* Character of Salvation." *Theron and Aspasio* remained popular well into the nineteenth century, though Wesley found Hervey's theology too Calvinistic and published an attack on the book.[47]

Before Asbury was ready to form his own opinion, he read a volume of Wesley's sermons and then picked up Humphrey Prideaux's multi-volume *The Old and New Testament Connected in the History of the Jews and Neighbouring Nations*, which remained in print until the mid-nineteenth century. After finishing the third volume of Prideaux, Asbury returned to Hervey's *Theron and Aspasio*.[48]

Hervey's book gave Asbury pause, leading him to reflect on the tension between Calvinism and Arminianism, between the sovereignty of God and human agency, one of the thorniest issues in Christian theology. Asbury's inclination was to look for a pragmatic solution rooted in experience. If Hervey was "in error by leaning too much to imputed righteousness, and in danger of superseding our evangelical works of righteousness, some are also in danger of setting up self-righteousness, and, at least, of a partial neglect of an entire dependence on Jesus Christ. Our duty and salvation lie between these extremes," Asbury concluded. Since the Bible contained apparently contradictory statements on the subject ("St. Paul says in one place, 'By grace are ye saved, through faith; and that not of yourselves, it is the gift of God.' In another place the same apostle saith, 'Work out your own salvation with fear and trembling,'" Asbury noted,) the solution had to be a combination of the two. "What God hath joined together, let no man put asunder," he concluded.

> And he having joined salvation by grace, with repentance, prayer, faith, self-denial, love, and obedience, whoever putteth them asunder will do it at his peril. But it is likewise true that others who see the danger of this, in order, as they imagine, to steer clear of it, go about to establish their own righteousness; and although they profess to ascribe the merit of their salvation to Jesus Christ, yet think they cannot fail of eternal life, because they have wrought many good deeds of piety towards God, and of justice and mercy towards man; and they would think it incompatible with Divine justice, to sentence them to eternal punishment, for what they call the foibles of human nature, after having lived so moral and upright a life.[49]

There is nothing particularly original here, but it is worth noting that Asbury's assessment of Hervey's book was less harsh than John Wesley's.

Wesley feared that Hervey's Calvinism would lead to a casual acceptance of human failings. In the thirteenth dialogue of Hervey's book, Aspasio tells Theron that "our present Blessedness does not consist in being *free* from Sin," to which Wesley replied, "I really think it does." Hervey had been one of the original Oxford Methodists, but Wesley believed he had "died cursing his spiritual father."[50]

Asbury could see little practical harm in Hervey's thinking. Asbury was capable of evaluating relatively dense theological questions, and he was certainly aware of Hervey's Calvinism, but theological exactitude didn't concern him as much as it did Wesley. Asbury cared more about institutional (one might say community) boundaries than someone like Joseph Pilmore, but his real affinity was toward the kind of "mere Christianity" espoused by Richard Baxter. Asbury tried hard to appreciate the more narrowly focused distinctions that were so important to Wesley and others, but his heart wasn't really in it. His purpose in reading was to feel the intellectual currents of the day, so that he could guide the movement to engage them.[51]

As a result, Asbury rarely took these kinds of theological reflections past the level of random notes in his journal, most much shorter than the one described here. Even when he had time to read and write, as he did in 1778 and 1779, he produced little for publication. Where Jonathan Edwards aspired to spend thirteen hours a day alone in his study (and very often succeeded) churning out a massive literary legacy, Asbury aspired to spend an equal amount of time preaching and conversing with fellow believers. Solitary scholarship "is not to me like preaching the Gospel," he realized. His intellectual talent was as a mediator between writers like Wesley and Hervey and the throngs of Americans who turned out to hear Methodist preaching.[52]

But for now, in the spring of 1779, he still had plenty of extra time, so he continued to read. In February he read Samuel Clarke's *A General Martyrology, Containing a Collection of All the Greatest Persecutions Which Have Befallen the Church of Christ*. That March Asbury read Thomas Watson's *A Body of Practical Divinity, Consisting of Above One Hundred and Seventy Six Sermons*, which runs more than seven hundred pages in most editions. Watson was somewhat a Calvinist, so it isn't surprising that Asbury concluded that "the general drift of it does not comport with my sentiments." Yet he thought that it "contains many good things," enough so that he "had a mind" to abridge two of Watson's sermons for American Methodists.[53]

On March 23, his "eyes being sore," he let Thomas White's children read to him a biography of John Bruen, written by William Hinde. Born into a wealthy family in Cheshire, England, Bruen (1560–1625) led a wayward life, until, after the death of his father, he set out to reform his household. His servants were known for their ability to quote scripture, and his house became a center of hospitality. Hinde (1568/9–1629) was a Puritan and the curate of nearby Bunbury parish. One of the lessons that Asbury took from Bruen was "that great blessings more frequently attended the labours of plain, simple preachers than of the more sublime and eloquent," leading Asbury to "fear that I had not been simple enough." He finished the month reading some of Wesley's writings on prayer, before, in April, turning once again to the multi-volume *Dissertation on the Prophecies* by Thomas Newton (1704–1782), the bishop of Bristol, England. During the first week of May, Asbury picked up a copy of Jonathan Edwards' *A Treatis Concerning the Religious Affections*, which, "excepting the small vein of Calvinism which runs through it," he found "a very good treatise, and worthy [of] the serious attention of young professors."[54] The pace of Asbury's reading remained fairly steady for most of 1779. For the rest of his career, his reading waxed and waned depending on how busy he was with traveling, preaching, and administrative responsibilities and what books he could get his hands on. But when he had the chance, he read, reflecting a sincere curiosity about the world around him.[55]

Holed up at the Whites', Asbury couldn't yet discern that the war would ultimately work to Methodism's advantage. It generally accelerated a process by which ordinary Americans became less deferential, less willing to accept traditional notions of hierarchy and patronage, more inclined to consider themselves inherently the equal of anyone else. This republican revolution extended beyond politics to include religion. Less inclined to accept the rule of a hereditary class of gentlemen in politics, common people also began to question the need for elite, college-educated clergy. The Methodists offered a clear alternative in this regard, drawing their preachers from the ranks of farmers and artisans who shunned formal theological training. In particular, the war signaled the demise of state-sponsored religion. Pennsylvania, Delaware, and New Jersey, which never had strong colonial traditions of establishment, prohibited establishments in their constitutions written during the war years, as did New York. The southern states of Maryland, Virginia, North Carolina, South Carolina, and Georgia disestablished the Church of England in the 1770s and 1780s, effectively ending tax support for churches. Only in New England did some semblance of religious establishment persist into the nineteenth century.[56]

With the end of legal establishment, much of the financial, political, and social advantage enjoyed by the Anglican Church in the South and Congregationalists in the North evaporated, though in other respects the legacy of New England Congregationalism remained strong. Among middling Americans, Anglicanism in particular stood in a precarious position as the war drew to a close. America's oldest denominations, so used to a favored status in society, had a difficult time competing with the Methodists and Baptists in post-revolutionary America's increasingly egalitarian environment. In the south Atlantic region, Methodism's earliest stronghold, the Episcopal Church's share of church adherents dropped from 27 percent in 1776 to 4 percent in 1850.[57] In contrast, almost everything about the Methodist movement—its Arminian theology, organization, and social makeup—worked to its advantage in post-revolutionary America. The dominant churches from the colonial period had few leaders like Asbury, who could readily identify with the new aspirations of common people and who weren't tied to older patterns of social hierarchy. Unlike the gentlemen clergy he so often encountered during his early days in America, and unlike even Wesley, Asbury was no gentleman, but this wasn't necessarily a disadvantage.

6

Leads to Another

The worst of the fighting might be over, at least in Delaware and Maryland, but the movement was still vulnerable from within. Over the course of the war, the preachers in the North (including Maryland and upper Virginia) had become increasingly isolated from those in lower Virginia and North Carolina. As he traveled more extensively in 1779, Asbury learned that the southern preachers were determined to follow Robert Strawbridge's example and begin administering the sacraments, particularly the Lord's Supper and baptism, on their own.

Debate over the sacraments had simmered since the previous two annual conferences. A week prior to the 1777 conference, a number of preachers met at the Goughs' Perry Hall mansion, where they debated "whether we could give our consent that Mr. Rankin should baptize, as there appeared to be a present necessity." They concluded "that this would be a breach of our discipline." A week later the full conference met in Harford County, Maryland, with Rankin presiding. The printed minutes make no mention of the sacraments, but the manuscript minutes include the question, "What shall be done with respect to administering the ordinances [?]" The answer: "In the present unsettled situation of the publick affairs it is highly expedient that the Preachers and people persue imvarably the Same plan that they have done from the beginning." Whether or not "alterations . . . in our original plan" were necessary would, the preachers hoped, be easier to discern in a year. The decision to table this question until the next conference was unanimous, according to William Watters.[1]

Complicating the preachers' deliberations at the 1777 conference was the uncertainty surrounding the British preachers. Watters writes that "several of our European preachers, thought if an opportunity should offer, they would return to their relations and homes in the course of the year." Everyone suspected that Rankin and Shadford would leave soon. Asbury indicated that he would stay, but left room for doubt. Two months before the conference, Shadford wrote to Asbury "intimating that, according to rule, the time was drawing near for us to return" home. Asbury wrote back "that as long as I could stay and preach without injuring my conscience, it appeared as my duty to abide with the flock. But I must confess Satan has harassed me with violent and various temptations." Even if Asbury remained, it wasn't clear to what extent he would be able to travel and lead. As a contingency, the conference appointed a committee of five—William Watters, Philip Gatch, Edward Drom-goole, Daniel Ruff, and William Glendinning—to "act in the place of the general Assistant, in case they [Wesley's missionaries] should all go before next conference." The printed minutes don't show a circuit appointment for Asbury, though the manuscript minutes put him on the Annapolis circuit. He preached in and around Annapolis for part of the year, before going into hiding at the Whites' the following March.[2]

The 1778 conference made little headway on the issue of the sacraments. Meeting at Leesburg, Virginia, in May, with William Watters presiding in the absence of any British preachers, the preachers again took up the question of administering the sacraments. Many argued that it was now time to begin doing so. "It was with considerable difficulty that a large majority, was prevailed on to lay it over again, till the next conference, hoping that we should by then be able to see our way more clear in so important a change," writes Watters.[3]

The 1778 minutes don't list Asbury in any capacity. He was given no circuit appointment, and his name wasn't included in the list of assistants, or senior preachers. By the spring of 1779, he was still unwilling to leave Delaware, except for a few brief excursions into Maryland, but he also realized that time was running out to deal with the southern preachers. The more comfortable they became with administering the sacraments, the less likely that they could be brought back into the Methodist fold.[4]

In April 1779, Asbury called a "preparatory" (and, in the eyes of many of the southern preachers, an illegal) conference of the northern preachers at Thomas White's in Delaware. They met a month in advance of the regular yearly conference, which was scheduled to meet at the Broken Back Church in Fluvanna County, Virginia. No precedent existed for this sort of preemptive conference, particularly since only the northern preachers (less than half the total) were invited. Asbury's only authority in this conference rested on his previous appointment from Wesley. Regardless, given the mood of the 1777 and 1778 conferences, he now realized that if he didn't act immediately the southern preachers would likely adopt some form of ordination, thereby separating themselves from Wesley and the movement's historical connections.

The sixteen northern preachers gathered at the Whites' tried to gain the initiative by voting to "guard against a Separation from the Church either directly or Indirectly." Since they "had great reason to fear that our brethren to the southward were in danger of separating from us, we wrote them a soft, healing epistle," according to Asbury. The conference also sought to fill the connection's leadership void by voting Asbury the title of General Assistant in America and granting him a veto over all conference proceedings (Asbury himself wrote these paragraphs in the manuscript conference journal). This was an extraordinary decision, considering that it was made by an irregular conference composed of less than half the connection's preachers. In case of Asbury's death or "absence," the conference appointed Daniel Ruff, Freeborn Garrettson, and Thomas McClure to act as "general Assistants for the Northrin Stations." The question now was would the southern preachers respect the judgment of Asbury and their colleagues to the north? It didn't take long to find out.[5]

The southern preachers, mostly Virginians, met for the regularly ap-pointed conference in Fluvanna County in May 1779. Only William Watters, who had taken it upon himself to mediate between the two sides, attended from the North. He was determined "to endeavour by every means in my power to prevent a division: or if that could not be done, to stand in the gap as long as possible." A month earlier, at the Delaware conference, Watters had urged Asbury to attend the southern meeting, but despite "all that I could say or do he could not be prevailed on." Asbury was still too worried about anti-loyalist violence to risk leaving "his present situation where he was well known," according to Watters.[6]

Despite Watters's efforts, the preachers meeting at Fluvanna chose to ignore the decisions and advice of the "preparatory" conference held in Dela-ware. They took no notice of Asbury's elevation to General Assistant, failing to even include his name in the minutes. Instead, they voted to ordain one another to administer the sacraments because, as Philip Gatch put it, "the Episcopal Establishment is now dissolved and therefore in almost all our circuits the members are without the ordinances." The southern preachers elected a presbytery of three preachers, Philip Gatch, Reuben Ellis, and James Foster, plus an alternate, Leroy Cole, who then ordained the rest by the laying on of hands.[7]

Southern Dissent

Why did southern Methodists choose this moment to break so radically from Methodist practice? Four factors pushed them in this direction: (1) the lingering influence of the Great Awakening and the rise of the Baptists, (2) deteriorating relations with the Church of England and its failure to keep up with population growth and territorial expansion in the South, (3) the lack of strong ties to Wesley, and (4) Methodism's rapid growth in the South.

The Great Awakening that swept through the colonies in stages from the 1720s to the 1740s had a lasting impact on American popular religion into the nineteenth century. Methodists readily identified with the zeal and activism of the awakening despite its largely Calvinist underpinnings. While on board ship to America in 1771, Asbury read Jonathan Edwards's account of the awakening in New England. Only days after the April 1779 conference in Delaware he was reading Edwards' *Treatise on Religious Affections* (1746), which he admired despite its "small vein of Calvinism." In 1776 Asbury first read Edwards's biography of David Brainerd, the famous missionary to the Indians in New England who died at Edwards' home in 1746, declaring of Brainerd, "my soul... longs to be like him." Asbury reread the Brainerd biography on several occasions, once remarking that Brainerd was "a man of my make, such a constitution, and of great labours; his religion was all gold, the purest gold." He also professed admiration for "that old saint of God, William Tennent," and "pious Mr. [Samuel] Davies," and was delighted to speak with the widow of Gilbert Tennent, whom he "revered." Like Edwards, all three were noted leaders of the pre-Revolutionary War revivals.[8]

The Great Awakening figure that American evangelicals most readily identified with was George Whitefield. In 1739 and 1740, Whitefield made a wildly successful tour of the American colonies from Georgia to New England, establishing himself as an American celebrity and focusing the message of the awakening into a simple, clearly identifiable formula. An early friend of the Wesleys at Oxford, Whitefield preached the necessity of the "New Birth" with a zeal that American Methodists, in spite of Whitefield's Calvinism, couldn't help but admire. Reading Whitefield's sermons as a teenager had stirred Asbury's curiosity about the Methodists. Hearing Whitefield preach for the first time had done much the same for Thomas Rankin. Rankin judged Whitefield to be John Wesley's equal, the highest compliment he could pay. Whitefield's criticism of the lifeless formality of the Anglican Church and the indolence of much of its clergy also rang true for many in the South. The Great Awakening provided a model of religious experience for American evangelicals largely independent of the Church of England and the social hierarchies it supported.[9]

Dissent from the Church of England in Virginia gained momentum during the 1760s, particularly among the Separate Baptists. Prior to 1760, there were few Baptists in Virginia, but by the American Revolution they had grown to nearly ten thousand, along the way fending off vigorous opposition from the predominately Anglican gentry. "The Baptists, who preceded us, had encountered and rolled back the wave of persecution," Philip Gatch wrote as he preached along the James River in southern Virginia in 1776. The Methodists and Baptists had much in common. Both offered plain preaching and close, supportive communities that freed believers from the obligation of imitating the gentry in excesses of drink, violence, and debt.[10]

The difference, of course, was that the Baptists could baptize. At times Methodists felt the Baptists nipping at their heels, following them from one preaching appointment to the next to beguile new converts with their trademark doctrines. As a result, the Fluvanna conference felt it necessary to fully define the Methodist position on baptism, agreeing to administer baptism by either sprinkling, or, in the case of adults, plunging, whichever the candidate preferred, but not to rebaptize converts, which would have represented an abandonment of infant baptism.[11]

Asbury was well aware of the Baptist challenge. On his first trip to southern Virginia, he had complained that "the Baptists endeavor to persuade the people that they have never been baptized. Like ghosts they haunt us from place to place. O, the policy of Satan!" While preaching in Sussex County, Delaware, in July 1779, he found that local Baptists were "fishing in troubled water, (they always are preaching water to people,) and striving to get into all the houses where we preach." (Asbury loved to use water metaphors when writing about Baptists.) "Must we instrumentally get people convinced, and let Baptists take them from us?" Asbury complained. "No; we will, we must oppose: if the people lose their souls, how shall we answer it before God?" What Asbury and the southern preachers differed on was how to meet the Baptist challenge.[12]

In this environment, it is hardly surprising that by 1779 Virginia Methodists would want to distance themselves from the Church of England. Joseph Pilmore had seen this coming. While in New York in the early 1770s, he wrote to Mary Bosanquet in England that "the chief difficulty we labour under is want of Ordination & I believe we shall be obliged to procure it by some means or other. It is not in America as it is in England, for there is no Church that is one Establish'd more than another." What was true in New York was even more so in the South, where obtaining the sacraments through the Anglican Church was difficult at best. Even where Anglican clergymen could still be found by 1779, they were rarely on friendly terms with local Methodists, as Asbury and others had discovered in their dealings with Samuel Keene and Robert Reade in Maryland. This was a serious liability for southern Methodists. A church bereft of the sacraments was at a serious disadvantage among people for whom the ordinances represented a major portion of what organized religion they knew.[13]

Southern Methodists also lacked strong ties to Wesley and his leadership structure. Before the war, Wesley's missionaries spent relatively little time in southern Virginia and North Carolina, choosing rather to concentrate on New York, Philadelphia, Maryland, and Delaware. With Asbury's retirement to the Whites' in early 1778, it is little wonder that the southern preachers felt justified in taking matters into their own hands. All of Wesley's preachers had abandoned America save Asbury, and he seemed little connected to their affairs.

During the remainder of 1779 and early 1780 the two sides drifted further apart. Methodism continued to grow in southern Virginia and North Carolina, which "confirmed the preachers in the belief, that the step they had taken was owned and honoured of God," according to Jesse Lee. In 1774, only about two hundred Methodists lived in southern Virginia and North Carolina. By 1779, more than half of the 8,600 American Methodists lived there. "At that time there was very little room to hope that they would ever recede from their new plan, in which they were so well established," Lee wrote. Asbury came to much the same conclusion after he received a copy of the minutes of the Virginia conference, which omitted his name and all but two of the circuits north of Virginia. The southern preachers "have been effecting a lame separation from the Episcopal Church," Asbury noted. "I pity them: Satan has a desire to have us, that he may sift us like wheat." Back in 1775, when Asbury had considered going to Antigua, he had held back in part because he wasn't ordained to administer the sacraments. "It is possible to get the ordination of a presbytery; but this would be incompatible with Methodism," he concluded at the time. His opinion remained unchanged.[14]

A Near Thing

Asbury could take some comfort from Methodism's solid foundation on the Delmarva Peninsula, which steadied his resolve to stand up to the southern preachers. He attended seven quarterly meetings on the peninsula between February 1779 and April 1780, observing Methodism's strength in the region. At a quarterly meeting near Dover in February 1779, he preached to some seven hundred people and afterwards "entertain[ed] great hopes that we shall see a gracious revival of religion." He saw similar crowds at meetings in April and August, and perhaps 1,200 people attended a quarterly meeting at Edward White's barn in November.[15]

As he formulated his plans, Asbury conscientiously worked to maintain his devotional life. Reading, especially from the Bible, was an important component of this, but prayer and meditation formed the foundation of the holy life. "It is plain to me the devil will let us read always, if we will not pray; but prayer is the sword of the preacher, the life of the Christian, the terror of hell, and the devil's plague," he wrote in September 1779. This wasn't a hasty judgment, considering that he had just emerged from fifteen months of relative isolation, affording him ample time to test the merits of reading and prayer for spiritual nurture. Asbury rarely had ecstatic experiences during his devotional times, unlike, for example, Freeborn Garrettson, who recorded visions and prophetic dreams in connection with his prayers. But if Asbury's devotional life was less dramatic than that of other Methodists, it was no less central to his life. Since his days were increasingly full with traveling, preaching, and other meetings, he tried to do his devotions in the morning, between 4:00 a.m. and 6:00 a.m., or, failing that, at night before bed.[16]

By late 1779, the chances for reconciliation looked bleak. In November 1779, Asbury received a letter from the Anglican minister Devereux Jarratt, who was "greatly alarmed," though Asbury feared it was "too late: he should have begun his opposition before." "Our zealous dissenting brethren are for turning all out of the society who will not submit to their administration," Asbury reflected. "I find the spirit of separation grows among them, and fear that it will generate malevolence, and evil speaking . . . they say, 'We don't want your unconverted ministers; the people will not receive them.' I expect to turn out shortly among them, and fear a separation will be unavoidable." He began to contemplate a tactical retreat. "If I cannot keep up old Methodism in any other place, I can in the [Delmarva] peninsula: that must be my last retreat," he wrote in April 1780, just before the meeting of the northern annual conference.[17]

The northern conference met on April 24, 1780, in the new Lovely Lane Chapel in Baltimore. Philip Gatch and Reuben Ellis attended as representatives from the South, hoping "to see if any thing could be done to prevent a total disunion, for they did not wish that to be the case," according to William Watters. Gatch and Ellis's credentials as Methodist preachers were above reproach. Gatch, one of the first American preachers to ride a circuit, had proven his mettle during the war when he had been tarred by a mob while preaching near Baltimore, the hot tar permanently damaging one of his eyes. The next day he barely escaped a whipping, but continued to preach. While riding the Sussex circuit in 1777, Gatch was attacked by two men who nearly dislocated both of his shoulders. In January 1778, he married and located, but continued to preach locally. Ellis was no less impressive. He had been preaching in southern Virginia since 1777, with a solid reputation for piety and devotion to Methodism.[18]

As the conference unfolded, Asbury tried to implement a compromise that gave both sides something. In response to "the step our brethren have taken in Virginia," he proposed five conditions for reconciliation:

I. That they should ordain no more.
II. That they should come no farther [north] then Hanover circuit [along the James River in southern Virginia].
III. We would have our delegates in their conference.
IV. That they should not presume to administer the ordinances where there is a decent Episcopal minister.
V. To have a union conference.

After "long debate," the majority of the preachers rejected this compromise as too lenient and too awkward. The plan called for the southern faction to cease ordaining new preachers, but not for those already ordained to quit administering the sacraments. Instead, the northern preachers voted to send a simple ultimatum: "we look upon our Virginia brethren who have dissented from us no longer as Methodists in Connexion with Mr. Wesley and us, till they return to us again." This left little room for negotiation. The northern preachers could hardly have expected Gatch and Ellis to agree to this, and they didn't. Gatch and Ellis "thought their brethren were hard with them," according to Watters, one of the few northerners who remained sympathetic to the southern position. A schism now seemed certain; "it was like death to think of parting," Asbury wrote.[19]

Then, according to Asbury's own account, "a thought struck my mind." This was for the southern preachers to suspend administering the sacraments for one year, "and so cancel all our grievances," for the time being. To this Gatch and Ellis, who "had been very stiff" up to that point, agreed, as did the conference as a whole, "without a dissenting voice," according to the minutes. The new plan was for Asbury, Freeborn Garrettson, and William Watters to attend the upcoming southern conference in Virginia, hoping to convince the preachers there to agree to the one-year moratorium. "I awfully feared our visit would be of little consequence," Watters wrote. "Yet I willingly went down in the name of God—Hoping against hope."[20]

Even with Gatch and Ellis onboard, the prospects didn't look good. Soon after the northern delegation's arrival on May 8, 1780, in Manakintown, along the James River in Virginia where the conference was to be held, Asbury looked up fellow Englishman John Dickins to get a feel for the mood of the southern preachers. He found Dickins still "opposed to our continuance in union with the Episcopal Church." Watters and Garrettson also "tried their men, and found them inflexible." For many southerners, the strongest argument in favor of their position was the recent growth in membership. This is what Watters had in mind when he noted that "to all their former arguments, they now added (what with many was infinitely stronger than all the arguments in the world) that the Lord approbated, and greatly blessed his own ordinances, by them administered the past year." "These people are full of the ordinances," Asbury concluded. "There [has already been] a separation in heart and practice."[21]

When the conference convened the next day, Asbury nevertheless set out to make his case. "I read Mr. Wesley's thoughts against a separation: showed my private letters of instructions from Mr. Wesley; set before them the sentiments of the Delaware and Baltimore conferences;" and read some of the correspondence that had passed between the two sides. They then took a break for public preaching, with Asbury attempting to preach "as though nothing had been the matter among the preachers or people." But when they reconvened, the southern preachers appeared "to be farther off; there had been, I thought, some talking out of doors," Asbury concluded. Asbury, Garrettson, and Watters now withdrew, leaving the southern preachers to debate the proposed one-year suspension among themselves. An hour later they had their answer, "which was, they could not submit to the terms of union."[22]

Asbury left the meeting "under the heaviest cloud I ever felt in America." It now appeared that American Methodism would be split into a smaller, more broadly Wesleyan faction in the upper South and North, and a larger, semi-Presbyterian faction in lower Virginia and North Carolina. Then, during the night, after much prayer a majority of the preachers unexpectedly had a change of heart. The next morning they voted to accept the suspension and refer the matter to John Wesley. They also agreed that Asbury should "superintend the work at large," North and South. This closely followed the northern conference's position, which required every preacher to annually obtain a license, signed by "bro. Asbury . . . in behalf of [the] Conference."[23]

It is amazing that the southern preachers reversed course so completely given all that had transpired between the two sides. Garrettson, Watters, and Edward Dromgoole (one of the few Virginia preachers who sided with Asbury) may well have played a role in the reversal, but everyone understood that Asbury was the northern faction's leader. Prior to the conference, most of the southern preachers hadn't met him in person. Some may have feared that he was an aspiring high churchman, like Joseph Pilmore, or that he opposed southern-style worship, like Thomas Rankin. Asbury was neither, as Methodists to the north had already learned. He had no interest in limiting the popular nature of southern Methodism beyond holding back on the sacraments. Though he had spent nearly two years laying low in Delaware, his piety was above reproach. His intentions seemed pure, even to those who disagreed with him. Asbury wasn't a crass political opportunist, and the southern preachers seem to have appreciated that he wasn't trying to provoke a showdown. Unfortunately, at Manakintown it had come to that, for which he partly blamed himself.[24]

Stepping back to take a broader perspective, was Asbury justified in thwarting the will of the southern preachers, so clearly expressed at Fluvanna in 1779? Methodist historians have debated this question from the nineteenth century on. The answer depends on what one holds most dear in this debate. For Nathan Bangs, who published a four-volume history of American Methodism in 1838, continuity with John Wesley was the most important thing. Bangs argues that Asbury's "preparatory" conference at the Whites' in 1779 was really the *"regular* Conference," since it was the one led by "the General Assistant," never mind that it was the same conference that gave Asbury that title. Asbury's ties to Wesley were what gave him an authority that none of the southern preachers could match.[25]

Edward Drinkhouse disagreed. For Drinkhouse, who published a *History of Methodist Reform* in 1898, Manakintown represented a "fatal compromise," a "lost opportunity" to nip episcopal tyranny in the bud and establish a more democratic church polity. "All the Scripture, all the methods of the primitive Church for two centuries, all the logic, all the rights of manhood Christianized, all the political sentiments of the American Methodists and revolutionary people, were on the side of" the Fluvanna reformers. At Manakintown, the preachers had tragically caved in "under the spell of Asbury's genius and magnetism." Drinkhouse had a point. The Wesleyan patterns articulated by Asbury did act to thwart some decidedly American tendencies. But Drinkhouse draws too sharp a distinction between Asbury's goals and those of the southern preachers. Asbury's objective in this debate was to mediate between Wesley and American Methodists, thus preserving what he saw as the best of both. "Once within the magic circle of his [Asbury's] personal presence" (to use Drinkhouse's words), the southern preachers agreed with the wisdom of this approach. The concerns of Methodist historians notwithstanding, the legality of the various conference proceedings weren't uppermost in the minds of the preachers at the time. North and South, they were most concerned with bringing people to salvation and teaching them to live holy lives. To this end, Asbury seemed a trustworthy guide.[26]

The Manakintown conference established a framework for reconciliation, but there was still a chance that the southern preachers would change their minds. To insure that this didn't happen, Asbury set out on a six-month tour of Virginia and North Carolina. If hiding out at the Whites' in Delaware had been Asbury at his most ineffective, his 1780 tour of the South was Asbury at his best. "There seems to be some call for me in every part of the work," he wrote as he rode across the region. The sacramental crisis had been a near thing, and Asbury blamed himself for having neglected the South for so long. "O! if a rent and separation had taken place, what work, what hurt to thousands of souls!" he reflected. "It is now stopped, and if it had not, it might have been my fault; it may have been my fault that it took place; but I felt a timidity that I could not get over."[27] He now set out to make amends.

Asbury spent May and the first half of June 1780 traveling through Virginia, before entering North Carolina, crisscrossing the state until he returned to Virginia in early August. Large crowds, by backcountry standards, gathered to hear him preach, often numbering in the hundreds. By the end of October, he had ridden more than 2,600 miles in six months and visited scores of towns and settlements. In Nansemond County, Virginia, he preached to three hundred people with "uncommon freedom." Afterward, the people "collected me money" and "a man offered me a silver dollar," but he refused both, "lest they should say I came for money." He hadn't come for money, but "to gain a general knowledge of the preachers and people" and vice versa, thereby "strengthen[ing] our union."[28]

The hardship of traveling in the backcountry was itself an act of atonement. "By constant traveling I may do good," he wrote in North Carolina in June. "My trials are great; riding twenty miles a day, or more; rocky roads, poor entertainment, uncomfortable lodging; little rest night and day," he added a month later. He still rose at 5:00 a.m. to pray for an hour when he could, at times making a point to pray for each preacher and circuit in America, north to south. But conditions made this routine difficult to keep up. "I am badly situated: and . . . have no place of retirement at some houses," he wrote while in North Carolina. At one home he tried to get away by walking into the woods, but gave up because "there are so many ticks, chiegoes [chiggers], and such insects at this season upon the ground." Long and difficult rides between appointments often required that he leave early, cutting short his morning prayers. "Have only time to pray and write my journal," he cryptically noted on one hectic morning. "Always upon the wing, as the rides are so long, and bad roads; it takes me many hours, as in general I walk my horse." This pattern persisted throughout his tour. "I can hardly get time and place to note down anything," he complained while in Virginia in August 1780. "I spent some time, at the quarter-meeting in the barn, alone. Oh! how good did that seem." It wore him out, but it also provided the connection that he was looking for. On one occasion he felt guilty "for telling humorous anecdotes" that may have gone "beyond the bounds of prudent liberty," yet southern Methodists clearly liked what they saw.[29]

If Asbury arrived a stranger in southern Virginia and North Carolina in May 1780, he didn't leave one the following October. His southern tour did much to solidify his leadership in the minds and hearts of American Methodists. Less than a decade after coming to America, Asbury understood its people—their hopes, tastes, needs, and fears—perhaps as well as anyone. The sacramental question wouldn't be finally settled until 1784, but it would never again threaten the movement's unity.

The Curse of Slavery

The winding down of the sacramental crisis brought more sharply into focus a far larger problem. African Americans had been part of American Methodism from the beginning, as Asbury was aware from his earliest days in New York. He regularly preached to and prayed with slaves and free blacks, respecting their spiritual equality, but otherwise taking little notice of the oppression they lived under. Even as he began to work his way south into Maryland and Delaware (beginning in 1772), and then Virginia (in 1775), he made few comments about slavery in his journal. It wasn't until June 1776 that he recorded his first extended reflection on slavery. After meeting the white class meeting at Fell's Point, near Baltimore, he "met the black people, some of whose unhappy masters forbid their coming for religious instruction. How will the sons of oppression answer for their conduct, when the great Proprietor of all shall call them to an account!"[30]

Asbury wasn't alone in only slowly coming to regard slavery as a moral problem. Methodists weren't part of the earliest protests against slavery, either in America or England. By the war years this began to change as Methodists joined a growing number of Americans and Britons in the belief that slavery was a great moral evil, radically at odds with the word of God. In 1774, the Continental Congress first resolved to end the slave trade, the same year in which Wesley published his tract, *Thoughts Upon Slavery*, insisting that "the African is in no respect inferior to the European," and that "liberty is the right of every human creature." As in much else, Thomas Rankin followed Wesley's views regarding slavery. Rankin met "many members" of the newly formed Congress in Philadelphia in August 1775 and "could not help telling many of them, what a farce it was for them to contend for liberty, when they themselves, kept some hundreds of thousands of poor blacks in most cruel bondage." The previous month Rankin declared to a congregation near Baltimore "that the sins of G[reat] Britain and her Colonies, had long called aloud for vengance" particularly "the dreadful sin of buying and selling the souls and bodies of the poor Africans." While confined to Delaware in June 1778, Asbury noted that Quakers in the area were "exerting themselves for the liberation of slaves." This, he now thought, "is a very laudable design; and what the Methodists must come to, or, I fear, the Lord will depart from them."[31]

By 1779, Asbury's opposition to slavery had become so strident that when his journals were first published in their entirety in 1821, the editors removed some of his more vivid denunciations. Unfortunately, the standard 1958 edition follows the 1821 volume in this regard. Asbury's manuscript journals burned in a publishing house fire in 1836, but portions of his journals published between 1789 and 1802 preserve his views on slavery from the period between 1771 and 1780. While still living at the Whites' in Delaware, Asbury wrote:

> I have lately been impressed with a deep concern, for bringing about the freedom of slaves, in America, and feel resolved to do what little I can to promote it. If God, by his providence hath detained me in this country, to be instrumental in so merciful and great an undertaking, I hope he will give me wisdom and courage sufficient, and enable me to give him all the glory. I am strongly persuaded, that if the Methodists will not yield in this point, and emancipate their slaves, God will depart from them.

A month later, in preparation for the upcoming April 1779 conference of the northern preachers, Asbury prepared a statement "against slavery...I trust it will be one of the means, towards gradually expelling the practice from our society. How would my heart rejoice, if my detention in these parts, should afford me leisure, in any measure, to be instrumental in so desirable a work." There must have been considerable opposition to this proposal, since no record of it is included in the minutes. Still, he apparently managed to win over some of the preachers. Two days after the conference, in another passage expunged from the 1821 and 1958 editions, he writes, "I was employed according to the desire of the conference, in preparing a circular letter, to promote the emancipation of slaves, and to be read in our societies." No copies of this letter survive, if indeed Asbury ever completed it. Nevertheless, the next year he pushed things further.[32]

In 1780, the same year in which Pennsylvania passed the first emancipation law in the United States, the northern annual conference held in Baltimore (the same conference that denounced southern Methodists for taking up the sacraments), also declared "slave-keeping" to be "contrary to the laws of God, man, and nature, and hurtful to society; contrary to the dictates of conscience and pure religion, and doing that which we would not others should do to us and ours." In an attempt to add teeth to this denunciation, the conference (under Asbury's direction) demanded that all traveling preachers emancipate any slaves they owned "on pain of future exclusion." The preachers agreed to read these pronouncements "in every Society," telling slaveholders that they had "but one year more, before we exclude them." Though approved only by the northern conference, these rules reflect growing abolitionist convictions—largely formed out of the ideology of the revolution—among Methodists in the North and upper South. Writing in 1806, William Watters lamented that his brother had died in Maryland in 1774 "before there was much, if any, talk amongst us about the impropriety of holding our fellow creatures in slavery," and therefore hadn't freed his slaves. Only six years later, slavery was a topic that couldn't be ignored.[33]

As African Americans began to pour into the movement, preachers increasingly commented in their journals and letters on the numbers of black Methodists and the integrity of their faith. Thomas Rankin wrote that during the 1776 revival in Virginia, "hundreds of Negroes" were among those joining in the meetings, "with the tears streaming down their faces." Similarly, while preaching in Calvert County, Maryland, in 1781, William Watters wrote that "the eagerness to hear and receive instructions amongst the poor blacks in these parts, is truly affecting, and exceeds any thing I have ever seen in any place." As he saw the spiritual integrity of African Americans, Asbury came to believe that they deserved a role in shaping the spiritual practice of their communities. While in Delaware in March 1779, he noted that "a black man, who had been liberated by Mr. Blades, gave such an extraordinary account of the work of God in his soul, and withal displayed such gifts in public exercises, that it appears as if the Lord was preparing him for peculiar usefulness to the people of his own colour."[34]

Yet as he journeyed through southern Virginia and North Carolina in 1780, Asbury could see trouble ahead. Antislavery ideas clearly weren't as popular here as in the North. On May 22, 1780, in Nansemond County, along Virginia's southern border with North Carolina, Asbury "laboured" to convince "brother Hill, to free his negroes," which Hill agreed to do that Christmas. The next day, Asbury preached to about three hundred people and then spoke to "our friends...about the freedom of their slaves; they acknowledge the evil," but argued that slaves given their freedom would only "be taken up and sold" again by someone else. On June 4, in Dinwiddie County, Virginia, Asbury again "spoke to some select friends about slave-keeping, but they couldn't bear it: this I know, God will plead the cause of the oppressed, though it gives offence to say so here." These experiences drove home just how intractable an issue slavery was in the South. A few weeks later, in North Carolina, he reflected that "there are many things that are painful to me, but cannot yet be removed, especially slave-keeping, and its attendant circumstances. The Lord will certainly hear the cries of the oppressed, naked, starving creatures. O! my God, think on this land."[35] At this point, the issue of slavery appeared like a cloud the size of a "man's hand," but Asbury was beginning to see that it might build into a storm capable of ripping Methodism and the nation apart.[36]

7

Looking Forward, Looking Backward

In the wake of the sacramental crisis, Asbury established a pattern of relentless travel across the continent that would define him and the church for decades to come. By the end of March 1781, he estimated that he had ridden nearly 4,000 miles over the preceding eleven months, ranging from North Carolina through Virginia, Maryland, Delaware, Pennsylvania, and New Jersey. Rather than sticking to places with established Methodist societies, he often chose to visit settlements that Methodism hadn't yet reached. "We must suffer *with*, if we labour *for* the poor," he wrote to Wesley in March 1784, after describing the difficulties preachers met with in their travels: "being often obliged to dwell in dirty cabins, to sleep in poor beds, and for retirement [in other words, privacy], to go into the woods." Yet how else would they find the people who most needed the gospel? "O how many thousands of poor souls have we to seek out in the wilds of America, who are but one remove from the Indians in the comforts of civilized society, and considering that they have the Bible in their hands, comparatively worse in their morals than the savages themselves," Asbury wrote while in western Virginia. On one occasion he preached three times and rode 40 miles, all in a day. After a "long cold ride" in December 1783, near the Virginia-North Carolina border, he "lodged where we had nothing to eat or drink but a little toast and water: I went shaking to bed as if I had an ague on me." At a "small house" on the Maryland-Pennsylvania border he slept three to a bed. At another cramped home on the Virginia–Pennsylvania border he slept "*Three* thick—on the floor." Yet the next day he had an audience of seven hundred "serious and attentive" people, more than compensating for the lack of a comfortable bed. In his travels he hoped not only to win converts, but also to set an unmistakable example for the other preachers to follow.[1]

The road acted as a tonic for Asbury. For the next several years, he remained in good health and spirits, which confirmed "that I am about the work I am called to, and the Lord gives me strength according to my day." In August 1783, he wrote to George Shadford in England that despite riding 4,000 miles a year in "all weathers," he enjoyed "more health than I have for twenty years back" (he was only thirty-eight at the time). Gone from his journal are the bouts of depression he experienced while confined during the war. "It is my constitutional weakness to be gloomy and dejected; the work of God puts life into me," Asbury observed.[2]

To get the most from his time, he began spending the winter in the South and the summer riding through the North, another pattern he followed for the rest of his career, which made sense for someone who spent so much of his time on horseback. Who would want to ride through New England in the dead of winter or South Carolina in the summer? Coupled with this was the decision to hold multiple annual conferences, beginning with the addition of a southern conference immediately preceding the annual Baltimore conference. By 1788, Asbury had expanded the annual conference system to include eight district conferences.

Reconnecting with places isolated by the war was part of this expansion. Traveling north on his annual tour, Asbury reached New York City on August 25, 1783, his first visit there in nearly a decade. The New York society was small, largely a result of the war, reporting only sixty members for the city (down from two hundred a few years before) and twenty-four for Long Island. During the British occupation from September 1776 to November 1783, the John Street Church (then called Wesley Chapel) fared better than most of the city's churches, many of which were taken over by the army and turned into prisons, barracks, stables, and hospitals, and their pews were burned for fuel. Presbyterian churches in particular were routinely seized and looted. Owing to Methodism's official status as a society in the Church of England and John Wesley's opposition to the American cause, the John Street Church remained open, though not without opposition. At a Christmas Eve service, a British officer dressed as the devil paraded down the aisle toward the pulpit until a man with a cane knocked his mask off, exposing his identity. Outraged, "his companions outside then commenced an attack upon the doors and windows" until the city guard arrived. This sort of harassment notwithstanding, preaching during the war continued under John Mann, a local preacher, and Samuel Spraggs, a

A British officer, dressed as the devil, interrupts a meeting at the John Street Church during the British occupation of New York City. (From Abel Stevens, *History of the Methodist Episcopal Church in the United States of America*, vol. 1 [New York: Carlton & Porter, 1867].)

former itinerant. Mann and Spraggs fled New York after the war, and the taint of loyalism led to a sharp post-war decline for the New York society.[3]

To reignite the work in New York, Asbury coaxed John Dickins out of retirement in April 1783. Born in London in 1746 or 1747 (he was never sure of the date), Dickins was, by some accounts, educated at Eton and in London before settling in America, though the Eton records, which are incomplete, don't list him. Whatever the source of his education, by the time he arrived in America he had some command of Latin and Greek and had read fairly widely in literature, science, and mathematics. Dickins probably taught school and may have come to America as a tutor. He joined the itinerancy in 1777, but then settled in North Carolina in 1780 following his marriage. Rejoining the traveling connection at Asbury's request, Dickins and his wife arrived in New York City in June 1783. Two weeks later, Dickins sized the situation up in a letter to Edward Dromgoole of Virginia: "Most of the people want fellowship with each other; & many want zeal & simplicity. They have had but little discipline among them for some time. I intend, through God's grace, to keep a tight rein." Though his initial "reception was rather cool," Dickins didn't back down. New Yorker John B. Matthias, a semi-literate carpenter in his early twenties, described "thundring John Dickons" as "a plain dreast man and When he spock it came with all his might, and it suted me very well, for I allways love'd to hear preashears spack as if thay whar in ernest." Dickins turned out to be a perfect choice for New York. He succeeded in attracting people like Matthias and reestablishing discipline, exactly what Asbury hoped he would do. By 1786, the New York City society was once again reporting more than two hundred members. It would soon serve as the jumping-off point for the rest of the Northeast.[4]

Leaving New York on September 1, 1783, Asbury made his way south through New Jersey and Delaware, and then on to Virginia and North Carolina for the winter. Decisions such as sending John Dickins to New York City eased any lingering doubts about Asbury's ability to lead. The 1782 Baltimore conference voted unanimously to "choose brother Asbury to act according to Mr. Wesley's original appointment, and preside over the American conferences and the whole work." American preachers began writing to Wesley in support of Asbury. "The preachers are united to Mr. Asbury, and esteem him very highly... and earnestly desire his continuance on the continent during his natural life; and to act as he does at present, (to wit), to superintend the whole work, and go through the circuits once a year.... [We] would not willingly part with him, or submit to any other to act in his place," Edward Dromgoole wrote to Wesley in May 1783. Asbury also lobbied Wesley on his own behalf, writing on September 20, 1783, that "no man can make a proper change upon paper, to send one here, and another [there] without knowing the circuits and the gifts of all the preachers, unless he is always out among them." Lest Wesley miss the point, Asbury reminded him that, "I have laboured and suffered much to keep the people and preachers together: and if I am thought worthy to keep my place, I should be willing to labour and suffer till death for peace and union."[5]

Wesley had already come to much the same conclusion. On October 3, 1783, before he could have received Asbury's letter of September 20, he wrote appointing Asbury General Assistant, the highest rank of any preacher in America, formerly held by Thomas Rankin, who was now in London. Wesley also wrote to other prominent American Methodists voicing his confidence in Asbury. "Bro: Asbury is raised up to preserve order among you, & to do just what I should do myself if it pleased God to bring me to America," Wesley wrote to Edward Dromgoole on September 17, 1783.[6]

By the time the Baltimore annual conference met in May 1784, "Asbury, by common consent, stood first and chief," according to Thomas Ware. "There was something in his person, his eye, his mein, and in the music of his voice, which interested all who heard him. He possessed much natural wit, and was capable of the severest satire; but grace and good sense so far predominated that he never descended to any thing beneath the dignity of a man and a Christian minister. In prayer he excelled." Ware's admiration for Asbury makes it all the more telling that he attributed some of Asbury's influence to his use of wit and satire, things that Methodists didn't usually associate with spiritual purity. Ware adds that had Asbury "been equally eloquent in preaching, he would have excited universal admiration as a pulpit orator." Here, again, is a picture of someone who was more at ease in small groups than in front of large audiences, whose ability to influence and inspire increased the closer people got to him.[7]

Though Asbury was not much of a performer in the pulpit, it was, paradoxically, his humor that helped create a bond with the younger preachers. Consider Thomas Ware's account of his first meeting with Asbury. Shortly after his conversion in 1780, Ware began to publicly exhort near his home in New Jersey. When Asbury passed nearby, he summoned Ware for an interview, beginning with questions on free will and Arminianism. "He then looked at me very sternly, and said, 'What is this I hear of you? It is said you have disturbed the peaceful inhabitants of Holly, by rudely entering the house where a large number of young people were assembled for innocent amusement," which included drinking, to invite them to a Methodist meeting. Ware stammered that his "zeal in this affair may have carried me too far," but that he only meant it for good. Without "relaxing the sternness of his look," Asbury next asked, " 'was it not bold and adventurous . . . for so young a Methodist to fill, for a whole week, without license or consultation, the appointments of such a preacher as George Mair?' " Not knowing Asbury any better, Ware thought that he was now in serious trouble. He tried to backtrack, explaining that his exhortations in Mair's absence were "generally very short, unless when the tears of the people caused me to forget that I was on unauthorized ground." At this point Asbury had Ware exactly where he wanted him. Embracing Ware, he told him that far from being angry with his "pious deeds," he was so impressed that he was sending him to take over the Dover circuit. "Here I was caught, and how could I decline?" Ware writes. Having just done everything he could to prove his sincerity, how could he now turn Asbury down? Asbury's humor won Ware over in a way that blunt demands might not have.[8]

Perhaps the only regret that Asbury had about his hectic schedule was that it often cut into his devotional life. He still tried to spend an hour in the morning and evening in prayer, but couldn't always find the time. "I am not so pious as I want to be; I pray much, but I do not watch and pray enough," he wrote in a journal passage typical of many from this period. His reading in particular fell off. Even if he had had the time, he could only carry a few books. "I have little leisure for anything but prayer; seldom more than two hours in the day, and that space I wish to spend in retired meditation and prayer: riding, preaching, class meeting, leaves but little for reading or writing," Asbury lamented (or boasted) on one of his tours through Maryland. He knew that Wesley read while riding in England, but the poor condition of roads in America, which jostled riders and demanded that they pay attention to what lay ahead, made it all but impossible for him to do the same.[9]

If he could read but little, Asbury could still take solace in his poverty. In June 1784, he wrote to his parents from Maryland, in response to the first letter he had received from them in seven years because of the war, that he had just sent them five pounds through Richard Sause, a prominent New York City Methodist, and had sent eleven guineas the fall before. He knew that it wasn't as much as his parents needed, but could only assure them that he wasn't spending much on himself either. He had always been "moderate in dress," and during the war he had sold many of his books to get by. His present allowance from the conference was $60 per year, plus traveling expenses, leaving little for extras. "I know not that I can call my one coat and waistcoat, and half a Dozen shirts, two Horses, and a few Books, my own, if the Debts were paid," he wrote. Opponents often accused him of grasping ambition, but rarely, and never convincingly, of misusing money.[10]

In the same letter, Asbury confided to his parents that he intended to remain in America "for life," which must have been a bitter pill for his mother. He also wrote that he was "inclined" to remain unmarried. One reason was "what once befell me in England," perhaps a reference to a brief romance with Nancy Brookes in 1768. Asbury gives few hints in his journal or letters about how he dealt with the complete absence of sexual romance in his life. The unhappy marriages of other Methodist preachers, including John Wesley and George Whitefield, could hardly have been inspiring. His sister's death, his parents' evidently rocky relationship, and his mother's possessiveness must have also served as warnings about the difficulties of marriage and children.[11]

Passions

The toll that repressing his sexuality took on Asbury is difficult to gauge. He turned thirty-nine in 1784. His grueling travel schedule seems to have been, in part, a mechanism he used to keep unwanted desires at bay. It consumed his energy and left him little time to fall into temptation and subsequent depression. Late in life, at about age seventy, he told his assistant John Wesley Bond "that he had experienced an intire death, to the 'Lusts of the flesh, the lusts of the eye, and the pride of life.'" Asbury attributed this "to the great sinking of the powers of nature: that [his] whole system being so long and so greatly broken by disease, its powers were so nearly ex[h]austed, that desire had failed." When exactly this happened he doesn't say, though almost from the beginning Asbury constructed his life in a way that precluded any temptation to compromise the itinerant life, particularly through marriage.[12]

For others, the decision wasn't so easy. While committed to preaching the gospel, most preachers also wanted to marry and have children. Many, like John Littlejohn, married and left the itinerancy after a few years. Those who stayed on often found themselves in a continual struggle with the flesh, as was the case for William Ormond. Born in North Carolina in 1769, Ormond was converted in 1787 and entered the traveling connection in 1791. His career was typical of most circuit riders, with the exception that he was more explicit about at least one of his struggles in the faith. "Last night I was greatly tempted; have I Sinned Lord shew me," he wrote in January 1796, while preaching on the Sussex circuit in Virginia, one of the largest in the state. Three weeks later he was "determined to oppose the Devil & the flesh more than ever." Exactly what was troubling Ormond becomes apparent in his April 18, 1796, journal entry: "I am more than ever convinced of the sin of Masturbation." A month later he wrote, "I find the Enemy very busy, my Flesh is an enimy to my Soul, how hard it is to keep my Body in subjection," followed a few days later by, "Last night I had a hard wressel with the Devil & my Flesh. I wish it may be the last time." It wasn't. The struggle continued for years to come.[13]

After moving to the Trent circuit in North Carolina, Ormond had a dream in July 1796 in which he proposed marriage to a widow, and she turned him down. Undeterred, Ormond decided to press his case. "I have been greatly temped this year; sometimes I fear I am not saved from Sin. O what an enimy my Flesh is to my Soul; the Apostle says it is better to marry than to burn—Nature is a mistery—Man is a riddle to himself." Unfortunately, his dream proved prophetic, and the widow did indeed turn him down. For a while Ormond's journal is silent on the issue of his temptations, but then on October 12, 1796, he wrote, "Last Night I was beset with my Old temptation; Lord when shall I be delivered." More than four dozen entries like this appear in Ormond's journal through the summer of 1803, even as he continued to successfully travel and preach. "Last night the Enemy was busy. Lord have I sinned[?] O when shall I become immortal & bidd adiew to trials & violent Temptations," he wrote on March 18, 1797. "I have my Trials, last Night Satan assaulted me with his Old Weapon," he wrote in December 1798. "I was grievously Tempted last Night. O! Lord save me from all Sin. My Flesh is an enemy to my Soul," he wrote on March 8, 1800, followed by "I was buffeted by Satan last Night," on March 9.[14]

Ormond wasn't really sure how much of a sin temptation alone was, but he was sure that the act itself was wrong and clearly embarrassed by it. He didn't have enough will power to completely repress his sexuality, so marriage seemed the only answer. While riding the Caswell circuit in North Carolina in the fall of 1800, he fell in love with Polly Moore and again proposed marriage. "O! how I love my precious Polly," Ormond confided to his journal. But it wasn't to be. After considering his proposal for almost two months, Polly turned him down. "How shall a Man know when a Woman loves him[?]" Ormond wondered. Following Polly's rejection, his "besetting Temptation" returned with a vengeance. Ormond never did find an answer to this problem. He died of yellow fever in October 1803, while stationed in Norfolk and Portsmouth, Virginia. We can only guess to what extent others knew of his nighttime struggles, but Ormond enjoyed a solid reputation among fellow Methodists. In a time when nearly all young adults married and extramarital sex wasn't tolerated among church people, it must have been obvious that voluntary celibacy was a trial for young Methodist preachers. The 1804 conference minutes eulogized Ormond as "quick in body and mind, but affectionate, fervent, and faithful: he was gracious and gifted; and upon the whole, was a good man, and a good preacher."[15]

There is no evidence that Asbury yielded to temptation as Ormond did, or that he engaged any other sort of sexual behavior that evangelicals of the time would have considered sinful. If he had, it would have been nearly impossible to hide from the many preachers and countless other people he traveled and lodged with, and opponents would no doubt have used it against him. But in this regard Asbury's poverty and purity were of a piece. The energy he might have used to fulfill his sexual desires and support a wife and children he instead poured into his ministry. The Methodist community was his only family in America, the salvation of sinners his only passion.

The celibacy of the itinerancy was a pragmatic expedient, not an attempt to undermine prevailing notions about marriage and sexuality. Asbury preferred unmarried preachers because they could devote more of themselves to their ministries, and because experience had taught him that Methodist communities resented having to support a preacher's wife and children. Yet everyone realized that celibacy was only a temporary commitment for most preachers. Methodists didn't expect their preachers to reject their sexuality, only to triumph over it for a time. Those who sought a more radical solution to the problem of sexual temptation were quickly shunned, as the case of Jeremiah Minter demonstrates.

Born in Powhatan County, Virginia, in 1766, Minter joined the itinerancy on trial in 1787. In 1789 he was assigned to the Brunswick circuit in southern

Virginia and in 1790 to the nearby Mecklenburg circuit, where Sarah Jones lived. Though Jones was older than Minter and married, the two developed an extraordinarily close friendship. For a time they exchanged almost daily letters, and Minter lent Jones his diary, which she pored over with enraptured intensity. "I love your soul my precious brother!" she wrote to Minter on January 25, 1790. "I am glad you were ever born to assist me, and steer me, and drive, and pull, and make me run to Heaven," she added that May.[16]

Suspicions predictably arose. Jones claimed that her husband approved of her correspondence with Minter and naively showed his letters to friends. There may in fact have been a spark between the two. "I have thought your spirit so much like mine, that I have thought I knew your temptations often, and think so yet," Jones wrote to Minter on one occasion. From the way events played out, however, it seems clear that things didn't go any further than the written and spoken word. There is no reason to doubt Jones's sincerity when she wrote to Minter, "I think either of us would die stone dead, and come to life again, and die again, before we would sin." Some years later she wrote to Minter, "Some have also thought (or said so) that there was an agreement between us,—that we waited for the death of my husband, to enter a state of marriage. Before God I positively denied the charge...I never on earth intended such a thing. I assert upon my honor that our union was only in Christian friendship, as a help to the heights of virtue and gospel holiness." Yet the gossip continued.[17]

Whether because he felt more temptation than Jones recognized, or because he hoped to quell the gossip surrounding their relationship, Minter did something drastic that shocked Virginia Methodists. Sometime in early 1791 he had himself surgically castrated. If he thought that this would end the controversy over his relationship with Jones, he was sadly mistaken. Had he not chosen castration, Asbury probably would have simply transferred Minter out of the district to avoid what was becoming something of a local scandal, if unfairly so. But Minter's actions now raised a more fundamental question. "Poor Minter's case has given occasion for sinners and for the world to laugh, and talk, and write," Asbury wrote in April 1791 while in North Carolina.[18]

Meeting in Petersburg, from April 20 to 22, the Virginia conference took up Minter's case. Neither Asbury nor Thomas Coke (more about him shortly) mention the ensuing deliberations in their journals, but Minter writes that they made him leave the room while the preachers debated behind closed doors. Their decision was to expel Minter from the traveling connection and send him to the West Indies, though in what capacity isn't clear. What they most wanted was to get rid of Minter for a while, hoping that the sensationalism surrounding his case would die down. Accordingly, Minter's name simply disappears from the 1791 conference records. Minter later wrote that Asbury, Coke, and James O'Kelly, the leading figures at the conference, had engaged in "witchcraft" against him. He also asserted that, while "in league with a devil," Asbury had used sorcery to haunt him "scores of times" in the form of evil spirits. These charges were still in the future in 1791, but Minter's colleagues must have sensed his drift toward nuttiness even then.[19]

Minter spent about six months preaching in Antigua and St. Vincent before returning to New York City, where Asbury refused to let him preach. Minter then sought readmission to the traveling connection at the General Conference that met in Baltimore in November 1792. After again deliberating behind closed doors, the conference turned him down, but allowed him to continue as a local preacher for the next seven years, until he eventually left the church. Giving Minter even this much leeway reveals his colleagues' ambivalence about what he had done. They agreed with his desire to avoid the "allurements and entanglements of marriage," but not his rejection of his sexuality.[20]

Over the next several years, Asbury consistently denied Minter's requests to rejoin the itinerancy without first admitting his error in making himself a eunuch. Minter flatly refused, eventually concluding that Asbury was a "wicked

Barratt's Chapel, Kent County, Delaware, where Coke and Asbury first met. (Photo by the author.)

and hypocritic" agent of Satan. As for Sarah Jones, Asbury never believed that her relationship with Minter amounted to adultery. "She has had a painful journey through life; but her persecutions and troubles are now at an end, and heaven will compensate for all," he wrote shortly after Jones's death in December 1794. Asbury preached Jones's funeral sermon from Job 3:17, "There the wicked cease from troubling; and there the weary be at rest," a passage Jones herself selected. "She was doubtless a woman of sense, vivacity, and grace," he concluded.[21]

On Sunday, November 7, 1784, Asbury preached to a "large congregation of people of different denominations" in the court house at Snow Hill, in Worcester County, Maryland, while working his way north through the Delmarva Peninsula. He was hurrying to meet Thomas Coke, who had just arrived on a mission from John Wesley, though as yet Asbury didn't know the details. Coke and Richard Whatcoat had arrived in New York on November 3, where Coke reported that "the whole country has been, as it were, expecting [me] and Mr. *Asbury* looking out for me for some time." Continuing north, Asbury headed for Barratt's Chapel, located about 10 miles south of Dover, Delaware, where he had arranged for about a dozen preachers to meet with Coke. Meanwhile, Coke and Whatcoat rode south, also heading for Barratt's. Arriving late for the Sunday service on November 14, Asbury walked in as Coke was preaching. Following preaching, Asbury was "greatly surprised to see brother Whatcoat assist by taking the cup in the administration of the sacrament." He knew that, of the two, only Coke was an ordained priest in the Church of England. So what was Whatcoat doing?[22]

8

A New Church in a New Nation

American Methodism expanded dramatically in the 1780s, built on the consolidation Asbury brought to the movement after the war. Suspicion about Methodist loyalties faded as the war wound down, and Methodists themselves began to feel more at home in the new social and political order of post-revolutionary America. The movement was still Wesleyan, but increasingly separated from Wesley himself. Membership in America rose from 8,500 in 1780 to 57,600 in 1790, and the number of preaching circuits increased from twenty-one to ninety-eight.[1] The culmination of this expansion and growing separation from England was the formation of an independent American Methodist church in 1784, with Asbury at its head.

Wesley had been weighing the problem of ordination for Methodist preachers for several years. On the one hand, he was committed to remaining in the Church of England, at least in principle. Though he maintained to the end of his life that he and the British Methodists hadn't separated from the Anglican church, he recognized that many Methodists didn't have access to the sacraments from an Anglican priest. If this was true in England, it was doubly so in America, as Asbury and others told him. The end of the war and Wesley's own advancing years (he turned eighty in 1783) led him finally in 1784 to take a decisive step. In that year, he legally incorporated Methodism and began ordaining preachers with his own hands. He hoped by these measures to maintain some kind of direct control over American Methodism and keep the American movement broadly within the Anglican tradition.[2]

The legal incorporation of Methodism in England was only loosely connected to the American situation. Wesley designed the Deed of Declaration to protect Methodist property and insure that the movement would go on by legally incorporating a conference of one hundred preachers to take over after he and his brother Charles were gone. When American Methodists first saw the deed, they took notice that there was "nothing said of Mr. A[sbur]y," though he was added later in 1784. One of the British preachers offended at being excluded from the "Legal Hundred" was Joseph Pilmore, who resigned and left for America, where he was ordained a deacon in the Protestant Episcopal Church by Bishop Samuel Seabury in November 1785.[3]

More important from the American perspective was Wesley's decision to ordain Methodist preachers. Early in his career, Wesley was so horrified at the prospect of lay preachers administering the sacraments that he told the 1760 Conference "He himself would rather commit murder than administer the Lord's Supper without ordination."[4] Unfortunately, only Anglican bishops could ordain. After one of his preachers was refused ordination in 1760, Wesley vented his frustration in his journal: "Our church requires that clergymen should be men of learning, and to this end have a university education. But how many have a university education and yet no learning at all? Meantime one of eminent learning, as well as unblameable behaviour, cannot be ordained 'because he was not at the University!' What a mere farce is this! Who would believe that any Christian bishop would stoop to so poor an evasion?" Wesley was not only convinced that many Methodist preachers were adequately learned, but that formal education was only part of the whole. "Which do you think is the safest guide," Wesley asked in 1768, "a cursing, swearing, drinking clergyman (that such there are you know), or a tradesman who has . . . diligently made use of all the helps which the English tongue has put into his hands, who has given attendance to reading, has meditated on these things and given himself wholly to them? Can any reasonable man doubt one moment which of these is the safest guide?"[5]

More recently, in August 1780, Wesley had written to the Bishop of London, under whose jurisdiction America fell, asking him to ordain a preacher to serve in Newfoundland. To the objection that the preacher couldn't read classical languages, Wesley replied, "but your Lordship did see good to ordain and send into America other persons who knew something of Greek and Latin, but who knew no more of saving souls than of catching whales." This tone wasn't likely to win the bishop's sympathy, and it didn't. He refused to ordain the preacher in question, confirming in Wesley's mind that there would never be enough Anglican priests of sufficient quality to serve the needs of American Methodists.

So, in 1784, with the war now over, Wesley took matters into his own hands. He had long believed that in theory presbyters of the church (of which he was one) had the same right as bishops to ordain. Acting on this conviction on September 2, while in Bristol, Wesley ordained Richard Whatcoat and Thomas Vasey deacons and then elders (the equivalent of priests). He then ordained Thomas Coke (already a priest in the Church of England) a superintendent, an office on the same level as, though in Wesley's mind distinct from, a bishop. Writing to the American preachers on September 10, 1784, Wesley explained why he no longer felt obligated to wait for the "English bishops" to act: "(1) I desired the Bishop of London to ordain only one, but could not prevail. (2) If they consented, we know the slowness of their proceedings; but the matter admits of no delay. (3) If they would ordain them now, they would likewise expect to govern them. And how grievously would this entangle us!"

Thomas Coke (1747–1814). (From Samuel Drew, *The Life of the Rev. Thomas Coke, Including in Detail His Various Travels and Extraordinary Missionary Exertions, in England, Ireland, America, and the West Indies: With an Account of His Death* [New York: Carlton & Porter, 1853].)

Since American Methodists were now "totally disentangled both from the State and from the English hierarchy, we dare not entangle them again either with the one or the other," Wesley wrote. Coke, Whatcoat, and Vasey sailed for America on September 18, 1784, the first of eighteen voyages across the Atlantic for Coke, with instructions for Coke to ordain Asbury a joint superintendent of American Methodism.[6]

Zealous and mercurial, eloquent and impetuous, Coke shared little in common with Asbury other than their Methodist faith. Coke, thirty-seven, was the son of an apothecary who twice served as bailiff (or mayor) of Brecon, Wales. Coke's upbringing was polite, if provincial, and far different from Asbury's or most other Methodists. In 1764, Coke entered Jesus College, Oxford's Welsh college, as a gentleman commoner, eventually earning a BA (1768) and a doctorate in Civil Law. He was ordained in 1772. As a gentleman commoner at Oxford, he enjoyed privileges not available to poorer students. As the university had for Wesley and many others, Oxford claimed a special place in Coke's heart, identifying him as part of an elite inner circle. Nevertheless, Coke's parish in South Petherton, Somerset, threw him out in 1776 for his growing Methodist sympathies. Casting his lot with the Methodists, Coke was based in London for the next seven years, becoming one of John Wesley's most trusted advisors. Coke's passion for foreign missions made him a logical choice for America.[7]

Coke was Asbury's mirror image in many respects. He was well-educated, urbane, and not above entering into political intrigue, as American Methodists would discover. Unlike Asbury, Coke was never content with the day-to-day management of any single project. While his vision was large, it never remained focused on one thing for very long. Thomas Ware, who met Coke for the first time in 1784, wrote that he "was not at first sight at all pleased" with Coke's appearance. "His stature, his complexion, and his voice, were those of a woman rather than a man; and his manners were too courtly for me, so unlike the grave, and as I conceived, Apostolic deportment of Mr. Asbury." (Coke stood just over five feet tall, short even by eighteenth-century standards.) But Coke had his strengths. "In public he was generally admired; and in private very communicative and edifying," Ware observed. For all his impetuousness, Coke wasn't usually arrogant or condescending toward his less refined brethren, a trait that won him many friends. He was also skilled at handling floor debates in conference, "the best speaker . . . on a conference floor, I ever heard," according to Ware. As a counterpoint to Asbury, Coke provided American Methodists a buffer against the criticism that they were devoid of education and refinement.[8]

Some American Methodists immediately embraced Wesley's new plan, including John Dickins, who learned of Coke's mission when he arrived in

New York City in November 1784. Given his earlier role in defending the southern preachers' ordinations in 1780, it isn't surprising that Dickins supported this latest development. He pressed Coke to immediately make his intentions public, since "Mr. Wesley has determined the point, and therefore it is not to be investigated, but complied with."[9]

Asbury was characteristically more cautious. The sacramental crisis had taught him that Wesley's word alone wasn't enough, particularly in the South. Wesley's plan to organize American Methodists "into an Independent Episcopal Church" couldn't be foisted on the American preachers; they would have to have their say. Asbury later wrote that, at the time American Methodists "were too jealous to bind themselves to yield to him [Wesley] in all things relative to Church government. Mr. Wesley was a man they had never seen—was three thousand miles off—how might submission, in such a case, be expected?" This was why Asbury had invited a group of preachers to join him at his first meeting with Coke at Barratt's Chapel. After discussing the proposal over Sunday dinner, Asbury, Coke, and the eleven preachers present decided to call "a general conference, to meet at Baltimore the ensuing Christmas."[10]

In order to have as many preachers present as possible (particularly from the South), Asbury and Coke sent Freeborn Garrettson to Virginia and North Carolina with the news. Over the next six weeks Garrettson rode 1,200 miles ("like an arrow from North to South," in Coke's words), calling the preachers to Baltimore. As he went, Garrettson preached nearly every day, which Jesse Lee later claimed prevented him from giving "timely notice to the preachers who were in the extremities of the work," including Lee himself, who missed the conference. Even so, Garrettson managed to get word to most of the preachers in the South for what promised to be an historic event.[11]

While Garrettson sped south, Asbury attended three quarterly meetings in Maryland, taking the pulse of the preachers and people. Only after gauging their enthusiasm for ordination was he content to follow Wesley's plan. In early December, Asbury rode to Baltimore to rejoin Coke, Whatcoat, and Vasey, having concluded that "the preachers and people seem to be much pleased with the projected plan; I myself am led to think it is of the Lord." About sixty-five preachers gathered at the Lovely Lane meetinghouse in Baltimore out of about eighty-three active itinerants. Coke and Whatcoat, neither of whom had experienced an American winter before, commented on how cold it was. Fortunately, local Methodists "were so kind as to put up a large stove," according to Coke.[12]

For all of its significance, the drama of the event was mostly implied. The preachers gathered in Baltimore voted unanimously to form an independent church, free of all ties to the Church of England, and elected Coke and Asbury superintendents of the new body. On successive days Asbury was ordained deacon, elder, and superintendent. He had two reasons for insisting on an election, rather than simply receiving Wesley's ordination. First, election gave him a measure of authority and legitimacy not mediated through Wesley. From this point on, he served at the pleasure of the American conference. Wesley couldn't recall him to Britain, as he had tried to do during the war, or appoint someone to supersede him without the approval of the American preachers. Second, Asbury understood the importance of elections in American society. Though conferences in 1779 and 1782 had already made him the leader of American Methodism, he knew that in the democratic context of the post-revolutionary years only the election of superintendents would place them above the charge of tyranny (and not always even then).[13]

Coke dispelled any doubt as to what Wesley's ordinations meant with regard to the Church of England in a sermon he preached at Asbury's ordination on December 27, 1784. The colonial Anglican church, Coke claimed, had been "filled with the parasites and bottle companions of the rich and the great. . . . the drunkard, the fornicator, and the extortioner, triumphed over bleeding Zion, because they were faithful abettors of the ruling powers." Coke argued that the Anglican clergy denied that believers could know for certain that their sins were forgiven by *"the witness of the Spirit of God,"* something that Methodists believed *"fundamental, yea, essentially* necessary to constitute a child of God." This sort of theological carelessness led to moral failure. "We *cannot* be ignorant," Coke declared, "that they [Anglicans] justify as innocent many of the criminal pleasures of the world— card playing, dancing, theatrical amusements, &c.—pleasures utterly inconsistent with union and communion with God."

Restraint was never one of Coke's virtues, but he didn't stop there. He also subtly recast the nature of his and Asbury's ordinations. At several points in his sermon Coke announced that he had come to ordain Asbury "a Christian bishop," setting, from the beginning, a precedent for replacing the title "superintendent" with "bishop." In his journal, published in the *Arminian Magazine* in Philadelphia in 1789, Coke wrote, "I ordained brother *Asbury* a bishop." It was clear to the preachers gathered in Baltimore that they were establishing an episcopal polity completely independent from the Church of England, and, ultimately, from Wesley himself. Coke would later have second thoughts, deciding that he had pushed things too far in this first wave of exuberance. But for the church as a whole, there would be no turning back.[14]

The process of electing and ordaining superintendents/bishops created uncertainty about the nature of the episcopacy. Were superintendents/bishops elevated to their positions by God, or merely appointed by their colleagues? The 1785 *Discipline* (a handbook of doctrine and practice for church members) authorized by the Christmas Conference, stipulated that a superintendent couldn't be ordained "without the Consent of a Majority of the Conference." In answer to the question, "To whom is the *Superintendent* amenable for his Conduct?" the *Discipline* answered, "To the Conference: who have Power to expel him for improper Conduct, if they see it necessary." And yet throughout his episcopal career, Asbury and most of his colleagues assumed that his office carried some additional, divine sanction. Removing him would have been a momentous thing, indicating that God had withdrawn his seal from Asbury's ministry. Democracy and episcopacy weren't easily reconciled, but for the moment Asbury and the preachers wanted the advantages of both.[15]

Though the vote to establish the new church was unanimous, some of the preachers still harbored doubts. Thomas Haskins wondered why the whole thing had to be done with such haste. He favored waiting until the following summer and inviting local Episcopal clergymen to attend and offer advice.[16]

Indeed, two Baltimore Episcopal clergymen, John Andrews, rector of St. Thomas's and St. James's parishes in Baltimore County, and William West, rector of St. Paul's Church in town, hurriedly arranged a meeting with Coke just prior to the Christmas Conference to propose a plan for consolidating the Methodist and Episcopal churches. On December 31, 1784, Andrews wrote to William Smith, Maryland's leading Episcopal clergyman, describing the outcome of this meeting. "At the appointed hour, which was six in the evening, he [Coke] did not fail to attend us; and brought with him Mr. Goff [Gough] and Mr. Asbury." While they drank tea, Coke "was full of vivacity and entertained us with a number of little anecdotes not disagreeably." "At length" Andrews and West revealed their plan, suggesting that Coke could be consecrated a bishop in the new, consolidated church. He was, after all, an Oxford educated priest of the Church of England and would trail large numbers of new members in his wake. While they plied Coke with this offer, Andrews and West essentially ignored Asbury. They assumed that Coke was the only person of consequence in the room, confirming for Asbury how misguided their proposal was. The clergymen were prepared to accept Coke as their equal, but past experience and their present conduct indicated that the same wouldn't be true for the rest of the Methodist preachers. According to Andrews, Asbury told them "that the difference between us lay not so much in doctrines and forms of worship as in experience and practice. He complained that the Methodists had always been treated by us, with abundance of contempt; and that for his own part, tho' he had travelled over all parts of this Continent, there were but four clergymen of our Church from whom he had received any civilities."[17]

Not willing to give up so easily, and again overlooking Asbury, Andrews went to see Coke a day or two later to renew the offer. Coke, of course, had no instructions from Wesley to consider any sort of consolidation and told An-drews so. "Thus ended our negotiation which served no other purpose than to discover to us, that the minds of these gentlemen are not wholly free from resentment, and it is a point which among them is indispensably necessary, that Mr. Wesley be the first link of the Chain upon which their Church is suspended," Andrews wrote to Smith. It wasn't the complete end of the affair, however. Several years later, after American Methodists had drifted away from Wesley in ways that no one could foresee in 1784, Coke had occasion to reconsider the offer he now felt obliged to reject.[18]

Predictably, others also decried American Methodism's final split from the Church of England. Charles Wesley blamed Coke for talking his brother into administering the "infamous" ordinations, though in fact Coke seems to have agreed to the plan with some reluctance and only after thinking it over for several months. When Charles heard of Coke's ordination of Asbury, he responded sarcastically in verse:

> A Roman emperor, 'tis said,
> His favourite horse a consul made:
> But Coke brings greater things to pass—
> He makes a bishop of an ass.

When Charles read Coke's ordination sermon for Asbury, preached in Balti-more, he wrote a pamphlet declaring that "as a *Methodist* he contradicts the uniform Declarations and Publications of the Rev. Mr. *J. and C. Wesley*, for near fifty Years." "Does not Ordination necessarily imply Separation?" Charles asked. The answer seemed obvious.[19]

Now age seventy-seven, Charles was one of the central figures in the early Methodist movement and for many years John's most trusted colleague. But Charles was also less of a populist than his brother. Early on, he was troubled by the growing influence of Methodist lay preachers who had not been ordained. "Unless a sudden Remedy be found *the Preachers will destroy the work of GOD*," he wrote in about 1751. The problem, in Charles's mind, was that many of the preachers had fallen into "idleness" as a result of leaving their trades to preach. "The unusual Respect they met with turned their Heads. The Tinner, Barber, Thatcher, forgot *himself*, with his Business & immediately set up for a Gentleman." To continue sending them out was to "act the Part of rash Enthusiasts" and, worst of all, to promote a schism from the Church of England. The solution, Charles suggested, was to return the lay preachers to their trades ("*All* of them, I mean, excepting a few whom we can entirely trust"), allowing them to preach only in their spare time.[20] John's loyalties were to Methodism first and the Church of England second, while Charles's were the other way around. More to the point, John was more willing to trust the judgment of ordinary people than Charles was. "Our different judgment of persons was owing to our different tempers, his all hope and mine all fear," Charles wrote in 1772.[21] Had Charles had his way, Asbury would never have entered the itinerancy in the 1760s or sailed for America in 1771.

Asbury wasn't surprised by the reaction of devoted churchmen like Charles Wesley, though he had long since stopped thinking of himself as primarily British or Anglican. Even more than John Wesley, Asbury was a Methodist first and an Anglican second. He was also increasingly an American. In the letter to his parents in June 1784, he wrote that he had sent "Eleven Guineas last fall," which must have puzzled them. The English used "autumn" when referring to the third season of the year, something that Francis had apparently forgotten.[22]

Joining Charles Wesley in censuring the ordinations was Joseph Pilmore, who Charles Wesley helped obtain his own ordination in the Episcopal Church the next year.[23] Pilmore wrote to Wesley on several occasions to thank him and express his hope that the breach between the Methodists and the Episcopal Church in America would soon be mended. But Pilmore was enough of a realist to caution Wesley that "*the Clergy and Laity here* will never more submit to any foreign power, either civil or Ecclesiastical." He knew better than anyone that there was little hope that the "misguided Methodists" would return to the Episcopal fold.[24]

The Methodist separation also exhausted the last of Devereux Jarratt's goodwill toward the movement. Writing to the Methodist preacher Edward Dromgoole in May 1785, Jarratt complained that he hadn't been invited to the Christmas Conference. "I cannot conceive how I have deserved to be treated so coldly, to say the least. Surely it proceeds from no good Spirit." Jarratt could be abrasive and short-tempered (he laughed when Coke showed him his ordination papers from Wesley), and for several years he largely blamed Asbury for his estrangement from the Methodists. "Once Mr. Asbury seemed to think Nothing could be done so well without me—but now he thinks I have done more harm than all the Preachers have done good . . . Franky ought to have been the last Man to say this," Jarratt wrote in 1788. Apart from separation from the Episcopal Church, Jarratt now believed that Methodism and American society in general had become too democratic and egalitarian. "In our high *republican times*, there is more *levelling* than ought to be," he concluded.[25]

Methodist historians have debated the legitimacy of the Christmas Conference since the nineteenth century. As is often the case in debates over the American Constitution, they have largely focused on the original intent of the principals involved. Writing in the 1820s, Alexander M'Caine argued that John Wesley never intended to create a separate, episcopal church in America, or make Coke and Asbury bishops. M'Caine was part of the movement to estab-lish the Methodist Protestant Church (founded in 1830), a breakaway denomi-nation that eliminated the episcopacy, the office of presiding elder, and allowed for lay representation in annual conferences. M'Caine's first book, *The History and Mystery of Methodist Episcopacy* (1827), in which the only mystery seems to be why anyone had ever accepted it to begin with, was answered that same year by John Emory's *A Defence of "Our Fathers," and of the Original Organization of the Methodist Episcopal Church*. Emory argued that Wesley, notwithstanding his later denunciation of Asbury for taking the title of bishop, clearly favored an episcopal church polity.[26]

Later authors largely followed the lines of argument laid out by M'Caine and Emory. Nathan Bangs (1840) and Abel Stevens (1867) argued that the Christmas Conference faithfully adhered to Wesley's intentions in establishing a separate, episcopal church. Stevens in particular argued that Wesley didn't object to the "Episcopal function," but only to the title of bishop, which in England had become associated with "pretentious ecclesiastical dignities." Edward Drinkhouse, writing in the 1890s, countered that Coke and Asbury manipulated the Christmas Conference to increase their own power at the expense of Wesley and the general desire of American Methodists. In this scenario, Coke and Asbury deliberately thwarted the plan for American Meth-odism that Wesley had entrusted to Coke by creating an episcopal structure that placed them above Wesley's reach, or indeed anyone else's. They were now bishops, a title even Wesley couldn't claim.[27]

Both sides in this debate shared the assumption that Wesley understood the American situation thoroughly and had a comprehensive plan in mind for dealing with it. What they disagree about is whether or not Coke and Asbury faithfully followed that plan. Asbury knew better. From his first meeting with Coke, he saw that Wesley's plan was ambiguous on several key points. He trusted Wesley's theology, but realized that he was far removed from events in America, where the war had tarnished Wesley's image. Specifically, Wesley's instructions didn't clearly delineate to what degree American Methodists were free in the future to appoint their own leaders and adjust their polity. The ambiguity soon led to a break between the American church and Wesley himself.

The Campaign Against Slavery

Not content to stop with Wesley's ordinations, the Christmas Conference out-lined a plan to rid the church of slaveholders entirely. "We view it as contrary to the Golden Law of God on which hang all the Law and the Prophets, and the unalienable Rights of Mankind, as well as every Principle of the Revolution, to hold in the deepest Debasement, in a more abject Slavery than is perhaps to be found in any Part of the World except America, so many Souls that are all capable of the Image of God," declared the *Discipline*, authorized by the conference and published by Asbury and Coke in 1785. Every Methodist slaveholder was given twelve months to execute a legal deed of emancipation, although the emancipations themselves could be delayed. Slaves between the ages of forty and forty-five were to be freed by the time they reached forty-five. Those aged twenty-five to forty were to be freed within five years; those between twenty and twenty-five, by the age of thirty; those younger than twenty, by the age of twenty-five at the latest. The preachers were instructed to keep written records verifying compliance; members who refused to follow the rule were to be expelled, as were any members who sold their slaves. The plan would have systematically rid American Methodism of slavery and brought freedom to thousands of African Americans, but it wasn't to be.[28]

Methodist opposition to slavery hadn't taken shape in a vacuum. White Methodists learned to appreciate the injustice of slavery largely through rubbing shoulders with the many African American converts pouring into the movement. In 1786, the first year black and white members were listed separately in the annual minutes, African Americans represented just over 9 percent of all American Methodists. By 1790, they accounted for 20 percent of the more than 57,600 members, a proportion that held steady through the turn of the century. In some places, African Americans made up an even greater proportion of members. On the Delmarva Peninsula, the district that Asbury knew best, they represented 30 percent of all members in 1787. Blacks not only joined in great numbers, but they also proved capable of leading and preaching. A good example is Harry Hosier, also known as "Black Harry."[29]

Little is known of Hosier's early life, though it is likely that he was born a slave in North Carolina about 1750, and later gained his freedom. By 1780, Hosier was preaching among Methodists in Virginia and the upper South, captivating audiences with his eloquence. Though illiterate, he had a good memory for scripture passages. The *New-York Packet* described him in September 1786 as "a very singular black man, who . . . has preached in the Methodist church several times, to the acceptance of several well disposed judicious people.—He delivers his discourses with great zeal and pathos, and his language and connection is by no means contemptible." In some settings Hosier preached only to African Americans, but in others he preached to mixed audiences. In 1781, he accompanied Asbury on a preaching tour of Virginia, traveling with him on several occasions thereafter. "The truth was, that Harry was a more popular speaker than Mr. Asbury, or almost any one else in his day," according to John Lednum, a nineteenth-century historian of American Methodism. The Methodist preacher Henry Boehm heard Hosier preach a sermon of "great eloquence and power" in Delaware in 1803. "He was unboundedly popular, and many would rather hear him than the bishops," marveled Boehm.[30]

Yet it is clear that Hosier wasn't treated the same as a white preacher. He apparently was never ordained and evidently posed as Asbury's servant in some places. After their initial meeting at Barratt's Chapel, Coke writes in his journal that Asbury had "given me his black (Harry by name) and borrowed me an excellent horse" for his upcoming tour of the connection. It is unlikely that Asbury referred to Hosier as "his black," but it is also clear that Coke didn't think of him as just another preacher. Asbury of course had no servant in the conventional sense of the word, though other preachers sometimes rode with him, acting as assistants. But Coke wouldn't have referred to them as if they were servants. Hosier was different only because he was black. After traveling with Hosier for a couple of weeks, Coke marveled at his preaching. "I sometimes give notice immediately after preaching, that in a little time Harry will preach to the blacks, but the whites always stay to hear him," Coke wrote on November 29, 1784. "I really believe he is one of the best Preachers in the world, there is such an amazing power attends his preaching." This was high praise, but it didn't gain Hosier equal treatment with white preachers. Most Methodists of this period had little trouble reconciling spiritual equality with some degree of social inequality. Still, Hosier's presence and that of thousands of other African American Methodists brought the issue of slavery to the forefront of Methodist thinking in the 1780s.[31]

Asbury had spent enough time in the South to know what they were up against. The year before, he had stopped for the night at the home of John Worthington, a Maryland Methodist who lived a short distance from Baltimore. At Worthington's he "beheld such cruelty to a Negro that I could not feel free to stay; I called for my horse, delivered my own soul, and departed." He didn't return to Worthington's again, though it remained open for preaching and quarterly meetings for nearly a decade. A week after his abrupt departure from Worthington's, Asbury stopped at the home of John Willson, another Maryland Methodist. Though the Willsons were "kind beyond measure," Asbury got into an argument with either Willson or his father, who "acknowledged the wrong done the blacks by taking them from their own country, but defended the right of holding them." "Our talk had well-nigh occasioned too much warmth," Asbury noted. Having already attempted in a small way to convince some southern Methodist slaveholders of the evils of slavery, he knew that implementing the new rules would be a bitter fight.[32]

Coke was still too new to the South to see this. Following the Christmas Conference, he set off on a tour of American Methodist sites, crossing into Virginia in March 1785. At one stop while he preached an anti-slavery sermon in a barn, "many of the unawakened" stalked out, waiting outside to "flog" him when he appeared. According to Coke, one "high-headed Lady" offered the "rioters" £50 if they would give "that little Doctor one hundred lashes." Protected by a group of prominent Methodists, including a "Colonel" and a justice of the peace who had recently freed fifteen slaves, Coke escaped without harm. From this point on, he mostly limited his anti-slavery efforts to private conversations, much as Asbury had done. When he crossed into North Carolina, Coke set aside his "Testimony against Slavery for a time . . . the Laws of this State forbidding any to emancipate their Negroes." When he did speak publicly against slavery after returning to Virginia, he was careful to begin by "addressing the Negroes in a very pathetic manner on the Duty of Servants to Masters," hoping that the whites present would then listen "without much offence, or at least without causing a tumult."[33]

Nevertheless, when the Virginia preachers met for a conference in early May, Coke and other antislavery advocates urged them to send the Virginia Assembly a petition calling for "the immediate or Gradual Extirpation of Slavery." Drawing largely on the ideology of the revolution, the petition argued that "Justice, Mercy, and truth, every virtue that can adorn the Man or the Christian, the Interest of the State, and the Welfare of Mankind, do unanswerably,—uncontroulably plead for the removal of this grand Abomination." Methodist preachers collected signatures across the state, from present-day West Virginia and northern Virginia through the center of the state to Halifax, Mecklenburg, Brunswick, and Greensville counties on its southern border.[34]

From the beginning Asbury suspected that the petition would raise a storm. Even as the conference drafted it, he "found the minds of the people greatly agitated with our rules against slavery," and in particular with the "petition to the general assembly for the emancipation of the blacks." Still, with the help of the abolitionist General Daniel Roberdeau, whom Asbury first met in 1772 and now lived in Alexandria and had signed the Methodist petition, Asbury and Coke arranged a meeting with George Washington at Mount Vernon a few weeks after the Virginia conference. Following dinner, the two asked Washington to sign the petition. Though they came away from the meeting believing that Washington supported the measure, he refused to sign, which isn't surprising given Washington's views on slavery. While he favored some sort of gradual emancipation in theory, Washington feared the prospect of a large, free African American population. Nonetheless, Coke and Asbury weren't that far off in believing that Washington was sympathetic to their cause. He was the only one of the Founders to free his slaves, doing so in his will. Indeed, his intention to free his slaves appears to have taken shape about 1789, a decade before his death and not long after his meeting with Asbury and Coke. In any event, Asbury remained fascinated with Washington for the rest of his life.[35]

The response to the emancipation petition was tragic, if predictable. Washington noted that when the petition was presented to the Virginia Assembly, it "could scarcely obtain a reading." Not only did the legislature reject it unanimously, it sparked a series of pro-slavery counter petitions presented to the legislature in 1784 and 1785. Originating in the same southern and central regions of Virginia where Methodists collected signatures for their petition and where Methodism was strongest, the pro-slavery petitions were signed by more than twelve hundred people from eight counties: Amelia, Brunswick, Halifax, Hanover, Henrico, Lunenburg, Mecklenburg, and Pittsylvania. Together, the petitions advanced four central arguments against emancipation revolving around property rights, social stability, biblical precedents, and independence from Great Britain.[36]

The pro-slavery petitioners argued that the American Revolution had been fought primarily to secure the right to private property, not, as the Methodist petitions claimed, to secure "liberty" for all "mankind." To protect their property, Americans had "risked our Lives and Fortunes, and waded through Seas of Blood," according to the petitions from Amelia, Halifax, Mecklenburg, and Pittsylvania counties, or, as the Lunenburg petition put it, "seald with our Blood, a Title to the full, free, and absolute Enjoyment of every species of our Property, whensoever, or howsoever legally acquired." Emancipating their slaves would deprive owners of their property and undermine social stability, leading to "inevitable ruin," according to the Lunenburg petition. It would result in "Rapes, Murders, and Outrages . . . inevitable Bankruptcy . . . Breach of public Faith . . . Loss of Credit with foreign Nations; and lastly Ruin to this now free and flourishing Country," argued the Halifax petition. Knowing that supporters for emancipation argued from religious principles, the pro-slavery petitions devote considerable space to examples from both the Old and New Testaments that supported bound labor. While anti-slavery advocates were "pretending to be moved by Religious principles and taking for their motives universal Charity," the Brunswick petition argued "That it was ordained by the Great and wise Disposer of all Things, that some Nations should serve others, and that all Nations have not been equally free." Finally, the petitions argued that those supporting a general emancipation were "Tools of the British Administration," as the Halifax petition put it.

On this point the Methodists were particularly vulnerable, considering their mixed record of participation in the revolution, even in Virginia. The petition from Lunenburg County explicitly made this point by expressing outrage at the sight of fellow Virginians "prostituting their [views] by uniting them with a proscribed Coke an imperious Asbury and other contemptible Emissaries & Hirelings of Britain in promoting and advocating a Measure which they know must involve their fellow Citizens in Distress & Desparation, not to be described, or thought of, without Horror; & their Country in inevitable ruin." The fact that the petition names Coke and Asbury indicates the degree to which the two had become lightning rods for the debate over slavery. What must have been especially discouraging for Asbury was that all of the pro-slavery petitions called for a repeal of the 1782 private manumission act, which allowed individual slaveholders to free their slaves. The Virginia House of Delegates subsequently defeated a bill to repeal the 1782 act, fifty-two to thirty-five, but it was clear on which side the sympathies of most leading Virginians fell.[37]

Slavery was a deeply divisive issue that cost the Methodists the support of many former allies. Edward Dromgoole, who rode the Brunswick circuit in southern Virginia during the 1785–1786 conference year, later wrote "the state of religion was brought very low in our circuit during 1785 and 1786. Some prejudices arose on account of the new minutes that were made, and new terms of communion proposed, chiefly with respect to holding Slaves." Dromgoole himself left the itinerancy in 1786 to become a successful Brunswick County planter and slaveholder. By 1798 he owned more than 800 acres of land and six slaves, and in 1803 the buildings on his property were valued at $2,050.[38]

Devereux Jarratt also broke with the Methodists at least in part because of the church's anti-slavery rules. Jarratt came from a relatively wealthy background of landed slaveholders. Relying largely on his wife's money, by 1782 Jarratt owned a 640-acre plantation and two dozen slaves; at his death in 1806 he still owned twenty-three slaves. When Coke and Jarratt first met in March 1785, Coke claimed that they discussed the new rules concerning slavery at length, but Jarratt "would not be persuaded." "The secret is, he has twenty-four Slaves of his own," Coke wrote. By May, Coke claimed that Jarratt had become "a violent assertor of the propriety and justice of Negro-Slavery." Despite his assertions to the contrary, Jarratt took an active role in undermining the anti-slavery movement. On May 31, 1785, he wrote to Edward Dromgoole, then stationed on the Brunswick circuit, complaining that the anti-slavery rules had become "destructive & divisive" among Virginians who "may be led, but not drove." Three years later he was still complaining about Methodists comparing slaveholders to "*horse thieves & Hogstealers, Knaves*, &c" and insulting them "at every turn with the odious Name of Oppressors, Rogues, & Men destitute of even heathen honesty." This helps to explain a portion of Jarratt's bitterness against the Methodists. Not only had they left the true church, but they had also challenged a fundamental pillar of southern society on which much of his wealth rested.[39]

Methodists had long faced opposition in Virginia, but the conflict over slavery drove resentment of the movement to a new level. Suspicions about Methodist loyalism during the war hadn't led to as much violent persecution in Virginia as in Maryland. Prior to the 1780s, Virginia Methodists were most often ridiculed for their supposed religious fanaticism and loud preaching. During the 1760s and 1770s the *Virginia Gazette* delighted in ridiculing the artisan origins of Methodist preachers, calling them "illiterate zealots, that leave their lawful callings for an employment to which it is manifest they are not called." The paper also ran stories on the wild-eyed enthusiasm of English Methodists, including accounts of a Methodist preacher running into a church and tearing up the Bible and Prayer Book and a Methodist ribbon weaver attempting to drown himself so that he might reach heaven all the sooner. Many white Virginians saw Methodists as "furious, ignorant, and illiberal zealots," as one correspondent to the *Virginia Gazette* wrote, but not particularly dangerous. Methodist abolitionism changed this, reaching as it did to the heart of Virginia culture.[40]

By the time the yearly conference met in Baltimore on June 1, 1785, a majority of the preachers, including Coke and Asbury, were ready to back down. When Asbury and Coke published the *Discipline* in 1785, they included a provision giving "our Brethren in *Virginia*" two years "to consider the Expedience of Compliance or Non-Compliance with these Rules." According to Coke, the conference voted to suspend the rules enacted less than six months before at the Christmas Conference, "on account of the great opposition that had been given it, our work being in too infantile a state to push things to extremity." It was a bitter defeat but not the last word. Opponents and defenders now turned their attention to local initiatives, beginning within Methodism a process of sectional division that would serve as a harbinger and catalyst of the Civil War. The Delmarva Peninsula and much of Maryland remained hotbeds of Methodist abolitionism well into the nineteenth century. Nevertheless, the topic of slavery disappeared from annual and general conference minutes for the next eleven years.[41]

Asbury's role in the controversy is best understood in the context of his larger commitment to preaching the gospel everywhere possible. He says comparatively little about the campaign against slavery in his journal, and he didn't champion the new rules in the South to the extent that Coke did. He had tried in the past to convince at least a few southern Methodists to liberate their slaves, without much success. Unlike Coke, whom Devereux Jarratt described as "a stranger in the land," Asbury knew how divisive the issue of slavery was among southerners. His commitment to the antislavery cause was genuine, but not as deep as his commitment to preaching the gospel as he understood it. The most important goal was to save souls for eternity, be they those of blacks or whites. All earthly cares were of secondary importance. Coke's reach often exceeded his grasp, but this rarely concerned him for long, since he constantly found new projects to engage his energies. Asbury was more single-minded in his commitments, more concerned with how individual decisions would fit together over the long term. His extensive travels through the South had given him a good feel for just what slavery meant to southern society. He realized that overturning it would take more than passing rules and sending petitions to state assemblies.[42]

Asbury had always been reluctant to challenge outside authorities and to take on political issues involving non-Methodists, particularly when he lacked a clear consensus within the church. In this sense, his response to the slavery controversy is similar to his reaction to the American Revolution. In order to preserve his opportunity to minister in America, he took an apolitical stance during the revolution, tacitly accepting its legitimacy once the outcome seemed certain. His goal was to emerge from the war in a position to preach the gospel and lead the Methodist movement, regardless of the war's political and military results. This had been possible since the revolution had a fairly clear outcome, one that nearly all white Americans remaining in the United States accepted at its conclusion. Slavery was another story. It would remain a perennial controversy for another eighty years, dividing Americans across a spectrum from northern abolitionists to southern fire-eaters. Sensing the intractability of the debate, Asbury chose to push the issue only in local settings where he thought he could see a workable solution. On a national level, there didn't seem to be one.

Even so, the bitterness with which Asbury later described the church's failure to combat slavery belies the logic of these decisions. Asbury knew that he was compromising with evil; there was nothing in his Methodist beliefs that could make that sit easy. His theology demanded that the eternal fate of souls take precedence over social justice, but slavery was still a moral tragedy, and he knew it.

A Methodist College

Coke's visit to the United States left another legacy, one that initially inspired but ultimately plagued Asbury and the church for years to come. Asbury had proposed opening an American school modeled after Wesley's Kingswood school as early as 1779. That November, while sitting out the war in Delaware, he "had some talk about erecting a Kingswood school in America" with Samuel Magaw, the Anglican minister at Dover, Delaware, with whom he was friends. When the northern preachers met for their yearly conference in Baltimore in 1780, they took up the question, "Will this Conference take into consideration the erecting a Kingswood School upon the plan Bro. Asbury has presented?" The answer was evidently yes, since Asbury continued to push the project forward. After meeting with Asbury in North Carolina in June 1780, John Dickins drew up a "subscription for a Kingswood school in America." By the time the northern and southern preachers had agreed to refer the sacramental crisis to Wesley in 1782, they had also approved Asbury's scheme. In November 1782, Thomas Haskins visited Abingdon, Maryland, where "the Conference is about to erect an academy and Chapel, a noble design if accomplished."[43]

When Coke and Asbury met at Barratt's Chapel in November 1784, they agreed to move forward with the school project, though on a grander scale. They chose the Abingdon site for the school because of pledges of land and financial support from local Methodists, including Richard Dallam and Henry Gough, who lived not far away at Perry Hall. Wesley's Kingswood school, founded in 1748 near Bristol, England, was intended to educate children "in every branch of useful learning," including "Reading, Writing, Arithmetic, French, Latin, Greek, Hebrew, Rhetoric, Geography, Chronology, History, Logic, Ethics, Physics, Geometry, Algebra, and Music." Designed to educate students in the classics, this would amount to a far more extensive curriculum than was available to most Americans attending common schools. Coke now convinced Asbury that the new American school should take this a step further by becoming a college, which meant a community of students and teachers living together to pursue an advanced curriculum, particularly in Latin.[44]

On November 14, 1784, Coke and Asbury met to discuss financing the new college. Coke optimistically reported that between them they had obtained about £1,000 sterling in subscriptions for the school. A few weeks later, Coke "gave orders that the materials should be procured for the erecting of the College." The following June, the Baltimore conference named the school Cokesbury, a combination of the bishops' names suggested by Coke. Asbury says comparatively little about all of this, in particular omitting any claim about the size of promised donations, which Coke overstated in his usual burst of exuberance at the beginning of a new project.[45]

Coke's own educational background, including his days at Oxford, must have had a lot to do with his desire for a Methodist college in America. His status as a gentleman had opened doors for him that were closed to Asbury and the other American preachers. Throughout his tour of the United States, Coke was entertained by leading citizens to a degree that Asbury never had been. Shortly after his arrival in America, he had coffee with the governor of New York and his wife, met with the city's Episcopal clergyman, and was subsequently entertained by elites north and south, including numerous "captains," "colonels," "doctors," state representatives, and other "gentlemen" and "gentlewomen" of "property," and "fortune," most of whom weren't Methodists. In so eagerly recording their titles in his journal, Coke was writing more for a British audience than an American one. He wanted to leave little doubt that America's pious gentry recognized him as an international religious leader, affording him the utmost respect. But he also intended for these encounters to serve as an example to American Methodists of what a more refined church could expect. Whereas Charles Wesley had wanted to keep uneducated preachers down, Coke wanted to raise them up, not suspecting that this might ultimately limit their access to common people if done on a grand scale.[46]

Asbury had no desire to make gentlemen of the preachers' sons who would attend Cokesbury, yet he wasn't averse to offering them the kind of opportunity that he had missed as a boy. He knew what it was to feel awkward and unlearned, but he really didn't understand what he was after. Having never attended a college, he had no idea how to run one. In theory, he saw little reason why learning and strict piety couldn't be combined, though in practice he would find this a difficult balancing act, as many others before and since have discovered.

On June 2, 1785, a day after the Baltimore conference ended, Coke sailed down the Chesapeake Bay on his way back to England, leaving the administration of the church once more in Asbury's hands. It is just as well that Coke left. Had he stayed, he and Asbury would undoubtedly have clashed over their different leadership styles. Coke would have been a disaster at stationing the American preachers and tending to the myriad details of managing the church. Still, his ability to see the big picture had been vital in establishing an independent American church, raising forthrightly the issue of slavery, and laying the foundation for a Methodist college in America. He would be back, but for now Coke only stayed long enough to see the first of these three visions through.

9

"Such a time ... was never seen before"

The Christmas Conference of 1784 was one of those events that changed everything and nothing at the same time. There was much that was new. American Methodism was no longer part of the Church of England, the state church of a nation with which the United States had just fought a war, nor was it as closely identified with John Wesley, whom few Americans had ever seen. Just as important, the church now had its own ordained preachers who could administer the sacraments. Yet much remained the same. The preachers were largely the same, and Asbury remained the church's most important leader. The movement's theology and culture were also little changed, as was its basic organizational structure. Thomas Ware later recalled that after 1784, "Every thing went on as it had before" with the "advantage" that Methodists now had the "delightful privilege" of "bringing our children to be dedicated in baptism at our own altars, and of receiving the sacrament of the Lord's Supper at the hand of our own ministers."[1] The changes of 1784 more resembled the orderly transition following a democratic election than a revolution.

This was certainly true for Asbury, whose daily life changed little. For several months he performed a steady stream of baptisms and administered the Lord's Supper more often than he later would, reflecting pent up demand. At one appointment in North Carolina, he agreed to plunge "four adults, at their own request, they being persuaded that this was the most proper mode of baptizing."[2] Otherwise he continued to travel much as he had since the end of the war, if anything increasing his pace to capitalize on the church's new momentum. In January 1785, while in Rowan County, North Carolina, he and a guide pushed on well after dark, crossing several "deep streams," so that he wouldn't disappoint a congregation that turned out to include only nine people. The next night he and two companions had to share a single bed. After Coke's departure for England in June 1785, Asbury turned west into western Virginia and Pennsylvania. By the end of July, his throat was painfully inflamed, but he decided not to stop for rest, even though he passed through the resort of Berkeley Springs. Instead he pushed on for the home of Prudence and Henry Gough outside of Baltimore, where he rested for two weeks in August. He then hurried to New York to complete his summer tour of the North. Travel, preaching, and prayer took up the bulk of his time, along with attending annual and quarterly conferences and seeing to the endless details of stationing preachers.[3]

As he made his way through New Jersey in September, Asbury stopped to buy a Jersey wagon for £44. Often used on stage routes to carry passengers, one traveler described them in 1783 as "neither convenient or neat." Even on the day he bought his wagon, Asbury wondered if it would "bring me into trouble in travelling, and in getting horses?" It did, and in early November, after he missed an appointment because of the cumbersome wagon, he traded it for a second-hand sulky, a light two-wheeled carriage intended for one passenger and drawn by a single horse. A few months later, outside Charleston, South Carolina, he abandoned even the sulky, remarking that the roads were so bad "I was thankful I had left my carriage, and had a saddle and a good pair of boots." Over the years he experimented with traveling in various kinds of light wagons, particularly when his health made riding a horse difficult. But he was always reluctant to sacrifice the speed and simplicity of traveling by horseback, or to limit himself to roads suitable for a wagon.[4]

Asbury turned south in November 1785 for his now familiar winter tour of southern Methodism. As had been his practice for several years, he attended two annual conferences in the South, the first in North Carolina in February 1786 and the second in Virginia in April, before heading north for the northern annual conference, held this year in Abingdon, site of Cokesbury College. He essentially repeated this process in 1787, with conferences in South Carolina (the first in that state) in March, Virginia in April, and Baltimore in May. The Baltimore conference had been scheduled for Abingdon in July, but Coke, who had returned to the United States by way of the Caribbean, switched the date and location, under Wesley's orders. Since Coke still had commitments to Methodism in Britain, he had decided to visit America every two years. Leaving England on September 24, 1786, bound for Halifax, Nova Scotia, his ship was badly damaged in a storm, limping into Antigua on Christmas day. After visiting several islands in the West Indies, Coke landed at Charleston, South Carolina, on March 1. He came with instructions from Wesley to ordain Richard Whatcoat a joint superintendent with Asbury. Wesley's presumption to make this kind of decision for American Methodists would test the meaning of what had happened at the 1784 Christmas conference.[5]

When Asbury learned of Wesley's plan from Coke, his response was characteristically cautious. He wrote to Whatcoat from Charleston that "Mr. Wesley has appointed you a joint Superintendent with me. I can, therefore, claim no superiority over you." He added that while the "mode" of Wesley's appointment "is not approved of" (a deliberate use of the passive voice), "many of us by no means object to the person." Asbury genuinely admired Whatcoat. His piety and simplicity of lifestyle were above reproach, and his loyalty to Methodism beyond question. Now fifty-one, Whatcoat was born in Gloucestershire, England, and raised in a pious Anglican environment. Though his father died while he was young, his mother had experienced conversion some years before his birth, which more or less mirrored Asbury's own childhood experience in the faith. At age thirteen, Whatcoat began an eight-year apprenticeship to an artisan who lived first in Birmingham and then in Darlaston, Staffordshire, only three miles from Asbury's home in Great Barr. At the end of his apprenticeship, Whatcoat moved to Wednesbury and began attending Methodist preaching. Whatcoat and Asbury were converted at about the same time and under the same preaching in the Wednesbury area. They must have known one another and probably attended class meetings together, though Whatcoat was some nine years older than Asbury. After Whatcoat's death, Asbury wrote that he was more "uniformly good" than anyone he had "known in Europe or America."[6]

Still, Coke's mission came as quite a surprise to Asbury, who, according to Coke, was "rather cool" at their first meeting. Under Asbury's influence, the South Carolina conference, held shortly after Coke's arrival, changed the superintendent's title to bishop. This certainly wasn't part of Wesley's directions and most likely came from Asbury as an initial response to Wesley's new attempt to control American Methodism. The change in title carried no explicit increase in power, but it was symbolically important, further distancing the American church from Wesley. Wesley had always been careful to insist that he had never separated from the Church of England and that his superintendents weren't usurping the role of the Church's bishops. "How can you, how dare you suffer yourself to be called Bishop?" he wrote to Asbury, addressing him as "my dear Franky," when he learned of the change. "I shudder, I start at the very thought! Men may call me a knave or a fool, a rascal, a scoundrel, and I am content; but they shall never by my consent call me Bishop! For my sake, for God's sake, for Christ's sake put a full end to this!"[7]

This was the last letter that Asbury received from Wesley, and it hurt him deeply (he called it "a bitter pill" in his journal). When he first came to America, Asbury wrote to his parents that he was "under Mr. Wesley's direction; and as he is a father and friend, I hope I shall never turn my back on him." All the same, he kept the new title. It was a more decisive break from Wesley than Asbury's decision to stay in America during the revolution. For his part, Wesley believed he had good reason to feel betrayed. He had sent Franky, the metalworker's apprentice, to America as a lay preacher, only to find him turned self-styled bishop. Who did Asbury think he was? And how could Wesley now answer critics in England, who accused him of encouraging a schism from the Church of England? From Wesley's perspective, Asbury had put him in a ridiculous position.[8]

Asbury and his supporters later claimed that they adopted the new title because it was less offensive to American ears than Reverend or Mr., since only God is addressed as "holy and reverend" in scripture (Psalms 111:9), and Mr. could be construed as a form of master, thus violating Jesus's command, "Neither be ye called masters: for one is your Master, even Christ" (Matthew 23:10). But at the time everyone knew that the real issue was Wesley's presumption to appoint the American church's leaders without consulting them.[9]

As the controversy over Whatcoat's appointment deepened, Asbury refrained from taking a direct role in the debate for three reasons. First, he genuinely respected Whatcoat and didn't want to shame him in public. Second, regardless of the issue, Asbury always disliked public controversies and tried to avoid them whenever possible. His instinct was always to look for some kind of backroom compromise. Third, in this case there was no shortage of people lining up to denounce Wesley's plan.

One of the most outspoken critics was James O'Kelly, whose influence in the independently minded South was pivotal. Writing in April 1787, prior to the meeting of the Virginia conference, O'Kelly compared Wesley's treatment of the American preachers to slaveholders and their slaves. Most likely born of Irish ancestry in Virginia, which he once called "my native country," O'Kelly served in the American army during the revolution. By 1778 he was itinerating on trial in Virginia. From 1779 to 1784 he rode the New Hope and Tar River circuits in North Carolina, and the Mecklenburg, Brunswick, and Sussex circuits in Virginia. At the Christmas Conference in 1784, O'Kelly was ordained one of the new church's first elders. He had little formal education, once referring to Asbury as "an utter stranger to a clasical education; being like me—born of poor parentage." A gifted and popular preacher nonetheless, O'Kelly built a large following in southern Virginia.[10]

With regard to Wesley's motives, O'Kelly asked, "Does he look upon our country preachers to be men of so low breeding as not fit to govern [themselves]? ... Or is there any political scheme in it?" American Methodists hadn't forgotten Wesley's open support of the British during the Revolutionary War (hence the reference to "any political scheme") and the persecution they had suffered as a result. "There is not a man in the world so obnoxious to the American politicians as our dear old Daddy," Asbury wrote to Jasper Winscom, a shopkeeper and local preacher whom Asbury had known on the South Wiltshire circuit in England. O'Kelly also didn't believe that Whatcoat was "adequate to the task, on account of his age" and because he was "a stranger to the wilderness of America." But "above all," O'Kelly urged that "two heads would produce two bodies." Either the church would be controlled by Americans (under Asbury) or by Wesley, but not both.[11]

Coke undoubtedly heard more of the same wherever he went. At the yearly conference in Baltimore, Asbury remained in the background while Coke pressed the preachers to follow Wesley's orders. It was a lost cause. According to Jesse Lee, the conference objected to Whatcoat's ordination for two reasons: "1, That he was not qualified to take the charge of the connection. 2. That they were apprehensive that if Mr. Whatcoat was ordained, Mr. Wesley would likely recall Mr. Asbury, and he would return to *England*." In fact, at the British Conference meeting in Manchester in 1787, Thomas Rankin reportedly declared that if he "had the power and authority of Mr. Wesley, he would call Frank Asbury home directly." Word apparently even reached Eliza Asbury, who wrote to her son that she hoped to see him in England soon.[12]

Unwilling to concede, Coke countered by pointing out that the Christmas Conference had pledged that "during the life of the Rev. Mr. Wesley, we acknowledge ourselves his sons in the gospel, ready in matters belonging to church government, to obey his commands." The preachers replied that either they hadn't been present at the 1784 conference, or "they did not feel ready *now* to obey his [Wesley's] commands." This must have come as quite a shock to Coke, who never did understand how democratic the foundations of American Methodism were. At one point Coke supposedly interrupted Nelson Reed, one of the American preachers, saying, "You must think you are my equals;" to which Reed replied, "Yes, sir, we do; and we are not only the equals of Dr Coke but of Dr Coke's king." Turning to Asbury, Coke remarked, "He is hard upon me." "I told you that our preachers are not blockheads," Asbury replied. It was the same mistake that Coke had made with regard to the emancipation of slaves, assuming that southern Methodists would simply do as they were told, freeing their slaves in obedience to him and the church. A gentleman at heart, Coke couldn't fully comprehend a society in which ordinary people refused to defer to their betters.[13]

Whatcoat says nothing about the whole ordination affair in his memoirs, confirming his reputation for humility and charity. No one grumbled when Asbury appointed Whatcoat elder over nine of the church's most important circuits on the Delmarva Peninsula for the next year. For Coke, however, the worst was yet to come. After rejecting Wesley's orders, the preachers heard complaints against Coke for changing the conference dates and "for writing improper letters to some of our preachers, such as were calculated to stir up strife and contention among them." With the tide against him, Coke agreed to sign a remarkable agreement abdicating much of his authority over the church:

> I do solemnly engage by this instrument, that I never will, by virtue of
> my office, as superintendent of the Methodist church, during my
> absence from the United States of America, exercise any government
> whatever in the said Methodist church. . . . And I do also engage, that I
> will exercise no privilege in the said church when present in the
> United States, except that of ordaining according to the regulations
> and law, already existing or hereafter to be made in the said church,
> and that of presiding when present in conference, and lastly that of
> travelling at large[14]

The conference also dropped Wesley's name from the minutes. It was reinstated in 1789, but not as before. In answer to the question "Who are the persons that exercise the Episcopal Office in the Methodist Church in Europe and America?" the 1789 conference answered, "John Wesley, Thomas Coke, and Francis Asbury." But to the next question, "Who have been elected by the unanimous suffrages of the General Conference, to superintend the Methodist connection in America?" the conference replied, "Thomas Coke, Francis Asbury." Indeed, Coke may have narrowly escaped having his name removed as well by signing the agreement given above. Thus chastened, he sailed for Ireland three weeks after the Baltimore conference. The whole affair worked to significantly strengthen Asbury's authority as the leader of American Methodism. James O'Kelly would later regret vesting so much power in Asbury, but for now he enjoyed the overwhelming confidence of the preachers.[15]

The affair over Whatcoat's appointment widened the gulf between Wesley and Asbury. Wesley believed that Asbury was largely responsible for the American conference's refusal to ordain Whatcoat a superintendent and its decision to remove his (Wesley's) name from the minutes. "It was not well judged of bro: Asbury to *suffer,* much less indirectly to *encourage* that foolish step in the late Conference," Wesley wrote to Whatcoat in July 1788. "Every Preacher present ought both in Duty & in Prudence to have said 'Brother Asbury, Mr Wesley is *your* Father; Consequently, ours, and we will affirm this in the face of all the world.'" Yet even if Asbury had been willing to submit to Wesley's control (which he wasn't), he had little choice in the matter. Wesley didn't understand that Asbury couldn't control the more democratically mind-ed American conference as Wesley did the British. "I know the Americans very well," Asbury wrote to Thomas Morrell. "I am fully convinced that it was not expedient for Mr. Wesley . . . to claim the shadow of power [or] authority" over the American church.[16]

The Whatcoat controversy also strained Asbury's relationship with Coke, but didn't ruin it. Much of the credit must go to Coke. Though quick to anger, he was also quick to forgive. Shortly after he returned to England in August 1787, Coke wrote to Asbury to tell him that he had seen his mother in Birmingham and had given her three guineas from Asbury and five guineas of his own, and "informed her that she might draw upon me for any thing she wants."[17]

Revival

For most Methodists, 1787 was remarkable not for the ruckus over Wesley's proposed ordination of Whatcoat, but for the number of revivals and the expansion of the church's borders. The overwhelming support that Asbury enjoyed had far more to do with how well the church was doing than with anything connected to Wesley. "Such a time for the awakening and conversion of sinners was never seen before among the Methodists in America," reported Jesse Lee. The largest revivals took place in southern Virginia, which, along with the Delmarva Peninsula, had long been a stronghold of Methodism. Between 1786 and 1788 membership increased from 18,791 white and 1,890 black members to 30,809 white and 6,545 black members, a 64 percent increase in white members, a 246 percent increase in black members, and an 81 percent increase overall. During the same period the number of circuits rose from fifty-one to seventy-six and the number of traveling preachers from 117 to 165.[18]

Asbury witnessed some of these revivals firsthand, receiving reports on others. In January 1788 he noted that Philip Cox, then riding the Sussex circuit in Virginia, "thinks that not less than fourteen hundred, white and black, have been converted in Sussex circuit in the past year; and brother [John] Easter thinks there are still more in Brunswick circuit." Cox claimed that ten thou-sand people attended a quarterly meeting in July 1787. Asbury wrote to

Thomas Coke that more African Americans would have joined the church if their "lordly masters" hadn't prevented them.[19]

The revivals were marked by emotional worship, passionate preaching, and long meetings. In southern Virginia, a series of quarterly meetings served as the focal point, often lasting five or six hours, and sometimes all night. At a quarterly meeting held July 25 and 26, 1787, at Mabry's chapel on the Brunswick circuit, "the power of God was among the people in an extraordinary manner: some hundreds were awakened; and it was supposed that above one hundred souls were converted," according to Jesse Lee. The meeting continued for two days, extending from Thursday through Friday evening. Many who had attended the Mabry chapel meeting hurried to the next quarterly meeting, held at Jones's chapel in Sussex County on Saturday and Sunday, July 27 and 28. As they rode in, they could hear shouting and weeping half a mile from the meetinghouse. The ensuing meeting was even more spectacular than at Mabry's chapel. On Saturday, according to Lee, "hundreds of the believers were so overcome with the power of God that they fell down, and lay helpless on the floor, or the ground; and some of them continued in that helpless condition for a considerable time." Jones's chapel couldn't hold all of the people, so the next day some of the preachers held meetings in the surrounding woods. As they took turns preaching, "the power of the Lord was felt among the people in such a manner that they roared and screamed so loud that the preacher could not be heard, and he was compelled to stop." The revival blurred racial and class boundaries as "scores of both white and black people fell to the earth; and some lay in the deepest distress until the evening. Many of the wealthy people, both men and women, were seen lying in the dust, sweating and rolling on the ground, in their fine broad cloths or silks, crying for mercy." Overall, Jesse Lee believed that the 1787 awakening exceeded the 1776 revival in scope and intensity.[20]

Freeborn Garrettson experienced the power of the revival while stationed on the Delmarva Peninsula from 1787 to 1788. "The people in this part of the country seem as if they would all be Methodists," Garrettson observed in May 1787. In his mind the extent of the revival was directly related to its emotional exuberance. "Those preachers whose labours the Lord particularly blest in this revival, were lively and powerful; and there was much of what some call wildfire among the people: the cries of the distressed were frequently so great, that the preacher's voice was drowned." While this disturbed some who objected to "hollowing meetings," Garrettson was firmly convinced that the revival wouldn't have continued without it. "I am never distressed in hearing convinced sinners crying for mercy; though they were to cry so loud as to be heard a mile," Garrettson concluded. Richard Whatcoat described the revival in much the same terms when he took Garrettson's place as supervising elder on the peninsula in 1788. At one quarterly meeting near Cambridge, Maryland, in April 1789, "the cries of the mourners, and the ecstasies of believers were such, that the preacher's voice could scarcely be heard, for the space of three hours," according to Whatcoat.[21]

When Thomas Coke returned to the United States on February 24, 1789, he noted a "great revival" taking place almost everywhere south of the Pennsylvania-Maryland border. In Annapolis, Maryland, according to Coke, rather than orderly singing or prayer by one person at a time, "the congregation began to pray and praise aloud in a most astonishing manner." This cacophony of unrehearsed prayer and praise to God shouted out by any number of people at the same time shocked Coke, just as the exuberance of southern revivals had shocked Joseph Pilmore and Thomas Rankin before him. At first he "felt some reluctance to enter into the business; but soon the tears began to flow, and I think I have seldom found a more comforting or strengthening time." Unlike Pilmore and Rankin, Coke soon accepted the legitimacy of what he saw. Writing to Ezekiel Cooper aboard ship after spending four months in America, Coke summed up his new position on the emotionalism of American Methodism: "the shouts in the congregations, which at first I reluctantly entered into, met with my full approbation in a little time. I saw in them the hand of God; and the signal and numerous convictions and conversions which took place at those times, were demonstrative proofs of the approbation of the Most High. And who was I, that I should fight against God?"[22]

Like Coke, Asbury was willing to accept what seemed to be a genuine outpouring of the Spirit, even if it meant giving up a degree of control and yielding to the emotions of an audience. While in North Carolina in June 1788, he noted that "preaching and praying is not labour here: their noise I heed not; I can bear it well when I know that God and Christ dwells in the hearts of the people." A year later he wrote to Jasper Winscom in England, "We have noise and shouting and you must have the same or you will not get the work revived. The work of God has been long trod upon" by those who urged that meetings not be "too long—too loud—so many minutes and all this is order, order but no souls converted to God." Though he was seldom remembered as a fiery preacher, the revival drew out even Asbury. He preached a "very alarming" sermon in Maryland in October 1788. "Seldom, if ever, have I felt more moved," he wrote. Reuben Ellis heard Asbury preach "the greatest Sermon that ever I heard from" Jeremiah 15:19 in February 1790 in Charleston. "The word was indeed with power. A cry arose...in different parts of the Church, where Mourners were crying for mercy, till near 10 O Clock."[23]

Shouting was part of the larger work of God but it couldn't be the whole of it. One of Asbury's chief concerns during this period was to incorporate new members into the church in such a way that they wouldn't fall away once the initial surge of emotionalism subsided. Writing to Ezekiel Cooper in December 1788, while Cooper was stationed in Baltimore, Asbury urged him to "visit from house to house, and that regularly once a fortnight for no other purpose, than to speak to each in the family about their souls, that they may be ready for your help." He also instructed Cooper to preach every other night, visit each of the approximately thirty class meetings every other week, organize more bands, and "remember the sick," "the poor Negroes and also the children." The goal was to keep the "work" in "motion" so that the people wouldn't "settle on their Lees." Community development and consistent discipline were familiar themes for Asbury, having always been at the heart of his conception of the Methodist system. Large, dramatic revival meetings might draw crowds of curious onlookers, but only a deeper level of integration would keep them. This placed a "very great" burden on the preachers, but no more than the punishing regimen Asbury held himself to.[24]

Indeed, far from resenting Asbury's guidance, Ezekiel Cooper pushed himself to live up to Asbury's expectations. Cooper, twenty-five years old in 1788, had been raised a nominal Anglican on Maryland's Eastern Shore. Freeborn Garrettson stopped at Cooper's home when he was thirteen and asked his mother if he could preach there. She agreed, even though Cooper's stepfather was an "officer of rank" in the militia and "a violent enemy to the Methodists as a people whom he supposed [were] enemies to the country." Garrettson's sermon left a deep impression on Cooper, who "felt the drawings of the spirit powerfully in my soul." But local suspicions that Methodist preachers were agents of the British kept Cooper from further contact with the movement for several years. "For some time" he had only "one of our negro men who was also concerned upon the subject" to talk to about his religious state. Eventually Cooper's religious convictions faded until he once again attended a Methodist meeting in 1780, at his mother's insistence. For much of the next year, in typical evangelical fashion, his convictions grew until one day as he walked alone in the woods, "I had such a confidence in the merits of Christ and mercy of God; that I layed hold of the promise; felt my burden remove; and a flood of peace, love and joy break forth in my soul." Following his conversion, Cooper joined a class meeting in the spring of 1782. "Class meeting I found one of the most profitable meetings I attended," Cooper later recalled.[25]

Soon after his conversion, Cooper began to feel a call to preach and "warn sinners to flee the wrath to come." Others first noticed his gift for words in his public prayers. Consequently "the brethren at length made it a constant practice to put me to prayer among them." While riding the Talbot circuit during the 1783–1784 conference year, Freeborn Garrettson made Cooper a class leader. Yet Cooper hesitated when it came to preaching, torn between the conviction that God had called him and the fear of embarrassing himself. Overcome with anxiety, he "fell into a lingering state of body, and a dull frame of soul," wasting away to "a mere skiliton." Friends feared he would die, but in early 1784 Cooper pulled himself together and began to exhort after others had preached. Though Cooper doubted his abilities, he was destined to become one of early Methodism's most erudite voices. His intelligence and zeal must have been evident even amid his own self doubts, prompting Asbury to appoint him to the Caroline circuit in Maryland in November 1784. Cooper reluctantly agreed, preaching his first sermon (as opposed to giving an exhortation) at his first appointment on the circuit. During the next three years, he rode the Long Island circuit in New York, and the East Jersey and Trenton circuits in New Jersey. At each appointment Cooper met with considerable success. Long Island membership tripled during his year there, and membership increased by one hundred on the East Jersey circuit and nearly two hundred on the Trenton circuit during his time on each. But these accomplishments paled in comparison to what happened next in Baltimore, where Asbury stationed Cooper in the fall of 1788.[26]

Cooper's appointment to Baltimore didn't begin promisingly, and Asbury's support wasn't initially much of an asset. Cooper later wrote to Asbury that at the Baltimore conference in September 1788, many of the city's Methodists "were much tempted against you, on account of some plain[,] severe reproofs which you gave, in such close and, as they thought, general terms, that they concluded, you called in question their sincerity in religion, and condemned them as hypocrites altogether."[27] To make matters worse, Cooper arrived in Baltimore in poor health, "a moving skiliton worn down to such weakness that I could hardly walk." It was at this point, in December 1788, that Asbury wrote urging Cooper to redouble his efforts. His health notwithstanding, Cooper "moved cautiously, but steadfastly," to enforce the full range of Methodist discipline "with exactness." He didn't have to wait long to see the fruit of his efforts. In February 1789, "the glorious work broke out like a fire, which had a long time struggled for vent, and blazes forth in a flaming conflagration," Cooper wrote. "Every evening in our congregation, which were uncommonly numerous, the power of God was like a rushing mighty wind. The citizens who never came to our church at other times, now flocked in abundance to see and hear, what some called, the 'methodistical rant and enthusiastical madness.'" Meetings "continued till 1, 2, or 3 oc in the morning," and at least one meeting in Baltimore drew an estimated four thousand listeners. Cooper preached and met classes almost every day (as Asbury had urged him to do), while class leaders and other lay people led a series of nightly prayer meetings in private homes. So many men and women spoke at these meetings that Cooper concluded "all the Lord's people are prophets." At one love feast, "there seemed to flow words of fire from every mouth, while one after another, full of rapture and love, arose and humbly declared the great goodness of God to their souls. It was as a penticost indeed, and like unto the very suburbs of heaven." About a hundred new members joined in the first month, and four hundred to five hundred joined within the year.[28]

No more an enthusiast at heart than Asbury, Cooper felt obligated to explain the extraordinary emotional outbursts associated with the revival. "Our meetings, 'tis true, were very noisy, with penitential cries and shouts of praise; many could not bear this, but reprobated it as insufferable madness in places of worship," he admitted. "As if their hearts were rending and their hopes sinking," mourners would cry out: "*Has the Lord no mercy for me?*" "*What shall I do?*" "*Am I a wretch undone and banished from God forever?*" ..."*Save! Save! Save! Lord save from the wrath to come! Save or I sink into hell!*" Cooper was, of course, pleased with the conversion of sinners, but he knew that many outsiders wondered why the same effects couldn't be achieved without all the shouting. His "reply was generally, I did not know how that might be, but this was certain, they were not produced before, and [I] doubted whether they would have [been], had not God worked in this extraordinary manner." He suspected that the real problem for those upset by the revival's noise was a desire for respectability in the eyes of the ungodly. "I am awfully afraid that many will lose their souls through fear of reproach," Cooper wrote to Asbury. "The cross is a mortifying thing to nature—a fathomable, honourable religion, allowing the maxims, customs, and pleasures of this world many would like; but when gospel holiness, the pure religion of Christ is preached and en-forced—that we must deny ourselves of all vanity, and walk the strait and narrow way of humility and meekness, love and obedience, they pray to be excused."[29]

Asbury's influence on Cooper is difficult to miss; they sound so much alike. Cooper described one of Asbury's sermons that September in Baltimore as "an affecting sermon indeed. The people were melted into tears abundantly. The word was like hammer and fire." As long as Asbury and the younger preachers agreed on so much—the need for personal piety and communal discipline, the dangers of seeking after wealth and worldly respectability, and, above all, the need to bring sinners to the crisis point of conversion—their support for him would remain strong. Cooper and several friends rode about 10 miles to hear Asbury preach a final sermon "before he got out of reach" on September 16, 1789. "Oh that good and gracious man[,] how I feel for him under his great charge. I pray the Lord to support & be with him while he has the care of the churches that he may govern to the glory of his master[']s name and the good of the cause of religion," Cooper wrote in his journal.[30]

For Asbury, success came at a price, bringing with it a heavier work load. The tide of new members and prospective preachers remained strong from 1787 into 1789, particularly in the South and West. He still stuck to his policy of visiting each region once a year, but as the church's borders expanded this became a more demanding task. "Brother Hagerty attempted to travel with me, but was soon glad to resign," Asbury wrote as he rode through Maryland in December 1787. Hagerty was an elder and a seasoned veteran, having joined the traveling connection in 1779, but few could keep up with Asbury for long. "I seldom mount my horse for a ride of less distance than twenty miles on ordinary occasions; and frequently have forty or fifty in moving from one circuit to another," he wrote while in North Carolina in January 1788. During the first three months of 1788, he crisscrossed Virginia, North Carolina, and South Carolina before arriving in Georgia on April 1. Returning north through the Carolinas, he crossed into Tennessee at the end of April. He then turned east, making stops in North Carolina, Virginia, and Pennsylvania before arriving in Maryland in September. Following the annual conference in Baltimore, he rode north through Pennsylvania, New Jersey, and New York before turning south once again into Delaware, Maryland, and Virginia. During 1788 alone he held six annual conferences in as many states. By the time of the Baltimore conference, he was complaining that he couldn't preach because "my mind was clogged by business with so many persons and on so many subjects."[31]

The rides got longer, and traveling conditions in the new frontier regions were at times even more difficult than what he was used to. "O how glad should I be of a plain, clean plank to lie on, as preferable to most of the beds," he wrote after an unpleasant week of traveling in western Virginia. He added: "and where the beds are in a bad state, the floors are worse. The gnats are almost as troublesome here, as the mosquitoes in the lowlands of the seaboard." In North Carolina he complained that while sleeping in an "unfinished" house that offered little protection against the weather, a horse "kicked the door open, and I took a cold, and had a toothache, with a high fever." Like most Americans of the time, Asbury had a pre-romantic view of nature. When he looked on the undeveloped backcountry, he saw hardship rather than grandeur, menace more often than beauty. He often complained about the prosperity and complacency that development brought to frontier regions, but he seldom lamented the destruction of the wilderness. Nature presented abundant dangers for those who lived their lives largely outdoors, and there seemed no end of it.[32]

As always, the roads were bad in the backcountry, and bridges were few, or so poorly maintained that they weren't worth the risk. He and his companions often had to wade or swim their horses across rivers and streams, at times soaking riders and their possessions, including books. When they took long detours to avoid crossing at dangerous spots, they increased the length of their journey, or, worse, lost the main path. Thomas Coke, who traveled with Asbury for several months in 1789, records one instance in which they were lost for 21 miles in the South Carolina and Georgia backcountry. "Frequently indeed we were obliged to lodge in houses built with round logs, and open to every blast of wind, and sometimes were under the necessity of sleeping three in a bed. Often we rode sixteen or eighteen miles without seeing a house . . . and often were obliged to ford very deep and dangerous rivers. . . . Many times we ate nothing from seven in the morning till six in the evening," Coke wrote. If all of this was a temporary adventure for Coke, it was a part of everyday life for Asbury (though in all fairness Coke knew other hardships, including long voyages at sea). The threat of injury while traveling in the backcountry was real, made all the more dangerous by the difficulty of getting good medical care, such as it was in the late eighteenth century.[33]

Asbury looked on this kind of danger, passively imposed by nature, as a challenge, a test of his faith. To survive under these conditions was an indication of God's approval. After spending a day crossing the Great Dismal Swamp in southern Virginia, which covered more than 600 square miles straddling the Virginia-North Carolina border between the James River and Albemarle Sound, he wrote that "our passing unharmed through such dangers and unhealthy weather, feelingly assures me that I am kept by the immediate interposition of His providence." God's protection notwithstanding, life on the road took an increasing toll on Asbury's body.[34]

10

"Alas for the rich! they are so soon offended"

Despite its growth, Methodism remained a poor person's church. Exhibit A was Cokesbury College. On June 5, 1785, less than a week after Coke sailed for England and ended his first American tour, Asbury preached the "foundation sermon" of the college. But it was more than two years before the school actually opened. Finding enough money to run it was always a problem. Asbury wrote to the preachers, urging them to do what they could "in collecting money to carry on the building of our college," a campaign that was only marginally successful. By May 1786 the main building still lacked a roof, and the project was already £900 in debt. To make up the chronic shortfalls, Asbury periodically went "begging for the college," which finally opened with twenty-five students on December 6, 1787. Difficult times still lay ahead. On August 10, 1788, while in western Virginia, Asbury "received heavy tidings from the college—both our teachers have left; one for incompetency, and the other to pursue riches and honours: had they cost us nothing, the mistake we made in employing them might be the less regretted."[1]

One of the teachers was Truman Marsh, a recent Yale College graduate who had been hired the year before to teach Latin for £80 a year. The next March, 1789, he was ordained an Episcopal priest by Bishop William White of Pennsylvania. The other departing teacher was Levi Heath, Cokesbury's president, whom Coke had recruited from England in early 1786 for £60 a year plus room, board, and other expenses. An Anglican priest, Heath doesn't appear to have attended a university, though he taught grammar school in Kidderminster, England, while also serving as curate of a local church. No sooner had he recruited Heath than Coke left for America without making sufficient provision for Heath's moving expenses. Though initially scornful of a Methodist college in America, Wesley took an interest in Heath and his family, advancing him enough money to keep him going until Coke returned in late June 1787. Heath arrived in Baltimore that September, but by the following summer he, like Marsh, had left amid charges of "neglect" and incompetency in Latin. Like Marsh, Heath became an Episcopal priest, preferring to remain in America despite Wesley's offer to pay his way back to England.[2]

The school struggled on with new teachers under the direction of Jacob Hall, a local physician, but its mounting debt weighed heavily on Asbury. Methodists believed that remaining free of debt was a moral responsibility, and to this point in his career Asbury had held steadfastly to this principle. Now Cokesbury threatened to undermine his reputation for fiscal restraint. Minimum annual expenditures for the college amounted to £200, while contributions remained "trifling." In November 1788, Asbury heard of an attempt to burn the college. Two weeks later he visited the school and learned that the report was true. Someone had set a fire in a closet, causing £100 of damage before it was discovered by students and extinguished. Compounding Asbury's dissatisfaction, he concluded that although some of the current students had promise as scholars, "they want religion."[3]

Be that as it may, when Thomas Coke visited Cokesbury with Asbury in May 1789, he could hardly contain himself. Coke was "highly pleased with the progress they have made towards the compleating of the building; the situation delights me more than ever." He was also "satisfied beyond a doubt" with the current teachers and all but one of the students, whom he and Asbury expelled for lack of piety. Best of all, according to Coke, the school's finances now allowed it to support four students fully and two in part, all of them preachers' sons and orphans. Yet Coke couldn't have been entirely oblivious to the school's true financial state. Shortly after he and Asbury visited Cokesbury, they had a subscription letter printed asking for donations to cover £2,000 (Maryland currency) in debt. Undeterred, Coke set in motion plans to establish another college in Georgia (it never materialized) and another in Kentucky. Ever the visionary, Coke, who habitually overextended himself and underestimated financial obligations, was seeing what he wanted to see. Free of the responsibility of actually raising the money for Cokesbury, he dreamed big, leaving Asbury to pick up the pieces.[4]

Despite Coke's optimism, Cokesbury was still £1,000 in debt in December 1791, when the trustees resolved to quit admitting charity students and told

Asbury to stop "beg[g]ing" for money on their behalf. Asbury attributed Cokesbury's troubles to the general "poverty of the people," which is a fair assessment. Cokesbury didn't fit the culture of early American Methodism. Fifty years later, as Methodists helped create the American middle class, they became avid college builders, founding more than two hundred schools and colleges between 1830 and 1860. But the Methodists of the 1780s weren't college people. They were farmers and artisans for whom a few years of common school were the norm. They didn't expect to send their children to college and therefore could see no good reason to give their hard-earned money to build one. Asbury should have known better, but his judgment was clouded by Coke's enthusiasm and his own ambition. Keenly aware that his education fell far short of Wesley's and Coke's, Asbury tried to vicariously atone for his shortcomings through Cokesbury. If he didn't have a university education, he would have the next best thing: a college to call his own.[5]

Cokesbury exposed the church's poverty, but this wasn't necessarily a bad thing. During a two-week stay at Berkeley Springs in August 1789, Asbury reflected that his "soul" had "communion with God, even here. When I behold the conduct of the people who attend the Springs, particularly the *gentry*, I am led to thank God that I was not born to riches." Bath was particularly bad in this regard, but it wasn't alone in reflecting the perils of prosperity. "To begin at the right end of the work is to go first to the *poor,* these *will,* the rich *may possibly,* hear the truth," he observed while in New York in June 1789. Like John Wesley, Asbury believed that wealth was inherently corrupting. When he first heard of the provisional treaty of November 30, 1782, that ended the Revolutionary War, he realized the new peace would present its own challenges. It would "cause great changes to take place amongst us; some for the better, and some for the worse. It may make against the work of God: our preachers will be far more likely to settle in the world; and our people, by getting into trade, and acquiring wealth, may drink into its spirit." A few months later in Philadelphia he thought he could see this happening: "The city is all in motion—stores full of goods, great trade going on; all things prosper but religion," he wrote on August 16, 1783.[6]

For now Asbury could mostly count on the support of the preachers when it came to decrying the debilitating effects of wealth. Reflecting on his decision to leave the traveling connection and locate in 1783, William Watters was careful to point out that he didn't do so to better himself in this life. "I never had a thought of settling to get riches, or any thing that the world can afford," Watters wrote. Rather, his decision was motivated by his poor health and the need to provide his wife and children with bare necessities. For several years he had suffered from a number of ailments, including an extended bout of malaria beginning in the fall of 1781 that lasted nearly two years. But he remained adamant that these difficulties hadn't led him to seek security in the things of this world. "I have never, since I first knew the Lord seen any thing in this world worth living an hour for, but to prepare and assist others to prepare, for, that glorious kingdom, which shall be revealed at the appearing of our Lord and Saviour Jesus Christ." Even after he located and took up farming, Watters remained convinced that "the love of money is the root of all evil." Those who coveted wealth risked falling from the faith and "pierc[ing] themselves through with many sorrows." Watters never did become financially comfortable, refusing to pursue business ventures that might injure his reputation as a local preacher. In 1801, after his children were grown, he re-entered the traveling connection for five years, locating for the final time in 1806.[7]

The only acceptable course was to live in a state of voluntary poverty, or as close to it as decency allowed. Writing to an English correspondent in August 1788, Asbury noted with satisfaction that he could hardly afford "one coat on my yearly allowance." "Our connection is very poor, and our preachers on the frontiers labour the whole year for 6 to 8 pounds," which, in Asbury's mind, was a good thing. His belief in the virtue of poverty was one of the reasons he clung to the practice of paying all of the preachers the same salary ($64 a year), whether probationers or bishops. This had the virtue of reducing competition for more affluent, usually urban, circuits, since the preachers assigned to those circuits couldn't expect to benefit much from the relative wealth of their congregations. Offering better salaries on circuits that could support them would have drawn more candidates into the ministry and kept others from locating, but only at the risk of making money a motivation for preaching.[8]

In general Methodists admired Asbury's financial restraint, but there were differences in the way that most viewed the problem of wealth. A life of voluntary poverty may have seemed ideal to Asbury and preachers like William Watters, but most Methodists hoped to do better. In their minds the root problem wasn't wealth, only how it was used. The gentry led immoral lives because they were corrupt at heart, with or without their money. Prosperity held its own dangers to be sure, but most Methodists dearly hoped that they would have the chance to prove that wealth and piety could be successfully combined. For now, they could only speculate on what it might be like to try. The gap between Asbury and the broader church in this regard would become important only after a sizeable proportion of Methodists obtained the kind of wealth that they could only dream of in the 1780s. Methodism already had a few wealthy members, families like the Goughs of Perry Hall, but as yet they didn't define the culture of the church.

Freeborn Garrettson and New York

Lack of money hadn't held back growth in the South, and it wasn't really the problem in the North. In eastern Pennsylvania and New Jersey, entrenched Lutheran and Presbyterian churches had managed to stamp out most New Light exuberance following the Great Awakening and still remained unfriendly to Methodist-style religion. Eastern Pennsylvania and New Jersey Methodists accounted for only about 7 percent of the church's membership in 1788. While Asbury was in Pennsylvania in early July 1789, he noted with "distress" that the church had fewer than a thousand members to show for twenty years of preaching in the state.[9]

New England, with its firmly rooted Congregational churches, presented a similar challenge. Methodists would eventually shake the foundations of organized religion in these regions, but it would always be slow going when compared to the South, where the Anglican church offered relatively little resistance, or the West, where there was often no organized religion to speak of before the Methodists arrived.

The one exception in the North was upstate New York, essentially a western frontier in the 1780s. Prior to the war, the Methodists hadn't ventured very far up the Hudson River, a task Asbury now set for Freeborn Garrettson. Bold, ambitious, and pleasantly stubborn, Garrettson was a pivotal figure in early Methodism and one of Asbury's most dependable assistants. A Marylander who had freed his slaves soon after his conversion, Garrettson's spirituality was as intense as Asbury's, though with a more mystical quality to it. A reputation for bizarre supernaturalism followed Garrettson and the Methodists to upstate New York, where it was rumored that Methodist preachers threw blue spiders on their victims to enchant them.[10]

Garrettson possessed a combination of intelligence, level-headed good sense, and fearless zeal that made him an ideal choice to send to difficult but strategically important regions. His parents were third-generation English settlers who owned a considerable amount of land in Harford County, Maryland. Their financial security allowed him to remain in school until age seventeen, acquiring a better than average education. At the Christmas Conference of 1784, Garrettson was ordained one of the church's first elders and then sent to Nova Scotia as a missionary to English settlers and former American loyalists. His success in Nova Scotia led Wesley to instruct Thomas Coke to ordain Garrettson the superintendent of the British North American provinces and the West Indies during Coke's 1787 tour of the United States (the same visit on which Coke tried to ordain Whatcoat a joint superintendent with Asbury). Garrettson had misgivings about the plan from the beginning, apparently reluctant to sever his ties with the American church. He later remembered asking Coke for a year to travel more broadly, particularly to the West Indies, before deciding. Coke either misunderstood Garrettson or decided that his uncertainty was answer enough, and the ordination was shelved. Instead, Garrettson spent the 1787–88 conference year as supervising elder for the four circuits and fourteen counties of the Delmarva Peninsula. The peninsula was an important district, but it didn't put Garrettson's talents to best use. Asbury had something more challenging in mind for him, making him the supervising elder over New York Methodism in 1788. A few years earlier, in 1783, Asbury had sent John Dickins to reinvigorate New York City Methodism. Now he hoped that Garrettson could do the same on a larger scale.

Far from representing a sort of exile (the Hudson River valley was hardly the Siberia of post-revolutionary America), Asbury's choice to send Garrettson to New York was based on a realistic assessment of what kind of leader the situation required. The state was an important population center in its own right, but it also represented the gateway into New England, a region that Methodism had yet to penetrate. Despite twenty years of preaching in and around New York City, the church had only about one thousand members in the state. Garrettson was the kind of person who worked best without much direct supervision, something that Asbury understood and factored into his choice. If Garrettson was something of a mystic, his genteel background and easy manner also gave him the skills necessary to handle urbane New Yorkers, as events would prove.[11]

One unintended consequence of Garrettson's new assignment was his romance with Catherine Livingston. The two were unlikely lovers, given their families and social roots. Born into the stunningly wealthy, politically powerful, and religiously respectable Livingston clan of New York, Catherine was raised amid the best that polite society had to offer. The combined fortunes of her parents, Judge Robert R. and Margaret Beekman Livingston, included 750,000 acres along the Hudson River south of Albany. Catherine attended parties with the likes of George and Martha Washington, Alexander Hamilton, foreign ministers, and French officers. Her brother Robert later served as U.S. Secretary of Foreign Affairs and delivered the oath of office to George Washington at his inauguration in New York City. Garrettson may have come from more respectable stock than most Methodists, but it was nothing compared to the Livingstons.[12]

Yet in their religious temperaments, Freeborn and Catherine (or Kitty) were much alike. She later recalled that during her childhood, "nothing could exceed the cheerfulness of our family circle, the happiness of Clermont [the Livingston estate] was almost proverbial." Nevertheless, as she approached adulthood she grew increasingly dissatisfied with the direction of her life.

"There was something wanting," she later recalled. While living in Philadelphia in 1782, she and a friend, Mary Rutherford, "would sit up after returning from brilliant Balls, and gay parties, and moralize on their emptiness, till it really became burdensome to accept of invitations, for such was the dissipation of the day that we had been asked to five private Balls in one week, but made it a rule never to go to more than one." Following the deaths of several close friends, including Rutherford, Catherine experienced conversion in the fall of 1787 while reading the Book of Common Prayer alone in her room. A servant introduced her to Wesley's writings, but for more than a year she remained alone in her pilgrimage of faith.[13]

Then she heard Freeborn Garrettson preach, and a new world opened up. During their courtship, Freeborn and Kitty read one another's journals and even had the same religiously inspired dreams. Their romance came as a shock to Margaret Livingston. A penniless Methodist preacher was no match for her daughter. She eventually relented, and the two were married on June 30, 1793.

Freeborn Garrettson (1752–1827). (From Abel Stevens, *History of the Methodist Episcopal Church in the United States of America*, vol. 2 [New York: Carlton & Porter, 1867].)

They enjoyed a supportive and happy marriage, but Catherine's close family ties meant that Freeborn could never really leave New York. Relying on money from Catherine's inheritance, the Garrettsons built a substantial mansion, known as Wildercliffe, or Traveler's Rest as Asbury called it, overlooking the Hudson River at Rhinebeck. Asbury stopped there whenever he could. He always admired the Garrettsons' faith, but regretted Freeborn's inability to leave the Livingston orbit and travel more broadly. Garrettson's daughter later wrote that all that was precious to her father was at Wildercliffe, yet in later years he felt guilty, believing that he should have traveled and preached more.

Those regrets were in the future, however. For now Garrettson had more than enough to do. When he first took charge of New York Methodism in 1788, he had twelve young preachers to cover a vast territory stretching from the outskirts of New York City north to Lake Champlain. He traversed this district every three months, riding about 1,000 miles and preaching about a hundred sermons on each round. During his first year in New York, membership in the

Catherine Livingston Garrettson (1752–1849). (From *The Ladies Repository*, vol. 24 [June 1864]).

district increased from 535 to 1,420. By May 1789, Asbury could report with satisfaction that "our work opens in New York State." That same month, while in New York, Thomas Coke wrote that "in the country-parts of this State, Freeborn Garrettson, one of our Presiding Elders, has been greatly blessed; and is endued with an uncommon talent for opening new places." Asbury expanded Garrettson's responsibilities to include ten circuits and nineteen preachers for the conference year 1789–90. For the next decade Asbury appointed Garrettson to supervise upstate New York districts. If Garrettson hadn't married, Asbury would certainly have moved him every few years to take advantage of Garrettson's talent at organizing new regions. But Catherine's family and social connections were too strong. With the exception of two relatively short appointments in Philadelphia, one for six months and the other for a year, Garrettson spent the remainder of his career in New York, serving a final stint as presiding elder from 1811 to 1815. Asbury had chosen well in sending Garrettson to New York.[14]

Politics

Despite his organizational genius, Asbury feared the broader political world. Since his youth near Birmingham, he had seen political force misused against Methodists, and he continued to suspect that it was almost always detrimental to true religion. America was no different in this regard.[15]

The only politician Asbury admired was George Washington, yet even with Washington he was initially cautious. After their first meeting in May 1785 at Mount Vernon, Asbury sent Washington "one of our Prayer Books," with an extra copy for Martha Washington, and a volume of sermons, presumably Wesley's, in April 1786. After Washington was elected president, Asbury, Coke, John Dickins, and Thomas Morrell (who had served as a major under Washington during the Revolution) met with Washington in New York on May 29, 1789. Asbury read an address from the church praising "the most excellent constitution of these states, which is at present the admiration of the world," and promising "our fervent prayers to the throne of grace, that GOD Almighty may endue you with all the graces and gifts of his Holy Spirit, that may enable you to fill up your important station to his glory, the good of his church, the happiness and prosperity of the United States, and the welfare of mankind." Morrell later remembered that Asbury read the address "with great self posses-sion . . . in an impressive manner." Washington in turn read an address thanking Asbury and his companions for their prayers and noting that "the people of every denomination" who regarded themselves "as good citizens, will have occasion to be convinced, that I shall always strive to prove a faithful and impartial patron of genuine, vital religion." The *Daily Advertiser* of New York reprinted both addresses on June 3, 1789, as did the *Arminian Magazine*.[16]

Yet it would be easy to read too much into this event, which Asbury didn't even record in his journal. His main concern at this meeting seems to have been preventing Coke from reading the address. "It was with great difficulty and peculiar delicacy, [that] I prevented the doctor from presenting the address," Asbury wrote to Thomas Morrell in September 1789. Too many Americans still remembered Wesley's opposition to the revolution and knew of Coke's close ties to Wesley. "It is impossible for Mr. Wesley ever to reconcile himself to this country" or for Coke to "satisfy the objections" his British connections raised "while he continues to be a non resident in this country," Asbury wrote to Morrell. In fact, a number of people wrote to New York papers after the address was published, complaining of what they saw as Coke's hypocrisy in now pretending to be a friend of America. Asbury's role in presenting the address raised no similar objections.[17]

Given Asbury's distrust of politics, it is ironic that by the early nineteenth century Methodism became a leading political force in several states, including Delaware, where Methodists were overwhelmingly Federalists, and Ohio, where they were predominantly Republicans. While the church didn't openly promote political activism, it taught members to be hard working and frugal, gave them confidence that as individuals they occupied a meaningful place in the world, and instilled in them the value of community involvement (as with the importance of attending class meetings) and the need for communal discipline. These habits were easily transferable from the spiritual to the secular world, giving Methodists a cultural foundation from which to move into the political realm. But such habits took time to bear fruit. The active involvement of Methodists in politics didn't really gain momentum until after 1800. By then, Asbury's apolitical orientation had given the church the character of a body without a head when it came to questions of political engagement.[18]

The Council

Garrettson's first year in New York ended with a summons from Asbury to come to Baltimore to attend the first session of the Methodist Council. The short-lived council represented Asbury's latest attempt to maintain order in the rapidly growing church. His experience in 1788 of holding six annual conferences stretching from Georgia to New York had convinced him that the church was growing too large for one person to administer face-to-face. And yet he was unwilling to call for the election of another bishop who, unlike Coke, would take a serious interest in running the church. Asbury didn't believe that anyone else was equal to the task, and the majority of the itinerant preachers agreed, preferring to trust their fate to an overworked Asbury than commit themselves to the judgment of anyone else. At the same time, Asbury realized that something had to change; as the church continued to expand his stamina would inevitably give out. The council was his first attempt to solve this problem.

The council consisted of the bishop and most of the presiding elders, a new term used to designate those elders who supervised a district consisting of several circuits.[19] The council was supposed to serve as the church's highest administrative body, with authority to set policy for the church as a whole. The regional annual conferences would continue to meet, though under the direction of the council. Hence, if Asbury were to miss any particular annual conference, he wouldn't entirely give up his control over it. Central to his thinking was his memory of the sacramental crisis of 1779 and 1780, when the southern preachers seceded from the rest of Methodism while he was stuck in Delaware.

But the council wasn't a democratically elected body, and this doomed it in the end. Religion is never a strictly democratic affair, and Methodists readily admitted that God's grace was beyond their control. They tacitly acknowledged that the office of bishop came with a prophetic mandate. But they also stubbornly insisted that bishops weren't infallible and that their decisions were subject to review. Just how stubbornly Asbury would soon learn.

The first council met from December 3 to 10, 1789, in Baltimore, the church's unofficial capital. Asbury and eleven presiding elders attended, representing the church's geographic regions from Georgia to New York. Asbury and Garrettson both believed that this first meeting went well, characterized, in Garrettson's words, by "sweet conversation," "harmony," and "sweet union with Jesus." The rules adopted by the council stipulated that all resolutions required the consent of the bishop and two-thirds of the elders present. The council also agreed that any resolutions they passed had to be approved by a majority of the itinerant preachers in each conference before they went into effect. With the rules set, the council passed a series of resolutions aimed at standardizing practices throughout the church. Sunday worship was to begin at ten or eleven o'clock in the morning and was to consist of "Singing, Prayer, and reading the Holy Scriptures, with Exhortation or reading a Sermon, in the Absence of a Preacher." The service was to be led by an "officiating Person" appointed "by the Elder, Deacon, or travelling Preacher." No more meetinghouses were to be built without the consent of the conference and the presiding elder unless they could be "finished without the least Debt remaining." The council also resolved that Cokesbury students would no longer be continued on credit, requiring them to pay at least a portion of their tuition in advance, and that deacons had to wait at least three years before becoming elders. Finally, the council asked all members for "Proposals" for "some Scheme for relieving our dear Brethren who labour in the Extremities of the Work," primarily on the western frontiers. "A spirit of union pervades the whole body, producing blessed effects and fruits," Asbury wrote at the end of the council's session.[20]

Yet even as the council met, opposition was brewing against it. Jesse Lee believed that the plan was "entirely new, and exceedingly dangerous." According to Lee, a majority of the preachers had voted in favor of creating the council before they realized how much it would increase the bishops' power. "The council was to be composed of the bishops, and the presiding elders; the presiding elders were appointed, changed, and put out of office by the bishop, and just when he pleased," which meant that the council would be controlled by the "bishops, and a few other men of their own choice," Lee wrote. To make matters worse, Lee contended that the constitution adopted by the first council was less democratic than the preachers had expected, in particular because it gave Asbury a veto over all council proceedings.[21]

Though a member of the first council, James O'Kelly likewise feared its influence. Writing several years after the fact, O'Kelly claimed that during their deliberations Asbury cunningly "duped" the elders, controlling the council's agenda so that the others "moved on in the dark, and groped as a blind man." According to O'Kelly, Asbury used apocalyptic imagery, reminding the preachers that "the Millenium was approaching, or coming fast on!" and prayers "that God would deliver the preachers from the curse of suspicion," to create a sense of urgency and coerce them into following his will. Particularly galling to O'Kelly was the prohibition against building new meetinghouses without approval, which he maintained was an "invasion" of the people's "civil, as well as religious liberties." Asbury and his supporters insisted that this measure was designed to prevent societies from taking on too much debt, but it was probably also intended in part to foil a movement O'Kelly supported aimed at incorporating church property in a way that removed it from the bishops' control. Following the meeting, O'Kelly "told Francis, that instead of counsellors, we were his tools; and that I disliked to be a tool for any man." O'Kelly later insisted that the council had been nothing but a "grand deception." Asbury and Garrettson hoped that the council would promote order and efficiency, but to O'Kelly and Lee it looked like blatant tyranny. Unfortunately for Asbury, the furor over the first council meeting was a harbinger of things to come. If the church had proved increasingly difficult to manage in the second half of the 1780s, the 1790s would stretch his resourcefulness to the breaking point.[22]

II

"Be not righteous over much"

One measure of the church's success was that it now had to deal with pretenders. By 1792 there were at least three cases of "infamous imposters" traveling through the country from Virginia to New York with forged preaching licenses, pocketing offerings, and in one case marrying "a young woman of a reputable family," even though the impostor already had a wife. When Thomas Ware rode north in the spring of 1793 to take charge of the Albany district, he discovered that the year before a young man had traveled the same route claiming that he was Thomas Ware. Ware's impostor told those he met that Asbury had sent him from the South to join Jesse Lee in New England, but he had lost his horse through misfortune. Several unsuspecting congregations took up collections to assist him. This sort of thing wouldn't have happened fifteen years before, during the revolution when no one wanted to be mistaken for a Methodist preacher. But by the 1790s the church had succeeded enough to attract its share of charlatans.[1]

The expansion of American Methodism during the 1780s had been remarkable, transforming it from a beleaguered sect of alleged Tories to a widely recognized, if not universally respected, church. Growth during the 1790s fell off. Between 1780 and 1790 American Methodism expanded from 8,500 members to 57,600, an increase of 578 percent. By 1800 membership had risen only another 6,070, an 11 percent increase for the decade. What growth existed was unevenly distributed. The church expanded into new areas, particularly west across the Appalachian Mountains and north into upstate New York and New England. The decline came mostly in the South, where membership among whites fell in Delaware, Maryland, Virginia, North Carolina, and Georgia. Black membership continued to grow in all these states except Virginia, but not enough to keep total membership from declining in each. "The Lord works westward and more northward, and eastward. We have great prospects about Boston, Connecticut and Rhode Island," William Watters wrote to Asbury in October 1793. Conspicuously absent from this summary was any mention of the South. Asbury was convinced that most of the problems in the South resulted from dissatisfaction with Methodism's longstanding opposition to slavery and the impact of dissidents, unhappy about a range of issues, who chipped away at Methodist unity from within. There had been little for Methodists to fight over in 1780. They had largely overlooked internal disputes in the interests of survival. But by 1790 the church had acquired enough resources and stability that those dissatisfied with Asbury's leadership no longer felt constrained to hold their tongues and wait.[2]

In January 1790 Asbury crossed into Virginia, working his way south for the winter. Riding through southern Virginia, he received an angry letter from James O'Kelly, the district's presiding elder, containing "heavy complaints of my power" and threats to "use his influence against me." In particular, O'Kelly demanded that Asbury give up his veto power over the council's proceedings for at least a year. O'Kelly's threats "greatly alarmed" him, and with good reason since he held sway over Southside Virginia, where he had preached for nearly a decade and served as a presiding elder since 1785. This, Asbury realized, gave O'Kelly a great "advantage" at Virginia conference proceedings. "All the influence I am to gain over a company of young men [i.e. the preachers] in a district must be done in three weeks," Asbury observed. "The greater part of them, perhaps, are seen by me only at conference, whilst the presiding elder has had them with him all the year." But there was nothing Asbury could do about it at the moment. His schedule required that he proceed quickly south through North Carolina and on to South Carolina for the year's first district conference.[3]

That conference opened in Charleston on February 14, 1790, proceeding "in great peace and love," according to Asbury. But the results of the conference's deliberations could hardly have given him much comfort. The preachers determined that Cokesbury and the church's printing business ought to "be left with the council to act decisively upon," which is no surprise since both were in debt. In all other matters they decided that the annual conferences ought to have the last word, with the council acting only in an advisory capacity. This, of course, defeated the whole purpose of the council as Asbury envisioned it. The problem with the organization of American Methodism was that no one body could act for the church as a whole. The annual conferences didn't meet together, though they were in theory one conference. No decision was binding until all the conferences had approved it. This left Asbury in the precarious position of having to shuttle from one conference to the next, attempting to hammer out compromises on various issues as he went. He attended thirteen district conferences across the nation in 1790 and again in 1791, and sixteen in 1792. Even given his powers of persuasion, the chances that all of the conferences would independently reach the same conclusion on any but the most basic issues weren't good. Asbury had hoped that the council could act as the church's highest central authority, formulating policies that the conferences would accept. He had erred, however, in assuming that the preachers would so easily give up their collective authority in the name of efficiency. Most of the preachers trusted Asbury, as events would prove, but they also knew that he wouldn't always be their bishop.[4]

Leaving Charleston, Asbury headed west for the Georgia annual conference. Traveling conditions were always difficult in the backcountry, and Georgia was no exception. He preached nearly every day while riding about 30 miles a day. "Frequently we have not more than six hours' sleep; our horses are weary, and the houses are so crowded, that at night our rest is much disturbed," he complained on March 4, after preaching near the banks of the Ogeechee River. "Jesus is not always in our dwellings; and where he is not, a pole cabin is not very agreeable." The Georgia conference itself was uneventful, and by March 26, he had left Georgia, ridden through South Carolina, and crossed into North Carolina. Pushing on, he reached western Tennessee in early April. There he was forced to stop rather than continue on to Kentucky.[5]

His health now reached a breaking point. At times he complained of swelling in his feet, an increasing number of "violent headaches," and "my old complaint—an inflamation in the throat." He was reading less, and, if his journal is a fair indication, spending less time in prayer and meditation. Now, in the spring of 1790, the furious pace of the past three months, combined with difficult traveling conditions and the stress of dealing with dissension over the council, proved too much. While in South Carolina in March, he complained of a "nervous headache, which returns once a month, and sometimes oftener." A few days later he noted that he was "still unwell with a complaint that terminated the life of my grandfather Asbury, whose name I bear; perhaps it will also be my end." The following month, in Tennessee, his stomach was so "unsettled" that it made "labour and life a burden." All of this brought on a bout of depression, leading him to "feel happy in the prospect of death and rest," if it weren't for the satisfaction it would give his opponents. "I could give up the church, the college, and schools; nevertheless, there was one drawback—What will my enemies and mistaken friends say? Why, that he hath offended the Lord, and he hath taken him away." Living to spite others isn't much of a reason for living, but such was the state of Asbury's mind.[6]

Stopping at a tavern run by Thomas Amis in eastern Tennessee, Asbury and his party prepared to cross into Kentucky. But when they turned their horses out to graze, they ran off. This, combined with Asbury's ill health, led him to wonder if God was providentially preventing them from continuing on. Others wondered the same thing. Jeremiah Abel, the preacher assigned to the West New River circuit in Tennessee, "sought the Lord by fasting and prayer, and had a strong impression that it was the will of God" that Asbury not press on to Kentucky. With an eye toward the threat of an Indian attack along the way, Asbury decided to heed Abel's advice. (Violence between Indians and white Kentuckians had been escalating since the mid 1780s and continued to intensify until Anthony Wayne's victory at the Battle of Fallen Timbers in 1794.) [7]

Staying at Amis's tavern was, however, out of the question. Apart from the cost, Amis ran a whiskey distillery, claiming to make £300 a year "by the brewing of his poison." Asbury gave "great offence" by "speaking against distilling and slave holding." He now decided to turn back into Virginia, proceeding to the home of Elizabeth Russell, one of the many "mothers in Israel" he turned to in times of need, where he was "nursed" back to health "as an only child." During the next three weeks Asbury regained his health while preaching in the western Virginia and eastern Tennessee region around Russell's home. Then, on May 3, he had what he considered a prophetic dream, which he told to Richard Whatcoat, who recorded it in his journal. "Last Night Bishop Asbury Dreamed that a Company was come to conduckt him...through the wilderness and that Two Sedate men Came up to him where he was: which was Exactly so." The next morning, ten men from Kentucky arrived, including the preachers Peter Massie and Hope Hull, the two sedate men just as Asbury had seen in his dream. The fulfillment of this dream was enough for Asbury to put aside other worries and start for Kentucky. He was no enthusiast on the order of Freeborn Garrettson, but he shared with nearly all Methodists a deep conviction that God still spoke directly to believers. The world of the supernatural wasn't remote or entirely hidden. Relying too much on dreams, visions, and supernatural impression could get one into trouble, but, when judged wisely, they could also be a valid source of divine guidance.[8]

The party traveling to Kentucky included sixteen men carrying thirteen guns. Along the way, Asbury carved his name and the date "May 1, 1790" into a powder horn. He clearly took the threat of Indian attacks seriously, sleeping little and recording several stories of previous attacks he heard along the way.

The journey would have been difficult even without the fear of Indians, following mountain tracks, fording rivers and muddy creeks, with few friendly homes to visit. All told, the party rode about 300 miles in six days. Once across the mountains, Asbury was again in his element, among rural people hungry for a religious experience that spoke to their everyday hopes and fears, who had little in the way of church property or institutional power to fight over. Debates over the council seemed far away. Crowds turned out to hear him preach, at one stop numbering more than six hundred, which made up for having to sleep outdoors under a tree that night. Despite the hardships of life on the frontier his health revived, a good indication that he was content with his circumstances. At the annual conference held near Lexington, "kind people" entertained Asbury in a "very comfortable house." The conference proceeded "in great love and harmony," including obtaining subscriptions of "upwards of three hundred pounds" in land and money to establish a new school (as opposed to a college) near Lexington, to be called Bethel. "I would not, for the worth of all the place, have been prevented in this visit," Asbury wrote as he prepared to leave Kentucky. "It is true, such exertions of mind and body are trying; but I am supported under it: if souls are saved, it is enough." Saving souls was always his highest priority, a thing best accomplished under the Methodist circuit plan. Asbury didn't relish the battles that he knew were coming over church polity, but experiences like those he had just had in Kentucky reinforced his conviction that the ability to send skilled preachers wherever they were most needed was key to Methodism's success. He was determined to preserve the itinerant connection if at all possible.[9]

The return journey from Kentucky to Virginia was much like the trip there, riding about 500 miles in nine days. Along the way, Asbury and Whatcoat held an annual conference in North Carolina, where the issue of the council dominated discussion. After debating the resolutions of the South Carolina conference, the North Carolina preachers added amendments of their own before sending Asbury on his way. From there it was on to southern Virginia, where O'Kelly was the presiding elder and opposition to the council was centered.[10]

One of the young preachers who was decidedly influenced by O'Kelly and opposed to the council was James Meacham. Meacham joined the itinerancy on trial in 1788, that year riding the Bertie circuit under O'Kelly's supervision. The next year he rode the Greenville circuit, also under O'Kelly, moving in 1790 to the Orange circuit in northern Virginia under Ira Ellis and Leroy Cole. Meacham's opposition to slavery also drew him to O'Kelly. He "took much delight" in reading O'Kelly's antislavery tract, *Essay on Negro Slavery*, which he first discovered in April 1790, admiring it so much that he immediately began distributing copies to anyone he thought it might persuade. It is hardly surprising that by the spring of 1790, Meacham sided with "my dear old Bro. O'K" against the council.[11]

The Virginia conference opened in Petersburg on June 14. Asbury met with "a warm reception" according to O'Kelly, and "all was peace" until the council came up, after which things quickly degenerated into partisan bickering. O'Kelly and Asbury both realized that the present system of allowing each annual conference to independently debate, amend, and vote on measures that the other conferences would then supposedly agree to without reservation would never work. "The cause of our ragged separation," according to O'Kelly, was that "the different districts adopted different constitutions!" Asbury likewise complained that any new proposal had "to be explained to every preacher; and then it must be carried through the conferences twenty-four times, that is, through all the conferences for two years." But while the two agreed on the problem, they fundamentally disagreed on the solution. For Asbury, the answer was to create a central body of the church's senior leaders, appointed at the bishops' discretion, to guide and direct the conferences. O'Kelly had a simpler solution: eliminate centralized authority altogether. He framed his arguments in republican terms and maintained that what he was really fighting against was Asbury's "spurious episcopacy" (spurious was O'Kelly's favorite term to describe Asbury's authority). O'Kelly couldn't see why the church needed a "High-Priest" at all. Asbury's "Ecclesiastical Monarchy . . . makes a bad appearance in our Republican world," he wrote. "Francis was born and nurtured in the land of kings and bishops, and that which is bred in the bone, is hard to get out of the flesh."[12]

O'Kelly could be a bitter critic, refusing to recognize any trace of goodwill in his opponents, but there was an element of truth in his accusations. A tension existed at the heart of American Methodism's organizational structure, an uneasy balance between American democratic ideals and Wesley's more hierarchical ecclesiology. In some respects Asbury exercised the same power that Wesley held in Britain, including the right to station each preacher where he saw fit. Yet Asbury exercised his authority only at the discretion of the church's itinerant preachers, embodied in their conferences. They had, according to the church's *Discipline*, the "Power to expel" a bishop "for improper Conduct, if they see it necessary." Just what "improper conduct" amounted to wasn't defined, but it wasn't limited to criminal or moral offenses. Wesley never suffered himself to be bound by similar rules. To the end of his life he maintained the right to admit or exclude people, preachers, and stewards as he saw fit, and to send preachers wherever he chose, telling them "when, where, and how, to labour." God had given him this authority, and none other could take it away. "As long as I live the people shall have no share in choosing either stewards or leaders among the Methodists," Wesley wrote in 1790. "We are no republicans, and never intended to be." The same wasn't true in America, where from the beginning the church rested on a more democratic foundation. Yet, as O'Kelly knew, the chances that all the conferences would agree to remove someone like Asbury were no better than that they would agree on anything else. In O'Kelly's mind, the bishops could more easily manipulate the conferences than vice versa. Up to this point Asbury and the conferences had worked reasonably well together, holding in balance the tension inherent in Methodist polity. But in Virginia things threatened to come apart.[13]

After the first day of the Petersburg conference, Asbury complained that the younger preachers "appeared to be entirely under the influence of the elders." He says little about what transpired, adding only that "I was weary, and felt but little freedom to speak on the subject." O'Kelly says more, claiming that on the second day of the conference nineteen of the twenty-one preachers present rejected Asbury's proposals concerning the council, whereupon, in a fit of anger, Asbury declared that they were "all out of the union." "Then, as one in distress, he gathered up his papers" and stormed out of the conference without even pausing for the usual closing prayer. Over the next several days, according to O'Kelly, the nineteen expelled preachers offered Asbury several proposals that would allow them to continue in the church while presenting their views to the other conferences, but Asbury rejected them all. Finally, as he prepared to leave Petersburg, the younger preachers begged him to appoint them under the "old plan." Asbury agreed, "but no regard was paid to O'KELLY," according to O'Kelly. There is probably some truth in O'Kelly's account, though it seems unlikely that the Virginians were all models of reasonableness and discretion while Asbury played the tyrant. Asbury hated these kinds of exchanges and often reacted by becoming sullen or distant. Nicholas Snethen later claimed that O'Kelly's account was "void of all truth," though he did admit that Asbury "said some things, which upon reflection he did not justify." In any event, the preachers all received appointments, including O'Kelly, whom Asbury reappointed the district's presiding elder. Yet everyone knew that the matter wouldn't go away. O'Kelly's district had become the weakest of the twelve links that formed the church's "chain of union."[14]

Following the Petersburg conference, Richard Whatcoat, who was traveling with Asbury, was "smitten with boils," so that Asbury believed he couldn't "go on." Whatcoat somehow managed to continue, but in the weeks to come Asbury himself came down with fevers and other ailments, leaving him in "great misery of body." He also pushed on, northwest through Virginia, preaching as he went, attending a quarterly meeting in Morgantown and holding a district conference, with Whatcoat, in Uniontown, Pennsylvania, in late July. From there Asbury rode back through Virginia, holding a district conference for northern Virginia at Leesburg beginning August 25. There, Asbury managed to get a vote in favor of the council with the support of the district's presiding elder, Ira Ellis. But many of the preachers remained in opposition. Unable to attend the Leesburg conference, James Meacham heard a report on its proceedings from Ellis when the two met on September 1, 1790. After arguing for nearly an hour, Meacham concluded that, despite Ellis's support for the council, "I am oppos'd to it, & so is all the South district of Virginia." Four days later Meacham received four letters from traveling preachers he knew in southern Virginia that seemed to confirm his view. "They are much oppos'd to the Counsil, Set, Yea fixt, against it, & their Elder with them," Meacham noted. "I think I can see a door for ill consequences."[15]

Following the Leesburg conference, Asbury rode north to Baltimore, where he held an annual conference amidst a revival sweeping through the city's societies. The main purpose of these conferences was to appoint the preachers to their circuits for the coming year, to ordain deacons and elders, and to share news and ideas from one conference to the next. If Asbury also hoped to use the conferences to stir up support against O'Kelly, he was disappointed. Following the Baltimore conference, Asbury rode east to Delaware for the Delmarva Peninsula conference, which opened on September 13. There he heard from "one or two of our brethren," who "felt the Virginia fire about the question of the council."[16]

Riding north to Philadelphia, Asbury opened the conference for the "poor Pennsylvania district" on September 22. Poor in this context had a double meaning. While spiritual poverty was bad, fiscal poverty was just fine. Pennsylvania had both. On the one hand, it had always been hard ground for Methodism, with few revivals like those seen in other districts. On the other hand, Asbury noted with approval that Philadelphia Methodists "are generally poor." "Perhaps it is well," he concluded. "When men become rich, they sometimes forget that they are Methodists." From Philadelphia, he crossed into New Jersey, holding the district conference in Burlington. Southern New Jersey was in the midst of a revival, with one account claiming that "six hundred souls had professed conversion," on the Flanders, Trenton, Burlington, Salem, and Bethel circuits during the past six months. Indeed, the conference minutes for 1789 and 1790 showed an increase of 615 members (from 1748 to 2363) on the New Jersey circuits for the year. Asbury experienced some of the force of the revival on the second night, when "we had a shout," followed by attacks from rowdies who "broke our windows" during the meeting. At a love feast the next day, "a genuine, sweet melting ran through the house" as members rose one after another to share their testimonies.[17]

After a few days in New York City for the New York annual conference, Asbury turned south for the winter. His immediate goal was Baltimore, where the council was scheduled to hold its second meeting in December. He knew that conflict of the kind he hated most was at hand, and at times it distracted him from his devotional life. "So many persons and things occupy my time, that I have not as much leisure and opportunity for prayer and communion with God, and for drinking into the Holy Spirit of life and love as I could wish," he groused while traveling through Maryland in November 1790. This led to occasional lapses into his old sin of "levity." On one occasion he "reproved" himself for "a sudden and violent laugh at the relation of a man's having given an old Negro woman her liberty *because she had too much religion for him.*"

Yet his core spiritual convictions had changed little during his nearly twenty years in America. Seeing that it looked like rain as he rode through Virginia in June 1790, he prayed that it would pass, "fearing its effects in my very weak state." In answer to his prayer, he was "mercifully preserved"; only a few drops fell on him even though it had rained "very heavily" just ahead. Likewise, while crossing a river in Maryland in November with the "wind blowing fiercely," Asbury prayed for calm. The result was that "when we had entered the boat, we had a sudden calm."[18]

Just as he believed that God still answered his prayers, he also urged others to follow the same basic devotional practices that he had learned thirty years before in England. In a letter to friends in England, Asbury asked, "What progress do you make in sanctification?" "Are you sure of heaven yet? Are you fit to die yet?" To assess whether or not their souls "be in a thriving case," Asbury proposed that his friends answer seven questions. First, do *"your appetites be more strong.* Do you thirst after GOD and grace, more than heretofore? Do your care for and desires after the world abate?" Second, do *"your pulses beat more even.* Are you still off and on, hot and cold?" Third, "do you lay out yourselves for the good of others? and are ye filled with zealous desires for their conversions and salvation? Do you manage your talk and your trade, by the rules of religion? Do you eat and sleep by rule? Doth religion form and mould, and direct your carriage towards husbands, wives, parents, children, masters, servants?" Fourth, Asbury asked, *"If the duties of religion be more delightful to you?"* and fifth *"If you are more abundant in those duties which are most displeasing to the flesh?"* Sixth, do *"you grow more vile in your own eyes?"* and seventh, do *"you grow more quick of sense, more sensible of divine influences, or withdrawings?"* The advice contained in the form of these questions could have been written at any point in Asbury's career, or by most any Methodist preacher or committed member. The degree to which Asbury or anyone else measured up to this standard varied, of course. But the standard itself changed little, providing Asbury with a firm spiritual and emotional foundation and an instant connection to believers he met wherever he traveled.[19]

The council's second meeting opened in Baltimore on December 1, 1790. Conspicuously absent was James O'Kelly, or any delegate from southern Virginia. Acting on O'Kelly's advice, the Virginia preachers sent only an "affectionate letter." Asbury says little about the council's proceedings in his journal, other than the perfunctory assertion that "we had great peace and union in all our labours." The council "*unanimously*" agreed to "consider themselves invested with *full* power to act *decisively* in all temporal matters." Yet they did little. The provisions they passed mainly concerned organizing the church's publishing ventures and arranging yet another loan for Cokesbury, this time for £1,000. O'Kelly was predictably unimpressed. He later complained that the entire focus of the council had been "money, money." He questioned where all the money went and had little doubt that Cokesbury was a waste of whatever funds it received. "I believe that God sent out the Methodist preachers, not to build colleges, but to build up a holy, simple-hearted people." Over the next several weeks Asbury encountered repeated opposition from "dissatisfied brethren" who agreed with the general thrust of O'Kelly's criticisms. "I am charged with dreadful things about the council," Asbury wrote on February 2, 1791.[20] He may still have hoped to weather the storm without scrapping the council, but things would soon take a turn for the worse.

Enter Thomas Coke. Coke arrived in Charleston, South Carolina, in late February, bringing with him a preacher from the West Indies, William Hammet, who would soon create his own schism in the church. But the immediate issue at hand was the council. Asbury and O'Kelly had each previously written to Coke to make their case. O'Kelly's letter isn't extant, but he had clearly put aside his earlier animosity toward Coke in hopes of gaining an ally against Asbury. Asbury's letter largely celebrates the movement's continued growth, begging the question of how such a popular system could be as flawed as O'Kelly insisted. To O'Kelly's charge that he had enriched himself at the church's expense, Asbury offered a flat denial: "All the property I have gained is two old horses, the constant companions of my toil, 6 if not 7000 miles every year.... As to clothing, I am nearly the same as at first; neither have I silver, nor gold, nor any property." There seemed little denying the truth of this, and opponents never gained traction on this issue. The real bone of contention had more to do with power than money, and on this point Coke now sided with O'Kelly.[21]

According to O'Kelly, at the Charleston annual conference Coke "pleaded" O'Kelly's "cause" and "withstood Francis to the face; [and] condemned his conduct." Asbury and Coke say little about these events, but Asbury did agree to Coke's demand for a general conference of all the preachers to meet later in Baltimore, indicating that at least to some degree Coke and O'Kelly won the support of the South Carolina preachers. Asbury and Coke then took separate routes to the Georgia conference, where Asbury was primarily concerned with the lack of zeal among the people. "The peace with the Creek Indians, the settlement of new lands, good trade, buying slaves, & c. . . . take up the attention of the people," he complained. Coke seemed more pleased with conditions in the state, though he bemoaned the many ticks that harassed him along the way. By the end of March, the two were in North Carolina for the state's annual conference. From there it was on to Virginia, where Asbury knew that "trouble" was "at hand." Predictably, as he approached Virginia his health worsened. By the time he crossed the border he was "constantly weak and feverish in body."[22]

At the Virginia conference, which opened in Petersburg on April 20, 1791, Coke stood solidly behind O'Kelly's assault on the council and Asbury's episcopal authority. "Methodism is gone," Coke wrote to O'Kelly. Together, he told O'Kelly, they could "overthrow the new institution [the council]" and restore things as they had been before. If Asbury didn't give in, Coke assured O'Kelly that he "would contend for a republican government." "Give me thy hand. Fear not. I am a friend to America," Coke wrote. Unfortunately for O'Kelly, he didn't know Coke well enough to suspect that he might have ulterior motives for taking sides against Asbury. If he had, he would have known that Coke was no republican at heart. He only sided with O'Kelly in an effort to weaken Asbury and thereby set the stage for what he planned to do next.

Even as the Virginia conference sat, Coke was launching a new intrigue. On April 24, without telling Asbury, Coke wrote a letter to Bishop William White of the Protestant Episcopal Church (the former Church of England in America) proposing reconciliation between the Episcopal and Methodist churches in America. Coke and Asbury were traveling together at the time, so there is no doubt that Coke deliberately kept the letter secret. What sort of mandate Coke thought he had for this is difficult to imagine, at least from the American perspective, other than a sense that the Methodists should never have separated from the church of his youth in the first place.[23]

Still, Coke, ever the visionary, pressed his case. He began by reminding White that he had been "brought up in the Church of England, & have been ordained a Presbyter of that Church," but "thro' a Variety of Causes and Incidents," had lost his first love. Consequently, for a time he had become "exceedingly biased" against the Church, and had therefore likely gone "further in the separation of our Church in America than Mr. Wesley ... did intend." In other words, the creation of an independent American church had been a mistake, one that he and Wesley would now gladly take back if they could. But why should the Episcopal Church want them back? Here Coke stressed the size of American Methodism, which could count "above 60,000 Adults" (actual membership in 1791 stood at 63,269 whites and 12,884 blacks). Moreover, this was only the tip of the iceberg with regards to Methodism's real audience, according to Coke. Adding in the nonmembers who "constantly" attended Methodist meetings and the children of members and sympathizers brought the total "which form our Congregations in these states" to 750,000, a ratio of more than twelve adherents for every one member. Coke wasn't alone in making these kinds of claims. A few years later, in 1805, Asbury estimated that membership stood at a hundred thousand, but that up to one million people "regularly attend our ministry." Thomas Wallcut, a New Englander traveling through the upper South in 1789, wrote to his Unitarian minister in Boston that "the spread of Methodism in Virginia & Maryland is unparalleled & astonishing—Some go so far as to say that full half the People are Methodists already." Wallcut was exaggerating, and Coke and Asbury probably were as well, though just how much is difficult to tell, especially since Coke and Asbury counted people who held membership in other churches while regularly attending Methodist meetings. Estimates like these inflate Methodism's audience, but they aren't as far off the mark as they might seem. Many people attended more than one church. The Methodist itinerant William Capers noted that in Charleston, South Carolina, in 1811, Methodist "preaching might be attended with great propriety, for almost everyone did so," though few actually joined the church since "it was vastly more respectable to join some other Church, and still attend the preaching of the Methodists, which was thought to answer to all purposes." Coke anticipated that a reunified church would be more successful in drawing these kinds of people into full membership. In addition to its membership, Coke also noted that American Methodism could boast 250 itinerant preachers and "a great Number of local Preachers, very far exceeding the number of traveling Preachers." Hence, reunion offered Episcopalians the opportunity to instantly and vastly increase the size of their church.[24]

There were of course obstacles in the way. To begin with, the current Methodist preachers would never give up their ordinations. Since none of the American preachers had a classical education, they would be suspicious that even if the current Episcopal bishops dropped the requirement that ministers demonstrate proficiency in "learned Languages," (primarily Latin and Greek) their successors might not. The obvious solution was to have a "Methodist" bishop included in the unified Episcopal structure, and Coke clearly had himself in mind. But the greatest obstacle to reunification was Asbury, "whose Influence is very capital," and who "will not easily comply; nay, I know he will be exceedingly averse to it," Coke wrote. He assured White that Wesley fully supported a reunion and "would use his Influence to the utmost . . . to accomplish that (to us) very desirable Object." Coke closed the letter by imploring White to keep their correspondence secret until they could meet in person. At this point he probably believed that Asbury would have to be forced out for his plan to succeed, which explains much of his interest in forming an alliance with O'Kelly. It is difficult to imagine that O'Kelly would have had any sympathy for Coke's reunification scheme. Having dedicated himself to weakening, if not eliminating, episcopal authority within Methodism, why would he then agree to place himself under the control of the Episcopal Church? If Asbury was a tyrant, what would the Episcopal bishops be, with their classical educations and social pretensions?[25]

John Wesley's death, which Coke and Asbury learned of while traveling through Virginia on April 28 or 29, 1791, threw all of Coke's plans into disarray. He immediately set off for England. Coke was in a hurry because he hoped to win election as "President of the European Methodists" on his return to Britain. (To his credit, when British Methodists refused to recognize him as Wesley's successor, Coke gracefully accepted the outcome.) A delay in Philadelphia allowed him to have tea three times with Bishop White, whose response to Coke's proposal was better than he had dared hope, to the point of suggesting that the Episcopalians might be willing to ordain Asbury a bishop along with Coke. Encouraged by White's response, Coke wrote to Protestant Episcopal Bishop Samuel Seabury of Connecticut on May 14, 1791, confessing that although he had earlier "promoted separation from" the Church of England, "within these two years I am come back again: my Love for the Church of England has returned." After repeating many of the same arguments from his earlier letter to White, Coke concluded by suggesting that if the Episcopal church "would consent to yr Consecration of Mr. Asbury and me as Bishops of the Methodist Society in the Protestant Episcopal Church in these United States," and give assurances that there would always be a "regular supply" of Methodist bishops, then "all other mutual stipulations would soon be settled." All of this was conjecture on Coke's part, and he had to admit to Seabury that "I do not fully know Mr. Asbury's mind on the subject. I have my fears in respect to his sentiments: and if he do not accede to the Union, it will not take place so completely as I could wish." Unfortunately for Coke, Seabury was more of a High Churchman than White; he and other leading Episcopalians weren't about to agree to these terms. It would be some time before Coke realized just how badly he had miscalculated. Before leaving America, he wrote to O'Kelly on May 4 urging him to "be firm, be very firm, and very cautious, and very wise, and depend upon a faithful friend in Thos. Coke." Just how matters would work out between the two would have to wait until Coke returned the following year.[26]

Coke and Asbury met at New Castle, Delaware, on May 16, 1791, the day that Coke boarded the *William Penn* for England. Asbury probably already knew of Coke's letter to Bishop White though he hadn't seen it. When the matter came up, Asbury "was decidedly against the re-union," according to Coke. He tried to make the scheme sound as innocent as possible, but, even so, Asbury didn't buy it. This is hardly surprising, not only because of Coke's alliance with O'Kelly, but also in light of the severity of Coke's criticisms of Asbury in recent weeks. In a funeral sermon preached for Wesley in Baltimore on May 1, Coke asserted that excluding Wesley's name from the official minutes in 1787 "was an almost diabolical act." Of those responsible "in Mr. Wesley's expulsion," two were already "dead and damned, and the others, with their patron, will go to hell except they repent." Their patron was, of course, Asbury. Before leaving America, Coke repeated this charge in several letters, including one written to Thomas Morrell as Coke sat aboard the *William Penn* in Delaware Bay on May 17. The "most cruel treatment" that Wesley "met with from five or six men in Baltimore in the year 1787" had, Coke asserted, "hastened the debilitated state of our honoured Friend's Body, and therefore probably his Death." Coke could hardly have brought more serious charges against Asbury. In effect, he accused Asbury of figuratively stabbing Wesley in the back and literally hastening his death, crimes worthy, Coke declared, of eternal damnation.[27]

For several months Coke remained convinced that a reunion between the Methodist and Episcopal churches might work. He would have known better if he had had more contact with Episcopal clergyman like Joseph Grove John Bend. As Rector of St. Paul's Church in Baltimore, Bend was in a good position to assess the Methodist onslaught, particularly since Baltimore Methodism had experienced several recent waves of revivals. Alarmed at Methodism's growth, Bend took a dim view of what he saw as Methodist enthusiasm and ignorance. In a sermon dated August 29, 1791, he used Ecclesiastes 7:16, "Be not righteous over much" (a favorite of Episcopal priests when dealing with Methodists) to lash out at those of "a warm & gloomy disposition, who abhor the lukewarmness . . . of the gay world; who deny themselves many innocent enjoyments; & who, indulging a heated imagination, become arrogant & censorious, thinking & speaking uncharitably of all those whose devotion is more tranquil." Bend was particularly troubled at the way that excessive religious zeal undermined social authority. "It is impolitic in those in inferior stations, to set themselves up, as teachers of those above them," Bend preached. If taken too far, religious zeal could undermine the stability of society by drawing workers away from their proper callings (another favorite topic of Episcopal clergy). "He, who indiscreetly spends in religious exercises to[o] large a portion of his time, as to break in upon ye allotted to honest industry, runs a risk of falling into poverty, of involving his family in distress, of neglecting the education of his children, & of becoming, with health & strength in his possession, a pensioner on the bounty of another," declared Bend. He repeated this sermon three times in Baltimore, continuing to hammer away at its themes for years to come. Methodists, Bend wrote to William Duke in November 1798, "are, for the most part, persons of the lower classes in life, & distinguished by ... ignorance." Asbury was in Baltimore a month after Bend first preached his "be not righteous over much" sermon, and he knew that Bend wasn't alone among Episcopal clergymen in his resentment of Methodism, the depth of which Coke evidently failed to gauge.[28]

In July 1791 Coke wrote from London to Joseph Benson in Birmingham, England, that Bishop White had "assured me that every concession would be made on their parts that was consistent with what they believed to be Essentials, in order to accomplish so desirable an End as a Re-union of the two Churches." Not long after, however, Coke realized that his plan was doomed. "Permit a friend to drop a caution to you. . . . when you visit this continent again, come with great care . . . for you are suspected, by some of your sincere friends, to have conducted yourself when last here with a degree of unkindness to this connection and especially to our ever worthy brother A[sbury]," Ezekiel Cooper wrote to Coke on August 11, 1791. "Nothing will touch the majority of our preachers sooner & more powerfully than to seek the unjust injury of him [Asbury] who has served them so long & so faithfully," Cooper warned.[29]

Once he realized his mistake, Coke could only hope to control the damage. In September 1791, he wrote to Asbury pleading that he overlook "the imprudence I was led into in preaching Mr. Wesley's funeral sermon" and "some other things which you might construe as unkindliness to you." Even Coke must have realized that his earlier accusations would be difficult to finesse. His letters to Asbury became desperate. "You must make allowance for me, considering the great influence Mr. Wesley had on my mind, and his great prejudice toward you," Coke pleaded. "Why don't you send me your minutes? Why don't you write to me?" Asbury's response, when it came, offered Coke little comfort. Writing to another preacher in September 1791, Asbury noted "I wrote to the Doctor [i.e. Coke] that if he came here again he would see trouble." This warning apparently prompted further backtracking on Coke's part. In December 1791 Asbury wrote to Edward Dromgoole that "the Doctor has made most humiliating concessions for his conduct at Charleston, Petersburg, and Baltimore, and promises nothing but peace, if he comes here." Indeed, writing to Ezekiel Cooper on November 21, 1791, from London, Coke assured him that when he returned to America it would be "as a Man of Peace. . . . The time for every thing else is past."[30]

New England

Following Coke's departure in May 1791, Asbury felt free to put concerns over the council aside and turn his attention to something more basic. He had always believed that the church's primary mission was to preach the gospel as widely as possible, continually pushing outward to engage the nation's rapidly expanding boundaries. One of these regions was New England. "My call this year appears to be easterly where I have long wished to go, and now providence calls loudly," Asbury wrote to the preacher Daniel Fidler just two days after learning of Wesley's death. Working his way north, Asbury held annual conferences in Baltimore, Philadelphia, New Jersey, and New York before crossing into Connecticut in early June 1791. No sooner had he crossed the border than he declared the region spiritually dead, reflecting his own prejudices toward America's older Calvinist churches. "We are . . . never out of sight of a house; and sometimes we have a view of many churches and steeples, built very neatly of wood; either for use, ornament, piety, policy, or interest—or it may be some of all these," Asbury wrote. "I do feel as if there had been religion in this country once; and I apprehend there is a little in form and theory left. There may have been a praying ministry and people here; but I fear they are now spiritually dead; and am persuaded that family and private prayer is very little practiced." The problem wasn't that people refused to listen; indeed they attended "in great multitudes." But the young laughed and played in the galleries, and the old seemed "heavy and lifeless." New Englanders, Asbury quickly concluded, "must be stirred up to expect more." It was the same wherever he went. In Rhode Island the people appeared "settled upon their lees," as also seemed to be the case in Boston.[31]

Asbury was, in fact, encountering New England Congregationalism at the end of long spiritual drought. The Great Awakening of the 1730s and 1740s had revitalized churches across the region, but this had been followed by decades of institutional torpor. During the 1790s, New England Congregationalism began to regain some of its earlier momentum, partly as a result of its encounter with Methodism, which challenged the religious status quo in a way that ultimately benefited both, at least in terms of growth. According to Samuel Goodrich, the son of a Connecticut Congregationalist minister, by the 1850s Methodism had so infiltrated the religious life of New England that "orthodoxy was in a considerable degree methodized, and Methodism in due time became orthodoxed." But the end point of this process was well in the future, and not at all obvious to Asbury in 1791.[32]

Why did Asbury go to New England, far from the church's center of power, at a time of roiling internal conflict? Considering that less than 1 percent of the church's membership lived in the region, there was no pressing need for him to make this trip. With the fight over the council still undecided, one could hardly have blamed Asbury if he had chosen to stay in Baltimore or some other centralized location where he could keep his eye on O'Kelly and actively work to counter his influence. But these weren't the kind of concerns that primarily motivated Asbury. Much as he had done a decade before in Virginia and North Carolina during the sacramental crisis, he felt compelled to meet the people for himself, making his own way through the cities and countryside of the land of the Puritans. In so doing, he set an example for the young itinerants who would follow him and for the people of the region, for whom "Bishop Asbury" now became more than just a name. If Methodism was a hierarchical organization, it was one in which the pyramid of power was indeed quite flat. This goes a long way toward explaining the trust that Asbury's colleagues had in him. Had he appeared more grasping, more concerned with the trappings of power, it would have been far easier for critics like O'Kelly to make their charges stick.

At New Haven, Connecticut, Asbury preached to a congregation that included Ezra Stiles, president of Yale, Samuel Wales, professor of divinity at Yale, and Jonathan Edwards, son of the great New England theologian and minister. But when Asbury finished, "no man spoke to me." He wished to tour the college grounds, "but no one invited me. The divines were grave, and the students were attentive; they used me like a fellow-Christian, in coming to hear me preach, and like a stranger in other respects." The snub cut deep. To the professors and students of Yale, he was still the son of a gardener, a metalworker's apprentice without a college education. In this context Asbury revealed part of the motivation that led him to pour so much time, energy, and money into Cokesbury College. "Should Cokesbury ... ever furnish the opportunity, I, in my turn, will requite their behaviour, by treating them as friends, brethren, and gentlemen," he wrote in his journal. Like so many religious leaders before and since, Asbury concluded that if he wasn't welcome at the best colleges of his day, he would simply create his own to take their place.[33]

New England reminded Asbury more of the land of his birth than any place he had been in America. But the comfort of a familiar landscape didn't make up for the loneliness that began to creep over him. When he tried to preach in Boston, he had to shout because "the sinners were noisy in the streets." He even had a difficult time finding lodging in Boston. "Of their hospitality I cannot boast," he wrote after several days in the city. Even on his first trip to "wicked Charleston," South Carolina, six years before, "I was kindly invited to eat and drink by many—here by none." He longed for Methodist-style hospitality. Its absence "made me feel and know the worth of Methodists more than ever." Inevitably, his health began to suffer, a sure sign that he was under stress: "My body is fatigued and listless—my spirit tried and tempted: infirmities cleave to me."[34]

Asbury prepared to leave New England in late July 1791 with mixed emotions. By the end of his tour, he was tired of preaching to unreceptive audiences and longed "to be with the Methodists again." The trip hadn't been easy (he had ridden about a thousand miles in two months), but he had learned what he needed to know. When he visited Massachusetts again the next year, he was told that New Englanders "are not to be moved." Asbury responded: "it is true, they are too much accustomed to hear systematical preaching to be moved by a systematical sermon, even from a Methodist; but they have their feelings, and touch but the right string, and they will be moved." He now had a better idea of which strings to pluck, specifically which preachers stood the best chance of reaching eastern audiences.[35]

The New England tour offered some respite from the turmoil over the council, but the problem hadn't gone away. In the immediate context, unity would be hard to come by. The church could make room for a great deal of individual initiative, but there were limits on how far its doctrinal and organizational grid could be stretched. If Asbury needed any additional proof of this, he did not have to look further than the recent cases of William Glendinning and William Hammet.

12

Schism

By the summer of 1785, William Glendinning was losing his mind. When he tried to sleep, "Let the night be ever so dark, all would appear like dismal flaming brimstone burning around me." Twice he tried to cut his throat with a razor, but couldn't bring himself to do it. Friends bound him and took him to a doctor against his will, to no avail. Soon he began to see the devil—not a vision of Satan, but Satan himself—lurking about at night, his face "black as any coal—his eyes and mouth as red as blood, and long white teeth gnashing together." At times Satan spoke to him, mocking his wretched condition and telling him that there was no "mercy for the wretch, that blasphemes the Holy One of Israel." Glendinning devotes much of his memoir to describing these encounters, which continued for nearly five years. He couldn't keep his hands still and lost all track of time. Sleep offered him no respite. In his dreams "the flaming pit" of hell "would be laid open to my view, burning all around me. . . . Then would I feel as if the fallen angels had me in their arms, and fastening the chains of misery round me." Eventually he tried to kill himself by tying one end of a rope around a large stone and the other end around his neck, and then dropping the stone into a deep pool. But the rope broke and a miserable Glendinning floated downstream to shallow water.[1]

He hadn't always been like this. Born in Moffatt, Scotland, in 1747, Glendinning entered an apprenticeship to a tailor at age thirteen, after the death of his father. Finishing the apprenticeship at seventeen, he "had a rambling mind," wandering from city to town in southern Scotland and northern England while working at his trade. Twice he had visions in which "the earth and all the elements appeared, to my view, as all in a flame of fire." When he was nineteen his mother died, leaving him a modest inheritance. Glendinning used this money to buy passage to America, arriving in Alexandria, Virginia, in June 1767. He soon moved to Annapolis, Maryland, where he became "outwardly wicked, and lost all fear of offending God." A year or so later he moved to Baltimore, where he again had the vision of fire consuming the earth. It was also in Baltimore that he first heard Methodist preaching. At first he stood "looking on, and laughing," but soon the preacher's words found their mark, filling Glendinning with "great terror and a deep sense of my lost state." After a subsequent meeting, Glendinning went into a field to pray and seek "deliverance" from "this deplorable condition," when "suddenly there shone (or seemed to shine) a light from heaven around me. I immediately felt the burden of sin removed, and my heart was put in possession of the PEACE, which cometh from GOD alone." He soon began to speak in public, joining the itinerancy in 1773 or 1774, teamed with Philip Gatch on the Kent circuit in Maryland. For the next decade he rode circuits, mostly in the South, paired with some of early Methodism's leading preachers. So far, his career seemed thoroughly typical. Much of Glendinning's story—a humble family background, limited education, apprenticeship at a trade, a restless spirit and thirst for travel, supernatural visions and prophetic dreams, a dramatic conversion, and a quick transition from convert to preacher—resembled that of most Methodist preachers.[2]

About 1784 Glendinning's story took a bizarre turn. While riding the Brunswick circuit, he began to question "whether the Scriptures were the truths of God or not?" These doubts "brought my mind into such a state of perplexity and confusion that almost every thing began to wear a gloomy aspect, by night and by day, awake or asleep." His "atheistical inquiries" took "such deep root" in him "that my mind got more and more darkened, and I lost sight of my reconciled God, and all spiritual comforts departed from me." "Darkened" in his "understanding," he "became wretched in my soul . . . so that every place, person, or thing, that I saw, or knew, was almost constantly an offence to me." Even so, Glendinning's colleagues had enough confidence in him to propose electing him an elder at the 1784 Christmas Conference. But Glendinning refused to have his ordination tied to any specific appointment, so the conference passed him over. Instead, Glendinning was reappointed to the Brunswick circuit. He soon overcame his "atheistical" doubts, but remained "the most miserable and wretched of all beings." In 1785 Asbury appointed Glendinning to the important Sussex circuit in Virginia, though by that time he was sleeping little and quickly coming unhinged. Haunted by fears that he was damned for all eternity, Glendinning quit traveling in June 1785, going to live with first one friend and then another.

Methodists across Virginia and North Carolina eventually learned of Glendinning's condition. In April 1790, while riding the Greenville circuit in North Carolina, James Meacham "heard from that poor Man Glendinning, he is still as bad as ever—no hope of his recovery." A few days later Meacham passed within three miles of Glendinning's residence, taking the opportunity to again comment on "the Shoking condition of W.G. . . . he is like a Man Fatally void of Rational reason[;] he is fearful." Others passed through fires of temptation and periods of doubt, but Glendinning's condition transcended the usual spiritual struggles. Methodists acknowledged that a loss of mental balance could be either spiritual or physiological in nature, but whatever its origin, Glendinning's state seemed extraordinary.[3]

Eventually Glendinning had what amounted to a second conversion experience, in which he "instantly knew" "the same comfort as when I was first brought to the Lord's pardoning love." But the five-year ordeal changed him forever. He now "clearly saw the great evil of people's laying so much stress upon their own particular systems of doctrine, forms of church government, and modes of worship." When he considered becoming a Methodist preacher again, he "saw I should not stand in that order," since abiding by the church's rules would only "hinder my usefulness." News of Glendinning's recovery reached Asbury. When the two met, Asbury told him that he would have to take a regular appointment if he wanted to preach in Methodist churches. Glendinning agreed to attend the upcoming annual conference in Petersburg in April 1791, but refused to take a circuit appointment. At the Petersburg conference, Thomas Coke took the lead in questioning Glendinning about his experiences and intentions, at one point telling him that his encounters with the devil "were only imaginary." Meeting again in December 1791, the conference wrote a letter to Glendinning, signed by twenty-one preachers, including Asbury and O'Kelly, informing him that they would no longer allow him to speak in Methodist churches.[4]

Why the conference turned Glendinning away isn't as obvious as it first seems. In response to Coke, Glendinning pointed out that Methodists held in high regard many people who claimed to have had, or at least believed in the possibility of, physical encounters with beings from the spirit world, including Richard Baxter and John Wesley himself. Wesley's *Arminian Magazine*, the monthly periodical of British Methodism, contains dozens of sensational stories of the supernatural in everyday life. At times it reads like a supermarket tabloid, with stories of ghosts appearing to reveal the identity of a murderer, convince an atheist of the error of his ways, and warn a duke of a murder plot against him. It includes accounts of a murder prevented by a prophetic dream, a boy who could identify the location of underground water, episodes of witchcraft, and so on. Closer to home, the church had recently published Freeborn Garrettson's journal, in which he claimed on one occasion to have wrestled in the night with the devil, who appeared as "a cat" or "a great rat." A couple of weeks before the Virginia conference wrote to Glendinning in 1791, Philip Bruce, presiding elder for northern Virginia, wrote, "We have a variety of books—but none more entertaining than Bro. Garrettson's Experience & travels—these will sell." Meanwhile, Garrettson served as presiding elder over the Albany district in upstate New York, one of the church's fastest growing and most important regions. In 1794, the British *Arminian Magazine* published excerpts from Garrettson's journal as its feature article for ten consecutive months, an honor granted to no other American.[5] Nor was Garrettson's account unique, as the experiences of preachers such as Benjamin Abbott (whose autobiography the church published in 1801) demonstrate.[6] To Glendinning, there seemed little reason why the church should reject his account, since it seemed to fall squarely within Methodism's supernaturalist tradition.

Yet there were differences. None of the other preachers had descended into anything like Glendinning's kaleidoscope world. After all, Wesley and Garrettson hadn't been confined to a small cabin for five years while they raved like a lunatic about Satan dragging them bodily into hell. Moreover, some still doubted Glendinning's mental stability. When Asbury heard him preach in December 1790, he concluded that Glendinning was still "not right in his head." What made Glendinning suspect wasn't that he claimed to have seen the devil, but that the experience dominated his life. He had lost his mind for five years, and not everyone was sure that he had it back.

For Asbury there was an even more important concern. The experiences of Garrettson, Abbott, and others like them had led them into the church, not out of it. If more than a few preachers followed Glendinning's lead and refused to take regular circuit appointments, the whole itinerant system would collapse. During one of their meetings, Glendinning recounts that Asbury told him, "The door was open for me to come in among them, but that their government could not give way,—for if they were all to plead as I did, what would become of their government?" Glendinning and Asbury exchanged a series of letters and met at least twice over the next three years, but the result was always the same: Glendinning refused to take a regular appointment and Asbury refused to sanction his preaching at large. The issue went to the core of Methodist polity. By his own admission, Glendinning felt compelled to tell anyone who would listen that the Methodist connection was "unscriptural," that the conduct of many of their preachers toward him was "unchristian," and that the power Asbury possessed as bishop "was too great for any human being."[7] For the next several years Glendinning repeatedly sought readmission to the itinerancy on an at-large basis, but the annual conferences consistently turned him down. Still, his protests clearly added fuel to the fire of dissent already smoldering in Virginia. In the end, Glendinning was the kind of well-intentioned but narrowly focused zealot that organizations always have a difficult time dealing with. Convinced that he had a commission directly from God, he expected everyone in his path to yield to the voice of the Lord.[8]

Hammet

While Glendinning fought the devil and Asbury in Virginia, William Hammet launched a similar campaign against episcopal Methodism in South Carolina. Thomas Coke had brought Hammet to Charleston, South Carolina, from the West Indies for fear that he would die if he stayed in the tropics. An Irish Methodist preacher, Hammet had come to the Caribbean after John Wesley ordained him in July 1786 for missionary work in the Americas. Originally appointed to Newfoundland, Hammet's ship was blown off course during a spectacular storm, landing him instead on the island of St. Kitts in January 1787.[9] For the next two years Hammet worked diligently to preach the gospel on the island. When Coke returned to St. Kitts in January 1789, he transferred Hammet to the island of Tortola. Hammet later continued on to Jamaica, where Coke found him in January 1791 with a raging fever, in an "immaciated state, with my face ulcerated," as Hammet later wrote. Determined that "nothing should be omitted that might any way contribute to save so valuable a life," Coke decided that Hammet should accompany him to the United States. After surviving a shipwreck on Edisto Island, the two arrived in Charleston on February 23, 1791.[10]

Hammet made such a favorable impression on the Methodists of Charleston that they quickly decided they must have him for their preacher. Asbury, who was in Charleston at the time, confided his misgivings in his journal on March 1, 1791: "I am somewhat distressed at the uneasiness of our people, who claim a right to choose their own preachers; a thing quite new amongst Methodists. None but Mr. Hammett will do for them. We shall see how it will end." At first Asbury resisted, but Hammet followed him up the coast to plead his case. He met Asbury in Philadelphia in May, bearing "a wonderful list of petitioners" requesting his appointment to Charleston. "To this, as far as I had to say, I submitted," Asbury noted in his journal. Rather than force the issue from a distance, he decided to give Hammet some slack and see how events would play out. Hammet continued on to New York City, returned to Philadelphia, and then spent six weeks preaching in Baltimore and Annapolis before finally arriving back in Charleston toward the end of July. There he discovered that the other two preachers appointed to Charleston, James Parks and the district's presiding elder, Reuben Ellis, considered him the third preacher in Charleston rather than the preacher in charge. Offended, Hammet left the church around Christmas 1791 and took to preaching in the town market.[11]

When Asbury returned to Charleston in February 1792, he found "a great commotion among the people, excited by the conduct of William Hammett, who has divided the society in Charleston, and taken to himself some chaff and some wheat," about twenty members in all. Asbury feared that they would soon gain control of the Charleston meetinghouse. "We are considered by him as seceders from Methodism!—because we do not wear gowns and powder; and because we did not pay sufficient respect to Mr. Wesley!" Asbury marveled. This last point, that American Methodists had disregarded Wesley, was the one that Hammet focused on in an upcoming pamphlet war with Thomas Morrell, John Dickins, and Thomas Coke. Hammet had traveled extensively with Coke in early 1791 when Coke was at the height of his opposition to Asbury's leadership. As a British Methodist, Hammet was probably predisposed to distrust Asbury anyway. To what degree Coke and Hammet influenced one another at this critical juncture is difficult to say, but once in America Hammet quickly came to believe that the American church was an illegitimate substitute for Wesley's authority. Hammet was amazed that American Methodists had allowed "themselves to be trammell'd with the most rigid Episcopacy in the world except that of the Church of Rome." His journal refers to American Methodism as "Mr. Asbury's connection," as opposed to "Mr. Wesley's connection." Professing himself to be "no friend of overgrown episcopacy, and an enemy to arbitrary power," he called on American Methodists to eliminate the offices of bishop and presiding elder, and to do away with the council in favor of a general conference of all the preachers. Presaging one of James O'Kelly's demands, Hammet also called for a rule allowing preachers to challenge their circuit appointments if they were unhappy, lest the bishop and elders "worry any man out of the itinerant connexion."[12]

John Dickins, head of the church's printing operations in Philadelphia, responded to Hammet's attack in a pamphlet, *Friendly Remarks on the Late Proceedings of the Rev. Mr. Hammet*, published in Philadelphia in September 1792. Dickins pointed out that in meetings with Asbury and others, Hammet had been vague about whether and when he might return to the West Indies, and he had also taken several months to return to Charleston from the North.

Was it not therefore prudent to appoint other preachers to Charleston? But Dickins's real concern was with Asbury's reputation, which he asserted rested more on the bishop's "actions" than on his "words only." Asbury's "diligent, laborious and constant mode of travelling has given to thousands an opportunity of knowing him well," evidence once again of Asbury's ability to connect with people at large. To Hammet's charge that Asbury acted arbitrarily in stationing the preachers, Dickins responded that considering Asbury had two hundred preachers to station each year, "we are left to wonder how he conducts the whole with so much ease, and so little appearance of changeability," or favoritism. Dickins's answer to Hammet's proposal that preachers be allowed to appeal their appointments is telling considering the storm that would soon break when O'Kelly made the same proposal. Dickins didn't argue that Asbury's appointments were always perfect, but that they were reasonable, and that the church's larger mission demanded that everyone sacrifice for the common good. Otherwise, "every one might object to his station, and what confusion would there be in a conference where every one is dissatisfied!"[13]

Meanwhile, Hammet went to work building a new denomination, which he called the Primitive Methodist Church. He built a large church in Charleston, enlisting at least four preachers who had briefly itinerated under Asbury: Philip Mathews, James Johnstone (or Johnson), Adam Cloud, and John Phillips, along with a former colleague from the Caribbean, William Brazier. Together they expanded the Primitive Methodist Connection into North Carolina and Georgia, and launched several missions in the Caribbean. Yet Hammet didn't get the widespread support from Methodists in America or Britain he hoped for. Coke, in particular, abandoned whatever commitment he may have had to Hammet in the wake of Wesley's death and his efforts to patch things up with Asbury, convincing the British Conference to do the same. In August 1792 the British Conference wrote to Asbury informing him that,"[we] esteem union and concord among brethren as one of the greatest blessings, and therefore do most deeply disapprove of the Schism which Wm. Hammett has made in the city of Charleston, and do acknowledge no further connection with him who could attempt to rend the body of Christ." When Coke returned to Antigua in February 1793 for the West Indies conference, he convinced the twelve preachers present to sign a similar declaration denouncing "the rent" that Hammet had created in the church and disowning "all connexion with him."[14]

Hammet responded in kind. In October 1792 he published a pamphlet accusing Coke of causing the death of two missionaries in the Caribbean by treating them "cruelly, unjustly and unchristianly," mismanaging the West Indies missions and buying slaves. The first two charges were a matter of debate, but the third wasn't. In 1791 Coke had sent a missionary, John Baxter, and school teachers, Mr. and Mrs. Joyce, to the island of St. Vincent. There they built a schoolhouse after the island's legislature gave the church 150 acres of land to create a mission to the native Caribs. Coke claims that he raised £1,500 in subscriptions and gave another £500 himself, but it still wasn't enough to support the mission. Reasoning that the land grant was "a providential gift," Coke agreed to purchase slaves (six to ten in all, according to Hammet) to plant coffee and cotton on the mission's land, reasoning that they "would certainly be treated by us in the tenderest manner." Even for Coke this was a remarkable decision, given his earlier strident opposition to slavery in the American South. Yet as was so often the case, he was swayed by immediate circumstances and those closest at hand. No sooner had he left the island than he began to have second thoughts. A few months later Coke wrote to the mission from Baltimore that they could not keep the slaves "on any consideration." Coke claims that he bore the cost of their emancipation, but the damage was done. "Dr. C has *printed* and *preached* against negro traffic, how consistent was he then, to give orders to purchase them upon any pretence whatever?" asked Hammet.[15]

Hammet's inconsistencies made him a less effective critic than he might have been. John Phillips, whom Hammet ordained in 1795, left the church in a matter of weeks. The next year he published his own account accusing Hammet of being an autocrat, drunkard, freemason, and slaveholder who "openly and avowedly declared *perpetual slavery* to be right." In fact, by January 1795 Hammet had purchased a slave of his own. When Coke visited Charleston in late 1796, he smirked that Hammet had now "gained a sufficiency of money" to buy a plantation and "stock it with slaves; though no one was more strenuous against slavery than he, while destitute of the power of enslaving." Hammet's early success quickly faded. "Poor *William Hammett* is now come to nothing," Coke wrote in late 1796. "When he began his schism, his popularity was such, that he soon erected a Church, nearly, if not quite, as large as our New-Chapel in *London*; which was crowded in the Lord's-day. But, alas! he has now upon Sunday evenings, only about thirty white people with their dependent blacks."[16]

Still, Hammet's schism grated on Asbury to the end of his life. For someone who struggled with insecurity anyway, it was bitterly disappointing to lose friends under the weight of Hammet's criticisms. Asbury characteristically responded by trying to win them back in person, one at a time, even if it took years. William Capers, who later became a Methodist preacher, noted that his father had been one of the earliest converts to Methodism in Charleston, joining the church in 1786. Asbury often stayed in Capers's home until he joined Hammet's schism in the 1790s. The elder Capers and Asbury weren't reconciled until 1808, when they met at a camp meeting near Camden, South

Carolina. Though it had been seventeen years since they had seen each other, Asbury remembered the names of Capers's children and asked after them "as if it had been a few months," according to the younger Capers. Asbury had forgotten none of it.[17]

Hammet and Glendinning were too unstable to successfully challenge Asbury's authority over the American church as a whole. But together they helped to set the stage for one who could, James O'Kelly, by creating an atmosphere in which Asbury's authority seemed vulnerable. For Asbury these were difficult times, but not without their lessons. Glendinning and Hammet were real-life examples of the risk of compromising the itinerant system. The danger posed by their demands served to focus Asbury's resolve to defend connectional preaching at nearly any cost. At stake, in his mind, were the souls of countless Americans who might not hear the gospel if he couldn't send preachers where they were most needed, rather than leaving them where they were most comfortable. Particularly alarming to Asbury was Hammet's demand to stay in Charleston on what amounted to a permanent basis. "It will never do for preachers to rise up in a district and never move out of it for three or four years," he wrote to Nelson Reed in January 1792 as he hurried from Virginia to South Carolina to deal with Hammet.[18]

O'Kelly

Asbury arrived in Baltimore four days before the opening of the first quadrennial General Conference feeling "awful." He had just completed an exhausting seven-month tour from Georgia through Kentucky to New England and back to Maryland. In Kentucky he was "seized with a severe flux," an eighteenth-century synonym for diarrhea. The pain was "as severe . . . as, perhaps, I ever felt," but still he pressed on. For relief he ate rhubarb and drank a bottle of "good claret." Worse was the turmoil building ahead of the General Conference. Even the dependable Garrettson gave Asbury an earful as the two traveled together across Garrettson's district the week prior to the New York conference. "We had some close conversation on church government. On this subject there is not a perfect unanimity of sentiment," Garrettson recorded in his journal.[19]

Not quite half of the church's 266 itinerant preachers showed up for the General Conference, which opened on November 1, 1792.[20] They arrived in a mood to do something to limit episcopal authority, insuring that they wouldn't have anything like Asbury's ill-fated council foisted on them again. No sooner had the conference convened than James O'Kelly launched his assault on Asbury's episcopal powers. On the second day O'Kelly put forward a motion that "After the Bishop appoints the Preachers at Conference to their several circuits, if any one think himself injured by the appointment, he shall have liberty to appeal to the Conference and state his objections; and if the Conference approve his objections, the Bishop shall appoint him to another circuit." At this point O'Kelly probably still expected Coke's support. Prior to leaving for England in May 1791, Coke issued a circular letter in which he called for the "abolition" of American Methodism's "arbitrary aristocracy," meaning Asbury's episcopal powers. Coke proposed that the district conferences elect the presiding elders rather than allow the bishops to appoint them, and that "an appeal [be] allowed each preacher on the reading of the stations." This was essentially the same proposal that O'Kelly now made. At the time of his 1791 circular letter, Coke was, in the words of one historian, "a radical of the radicals." "A good superintendent is but a man, and a man is fond of power...[and] may become a tyrant, or be succeeded by one," Coke wrote in May 1791.[21] But by the fall of 1792 he had completely changed course, as O'Kelly now learned. He later wrote that Coke's arrival in Baltimore had "revived me, for I thought my best *friend* had come to town." But he quickly discovered "that Thomas had taken the alarm!... he had stepped over to the strongest side, and left me to suffer."[22]

Even without Coke's backing, O'Kelly could still count on considerable support. As debate raged over the next three days, a number of preachers took the floor to defend O'Kelly's motion, including Hope Hull, who had just spent five months traveling with Asbury from Georgia to Connecticut, William McKendree, a rising star who had preached under O'Kelly's supervision for the past five years, and Freeborn Garrettson. Characteristically, Asbury took little part in the public debate, preferring instead to work "*behind* the screen," as O'Kelly later put it. Early on, it looked as though the majority of the preachers would vote in O'Kelly's favor. They assumed there would be few of the kind of appeals that O'Kelly's motion allowed for. "For myself, at first I did not see any thing very objectionable in it," Thomas Ware later recalled. Ware had never liked the council. The present motion appealed to him because it reaffirmed the authority of the conferences and their right to pass judgment on the bishops' decisions.[23]

Complaining of a cold, Asbury withdrew from the conference early on, sending a letter of explanation. In it, he urged the preachers to look beyond themselves, especially in the matter of circuit appointments. "Are you sure that, if you please yourselves, the people will be as fully satisfied?" Asbury asked. "They often say, 'Let us have such a preacher;' and sometimes, 'we will not have such a preacher—we will sooner pay him to stay at home.' Perhaps I must say, 'his appeal forced him upon you.'" This was, of course, the crux of the matter with regard to the effectiveness of the itinerant system, as the majority of the preachers now realized. If the preachers were allowed to look to their own comfort, "easy and wealthy circuits" might become "crowded with preachers, while poor circuits would be left desolate," seriously compromising the church's ability to continually push outward, as one of the preachers pointed out during the debate. Sending a letter rather than appearing in person was predictable on Asbury's part. A simple cold would hardly have slowed him down on most occasions, but large assemblies were a different matter, particularly when they promised public debate with quick-witted opponents. He simply couldn't bring himself to face the prospect, no matter the consequences.[24]

As the debate progressed, the tone of O'Kelly's supporters soon alarmed Ware and many of his colleagues. Had the motion been "differently managed," Ware believed that it might have passed. "But when it came to be debated, I very much disliked the spirit of those who advocated it, and wondered at the severity" that those "who spoke in favour of it indulged in the course of their remarks." "O Heavens! Are we not Americans!" Hope Hull exclaimed at one point. "Did not our fathers bleed to free their sons from the British yoke? and shall we be slaves to ecclesiastical oppression? What, no appeal of an injured brother? Are these things so? Am I in my senses?" "We are far gone into POPERY!" added Stephen Davis, another of O'Kelly's allies. As he listened to this debate, John Kobler's reaction was similar to Thomas Ware's. "I was struck with fear that some of the brethren was rather too warm, & by the delivering their arguments, was giving way to a false zeal," Kobler wrote in his journal. What at first had seemed a straightforward proposal to assure that everyone received fair treatment now took on a more ominous cast. Many now realized that what O'Kelly really intended was to do away with the present itinerant system, remaking Methodism into a loose confederation of nearly autonomous districts. In particular, he was determined to secure his grip over the circuits of Southside Virginia, where he had preached for more than ten years and served as presiding elder since 1785, with as many as twenty-eight preachers under his supervision. "A consolidated government is always bad," O'Kelly wrote to a friend shortly after the General Conference. Realizing this, the preachers voted overwhelmingly to reject O'Kelly's motion on the evening of the fourth day.[25]

In the end, it was Asbury's conception of the itinerancy that the preachers voted to protect. "The sacrifice that a preacher makes in giving up his choice, and going wherever he is appointed, is not small. But no one is worthy of the name of a travelling preacher, that does not cheerfully go any where he can, for the general good," William Watters wrote with this issue in mind. "Better many individuals suffer, than the work at large." This was more than idle speculation on Watters's part. Like nearly all itinerants, he had endured appointments not at all to his liking. In 1782 Asbury had appointed Watters to the Fluvanna circuit in Virginia, far from his wife and home in Maryland, despite the fact that Watters had been battling malaria for most of the past year. He continued in poor health all that year and into the next, when he was appointed to the Hanover circuit, "as far from home, and nearly as laborious, as the one I just left." "I have often thought my going to those appointments, amongst the unhappiest circumstances in my life," Watters later reflected. But even this experience didn't diminish his faith in the itinerant system. Those who opposed O'Kelly did so not because they feared democracy, but because they sensed that following O'Kelly's path risked fragmenting the church. No one wanted to be responsible for creating more Hammets or Glendinnings. O'Kelly was right about the council, as just about everyone except Asbury realized from the start, but his solution was no better.[26]

The day after losing the vote on his motion, O'Kelly and three of his supporters, including McKendree but not Garrettson, left the conference. O'Kelly sent a letter to the conference, saying that "he was always afraid our Superintendents was on a stretch for power," according to John Kobler. "This breach gave a Sudden Shock to the whole body and every member I believe bore its part; tears flowed from every face," Kobler recorded in his journal. The conference appointed a committee of three, including Garrettson, to try to talk O'Kelly into coming back, but to no avail. "Many tears were shed, but we were not able to reconcile him to the decision of the conference," Garrettson wrote in his journal. "His wound was deep, and apparently incurable."[27]

The drama wasn't over, however. Garrettson and his committee reported back to the conference that though they hadn't convinced O'Kelly to return, they still believed that "God was with" him. Angered by even this limited show of support for O'Kelly, Coke, acting as the conference president in Asbury's absence, declared that the dissidents had "done violence to their public faith" by splitting the church. When someone challenged this reading of events, Coke "in great warmth . . . offered to stake his salvation, on pain of damnation, to the truth of his assertion." Hearing an account of this exchange, O'Kelly wrote a note to Coke accusing him of betraying "thy trust to me and others" and demanding "Christian satisfaction." The charge was largely true, of course, and Coke responded by meeting with the Virginia preachers that night to apologize for his "false zeal." Quick to anger, Coke was equally quick to admit his mistakes. But the damage was done, and O'Kelly remained alienated from the church.[28]

Asbury was different from either Coke or O'Kelly. All three were men of deep and abiding faith, but each had a different sense of his place in Methodism and public life. For all of his zeal, O'Kelly's writings convey a deep sense of personal grievances long nurtured. Unimpressed by the aristocracy of wealth, he never caved in to the allure of respectability, even to the degree that Asbury did in supporting Cokesbury College. Yet for all his populism, O'Kelly craved personal recognition. His writings about the events leading up to the General Conference say little about the people or the place of Methodism in their lives. Everything is construed as a struggle between the preachers and the bishops, or, more specifically, between himself and Asbury. Episcopal Methodism was flawed not because it failed to take the gospel to the lost (its core mission), but because it threatened to subordinate O'Kelly's role in that enterprise. He would later complain, in 1801, that he had "spent the *prime* of my days for the salvation of an *unthankful* people."[29]

Coke was less self-absorbed than O'Kelly, but more aristocratic. Only Coke could have been so insensitive to the opinions of ordinary Methodists to believe that there was any chance of a reunion with the Episcopal Church. A gentleman at heart, Coke believed that others would listen to him out of respect for his education and social standing. They often did, but there were limits. For all his good intentions, Coke was an interloper in America who never stayed long enough to really understand the church he pretended to lead. His propensity to change his mind only made it that much more unlikely that American Methodists would trust him. They respected his piety and education, but not always his judgment. Where O'Kelly was a localist whose interests didn't extend past a slice of the South, Coke came off as an international gadfly.

Asbury jealously guarded the itinerant system and had little patience for critics on this point. He was too stubbornly single-minded to allow that anything mattered more than preaching the gospel; but so long as Methodists accepted this, he had their support. His willingness to withdraw from key debates had a lot to do with how much the preachers trusted him. If he was a tyrant, it was in the most subtle of ways, as even O'Kelly acknowledged. After reading the published portion of Asbury's journal in September 1795, James Meacham, a former ally of O'Kelly's, concluded that its "whole tenor" depicted "an upright soul." If Asbury asked some preachers to take difficult backcountry circuits, they could hardly complain that he was asking more of them than of himself. Asbury's poverty was apparent to all, and those who suggested that he was secretly hoarding funds (as O'Kelly had) only damaged their credibility. "Where is all that he has been heaping up for near these forty years?" asked William Watters in 1806, though the question would have worked just as well in 1792. "Of all men that I have known he is in my estimation, the clearest of the love of money, and the most free to give away his all, in every sense of the word."[30]

The preachers also trusted Asbury's hard-won organizational wisdom. He knew more about not only Methodism but rural America than probably anyone alive. Who else had traveled the back roads of the nation as extensively for so many years? Coke and O'Kelly clearly surpassed Asbury as public speakers and might have matched him in piety and zeal, but they didn't know America or American Methodists as he did. Equally important, Asbury had a remarkable ability to accurately assess what each community needed. The people of any region had "feelings," as Asbury had noted in New England. The secret was to "touch the right string" so that "they will be moved." It was a thin line to walk, and Asbury sometimes failed in the attempt (as with the rules against slavery in the South), but few imagined that anyone else could have done better. The preachers didn't always like their appointments, but most knew that no one else could have made better choices on the whole. Asbury had reached too far with the council, but considering the inefficiency of the annual conference system it was easy to see why. Having reasserted the authority of the conferences, the preachers were satisfied to leave the day-to-day management of the church in Asbury's hands, content to watch him work himself to death on their behalf.

Neither side really wanted a schism, but over the next several months misunderstanding and distrust grew on both sides. Since O'Kelly was "almost worn out," at Asbury's suggestion the Virginia conference, which met near Petersburg in November 1792, agreed to pay him £40 a year and allow him to continue preaching in Methodist churches, provided he was "peaceable, and forbore to excite divisions among the brethren." O'Kelly saw these conditions as yet another indication of Asbury's deceitfulness. "Here we discover the unscriptural degree of power over the people," O'Kelly wrote. "If Francis gives a grant to any minister to preach...their doors must be open. Then, if Francis sends his authority to shut the doors against the same minister, none must open. This is 'the power of the keys.'" O'Kelly said that he accepted the offer of the pulpits, but not the money. Later, he claimed that Asbury sent him £10, which he considered a gift and used to buy a horse. Others claimed that O'Kelly drew the money from the book funds, knowing that it was part of the £40 salary. When an elder (probably Ira Ellis) accused O'Kelly of stirring up discord while taking money from the church, O'Kelly replied that "surely...'you did not intend it as hush money.' The people will ask, and I shall teach." Whatever the source of the money, O'Kelly had a point. Asbury's attempt to influence him indirectly, in this case using money, was exactly the kind of manipulation that had infuriated O'Kelly so often in the past. But O'Kelly was equally unrealistic if he expected the church leadership to publish his preaching appointments and open their meetinghouses so that he could condemn them from their own pulpits.[31]

By late 1793 there seemed no alternative short of separation. That December, O'Kelly and his followers met in conference, agreeing to form a new church on a more democratic footing. Calling themselves the Republican Methodist Church, they drew in as many as 1,000 former Methodists. "Republican" was a popular term in Virginia politics; at the same time that O'Kelly launched his revolt against Asbury, Thomas Jefferson's and James Madison's Republican party was taking shape in opposition to the Federalists. What could be more American (or at least more Virginian) than a republican church? The new church, led by O'Kelly and the former Methodists preachers John Allen, Rice Haggard, and John Robertson, "formed our ministers on an equality; gave the lay-members a balance of power in the legislature; and left the executive business in the church collectively," according to O'Kelly. But what exactly did that mean in practice? To answer this question, the Republican Methodists met again in August 1794 in Surry County, Virginia, where O'Kelly had owned a farm before entering the itinerancy and where his wife had grown up. They agreed to "lay aside every manuscript, and take the word of God, as recorded in the scriptures" as its guide. They also rejected the office of bishop ("The bishop was more despised by them, than any other man," Jesse Lee noted), but kept the office of elder, rejoicing to discover that the "primitive [meaning New Testament] church government, which came down from heaven, was a republic."[32]

One of the young Virginia preachers who might have followed O'Kelly was James Meacham. He had spent most of his career under O'Kelly's supervision and admired his opposition to the council and slavery. After the General Conference, Meacham took up his appointment on the Mecklenburg circuit, in the heart of O'Kelly's territory, and occasionally traveled with O'Kelly and heard him preach. Yet by March 1793 Meacham had concluded that O'Kelly and his followers were guilty of "Gross inconsistency" in their "protest against . . . against Mr. A[sbur]y . . . which I cannot reconcile to my reason."[33]

By July 1794 James Meacham had begun referring to O'Kelly's followers as "the schismatics." He was particularly dismayed at the way the Republican Methodists attempted to draw a connection between politics and religion. Following their conference in August 1794, Meacham dined with a man who "told me that it was fully believed by many (from the conduct & conversation of Mr. O'K) that the Original Methodist[s] could not be any thing else but (in fact) enemies to the Constitution of the States. . . . O! the Maliciousness of men," fumed Meacham. Apart from using politics, Meacham also believed that the Republican Methodists had begun to compromise their opposition to slavery. On July 31, 1795, Meacham preached at the home of the itinerant Henry Willis's father. There he met Abel Olive, who the year before "came to our conference and offered to travel . . . but he being interrogated closely on Slavery he took umbrage & left us & now is in connection with Mr. O'K." By this time the deep respect that Meacham had once felt for O'Kelly was gone.[34]

What dismayed Meacham amused the Episcopal priest Devereux Jarratt. Writing to a friend in March 1794, Jarratt took undisguised glee in noting the growing hostilities between the rival Methodist groups in southern Virginia. "O'Kelly does great things in the devisive way and I dare say he will make Asbury's Mitre set very uneasy on his head, so as to give sensible pain to his heart, and it may be to such a degree, that he may sincerely wish Dr. Coke had never given him a Mitre at all," chuckled Jarratt.[35]

O'Kelly and most of his followers soon changed their church's name from the Republican Methodists to the Christian Connection or Christian Church (though some kept the old name and left to form a separate group), gaining as many as 20,000 members in the South and West by 1809, though for the most part they remained centered in southern Virginia and northern North Carolina. For the moment O'Kelly's challenge was a serious blow to the Methodist Episcopal Church. Largely as a result, Virginia membership fell from a peak of 17,605 in 1793 to 13,288 in 1799, a loss of more than 4,300 members. Yet in the long run, the impact of the O'Kelly schism was less dramatic than it appeared at the time. While the Methodist Episcopal Church continued to expand across the nation as a whole, the O'Kelly-ites remained geographically confined. By 1810 Jesse Lee believed that their numbers were declining. O'Kelly's new church may have been more strictly democratic, but as a result it was also less able to distribute its resources widely and more prone to bogging down in local controversies.[36]

One final thread worth following in the O'Kelly story concerns William McKendree. Born in King William County, Virginia, on July 6, 1757, McKendree volunteered to fight on the American side during the revolution. He was at Yorktown when Cornwallis surrendered, though he was always reluctant to discuss his war experiences. Awakened during the Virginia revival in the second half of the 1770s, he was finally converted during the powerful 1787 revival that swept through the Brunswick circuit, where McKendree lived. In 1788 he joined the traveling connection on trial and was appointed to the Mecklenburg circuit in O'Kelly's district. From then until 1792, McKendree served exclusively under O'Kelly. During these years O'Kelly convinced McKendree, as McKendree later wrote to Asbury, "of the imminent danger of near-approaching ruin which our then flourishing Church would in all probability suffer" because of "the want of religion in a party of leading characters," principally Asbury, "whose unbounded thirst for power and money, as I understood him, was to pull down destruction on the Church of God." As a result, McKendree was one of the preachers who pulled out of the 1792 General Conference and rode out of town with O'Kelly.[37]

McKendree didn't attend the Virginia district conference held in Manchester a few weeks later. Instead, he sent a letter of resignation to Asbury, declining to take a circuit appointment for the coming year. Yet it wasn't long before he began to have doubts. Reminiscent of John Dickins more than a decade before, shortly after the Manchester conference Asbury invited McKendree to ride with him for awhile. After a few days, McKendree began to have second thoughts about Asbury, O'Kelly, and their respective motives. Asbury just didn't seem the tyrant and fraud that O'Kelly made him out to be. As a result, McKendree agreed to take the Norfolk, Virginia, station for the coming year. The next year McKendree volunteered to travel with Asbury for three months before taking up his appointment on the Union circuit in South Carolina. By the end of this time, whatever doubts he may have had about Asbury's character and intentions were gone. McKendree would go on to offer vital service to Asbury and the church.[38]

13

Reconnecting

While in New York City in September 1793, Asbury wrote to his parents, telling them that he had sent "a small sum of money" by way of Methodist merchants in New York. He wished that he could do more, but, as he reminded them in a similar letter the next year, his annual salary was still only $64 a year. He might have been able to save more if "the wicked world and those that leave our connection" (O'Kelly and his followers) hadn't "Blacken[ed] my character By saying I have the profits of Books at my command, and profits from the College [Cokesbury]." Neither had ever turned a profit, of course, certainly not Cokesbury. But Asbury preferred to avoid the issue entirely by continuing to keep himself poor. "The coat and waistcoat I now have on I have worn 13 months, and I would not carry a second shirt if I could do without it," he wrote to his parents in October 1795. "As my Father and Mother never disgraced me with an act of dishonesty, I hope to echo back the same sound of an honest, upright man."

Still, it troubled him that his parents might go wanting, so he advised them to "sell any useless property you have, and live upon the proceeds. I shall never want or possess anything you have." He hadn't forgotten "old England" but would never "reside there" again. He must have known that this would be bitter news to his parents, but there it was. He was forty-eight years old and responsible for about 270 traveling preachers and another seven hundred local preachers, spread over an area 1,400 miles from north to south, and 1,000 miles east to west. With so much to do, how could he ever turn his back on America? Having weathered challenges from O'Kelly and Coke, Hammet, and Glendinning, Asbury was at the height of his authority over American Methodism. Even Wesley was gone, eliminating any real threat of interference from Europe. His previous life as Franky, the metalworker's apprentice, must have seemed like someone else's story that he had once read. The formative experiences of his childhood had shaped him in ways that he could no longer admit or probably even discern, and he had no desire to return to the world from which they came. Methodism had allowed him to remake himself in ways that he never doubted were for the better; to turn back now would be to risk the very salvation of his soul.

Bringing his parents to America also seemed out of the question. He wouldn't have been able to spend much time with them in any event, leaving them far from everything that was familiar and little closer to him. "My hands are very full," he reminded them. "I am here, and there, and every where, upon the continent." He had no time for a possessive mother and an embarrassingly flawed, if good-natured, father. Both sides seem to have realized this, never seriously pursuing plans for the elder Asburys to move to America. Should his father die, his responsibility to his mother would increase, perhaps necessitating that she move to America. "I do most earnestly wish, if my mother should outlive my father, she would come to me, if able," Asbury wrote to his parents. Until then, things were best left as they were.[1]

Asbury responded to the outcome of the O'Kelly affair in the same way that he had responded to similar events (the aftermath of the sacramental crisis in 1780 comes to mind) throughout his career. Rather than taking time off for recuperation, let alone celebration, he threw himself into his work, eventually at tremendous personal cost. He began the year in Charleston, at the South Carolina annual conference. From there he rode down the coast to Savannah to hold the Georgia annual conference, stopping at the site of George Whitefield's former orphanage along the way. "A wretched country this!" Asbury reflected as he surveyed the orphanage ruins. Anglicans, Baptists, and Independents had all come to a bad end there, yet the Methodists couldn't give up on a region that contained "souls, precious souls, worth worlds." By the time he made his way back to South Carolina, he had ridden 650 miles in a month. Riding north through the Carolinas, he made his way to eastern Tennessee in time to convene the first annual conference held in the state on April 2, 1793. Over the next four weeks he rode another 500 or 600 miles, traveling north to Kentucky to hold that district's annual conference before returning to Tennessee in May. From there he turned northeast, holding annual conferences in West Virginia and western Maryland before crossing into Pennsylvania in late June. As he rode he had to plan for each conference, particularly where to station the preachers for the coming year.[2]

He arrived in New York in July, "tired down with fatigue and labour," having already suffered several bouts of "rheumatism" in his chest earlier in the year. This was probably rheumatic fever from streptococcocal throat infections, which can affect the heart valves and lead to congestive heart failure, sometimes called dropsy. It was an old complaint of Asbury's. "I was subject, when in England, during the winter's cold, and in the Northern States, likewise, to a heavy cough and continual tickling, frequent sore throat, and rheumatic complaints," he wrote to Thomas Morrell in February 1791. He also had occasional toothaches from untreated cavities (a common condition), at least one of which he treated by placing tobacco "in" the tooth. Abscessed teeth can also lead to infections that damage heart valves. For treatment, Asbury sometimes had himself bled, which may have provided some real relief. Blood letting can reduce the fluid overload caused by congestive heart failure and allow the swollen heart chambers to return to a more normal size, thereby improving the strength of contraction. Congestive heart failure would eventually prove the death of him, but only by slow degrees.[3]

Jesse Lee and New England

Still, he didn't rest, pushing on to hold an annual conference near Albany before turning east to New England. Conditions in upstate New York seemed especially promising, since O'Kelly and the other dissidents had never had much influence there, and there was no threat of Indian wars. Had Asbury thought about it, he might have added that there was also little conflict over slavery. About two hundred people had been converted in the past year alone. New England was another story. As he made his way through Connecticut and Massachusetts in July and August, he realized that they didn't offer the same opportunities. Methodist preaching in New England drew enough hearers to keep seven or eight preachers busy, but only about three hundred had joined the church.

Part of the problem was that Methodists didn't enjoy government support. The revolution had set in motion a wave of opposition to tax-supported religion across the United States, but in New England, where government support of religion had been strongest during the colonial period, establishments were generally modified rather than scrapped after 1776. During the 1780s Massachusetts, Connecticut, and New Hampshire adopted constitutions allowing for multiple establishments, in which local communities could vote on which church would enjoy the benefits of money that was collected from all taxpayers, with few exceptions, regardless of individual religious beliefs. In most towns and parishes this meant that the Congregationalists, who were usually in the majority, could still count on tax support. But the new system also held out the possibility that Anglicans, Baptists, Quakers, and others could vote themselves tax support in places where they held the majority. In Massachusetts, some urged the Methodists to do exactly this. At least for now the preachers "absolutely refused this plan," for which Asbury "commended them." Taking the government's money meant becoming entangled in the corrupt and unawakened world of politics, something that Asbury had always avoided. Having seen the collapse of state-sponsored religion in the South, Asbury and the preachers he imported from there brought a broader perspective to New England's debates over separation of church and state. They realized that state-sponsored religion was a step backwards, even if not all New Englanders could see it that way yet.[4]

Among the most strident opponents of Methodism in New England were the Congregationalist ministers, another product, Methodists believed, of the corrupt bargain between church and state. Ezekiel Cooper, who arrived in New England for the first time in 1793, concluded after a nine-month tour of the region that "the standing ministers I apprehend are our greatest foes. They fear the craft is in danger, and if . . . itinerant men [preachers] are encouraged, the salery of many will come down. Nothing makes men so zealous as trade, so those men, many of them, make a perfect trade of the ministry, & are more zealous to keep us away, than to get the people converted." Money was the root of the problem, a theme Cooper returned to again and again. "I cannot refrain thinking they [the established ministers] are like articles set up at vendue. The highest bidder takes them," Cooper lamented. "Whatever parish gives the greatest offer, gives the loudest call, & they strike themselves off to them; so that they are bought and sold."[5]

Jesse Lee, who had been instrumental in taking Methodism to New England in 1789, agreed. Even though he could count twenty preaching houses within the bounds of his two weeks', 130-mile circuit, he "feared that many of the Ministers are not ingaged in the work," as he wrote to Cooper in August 1789. "The Presbyterians are the Established religion, & every person is obliged to pay to them, unless they have a Certificate from some other society," Lee wrote to Cooper. Despite the difficulties this created, Lee was certain that he "was just where God would have me to be."[6]

Four years later Lee was still certain of this, but Asbury had his doubts. What to do with Lee posed a dilemma. Lee had long craved a more substantial role in the church, but Asbury was never satisfied that he would make a good bishop. Now it seemed that even New England might be too much for him. Lee had served as elder of the district since 1790, but when Cooper arrived there in

February 1793, he discovered that Lee hadn't consistently enforced Methodist discipline. Cooper, one of early Methodism's most erudite public speakers, had spent much of 1792 in Charleston, South Carolina, before leaving the city because of his health. Intelligent, calm, and efficient, Cooper was a peacemaker by temperament, with a bearing that could impress even sophisticated urban audiences. Asbury had sent him to Charleston to help quell the Hammet schism; now he dispatched him to New England for a similar task.[7]

When Cooper visited Lynn, Massachusetts, Lee's headquarters for the past two years, he discovered that "my dear brother Lee had not enforced the discipline in this place." Lee hadn't required members to kneel when praying, or stand when singing. Worse, "any one who choose may come to the classes, and as long as they please, without joining. 6 months, 9 months, nay a year & not join," Cooper wrote. Lee's insensitivity to local customs, particularly his refusal to allow the singing of fugue tunes, had also angered many in Lynn, such that they were threatening to return to the Congregational church. Lee predictably took quick exception to what he saw as Cooper's meddling and refused to change his ways. There was little that Cooper could do since Lee was the district's presiding elder. The responsibility to deal with Lee fell to Asbury, who wondered how he could remove Lee without completely alienating him and without knowing where to send him next. In June 1793 Asbury wrote to Thomas Morrell, then stationed in New York City, that he might send Lee there "if you could cure him of his obstinacy." But a month later he reconsidered, worrying that if Lee went to New York he might "get in with the wrong heads." Virginia was also out of the question since Asbury feared that there Lee would "join the faction," meaning O'Kelly and his followers.[8]

As Asbury laid his plans for the conference scheduled to meet in Lynn that August, he had reason to suspect that the inevitable confrontation with Lee would be acrimonious. At the 1792 General Conference in Baltimore, which precipitated the O'Kelly schism, Lee "strove very hard to have several parts of the discipline altered & the Bishops power reduced," though without success, according to Cooper. He believed that Lee did this specifically so that he could keep his appointment in Lynn. Before he could remove Lee, Asbury first had to line up his replacement. On the way to the Lynn, Asbury fell in with Cooper. As they rode, Asbury convinced a reluctant Cooper to take the eldership of the district. That settled, when the conference opened on August 1 Asbury first tried to station the district's other preachers before dealing with Lee, but even this proved difficult. In particular, Asbury wanted to send Menzies Rainor, a relatively new preacher who had joined the itinerancy in 1790, to New York, but Rainor initially refused. "This was a matter of considerable trouble," Cooper noted, though eventually Rainor agreed to go.[9]

Asbury next tried to appoint Lee to New York City, but Lee also refused, initially claiming that he needed at least three months to tie up loose ends in Lynn. When Asbury finally agreed to this, Lee equivocated, refusing to give any "assurance or real satisfaction that he would go to [New] York at all," according to Cooper. Finally, Lee proposed going to Maine to pioneer a new circuit, but only if the town of Lynn were added to his charge, even though another preacher, Jordan Rexford, had already been appointed to the Lynn circuit. It was also customary for the district's presiding elder to use Lynn as his base (as Lee had done), meaning that there would in effect be three preachers assigned at least in part to Lynn. Despite the potential for conflict, Asbury finally agreed, realizing, as Cooper concluded, that if Lee weren't accommodated he would "resent it so highly" that he might "take some improper step." "I truly wonder at a man of sense, to be so troublesome and unreasonable & ungovernable—so stiff & set," Cooper wrote. "He complains that the Bishop never consulted him—but it seems that he never advised with the Bishop, never gave him information of the state and condition of his district & the preachers. . . . He may think that the Bishop was absolute & delt hard with him. But I cannot see one absolute step. He yielded and yielded. . . . But brother L[ee] yielded in hardly any thing."[10]

In all, the Lynn conference was "more painful than any one conference beside," in Asbury's estimation. Cooper agreed. "Of all the Conferences I ever attended this was the most troublesome and trifling. So much accusation, cross questions, dispute, and opposition that I confess I was grieved & ashamed," Cooper wrote in his journal. In Cooper's mind, this was no accident. "There appears to have existed a long jealousy between br A[sbury] & br L[ee]," he concluded, though Cooper clearly blamed Lee more than Asbury. Lee doesn't discuss the Lynn conference in his published history of early Methodism, but he didn't quickly forget its results. A few months later, in December 1793, Cooper and Lee had another run-in at which Cooper accused Lee of "trampling" the authority of the conference. "He appears to be resolved to oppose the regular government of our church, and I am more & more satisfied that he only wants power & influence & [that] all would bend before him," Cooper fumed in his journal. "He delights to exercise authority when & where he can; but cannot bear to be ruled or governed." By January 1794 Lee had written to a friend in Baltimore that Asbury had "no religion." "Lord, help me, I have but little," Asbury wryly replied.[11]

For all the bickering and hard feelings, the Lynn conference speaks volumes about Asbury's leadership style. In the end, he managed to remove Lee without completely alienating him, as later events would prove, and install a skilled, if reluctant, new elder in his place. By the next New England conference, which met in September 1794, also in Lynn, Asbury had enough confidence in Lee to reappoint him presiding elder over the district. Cooper and Lee also patched up their differences, such that by October 1794 Cooper could write that he and Lee were "quite comfortable together. Altho' there was a great trial between us some time ago, yet now we are as friendly as ever, having made up our difference." Lee could be stubborn and incorrigible, but Asbury realized that he was also a bold and effective preacher. Asbury's tolerance for strong-willed colleagues made it possible to accommodate Lee, thereby preserving the services of a valuable preacher for years to come. Even so, Lee was only one of the 269 preachers Asbury had to station in 1793. What's remarkable isn't that the O'Kelly and Hammet schisms happened, but that there were so few like them.[12]

Worn Down

Despite its accomplishments, the 1793 New England tour left Asbury exhausted. To make matters worse, on the way into New York City in late August he was thrown from his horse, injuring his shoulder. "I have been sick upwards of four months," he reckoned, during which time he had ridden more than 3,000 miles, held six district conferences, attended numerous quarterly meetings, and preached often. Now he caught the flu, and it was all that he could do to get through the business of the conference presently meeting in the city. What he badly needed was a break, but for now, with eight more conferences scheduled before year's end, all he could do was push on.[13]

While in New York Asbury learned that yellow fever was sweeping through Philadelphia. The epidemic slowed his progress toward the city, where he was scheduled to hold an annual conference during the first week of September. In less than three months yellow fever killed 4,000 of the city's 50,000 inhabitants, spreading panic from Boston to Virginia. The yellow fever virus invades the liver, leading to necrosis of the liver and jaundice. Characterized by violent headaches, joint aches, high fever, vomiting progressively tinged with blood until it turns black, and a yellowish cast to skin and eyes, yellow fever was brought to Philadelphia, along with the *Aedes aegypti* mosquito that spread it, from the Caribbean. Benjamin Rush, the most famous physician of his day, quickly recognized the presence of the disease in Philadelphia, but without the benefit of modern understandings of how viruses work, he had no effective means to contain or treat it. Most doctors believed that marsh miasmas and putrefying vegetable matter could poison the air, leading to yellow fever and other diseases. Rush was convinced that a shipment of waterlogged coffee left to rot on the wharf was the cause of this most recent epidemic.[14]

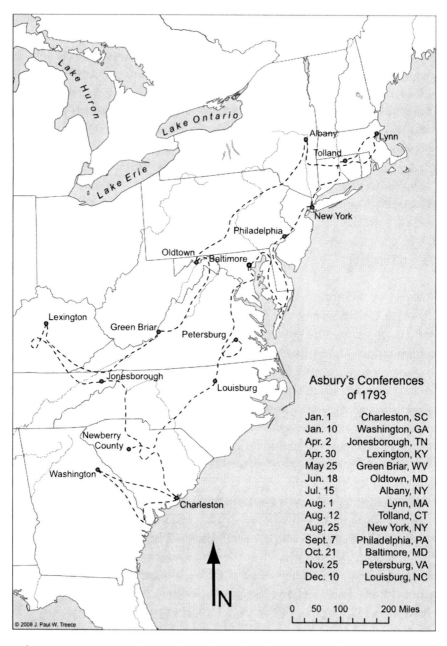

Asbury's Conferences of 1793

Jan. 1	Charleston, SC
Jan. 10	Washington, GA
Apr. 2	Jonesborough, TN
Apr. 30	Lexington, KY
May 25	Green Briar, WV
Jun. 18	Oldtown, MD
Jul. 15	Albany, NY
Aug. 1	Lynn, MA
Aug. 12	Tolland, CT
Aug. 25	New York, NY
Sept. 7	Philadelphia, PA
Oct. 21	Baltimore, MD
Nov. 25	Petersburg, VA
Dec. 10	Louisburg, NC

© 2008 J. Paul W. Treece

Asbury's 1793 tour covered more than 3,600 miles, beginning in Charleston, South Carolina and ending in Newberry County, South Carolina. (Map by J. Paul W. Treece, University of Missouri Geography, 2008.)

As he struggled to treat the sick, Rush left a detailed account of his efforts in a series of sixty letters written between August and November 1793 to his wife, who had fled to New Jersey. After experimenting with several treatments, Rush convinced himself that he could cure the disease using calomel, a compound of mercury and chlorine, combined with jalap, a Mexican root that acted as a violent herbal cathartic. Together they induced vigorous vomiting and purging of the bowels. The efficacy of these purges could be enhanced, Rush believed, by combining them with aggressive, daily bleeding (taking up to 80 ounces of blood at a time) and cold baths. Rush extracted 144 ounces of blood in six days from one patient, while at the same time giving him 150 grains of calomel and about the same of jalap, but the man survived anyway. Of course, Rush's efforts did little to stem the tide of the disease, and the treatments suggested by others proved no more effective (there is still no cure for yellow fever though a vaccine was developed in 1937). As the death toll mounted, many who had the means fled the city, including the state legislature, which did so on September 5, the day before Asbury rode into town. "I judge the people die from fifty to one hundred in a day: some of our friends are dying, others flying," Asbury wrote as he entered the city. His estimate was fairly accurate. By September, Rush also estimated that people were dying at a rate of up to one hundred per day.[15]

If Asbury feared catching the disease, he didn't show it. Since no one really understood what caused diseases like yellow fever, many, including at times Rush himself, saw them as divine judgments. When Catherine Garrettson arrived in the city that summer, she described the "fearful Epidemic fever" as "a dreadful visitation from above." Like many who had the means, she and her husband, Freeborn Garrettson, the district's new presiding elder, fled the city for several months, spending part of the time in Maryland. But Asbury wasn't so easily intimidated by the threat of sickness and never really had been. Since believers had nothing to fear from God's judgments, they not only had little reason to flee, but an obligation to proclaim the gospel to those who remained and might be on the brink of death. Even though his "strength was gone," on his first Sunday in the city Asbury preached twice in between conference sessions. "The people of this city are alarmed; and well they may be," he observed. He chose as one of his Sunday sermon texts Isaiah 58:1, "Cry aloud, spare not, lift up thy voice like a trumpet, and show my people their transgressions, and the house of Jacob their sins." Realizing that nothing served to focus people's attention on the fate of their souls like the prospect of death, Asbury seized the opportunity to remind those who remained in the city that they stood on the edge of eternity. Given his own precarious health, Asbury probably stood as close to the brink as anyone in Philadelphia. He nevertheless escaped unscathed, departing the city on September 11.[16]

After leaving Philadelphia, he made his way south through Delaware, northern Virginia, and Maryland, arriving in Baltimore for its annual conference on October 20. Along the way he attended seven quarterly meetings and visited Cokesbury College, which was, as always, struggling, "£500 in debt, and our employees nearly £700 in arrears." Following the Baltimore conference, Asbury rode to Petersburg for the Virginia conference on November 24. This was the heart of "the divisive spirit" created by the O'Kelly schism, and Asbury had "some difficulties" stationing the fifty-five preachers present.[17]

In all, the Virginia conference was exhausting for Asbury, allowing him only sixteen hours of sleep over the course of four nights. Yet, as had been the case throughout the year, there seemed little choice but to push on to the next annual conference, this time in North Carolina only two weeks away. Something had to give, and it did. Since the first of the year, he had conducted thirteen annual conferences, from Georgia in the South, to Tennessee and Kentucky in the West, to Massachusetts and Connecticut in the North, pushing himself to exhaustion along the way with quarterly meetings, regular preaching, long rides, and hard fare. He arrived in South Carolina in late December 1793 dangerously ill and low in spirits. "I am sometimes tempted to wish to die," he confessed in his journal. As the annual conference met on January 1, 1794, he "was seized with a severe chill, an inveterate cough and fever, with a sick stomach." The only place available to rest was a room without a fire where another preacher, Philip Bruce, was struggling through an attack of dysentery. With Bruce "moving so frequently" and a constant traffic of people coming and going, Asbury got little rest. Sick as he was, he got out of bed to ordain four elders and six deacons. Afterward he took a "powerful emetic," had himself bled, and drank betony tea, whose high tannin content made it somewhat effective against diarrhea (the tea was probably on hand for Bruce's benefit). Unfortunately, too much betony tea is toxic to the liver and an irritant to the gastrointestinal tract. Taking it with the emetic probably wasn't a good idea.[18]

The combined results of his illness and treatments nearly killed him. For the next two months, Asbury got no further than Charleston, where he spent most of his time reading and slowly recuperating. As he mended, he came to the obvious conclusion that he could no longer attend all of the annual conferences each year and that he would have to delegate some of this responsibility to others.[19]

He had seen this crisis of leadership coming in the 1780s, leading him to institute the short-lived council of elders in 1789. After the preachers rejected that plan, he doggedly tried to return to his old pattern of presiding over all the annual conferences, but the strain was inevitably too great. Now there was no alternative but to find some way to delegate more responsibilities to others.

Knowing that he wouldn't be well enough to cross the Appalachian Mountains in the spring, he wrote to the presiding elders of the western-most districts advising them to run their own conferences and station their own preachers. From Charleston, he wrote to John Kobler, presiding elder of the Holston district in Tennessee, informing him that he had "enjoyed very little Health since the first of August, having had Inflammation, lameness, influenza, Fevers & Colds." Since traveling to Tennessee in the spring was out of the question, Asbury authorized Kobler to "take the Precidency of the Conference" and enclosed "a Plan of the Stations of the preachers which I should be glad should take place." But Asbury also gave Kobler the freedom to "do as well as you can" with whatever "Contingencies" might arise. He sent a similar letter to Francis Poythress, presiding elder of the Cumberland district, encompassing circuits in Tennessee and Kentucky. He advised both men to meet him at the conference scheduled for May in Botetourt County, Virginia. Asbury hoped in this way to keep abreast of what he knew was a rapidly developing area. It was a strategy that he would employ more and more frequently in the coming years.[20]

Asbury was fortunate to have John Kobler to act on his behalf for the Holston district. Now twenty-six, Kobler had experienced conversion at nineteen and joined the itinerancy at twenty-one. His abilities quickly impressed Asbury, who moved him rapidly through the ranks. In 1790 and 1791 Kobler served under James O'Kelly in Virginia. Completing his probationary period in 1792, Kobler was received into full connection, moving to the Greenbrier circuit in western Virginia under Poythress. By the following year, he was an elder in charge of the Holston circuits and fiercely loyal to "our dear Bishop" Asbury. As presiding elder, Kobler drew up "rules for daily observation" for his preachers:

1. Let every preacher who is in health, rise in the morning by light.
2. Before he starts to his appointment reserve an hour at least for retirement to be spent in prayer & reading the bible.
3. Preach & Meet the class.
4. From the time of public service till evening retirement spend an hour & half in the most useful Improvements retired from Company.
5. From evening retirement till family prayer, to be spent in Reading, Singing and Godly Conversation with the family.
6. Visit the Sick whenever we can, whether they send for us or no.

Asbury could hardly have asked for a more dedicated assistant.[21]

Poythress was more experienced than Kobler and also proved effective at the time, though he later met a tragic end. Born in Virginia to relatively wealthy parents (by Methodist standards), Poythress experienced conversion under the preaching of Devereux Jarratt. Caught up in the first Virginia revival, Poythress joined the itinerancy in 1775, riding the first circuit in North Carolina in 1776 along with Edward Dromgoole. Poythress spent the next nine years riding circuits in Virginia, North Carolina, and Maryland before becoming a presiding elder in Virginia in 1786 and North Carolina in 1787. In 1788 Poythress moved across the Appalachian Mountains as elder for the Kentucky circuits. There he remained until 1800, directing much of the church's growth in the trans-Appalachian West. In 1794 membership on the circuits under Poythress's direction totaled more than 3,700; Asbury was impressed enough to recommend that Poythress be made a bishop in 1797. In 1800 Poythress finally left the West to become presiding elder over much of North Carolina. But somewhere along the way he began to lose his mental grip, "shattering his nerves," as one friend observed. The next year he returned to Kentucky, but "the light of the temple was gone." He "now stared upon the faces of old, loving, long-tried friends as though they were strangers." Poythress left the connection in 1801 and never preached again. In 1810 Asbury found him living with his sister near Lexington, Kentucky. "This has been an awful day to me," Asbury reflected in his journal on October 15, 1810. "I visited Francis Poythress: 'If thou be he—but O, how fallen!'" "He [Poythress] *has been for ten years in a state of insanity, and is still in a distressed state of mind,*" added Henry Boehm, who was traveling with Asbury at the time.[22]

This was all in the future, however. In 1794 Poythress's collapse was still six years away, and he, like Kobler, appeared up to the task of running his district without much direct intervention from Asbury. Both were respected preachers who knew their territories better than anyone else in the connection. What they lacked was Asbury's broader vision of the church as a whole.

From 1794 through 1796, Asbury adopted a reduced version of his customary annual tour, beginning in Charleston in January, proceeding northwest along the frontier in the spring, on to New England in the summer, and then south along the East Coast, arriving back in Charleston by the first of the next year. It was still a demanding schedule, and he still insisted on pushing himself relentlessly. In less than three months between March and June 1796, for example, he rode 2,300 miles from Charleston, South Carolina, through Georgia, North Carolina, Tennessee, Virginia, and Maryland before finally arriving in Baltimore. "Were I to charge the people on the western waters for my services, I should take their roads, rocks, and mountains into the account, and rate my labours at a very high price," he wrote while in western Virginia during this swing. Yet if the basic outline was the same, the overall scope of his travels was significantly reduced. After his physical breakdown in January 1794, he didn't return to Tennessee until April 1795, Georgia

Francis Asbury, by Charles Peale Polk, 1794. (Courtesy of Lovely Lane Museum and Archives, Baltimore, Maryland.)

until March 1796, western Pennsylvania until June 1796, and didn't set foot in Kentucky at all during this period. He presided over eight district conferences in 1794, seven in 1795, and another seven in 1796, down considerably from the fourteen he conducted in 1793.[23]

Less traveling meant more free time. What was he to do with it? One possibility was to establish a more permanent headquarters in a centrally located city like Baltimore. From there he could more easily maintain contact with the movement's various regions, summoning presiding elders for periodic conferences. This might accomplish informally what the council failed to do. Asbury was already writing hundreds of letters a year; supervising the districts from a distance would only require expanding a correspondence network already in place. Baltimore was an ideal location from which to do this, located as it was in the church's strongest region—62 percent of Methodists lived in

Maryland, Virginia, and North Carolina in 1796—and relatively accessible from other areas of the nation.

There is no indication that Asbury ever entertained such a plan. Doing so would have meant rejecting much of what he had sought to instill in the movement for more than twenty years. His breakthrough contribution to American Methodism in 1771 had been realizing that the movement was never going to thrive if the preachers didn't go to the people, most of whom lived outside the cities of the eastern seaboard. Pilmore and Boardman's error had been limiting themselves to New York and Philadelphia, only vaguely aware of the movement's new growth in the South. Asbury wasn't about to repeat their mistake. "I have one rule, not to do great things in haste; another, not to act at a distance, when I can come near," he wrote to Thomas Morrell in June 1793.[24]

Instead, he used the freedom that a reduced travel schedule provided to return to more basic pastoral duties. He did this not only to serve as an example to others (which he clearly intended), but also as an expression of his own convictions. No Methodist preacher was above the care of individual souls. The church's *Discipline* reminded preachers that "Family-Religion is wanting in many branches." Public preaching alone couldn't remedy this, "though we could preach like Angels." The solution was for "every travelling preacher" to "instruct" members "from house to house. Till this is done, and that in good earnest, the Methodists will be no better" than other people.[25]

These weren't to be merely social calls, as Asbury reminded Ezekiel Cooper, then stationed in New York, in January 1795. "Your attention ought to be paid to discipline, and visiting from house to house, but not to Eat and Drink," Asbury wrote. "We ought to visit as Doctors or as persons to plead the cause of their souls; not as guests to eat and drink, but [as] Divines for souls." Asbury tried to devote as much time as he could to these base-line duties, particularly when he wasn't traveling. While in Charleston, he spent time visiting people in their homes in the afternoon and sitting in on class meetings, especially the African-American and women's classes. During one two-month stay in Charleston, he preached eighteen sermons, met fifteen classes, wrote eighty letters, and visited thirty families "again and again." He did much the same during a week in Baltimore in May 1795. Wesley and the *Discipline* commanded preachers to "Go into every house," Asbury observed on this occasion. "I would go farther, and say, go into every kitchen and shop; address all, aged and young, on the salvation of their souls." In New York the following July, he met the black classes (there were eight) and two men's classes on one day, and another nine classes the next. In this way he reckoned that "I have now spoken to most of the members here, one by one." He did much the same in Philadelphia in July 1796, in Elizabeth-town, New Jersey, in August 1796, and again in New York City that same month.

"I was taken up in meeting classes and visiting from house to house a good deal of my time in the day," he noted on this last occasion.[26]

A reduced traveling schedule had the potential to marginalize him from the life of the districts he failed to visit each year, but it also offered the opportunity to reconnect with the more fundamental workings of the movement. Most members, and most preachers for that matter, spent little of their time concerned with the workings of annual conferences. Their spiritual lives revolved around class meetings, neighborhood preaching, and community discipline. For most, quarterly meetings, with their attendant sacramental services and love feasts, were the extent of their involvement in the wider Methodist world. The circuit riders traveled more extensively of course, but most of their time was nevertheless devoted to these same kinds of activities.

A case in point is Ezekiel Cooper. At the same time that Asbury was pushing himself to the breaking point in 1793, Cooper was settling in to his new appointment in New England. Apart from acting as Asbury's agent in dealing with Jesse Lee, Cooper threw himself into the work of ministering to locals. Even as a presiding elder with the responsibility of supervising the district's preachers, Cooper kept up a regular schedule of attending class meetings and visiting families in their homes in Lynn, his unofficial headquarters, and the surrounding villages. He began one week in July 1794 by meeting a class on Monday evening about two miles from where he boarded in Lynn. The next morning he crossed the countryside to the village of Swampscott, a mile or two east of Lynn, visiting four families along the way. Making his way to Woodend, he met a class at 5:00 p.m., and another at 8:00, spending the night at this last home. The next day, July 16, he walked to the village of Gravesend, where he visited seven or eight families "from house to house." That afternoon he took tea at deacon Farrington's, "with a number of Ladies, who were upon a visit at the Deacon[']s." In the evening he met a class at "friend Johnsons," where "we had a lively time," as Cooper noted in his journal. "I dont know that I have been more happy for a long time." The next day, Thursday, he "pursued my visiting," then met a class at three o'clock and preached at night. On Friday he "walked and visited the people so much that I was quite tired before night." Nevertheless, at five o'clock he attended a funeral and then visited three more families before calling it a day. On Saturday, Cooper "went on visiting," meeting ten or twelve families before four o'clock, when he met with a group of children. Afterward he called on two or three more families. In all, it was "a fatiguing week to my body & mind," Cooper wrote.[27] Most itinerants had further to ride between preaching places and class meetings than Cooper did in Lynn, but otherwise the rhythm of their lives was much the same. Devoting more time to these kinds of basic duties offered Asbury the chance to reconnect with some of the church's core values in a way that events of the past several years hadn't allowed.

Romance and Respectability

This kind of ministry was exhausting in its own way, and not everyone could take it for long, particularly when a romance came along. "Married or single," preachers "leaving the work, is my destress," Asbury wrote to Ezekiel Cooper in November 1793. Asbury had Cooper specifically in mind. He knew that Cooper was discouraged by his continuing struggle with Jesse Lee for control of the New England district. By January Asbury suspected that "Brother Cooper will decline this year; it is what I have long feared." In fact, in early 1794 Cooper fell in love with Polly Bemis, the daughter of Abraham Bemis, a tavern keeper who, along with his wife, was one of the leading Methodists of Waltham, Massachusetts. Cooper immediately wrote to John Dickins in Philadelphia asking his advice, perhaps hoping for a sympathetic answer since Dickins himself was married and had children. Dickins's reply could hardly have been much comfort to a young man in love. "If I may be permitted to speak my mind freely and affectionately in respect to your quitting the traveling connection, I must say it appears to me you are under a temptation. You are convinced that you have been in the way of duty. But are you as sure that you would be in the way of duty then?" Dickins wrote in April 1794. "I am apprehensive, that this is a particular time in which every preacher who loves the connexion, should endeavour as far as circumstances will possibly permit, to continue in the work; for I hear of several that have declined, and others who intend it. O my brother! if you are under no necessity to marry, stick by the work till nature is worn out." There was no mistaking Dickins's meaning.[28]

But Cooper couldn't help himself. He and Polly exchanged frequent letters, as was typical in romances of the time, and saw each other whenever Cooper's circuit allowed him to stop at Waltham. Polly's letters were "like a barbed dart to my very heart," Cooper confessed in his journal. How could he resist "one whose good sense and fine accomplishments are joined to a virtuous irre-proachable reputation, an agreable person & excellent disposition. Whose purity is conspicuous to all who know her, & joined with more than a common education. The only daughter and child of her parents, possesed of a consider-able property, and thriving in the world." For the bookish, contemplative Cooper, who had been raised in a relatively well-to-do family, Polly seemed nearly perfect. "I am affectionately and warmly attached to her. I think I could be happy with her," he wrote on June 20. On August 7, Cooper proposed to

Ezekiel Cooper (1763–1847). (From Abel Stevens, *History of the Methodist Episcopal Church in the United States of America*, vol. 3 [New York: Carlton & Porter, 1867].)

Polly that they "take each other for life in the bonds of union, no more to be twain," and she accepted.[29]

So everything was settled. Or was it? Cooper knew that he would be leaving New England that fall, and apparently he didn't intend to marry Polly until he returned at some later, unspecified date. When the couple talked again on September 12, Cooper recorded that Polly, "expresses a fear that I am not settled & fixed in my intentions about returning to this part of the world. I in a plain manner related the uncertainty of it, and told her that I apprehended there was no dependence to [be] made on it. That I might return in the Spring, in the summer or in the fall or not at all." For the next several weeks, Cooper was in "exquisite pain of mind." To complicate matters, a rival for Polly's hand tried to slander Cooper's reputation with her family, but her parents still backed Cooper. In the midst of this turmoil, Cooper made up his mind to locate, writing a letter to that effect to Asbury on October 1. But he couldn't bring himself to put it in the mail, knowing how disappointed Asbury would be. Finally, on October 17, the couple had a long talk in which Cooper suggested they drop their formal engagement until he returned (if ever). Polly, however, "wished that it might stand as it was." Their final parting two days later was about as painful as it could be. According to Cooper, "her last word was 'O you must return if you can,' which she uttered in such a way, that showed the full feelings of her dear heart, to which I replied, 'I will endeavour so to do.' And so in tears we parted." They never saw each other again.[30]

How much of all this Asbury knew is difficult to tell, but he never again assigned Cooper to New England. Cooper pined for Polly for several months as he took up his new duties in New York City, but his longing for her couldn't overcome his commitment to the ministry. He couldn't see how a traveling preacher could have it both ways, a view held by almost all Methodists of the time. As Dickins advised and Asbury hoped, Cooper never did marry. Even so, the idea of a celibate ministry ran counter to one of the core tenets of American culture, that eligible young men and women should get married and have children. As Methodists became more comfortable with the world around them, they found celibacy as a countercultural ideal more difficult to sustain. Eventually, Cooper's decision to forgo marriage in service of the gospel proved the exception.[31]

More often than not, preachers did eventually find wives and leave the itinerancy. However much Asbury regretted the loss of talented preachers, there was little he could do when a circuit rider wed, other than offer a less than heartfelt blessing. Marriage was, after all, an honorable Christian institution. In April 1795, while in Tennessee, Asbury spent a night with Mark Whitaker, who had married two years before and settled in nearby Virginia. "I wish his wife may not love him to death," was all the enthusiasm Asbury could muster for Whitaker's new life. Asbury's assessment of Reuben Ellis's marriage the following November was more positive, though still far from enthusiastic. "Brother Reuben Ellis is certainly married, for the first time; may it be for the glory of God, and the good of his Church, and comfort of the dear man and his wife." Asbury hoped that Ellis would remain active in the ministry, but in fact he died the following February.[32]

Closely related to the problem of preachers marrying and locating was a tendency for those who remained to cut a more refined figure in polite society. "I fear I do not see as much simplicity in our young brethren now as in years past. The love of shining dress and talents appears to be too prevalent," Asbury wrote to the preacher Daniel Fidler in June 1793. Young preachers increasingly seemed less willing to make the same sort of sacrifices that their older colleagues had. They appeared less countercultural, more concerned with making a good impression, especially in the cities. As with preachers leaving the itinerancy, this wasn't a new problem. But it took on increasing significance as younger preachers began to sense the possibility that they might succeed in winning a more respectable place in society where their predecessors had, with few exceptions, failed. Asbury knew that this would happen only at the loss of Methodist "simplicity." "We have had few City preachers but what have been spoiled for a poor man's preacher," he wrote to Ezekiel Cooper in January 1795. What was true of the preachers was true of the broader church. Writing to Martha Haskins of Philadelphia, Asbury bemoaned the fact that there were so few women's prayer meetings in that city. "Oh that the sister would establish prayer meetings once a week.... if we had a spirit of wrestling prayer we should see great very great things." But the trend seemed sadly in the opposite direction, away from discipline and self-sacrifice and toward the false light of high society. For the first time, Asbury began to sense that a significant segment of the church was moving beyond his core values. "It is low times with the new sort of methodists," he lamented to Haskins.[33]

The feeling was still fairly vague, lurking in the back recesses of his mind, but it was enough to make him wonder about his future in America. "My mind is variously exercised as to future events—whether it is my duty to continue to bear the burden I now bear, or whether I had not better retire to some other land," he mused in May 1796. At the time he was riding through eastern Tennessee on his way to Virginia, the center of his most strident opposition. On this occasion, however, he wasn't thinking of O'Kelly, but of the growing allure of respectability that beckoned the movement away from its highest calling. "I am not without fears, that a door will be opened to honour, ease, or interest; and then farewell to religion in the American Methodist Connexion." What hope did he have left? That "death may soon end all these thoughts and quiet all these fears." Death, of course, wasn't something a believer need fear; indeed, it offered entrance into a better life. Even so, this was a decidedly gloomy outlook on the future of the church. Despite all its successes, Asbury feared for the future of American Methodism.[34]

14

"Weighed in the balances"

Asbury's physical breakdown also offered him an opportunity to reconnect with a group that he had neglected for several years: African American Methodists. For more than a decade Asbury had been opposed to slavery and supportive of the church's efforts to reach out to African Americans, both slave and free. But in recent years he had been absorbed in fending off challenges from O'Kelly and others, and managing the church's expansion west across the Appalachian Mountains and north into upstate New York and New England. Gradually, as his pace slowed and he spent more time in local community settings, Asbury came to a new appreciation of black Methodism on two levels. First, his increased opportunities for worship with African Americans gave him a new appreciation for their spirituality; they often attended when whites wouldn't, worshiped with greater fervor, and practiced more consistent discipline. Second, slowing down forced him to more fully confront the injustices of slavery and the intransigence of whites.

There was no shortage of evidence on either count. While on his way to Charleston in February 1793, he found that some whites not only refused to provide him lodging in their homes, but also refused to let him sleep in their slaves' quarters, fearing that he might spread antislavery views. A few days later a man agreed to guide Asbury through a swamp, but when he discovered that the man owned slaves, Asbury lectured him on "his folly and the dangerous state of his soul." Offended, the man abandoned Asbury to find his own way through the swamp, apparently unmoved by warnings against the spiritual morass of slaveholding. When Asbury reached Charleston the next day, he couldn't help but notice that of the five hundred Methodists in the city, three hundred were black. As he recuperated there in early 1794, African Americans visited him regularly, and when he preached, they formed the majority of his audience. At a love feast in 1794 Asbury noted that "the poor Africans spoke livingly of the goodness of God." Whites, on the other hand, could scarcely endure his preaching. When he "let loose" while preaching in Charleston in February 1794, the one hundred whites in attendance "fled" the house; "they cannot, they will not, endure sound doctrine," Asbury concluded. By January 1795, his white audience in Charleston had declined to only seventy people. That December, in nearby Georgetown, he reported that "we have nearly one hundred Africans in society, while we have only seven or eight whites, our doctrine being too close, and our discipline too strict." With more time to think about it, the magnitude of African American Methodism and the tension it caused among whites became more obvious to him, leading Asbury to reason more closely on the issue than he had for some time.[1]

There was, of course, danger in pursuing an antislavery agenda single-mindedly. At the South Carolina conference meeting in March 1794, some of the preachers warned Asbury "that if we retain none among us who trade in slaves, the preachers will not be supported." This was a conundrum that wouldn't go away, and even Asbury had to admit that it was becoming increasingly difficult to find enough preachers to supply the state. Opposition to Methodism's tacitly antislavery message at times turned violent. In January 1795 a group of rowdy young men in Charleston "made a riot, broke the windows, and beat open the doors" of the church while Asbury preached inside. "The desperate wickedness of this people grieves and distresses my soul," he wrote after this event. A few weeks later he was "insulted on the pavement with some as horrible sayings as could come out of a creature's mouth on this side of hell. When I pray in my room with a few poor old women, those who walk the streets will shout at me." The reality of this left him "deeply dejected." "I have been lately more subject to melancholy than for many years past; and how can I help it: the white and worldly people are intolerably ignorant of God; playing, dancing, swearing, racing; these are their common practices and pursuits," he lamented in February 1795, after spending more than a month in Charleston. While "the women and Africans" turned out for meetings, "our few male members do not attend preaching; and I fear there is hardly one who walks with God," he wrote. "I have thought if we had entered here to preach only to the Africans, we should probably have done better," he added the next February while in Charleston. Pompous displays of wealth mixed with cruelty to slaves led Asbury to label Charleston "the seat of Satan."[2]

Charleston wasn't alone. While riding through South Carolina's rice country in March 1794, he drew a comparison between rice plantations and British warships. "If a man-of-war is 'a floating hell,' these are standing ones: wicked masters, overseers, and Negroes—cursing, drinking—no Sabbaths, no sermons." In North Carolina, Asbury confessed that his "spirit was grieved at the conduct of some Methodists, that hire out slaves at public places to the highest bidder, to cut, skin, and starve them; I think such members ought to be dealt with: on the side of oppressors there are law and power, but where are justice and mercy to the poor slaves?"[3]

Even preachers owned slaves in parts of the South. For several weeks in late 1797 Asbury stayed at Edward Dromgoole's, where he feared he "had or should say too much on slavery." A veteran preacher from the 1770s, Dromgoole left the traveling connection in 1786. He remained active as a local preacher while acquiring more than 800 acres of land and six slaves in Brunswick County, Virginia. Since local preachers answered only to their quarterly conferences, Asbury had no direct authority over Dromgoole. With nowhere else to turn, he vented his frustration in his journal: "O! to be dependent on slaveholders is in part to be a slave, and I was free born. I am brought to conclude that slavery will exist in Virginia perhaps for ages; there is not a sufficient sense of religion nor of liberty to destroy it; Methodists, Baptists, Presbyterians, in the highest flights of rapturous piety, still maintain and defend it."[4]

The contradiction became more glaring as opposition to slavery rose among Methodists farther north. Nearly one thousand slaves were freed in three counties on the Delmarva Peninsula between 1791 and 1799, mostly by Methodists, with another thousand freed between 1800 and 1819. This helped increase the proportion of free African Americans in Maryland's Caroline, Dorchester, and Talbot counties from about 15 percent of all African Americans in 1790 to more than 33 percent by 1810. Among the Delmarva Methodists who freed their slaves was Judge Thomas White, Asbury's protector during the revolution. In his will, White liberated all twenty-one of his slaves, writing, "I think it wrong and oppressive and not doing as I would be willing to be done by, to keep negroes in bondage or perpetual slavery." The contrast troubled Asbury. While "our southern friends are battered on the subject of slaves," northern Methodists lived in "peace," Asbury observed. "It will not do; we must be Methodists in one place as well as another."[5]

One of the things he had come to realize was that African Americans in the South were better off meeting by themselves, apart from white supervision. As he traveled through the South, he met separately with African Americans

when he could, sometimes attending a black meeting instead of a simulta-
neous white one, as in Charleston in January 1796 when he met with "the poor
slaves in brother Wells's kitchen, whilst our white brother held a sacramental
love feast in the front parlour upstairs." After meeting with a group of slaves in
North Carolina, Asbury noted that "we lose much by not meeting these people
alone," even if their owners were "professors of religion." One solution was for
black Methodists to have their own preachers, perhaps even their own
churches. As he prepared to leave Charleston in 1795, Asbury wrote that "the
poor Africans brought their blessings, and wishes, and prayers. Dear souls! May
the Lord provide them pastors after his own heart!" In fact, Asbury soon began
ordaining black preachers, even before he had conference approval to do so.[6]

Richard Allen

Philadelphia offered an example of what African American Methodism could
accomplish in a more tolerant setting. The catalyst for this renewal was Richard
Allen. Born a slave to Benjamin Chew of Philadelphia on February 14, 1760,
Allen eventually became the leading African American Methodist of his generation, Asbury's counterpart for black Methodism. A prominent Philadelphia
lawyer and attorney general of Pennsylvania at the time of Allen's birth, Chew
also owned a 1,000-acre plantation near Dover, Delaware, where the Allens
lived and worked. Chew had been a Quaker until 1758, when he quit the Friends
to join the Anglicans, who were conveniently more tolerant of slaveholding.
About 1768, Chew sold the Allen family to Stokeley Sturgis, a planter and
neighbor of Chew's, though of far less wealth and social status. Allen later
recalled that Sturgis was "what the world called a good master. He was more like
a father to his slaves than anything else. He was a very tender, humane man."
For all his kindness, Sturgis sold Allen's mother and three of her children,
probably about 1776, when his finances took a turn for the worse, retaining
Richard, his brother John, and a sister near Richard's age. Allen records little
else about his family and early life in his short autobiography, perhaps blocking
out memories too painful to recall, or because his experiences were so common
among slaves that they seemed to warrant no further explanation.[7]

What Allen does record at some length is his conversion experience. After
hearing a Methodist preach at about age sixteen, he felt "awakened and brought
to see myself, poor, wretched and undone, and without the mercy of God." In a
pattern familiar to all Methodists, he struggled over his sins until "one night
I thought hell would be my portion. I cried unto Him who delighteth to hear the
prayers of a poor sinner, and all of a sudden my dungeon shook, my chains flew

Richard Allen (1760–1831), from a steel engraving by John Sartain of Philadelphia. (Courtesy of the Billy Graham Center Museum, Wheaton, Illinois.)

off, and, glory to God, I cried. . . . Now my confidence strengthened that the Lord, for Christ's sake, had heard my prayers and pardoned all my sins." His brother and sister also "embraced religion," and Allen joined a class meeting at Benjamin Wells's farm, less than a mile from Sturgis's home. After their conversion, Allen and his brother, exhibiting the kind of drive and determination that would characterize so much of Allen's life, "held a council together, that we would attend more faithfully to our master's business, so that it should not be said that religion made us worse servants; we would work night and day to get our crops forward." Allen also began holding family prayer in Sturgis's kitchen. Sturgis and his wife eventually joined in, inviting Allen to move from the kitchen to the parlor. Sturgis was so impressed with the Allens' newfound piety that he encouraged the brothers to attend Methodist meetings and allowed Allen to invite preachers to his home. Asbury preached at Wells's farm on August 13, 1779, afterward meeting the class, presumably including Allen, and then in the evening preached at Sturgis's. Perhaps it was here that Allen first impressed

Asbury with his remarkable abilities. In 1778 or 1779 Freeborn Garrettson also preached at Sturgis's from the text, "Thou art weighed in the balances, and art found wanting" (Daniel 5:27). As a former slaveholder who had freed his slaves, Garrettson's words struck home as he declared that slaveholders would be among those found wanting in God's balance at the final judgment. Afterward, "my master believed himself to be one of that number, and after that he could not be satisfied to hold slaves, believing it to be wrong," Allen recalled. Sturgis agreed to sell Allen his freedom for £60 gold and silver, or $2,000 continental money, to be paid off in five yearly installments.[8]

To earn his freedom money, Allen cut wood (up to two cords a day), worked in a brickyard for $50 a month, and drove wagons loaded with salt, preaching at stops along the way. Allen pushed himself relentlessly, knowing that if Sturgis, then in his sixties, died before he could complete the bargain, he was "liable to be sold to the highest bidder, as he [Sturgis] was much in debt." Through extraordinary diligence, Allen was able to pay off his manumission in August 1783, a year and a half early. According to a testimonial written two years later, Allen was so successful as a salt dealer that he "got considerably by it both with Regard to Money and Reputation."[9]

Allen eventually made his way to Maryland, where he briefly rode the Harford circuit before finally settling in Baltimore in 1785, where he worked with Richard Whatcoat. Here Allen again met Asbury, who invited Allen to travel with him, but only under the condition that in southern states Allen would have to avoid mingling with slaves and sleep in the carriage. Allen refused on the grounds that if he got sick, there would be no one to care for him. Asbury's needs "would be taken care of, let his afflictions be as they were, or let him be taken sick where he would," but Allen "doubted whether it would be the case with myself." For all the development in his thinking, Asbury still had little understanding of the special challenges that African American preachers faced. He wanted to take Allen with him mainly to impress white audiences, without really understanding what the experience would mean to Allen.[10]

Returning to Philadelphia in February 1786, Allen joined the society at St. George's church and began preaching to the city's African American population as a local preacher, often preaching twice a day on weekdays and more often on Sundays. Philadelphia offered an inviting setting, with its rapidly growing but largely unchurched free African American population. During the American Revolution the city's black population had declined from fifteen hundred to about nine hundred, but by 1790 there were twenty-one hundred African Americans living in the city, less than three hundred of whom were slaves. Allen soon pulled together a "society" of forty-two African Americans, which met with the white Methodists at St. George's and included Absalom

St. George's Church, Philadelphia. The Methodists purchased the building in 1769 and remodeled it, with the addition of a gallery, in 1792. (Photo by the author.)

Jones. Like Allen, Jones had been born a slave in Delaware, later moving with his master to Philadelphia where he gained his freedom. At about the same time that Allen arrived in the city, Jones had quit attending Anglican services at St. Peter's Church and turned instead to the Methodists. But when Allen, Jones, and other leaders of the black Methodist community approached the district elder about opening a separate church, he refused, using "very degrading and insulting language." As an alternative, Allen joined with Jones and other black leaders to form the Free African Society in April 1787. Members had to live "orderly and sober" lives and contribute a shilling a month to help widows, orphans, and others in need.[11]

As the society laid plans for a "union" African church, the number of African Americans attending St. George's continued to increase. White leaders moved the black members, whom they considered a "nuisance," according to Allen, to seats along the walls, but even this failed to alleviate the crowding. To handle the growing numbers, church officials built a gallery, or balcony, the length of the church's two side walls in the spring of 1792. When the building was reopened, a sexton stood at the door to direct the black members to the gallery. Once there, they apparently chose the wrong seats. No sooner had they knelt to pray than a white trustee approached and took "hold of the Rev. Absalom Jones, pulling him up off of his knees, and saying, 'You must get up—you must not kneel here.'" Jones asked the trustee to at least wait until prayer was over, but he replied, "No, you must get up now, or I will call for aid and force you away." When Jones again refused to move, another trustee joined the first and together they began pulling black worshipers to their feet. By this time prayer had ended, and, according to Allen, "We all went out of the church in a body, and they were no more plagued with us in the church." The event "raised a great excitement" among the white members, and Allen later specu- lated that "they were ashamed of their conduct," but the damage was done. Later, the district's presiding elder, John McClaskey, threatened to "read you all out" if Allen and his friends didn't abandon their plans for a separate African Church and submit to McClaskey's supervision, but they refused. McClaskey's threats to "disown you all from the Methodist connection" carried little weight, since, as Allen put it, "we did not mean to go to St. George's church any more, as we were so scandalously treated in the presence of all the congregation present." Allen wasn't yet through with Methodism, but he meant to have a separate place of worship.[12]

Plans for the new church continued apace through 1792 and early 1793. At the ground breaking in March 1793, Allen was accorded a special place of honor. "As I was the first proposer of the African church, I put the first spade in the ground to dig a cellar for the same," he later recalled. But no sooner had construction begun than calamity struck in the form of the 1793 yellow fever epidemic. Fear of the disease sent shock waves of panic through the city's population. Writing in September 1793, as the epidemic was just gaining momentum, Benjamin Rush noted that "many die without nurses. Some perish from the want of a draught of water. Parents desert their children as soon as they are infected, and in every room you enter you see no person but a solitary black man or woman near the sick. Many people thrust their parents into the streets as soon as they complain of a headache." Rush had been one of the principal backers of the Free African Society and the African Church, and now, overwhelmed by the number of yellow fever cases under his care, he called on Allen to mobilize the African American community to attend the sick, assuring him that the fever had no effect on "persons of your color." There were, of course, many reasons why Allen and his colleagues might have refused, but Rush had proven himself an invaluable ally in securing funding for the African Church, and they were "sensible that it was our duty to do all the good we could to our suffering fellow mortals." Rush put Allen and his friends to work bleeding the sick and administering calomel purges; before the epidemic ran its course they bled some eight hundred patients. They also drove the death carts and buried the dead. In the process they quickly learned that assurances "that people of our color were not liable to take the infection" were nothing but wishful thinking. By September 25, Rush himself realized his error, writing to his wife that "the Negroes are everywhere submitting to the disorder," adding "Richard Allen, who had led their van, is very ill." Allen recovered, but by the time the scourge passed in November 240 African Americans had died, about 10 percent of Philadelphia's black population, a higher proportion than had perished in the white community.[13]

In the aftermath of the yellow fever epidemic, the leaders of the African Church decided to affiliate with one of the city's established churches. When the vote was taken on which denomination to join, only Allen and Jones stood by the Methodists, while a large majority chose the Episcopalians. This isn't much of a surprise given the recent experiences of Philadelphia's African Americans with both denominations. After all, many of the principal white supporters of the African Church were Episcopalians, including Rush and, ironically, Joseph Pilmore, while Methodists were among its worst opponents. While some Methodist leaders, including Freeborn Garrettson, had fled the city during the yellow fever epidemic, Pilmore had remained, going "everywhere where there is sickness or distress," according to Rush.

The decision presented Allen with a dilemma. Joining the Episcopalians offered him the chance to substantially raise his social standing. Only two years before Thomas Coke had dreamed of reuniting all of American Methodism with the Episcopal Church; now Allen had the opportunity to accomplish for African American Methodists what Coke had failed to do for the mostly white church. Had he chosen to do so, Allen could have become the minister of what seemed sure to be Philadelphia's leading African American church and the first ordained black Episcopalian in the nation.[14]

Yet Allen couldn't bring himself to leave the Methodists. Despite being "violently persecuted" by a string of elders, Allen remained "confident that there was no religious sect or denomination [that] would suit the capacity of the colored people as well as the Methodists; for the plain and simple gospel suits best for any people." For Allen, this was primarily a religious, not a professional or financial, decision. The Episcopal Church offered many rewards, but it didn't, in his opinion, provide the best setting for preaching the gospel. "The Methodists were the first people that brought glad tidings to the colored people. I feel thankful that ever I heard a Methodist preach. We are beholden to the Methodists, under God, for the light of the Gospel we enjoy; for all other denominations preached so high-flown that we were not able to comprehend their doctrine," Allen later recalled. Despite all that the Episcopal

Church could offer, he informed the other leaders of the African Church that he "could not be anything else but a Methodist, as I was born and awakened under them."[15]

Asbury's support of Allen probably played a crucial role in his decision to remain a Methodist. There were a number of reasons why Asbury might have objected to Allen's church. The district's presiding elder at the time of the St. George's incident, John McClaskey, opposed it, as did other leading Philadelphia Methodists. No doubt they had done all that they could to convince Asbury that Allen was misguided and ungovernable. Moreover, Asbury had always resisted attempts by white preachers, be they William Hammet, James O'Kelly, or William Glendinning, to exercise more authority than their appointments allowed, as Allen, a local preacher, had done by defying the orders of more than one elder. Yet it was also clear that Allen hadn't set out to create a schism; he hadn't chosen to be dragged from his knees while at prayer. Disowning Allen, who clearly wanted to remain a Methodist, would have meant abandoning the church's mission to much of Philadelphia's black population.

To see that this didn't happen, Asbury reconfigured the leadership of Philadelphia Methodism in Allen's favor. In July 1793, he removed McClaskey, whom he had appointed the district's presiding elder only the year before, sending him to Baltimore and replacing him with Freeborn Garrettson, the very preacher responsible for convincing Allen's former master of the injustice of slavery. Married only a few weeks before, Freeborn and Catherine Garrettson arrived in Philadelphia just as the yellow fever epidemic broke. They stayed only until the spring of 1794, when Catherine's pregnancy prompted their return to Rhinebeck, New York. Nevertheless, Garrettson was present during the critical period when Allen had to decide whether to become an Episcopalian or stay with the Methodists. Garrettson was early American Methodism's foremost abolitionist, and it seems unlikely that anyone could have missed the significance of his appointment at this critical juncture. The assignment must have carried special significance for Garrettson, enough to lure him away from New York, where he had been firmly rooted since 1788. From that date until the end of his career, Garrettson accepted only two appointments outside New York, both to serve as elder of the Philadelphia district during periods of turmoil among the city's Methodists, first in 1793 and again in 1799. After Garrettson left in 1794, Asbury continued to support Allen by appointing preachers friendly to black Methodism to Philadelphia, including Ezekiel Cooper in 1795 and 1796. How typical of Asbury to work behind the scene rather than out in front of the audience.[16]

With a small group of followers, Allen moved a former blacksmith's shop that he had purchased for $35, to a lot he had acquired on Sixth Street near

Lombard Street. He then "employed carpenters to repair the old frame, and fit it for a place of worship." Asbury arrived in Philadelphia in late June 1794, just in time to preach the dedication sermon for the new church, called Bethel. His presence provided unmistakable institutional recognition for Allen and his congregation. "Many hearty 'amen's' echoed through the house," Allen records, as Asbury preached. From the outset, Bethel was home to the Methodist style of worship that would have been frowned upon at St. Thomas's Episcopal Church. Allen and his followers were committed to "the liberty of extempore prayer" and to the right of "any that are moved thereto by the Spirit of God" to speak forth in public. In contrast to the meeting at Bethel, Asbury noted that later that evening "we had a cold time at the great church," meaning St. George's.[17]

Still, Asbury's support for Bethel came with certain expectations. He agreed to back Bethel only after Allen assured him that "our coloured brethren are to be governed by the doctrine and discipline of the Methodists." In November, Bethel's trustees published a statement affirming Asbury's under-standing of the new church's status. Avoiding inflammatory language, the statement began by pointing out the mutual benefits of a separate black church. For whites, it would "obviate any offence our mixing with our white brethren might give them." For African Americans, it would "preserve, as much as possible, from the crafty wiles of the enemy our weak-minded brethren, from taking offence at such partiality as they might be led to think contrary to the spirit of the Gospel, in which there is neither male nor female, barbarian nor Scythian, bond nor free, but all are one in Christ Jesus." The hoped-for result was that both communities "might the more freely and fully hold the faith in unity of spirit and the bonds of peace together, and build each other up in our most holy faith." The trustees claimed the right to hold their own elections for church officers, to limit membership to "descendants of the African race," to license their own exhorters and local preachers, and to manage their own "temporal concerns." Beyond that they agreed to continue "in union with the Methodist Episcopal Church, subject to the government of the present Bishops . . . as long as the present articles, creeds and discipline of said Church remain unaltered and unchanged." Asbury could hardly have asked for more. He was keenly aware that many white Methodists had shown far less loyalty to the church, leaving it over issues that seemed trivial compared to the kind of harassment that Philadelphia's African American Methodists had endured.[18]

Race clearly separated Allen and Asbury, but in other respects the two were much alike. Though Asbury would never fully comprehend the realities of slavery and racism, he and Allen could work together because their religion formed a stronger bond than race. The two shared a sense of loyalty to the church that first brought them to conversion and a zealous commitment to promoting plain Methodist doctrine. Neither was a particularly gifted or persuasive public speaker, nor an intellectual by training or temperament. Yet both were concerned with building disciplined communities of faith where members could be nurtured beyond the limits of simple conversion. Toward that end they were indefatigable in their own spheres of influence.

15

"We were great too soon"

Flames lit up the sky over Abingdon, Maryland, on December 4, 1795, as Cokesbury College burned, causing the roof to collapse and gutting the interior, leaving the outer walls standing naked and scarred. The fire marked the end of an era for Asbury and the church, dashing his hopes for a Methodist college but also relieving him of a considerable burden. Cokesbury had never lived up to his expectations, and it chewed up time and money while drawing attention away from other projects that might have offered better returns. From its inception the school had consumed £10,000, and now it was all reduced to ashes. Many, including Thomas Coke, suspected arson; two years later Asbury was still convinced that the burning of Cokesbury "was done wickedly." Maryland's governor offered a $1,000 reward for information leading to an arrest, but the case went unsolved. For Asbury, the loss of the school's library was especially tragic.[1]

The school had struggled to keep going for years. Much of the money collected for Cokesbury went toward construction of the Georgian-style main building, which by late 1789 had cost nearly £4,000 and was still incomplete, with a good deal of interior carpentry, plastering, and painting unfinished. Built on a hilltop with an impressive view, it measured 108 feet east to west, 40 feet wide, and three stories tall, with room to house one hundred students. Many thought it an impressive structure, though the Episcopalian Devereux Jarratt described it as a "vast pile."[2]

After the departure of Cokesbury's first teachers, Levi Heath and Truman Marsh, in 1788, local physician Jacob Hall took over running the school with new teachers. Hall was an Episcopalian with a degree from the University of Pennsylvania who had studied medicine at the University of Edinburgh, Scotland, Europe's leading medical institution. Cokesbury's initial curriculum had followed Wesley's Kingswood method, including an emphasis on reading Latin, some contact with Greek and Hebrew, arithmetic, geography, history, and large doses of devotional literature. Students were required to rise at 5:00 a.m., go to bed by 9:00 p.m., and study for seven hours a day. Play was strictly forbidden; in its place students were supposed to learn manual skills, particularly gardening. Under Hall the curriculum veered away from Wesley's plan, taking on the character of a more typical eighteenth-century academy. When Coke and Asbury stopped at Cokesbury in May 1789, they heard two students recite by memory chapters from Thomas Sheridan on elocution and a younger student recite a speech from Livy. Asbury gave the two older boys a dollar each, and Coke presented the younger student with a small gold coin. Asbury also rewarded three boys who "excelled in gardening" with a dollar each. The bishops may have been reasonably satisfied on this occasion, but others weren't pleased with the more secular curriculum. The itinerant William Colbert attended a public exhibition in the college hall in November 1791. "Part of it I liked much—and part, I think was too Theatreacal, for to be allow'd of in the College of a people that make so high a profession of religion as the Methodist do," Colbert sourly noted.[3]

By 1792 Hall was pushing for the school to become an independent public corporation with a charter from the state. This angered Jesse Lee and others who saw the church losing control of Cokesbury, but the school's financial state made keeping it equally problematic. Tuition, room and board were initially set at £30, though Asbury hoped that gifts would eventually allow much of the student body to consist of charity students who wouldn't otherwise be able to attend. But such hopes were never realized. Writing from Cokesbury in October 1793, student Thomas Dromgoole reminded his father Edward "that every Boy has to find his own Wood & Candles to Burn . . . or be turned away from the Fire."[4]

By the spring of 1794 the school had reached another crisis point, with enrollment falling by half. On September 28, 1794, Asbury and the New York conference, meeting in New York City, resolved "that nothing but an English free day school should be kept at Cokesbury." Asbury then rode south, crossing the Susquehanna and arriving at Cokesbury on October 16. There he found the school £1,200 in debt, with £300 due immediately. The next day Hall resigned as president of the college, and the school closed. "Our collegiate matters now come to a crisis," Asbury wrote on October 21. "We now make a sudden and dead pause;—we mean to incorporate, and breathe, and take some better plan. If we cannot have a Christian school (that is, a school under Christian discipline and pious teachers) we will have none." That December Cokesbury incorporated under five clergy and ten lay trustees with a charter from the state. Giving up control of the school was bittersweet for Asbury, who concluded to "let it go, we were great too soon." The trustees spent much of 1795 paying bills and reorganizing. No sooner had they done so than fire reduced all their efforts to ashes that December.[5]

Abandoning Abingdon for Baltimore, the school reopened in May 1796, where it was known as the Baltimore Academy. The new school included departments for boys and girls, while jettisoning what remained of Wesley's Methodist piety from the curriculum. That June Asbury noted that the academy had five teachers and two hundred students. The building, originally constructed to hold balls, concerts, and card parties, was an impressive brick structure located near the Light Street Methodist Church. But a year to the day after the burning of Cokesbury, tragedy struck once again when the academy also went up in flames. It never reopened.[6]

For Devereux Jarratt the failure of Cokesbury came as no surprise. Though he "felt for Mr. Asbury," Jarratt "never expected any great things, or good purposes," from Cokesbury. "Indeed, I see not, how any considerate man could expect any great things from a seminary of learning, while under the supreme direction and controul of tinkers and taylors, weavers, shoemakers and country mechanics of all kinds—or, in other words, of men illiterate and wholly unacquainted with colleges and their contents," Jarratt scoffed less than two months after Cokesbury burned. For Asbury, Cokesbury's demise came mostly as a relief. "As to the college," he later wrote, "it was all pain and no profit." He uncharitably tried to shift much of the blame for Cokesbury's overall failure to Coke. "Would any man give me £10,000 per year to do and suffer again what I have done for that house [Cokesbury], I would not do it," Asbury wrote in January 1796. "The Lord called not Mr. Whitefield nor the Methodists to build colleges. I wished only for schools—Doctor Coke wanted a college."[7]

About a month before the Baltimore Academy burned, Asbury joined 120 preachers in Baltimore for the second quadrennial General Conference. Thomas Coke arrived only a day or two before the conference began, after a voyage from London in which the weather was fair but the ship's crew the worst he had ever seen for "obscenity and blasphemy."[8]

The 1796 conference didn't have near the drama of the 1792 meeting, at which James O'Kelly stormed out of the church, but it did enact provisions that would have far reaching implications for Asbury and the church. It fixed the boundaries of six permanent annual conferences—New England, Philadelphia,

Baltimore, Virginia, South Carolina, and the Western conference—a significant reduction from the twenty conferences scheduled for the 1793 conference year. This would allow the bishops "to attend the conferences with greater ease, and without injury to their health," according to the conference minutes. Everyone realized that the strain on Asbury had become too great. The new system also made it more difficult for a dissident like O'Kelly to gain control over an entire annual conference. The majority of the preachers saw this as a positive step, though they must have realized that it had the potential to limit innovation.[9]

Between the General Conferences of 1792 and 1796, 106 itinerant preachers located and left the traveling ministry. Though most remained active as local preachers, their departure from full-time preaching represented a significant loss. "None . . . will doubt that we have sustained much injury by the location of so many of our ministers, at a period, when they were best qualified to be useful, and the necessity of supplying their places by young and inexperienced men," reflected the itinerant Thomas Ware, who attended the conference. This wasn't a new problem, of course. Asbury frequently had to scramble to fill circuits in every region, and circuits sometimes went begging for a preacher altogether, particularly in more remote areas. When he rode through the Swannanoa circuit in the Blue Ridge Mountains of western North Carolina in March 1794, he was shocked to learn that "neither preachers nor elders" had visited the circuit in six months, despite that fact that it contained about two hundred members. A few weeks later he learned the reason: one of the preachers appointed to the circuit had taken sick, while the other had married. To fill the opening Asbury moved Philip Sands from the Guilford circuit to Swannanoa, temporarily leaving Guilford with only one preacher. The urgency to provide someone for Swannanoa notwithstanding, some grumbled that Asbury was a "despot" for moving Sands in the middle of the conference year.[10]

The General Conference responded to this general problem by embracing the Chartered Fund that Asbury had drawn up the previous August in Philadelphia. Legally incorporated in Pennsylvania in January 1797, the fund was designed to take in voluntary contributions, distributing them to those in need. The articles of association permitted the fund to give up to $64 a year to "itinerant, superannuated, or worn-out single" preachers, twice that to married preachers, $64 a year to preachers' widows, and $16 a year to children or orphans of preachers, minus whatever they received from their home circuit. These weren't lavish sums, but most preachers and their families would have been glad to get even this. Often they didn't. Asbury estimated that only about one quarter of the preachers in Virginia received their full $64 a year, with things no better in other regions. The General Conference stipulated that the fund would operate as an endowment, withdrawing only the accumulated interest each year, beginning in August 1798, and it was clear that the fund wouldn't be adequately endowed any time soon. "No adequate means are devised to raise it," Thomas Ware concluded.[11]

Asbury's support for the Charted Fund represents a subtle shift in his thinking. Up to this point, he had taken comfort in the poverty of his preachers, believing that it would keep them pure from worldly ambition. But too much poverty could be equally problematic, particularly when the variable of marriage was added. Young men would marry, whether he wanted them to or not, and then they would become concerned for the security of their wives and children in a way that they hadn't been for themselves alone. The choice, Asbury now realized, wasn't simply between a poor ministry and a worldly one. It was between a destitute ministry populated mostly with inexperienced young men and a humble ($64 a year wasn't a lot of money) ministry that could count on support for their families, especially in old age. If the strength of the itinerant system was its ability to reach large numbers of people spread out over vast geographical areas, its weakness was that it wore preachers out so quickly, leaving the church dependent on an endless string of inexperienced young men. "I want some older heads in our ministry," Asbury wrote to William Watters, a veteran from the 1770s, but he rarely got them.[12]

Thomas Coke was equally concerned with the plight of married preachers, and less inclined to fear the danger of creeping affluence. When he learned that the Baltimore Academy had burned, he lamented that the £10,000 invested in Cokesbury and the academy hadn't been "laid out for the support of a married ministry." "I have long groaned in spirit on acct. of the loss we have suffered by the withdrawing of our married ministers on this Continent from the general work for want of support. The evil sustained by this is unmeasurable," he wrote to Ezekiel Cooper in December 1797. Coke instructed Cooper to find up to three married preachers who were considering leaving the itinerancy and offer them £20 a year in Coke's name. This was a generous offer, but it could hardly meet the larger need. To avoid a wave of pleading, Coke, in typically Coke fashion, urged Cooper to keep all these arrangements secret, even from Asbury. The following December, Coke again wrote to Cooper advising him "that the work will never flourish as extensively and permanently as we could wish, till you have further provision for a married ministry. . . . It is contrary to the Word of God & the reason of things, to suffer the married Preachers to drop off as they do for want of food for themselves and families." This was a problem that was only beginning to erode the foundations of the itinerant system, but Asbury and Coke could see that if it wasn't stopped soon, the whole structure might collapse.[13]

Everyone at the 1796 General Conference could see that Asbury's health was failing. If he should die, who would take his place? Could they depend on Coke? Some of the preachers knew about Coke's secret overtures to Bishop White offering to combine the Methodist and Episcopal churches in 1791, though the full details of the affair only came out later. "Some said they thought it a wicked attempt; and were not willing to admit that it was for the best, nor to take circumstances into the account," William Phoebus noted. Beyond the question of Coke's integrity, many were reluctant to dilute Asbury's authority while he yet lived, but they also realized that he wouldn't live forever. With this in mind, the majority voted to elect another bishop alongside Asbury, deciding that it was too great a risk to leave things as they stood. But before the conference could vote on candidates, Coke "begged that the business might be laid over until the afternoon." When the conference reconvened, Coke once again promised his services to America, "to live or die among [you]." Aside from his secret proposals to Bishop White, the extent of Coke's commitments in Europe and the West Indies made it seem unlikely that he could devote enough attention to America. Everybody knew that Coke habitually spread himself too thin. Jesse Lee took the lead in opposing Coke, whom he considered unreliable and not as well qualified as several of the American preachers present, himself included. Coke still had many supporters among the preachers, but Lee was a powerful presence. The debate might have gone against Coke if Asbury hadn't intervened. Standing before the conference, Asbury insisted that all past grievances should be buried so that "friends at first are friends at last, and I hope never to be divided." He had gone out of his way to keep Lee in the church in 1793, and he now did the same for Coke.

Following Asbury's advice, only seven of the 106 preachers present voted against Coke. Still, the preachers demanded a written pledge from Coke, recognizing not only his commitment to America, but also his subordinate status to Asbury:

> I offer myself to my American brethren entirely to their service, all I am and have, with my talents and labours in every respect; without any mental reservation whatsoever to labour among them, and to assist bishop Asbury; not to station the preachers at any time when he is present; but to exercise all the episcopal duties, when I hold a conference in his absence, and by his consent, and to visit the West Indies and France when there is an opening, and I can be spared.

In effect, Coke became the church's reserve bishop, to assume full episcopal power only in Asbury's absence. The printed conference minutes contain neither the debate, nor the vote, nor the written agreement, perhaps in deference to Coke, who says nothing about these events in his journal, noting only that "all was unity and love. There was not a jarring string among us."[14]

Asbury and Coke nonetheless managed to come away from the 1796 General Conference with opposite interpretations of what had happened. Coke believed that he and Asbury were to function as entire equals, if in slightly different roles, notwithstanding all that had been said against him at the conference and the wording of his pledge. Shortly after the conference, Asbury proposed that the two divide their responsibilities. He would take the South while Coke took the northern annual conferences from Philadelphia to New England. This was an important and expanding region, particularly with regards to New York, though to be fair it contained only 12,000 of the church's nearly 63,000 members. Coke was astonished, seeing the proposal as nothing short of an insult. He later wrote:

> I did not see in this plan any thing which related in the least degree to my being a Coadjutor in the Episcopacy, or which at all served to strengthen it; though it was for that purpose as the primary point, that it was thought eligible by the General Conference that I should reside for life in America. Bishop Asbury was to hold the three Southern Conferences entirely by himself; & I was to spend my whole time *merely* as a preacher; & on a plan upon which I should spend the chief part of my time in preaching to very few. The Northern States would be covered with snow. I should have Mountains of Snow to ride over, only to preach in general (a few Towns excepted) to the Family where I was, and a few of their neighbours. When Bishop Asbury retired, I fell on my face before God, & said, "O my God, what have I done?"[15]

It is difficult to imagine that Coke could have endured this arrangement for long, but he never even tried. Before he could head north, word arrived that he had been appointed to preside over the Irish conference. With this news Coke decided to return home after attending the southern annual conferences. Accordingly, he and Asbury presided over the Virginia conference meeting near Richmond in mid-November 1796, where they learned that collections fell short of meeting the preachers' salaries by £194. Coke and Asbury then took separate routes to South Carolina, meeting in Charleston for the conference's annual meeting, which convened on January 1, 1797. The time apart did little to quell Coke's resentment, especially considering that Asbury still refused to ask his advice. Despite his long absences in Europe and his relative unfamiliarity with the rank and file of the American preachers, Coke expected Asbury to consult him before drawing up the yearly appointments. "But to my astonishment I was not consulted in the least degree imaginable concerning the station of a single preacher," Coke later complained. "In short I neither said nor did any thing during the whole tour which had any usefulness attending it, as far as I can judge, but preach." Of course, Coke could have had the privilege of stationing the northern preachers had he chosen, but it is probably just as well that he didn't. What trouble might he have caused by insisting on particular appointments without much knowledge of the preachers involved or responsibility for the long-term consequences? For all of his energy and vision, Coke had a tendency to meddle and intrigue that Asbury had learned to distrust. Coke sailed for home in February, but he wouldn't soon forget the indignity he had suffered at Asbury's hand.[16]

Despite the tension between the two, the bishops managed to cooperate on one substantial project just before Coke left, spending much of January and February together in Charleston revising the *Discipline*. The first version of the *Discipline*, a handbook of Methodist doctrine and practice, had been published in 1785 and largely followed its British equivalent, Wesley's so-called "Large Minutes." The eighth edition, published in 1792, bore the title *The Doctrines and Discipline of the Methodist Episcopal Church*, which remained the title into the twentieth century. Largely with an eye toward answering the O'Kelly-ites, the 1796 General Conference asked Coke and Asbury to annotate a new edition of the *Discipline*.[17]

Published in 1798, the bishops' notes more than doubled the length of the first two sections of the *Discipline*, though most of the notes amount to little more than adding proof texts from scripture to the existing statements of doctrine and practice. The exception had to do with the episcopacy and the closely connected office of presiding elder, which Coke and Asbury defend at length. After noting the biblical precedents set by Timothy and Titus, who were "*travelling bishops*," Coke and Asbury argued that "every candid person, who is thoroughly acquainted with the New Testament, must allow, that whatever excellencies other plans may have, *this* is the primitive and *apostolic plan*." The 1798 *Discipline* also restored a section on slavery, with Coke and Asbury at one point writing, "The buying and selling the souls and bodies of men . . . is totally opposite to the whole spirit of the gospel. It has an immediate tendency to fill the mind with pride and tyranny, and is frequently productive of almost every act of lust and cruelty which can disgrace the human species." This went further than the church's previous condemnations of slavery by acknowledging, however vaguely, the sexual exploitation thinly concealed across the South.[18]

Coke did most of the writing, though Asbury provided him with notes he had "drawn up." Both bishops were satisfied with the result. "If I ever drew up any useful publications for the press, this was one of them, and perhaps the best," Coke later wrote. "I am sure I am right in my desire of printing the notes on the discipline," Asbury wrote to Ezekiel Cooper in October 1797, not long after he and Coke had completed their work. "You in your Annual distant station can hardly conceive the mischief and abuse we meet with from unchristian and illiberal minds." Regardless, on the whole the notes failed to impress readers. The eleventh edition of the *Discipline* (1801) dropped them entirely. Perhaps their greatest importance lies in the fact that they were written at all, by two men who could easily have refused to speak to one another. They were driven men, but their ambition expressed itself as a desire to excel at Christian charity and forbearance. Even with someone as exasperating as Coke. Even with someone as stubborn as Asbury.[19]

16

"Down from a *Joyless height*"

Sickness and death cast a shadow over Asbury as the century drew
to a close. While in Charleston in January 1797, he was seized with
the first of a string of fevers and other ailments that dogged him
through 1798. Fevers were to the eighteenth century what cancer is
today: a killer of otherwise healthy adults. As always, there was a
discernable connection between Asbury's emotional and physical
state. He "laboured under uncommon dejection" on January 17, and
the next day his "serious gloom continued." By the 26th a fever had set
in, confining him indoors for three days. He was back in bed on
February 17 with another fever, which he attributed to his long stay
in Charleston: "I feel pain to be gone, and do not expect much peace
of mind, or health of body, until I go to my old solitary country life."[1]

He still had a fever on Monday the 27th, but "rejoiced to
leave Charleston" anyway. The road failed to provide the relief he
hoped for. After crossing into North Carolina in March, his leg became
"inflamed by riding." For relief he applied a poultice. Another fever
started the next day after he was caught in the rain, continuing
intermittently for a week. He was still determined to go to Kentucky
and made it as far as eastern Tennessee in late March. There, "the
general advice of the preachers" was that his body couldn't stand
"the wilderness." Instead, Asbury once again sent John Kobler with
"letters of direction" to take his place at the Kentucky conference. In
early April another fever seized him in Virginia. His system was so
drawn down that he could only tolerate tea, potatoes, "Indian-meal

gruel," and chicken broth. For the next five months he uncharacteristically wrote little in his journal, skipping whole weeks without comment. Nevertheless he continued to travel, riding some 2,000 miles on horseback through Maryland, Pennsylvania, and New Jersey, arriving in New York in early September. By that time, he was suffering from "swelling in the face, bowels, and feet." His feet were so sore that he couldn't "set them to the ground" for two weeks.[2]

For relief, such as it was, he applied "leaves of burdock and then a plaster of mustard, which drew a desperate blister." Following the common medical advice of the day, he also "took cream of tartar and nitre daily, to cool and keep open the body." Cream of tartar acts as a laxative while nitre, or potassium nitrate, acts as a diuretic. He also "made use of the bark." As early as the 1630s, missionaries in the Andes Mountains of South America had learned that the bark of the cinchona tree, which contains alkaloid quinine, proved effective in treating malaria. The Jesuits soon became active promoters of the "Peruvian bark," leading some to call it "Jesuit's bark." By the late eighteenth century, it was understood that the bark was ineffective on "continuing" fevers of the kind that Asbury now had. He took it anyway, desperate for a cure. Always one who enjoyed the company of friends, he now found himself "left too much alone. I cannot sit in my room all day, making gloomy reflections on the past, present and future."[3]

One source of medical advice that Asbury surprisingly didn't turn to was John Wesley's *Primitive Physic, or An Easy and Natural Method of Curing Most Diseases*. First published in 1747, it went through thirty-six editions, twenty-three in Wesley's lifetime, including several published in America. The 1789 edition published in Philadelphia contains more than 900 recipes to treat 289 ailments. Some of Wesley's cures are harmless, some absurd, but no more so than the common practices of the day. For "extreme fat" (hardly Asbury's problem), Wesley sensibly recommended "a total vegetable diet" for a year. But to cure asthma he recommended drinking a pint of seawater every morning or living for a fortnight on only boiled carrots. For a fever he prescribed drinking "a pint and a half of cold water lying down in bed: I never knew it do hurt." He also counseled the usual vomits, purges, and bleeding. Coke and Asbury wrote a short preface to the 1789 edition recommending it to American readers, but Asbury didn't carry a copy with him. Despite the book's many printings, it held no special attraction for American Methodists, who regarded it with the same skepticism as other medical guides of the day.[4]

For eight weeks Asbury didn't preach. As he lay sick, he had "much time to think of and review my whole life." One conclusion he came to was that he needed to line up reliable successors. He first thought of Thomas Coke. Asbury had already given him a letter the previous February, before Coke sailed for

Ireland, urging him to live up to his commitment to the American church. "When I consider the solemn offer you made of yourself to the General Conference, and their free and deliberate acceptance of you as their Episcopos . . . You cannot, you dare not but consider yourself as a servant of the church, and a citizen of the continent of America." Asbury uncharitably dismissed Coke's work in the West Indies, writing "If you are a man of a large mind, you will give up a few islands for a vast continent, not less than 1400 miles in length, and 1000 miles in breadth."[5]

Despite this reminder, when he reached New York City in September 1797, Asbury received a letter from Coke confirming what Asbury must have expected. Coke had gone from Ireland to England and probably wouldn't return to America before spring, if at all before the 1800 General Conference. Asbury now decided that the church needed to elect a third bishop. "I am sensibly assured the Americans ought to act as if they expected to lose me every day, and had no dependence upon Doctor Coke; taking prudent care not to place themselves at all under the controlling influence of British Methodism," he wrote in his journal. "I feel like a man leaving the world and think every place is my last," he wrote to the preacher Daniel Smith on October 5, 1797.[6]

The preachers gathered for the Philadelphia conference the second week of October 1797, took one look at Asbury, and came to the same conclusion. Knowing that he would not stop, they unanimously agreed that Jesse Lee should become his full-time traveling companion. Asbury had had many traveling companions through the years on a less formal basis, usually preachers whom he invited to accompany him for a few weeks or months at a time. Together Asbury and Lee made their way south to Baltimore, where, despite an outbreak of yellow fever, they opened the region's annual conference on October 21. Asbury stationed the preachers, but Lee took care of almost everything else. "All the preachers, but myself, satisfied with their stations," Asbury wryly noted at the close of the conference.[7]

From Baltimore Asbury and Lee crossed into Virginia, making for Lane's Chapel in Sussex County, where the Virginia conference was scheduled to meet in late November. Along the way "who should meet us but Bishop Coke," riding a borrowed horse. Much to Asbury's surprise, Coke really had been tying up his affairs in Europe to make possible a quick return to America. "I have found it indispensably necessary to bring my long voyages across the Atlantic to a conclusion, and for that purpose to determine on which side of the Ocean to spend the remainder of my days," Coke had written to Thomas Williams in Wales the previous April. "After most mature consideration" he had "resolved in favour of the States of America. . . . My engagements to our American Connexion are irrevocable." He had at last made up his mind. At least for the moment.[8]

Coke had his enemies in England, but he also had his friends. They were distressed at the thought of losing his energetic presence for good, particularly with regard to foreign missions. Belatedly, the British preachers elected Coke president of their conference and pressed him to carry a letter to America requesting "the return of our friend and brother, the Reverend Doctor Coke. He has often been a peace-maker amongst us." Coke brought this letter with him, arriving after his ship was captured by French privateers, who seized most of his possessions before allowing him to board another ship bound for the states.[9]

When Asbury arrived at the Virginia conference in November 1797, the preachers were stunned at how bad he looked, much as the Philadelphia preachers had been, and voted that he ought to rest there until the next April. Unable to continue, Asbury sent Lee to take his place at the South Carolina conference in Charleston and sent "directions [on] how to station the preachers" to Jonathan Jackson, the presiding elder of the Charleston district.[10]

Meanwhile, Coke had again changed his mind and decided to return to Britain. Even though he would soon depart, he took it as a snub that Asbury appointed Lee and Jackson to handle the South Carolina conference, and perhaps it was. A year earlier Asbury had been unwilling to even consult Coke about the appointments when the two were together in Charleston. He now had no intention of turning Coke loose on his own, with his episcopal powers unfettered, to station thirty-one preachers he hardly knew. But Coke didn't see it that way. Having to give way to Asbury in his presence was bad enough, but to be ignored even when Asbury was incapacitated was too much. What was the point of being a bishop in that case? "What astonished me, I think I may say, almost beyond expression was the following mysterious circumstance—Bishop Asbury was so weak in Body at that time, that he was convinced he could not reach Charleston in time to hold the Southern Conference, & therefore he did not attempt it. I offered my services, as it would have been equally the same to me to have sailed from Charleston as from New York. But he refused me; & appointed Brother Jackson to station the preachers & Brother Jesse Lee to sit as moderator in the Conference," Coke later wrote. Asbury's treatment foreclosed any inclination Coke might have had to change his mind once again. He would be gone for the next three years, submerged in the affairs of the British connection and its foreign missions.[11]

The controversy with Coke only added to Asbury's gloom. From November 1797 to April 1798 he remained in Virginia, trying a number of cures, including more cinchona bark. Since iron was generally considered a tonic or an astringent, he began putting nails in his drinks. On January 1, 1798, he embarked on "an extraordinary diet—drink made of one quart of hard cider, one hundred nails, a handful of black snakeroot, one handful of fennel seed, one handful of wormwood, boiled from a quart to a pint, taking one wine glass full every morning for nine or ten days, using no butter, or milk, or meat." This was supposed to "make the stomach very sick, and in a few days purge the patient well," which it no doubt did, though some of the ingredients may have been beneficial in other ways. Black snakeroot was used to treat arthritis, diarrhea, dyspepsia (upset stomach), kidney problems, malaise, malaria, sore throat, and serve as an insect repellent (hence it was also known as bugbane). Fennel contains essential oils that can improve digestion, and wormwood was thought to reduce pain, lower fevers, and act as a sedative. By January 14 Asbury was back to taking tartar emetic, "kill or cure." He coughed up blood on March 10, but by May he was beginning to mend, aided by a vegetarian diet that had a "salutary influence upon my system, much more so than medicine" (little wonder there). For the next several months he lived "wholly upon vegetables" and wore only flannel.[12]

The duration of Asbury's illnesses may seem strange now, but prolonged and debilitating sicknesses were common in this period. Infections from viruses, bacteria, and parasites might linger for weeks or months at a time, often made worse by the treatments patients endured. Consider the case of the itinerant William Ormond, who was seized with an unspecified illness while preaching in North Carolina in December 1791. For a cure, he took a stewed mixture of ginger, sugar, alum, butter, vinegar, black pepper, and rosemary. In March 1792 he took another reduced mixture of alum, saltpeter (potassium nitrate, an oral diuretic), and honey, supposedly to combat scurvy, and that May he was bled. Then in July he was "taken very Poorly" and feared that he was "near the other world." In desperation he sent for a doctor named Bloodworth, who "gave me a few trifles, took his fea & left me (not knowing my disorder I fear)." Sister Blan then gave him a "Portion of Tartar," a typical emetic. Two weeks later he "heard of Tullisons-Drops," one of the dozens of patent medicines available at the time, and sent for some. Next he took fifteen drops of laudanum, a tincture of opium that became increasingly popular as a cure-all during the nineteenth century. A few days later Sister Hill gave him camphor and one of "Andersons pills," another patent medicine.[13]

By late August 1792 Ormond began to feel better, but then on the 26th he was "Suddenly taken with an ague in the night," followed by another "violent feaver & pain in the Head." He put pokeroot, which can act as an emetic and purgative and was also used to treat rheumatism, on the soles of his feet. Again he "thought Death was come," but soon recovered, until September 15 when he was again "taken with a violent fitt of the burning Ague" that lasted a week. "I have taken many things but no relief," Ormond lamented. More relapses and treatments followed till the end of the year, when he appeared to break free of whatever he had.[14]

Ormond remained fairly healthy until March 1801 when he contracted "hoarseness & Cold." For treatment he took calomel (mercurous chloride) and jalap "to correct the humor in my blood." This made him salivate freely, a symptom of acute mercury poisoning. Alarmed, Ormond "took a portion of Sulphur to kill the Murcury. The change was so great & powerful nature fail'd & I had very strange feelings all over." The combination nearly killed him. Sulphur was known as a laxative and for promoting sweating, and he continued to take it for several days, sometimes with castor oil, another cathartic. Though he was sure he would die, within a couple of weeks he again recovered. To cure a common cold, Ormond had done his best to kill himself and nearly succeeded. His experience with illness and cures is fairly representative of this period, paralleling Asbury's. The difference is that Asbury was more cautious about trying heroic remedies, even though he suffered more frequent and severe illnesses, pushing himself beyond what his body could tolerate.[15]

As he struggled to keep going, Asbury began to think about his larger legacy. While laid up in Virginia, he read through his journal, or had it read to him when he was too weak, with an eye toward publishing at least some of it. "It is inelegant," he concluded, yet "it is well suited to common readers; the wise need it not." As the church grew and his travels decreased, publishing his journal offered the chance to educate the many Methodists whom he might never meet. "I am only known by name to many of our people and some of our local preachers; and unless the people were all together, they could not tell what I have had to cope with," Asbury reasoned. "I make no doubt the Methodists are, and will be, a numerous and wealthy people, and their preachers who follow us will not know our struggles but by comparing the present improved state of the country with what it was in our days, as exhibited in my journal and other records of that day."[16]

Asbury had probably always intended to publish his journal, a precedent established by John Wesley and George Whitefield. In fact, the first two editions of the short-lived *Arminian Magazine* published in Philadelphia in 1789 and 1790 carried extracts of Asbury's journal from August 1771 to April 1773. Another portion was published in 1792, and the church published Freeborn Garrettson's journal in 1791. Realizing that he was no scholar on par with Wesley or even Coke, Asbury sought to convey much of his understanding of the faith through short outlines of sermons in his journal. This was certainly a reasonable approach, since sermons were the most important medium for communicating theological ideas in early Methodism. Typical Methodists might only read one or two of the church's publications each year, but they all heard sermons and plenty of them. From 1793 through 1796, Asbury recorded twenty-three sermon outlines, adding another thirty-nine from 1797 through 1800. The problem with these outlines is that most give only a focal scripture verse and three or four topic heads, with minimal development, usually occupying less than a third of the total printed page. A skillful preacher could have preached a successful sermon from these synopses, but only if he understood all that lay behind the subject headings. Many itinerants kept notebooks filled with these kinds of outlines, as a way to remember good sermons or keep track of what they had preached at each stop (thereby avoiding the embarrassment of repeating a sermon in the same place), but Asbury had loftier goals than this for his journal. Unfortunately, the outlines don't add up to much, and he mostly stopped recording them after 1807.[17]

By April 1798 Asbury was well enough to leave Virginia, traveling in a carriage, usually a two-wheeled sulky. He continued to use a carriage for the next several years, riding horseback only when the roads proved too rough. Later, when traveling with the aged Richard Whatcoat, the two took turns in the carriage, while the other rode horseback.[18]

Arriving in Philadelphia on June 2, Asbury heard that his father was dead, or very close to it. Two weeks later in New York he learned that his father was indeed "no more an inhabitant of this earth." As soon as he heard the news, he sat down to write his mother. His grief at the loss of his "venerable father" was real, but he offered her only sympathy from a distance. "At present, I have neither health, nor purse, nor inclination, nor confidence, to re-cross the seas," he told her. While he "dare not forbid your coming to this Continent," he urged her to "stay, to support the cause of Christ in your house, to the latest hour." For "company, and consolation" he advised her to "take a pious prudent woman to live with you," perhaps recalling what had happened after the death of his sister, when his mother had slipped into a prolonged depression. He promised to continue sending what little extra money he had. Though he hadn't seen his mother in nearly thirty years, she still exerted a powerful influence over him. "I have formed no other connection," Asbury wrote, referring to the fact that he remained unmarried. "This might give you some assurance that I am still your son." Eliza Asbury probably expected no more than this from her Frank. When she wrote informing him that she would remain in England, he replied that he could "gladly consent to your refusal to come to America," as if he had really offered her a choice. Asbury says nothing more about his father, other than to record a short account of his death sent to him by a Mr. Phillips of Birmingham.[19]

The absence of any reflection on his father's life is striking. Whatever worked to pull them apart in life continued in death. When Asbury was asked to baptize a child named Joseph Asbury Reynolds more than a decade later, he expressed "surprise" but didn't say why.[20]

From New York he pushed himself into New England in mid-July 1798, accompanied by Jesse Lee. Asbury was just now learning the details of O'Kelly's first book on the 1792 schism, *The Author's Apology for Protesting Against the Methodist Episcopal Church*, published in Richmond, Virginia, under the pseudonym "Christicola," though everyone knew that O'Kelly was the author. O'Kelly wrote that Asbury was a "long-headed Englishman" who continued to insist on the "slavish subjection" of fellow Methodists. Not only was episcopacy "the *root* of popery," but also Asbury wasn't even a real American, since he "came over from the land of Monarchy, before the revolution" and was still a British subject in his heart "to this day." "What can be the cause of all this ill treatment which I receive from him? Was it because I did not, I could not settle him for life in the south district of Virginia?" Asbury complained. Ultimately it had been Coke who led the opposition against O'Kelly in 1792 and the General Conference that had voted him down, but "only I am the grand butt of all his spleen," Asbury wrote. The bite of O'Kelly's criticism deepened what was becoming the darkest moment of Asbury's career.[21]

Asbury didn't respond to O'Kelly in print, leaving this to Nicholas Snethen, a thirty-one-year-old preacher from New York. Snethen was commissioned by the General Conference of 1800 to write *A Reply to an Apology for Protesting Against the Methodist Episcopal Government* (1800). O'Kelly answered Snethen with *A Vindication of the Author's Apology* (1801), followed by Snethen's *An Answer to James O'Kelly's Vindication of His Apology* (1802). O'Kelly had been right about one thing. No matter how hard he tried, he couldn't get Asbury to step out from "behind the screen."[22]

As he made his way north in late summer, Asbury was well enough to travel, but not by much. "I have been very low, and weak, and feverish of late: I can hardly write, think, read, ride, or talk to purpose," he wrote on his way through Rhode Island. Normally, the company of a few close colleagues on the road would have been just the thing to revive him. But not this time: "It is a little trying to be with people who are healthy, active, and talkative, when you cannot bear a cheerful part with them." A few days later in Massachusetts he was "greatly outdone" by the heat, "rocks, hills, and stones! . . . there is no purchase for this day's hire but souls."[23]

By late August Asbury and Lee had pushed their way up the coast of Maine and then inland to Readfield, where the first conference held in Maine opened on August 29, 1798. In all they had traveled more than 500 miles since leaving New York in July. Only ten preachers were present for the conference, including Asbury and Lee, but membership on Maine's six circuits was up 51 percent over the past year and more than one thousand people turned out for public preaching and ordinations on the 30th. The building was so overcrowded "owing to the people's wish to gratify their curiosity" that planks and supports in the gallery could be heard cracking and breaking during the meeting. Fortunately, the balcony didn't completely collapse, and "no person was killed or wounded." In keeping with the ordinations he had just performed, Asbury preached on the nature of Christian ministry, taking for his text 2 Corinthians 4:1–2, which begins, "Therefore seeing we have this ministry, as we have received mercy, we faint not." He concluded his sermon with a reflection on fainting not. "A person that fainteth loseth all action; is pale and dispirited: it is a near resemblance of death, and sometimes terminates in death. Unhappy the man who is dead and useless in the ministry!" This was as much a commentary on his own situation as anyone else's. To quit was to die; he had no choice but to press on.[24]

Now more than ever, he leaned heavily on the movement's women, particularly the many widows who opened their homes to him. Leaving Readfield after the Maine conference, he lodged at the widow Roe's near Lewiston, where he had also stayed on the way to Readfield. The next day he "preached in the widow Boynton's back room to about twenty-five persons, chiefly women." Later that month he came to the widow Abigail Sherwood's in New Rochelle, New York, "where I lay sick last year: it is still like a home [to me]." From 1797 to 1800 Asbury records lodging or preaching at the homes of widows thirty-four times in his journal. At other places married women made it their business to see to his comfort and care. Asbury's preachers were all men, but women were among his strongest supporters. He couldn't have continued traveling in his present physical condition without their constant attention. Yet it is difficult to learn much more about them since they rarely kept journals, exchanged letters with Asbury, or appear by name in church records. The bond that he shared with these women, forged around late night talks by the fire and family prayer after breakfast, must have been significant but remains elusive.[25]

Dickins, Cooper and the Book Concern

"What I have greatly feared for years hath now taken place. Dickins, the generous, the Just, the faithful, skillful Dickins, is Dead!" Asbury wrote on October 4, 1798, to Ezekiel Cooper, who was then stationed in Wilmington, Delaware. Dickins had remained in Philadelphia as yellow fever swept through the city in 1798, as he had in 1793 and 1797, "afraid of indulging any distrust" in God's providence, as he wrote to Asbury in early September. Dickins's sixteen-year-old daughter Betsy died of yellow fever on September 26; the next day Dickins was also gone. Cooper must have read on with some trepidation, guessing what was coming next. What Asbury had in mind was for Cooper to take over running the church's printing business. It wasn't yellow fever Cooper feared; it was the book business's debts.[26]

Dickins had done more than anyone to establish Methodist publishing in America, including using £300 from his wife's family to get the business going in the 1780s. By the late 1790s he had invested so much of his own money in the Book Concern, while simultaneously running an independent bookshop in the same building, that it became almost impossible to separate his debts from the book business's. To make matters worse, in 1790 the Preachers' Fund, predecessor to the Chartered Fund, had been invested in the Book Concern, intermingling the two accounts. By 1796 the Book Concern owed the Preachers' Fund £419. No one doubted Dickins's honesty or integrity, indeed everyone familiar with the Book Concern knew that he took a beating to keep it going. In 1792, the committee charged with overseeing the book business wrote that "too much praise cannot be given to Mr. D. when it is known with what disadvantages he has laboured from the commencement of the business to the present." Dickins had "put at Stake his own capital & risqued his all for . . . no compensation." The committee recommended raising his salary by $200 a year.[27]

Part of the problem lay in the way books were sold. The itinerant system offered a ready-made marketing network, though one that emphasized distribution over profits. Dickins sent books to hundreds of preachers, knowing that many would fail to repay him. Circuit riders were sent to preach the gospel, not keep accounts. Since the preachers' own money wasn't at stake, most proved more willing to distribute books than to collect money for them. Accounts inevitably became jumbled as preachers moved from one circuit to another, leaving books behind for their successors to dispose of. Amos G. Thompson wrote to Daniel Hitt in November 1792 to let him know that he had been transferred to Boston and was leaving his book account £10 in arrears. Thompson had been the presiding elder over western Pennsylvania and parts of western Virginia and Ohio, where Hitt remained. "If you ask where is the money? I answer, I have used it for want of Quarterage, &c. & must pay it, when I can get it to Jno. Dickins." Hitt, one of the few preachers who kept his accounts in good order, eventually straightened out the mess Thompson left behind, for which Dickins was grateful. "If every one with whom I deal were to show the same diligence, I should not be embarrassed as I am," Dickins wrote to Hitt in May 1794. As it was, "I am obliged to keep myself near £3000 in dept." Despite these problems, Dickins would be a hard act to follow. In his funeral discourse for Dickins, Cooper described him as "the wise, the worthy, the skilful, the generous, and the pious Dickins."[28]

Cooper was a logical choice to succeed Dickins. Since October 1797 he had been chair of the standing committee that oversaw the Book Concern, advising Dickins on what to publish and in what numbers. Cooper was bookish, eloquent, and comparatively well educated. A debate recorded in his journal gives some indication of this. One evening in December 1797, Coke visited Cooper in Wilmington, Delaware, along with the preacher James Moore and Judge Richard Bassett, who later served as a U.S. Senator from Delaware and the state's governor. As they sat in Cooper's boardinghouse room, they fell to debating whether Christ's reign during the thousand years of the millennium would be "personal" or "spiritual." Coke and Bassett argued for the former, that Christ would physically reign on the earth during the millennium. In this sense they took a pre-millennialist position, arguing that Christ would return before (hence the pre-) the thousand years of peace and prosperity described in Chapter 20 of Revelation. Cooper took a more post-millennialist position, arguing against the personal interpretation on the grounds that "the first Fathers of the Church did not hold it, and that none of the fathers during the first century ever advanced the idea. *Ignatius*, of *Antioch*, *Dionesius the Areopagite* of Athens, *Clemens Romanus*, *Polycarp* of *Smyrna*, and their contemporaries held no such doctrine." Moreover, "according to *Eusebius of Cesarea*, in his *Bibliotheca Patrum*, one *Papius* was the first who introduced that doctrine. True, after him, others of the fathers held it, and it has been called by some the '*Dotage of antiquity*,' according to Dupin[']s history of the fathers." Cooper also argued that if Christ returned both at the beginning of the millennium and later at the day of judgment, "then there are two comings yet to be expected, which will make three comings in all," a notion that to Cooper the Bible didn't support. Whatever the validity of Cooper's interpretation, few Methodist preachers had read widely enough to even venture these kinds of arguments. Cooper also had considerable personal savings and made a good impression in polite society, as Asbury knew.[29]

The problem was that Cooper didn't want the job. While everyone else seemed to think he belonged in one of the big cities, he had other ideas. Earlier, in October 1796, he had pressed Asbury to send him to the rural Pittsburgh circuit. Asbury initially agreed, but, according to Cooper, "the Trustees of the Society in this City [Philadelphia] united in a petition so strong to the Bishop, for my continuance" that Asbury changed his mind. The following April, Cooper bought a horse and again made plans to go to Pittsburgh until "the Society rose almost in arms against my leaving them." After a brief stint in Wilmington, he again faced the prospect of an appointment in Philadelphia. Dickins's death was probably the only thing that could have persuaded him to return to the city.[30]

What he found was even worse than he expected. For two weeks after his arrival on December 1, 1798, he negotiated with the executors of Dickins's estate, who refused to give him the property on hand unless he assumed the Book Concern's entire debt of more than $4,500, an amount equal to the annual salaries of seventy itinerant preachers. Cooper was understandably unwilling to "engage to pay a large debt upon the credit of debts due to the concern scattered abroad from New Ham[p]shire to Georgia—and some of it in very doubtful hands and of many years standing." He wrote to Asbury, then in Charleston, South Carolina, asking how much money he could count on from the Philadelphia conference. From that distance, there was little that Asbury could tell him. "I anticipated the difficulties, that would come in your way, of conducting the Book concern," Asbury replied on January 8, 1799. "We cannot desire any person to do our work for nothing; Yet we want it punctually done. . . . what you shall have for your service you must leave to the Conference." Cooper had the minutes printed but published nothing else until June.[31]

Before much else could be accomplished, Asbury had to convince Cooper to take the job for the long haul. Cooper was still under the impression that his appointment was only temporary, but he learned otherwise when the Philadelphia conference (which had oversight of the book business) met in early June 1799. With Asbury presiding, the conference elected Cooper editor and general book steward with only two dissenting votes, one of them Cooper's. "I submitted to the desire of my brethren with much reluctance, and take it as my cross. I only engage for one year at a time," Cooper ruefully noted in his journal.[32]

As it turned out, Cooper was a better administrator than Dickins. Where Dickins had relied on informal relationships, Cooper demanded uniformity and written records. He outlined his new policies in a letter printed in the annual minutes shortly after his election at the Philadelphia conference. Cooper reminded the preachers that while the Book Concern played a vital role in the church's mission, capable of doing much good, it was deeply in debt. "When I engaged in the business I had not one dollar of cash in hand belonging to the Concern, and have received but few remittances since. There are large sums due, and I most earnestly solicit the brethren to diligence and punctuality." Cooper didn't mince words when it came to assigning blame: "Some of our brethren have acted laudably and praiseworthy in this business. I wish the same could be said of them all." When changing circuits, preachers were to complete "an exact inventory" and then send him a receipt noting who was responsible for what. From now on, accounts would be kept in dollars and cents, rather than pounds, shillings, and pence, which varied in value from state to state.[33]

If Cooper was demanding of others, he, like Asbury, was equally demanding of himself. To wrest control of the book business from Dickins's estate,

Cooper loaned the Concern $800 of his own money. He wasn't pleased with the position Asbury had placed him in, but how could he complain, knowing how little Asbury kept for himself. Asbury always had this moral advantage over others—no one sacrificed more for the good of the church and the salvation of souls. Besides, Cooper knew that there really wasn't much more Asbury could do. "We will do what Little we can to Collect for you but we might as well climb up to the moon as attempt to get some of those debts," Asbury wrote in January 1801, from Camden, South Carolina, where the district conference was meeting. "I only wish that those that think hardly of you or me could . . . be only punished with our places they so much envy." Despite the odds, Cooper continued to expand the Concern's output, publishing more than 169,000 books and pamphlets between 1799 and 1804. At the same time he succeeded in pulling the book business out of debt, increasing its net worth to $45,000 by 1808.[34]

"Weak enough"

Accompanied by Jesse Lee, Asbury left Charleston at the end of January 1799 for his annual tour, though in truth he was in no condition for the road. On April 8 in Virginia, he had "two pounds of blood" drawn, or about a quart. The preachers of the Virginia conference, which met the next day, urged him not to preach again until he reached Baltimore, and a week later he coughed up blood.

By this time Asbury's congestive heart failure, most likely the result of rheumatic fever and episodes of streptococcal pharyngitis (strep throat), was increasingly evident. Rheumatic fever also causes polyarthritis, which, combined with edema resulting from his weak heart, made his feet swollen and sore, hence his preference for riding in a sulky rather than on horseback. Poor circulation to his feet would also have caused wounds to heal slowly. Putting nails in his drinks might have helped some, providing a source of iron needed to restore his blood cells, and his active lifestyle probably also helped him to survive longer, masking the early stages of his decline. But decline he did. "It is upwards of twelve years since I began the wreck of my constitution, when I became more immediately the superintendent of our community in America," Asbury wrote to a friend in August 1797.[35]

Following the Baltimore conference, which began on May 1, 1799, Asbury and Lee headed north for Philadelphia. At Salisbury, Maryland, Asbury again had himself bled. The next day his horse "began to sweat, swell and tremble—and died upon the road." Unfortunately, he had no money to buy a new one. Instead, he harnessed the horse of another preacher, Levin Moore, who happened to be traveling with them to Delaware, to the sulky, and the two rode to Samuel Smith's. There Asbury borrowed a horse from Smith, but two days later had to return it. The only alternative was to harness the horse of William Hardesty, another preacher traveling with the group, to the sulky and "wedge ourselves [in] with all our baggage together." Under these conditions Asbury plodded north. "I have had great dejection of mind, and awful calculations of what may be and what may never be," he wrote as he crossed into Delaware on May 26. There, three doctors examined him, advising "a total suspension from preaching, fearing a consumption or a dropsy in the breast" (consumption is an old name for pulmonary tuberculosis; dropsy of the chest, or hydrothorax, is a form of pleurisy, characterized by an accumulation of fluid in the pleural cavity, the membrane surrounding the lungs, and shortness of breath). His eyes were now "weak enough, even with Glasses."[36]

Knowing that he couldn't ignore his failing health for long, he began to make plans to resign the episcopacy. He arrived in Philadelphia in time to open the conference's annual meeting on June 6, 1799. This was the conference at which Ezekiel Cooper was officially appointed to run the Book Concern, but Asbury actually spent little time in the meeting, resting instead at the nearby Eagle Iron Works, owned by Henry Foxall. In answer to a note from Cooper, Asbury wrote on June 10 that his doctors had advised "rest, Rest or Death, or great Danger! I have resigned the pulpit—I am weaning the conference—I am absent Whole Days at a time; I keep no minutes now, never Preside, seldom speak in conference, only when called upon in a special manner." "I may shortly come to this, that I cannot serve the Connection, without sacrificing, my health, my Life, or my Conscience." These were desperate words, but he could see little choice.[37]

Following the Philadelphia conference, Asbury and Lee rode to New York for a joint meeting of the New York and New England conferences. Afterward Asbury was seized with "violent pain in my knee" and a high fever. "I never felt so great a resolution to resign the general superintendency as I do now ... my prayers and counsel will be turned this way until next General Conference," he wrote in his journal on July 1, 1799. The next month he wrote to Thomas Morrell, then stationed in Baltimore, informing him that "I have only to say I am writing my resignation ... to the General Conference. ... I firmly believe I have delayed my resignation too long, it is time they were put upon ways, means, and persons for the better organization of so great a Body of people.... I wish the preachers and people to take warning I am about to come down from a *Joyless height* and stand upon the floor with my Brethren." Several had already read his letter of resignation and "in general approve the design."[38]

Though sick most of the time, he continued to press south from New York through New Jersey, Pennsylvania, Maryland, Virginia, the Carolinas, Georgia, and then back to South Carolina as summer gave way to fall and then winter. He was often sick to his stomach, troubled by intestinal pain, and worn down by the labor of travel. "I need much faith and good water," he wrote while in Virginia that August. In September he placed two blisters on his chest, which predictably did him little good. One of his few consolations during this miserable tour was that he and Jesse Lee drew three thousand to six thousand people a week to hear them preach. "Thus, if no more, I can say that my travelling hath brought thousands to hear the Gospel, who, probably, would not otherwise have heard it." Yet this did little to change his mind about resigning. "I think of nothing less than the resignation of my office of superintendent at the general conference," he wrote that August in Virginia. The thought, he noted two months later in North Carolina, of "having to ride about six thousand miles annually; to preacher from three to five hundred sermons a year; to write and read so many letters . . . all this and more, besides the stationing of three hundred preachers . . . and spending many hours in conversation by day and by night, with preachers and people of various characters, among whom are many distressing cases," was now more than he could bear. He had been in America twenty-eight years. Did he "wish to live them over again? By no means . . . I could not come up to what I have done; I should be dispirited at what would be presented before me." He had spiraled so far down that it seemed impossible to recover.[39]

Asbury's declining health accelerated a shift in the nature of his relationship with the church. At the same time that it was growing in numbers and expanding its borders, his own travels and contact with the preachers and people declined. He did his best to stay connected, but it was a losing proposition. In addition, Methodists in general were becoming increasingly successful, confident, even comfortable. If they weren't careful, spiritual complacency was just around the corner. If his health had been better, Asbury might have seen the problem sooner and defined his opposition more clearly. As it was, he was at risk of becoming something that he had never been before in America: irrelevant.

17

"Feel for the power"

If 1799 ended dismally for Asbury, 1800 would offer a new beginning, with unexpected revivals and the election of a new bishop. But as winter gathered somewhere north of the Mason-Dixon line and Asbury hurried south to escape its onslaught, he couldn't yet see this. His greatest challenge remained supplying the circuits with competent preachers. Of the approximately 820 preachers who had entered the traveling connection between 1773 and 1799, only 263 remained in the saddle. Most of these were young, single men with little formal education. Of the active preachers, only thirty-six, or 13.6 percent, had been riding circuits for more than a decade. More than half (141 preachers) had traveled for less than five years, and more than a third (ninety-two preachers) for less than three years. The 263 itinerants of 1799 were responsible for 156 circuits spread across sixteen states, vast stretches of the western territories, and parts of Maine and Canada, containing 61,351 members (a ratio of 233 members per preacher) and perhaps three or four times as many listeners. Seventeen of the preachers served as presiding elders, Ezekiel Cooper was the book editor, Thomas Coke was in Europe, and Jesse Lee traveled with Asbury, leaving 242 itinerants to ride 156 circuits. This meant that nearly half of the circuits had only one preacher, rather than the expected two. Four circuits went without an itinerant preacher entirely. Shortages of preachers were most evident in the South (partly owing to the O'Kelly schism), the frontier regions of the West, and New England. Experienced presiding elders like

Freeborn Garrettson, who had been preaching since 1776, were invaluable resources, but there were few enough of them to go around.[1]

Following the claims of James O'Kelly, accounts of this period often imply that Asbury ruled the preachers with an iron fist, appointing them wherever he chose, without much regard for their opinions or those of the people more broadly. From this point of view Asbury's authority is a paradox: Why did such a democratically minded people put up with such a tyrant? In fact, most Methodists didn't see it this way. At some basic level, Methodists trusted Asbury because of his personal discipline and the example he set: no one sacrificed more for the gospel or better represented what Methodism ought to look like. But specifically with regard to the preachers, Asbury's authority rested more on his unparalleled knowledge and his subtle judgment, demonstrated over the years in a range of difficult circumstances. Most of the preachers were young, lacking experience beyond their home region. Given the limits of communication at the time, they knew little of events outside the area they traveled. They trusted Asbury because they believed he understood the church as a whole better than anyone.

Asbury would have preferred to circulate the preachers more widely, moving them from region to region as they matured, so as to increase their range of experience. But circuit preaching was a daunting enough challenge even on familiar ground, and few of the young men who entered the itinerancy were prepared to immediately leave their home region. Some eventually matured enough to do so, but most didn't last long enough to try. Of the ninety-two itinerants who began their careers between 1797 and 1799, only eighteen were still riding circuits in 1810, less than 20 percent. Of the rest, fifty-three had located because of marriage or poor health, eight had died, seven had dropped out before completing their two-year probationary period, four had withdrawn from the connection, and one had been expelled.[2] Thomas Lyell was only fifteen years old when he preached before a crowd of four thousand to five thousand people at a quarterly meeting in 1790. After saving enough money to buy a horse, Lyell joined the traveling connection in 1792. His first appointment was on the Frederick circuit in Virginia with Thomas Scott, who was only twenty-one or twenty-two and who had joined the traveling connection three years before. Between them, "a circuit of very considerable extent, and of very great importance was committed to the supervision and care of two youths—or rather a youth and a boy," Lyell later remembered. Membership increased by two hundred within the bounds of the circuit during the year, but this success notwithstanding Scott located in 1795.[3] Itinerant preaching was a young man's calling. No wonder Asbury commanded such wide respect. Few young men could match his perseverance even for five or ten years.

Asbury did what he could to balance the concerns of the preachers with the needs of the societies. Since he was always scrambling to supply the circuits and keep enough preachers in the field, he couldn't afford to push young preachers beyond what they could endure. But he also had to avoid damaging a circuit or city station with a poorly matched preacher. Coaxing often worked where an ultimatum might not. After the South Carolina conference annual meeting in early January 1800, held in Charleston, Asbury was still searching for someone to fill the Charleston appointment for the coming year. On January 8 he wrote to George Dougherty, who hadn't attended the conference and was then stationed on the Oconee circuit in Georgia, that Nicholas Snethen would be leaving Charleston. "It is imprest upon my mind that you are the only person of my choice to supply this critical but important station. These are to request you if life permits, to be in Charleston on February 7th as I must go hence the 10th," Asbury wrote. His assessment of Dougherty was based on conversations with other South Carolina conference preachers, since Dougherty had only joined the itinerancy on trial the year before and he and Asbury had spent little time together. At first glance Dougherty didn't look like a good match for Charleston. He was tall, thin, and gangling, with an awkward walk and a high, reedy voice. He had lost one eye to small pox, which also disfigured the rest of his face, and generally dressed shabbily. Nevertheless, Asbury had done enough checking around to know that there was more to Dougherty than met the eye. Charleston Methodists soon discovered that Dougherty had a subtle mind capable of constructing moving sermons that were intellectually and emotionally gripping. A preacher who later heard Dougherty preach found himself "absolutely enchained by a burst of elo-quence, a mellow blaze of rich thought as rare as it was overwhelming."[4]

Anticipating Dougherty's possible objection that another South Carolina preacher, James Jenkins, would be better qualified to fill the appointment, Asbury wrote to Dougherty that "Brother Jenkin[s] I am told will upon no consideration take this station." To add weight to his request Asbury pointed out that John Harper, the other preacher on the Charleston station, "highly approves the appointment and [agrees] that you must have the charge by all means." Asbury evidently sensed that he had to be diplomatic with Dougherty, rather than simply inform him of the appointment or leave it to the district's presiding elder to do so. The tactic worked. When Jesse Lee returned on February 7, 1800, from a tour of Georgia, which Asbury had been too sick to take, he had Dougherty in tow, ready to begin his ministry in the city. In fact, Lee, who was riding Asbury's horse, probably delivered the bishop's letter to Dougherty in person, perhaps further encouraging him to take the Charleston post. Asbury's decision to appoint Dougherty to Charleston and his efforts to convince the young preacher to take the assignment were worked out in a broad organizational context, relying on the opinions and support of a number of locals.[5]

Asbury's reduced traveling schedule coupled with the church's continuing expansion meant that he increasingly had to manage competing concerns from a distance. In late September 1800, he crossed the Holston River in eastern Tennessee, stopping at Benjamin Van Pelt's to leave his carriage before proceeding on horseback to Kentucky. Earlier in the year he had missed the Holston conference meeting, which was held in April while he was in eastern Virginia, on his way instead to Baltimore. Now he learned that at the conference John Page had been moved from Tennessee's Cumberland circuit to the Holston, Russell, and New River circuits in Virginia, despite a petition from the Cumberland people to keep Page another year. To Asbury's thinking, the Cumberland petition should have been heeded. "Had I attended at the last Holston Conference, you should have returned immediately to Cumberland," he wrote to Page from Van Pelt's. "I hope that you will now hasten to that charge as soon as possible." Page had been instrumental in directing a revival then sweeping through northern and middle Tennessee and southern Kentucky, including the Cumberland circuit. Asbury was anxious not to interrupt its progress, especially since Methodism had seen slack times in the West in recent years. Between 1792 and 1800, membership in Kentucky actually fell from 1,808 to 1,742 while the state population more than doubled, from less than 100,000 to more than 220,000. Much of the decrease was the product of the O'Kelly schism and opposition to the church's rules against slavery. Now the tide seemed to be turning, and Asbury didn't want to miss it. Page wasted no time in complying with Asbury's new instructions. After receiving the bishop's letter, he paused only long enough to eat dinner and then set out for Tennessee.[6]

To accomplish Page's transfer halfway through the conference year, Asbury proposed moving James Hunter from the Green circuit to join John Watson on the Holston, Russell, and New River circuits, taking Page's place. Watson wasn't the kind of preacher who could be left alone on such a vast charge. A colleague later recalled that he "was devoted to his work," and "few men understood our doctrines and discipline better than John Watson." But he "had a bad delivery and was never a very agreeable preacher." Green would temporarily be left without an itinerant, though Asbury hoped that either Benjamin Young or John Granade (one of early Methodism's most electrifying and eccentric preachers) could shortly "be spared to come to Green." Granade had never had a circuit appointment before, but Asbury had met him at a recent quarterly conference, quickly recognizing his unique abilities. These changes might have been managed by a presiding elder, except that none had been appointed that year for lack of a qualified candidate. As it turned out, at the next annual conference in 1801, Young joined Page on the Cumberland circuit, Hunter remained on the Holston and Russell circuits and Watson on New River. Samuel Douthet and Ezekiel Burdine transferred from the Little Pee Dee and Anson circuits in South Carolina to ride the Green. Meanwhile Asbury appointed William McKendree, one of the church's most capable younger preachers, presiding elder of the district. (The district was so big, encompassing parts of Virginia, Tennessee, Kentucky and Ohio, that McKendree later quipped he could only cover it if Asbury gave him an "immortal horse.") This was a lot of trouble to accommodate Page and the people of the Cumberland circuit (if it's confusing to read, think how difficult it was to arrange on the ground), but Asbury believed that the inconvenience was worthwhile. He couldn't please everyone, but within the confines of the system he worked tirelessly to find the best fit for the preachers he had. Page remained on the Cumberland circuit for four years until he was appointed presiding elder of the newly created Cumberland district in 1803. Unfortunately, that same year his health gave out and he located.[7]

At times itinerants simply refused to follow Asbury's directions, leaving him to work around them. He appointed John Kobler to the Cumberland circuit for 1798, but when it came time for him to "take my place by the bishops desire," he instead "held a counsel" with a group of Kentucky preachers, "and it was thought most advisable . . . for me to go over the Ohio to the Western Territory to form a circuit in that remote corner." Ignoring Asbury's directions, Kobler spent the year in Ohio, though the minutes show him on Cumberland. In September 1799 Henry Smith left Kentucky to form the Scioto circuit in Ohio. The next year Asbury wanted to move Smith, telling him "You have been there long enough." Smith disagreed. As he later recalled, since Asbury "could get no person that I thought would suit the place, I went back, and continued there until the fall of 1801." Asbury relented, assigning Smith to Scioto for 1800 and 1801. When Asbury appointed McKendree presiding elder over the Kentucky district in October 1800, he tried to persuade William Burke, then stationed on the Hinkstone Circuit in Kentucky, to take McKendree's former post as a presiding elder in Virginia. Burke flatly refused. "I told him it was out of the question; that I had returned to Kentucky, at his request, from Baltimore, in the spring; that I had rode down my horses; that I had worn out my clothes; that I was ragged and tattered; and last and not least, I had not a cent in my pocket." Once again, Asbury gave in, appointing Burke back to the combined Hinkstone and Lexington circuits. And this was just in the West. There was a kind of porosity to the system that Asbury, or anyone else for that matter, couldn't entirely control. It necessitated endless shuffling of appointments to fill voids and mend cracks, but what else could he do? He needed every preacher he could get.[8]

The Power of the Word

If the majority of the preachers were young and relatively new to circuit preaching, they still resembled their predecessors in several important ways. Like the preachers of Asbury's generation, they came from families of modest means. Had they not turned to preaching, they would have taken up farming or laboring with their hands. Most had only a few years of common school behind them, having never darkened the door of a college. Like their predecessors, they aspired to preach with what the itinerant Henry Smith, who took up his first circuit in western Virginia in 1794, described as an irresistible "holy 'knock-'em-down' power." Anning Owen, who began his preaching career in upstate New York in 1795, was known as "Bawling Owen" because of his impassioned preaching style. When South Carolina's Jimmy Jenkins prayed, his "soul, voice, strength, all went in. The sound was as the roar of a tempest, ablaze with lightning, and pealing with thunder." No matter what region they came from, Methodist preachers aspired to preach bold, extemporaneous sermons that stirred the hearts of their listeners. The eternal fate of lost souls deserved no less.[9]

Most of the circuit preachers were literate, but given their limited formal education and the press of their schedule, preaching as they did nearly every day, they had little time for extensive preparation. They lived their sermons and preached from their daily experience, for better or worse. They were "close home" preachers, as one circuit rider put it. Each sermon began with the preacher taking, or reading, a text of scripture. As they expounded on their texts, they relied heavily on anecdotes and analogies from everyday life. At the end of his forty-year preaching career, Henry Smith boasted that he "never wrote a sermon in my life," relying instead on the leading of the Spirit and his feel for an audience whenever he rose to speak.[10]

This was exactly the kind of preaching that Asbury had been converted under and that he continued to practice. Henry Boehm, who later traveled with Asbury as his assistant from 1808 to 1813, claimed to have heard him preach 1,500 times. Boehm's manuscript journal demonstrates that Asbury preached more often than he records in his own journal. Wherever he went, he preached at almost every opportunity, from camp meetings with crowds in the thousands to cramped frontier cabins with a few dozen people. Preaching was "his element, his life, he could not live long without," according to Boehm. Asbury chose his scripture texts carefully (Boehm describes his sermons as "scripturally rich") and reasoned through them in detail. Yet like all Methodist preachers, he made liberal use of anecdotes and examples gleaned from his experience. "He had a remarkable method of making an unexpected use of observations he had dropt in preaching," noted John Wesley Bond, who traveled with Asbury during the last two years of his life. "There was a rich variety in his sermons," added Boehm. "No tedious sameness; no repeating old stale truths."[11]

What impressed both Boehm and Bond was Asbury's subtlety, a quality perhaps lost on some listeners. Bond recalled that once when preaching in New York City to a mixed congregation of African Americans and whites, Asbury "anticipated" the way that the whites might use his sermon to criticize African Americans. He had evidently been preaching on the dangers of prosperity, pausing to observe that some whites might be thinking, "these people [African Americans] cannot stand prosperity.—good useage spoils them." "I don't know that they can bear prosperity as well as they can poverty or affliction—Have *we* borne it?—Are *we* as *humble* and as much *devoted* to *God, now*, as when we were *poor?*" These "words had a very striking effect on the audience," Bond remembered. Like all Methodist preachers, in his delivery Asbury relied "much on the divine influence," according to Boehm. Once, when Samuel Thomas stood to begin his sermon, Asbury, who was sitting nearby, tugged at Thomas's sleeve, whispering to him, "Feel for the power, feel for the power, brother." Any Methodist preacher would have understood what this meant. It was advice that Asbury himself tried to follow, though not always successfully. "He often felt for the power himself, and when he obtained it he was a kind of moral Samson," Boehm wrote. But "when he did not he was like Samson shorn of his strength."[12]

Despite his ability to persuade people face-to-face and his deep piety, Asbury never became a great preacher. Even John Dickins, one of his staunchest supporters, admitted that a fair number of the church's preachers "far exceeded" the bishop "in the judgment of the populace as public speakers." In particular, if "Mr. Asbury sought the applause of men, and was jealous lest others should eclipse him in a public character, he never would have, which he oftimes has, permitted preachers to travel with him for weeks and months together, who have far exceeded him in the judgment of the populace as public speakers," Dickins wrote in 1792. Dickins meant this as a compliment, but it also reveals Asbury's limits as a preacher.[13]

As his administrative responsibilities increased after 1800 and his health declined, Asbury's preaching became more disjointed. At their best "his addresses were generally, plain and simple; yet energetic . . . and, most commonly, consisted in a judicious selection of choice matter to suit the occasion," Ezekiel Cooper recalled. Yet all too often his delivery was "rather abrupt and obscure, owing to the suddenness of his transitions and digressions; and his method, frequently bore the appearance of the want of attention, and correct arrangement," Cooper added. Nicholas Snethen, who traveled with Asbury for several years beginning in 1800, agreed. Asbury "was a practical preacher; never metaphysical or speculative; never wild and visionary; never whining and fastidious. No exception could be taken to the general purity and dignity of his language. His enunciation was excellent," Snethen wrote in 1816. Yet "strangers" didn't generally find him "edifying." "This was owing, in part, to his laconic and sententious style, and the frequent concealment of his method; and in part, also, to his natural impatience of minuteness and detail, which was always heightened by the pressure of disease. He belonged to that class of preachers, who are said to wear well; who, the oftener they are heard, the better they are liked," Snethen noted.[14]

This was more or less what everyone said about Asbury's preaching. Nathan Bangs heard him for the first time at the New York conference in June 1804. "His preaching was quite discursive, if not disconnected, a fact attributed to his many cares and unintermitted travels, which admitted of little or no study. . . . He slid from one subject to another without system. He abounded in illustrations and anecdotes." Nonetheless, Bangs left the conference "filled . . . with admiration" for Asbury because "he presided with great wisdom, dispatch, and dignity, and treated the young preachers as a father." Once, when Asbury and Jesse Lee were traveling together, they stopped to preach near Philadelphia. Feeling unwell, Asbury asked Lee to preach in his place, without informing the congregation of the switch. After Lee's sermon, Asbury gave a short exhortation. When it was all over, "some said they liked very well what the bishop preached, but they did not like what that old man said after him," according to one observer.[15]

His own failings aside, Asbury pressed his preachers to devote themselves to the ministry of the word. In their notes to the 1798 *Discipline*, Coke and Asbury reminded preachers that their duty was to "shew the sinner how far he is gone from original righteousness" and to "describe the vices of the world in their just and most striking colours, and enter into all the sinner's pleas and excuses for sin, and drive him from all his subterfuges and strongholds." All the same, hell fire and brimstone alone wasn't enough. A preacher "must say nothing which can keep the trembling mourner at a distance: he must not provide for him a rich feast, and hand it up to him in dishes too hot to be touched." God's grace must never slip from view. "There must be nothing now held forth to the view of the penitent but . . . the mercy which is ready to embrace him on every side." If this weren't enough, preachers also had to consider the needs of new believers for "the pure milk of the word," and of mature Christians for "strong meat." It was a delicate balance, but it was the responsibility of every preacher to strike it as best he could.[16]

The preachers generally did their best to comply. William Ormond's journal contains one of the most complete records of sermon texts left by an itinerant of this period. Converted in December 1787 and sanctified in March 1790, Ormond took his first circuit appointment in 1791, when but twenty-one years old. For the next twelve years he rode circuits in North Carolina and southern Virginia, with one year in Georgia. He died of yellow fever in October 1803 while stationed at Norfolk and Portsmouth, Virginia. In his journal, which runs from July 1791, shortly after he began itinerating, to October 1803, a few months before his death (with the exception of a missing volume for December 1792 to August 1795), Ormond records 1,823 sermons from 262 identifiable scripture passages. His twenty-seven favorite texts, from which he preached at least twenty times each, account for 56 percent of all his sermons. Most of the Old Testament and much of the New never found their way into his preaching. Excluding Ormond's ten favorite Old Testament passages, the remaining Old Testament texts account for only 18 percent of his sermons. He preached on only four passages from Acts, only twenty-two times from Romans, but eighty-six times from Revelation, 117 times from 1 Peter, and 126 times from Isaiah. Ormond clearly knew many of his favorite texts by heart, often quoting them in his journal rather than giving the chapter and verse reference. Considering that he changed circuits every year, he probably never preached the same sermon twice in the same place. But he made little attempt to guide his listeners systematically through the Bible. Relying so heavily on Revelation, 1 Peter, and Isaiah suggests that Ormond's preaching mostly depicted a people under siege and the church as an insurgency.[17]

Asbury preached from a wider array of scripture texts over the course of his career with fewer favorites. He records preaching from 1,029 biblical passages in his journal (doubtless only a fraction of the total), only nine of which are repeated more than a dozen times. Yet, like Ormond, Asbury didn't strive for any kind of systematic organization to his preaching. Early Methodist preaching, as Asbury and his preachers understood it, was geared more toward dealing with immediate personal experience and the demands of everyday faith. The circuit riders had a sense of themselves as something new, as emissaries of a spiritual revolution sweeping the nation. They offered new wine to a thirsty multitude; there simply wasn't time to let it age.[18]

If he wasn't the best preacher in the connection, Asbury saw himself as a sort of Methodist George Washington. In the popular imagination Washington was austere, disinterested, standing above the fray of petty partisanship, concerned only for the welfare of his country, qualities that Asbury hoped others saw in him with regard to the church. Washington may not have been a great speaker, as Asbury wasn't a great preacher, but there was more to leadership than that. Asbury met Washington on two occasions, so it was with a measure of real loss that he learned on January 4, 1800, that Washington had died three weeks earlier. Though he didn't generally comment on political figures or events, he couldn't resist eulogizing Washington, that "matchless man!" in his journal. Washington's religious convictions, such as they were, tended toward moderate Anglicanism, but Asbury managed to convince himself that the president was an evangelical at heart. In particular, he noted that Washington provided for the manumission of his slaves in his will, "a true son of liberty in all points." "At times he acknowledged the providence of God, and never was he ashamed of his Redeemer: we believe he died, not fearing death." To die at peace, knowing that you were bound for heaven was the mark of the truly converted. Assigning these religious convictions to Washington was a stretch, but given his respect for Washington's public character, Asbury couldn't help himself.[19]

Hand to the Plow

On a bitterly cold day in February 1800, Asbury and Nicholas Snethen (the bishop's new traveling companion) left Charleston headed north. The roads were treacherous, and Asbury's carriage got stuck in the mud, breaking some of the rigging. They didn't reach their lodgings until 8:30 p.m. that night. Conditions remained difficult for days stretching into weeks as they made their way north. In North Carolina it snowed 18 inches and then rained. Snethen did most of the preaching as Asbury's health took a turn for the worse. By mid-March he was suffering from great "distress" in his "bowels." For relief he took a patent medicine, Stoughton's bitters. On March 15 Asbury and Snethen crossed into Virginia, having ridden 500 miles in four weeks. There a "friend" asked to borrow £50 from Asbury. "He might as well have asked for Peru," Asbury joked. "I showed him all the money I had in the world—about twelve dollars, and gave him five . . . I will live and die a poor man." Pushing himself, his horse, and carriage to the limit, Asbury arrived in Baltimore on May 5, completing a journey of 1,100 miles from Charleston. It had been imperative that he reach Baltimore before May 6, 1800, the day that the general conference was set to open and where he had every intention of resigning from the episcopacy.[20]

His colleagues had something else in mind. The conference opened with Thomas Coke, now fifty-two, who had just returned from Europe, reading an address from the British conference pleading for his return. This, of course, wasn't the first time this had come up. In 1797 Asbury and the Virginia conference had released Coke to serve in Europe, pending the decision of the 1800 General Conference. Now that it came to it, what were they to do with Coke? He still commanded a great deal of respect among the American preachers because of his learning and piety, and he still corresponded regularly with some of the more senior American preachers, including Ezekiel Cooper and Richard Whatcoat. He had taken great risks in the West Indies and promoted the mission tirelessly at home. Recently he had spent several months calling on political connections on behalf of preachers in Ireland and the Channel Islands (located in the English Channel off Normandy). Coke had contacts and a level of experience that few American preachers could match. Equally important, he represented an important link to the church's past, the more so considering that so many of the 116 preachers present at Baltimore were under the age of thirty and had been preaching for less than five years. Still, the West Indies and Ireland were British projects, with no real connection to America. Everyone realized that Coke's loyalties were divided and that he hadn't spent enough time in America to keep up with the church's rapid expansion. After two days of debate, the conference wrote to the British Methodists that Coke's commitments in Europe and the West Indies "turned the scale at present in your favour. We have, therefore . . . *lent* the Doctor to you for a season." Coke was to return to the United States for the 1804 General Conference at the latest. It was anyone's guess what his role in the church would be by then.[21]

With Coke's situation settled, the conference turned to three major issues: Asbury's status and that of the episcopacy more broadly, the support of married preachers and their families, and slavery, that most vexing of issues. When asked what his plans for the future were, Asbury replied "that he did not know whether this General Conference were satisfied with his former services." His "affliction" since the last General Conference had been such that he had needed a colleague to travel with him, he had been forced to stop and recuperate for weeks or months at a time, and for the most part he had been limited to riding in a carriage, reducing the scope of his travels. But when it came to it, Asbury simply couldn't say the words, couldn't bring himself to actually resign. So he asked the preachers to do what he couldn't do himself, to set him aside in favor of someone else. Did the conference still want the services of such an infirm old man, now fifty-four? The reply came in the form of a motion by Ezekiel Cooper that the conference "consider themselves under many and great obligations to Mr. Asbury, for the many and great services he has rendered to this connexion . . . [and] do earnestly entreat a continuation of Mr. Asbury's services." And that was it. The motion passed without dissent. Asbury had underestimated his own reputation. No one could imagine the church without him as long as he yet lived. (Cooper must have taken some satisfaction in making this motion considering the way that Asbury had maneuvered him into running the Book Concern.)[22]

Still, Asbury clearly needed help. William Burke proposed electing two additional bishops, but "a very great majority" favored adding only one, to be elected by the conference as a whole. Two leading candidates emerged for the post: Jesse Lee and Richard Whatcoat. Other potential candidates included Freeborn Garrettson and Ezekiel Cooper, but Garrettson was unwilling to travel far from his family and beloved home on the Hudson River, and Cooper was already occupied as the church's book agent, a role that suited him better. A few years earlier Francis Poythress would have been a strong candidate, but he was now sinking into insanity. Lee and Whatcoat offered the conference contrasting choices. Lee was capable, strong willed and experienced. He had joined the itinerancy in 1783, preaching extensively in Virginia, Maryland, New York, and New England. Most recently he had traveled with Asbury, meeting many of the connection's preachers across the country. If the preachers wanted a strong leader to balance Asbury's hand, then Lee seemed the obvious choice.[23]

Richard Whatcoat was altogether different. Born in Gloucestershire, England, in 1736, Whatcoat began preaching in 1763 and came to America with Coke in 1784. John Wesley had wanted to make Whatcoat an American bishop (Wesley would have said superintendent) in 1787, but the American preachers rejected the appointment under biting criticism of both Wesley and Whatcoat from James O'Kelly and, to a lesser but still significant extent, Jesse Lee. Whatcoat bore the whole affair with characteristic humility. During his sixteen years in America, he had traveled and preached extensively across the nation, but he had never entered into any of the church's controversies. Already in his mid sixties, his health periodically faltered under the hardships of itinerant ministry, yet he never complained. Indeed, what everyone admired about Whatcoat was his soft-spoken perseverance and deep, introspective piety. "I think I may safely say if I ever knew one who came up to St. James' description of a perfect man,—one who bridled his tongue and kept in subjection his whole body,—that man was [Richard] Whatcoat," the itinerant Laban Clark later recalled.[24]

The election was held on Monday morning, May 12, with Lee and Whatcoat tying on the first ballot. Whatcoat won on the second ballot by four votes,

Richard Whatcoat (1736–1806). (From Abel Stevens, *History of the Methodist Episcopal Church in the United States of America*, vol. 4 [New York: Carlton & Porter, 1867].)

fifty-nine to fifty-five. With characteristic humility, he referred to the election only in passing in his journal: "I was voted to the Office of Bishop," is his only comment. Lee, on the other hand, came to believe that a rumor circulating among the preachers had been instrumental in preventing his election. The story, according to Lee, was "that Mr. Asbury said that brother Lee had imposed himself on him and the connexion, for eighteen months past, and he would have got rid of him long ago if he could." When Lee confronted Asbury with the story, he denied having anything to do with it. At Lee's request, Asbury stood before the conference to disavow the rumor and express his gratitude for Lee's "past services." Lee later claimed to have traced the rumor's origin to a preacher independent of Asbury. Considering the trust that Asbury had placed in Lee over the past year and a half, it seems improbable that Asbury had anything to do with the alleged rumor. Still, it is worth reflecting on the ease with which Lee entered into these kinds of disputes. If he and Asbury had served as bishops together, they would almost certainly have had run-ins of the kind that characterized Asbury's and Coke's relationship, with the added complication that Lee would never have left. Their relative authority would have been ambiguous, doubtless giving rise to misunderstandings. Lee wouldn't have been able to bear any sort of subordinate status for long, nor would Asbury endure Lee's contentiousness. Whatcoat's election was a near thing, but the preachers chose a man of unquestioned piety who by personal inclination would function as something of a bishop-in-reserve for Asbury. What would happen in the event of Asbury's death was anybody's guess, but they could deal with that when it happened. For now, things would go on as they had before, with Asbury pressing himself to the limit of his endurance and Whatcoat filling in when he couldn't go on.[25]

Even before Whatcoat's election, the conference paused to consider the preachers' salaries, which were still fixed at $64 a year. On the morning of the 9th, James Tolleson proposed that whereas "the annual salary of our preachers being very justly considered too small—as almost every article of our consumption comes now at nearly fifty per cent higher than when the salaries were fixed," they should be increased (passed by five votes) to $80 a year (passed by an unspecified majority). The fact that the first motion passed by only five votes reveals how much the preachers still clung to Asbury's pattern of voluntary poverty. Among those who opposed the measure was South Carolina's James Jenkins. He "was willing that the married preachers should receive more than sixty-four dollars, but thought the single ones might make out" with less. Opposition to the increase also reflected the reality of church finances. Since many of the preachers didn't get the $64 due them now, why raise the salary further? Alas for Tolleson, he didn't live long enough to enjoy the extra money. He died that August in Portsmouth, Virginia, of yellow fever.[26]

Four days after Whatcoat's election, the conference took up the perennially divisive issue of slavery. No one spoke in its favor, but the conference's rejection of a number of antislavery proposals indicates the depth of the divide that separated Methodists. Nicholas Snethen's motion that "from this time forth no slaveholder shall be admitted into the Methodist Episcopal Church" was defeated (the minutes don't record the tally), as was John Bloodgood's motion that children born into slavery after July 4, 1800—a date chosen for its obvious significance—must be emancipated when they reached a certain age (left unspecified). Next, James Lattomus proposed that within the year every slaveholding member "shall . . . give an instrument of emancipation for all his slaves; and the quarterly meeting conference shall determine on the time the slave shall serve, if the laws of the state do not expressly prohibit their emancipation." This was the system that many quarterly conferences in border states had adopted, but here it was voted down, presumably by the southern preachers.[27]

With these defeats in mind, Ezekiel Cooper made what must have seemed a modest proposal "that a committee be appointed to prepare an affectionate address to the Methodist societies in the United States, stating the evils of the spirit and practice of slavery, [and] the necessity of doing away [with] the evil as far as the laws of the respective states will allow." The motion passed, probably because southerners saw it as a small price to pay to give the anti-slavery faction something to feel good about. After all, the conferences weren't required to do anything but read the address. Time would prove them wrong.[28]

"We have long lamented the great national evil of NEGRO SLAVERY," began the one-page address that the committee, appointed in response to Cooper's motion, brought in a few days later. Joining Cooper on the committee were William McKendree and Jesse Lee, both southerners but neither a friend of slavery, though Lee was the more ambivalent of the two. The address attacked slavery on two levels: as an affront to civil liberty and as a contradiction to Christian morality. As a civil matter, slavery was "repugnant to the unalienable rights of mankind, and to the very essence of civil liberty." In a nation "jealous" to protect its freedom, slavery represented "an inconsistency which is scarcely to be paralleled in the history of mankind!" Religiously, "the whole spirit of the New Testament militates in the strongest manner against the practice of slavery." Hence, "at this General Conference we wished, if possible, to give a blow at the root to the enormous evil . . . to rouse up all our influence, in order to hasten, to the utmost of our power, the universal extirpation of this crying sin." Strong language, but if southerners were alarmed, they could reflect that it only mirrored wording contained in the *Discipline* for several years. The annual conferences were urged to send addresses to their state legislatures demanding the "gradual emancipation" of all slaves. "O what a glorious country would be ours, if equal liberty were every where established, and equal liberty every where enjoyed!" Following the conference, Cooper printed and began circulating copies of the address, signed by the bishops, which soon found its way into newspapers north and south.[29]

Asbury had few illusions about the address changing the minds of many slaveholders or their sympathizers. He had spent too much time among slaves and masters, observing the growing inflexibility of many whites. His only contribution to this debate was a pragmatic proposal to provide for the ordination of "black and coloured people," something that he had already begun to do, though most of the preachers didn't know it. The conference responded by granting the bishops "leave . . . to ordain local deacons of our African brethren, in places where they have built a house or houses for the worship of God," so long as a qualified candidate was available. The candidate also had to "obtain an election of two-thirds of the male members of the society to which he belongs," along with a recommendation from the circuit preacher or preachers, all of which still granted a measure of control to local whites. Despite these controls, southern preachers were still "much opposed" to the new measure, according to Jesse Lee. They managed to pass a motion that the new rule would only be entered into the General Conference journal (which wasn't published until 1855) and not in the *Discipline*. As late as 1810, Lee claimed that "this rule is at present little known among the Methodist preachers themselves, owing to its having never been printed." Nevertheless, the rule provided new opportunities for the growing number of African American preachers.[30]

In fact, Asbury had already ordained Richard Allen the first black deacon in the Methodist church on June 11, 1799, though he didn't record the event in his journal. Asbury increasingly realized that if African Americans were to be converted, it would be under the guidance of their own preachers. Before his death in 1816, he recorded ordaining at least eight African American preachers, including James Varick, cofounder of the African Methodist Episcopal Zion Church in New York City, and Daniel Coker, a prominent Baltimore preacher, who, along with Richard Allen, founded the African Methodist Episcopal Church in 1816. Doubtless there were many more ordinations that, like Allen's, Asbury didn't record in his journal, as was usually the case with white preachers as well. Most of the ordinations of African Americans that Asbury does mention took place in Philadelphia or New York, though he occasionally ordained free African Americans farther south. In February 1812, near Richmond, Virginia, he noted that, "A charge had been brought against me for ordaining a slave; but there was no further pursuit of the case when it was discovered that I was ready with my certificates to prove his freedom."[31]

Backlash

Revitalized by the events of the General Conference, Asbury left Baltimore on May 20, 1800, for a tour ranging north to New England through the summer and west to Kentucky and Tennessee in the fall before turning south through the Carolinas for the winter. His health, usually a good barometer of his outlook, was "better than when [the General Conference] began." By the time he arrived in South Carolina in mid-November, he had ridden 1,000 miles in two months and kept twenty preaching appointments. Along the way, he slept under twenty unfamiliar roofs at the exorbitant cost of $50. It was a grueling schedule, but news of extensive revivals across the country buoyed his spirits.

Almost as soon as he crossed the border into South Carolina, he realized that things weren't going as well there as elsewhere. The "sickly state of the South, in both senses"—by which Asbury meant the region's unhealthy physical environment and its morally debilitating dependence on slavery—meant that it was unable to spare preachers for the growing West. Indeed, he predicted that five or six South Carolina preachers would locate that year. Two days later, as if in fulfillment of this prophecy, Asbury met Benjamin Blanton, the district's presiding elder, on the road. "He is now a married man," Asbury lamented. "Like others of his Southern brethren, after he has faithfully served the connexion about ten years, he talks of locating." This indeed proved the case, as Blanton soon left the traveling ministry for good.[32]

If Blanton's departure was distressing, it was nothing compared to what Asbury soon learned. In Charleston the address on slavery had become a target of pro-slavery advocates. The address's timing could scarcely have been worse. It appeared in the South within weeks of Gabriel's plot to stage a slave uprising in Richmond, Virginia, an event that sent shock waves through the region. Asbury now heard that John Harper and George Dougherty, the two preachers stationed in Charleston, had been assaulted. Harper wrote to Ezekiel Cooper, "We have lately had a good deal of Trouble, on acct. of the address from the G [eneral] Conference on the subject of emancipation." When the controversy first broke, Harper's house was "beset" by "two hundred angry men, with a Lawier of note at their Head, who uter'd great Threats." A few days later, while on his way home after preaching, Harper was surrounded by "a numerous Band of the *Champions of Liberty*," as he sarcastically referred to the pro-slavery mob. He was defended from the crowd's "rage by some Friends," who were themselves attacked and "now bear the marks of hard Blows."[33]

George Dougherty received even rougher treatment, at least in part because he had opened a school for African American children. After a prayer meeting Dougherty was seized by a mob and held under a pump till "almost deprived . . . of breath." He was saved from drowning when Martha Kugley, a Methodist, rushed into the mob and stuffed the folds of her dress (some accounts say her apron) into the spout of the pump, stopping the flow of water. After Dougherty's pumping, Harper published a letter in the local paper claiming that he had only seen accounts of the address in newspapers (neither Harper nor Dougherty had attended the General Conference) until on September 8, "a few" unsolicited copies arrived in a box of books from Cooper in Philadelphia. When word got out that Harper had copies of the address, a city official showed up at his door, demanding that he burn them. Harper complied, pleading in his published letter that he had never "desired to see that which the address recommends come into effect by any other than lawful, honorable and innocent means, and not by mobs, tumults, insurrections, or any means of so unhappy a tendency." Harper had arrived in America from the West Indies in 1795, but had spent most of his time in the North, much of it in Baltimore. Fearing for the safety of his wife and six children, he now made plans to flee the South at the first sign of another mob.[34]

Dougherty wasn't so easily intimidated. He was still operating his school the next spring, writing to Asbury that "My black school has increased to upward of forty, several of whom have discovered an excellent capacity in learning. But you will readily believe that this has no tendency to remove the reproach of the cross. The epithet of negro school-master, added to that of Methodist preacher, makes a black compound sure enough." Yet Dougherty managed to hold the society together. By May 1801, he could report that "the congregations are as large and serious as they were at any time since I came to Charleston. The number of blacks that attend on the Sabbath is truly pleasing." For all of the trouble in Charleston, Asbury could reflect that he had chosen well in bringing Dougherty there.[35]

The larger controversy further alienated Charleston's elite. In particular, it focused public attention on the sections of the *Discipline* respecting slavery that most South Carolinians had overlooked till now. That quickly changed. According to Harper, public figures of "the highest authority" now found the church's policies "to be highly Inimical to the Tranquility of the Country. Some Magistrates of the highest Respectability, have given it as their opinion, that we need not expect peace in this state, unless we abjure our principals respecting slavery, contained in the form of Discipline." A few weeks later, in December 1800, Asbury met a member of the South Carolina General Assembly who informed him that the address "had been read and reprobated" in the legislature, and "that it had been the occasion of producing a law which prohibited a minister's attempting to instruct any number of blacks with the doors shut; and authorizing a peace officer to break open the door in such cases, and disperse or whip the offenders." In fact, the law, which had the governor's support, prohibited any slave assembly without whites present and forbade whites from meeting with slaves in a "confined or secret place of meeting," or at night for "religious or mental instructions." Patrols that discovered an illegal meeting could break it up using the whip, as Asbury had heard. With tensions running so high, Harper wrote to Cooper, "It is the General opinion that if Mr. Asbury comes here it will be at the Peril of his Life." Asbury took the threat seriously, barely setting foot in Charleston until 1803. It was never his style to provoke a public confrontation.[36]

Yet confrontation he would have. As winter waned, Asbury and Whatcoat made their way through the Carolinas, arriving in Virginia in late March 1801.

Often they got nothing to eat between an early breakfast and a late dinner, with a ride of 30 miles in between. Along the way, they continued to encounter fallout from the address on slavery. Before crossing into North Carolina in late January, Asbury observed that he was "Sure nothing could so effectually alarm and arm the citizens of South Carolina against the Methodists as the *Address of the General Conference*. The rich among the people never thought us worthy to preach to them." In the past they had given "their slaves liberty to hear and join our Church." "Now it appears the poor Africans will no longer have this indulgence. Perhaps we shall soon be thought unfit for the company of their dogs." Two weeks later, he ran into a certain Solomon Reeves, who "let me know that he had seen the *Address*, signed by me; and was quite confident there were no arguments to prove that slavery was repugnant to the spirit of the Gospel; what absurdities will not men defend!" Asbury wondered. "If the Gospel will tolerate slavery, what will it not authorize? I am strangely mistaken if this said Mr. Reeves has more grace than is necessary [for salvation], or more of *Solomon* than the name." The address of course wasn't the root of the problem. It had only "lanced" the abscess "of deep rooted enmity, that has been swelling for years," Asbury wrote to Thomas Morrell, then stationed in Baltimore, that February.[37]

However little sympathy Asbury had for slaveholders, he had to admit that Methodist preachers now had less "access" to slaves. "Our way is strangely closed up at present in consequence of the *Address*," he noted a few days after his confrontation with Reeves. The storm raised by the address had a particularly chilling effect on Methodist activities in South Carolina, spreading outward from Charleston. At Manchester, on the Santee and Catawba circuit, a mob chased the itinerant Levi Garrison, who only escaped by taking "to the bushes." When Garrison's partner on the circuit, James Jenkins, visited the village soon afterward, he "expected hot work, for I was resolved to stand my ground." A mob again formed and broke up Jenkins's meeting, ordering the slaves to leave the house and seizing the bread Jenkins was using for communion. The leaders then ordered Jenkins outside where they planned to whip him, but he was made of sterner stuff then they expected, and calmly faced them down. Still, for all his bravery Jenkins regarded the address as a monumental mistake. By provoking the law passed by the South Carolina Assembly, the address "had well nigh taken the bread of life" from the "wretched, hungry, starving souls," of the slaves Jenkins was accustomed to ministering to. It had also "waked up the spirit of persecution against our people generally, and especially against the preachers; many of whom, and myself among them, suffered some gross insults repeatedly." Five years before, Asbury had noted that Charleston's few male Methodists "do not attend preaching." Instead,

Methodist congregations were mostly made up of "women and Africans . . . and some few strangers." According to Jenkins, this latest episode reduced even this attendance. He visited Charleston shortly after the controversy broke, writing that "I had been accustomed to see the galleries filled with coloured people, and to hear the most cheerful and delightful singing from these willing worshippers; but now there were not exceeding two or three heads to be seen . . . It did not seem like the same place. So much for the addresses from the General Conference." By May 1801 Dougherty reported a rebound in black attendance, following a relaxation of the law forbidding assemblies of slaves, but in Jenkins's mind the damage was done.[38]

Over the next few years tension between Methodists and planters decreased somewhat, but it never completely abated. While in New York in July 1802, Asbury heard that "persecution" had "ceased in Charleston." Yet when he returned to the state later that year, he learned that this wasn't entirely true. Methodist preachers still hadn't "gain[ed] the confidence of the lowland planters (if indeed that time shall ever be)" with the result that "thousands of the poor slaves" still didn't have access to the gospel. Much the same was true in Richmond, Virginia, where only four or five whites out of the city's seventy-odd Methodists attended meetings in September 1802, according to the city's stationed preacher, Alexander M'Caine. Methodism was "despised by the great, complained against to the Civil Magistrates by the Middle, & persecuted & stoned by the lower Classes—they have strove by every method to stop our night meetings," M'Caine wrote to George Roberts. After "repeated complaints," the city's Mayor "said he would stop the blacks, and if there were five people of colour after dark in our Meeting he would fine me & the rest 3 Doll[ar]s p[er] head, or I must receive 30 lashes on the bare back." Under these threats M'Caine felt compelled to "forbid the blacks from coming as there was a law against it—such a place I never was in before." What freedom Methodists had to preach across much of the South rested on an unspoken truce with proslavery whites. Carolina Methodists continued to expel members who traded slaves (Asbury mentions two in March 1801), but they never again participated in an appeal to state legislatures for the general abolition of slavery.[39]

The fallout over the General Conference's address made clear how far apart opinions among Methodists north and south had drifted. Where northerners, like Ezekiel Cooper, still hoped to force an end to slaveholding among Methodists, Jenkins-style southerners hoped only to work within the system, converting as many slaves as possible but taking no interest in their emancipation. To Cooper, slaveholding was a sin that no expediency could justify; for Jenkins, any hint of abolitionism meant an end to the church in the South. Asbury agonized over this conundrum for the rest of his life, unable to find a way out.

To make the anti-slavery movement seem less American, nineteenth-century southern Methodist historians invented the idea that it had all been Thomas Coke's doing. Describing the events of 1800 from the vantage point of 1856, Francis Asbury Mood, historian of Charleston Methodism, claimed that it was "the indiscreet interference of Dr. Coke with slavery" that had "aroused hostility against the Church in all quarters." So firmly rooted was this interpretation by 1884 that M. H. Moore could write that "the insane zeal of...Dr. Coke in particular" had "excited" the troubles of 1800. Moore even claimed that Dougherty had been seized and nearly drowned by mistake, having actually done nothing to indicate he had any qualms about slavery. Unfortunately, later historians have often carried this myth forward. In fact, after 1784 Coke had relatively little to do with Methodist abolitionism. It was instead American preachers like Ezekiel Cooper who pushed the issue to the breaking point. Asbury took a secondary role in this debate, except for the provision concerning ordination, which in the long run yielded much greater benefits for black Methodists, but he was still more centrally involved than Coke.[40]

18

"The garden of God"

"This night, this memorable night, never to be forgotten, excelled all I had ever seen," Thomas Smith wrote on New Year's Day 1801. When Smith arrived at the home of Captain Thomas Burton on the eastern shore of Virginia, he could hardly get into the yard, "the press of people was so great." "At the very commencement of the meeting the Spirit of the Lord came as a rushing, mighty wind—the people fell before it, and lay in heaps all over the floor. The work continued all night, nor did it stop in the morning, but continued for thirteen days and nights without interruption; some coming, some going, so that the meeting was kept up day and night." When it was all over, Smith took in ninety-five new members, forming fifty-five whites into one class and forty African Americans into another. Throughout the year, Smith recorded meeting after meeting lasting far into the night, with people falling "in all directions," crying out for mercy. "Our societies are getting so large I know not how we are to meet them," he wrote in November 1800. Indeed, Smith and his colleague on the Northampton circuit took in 607 new members that year alone.[1]

Smith's experience was part of a revival sweeping across America on a scale not seen since the 1780s. It was almost more than Asbury could have hoped for. Writing to Thomas Coke in August 1803, he reflected, "I thought once, should I live to see preaching established in all the states, and one hundred in society in each of them, I should be satisfied." Now he dreamed not of hundreds, but of "millions." His personal renown had also grown beyond what he could have imagined as a younger man. He was so well known that letters from Europe could be sent to him "in any publick town or city upon the continent," addressed simply to "Francis Asbury." A town had been named for him (Asbury Town, New Jersey), and parents across the nation named their children after him. No one of his generation was better known face-to-face across the nation.[2]

And yet Asbury couldn't and wouldn't allow himself to relax. The Methodist way of salvation demanded that one push on to the very end; there could be no rest short of the eternal rest of death. Eventually something had to give, either when his health failed or the church changed under his feet, demanding a new style of leadership. The day would come when both happened, but not yet.

After a quarterly meeting near Abingdon, where Cokesbury lay in ruins, Asbury and Whatcoat rode to Duck Creek, Delaware, for the Philadelphia conference annual meeting, which opened June 2 and continued for four days. With sixty-four preachers present, the annual conference became an extension of the revival sweeping through the Delmarva Peninsula. "The people would not leave the house day nor night," Asbury noted. "At one point, the meeting in the meeting-house continued without intermission for 45 hours," alternating between preaching, singing, and prayer, according to Jesse Lee. The people shouted so loud at times "that the speaker could not be heard." People went home only to sleep a little, hurrying back as soon as they awoke "at any hour of the night." "Such a time I think I never Saw before," Whatcoat concluded. "The people Scarcely left the preaching house Day or night." "Many of the saints, as well as sinners would tremble, shake, and fall helpless on the floor, and remain in that condition for a considerable time," Lee recorded. "The probability is, that above one hundred souls were converted to God," Asbury added. His estimate was confirmed two weeks later by George Kinard, who wrote to report 117 new members at Duck Creek.[3]

Despite great difficulty in stationing the preachers, in which Whatcoat took little part, the many conversions at the Duck Creek conference buoyed Asbury's spirits. By the time he reached Philadelphia, he could report that "My health is restored, to the astonishment of myself and friends." Among those who noticed the change was Whatcoat, who wrote to Asbury's mother that "the Hand Divine" had "marvelously prolonged" her son's life, "and restored his health, as well as my own." From Delaware they rode to New York City for the district's annual conference on June 19, then to Lynn, Massachusetts, for the New England conference on July 18.[4]

By late September Asbury and Whatcoat had reached the Holston River in eastern Tennessee. Asbury got his chaise over the river by straddling it between two canoes and then swimming his horse across. After leaving his horse and carriage at Benjamin Van Pelt's, he crossed into Kentucky to hold the district's annual conference at Bethel School. Though signs of a revival were on the horizon, it hadn't yet penetrated far into Kentucky. "It is plain there are not many mighty among the Methodists in Kentucky," Asbury wrote.[5]

As he crossed back into Tennessee, he could sense that things were different. Here the awakening initiated by John Page and others was already well under way. At Nashville more than one thousand people turned out to hear Asbury preach. The next day, October 20, 1800, he attended what amounted to his first camp meeting, though no one yet called them that, at Drake's meetinghouse. Since the church wasn't large enough to hold all the people, a preaching stand was set up "in the open air" among "a wood of lofty beech trees." There "the ministers of God, Methodists and Presbyterians, united their labours" and "mingled" together. Preaching, singing, and praying continued all day, and at night "fires blazing here and there dispelled the darkness and the shouts of the redeemed captives, and the cries of precious souls struggling into life, broke the silence of midnight." Two weeks later Asbury preached to another seven hundred people near the North Carolina border.[6]

By 1801 the revival had two epicenters from which it radiated outward, one in the Cumberland region of Tennessee and Kentucky and the other on the Delmarva Peninsula and western shore of Maryland. In late August 1800 Asbury learned that six hundred new converts had joined in the Baltimore district that summer alone. By fall, people packed Baltimore area churches. In November, George Roberts, then stationed in Baltimore, wrote to a friend in New York that they had just held the largest and loudest love feast the city had ever seen. "Such a general shout I hardly ever heard & when I tell you that near a thousand were presant you may form some Idea how great was the noys." Asbury also learned that a "work" was under way in Annapolis; "Indeed it begins to be more and more general in the towns, and in the country." This "revival upon the western shore of Maryland" and elsewhere was exactly what he had been "agonizing for . . . for many years."[7]

Soon the revival extended north, reaching New England and upstate New York. New England presiding elders Shadrach Bostwick and John Brodhead wrote to Asbury reporting awakenings on nearly every circuit. At one quarterly meeting in Connecticut, "many were struck and fell from their seats prostrate upon the floor, crying in bitter agonies, some for converting, and others for sanctifying grace," according to Bostwick. The revival also spread south through Virginia. In September, Asbury received a letter from Jonathan Jackson, presiding elder over the southeastern Virginia district, informing him that "great and powerful times" prevailed across the district, with two hundred added to the church that summer.[8]

Even in its early stages, Asbury was beginning to sense the possibility of this new work. The church as a whole had gained only six thousand members during the 1790s, and membership had actually declined in the South. During the decade from 1800 to 1810, membership would explode, nearly tripling from 63,700 to more than 171,700, with sustained growth in every state. In a familiar pattern, Asbury's perception of what was now possible worked like a tonic for mind and body, at least in the short term. "Here let me record the gracious dealings of God to my soul in this journey," he wrote on October 30 as he prepared to leave Tennessee and cross over into the Carolinas for the winter. "I have had uncommon peace of mind, and spiritual consolations every day, not withstanding the long rides I have endured, and the frequent privations of good water and proper food to which I have been subjected; to me the wilderness and the solitary places were made as the garden of God."[9]

Following the South Carolina conference at Camden in January 1801, he left for the North, intending to ride 5,000 to 6,000 miles during the next ten months. Richard Whatcoat, "my never-failing friend," as Asbury described him, again rode with him. By now much of Asbury's work had to be coordinated through the mail. Letters from Whatcoat and Asbury took on a pattern in early 1801. Asbury would write to give specific directions as to which preacher should be stationed where, when meetings should be held, and so on. Whatcoat would then add a short postscript, giving spiritual comfort and encouragement. It was an arrangement that accurately reflected the personalities and perceived responsibilities of both men. Whatcoat seemed to feel no resentment at his secondary status, though he was the older of the two. The year before he had written to Asbury's mother, Eliza, that he and Asbury "are like David and Johnathan, united to live, Travel and Labour together." The reference is to the biblical story of King Saul's son Jonathan, who risked his life to befriend and protect David, even though it meant that David would one day be king in his place. There was more than a little of Jonathan in Richard Whatcoat.[10]

When they reached the Kent circuit, they learned that nearly three thousand had joined the church on the Delmarva Peninsula during the past year. "There has been a most glorious revival of religion in this Peninsula," Whatcoat noted. At Dudley's meeting house in Queen Anne's County, Maryland, fifteen hundred blacks and whites turned out for a love feast. Eight days later at Dover, Delaware, so many people showed up to hear Asbury preach on a Monday that the meetinghouse couldn't hold them all and the meeting had to be moved to the nearby capitol building. Despite the success indicated by these crowds, the press of his schedule began to gnaw away at his sense of well-being, undermining the stamina he had enjoyed over the past year.[11]

Less Than Brotherly Love

He finally broke down after reaching Philadelphia on May 30, 1801. Two and a half weeks earlier, at the close of the Virginia conference, he had a "wart, cancerous in appearance," removed from his foot. The wound never really healed and now, accompanied by intermittent fevers, it incapacitated him. In Philadelphia the curiously named doctor Philip Physick took up Asbury's treatment. Physick had studied medicine in London and Edinburgh, and has been called the father of American surgery, though nothing he did for Asbury deserved such a lofty title. Physick diagnosed Asbury with a "sinew strain," concluding that the "dead part of the sinew" had to be burned away with round after round of a "caustic." The resulting pain must have been excruciating, but Asbury tried not to murmur. Disease was a product of God's providence, sent to test one's faith. Early Methodists rarely prayed for divine healing, a concept that would only gain prominence in America with the Mormons in the mid-nineteenth century and in the late nineteenth-century Holiness and Pentecostal movements. As he endured his treatment, Asbury made only spotty entries in his journal for seven weeks. "Why should I continue my journal while here? What would it be but a tale of woe?" he wrote in late July. He felt "shut up in Sodom, without any communication with the connexion at large."[12]

To make matters worse, the Philadelphia church was embroiled in a bitter controversy that Asbury was forced to mediate, unable to escape. Unlike the O'Kelly schism of a decade before, the Philadelphia split wasn't about core doctrine or polity. It began as a division between a wealthier minority and a poorer majority within the church. From there it spiraled into a clash of personalities and a blatant power struggle, just the sort of squabble Asbury regretted most.

In 1799 membership in Philadelphia stood at 411 whites and 211 African Americans, with three itinerant preachers assigned to the city. In the spring of 1800 Asbury stationed only one itinerant preacher, Lawrence McCombs, in the city after white membership declined to 407 and black membership increased to 257, many under Richard Allen's leadership at Bethel. As a result, Ezekiel Cooper and other local preachers became more heavily involved in the affairs of the city's Methodist churches. At the same time a deep division formed between a small group of what Cooper called "the most wealthy and respectable members" on one side, and "the poor" majority on the other. The catalyst for the split was the revival of 1800–1801, which swept some three hundred new white and nearly two hundred new black members into Philadelphia Methodist churches by the spring of 1801. Overwhelmingly these new members were artisans and laborers. Historian Dee Andrews calculates that by the spring of 1801, "at least 953 of the 1,117 members meeting at the four chapels in Philadelphia (more than 85 percent) were women, blacks, and laboring men." Alarmed, the "wealthy and respectable" faction, which included a disproportionate number of merchants and professionals, began looking for ways to solidify their control over St. George's church.[13]

To make matters worse, McCombs threw in his lot with the wealthier faction. He removed several class leaders aligned with the poorer faction, including Henry Manley, who was charged with "usury" and "disturbing the peace of the society," and replaced them with leaders from the other side. The displaced leaders appealed to Joseph Everett, the district's presiding elder. Meeting in late August 1800, Everett and the Philadelphia quarterly conference judged McCombs's actions "a stretch of power" and ordered Manley's membership restored and the removed leaders reinstated. McCombs refused. So, on October 27, Everett ordered him to another circuit and replaced him with another itinerant, Richard Sneath. But McCombs refused to leave the city, and the conflict simmered on.[14]

Sneath's appointment was clearly calculated to favor the laboring faction. He had little sense of social ambition and found the annual and general conferences he had attended "tedious." He much preferred the company of plain, zealous believers who liked their religion hot. On previous visits to Philadelphia, he preached several times at the two African American churches, Richard Allen's Bethel church and Zoar chapel, but only once at St. George's. Once stationed in Philadelphia, he divided his time evenly between the city's four Methodist churches: St. George's, Bethel, Zoar, and Ebenezer. There was no chance that Sneath would continue McCombs's pattern of favoring Philadelphia's more elite Methodists.[15]

Like Asbury, Cooper found the schism exasperating and complex, with layers of conflict on both sides. One of these layers involved the estrangement of McCombs and Everett. Between February 21 and March 5, 1801, McCombs and Cooper exchanged at least thirteen letters in which McCombs claimed that he had acted only to bring about a balance of power between the two sides and that Everett had interfered where he didn't belong. In his last letter to Cooper, McCombs threatened to "bring the matter to" the upcoming Philadelphia conference, so that "the preachers would the better know the *authority and power*, of a presiding Elder." "If a preacher is to be jostled out of his station ... at the nod, or whim, of the presiding Elder, it is a thing I never knew."[16]

Initially Cooper tried to remain neutral, believing that "each party was disposed to strain the questions altogether on their own side, and in their own favour right or wrong." But over time he became disgusted with the "temper and spirit of the ... wealthy and respectable party." They "gave way to such a bitterness of spirit, and to such an abusive principle and practice of evil speaking, and persecution that I more than ever was convinced that their motives were not pure, and their designs were not good." It dismayed Cooper that McCombs resisted any attempt to negotiate a reconciliation between the two sides that didn't include his own reinstatement in Philadelphia. To Cooper this smacked more of personal ambition than Christian charity. In the end, he could only "wish every old point of strife was buried between all parties—I believe things are & have been exagerated."[17]

Asbury first learned of the schism while in South Carolina in December 1800. He received several letters from the North which he likened to the messengers who brought news to Job of the destruction of his family and property. "While he was yet speaking there came also another . . ." Among the letters was a petition from "eighty male members of the society in *the city of brotherly love*, entreating me to do what I had no intention of doing—that was, to remove brother Everett from the city." He couldn't see that Everett had done anything wrong, and he must have been generally pleased with the appointment of Sneath, whom he had met the previous August. Moreover, the city was now in the midst of a revival, with "great congregations, great shoutings" and nearly one hundred new members, all an indication that "God was with them." The awakening gained further momentum in early 1801 under Sneath's leadership. Like the revival to the south on the Delmarva Peninsula, meetings often continued well into the night with "jumping and shouting" and people falling to the floor, unable to rise, crying out for mercy. At one meeting at Zoar chapel, Sneath reported that "the people shouted so loud that I could not hear myself speak." In late January 1801 Sneath found it necessary to divide one of the St. George's class meetings into three, still leaving one of the three new classes with forty members. The next day he took in twenty-four new members at St. George's and the following day another eighteen at Ebenezer.[18]

That June the Philadelphia conference refused to reverse any of Everett's decisions, whereupon McCombs relented, and he and Everett "made up," according to Cooper. This still left open the larger problem of the class division within the Philadelphia church. The conference asked the bishops to write a letter addressed to both parties, recommending that "all sides . . . drop every point of dispute, and return to peace and quietude," according to Cooper. The resulting letter, signed by Asbury and Whatcoat, contains no specific recommendations. It simply implores both sides "to have peace and unity re-established among you." Asbury had always been loath to interfere in local church affairs beyond stationing the traveling preachers. Now he and Whatcoat reiterated this policy, noting that they considered "each society as standing in its own accountability." Asbury would have been glad to been shut of the whole affair, but his injured foot prevented him from leaving the city.[19]

Rather than soothing overheated tempers, the bishops' address only added "offense to the dissatisfied party," meaning the wealthier faction, according to Cooper. Shortly after the Philadelphia conference, a group of fifty to sixty people resigned their memberships and set up a rival church. They purchased the north end of the Philadelphia Academy, a building originally built to accommodate the preaching of George Whitefield and lately owned by the University of Pennsylvania. The local preachers who joined the breakaway group, including former itinerants Charles Cavender and Thomas Haskins, refused to take preaching appointments from Sneath, setting up their own schedule of meetings instead. The group also included local preacher John Hood, who joined the first Methodist society in Philadelphia in 1768, Lambert Wilmer, at whose home Asbury stayed during his second visit to the city in May 1772, and Jacob and Hannah Baker. Jacob was a successful merchant, and the Bakers had been Methodists for nearly thirty years. Joining this group of venerable members were merchant and local preacher Samuel Harvey and physician William Budd, at whose home Cooper had recently boarded. This was a formidable group to lose, but Asbury's sentiments still remained with the poorer majority. Calling themselves "The United Societies of the People called Methodists," the new church grew to eighty-three members in its first year.[20]

On August 18, 1801, the United Societies drew up an independent constitution, which nevertheless remained decidedly Methodist in character. The "Articles of Faith" section is condensed but otherwise drawn almost word for word from the 1798 *Discipline* (the most recent edition) minus Coke and Asbury's explanatory notes, or any references to bishops or presiding elders. Where the ritual section of the *Discipline* called for the bishop to preside (for example at the ordination of elders), the new constitution substituted a "President Pastor." Conspicuously absent from the new constitution is any condemnation of slavery or the *Discipline*'s prohibition against "The buying or selling of men, women, or children, with an intention to enslave them." The United Societies saw themselves as genuinely Methodist, but under no obligation to Asbury or his presiding elders. Their concerns were those of Philadelphia's wealthier Methodists alone. What they wanted most was the authority to impose a degree of refinement on the city's Methodists, at least at the academy.[21]

Complicating the Philadelphia schism for Asbury was the fact that he had asked Thomas Haskins to edit his (Asbury's) journal for publication. Asbury wrote to Haskins on June 26, 1801, even as Haskins was preparing to leave the church, that he could still promise Haskins $100 for editing the journal. As if working with Haskins wasn't tricky enough, Asbury had to consider that Ezekiel Cooper, the church's book agent and an opponent of Haskins's faction, would ultimately be responsible for publishing the journal. Asbury was never entirely satisfied with Haskins's efforts, and a year later he concluded that he had seriously overestimated Haskins's "literary abilities." Early in 1802 Cooper published the portion of Asbury's journal covering the period January 1, 1779, to September 3, 1780, but Asbury wasn't pleased with the result. "If I had left him [Cooper] at liberty it would have been done better," Asbury wrote to George Roberts, then stationed in Philadelphia, in August 1802. As it stood, the journal was "very incorrect: had I had an opportunity before it was put to press, I should have altered and expunged many things." Two years later Asbury wondered whether further portions of the journal "will ever be published before or after my death."[22]

Still, he wanted a record of the church's progress, all the more so as the revival swept in crowds of new members. Since his journal had proved disappointing, he turned to the preachers, badgering the presiding elders to send him detailed accounts of revivals in their districts at least once a year. He hoped that these could then be edited "for the press" and published on a regular basis. "I wish that when any of my brethren write to me, that they would give me all the information they can of the work of God, it cheers my soul, and I can communicate it to thousands," he wrote to Thornton Fleming, presiding elder of the Pittsburgh district. He advised Fleming to "keep a small Journal at hand, and select at least one narrative of all the extraordinary things of the great meetings, and of the number of souls professing awakening, Justifying, Sanctifying, or reclaiming grace," to send to him. Alas, the elders generally failed to supply the kind of regular reports that Asbury was looking for. A few collections of letters and accounts from this period were eventually published, but not the kind of broader history that Asbury was hoping for.[23]

"The lame and the blind"

By early July 1801 Asbury longed to leave Philadelphia, which he alternately referred to as this "unhappy place," and "the city of strife, unmeaningly or ironically called Philadelphia," but the condition of his foot wouldn't allow it. "I only regret that I had anything at all to do with the Philadelphia fire and still I am here and cannot with safety get away," he complained to George Roberts. "You will judge of my case to sit from morning to evening in a disagreeable attitude in the heat of the weather and division in the middle of the city." By the end of the month, he was determined to leave, sore foot or not. Traveling south he made his way into Maryland, where he met Richard Whatcoat and his current traveling companion, Sylvester Hutchinson, in Frederick County. By necessity, Whatcoat had taken up Asbury's usual episcopal duties (ordaining deacons and

elders and stationing the preachers) at the New York and New England conferences that summer. But Whatcoat, generally known among the preachers as "Old
Father," was also ailing. Earlier Asbury had worried that Whatcoat would "lose his
sight in part or whole, he will ride and preach himself blind." Now it appeared
that he was indeed "almost blind," only able to "see dimly with one eye." Since
both bishops were in poor health—"the lame and the blind," as Asbury referred to
himself and Whatcoat—they decided to divide the work between them and meet
at the end of the year in South Carolina.[24]

Asbury and Snethen made their way across Virginia in September, arriving in eastern Tennessee late in the month to hold the Western conference
annual meeting. They were too late to attend the now famous Cane Ridge
camp meeting, which had been held in early August in central Kentucky, but
Asbury heard reports about it, including that "one thousand if not fifteen
hundred fell and felt the power of grace." Only twelve Western conference
preachers attended the Tennessee conference, the rest pleading that they
couldn't leave their circuits at this critical juncture because of "the greatness
of the work of God." Unfortunately, it was too late in the year for Asbury to
venture farther west and north across the mountains into central Kentucky and
Tennessee to see for himself, so he turned southeast into North Carolina. As
always the roads in the West were "equal to any in the United States for
badness," testing the limits of his "lame feet and old feeble joints." By October
he had walked or ridden more than 800 miles since leaving Philadelphia, an
average of about 100 miles a week. Weak as Asbury was, Snethen did most of
the preaching. Asbury usually then followed with an exhortation, or by reading
letters he had received describing the revivals on the Delmarva Peninsula or in
the Cumberland region.[25]

Crossing into South Carolina, Asbury was disappointed, but not really
surprised, to learn that there was little appearance of revival in the state.
"I cannot record great things upon religion in this quarter; *but cotton sells
high*," he sarcastically wrote as he crossed between the Tyger and Enoree rivers.
"I fear there is more gold than grace—more of silver than of 'that wisdom that
cometh from above.' "[26]

The three months of traveling since leaving Philadelphia had been spiritually rewarding but physically draining for Asbury. In September he wrote
from Virginia to George Roberts that "I am obliged to ride down the high
mountains because I cannot walk, and Jane [his horse] does not know how to
crook her joints down these precipices" as horses raised in the mountains
apparently did. Each step jolted him, causing pain "in the hip on the lame side
in riding." As always, decent lodging was hard to come by. Most frontier cabins
had only "one room and fireplace," into which the family crowded, "not usually

Daniel Killian's home, near Asheville, North Carolina, one of Asbury's favorite stopping places 1800–1813. (From R. N. Price, *Holston Methodism. From Its Origin to the Present Time*, vol. 1 [Nashville: Smith & Lamar, 1903].)

small in these plentiful new countries," along with the "half a dozen . . . strangers" that Asbury's visits always seemed to attract, "making a crowd," he observed. "And this is not all; for here you *may* meditate if you can, and here you *must* preach, read, write, pray, sing, talk, eat, drink, and sleep—or fly into the woods." What made it worthwhile were the dramatic revivals that he witnessed sweeping across the West.[27]

Arriving in Camden at the end of the year, Asbury received some unexpectedly good news. Since he had left Philadelphia, St. George's church had actually managed to retire a large debt despite losing its wealthiest members in the recent schism. At the time of the split, the church was "near three thousand Dollars" in debt for recent renovations, according to Ezekiel Cooper. He believed that those who left the church were actually encouraging creditors to sue for control of the building so that they (the separating faction) could buy it back. Whether or not this was true became a moot point when the remaining members managed to raise $4,000 in less than a year. "O Zeal! Zeal! what will it not do when made Elastic by opposition," Asbury wrote when he heard the news. Writing to Cooper, he recommended that the church use any surplus funds to buy or build a house for the city's preacher, making it easier to station a married preacher there.[28]

It was something to feel good about as he headed north in early 1802. He would soon receive news he had long feared.

19

"Like a moving fire"

His mother was dead, which inevitably came as a shock. She died
on January 6, 1802, though word only now reached him in early April in
Baltimore. The death of his father had produced only a few lines in his
journal, but his mother's led to an initial reflection of more than four
hundred words, with follow-up entries and a spate of correspondence
with friends and relatives in England. After recounting her family
history and conversion—her Welsh ancestry, how she had "lived a
woman of the world" until the death of her daughter, Sarah, how that
"hopeless grief" had eventually led to her conversion—Asbury recalled
how for fifty years "her hands, her house, her heart, were open to
receive the people of God and ministers of Christ; and thus a lamp was
lighted up in a dark place called Great Barre, in Great Britain." In death
all of his mother's faults were forgotten and only her strengths
remained, particularly her outgoing personality, which drew together a
society of believers in her village. "As a woman and a wife she was
chaste, modest, blameless; as a mother (above all the women in the
world would I claim her for my own) ardently affectionate." In other
words, Eliza was an ideal Methodist woman, a true "mother in Israel."
Where he *hoped* for his father's salvation, he was confident of his
mother's, as confident as his Arminianism would allow.[1]

Eliza's death was ultimately a blessing, as it was for all believers
who left this world of woe for a better place, but it still didn't rest
easy with her son. The effusiveness of his praise belied a measure of
guilt that he had never returned to England or brought his parents

to America. For all of his accomplishments, he had in some measure failed his own family. The obligation of children to their parents was on Asbury's mind the year before when he advised the itinerant Thomas Morrell to return home to his ill father. Morrell had been stationed in Baltimore in 1799 and 1800, participating in the thick of the city's recent revival. Learning that his father, who lived in Elizabeth, New Jersey, was ill, Morrell asked Asbury for an appointment closer to home. Asbury responded by stationing Morrell in New York City for the next three years, 1801 to 1803. Like Asbury, Morrell was the only living child of a lone surviving parent, his mother having died in 1796. "I should advise the preachers at such seasons to go and see their Parents," Asbury wrote to Morrell when he first learned of his father's illness in February 1801. "I am well persuaded that you ought to take a Station in [New] York . . . and when health, and weather will permit, if it was every week, visit your Father, and spend as much time as you can, a Day or Two; I am clear with Mr. Wesley, the obligation of children to parents never ceaseth but with life."[2]

When he returned home in 1801, Morrell found his father had indeed "declined much in health—so that I cannot see it my duty to leave him. I consequently must locate myself at least for a season." Morrell's journal reveals that during 1801 and the first half of 1802 he lived in Elizabeth and preached there almost exclusively, though the town already had two stationed preachers and his appointment was technically to New York City. But Asbury and the district's presiding elder overlooked this, making considerable allowance for Morrell's devotion to his father. "You ought to cheer the setting hour of your Father's life; hold and stay long," Asbury advised Morrell in February 1801. "My dear mother is going swiftly, if not gone . . . I have often thought very seriously of my leaving my mother, as one of the most doubtful Sacrifices I have made." What he couldn't do for his own mother he did for Morrell's father. In 1804 Asbury appointed Morrell to Elizabeth and the following year Morrell located there, leaving the traveling connection. His father died that September in 1805.[3]

Allowing Thomas Morrell to sit by his father's side vicariously assuaged some of Asbury's guilt, but it didn't absolve him of all regret. In particular he wanted details of his mother's last hours, which he hoped would show that she had died triumphant, confident in her faith. His cousin John Rodgers wrote from Walsall, Staffordshire, with some particulars, but not the kind of detailed deathbed account that Asbury was looking for. As to his mother's property, "I never expected or desired a farthing," he wrote to Rodgers. Still, he was disappointed to learn that "a certain Mr. Emery has taken all her property." Elizabeth had evidently signed everything over to Emery after her husband's death, so that she could live rent-free in their cottage, Asbury's boyhood home. Emery was likely the landlord of the Malt Shovel pub, and use of the cottage was probably tied to Joseph's employment at the malt house or farm. In essence, Elizabeth had died penniless, in hock to a tavern keeper, not the kind of end Asbury wished for his mother. At any rate, his last remaining tie with England was now broken.[4]

From Baltimore, Asbury and Whatcoat made their way through Maryland and the Delmarva Peninsula toward Philadelphia in the spring of 1802. Along the way they heard numerous reports that the region's awakening was "spreading along like a moving fire." Over the past eleven months the Baltimore and Philadelphia conferences, which included the peninsula, had added about ten thousand new members. Learner Blackman and William Bishop took in more than one thousand new members on the Dover circuit alone, an increase of 591 whites and 416 African Americans. "This was a gracious year to my soul," Blackman noted. "Some times I preached from 6 to 10 and 11 times a week and met large classes almost every day." As he traveled across the region, Asbury sometimes preached, but more often gave only an exhortation, or read letters giving accounts of the revival in various places. He would have preferred to stay in the Chesapeake, soaking up the church's success, but he couldn't favor the strong over the weak, the latter of which included Philadelphia.[5]

This year, however, things were even looking up in the city of brotherly love. Much to Asbury's surprise, the breakaway Academy church requested readmission as a regular appointment under the city's stationed preachers, George Roberts and John McClaskey. Still, the Academy members, whom Asbury referred to as the "separates" or "malcontents," continued to see themselves as different (read better) than Philadelphia's other Methodists. A month later Asbury learned that the Academy members wanted the eloquent Roberts to preach to them exclusively. "I utterly disapprove the motion," Asbury wrote to Roberts in June. "What, you confined in your labours to 100 in society and 1000 in congregation when you may preach to 10,000 or more by going into other churches?" Two weeks later Asbury further instructed Roberts "to preach but twice in the Academy Church, upon Sabbath Days, that will be sufficient, then you can go to St. Georges, Ebenezer, or Bethel." He threatened to move Roberts to New York rather than see him tied to the Academy alone, but the Academy members relented, and Roberts remained in the city.[6]

What most annoyed the Academy Methodists was the emotional energy that the revival brought to Philadelphia's churches, as the itinerant Thomas Sargent discovered when he took up his appointment in the city. In June 1803 Sargent attended a Monday evening love feast at the Academy as part of Asbury's instructions that the church accept the ministry of all the city's stationed preachers. "Nothing remarkable" happened until the meeting was dismissed and he left the building, Sargent wrote to Thomas Morrell a few days later. Standing in the yard, Sargent was startled to hear "several very loud shreakes." Rushing back into the building, he ran into several people "opposed to a noise" who were fleeing in the opposite direction "as if the old one [the devil] was after them." Among these was "a fine dressed lady, endeavoring to make her escape, [who] came up full drive against me," nearly bowling Sargent over. "My God what shall we do. It's just like St. Georges. We are ruined, we are ruined," the woman cried. She had attended all of the church's past love feasts, but "this is the first time I have seen them dance." When the woman asked Sargent if he thought this proper worship, he replied, "Oh yeas madam . . . it will do very well." Shocked, the woman "repented that she had ever been in the Academy. And so quit the ground." Clearly there was a divide between Sargent's style of Methodism (and Asbury's for that matter) and that of the Academy members. They still wanted to be Methodists, but without the shouting, falling, and dancing that accompanied the awakening in Philadelphia's other Methodist churches. They were too refined for such carrying on. Asbury was willing to accommodate the Academy Methodists, but not if it meant creating a separate elite brand of urban Methodism. His sympathies clearly rested with the city's poorer, shouting Methodists. The issue would come up more frequently in years to come, as an increasingly powerful minority of urban Methodists sought to fashion a church several degrees removed from its shouting roots.[7]

Traveling from Philadelphia to New York, Asbury received "a variety of letters, conveying the pleasing intelligence of the work of God in every State, district, and in most of the circuits in the Union." As in Philadelphia, at the New York conference a large number of new itinerant preachers joined on trial, in this case twenty-two, bringing the total for the last six conferences to sixty-three. This was certainly an encouraging development, though some charged Asbury with giving in to favoritism in stationing the preachers. The "care, and tumult, and talk, experienced in the noisy, bustling city," wore him down, as did the "passions, parties, hopes and fears" of preachers and people. While one preacher worried that he might be sent to New Hampshire or even Canada, another "wishes to go where [his brother] dreads to be sent, and smiles at the fears of his more timid brother." At the same time, the people complained that "such a one will be too strict, and may put us out of order—a second will not keep the congregations together; and our collections will not be made—a third will not please; because he is not a lively preacher, and we want a revival of religion."[8]

One result of this bickering was that the conference asked Asbury to go to the New England conference, scheduled to meet July 1 in Monmouth, Maine, unconvinced that Whatcoat could handle things on his own. This meant that

Asbury had to send Nicholas Snethen to the West alone to take his place, forgoing his chance to see the western awakening for yet another year. As always, he gave in to the collective will of the conference, shouldering his responsibility to the church as a whole. In all, his tour of New England was little better than he expected. "Should I live to be as old as Mr. Wesley, and travel as long as he did, yet shall I never see a Maryland in Connecticut," Asbury groused. At one appointment in Massachusetts, "an old drunkard" repeatedly interrupted his sermon. "My spirit has been greatly assaulted, and divinely supported in . . . the hope of *rest, rest, rest, eternal rest.*" New England had that effect on Asbury, making him look forward even to death.[9]

As he made his way south from New England, Asbury continued to hear news of the revival still sweeping the nation's middle corridor, from Delaware to Kentucky. Crowds at an annual meeting in Dover, Delaware, swelled to between five thousand and seven thousand over five days, and both Richard Bassett and Thomas Smith wrote that some one hundred people were converted. At the end of August 1802, Asbury witnessed the revival fire at a three-day meeting in Harrisonburg, Virginia. During the love feast on Sunday, "there was great shaking, and shouting, and weeping and praying." The outcry was so intense that "it was thought best not to stop these exercises by the more regular labour of preaching." Three weeks later he attended a camp meeting (the first he called by that name) in eastern Tennessee. Some fifteen hundred attended over four days, during which Asbury read accounts "of the work at Dover" to the crowd. Shortly thereafter, a letter arrived from Jesse Lee saying that the awakening had taken hold in southern Virginia, in the same circuits that had been the center of the 1787 revival. Indeed, many of those awakened were children of converts from the earlier revival.[10]

Writing separately to Ezekiel Cooper, George Roberts, and Thornton Fleming in December 1802, Asbury rejoiced that "upwards of 3000" new members had been added in the Western conference. Altogether he hoped for an "increase of 21,000 in the seven conferences" for the year. In the end, membership increased by 13,860 in 1802 and another 17,336 in 1803, a stunning achievement. He was particularly impressed with the efficacy of camp meetings, which were fast becoming a central feature of the awakening. Writing to George Roberts at Philadelphia, Asbury urged him to "have a camp meeting at Duck Creek, out in the plain, south of the Town, and let the people come with their Tents, waggons[,] provision, and so on, let them keep at it, night and Day." His advice to Thornton Fleming, presiding elder of the Pittsburgh district, was that camp meetings "have never been tried without success. To collect such a number of God's people together to pray, and the ministers to preach, and the longer they stay, generally, the better—this is field fighting, this is fishing with a large net."[11]

The exact origin of camp meetings is a matter of debate. In hindsight, Presbyterians, Baptists, and Methodists could all claim some priority to the practice, though the term wasn't generally used before 1802. For Presbyterians, camp meetings represented an extension of the tradition of multi-day sacramental meetings brought to America by Scotch-Irish immigrants decades before. Baptist associational meetings also sometimes lasted several days, drawing people from a wide geographical region.[12]

For Methodists, camp meetings represented a logical extension of the quarterly meeting, which had been used to draw together the preachers and people of a given circuit four times a year (as the name implies) for more than thirty years. Quarterly meetings fostered connection, that all-important word for early Methodists. Beginning in 1776, quarterly meetings in Virginia were expanded from one-day to two-day affairs, usually over a Saturday and Sunday. People traveled considerable distances to attend, and in revival seasons crowds in the hundreds and even thousands were common on some circuits. "Quarterly-meetings on this Continent are much attended to," Thomas Coke wrote as he made his way through southern Virginia in April 1785. "The Brethren for twenty miles around, and sometimes for thirty or forty, meet together. The meeting always lasts two days. All the Travelling Preachers in the Circuit are present, and they with perhaps a local Preacher or two, give the people a sermon one after another, besides the Love-feast, and (now) the Sacrament." As they developed in the 1780s and 1790s, quarterly meetings came to have a well-defined pattern. Fridays were observed as a day of fasting in preparation for the meeting. Preaching began Saturday morning and continued till early afternoon, when the business session convened. Here preachers and local leaders met to deal with disciplinary cases, license local preachers and exhorters, make recommendations to the annual conference, and discuss finances and other administrative concerns. Preaching continued Saturday night, followed by prayer meetings in nearby homes. Sunday morning began with a love feast, followed by sermons and exhortations from the presiding elder and circuit preachers. The sacraments of baptism and the Lord's Supper followed either at the close of the morning service or in the afternoon. Sunday evening concluded with more preaching, singing, and praying.[13]

The numbers who thronged quarterly meetings often strained resources despite the determined hospitality of locals. Such were the crowds that "we knew not what to do with the thousands who attended our quarterly meetings," Thomas Ware wrote, reflecting on the Delmarva Peninsula in this period. In southern Ohio, where settlement was still relatively thin, Philip and Elizabeth Gatch, along with two other families, began hosting quarterly meetings at their homes near the forks of the Little Miami River in 1800. "Women would walk twenty and even thirty miles to attend," Gatch wrote, "and it was [a] matter of astonishment to see the numbers that attended." Each family boarded fifty to one hundred people in their home, with the men sleeping in the barns where meetings were also held. In the summer of 1801 Abner Chase attended a quarterly meeting on New York's Saratoga circuit at which he and thirty to forty others stayed at the home of William Bentley. "As was the custom of those days, the brethren from abroad were entertained by the families in the vicinity of the meeting, not in pairs but by dozens." Services were also held in a barn at this meeting, with women sitting on the floor and men in the loft. In September 1802 Edward Talbot hosted a quarterly meeting at his home, about four miles from Shelbyville, Kentucky. Along with boarding forty to fifty people in his home, Talbot stabled their horses and donated an acre of corn for feed. Whether it was in Ohio, New York, Kentucky, or on the Delmarva Peninsula, quarterly meetings brought believers together in numbers that no other community event could match.[14]

What quarterly meetings did for a circuit, annual conferences did on a much larger scale, bringing together more preachers and people from a wider geographical area. The transition to camp meetings was easy for Methodists, who had a long history of holding extended two- or three-day meetings. The only real innovation was the camping itself. Even someone as well informed as Jesse Lee, writing in 1810, "never could learn whether they [camp meetings] began in the upper parts of South-Carolina, in Tennessee, or in Kentucky." When the first camp meeting was held and whether the concept was invented by Presbyterians, Methodists, or Baptists is really beside the point.[15]

That said, camp meetings did represent an important progression in the Methodist program to evangelize the nation, though it had little to do with a shift in theology or doctrine. Camp meetings took the familiar Wesleyan message of repentance, conversion, and sanctification and presented it in a new, more culturally accommodating setting. Nonmembers hadn't generally traveled long distances to reach quarterly meetings (how could they have expected to impose on the hospitality of strangers when they weren't even members?), but camp meetings created more public space, inviting nearly anyone who could bring provisions and a tent to attend. Almost immediately this new openness required organizers to create security details to keep out rowdies and peddlers. Asbury advised Daniel Hitt, presiding elder of the Alexandria, Virginia, district in August 1804, to appoint sixteen to twenty watchmen at an upcoming camp meeting, carrying "long, white, peeled rods, that they may be known by all the camp." This was a small price to pay for the opportunity to reach a much broader audience. No longer would multi-day meetings be limited by the floor space of local families.[16]

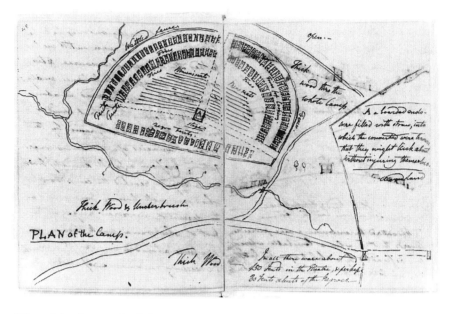

"Plan of the Camp," sketch by Benjamin Henry Latrobe, 1809. The tents are arranged around a perimeter, with the "Negro tents" located behind the preaching stand. Benches for men and women are on either side of a center aisle. In front of the preaching stand is "a boarded enclosure filled with straw, into which the converted are thrown that they might kick about without injuring themselves." Two streams border the camp to supply water. (Courtesy of the Maryland Historical Society, Baltimore, Maryland.)

Asbury's enthusiasm for camp meetings at this juncture is in some respects surprising, considering that he had only attended one by that name prior to 1803. The theatrical nature of camp meetings, with their nighttime preaching under the somber glow of torches, accompanied by the shrieks and groans of seekers, was a far cry from Asbury's own public manner. While others preached, shouted and fell, Asbury usually worked quietly behind the scenes, planning ahead, resolving disputes and talking closely with a handful of friends. He rarely wept, cried out, or had the kind of visionary experiences that many preachers and exhorters reported. Yet, much as he had recognized the centrality of southern emotionalism three decades before and defended it against the criticisms of Thomas Rankin, Asbury now perceived a unifying thread in the mass meetings of the current awakening. Camp meetings provided a link to popular culture that could be turned in favor of preaching the gospel. For whatever reason, and Asbury didn't speculate on what it was, people responded to these gatherings in a way that they didn't to ordinary church meetings.[17]

Camp meeting, lithograph (c. 1820) after a painting attributed to A. Rider.
(Courtesy of the Billy Graham Center Museum, Wheaton, Illinois.)

The force of the awakening continued unabated through 1803. On the
Delmarva Peninsula, the church continued to make converts at an astonishing
rate. "It seems as if the whole Peninsula must be *methodised*," Asbury wrote in
April as he made his way across the region. By 1810, Methodists represented 21
percent of the peninsula's adult population, with the church's broader influence extending further still. "Twenty-five years of faithful labours, and the
consistent lives of our brethren, generally have worn down prejudice; so that
many who will not *live* will, nevertheless, when they are sick, send for the
preachers, that they may *die* Christians," Asbury wrote. What was true on the
peninsula was also true in the West. In the summer and fall of 1803, he finally
had the chance to travel through western Pennsylvania and Ohio and then
down into central Kentucky. Near Pittsburgh he preached to two thousand at a
camp meeting in August, "the first of its kind attempted in this country." A
month later, two thousand attended the Western conference meeting, where
there was "preaching every day" and continual "singing and prayer, night and
day, with little intermission."[18]

Camp meetings produced displays of religious excitement that no one
could recall witnessing before. Huge crowds created a festival atmosphere
centered on preaching, worship, and prayer. In August 1803 Asbury met a

Presbyterian near Pittsburgh, Pennsylvania, who "asked my opinion" of people falling down during preaching. "I replied, that in my judgment, any person who could not give an account of the convincing power of God, might be mistaken." By itself, "falling down would not do." Yet Asbury was quick not to dismiss the phenomenon altogether, since it could be a sign of genuine conviction. Only a week before, he was pleased that "A woman, noted for being a mocker, fell down, and cried for mercy, confessing her sins before all the people," during one of his sermons. Those overcome "often uttered several piercing shrieks in the moment of falling," one participant later remembered. Some could speak, though unable to stand, while others lay motionless for hours, even days, with a weak pulse and cold skin. James Finley claimed that those who fell "uniformly testified that they had no bodily pain, and that they had the entire use of their reason and powers of mind." Another preacher wrote that some of the stricken experienced trances and visions in which they "professed to have seen heaven and hell, to have seen God, angels, the devil and the damned; they would prophesy, and, under the pretense of Divine inspiration, predict the time of the end of the world, and the ushering in of the great millennium."[19]

Foreign travelers couldn't resist treating the intense emotionalism of camp meetings as a tourist attraction. Their analyses reflect wider patterns of criticism of the revival. While traveling in Kentucky in 1802, Francois Andre Michaux attended a camp meeting near Lexington, noting that during the course of "vehement" preaching sometimes two hundred or three hundred people were overcome and fell. "This species of infatuation happens chiefly among the women, who are carried out of the crowd, and put under a tree, where they lie a long time extended, heaving the most lamentable sighs," Michaux reported. This was a common criticism of the awakening: that it preyed upon the more susceptible emotions of women and the poorly educated. While in Georgia in 1806, British traveler John Melish acknowledged that the Methodists had done some good by "enforcing the principles of morality amongst their votaries." But he questioned whether "the evil attending" camp meetings "does not overbalance the good." "I can see little sense in the practice they often have of thumping and making a noise in the time of divine service, thereby converting the temple of the Lord into a scene of confusion and discord, exciting the laughter of the profane, and distracting the serious."[20]

Even Methodist preachers, long accustomed to seeing people cry out and fall in a swoon, scarcely knew how to account for the new "exercises." Soon after he began circuit preaching in 1803, Peter Cartwright encountered the running, jumping, and barking exercises, and, most dramatically, the jerks, at camp meetings. Saints and sinners alike would be "seized with a convulsive jerking all over, which they could not by any possibility avoid, and the more they resisted the more they jerked," Cartwright later remembered. "I have seen more than five hundred persons jerking at one time in my large congregations." When Lorenzo Dow first heard of the jerks in February 1804, he assumed that reports describing them were "vague and false," until he observed hundreds of Presbyterians, Methodists, Quakers, Baptists, Episcopalians, Independents, and at least one circuit rider seized with the bizarre exercise. At one camp meeting site Dow noticed that fifty to one hundred saplings were cut breast-high, which seemed "slovenish" until he learned that they had been intentionally left that way for people seized with the jerks to grab.[21]

At the moment, the stakes seemed high. Predictably, the visibility of camp meetings was such that they "roused a spirit of persecution against us," according to Asbury. In July 1806 William Chandler, presiding elder for the Delaware district, wrote that at eight camp meetings since spring, "2293 have been Converted and upwards of 900 Sanctified." That December Asbury received more "good news" from Chandler, though mixed with word of fresh opposition. "The work of God is wonderful in Delaware," Asbury wrote. "But what a *rumpus* is raised! We are subverters of government—disturbers of society—movers of insurrections. Grand juries in Delaware and Virginia have presented the noisy preachers—lawyers and doctors are in arms—the lives, blood, and livers of the poor Methodists are threatened: poor crazy sinners!" Whatever the fate of their livers, he had reason to be alarmed. The following July, Joseph Everett wrote to Ezekiel Cooper that a Virginia court had fined Chandler and others $2,000 in connection with revival meetings.[22]

While some took Methodists to court, others harassed them on the ground. On the closing Sunday of a camp meeting in upstate New York's Tioga County, "some intoxicated young men seated themselves by the women, and refused to move until compelled; they fought those men who came to take them away, and when the presiding elder interfered they struck at him," according to Asbury. In the fray, the local "gentry fled away cackling falsehood like wild geese." The next day one of the rowdies had the preacher Anning Owen arrested for "*Sabbath breaking*, drunkenness and fighting." Even Asbury was charged with fighting, though he claimed he wasn't on the ground at the time. Given Asbury's aversion to public conflict and his frail health, it's hardly conceivable that he would have leaped into a brawl even had he been there. "All Earth and hell is roused against field meetings, but we will endure fines[,] imprisonment, and Death sooner than we will give them up," Asbury wrote to Stith Mead two weeks after the incident. Camp meetings were messy affairs, involving a number of risks, from runaway enthusiasm among the worshippers to violent attacks from rowdies. "These meetings exhibited nothing to the spectator unacquainted with them but a scene of confusion, such as scarcely could be put into human language," recalled one Methodist preacher. But they could also be scenes of sincere spiritual awakening and discovery, and for this Asbury willingly hazarded all other difficulties. When George Dougherty wrote from South Carolina's Camden district in the summer of 1805 that they had "all manner of...jerking, dancing, etc." Asbury could only comment, "yet the work goes on." "One thing appears to be certain," Jesse Lee later wrote, "that there never was a time among the Methodists, in any part of the United States, where so many professed to be converted in a few days."[23]

Why this revival at this time is a question observers generally answered in two ways. Participants who supported the awakening ascribed it to the merciful hand of God and the efforts of those who preached, prayed, and welcomed people into their homes. Given their Arminian theology, Methodists were comfortable with the idea that the revival was a cooperative effort between God and his people. Those who despised the revival tended to attribute it either to the devil or the work of delusional fanatics, a mirror image of the reasoning of the revival's supporters. Recalling his upbringing in Kentucky from 1785 to 1800, Daniel Drake described the Methodists he knew as "lamentably ignorant." "The high and disorderly excitement which characterized their worship was equally lamentable. Their camp meetings in the woods, which I sometimes attended, presented scenes of fanatical raving among the worshipers, and of levity and vice among the young men who hung about the camp."[24]

More recent observers have often explained the revival as the opening act of the Second Great Awakening. In this interpretation, the awakening is often depicted as beginning on the western frontier about 1800 and then moving east and north, culminating in the ministry of Charles Finney in upstate New York and along the Atlantic seaboard in the 1830s and 1840s. Some have seen the revival as a form of social control (the notion that religion can be used as a tool to surreptitiously control the unwashed masses), others as a response to conditions on the American frontier or the market revolution, and still others as an "isomorphic" congruence between popular religion and culture. The main problem with all of these explanations is that they obscure much of what Asbury and the Methodists actually did, primarily by assuming that Methodism was mostly experienced in short, violent bursts of "camp-meeting hysteria," as one author puts it.[25]

Interpretations linking Methodism to the early nineteenth-century frontier have been particularly influential in this regard. Following Frederick Jackson Turner's famous frontier thesis, historians long argued that the frontier created an environment uniquely receptive to camp meeting revivalism. A spate of books from the 1920s through the 1950s by William Warren Sweet (the dean of Methodist studies during this period who taught for two decades at the University of Chicago), Walter Brownlow Posey, Charles A. Johnson, Catharine Cleveland, Bernard A. Weisberger, and others placed the "Great Revival" of the early nineteenth century solidly on the frontier. The trans-Allegheny West was, in this interpretation, a scene of "brawling, debauchery, and drunkenness" (Johnson), where "every frontier community was a Sodom unredeemed" (Weisberger). Things might have continued this way if not for the Methodists, wielding the sword of the camp meeting. "Among all of the weapons forged by the West in its struggle against lawlessness and immorality, few were more successful than the frontier camp meeting. This socioreligious institution helped tame backwoods America," Johnson writes. Otherwise sophisticated studies in the 1960s and 1970s expanded this thesis to include "the South," but often still retained a focus on the frontier and camp meetings. More recent scholarship on southern religion and Methodism has taken a different turn, but the connection between the frontier and Methodism remains strong in textbooks and general histories.[26]

The problem with the frontier thesis is that most of the awakening didn't take place on the frontier. One center of the revival for Methodists was the Delmarva Peninsula and western shore of Maryland, an area long since settled. The proportion of American Methodists living on the peninsula jumped from 13 percent in 1800 to almost 19 percent in 1804, making it one of the church's fastest growing centers. Even most of the regions of Kentucky that were deeply involved in the revival were some twenty years removed from their initial phase of white settlement, as Ellen Eslinger has shown. Back in 1797, the itinerant John Kobler wondered whether it was worth it to go to Kentucky at all since "there is such a number of preachers there of all denominations, that I fear one so Insignificant as myself will be of no service" (Kobler went instead to Ohio in 1798). As the revival spread to southern Virginia, it encompassed regions settled several generations before that had already experienced awakenings in 1776 and 1787. There is simply no good reason to see this latest revival as fundamentally rooted in the frontier experience, at least as it took shape among Methodists.[27]

Nor is it the case that the revival fostered a sort of rugged individualism. In fact, one of the prerequisites for the revival seems to have been the formation of stable, settled communities. No organized religious group had much success in Kentucky in the 1790s, including the Baptists and Presbyterians. It wasn't until after two decades of settlement and the formation of stable communities that churches finally took root in much of the state. The revival also coincided with a marked decrease in the kind of Indian hostilities that Asbury had worried about during his western travels in the 1790s and a decline in violence in general. There seems little justification for arguing that the revival was a response to the loneliness and social deprivation of frontier life.[28]

Theories predicated on social control and the frontier fail to adequately account for Methodism in general and Asbury in particular. Part of the problem with Asbury is that he doesn't fit into familiar categories. He wasn't a dynamic public speaker like Charles Finney, Lorenzo Dow, or Peter Cartwright, nor was he an intellectual on par with New England's Timothy Dwight, Lyman Beecher, or the theologian Nathaniel W. Taylor. Yet, directly and indirectly, Asbury played a central role in the awakening's development. Indirectly, he helped guide Methodism through the difficult 1790s, keeping the circuit system intact, with its itinerant preachers, class meetings, quarterly meetings, heartfelt worship, communal cohesion, discipline, and emphasis on local initiative and lay leadership, against just the kind of opportunity that now appeared. More directly, Asbury strategically deployed the preachers, sending his most capable preachers where the prospects seemed brightest. His knowledge of the West, based on his travels and extensive correspondence network, made a quick response there possible. Recall that when a revival broke out on Tennessee's Cumberland circuit under John Page in 1799, Asbury reworked the 1800 appointments to keep Page there. Shortly afterward he made William McKendree, one of the church's rising stars, presiding elder over the Western conference. At the same time he placed other preachers in locations matched to their abilities: fearless George Dougherty in Charleston, eloquent George Roberts in Baltimore and then Philadelphia, indefatigable Thomas Smith and Learner Blackman on the Delmarva Peninsula (Blackman later moved to Kentucky), electrifying John Granade in Tennessee, and so on. All of this planning now paid off.

Asbury also publicized the revival from Georgia to Maine, Delaware to Tennessee, through his correspondence, collecting as many accounts of dramatic conversions and huge meetings as he could, and then reading them to congregations wherever he traveled. When he read accounts of the awakening in cities like New York, they had an electrifying effect on the people. This is another reason that Asbury badgered the presiding elders and circuit preachers to keep him informed of the revival's progress. No one had more extensive contacts throughout the nation, and no one was in a better position to shape public perception of the awakening. Unfortunately for Asbury, the success of the revival accelerated a process of subtle change within the church, eventually leaving him behind to defend abandoned ground.[29]

The revival also drew energy from the ecumenical cooperation of Methodists with Presbyterians, and to a lesser extent Baptists, which Asbury did all that he could to promote. Asbury, McKendree, and Whatcoat preached at a

Presbyterian sacramental gathering in October 1800, in the revival's early phase, presided over by some of the West's most influential Presbyterian ministers, including William Hodge, John Rankin, William McGee, and Thomas Craighead. Asbury later returned the favor by inviting Hodge and McGee to preach at the Western conference's annual meeting in Tennessee. Though they were never entirely comfortable with the Methodist presence, Presbyterians looked to Methodists for guidance on handling the falling, shouting, and weeping the revival produced. While in South Carolina in January 1801, Asbury received descriptions of the revival highlighting cooperation between Methodists and Presbyterians. He immediately wrote letters to Daniel Hitt, presiding elder of Virginia's Alexandria district, George Roberts in Baltimore, and Thomas Morrell, also still in Baltimore, informing them of the "most glorious work in Cumberland, in the Tennessee State, in the union of the Presbyterians and Methodists," which gave him "most animated pleasure and felicity." That fall Asbury received more accounts "of the revival of religion amongst the Presbyterians and Methodists in Cumberland," which he read to congregations wherever he went and passed along in letters to his many correspondents.[30]

Cooperation cost the Methodists little, while expanding their field of potential converts. For Presbyterians, the revival ultimately proved more problematic, with its implied Arminianism, raw emotional energy, and lack of focus on education. But for a brief season many Presbyterians in the West and South were willing to lock arms with the Methodists, an offer that Asbury gladly accepted. He enjoyed sharing meals and table talk with Presbyterian ministers who were friendly to the awakening. In Sparta, Georgia, in November 1801 Asbury encountered a "Presbyterian-Methodist woman" who "shouted and warned the Spartans to flee from the wrath to come" as he read a letter from James McGready to the congregation. Writing to a British correspondent in June 1803, Asbury claimed that "the Presbyterians, over half the Continent, are stirred up, and are in church and congregational union with the Methodists."[31]

Yet the "union" of Presbyterians and Methodists wasn't an entirely equal exchange. While Asbury and his preachers didn't set out to steal away nominal Presbyterians, it worked out that way more often than the reverse. Among Presbyterians "the walls of prejudice are falling," Asbury wrote to George Roberts in December 1802, with the result that "many young people and some elders come over to us." On another occasion near St. Matthews, South Carolina, he noted that while much of the local population were "originally . . . Dutch Presbyterians . . . many have joined the Methodists." He never had occasion to complain of the opposite.[32]

The Presbyterian orientation toward education and a calm, rational approach to all things religious soon drove a wedge between them and the
Methodists. "To all but the Methodists the work was entirely strange," James
Finley later recalled. After the initial revival wave, Asbury still sometimes met
with Presbyterian ministers, as when he "breakfasted with Rev. Mr. George
Newton, Presbyterian minister, a man after my own mind," on October 17,
1805, in North Carolina. But this became less frequent over time. "Friendship
and good fellowship seem to be done away with between the Methodists and
Presbyterians; few of the latter will attend our meetings now," Asbury noted
while in western Virginia in August 1806. "As to Presbyterian ministers . . . I
will treat them with great respect, but I shall ask no favours of them: to humble
ourselves before those who think themselves so much above the Methodist
preachers by worldly honours, by learning, and especially by salary, will do them
no good," Asbury added after meeting with several Presbyterian ministers in
Georgia that December. By 1809 his judgment of Presbyterians had become
even harsher: "O, the terrors of a camp meeting to those *men of pay and show.*"[33]

The Baptists were another story. From the start of the revival, there was
less cooperation and more direct competition between Methodists and Baptists. Methodist preachers across the West frequently complained that after
they had done the hard work of awakening sinners, Baptists would move in to
"reap the fruit." "As to John's people," (a play on John the Baptist's name) "they
are contrary to all people," Asbury complained in December 1802. No sooner
did "young people" get converted at Methodist meetings than the Baptists
came along to "sweep [them] into the water." In all fairness, each side poached
the other's converts. But it was the contentiousness and exclusivity of Baptists
that most annoyed Asbury, convincing him that Methodists needed to preach
more consistently on infant baptism and Christian perfection, the church's
signature doctrine.[34]

In the midst of this remarkable expansion, Asbury saw, or thought he
could see, a corresponding degree of Methodist unity. "I never saw the Connection more united and cheerful, and determined to go on while Liberty,
equality, and good order prevails, and the work of God goeth on with increasing
rapidity, in every Conference, District, and Circuit more or less," he wrote to
Ezekiel Cooper from New York in July 1805. "I am happy to find one spirit
animates the whole, for seventeen hundred miles: the same hymns, prayers,
and language salute my ears and heart," he wrote to Daniel Hitt later that
month. The revival spread Methodist culture more uniformly across the nation, expanding communication networks and mobilizing a new wave of
converts.[35]

20

Limits

The revival in the Chesapeake and the West was immensely satisfying for Asbury, but it introduced new complexities as the church continued to expand. In 1789 he had fewer than two hundred itinerant preachers in a dozen states. Now he had nearly four hundred traveling preachers in some twenty states and territories, including a large new component west of the Appalachian Mountains. Dividing and managing the work would have been difficult enough in good health, but Asbury and Whatcoat were both ailing. At the Western conference, held in the Cumberland region of Tennessee in October 1802, Asbury couldn't walk, and his "stomach and speech were pretty well gone." He had himself bled three times and on October 8, following the advice of a local doctor, applied bandages with "sugar of lead" (a toxic form of lead acetate that acts as an astringent) to his feet. The next day he "was attacked in the knee with a most torturing pain, attended with a swelling." The pain in his knee and feet brought on "a powerful rheumatic shock, such as I never had in my life." Incapacitated, he left William McKendree to examine and station the preachers. Following the conference, Asbury dispatched John Watson to meet Nicholas Snethen and send him to Georgia to fulfill his appointments there. Though in excruciating pain, he then pushed on through the backcountry of eastern Tennessee, determined to make the South Carolina conference meeting at Camden on January 1, 1803. McKendree traveled part of the way with him, lifting Asbury to and from his horse "like a helpless child."[1]

By day he could only preach by kneeling on a chair, and by night he could sleep only after taking laudanum, a tincture of opium. He may have developed an addiction to laudanum if he took it daily for more than a week at a time (his journal is unclear). If so, the narcotic withdrawal symptoms he would have experienced after quitting might explain some of his periodic complaints, including intestinal cramping and diarrhea. On occasion he also took patent medicines containing opium, including Bateman's Drops, which he obtained in western Virginia in May 1796 along with paregoric, another tincture of opium. All of this was quite common at the time. Doctors regularly prescribed opium, and the word addiction hadn't yet taken on its modern connotation.[2]

Spending much of the winter in South Carolina allowed Asbury to recover somewhat, but his health was still fragile as he set out for the north in February 1803. By the time he arrived in Philadelphia in May, he was "in a low state of bodily health," according to Richard Whatcoat. He nevertheless completed an ambitious circuit that year, taking in the Virginia conference in March, the Baltimore conference in April, the New England conference at Boston in June, the New York conference at Ashgrove in July, and the Western conference, north of Lexington, Kentucky, in October. He held up fairly well for most of the tour until he came down with "wasting dysentery," probably contracted from contaminated food or water, near Strasburg, Pennsylvania. Yet his pace hardly slackened. For relief he used wine, barks, and some "most excellent laudanum." Before crossing into Kentucky, he took his first extended tour of Ohio, a state that would figure prominently in Methodism's future development. At the Kentucky conference, he formed the Ohio circuits into a district and sent two missionaries to Natchez, Mississippi, and one to Illinois, places he would never see.[3]

While Asbury's health generally held out for most of 1803, Richard Whatcoat wasn't so fortunate. At age sixty-seven, he had ridden more than 3,700 miles during the past year. Whatcoat and Asbury traveled together for much of the spring and summer of 1803 until July, at Philadelphia, when it became apparent that Whatcoat couldn't go on. He had blood in his urine, the result, he suspected, of "gravel," or granular deposits of mineral salts, somewhat smaller than so-called kidney stones. To go on would be to "die by inches," according to Asbury. Following Asbury's advice, Whatcoat slowly made his way to Baltimore, where he remained from August 1803 to July 1804, usually only preaching once on Sundays. Whatcoat's latest setback almost guaranteed that new proposals would be floated at the upcoming General Conference to deal with the church's growing administrative complexity, something that Asbury anticipated with a measure of dread.[4]

Coke returned from Britain for the General Conference, sailing from England on September 21, 1803, and arriving in Norfolk, Virginia, at the end of October. Shortly before leaving for America, he wrote to Ezekiel Cooper, "The Lord has opened my way wonderfully & clearly (I was going to say, that he is written it on my mind as with a Sunbeam) to be wholly yours." One reason he now felt content to stay in America permanently was that God had "endued" the British Conference with "the True Missionary Spirit" to the point that they could be counted on to support the West Indies missions in Coke's absence. "I am now going to spend the remainder of my life with you," Coke wrote. He repeated this pledge shortly after his arrival in a letter to Richard Whatcoat. "I am now come to be yours entirely. Every shackle, every engagement, every obligation, in Europe, has been loosed or discharged; and my destination for life on this Continent is written by the Lord as clearly as if it was with a Sunbeam." His luggage certainly gave the impression that he was serious about staying. He brought "nineteen chests, boxes, & trunks, containing all my papers, most important books, &c."[5]

Yet, as was often the case, Coke hedged his bet. He was understandably more wary of his reception in America than his letters to Cooper and Whatcoat let on. Prior to his departure from England, he wrote to Alexander Sturgeon in Sligo, Ireland, assuring him "In respect to my return to Europe, I can only say to you what I said the other day to the English Conference ... that nothing will keep me in America but the clearest and most indubitable light that it is the will of God I should remain on that Continent." Coke asked Sturgeon to move the date of the Irish conference to the second week of July, so that he would have time to return to Ireland after the General Conference in Baltimore if he so decided. "Nothing but an indubitable assurance that the will of God requires me to continue there [in America], shall prevent my return," Coke assured another English correspondent.[6]

After learning of Coke's arrival, Asbury proposed that he take a 5,000-mile tour of the seven annual conferences, which would have carried him through the summer. This essentially was what Asbury did each year, if his health permitted. Coke had other ideas. He had already written to Whatcoat that he hoped to finish his *Commentary on the New Testament* (he had made arrangements with a printer in London to publish it before leaving for America) prior to the General Conference. To accomplish this, he planned to spend most of the intervening six months in Baltimore. "I must so contrive my Plan till the General Conference, that I may have a great deal of time to spend in retirement in order to finish," Coke wrote. Yet, after further consideration, he realized that it wouldn't look good for him to remain entirely in Baltimore. A sudden "impression" that he "should go to Georgia, to meet Bishop Asbury at the Georgia Conference ... completely robbed me of a night's rest." Two days later he set off for Georgia, surprising Asbury, who didn't know that he was coming, in Augusta.[7]

The meeting in Georgia was pivotal, and it didn't go well. Coke later claimed, in a public circular letter, that he was "amazed . . . to find, that every thing was in the same situation" as on his previous visit. "So far from my having any opportunity of strengthening the Episcopacy, according to your solemn engagements . . . when you accepted me as one of your Bishops, I was not consulted on the station of a single Preacher." Coke claimed that he wasn't even allowed to see the appointments at the close of the conference. "I then saw the will of God concerning me—that I ought not to labour in America, unless the General Conference would consent to comply in some degree with its engagements." He reiterated that he had no desire to take Asbury's place. "But every Bishop ought to have a right of giving his judgment on every point, or he is but the shadow of a Bishop." His treatment in America was especially galling since in Europe "my judgment has considerable regard paid to it." Coke concluded with his oft-repeated statement that he wouldn't "spend my life in America . . . *merely* to preach."[8]

Had Coke been willing to serve a kind of apprenticeship under Asbury, as Whatcoat had done, in time he might have become Asbury's equal in the church. But Coke was a gentleman, not an apprentice. Asbury had divided the work nearly equally with Whatcoat before the latter's health broke, and he increasingly relied on trusted elders to station the preachers when he couldn't attend an annual conference because of his own fragile health. "If I must bear the burden now laid upon me, I can call forth men of our own to help me, in or out of conference, men that know men and things by long experience," Asbury wrote to Daniel Hitt in January 1804, following the Georgia conference. With patience Coke might have won Asbury's trust, and that of the preachers more generally, but patience was never Coke's long suit, as it was for Whatcoat.[9]

Asbury sensed almost immediately after the Georgia conference that Coke would return to Europe. Following the conference, Coke reluctantly set off from Charleston, South Carolina, for a tour of New England before the General Conference. At the same time Asbury wrote to Daniel Hitt that Coke "cannot well be spared from the Irish and English Connection without irreparable damage; and I suppose he is better fitted for the whirl of public life, than to be hidden in our woods." Other observers came to the same conclusion. Isaac Robbins wrote to Hitt that he had the "satisfaction" of meeting Coke and hearing him preach in Fredericksburg, Maryland, in February, while Coke was on his way to Boston. "Brother Essex & myself rather suspect . . . by the answer he makes, when any one asks him with respect to his future residing with us, that he contemplates on returning to England," Robbins speculated. Whatever else the General Conference might do with regard to the episcopacy, Coke wouldn't be part of the equation.[10]

The 1804 General Conference, which convened on May 7, was more contentious and accomplished less than any of the previous quadrennial conferences, though it set some important precedents for the future. Of the 204 eligible preachers (those who had traveled at least four years), only 111 or 112 attended, more than half of whom were from the Baltimore and Philadelphia conferences. The New England, Western, and South Carolina conferences sent only twelve delegates between them. By the end of the two-week gathering, only seventy preachers remained. Asbury said little and Whatcoat said even less. He only spoke once, to "recommend the suppression of passion or ill-will in debate." Coke was more loquacious, speaking on a wide range of issues.[11]

The low point of the conference was a tedious paragraph-by-paragraph revision of the *Discipline*, during which many of the preachers gave up and left town. Intermixed with these tiresome proceedings were a number of votes on measures with far-reaching consequences. A motion by George Dougherty was passed prohibiting itinerant preachers from remaining on the same circuit for more than two years, as Asbury had sometimes allowed married preachers and others with special needs to do (a motion to recognize these special needs was defeated). The conference voted to move the Book Concern, which now had a net worth of $27,000, to New York City, whereupon Ezekiel Cooper resigned as editor. He was reelected anyway. Cooper had worked wonders with the book business, and by 1807 it had a net worth of more than $59,000. Growing Methodist prosperity, the recent revival, and friendlier relations with other denominations worked to open new markets. "If you had a Thousand more [books] to send into every District than you have sent they would soon be sold," Asbury had assured Cooper back in December 1801. "The Presbyterians, and others will purchase our Books." The profits from the book business were regularly tapped to make up for shortfalls at the annual conferences, as was the Chartered Fund, which remained in Philadelphia.[12]

The conference also took up the perennially divisive issue of slavery, but reached no easy consensus. After "a variety of motions" and "long conversation," Freeborn Garrettson proposed "that the subject of slavery be left to the three bishops, to form a section to suit the southern and northern states, as they in their wisdom may think best." The motion passed, but Asbury refused to go along. He knew he couldn't please everyone and risked charges of tyranny if he tried. How could an episcopal decree with any teeth in it succeed where so many previous efforts had failed? The conference should have known better. All else having failed, they naturally formed a committee, consisting of George Dougherty, Philip Bruce, William Burke, Henry Willis, Ezekiel Cooper, Freeborn Garrettson, and Thomas Lyell. Most of the members of this group had at

one time been dedicated abolitionists, but they failed to do anything of significance. Instead, the conference voted to suspend the rules on slavery in North
Carolina, South Carolina, and Georgia, and to print a separate version of the
Discipline without the rules on slavery for the southernmost states. "I think
never did a General Conference sit longer with more ado, and do less; and
perhaps the less the better," Asbury wrote when it was all over. He suspected
that Coke would be back in America in less than a year, but he was wrong. Coke
never returned.[13]

"If they want to go, let them go"

On June 2, 1804, Asbury's horse, Jane, was "horned by a cow, and lamed" at
Radnor, Pennsylvania. Jane's injury meant that she had to be left behind, which
he regretted. He loved his horses, named them, and cared for them as best he
could. Besides, "supple joynted Jane" represented "half of my personal estate."
After buying a new horse for $80, he rode to Philadelphia where he discovered
that Richard Allen had heard about Jane and bought him a horse for $90. Not
needing two horses, he sold one at a loss for $60. Jane recovered, but too late
for this tour, though Asbury later got her back. He wasn't so fortunate with
Spark. Asbury was forced to sell the horse in 1811 when he went lame in
Pennsylvania. As Asbury left Spark for the last time, "he whickered after us;
it went to my heart." Asbury's attachment to his horses wasn't unusual among
Methodist preachers. When William Ormond was forced to sell his horse in
1803 because he was moving to a city station, he took comfort from the belief
that they would be reunited at "the G[eneral]. Resurrection[,] then I shall
(I believe) see him in an immortal State never more to suffer."[14]

Leaving Philadelphia for the New York conference in June and the New
England conference in July, Asbury learned that George Roberts might refuse
to take his appointment in Baltimore. Roberts had entered the traveling
connection in 1789, serving from 1791 to 1794 in New England. In 1795 he
moved to New York City, where he remained first as a presiding elder and then
a preacher until 1799, when Asbury finally moved him to Annapolis and then
Baltimore. Roberts had "stayed an unwarrantable time in New York," Asbury
wrote to Ezekiel Cooper in June 1799, because no other station except Baltimore could support him. Writing later that month to two prominent Baltimore
Methodists, Asbury admitted that because Roberts was married, he would "be
more expensive than a single man," but Asbury assured them that "his address
will command a congregation, and draw support." Indeed, after hearing Roberts preach at the 1796 General Conference, William Colbert described him

as "an excellent speaker." According to Thomas Morrell, Roberts' colleague in Baltimore in 1800, he "was one of the most excellent of men. I think superior in every point of view to any I had ever been stationed with."

Roberts got on well with Maryland Methodists from the start, but he still had trouble maintaining his family. Still he didn't blame Asbury for his troubles. What else could the bishop have done? "We do not feel a murmer in our hearts against the providence of God," Roberts wrote to a friend in November 1799. "Why should we, when the least that we enjoy is infinitely more then we deserve [?]" Eventually, however, the pressures of raising a family on an itinerant's salary wore Roberts down. Asbury sent him to Philadelphia in 1802, where he wanted to stay, but the new two-year rule prohibited Asbury from leaving Roberts there in 1804. Besides, Asbury had already made other appointments for Philadelphia. "How many stock bricks must I take out of the wall before it is finished?" he asked Roberts. Instead, Asbury sent Roberts back to Baltimore. Roberts went, but only reluctantly. "George the first has just arrived with all the Royal family," wrote Thomas Sargent, another Baltimore preacher, when Roberts arrived in July 1804. Roberts must have heard a lot of this sort of sarcasm. While in Philadelphia, he had met Benjamin Rush, who advised him to study medicine. After his two-year appointment in Baltimore, Roberts located in Philadelphia in 1806 to practice medicine and presumably avoid another transfer and more complaints about his family, despite Asbury's best efforts to keep him in the itinerancy. "Perhaps it is best to let alone G. Roberts," Asbury wrote to Daniel Hitt, Roberts's presiding elder, in July 1805. "If they want to go, let them go . . . let us have volunteers."[15]

Though Roberts didn't quit until 1806, his discontent was evident in 1804, presaging a string of high-visibility defections. During the General Conference, Asbury had suspected that Thomas Lyell planned to leave the church to become an Episcopalian. No sooner had Asbury dealt with Roberts than a letter arrived from Lyell indicating as much (Lyell was ordained in the Episcopal Church on June 14, 1804, by Bishop Thomas Claggett of Maryland). Two months later, when he returned from New England, Asbury heard that Lyell had become rector of Joseph Pilmore's old congregation in New York City, two blocks from the John Street Methodist Church, at £450 a year. Lyell's salary was actually £500 a year plus a house, though he felt cheated when he discovered that Pilmore had made £600. At any rate, it was more than the $80 a year he was entitled to as a Methodist preacher. Now able to support a family with ease, Lyell married on April 15, 1805, and settled into a long tenure in New York City. "So, farewell to Tommy Lyell!" Asbury wrote.

As had been the case with George Roberts, Asbury had gone out of his way to keep Lyell, who was a graceful and urbane preacher, in the connection. "He

[Lyell] is a man of so much address that for many years [he] hath obtained that indulgence from the episcopacy, and people, no other man hath had," Asbury wrote to Epaphras Kibby shortly after Lyell's resignation. Lyell had also been one of the most frequent speakers at the General Conference only weeks before—no one save Thomas Coke and Ezekiel Cooper took a more public role in the conference proceedings—and had served on three important committees even as, it now appeared, he made plans to leave the connection. The spring after Lyell left the church, Ralph Williston did the same. Like Lyell, Williston had actively participated in the 1804 General Conference and, like Lyell, he became an Episcopal minister, eventually taking a church in New York City begun by another former Methodist preacher, George Strebeck, in the 1790s.

Asbury tried to put a positive spin on this trend and distance himself from it. "When any man leaveth our connection he leaves the conference, not me, I would not have it thought I am any thing in the business," he wrote to Ezekiel Cooper in July 1805. Asbury only regretted, or so he told Cooper, that departing preachers "should loose [lose] their first love; and give the world cause to say the methodist preachers will be bought with money as well as others. [F]or my part, I am glad they are gone, and so the judicious part, preachers and people, will say[,] let them go, and welcome." But it wasn't so easy, and Asbury knew it. Though seventy new preachers joined the traveling connection in 1804, forty-two located, two were expelled, and four died, yielding a net increase of only twenty-two. "Some want to localize the Connection, but find themselves disappointed and fly like Lyell and Williston, or locate like others, that cannot always be indulged," Asbury complained to Jacob Gruber in July 1807.[16]

Asbury wasn't the only one to sense the danger here. "I suppose the plain truth is this, he wishes to be greater, than the Methodists wish him to be," Enoch George wrote of Ralph Williston in August 1805. What if Lyell and Williston represented only the beginning of a trend that would continually rob the church of its seasoned and most competent preachers? In its early days the church had been shunned and even persecuted by more respectable churches. Now the Methodists were paying for their success as these same churches poached their most polished preachers. "I would wish my good Bro. that you would abide fast by the traveling connexion, for a great many of the old pillars have already given it up, and if all of them should desert it [the church] will totter and fall," Samuel Coate wrote to Ezekiel Cooper in March 1805. Coate himself had been "strongly solicited to settle down and take a parish close by my father in laws, where there is a church and no minister as yet." He knew he could command a substantial salary if he left, but "It is no temptation to me as long as I am able to act the part of a traveling preacher . . . rest, and ease, are desirable things but where we must purchase them at the expense of letting our little ark totter and perhaps fall they are dearly purchased." As a married preacher, Coate understood the pressure to settle down at a comfortable salary. He also realized that Cooper was just the kind of preacher that a respectable urban church would covet. In the end, however, it was Coate who left, locating in 1810, while Cooper remained in the ministry for another forty years. The problem of veteran preachers leaving to join more socially prominent churches made it that much more difficult for Asbury to battle the creeping affluence he now saw infecting the preachers.[17]

"Nothing is hidden"

Returning from New England, Asbury made his way into western Pennsylvania by the end of August 1804. There Richard Whatcoat caught up with him, having ridden slowly west from Baltimore after the General Conference. "I am so weary withall; I cannot write sense," Asbury confessed in the middle of a rambling, nearly incoherent letter to Daniel Hitt on August 22. After leaving Uniontown and crossing the Monongahela River, he contracted a "burning fever" and "most inveterate cough," leaving a thirty-four-day gap in his journal. He used emetics twice and had himself bled and blistered four times, which did him little good. Local Methodists "despaired" of his life, as James Henthorn wrote to Hitt. In the midst of his sickness, Asbury "was led into the visions of God; I shouted his praise."

Whatcoat stayed with Asbury through his illness, expecting to accompany him west when he recovered. The two set out for Ohio on October 10, though Asbury still wasn't well. Whatcoat, ailing himself, was unable to ride "at a greater speed than a walk," so Asbury exchanged his gentler mare for Whatcoat's larger horse. But the "great beast jolted me in such a manner as I could not have borne in health: I was pressed above measure, so that I despaired of life, or health." The road ahead looked dismal. On their present course, they still had a journey of 1,500 miles before reaching Charleston, South Carolina, in December.[18]

Whatcoat and Asbury were only eleven days along when Asbury again came down with a fever, forcing him to turn back. Acting as "my own doctor," he decided to "breakfast upon eight grains of ipecacuanha," or syrup of ipecac, an emetic and expectorant that "cleansed my filthy stomach, and so broke up my disease that a fever of fifty days fled." Asbury may have been suffering from amebiasis, an intestinal parasitic infection caused by drinking contaminated water, which can result in liver abscesses, fevers, and night sweats. Syrup of ipecac contains emetine that could have broken his fever by killing off the amoebas in his intestinal wall and liver. Unfortunately, emetine can damage the heart, contributing to his progressive congestive heart failure. A hacking cough still tormented him at night. Since Asbury couldn't continue, Whatcoat resolutely set out "wandering alone through the wilderness," according to Asbury. Mostly blind by this time, Whatcoat crossed southern Ohio to Chillicothe and then proceeded south across the Ohio River into Kentucky. By early November he had reached Lexington, and the following month he was in South Carolina.[19]

Asbury now gave up on accomplishing much for the remainder of the year other than reaching Charleston alive. Crossing into Virginia in early November, he attended a quarterly meeting at Newtown (now Stephens City), where "above all, I wished to see Daniel Hitt," presiding elder of Baltimore district. Asbury needed to ask Hitt for traveling money, since he was down to his last two dollars. He also gave Hitt a letter concerning next year's Baltimore conference (scheduled for April 1805), in case Asbury himself couldn't attend. The letter authorized Hitt to "preside in the Conference as I have done, and do all things with a single eye to the glory of God. Admit, examine, elect, and station the preachers." A postscript reminded Hitt to "*Mark well!* Should Bishop Whatcoat be present, his want of sight is such, he cannot preside, but he will be as counsellor, and may ordain." Once again Whatcoat was reduced to a subordinate position, this time by his health. Whatcoat and Asbury met in South Carolina at the end of the year, both in better health than when they had parted. Each was surprised to see the other alive.[20]

The church's sudden expansion was like being driven before a storm, but it was better than sitting becalmed in a sullen sea. Asbury's role in this expansion increasingly came down to managing the conferences. But even here he left much of the detail to the preachers themselves. The 1805 Virginia conference, typical of the many Asbury presided over during these years, opened with twenty-seven preachers present (four of whom arrived late), plus the two bishops. Financially, the conference finished the year owing the preachers $507.30 in unpaid allowances, $449.39 of which was made up from various sources, including $120 drawn for the Chartered Fund and $100 from the Book Concern. Annual conferences frequently had to deal with accusations brought against preachers, and this one was no exception. One of the first orders of business was to deal with the case of James Taylor, who was still traveling on trial when he fell into debt. Telling his presiding elder in North Carolina that he wished to return to the Virginia conference, Taylor instead "went courting from place to place, till at length he got a wife." Learning this, the conference dropped Taylor, leaving him without an appointment for the coming year. Next, Enoch Jones's presiding elder, Alexander M'Caine, brought "charges" against Jones for "obstinate conduct, and improper language to him." This was Jones's first year of circuit preaching, and evidently he was having a difficult time adjusting. The conference agreed that Jones should "be call'd in & talk'd to before the Conference," after which a "large majority" voted that he should remain on trial. Notice that it was the conference as a whole, not Asbury alone, that decided Jones's fate, a pattern repeated at other conferences.[21]

Less than a month later, Whatcoat and Asbury attended the Baltimore conference, which had a similar set of disputes to iron out. In one of these cases the conference appointed a committee of five preachers to "hear & examine" a complaint brought against William Brandon. After "weighing the evidence and circumstances," the committee unanimously found Brandon "guilty" of "unchristian & immodest conduct towards two young women" and later changing his story. The conference expelled Brandon, without comment from Asbury.[22]

Though Asbury attended nearly all of the annual conferences, surviving minutes indicate that he never dominated their proceedings. In 1802, with Whatcoat and Asbury present, the Virginia conference heard complaints that Jeremiah King had "neglected his appointments & . . . was seen huging the young women & also Given too much to a spirit of Levity." A committee, not including Whatcoat or Asbury (who were both present), determined King "Culpable, & directed that one of the Bishops should reprove him before the Conference, Which was done," though it isn't clear whether Whatcoat or Asbury did the reproving. (If Whatcoat, it's difficult to imagine anything too severe, though his saintly demeanor may have been rebuke enough.) King continued to travel and preach in the Virginia conference until he located in 1805, perhaps marrying one of the young women he was so fond of embracing. The year after King's case, the conference received "second hand" information "that Br. Thomas Fletcher sold a Negro." Fletcher was leaving the traveling connection to locate anyway and wasn't present at the conference, but the sale of a slave by an itinerant preacher was still a serious matter. His case was tabled "untill the matter can be clear'd up," though subsequent minutes give no further details. The larger point is that the conference as a whole took part in adjudicating disciplinary cases. Asbury's opinion presumably carried weight, but he seems rarely to have controlled conference deliberations.[23]

The 1805 Virginia conference also admitted fourteen new preachers on the recommendation of their quarterly meetings and approved the requests of four preachers to quit traveling and locate. Prospective itinerants were expected to bring a recommendation from their local quarterly meeting. In most cases applicants had already served as class leaders, licensed exhorters, or local preachers. The conference as a whole then examined the candidate and voted on whether or not to admit him to the traveling connection. Once again, the decision wasn't Asbury's alone, and, if the conference minutes are a fair indication, he often said little during these discussions. Outside of the circuit appointments, his was more of a partnership with the preachers and people than his critics allowed. Who did or did not become a circuit rider was left largely to the preachers as a body to decide. Their decisions, in turn, were largely determined by who the quarterly meetings chose to recommend to the annual conferences. If the people of a society or circuit didn't approve of a young man's abilities, he wasn't likely to ever appear before an annual conference. In this way Methodists got the preachers they wanted, or deserved.[24]

"Awful as death"

Just before the New England conference in July 1805, Asbury received a letter from Thomas Coke "announcing to me his marriage, and advising me, that he did not intend to visit America again as a visitor." Coke would return, Asbury wrote to Stith Mead, only "if his work can be pointed out and all be made safe and easy before he comes." "Marriage is honourable in all—but to me it is a ceremony awful as death," Asbury wrote, in one of his better-known journal entries, the day he received Coke's announcement. "Well may it be so, when I calculate we have lost the travelling labours of two hundred of the best men in America, or the world, by marriage and subsequent location." At the 1804 General Conference Asbury had guessed that Coke would soon marry, and now it had happened. Coke promised that he would no longer be a burden on the connection's finances, from which Asbury guessed that his new wife was "a lady of fortune." Coke's marriage set in motion the endgame of his connection to the American church.[25]

At fifty-seven, Coke had married Penelope Goulding Smith, heir to a substantial fortune, as Asbury surmised. They met in the fall of 1804, while Coke was collecting money for overseas missions, and were married the following April 1 in front of fifteen hundred people. "I am almost too happy in the possession of my God and my Penelope," Coke wrote to Samuel Bradburn four days after the wedding. "We love each other as much as, I think, two created Beings ought—I was almost going to say *can*." By all accounts it was a happy marriage. In her mid-forties when they married, Penelope Coke was cheerfully committed to traveling with her husband. They bought a carriage into which they stuffed piles of luggage and from which they tossed religious pamphlets to people on the streets. But Penelope's health was fragile, and Thomas knew there were limits as to what she could endure, especially with regards to crossing the Atlantic. A month after his marriage he wrote to Whatcoat that if he returned to America during Asbury's lifetime, "it will be necessary for the plan of our Episcopal labours to be fixed *on a permanent & unalterable basis.*"[26]

Coke continued his campaign to get a clear mandate from the American church with a June 1, 1805, circular letter sent to preachers across the connection. In it Coke rehearsed his understanding of the commitments made on both sides. He then proposed that he and Asbury divide the seven annual conferences "betwixt us, three and four, and four and three, each of us changing our division annually." As to his recent marriage, Coke assured the American preachers that "my wife is one of the best of women: she breathes the genuine spirit of a Christian pilgrim, and would go with me anywhere, yea, through fire and water." But he added a caveat: "The constitution of my beloved wife is a very delicate one. . . . She has been indeed brought up in a most tender and delicate manner, and therefore needs conveniences through life, which others not brought up in the same tender way have no need of." Almost as an afterthought Coke added that he didn't intend "to derogate, in the smallest degree, from the worth and integrity of my old, venerable, and worthy friend, Bishop Whatcoat." But he could see little meaningful role for the feeble elder bishop.[27] Most of the preachers hardly knew Coke outside his participation at the quadrennial general conferences, where he had often seemed of two minds regarding America. What were they to make of his offer?

Unfortunately for Coke, not much. One after another, the annual conferences sent replies to Coke "in a manner that will not please him," as Asbury put it. These responses were drawn up by committees, none of which included Asbury, and approved by each conference as a whole. In March 1806 the Baltimore conference appointed a "select committee" of five preachers, Daniel Hitt, Alexander M'Caine, George Roberts, Enoch George, and Nelson Reed, to reply to Coke. The lengthy letter they drafted left little doubt where they stood. "Notwithstanding your declarations that you have never broken your engagements to us in the smallest instance, we think you have widely departed from them," the committee wrote. Despite promises to "make America your home," once back in England Coke had "entered into" conflicting "engagements, without our knowledge or consent." "Our Discipline is as binding on the Bishops as it is upon the other Orders among us, and we think no Preacher ought to desert his post without being accountable to his brethren." Coke's proposal to divide the annual conferences with Asbury represented a dangerous "innovation" that would wound "the Itinerancy in the vitals," and weaken "the Machine in one of its main springs." Coke seemed to think that a bishop's authority was irrevocable, or nearly so, but the Baltimore conference said otherwise. "It is not our wish to debar any of our Bishops or Preachers from entering into matrimonial or other engagements if they think it right; but if they do, and thereby disable themselves from serving us in the respective relations, it is a right which we hold sacred, and which we will not voluntarily give up that we will dismiss them from those relations and cho[o]se others to fill their place."[28]

Coke believed that he and Asbury were equals in the episcopacy (though not Whatcoat), but the conference disagreed. "We think it our duty to inform you that in case of the death of Bishop Asbury, we do not believe the General Conference would ever invest any man with the same power," the conference stated. "He has been with us from the beginning... and in every instance he has conducted himself as such in adversity and prosperity—in fulness and want: he knew us when we were scarcely a people, and he has travel'd on with us through all our difficulties and dangers without ever flinching, till we have become more than One Hundred Thousand in number." What a contrast to Coke. From the preachers' perspective, Asbury's authority was based largely on his unparalleled record of service, the nature of which no one could ever duplicate. The conferences' replies to Coke made it clear that no one, not even Asbury, could "desert his post," and still remain in power. It was the General Conference, and not the bishops, who wielded the ultimate authority. Wesley had never allowed anything of the sort, and Coke had yet to grasp that things were different in America.[29]

It is a wonder that Coke continued to press his case, but he did. He responded during 1806 and 1807 with a series of letters to the annual conferences largely expanding on explanations and grievances from his earlier correspondence. In a letter to the Baltimore and Philadelphia conferences, dated January 6, 1807, Coke reiterated that "My dearest wife... can bear travelling... five thousand miles a year; & I can bear to travel 10,000 miles annually." This was clearly an exaggeration—even in good health Asbury could only manage about 5,000 miles a year—and the American preachers knew it. After all, they spent their lives traveling. Coke also felt it necessary to reminded the preachers that "in the circumstances in which the Lord has been pleased to place me I could not, as the Servant of Christ, sacrifice my considerable influence in Europe for a Sphere comparatively so small as that of a mere preacher in America." What were mere preachers supposed to make of this? Coke seemed unaware that his high-handed tone might offend. He understood the constitutional hierarchy of American Methodist polity, but not the democratic spirit that underlay it. Where Coke demanded his rights before he would serve, Americans expected him to earn his authority as a product of his service, as Asbury had always done. "As to Doctor Coke's business; I think it is time to talk strong & plain too, & let the good Doctor know that Americans are men of sentiment and principles," the preacher James Quinn wrote in May 1806.[30]

As Coke's stock fell, Asbury predicted that the next General Conference would consider "dissolving the union with Doctor Coke." Coke was getting what he deserved, but Asbury was characteristically reluctant to see him go. "Can we ever forget the days and nights we have sweetly spent together; spirits sweetly joined, and not a jar," he wrote to Coke in May 1806. "You have never had more undissembled friendship shown to you than in America." Yet Asbury was unwilling and unable to give Coke what he wanted: unwilling because he didn't believe that Coke was adequately prepared to lead the American preachers and unable because the preachers didn't trust Coke. Two months later, Asbury wrote to Bennet Kendrick, "Dr. Coke has made proposals to serve the connection on a different ground, the conferences, all that have heard, have rejected the Doctor's letter . . . every conference has written. Nothing is hidden." On the contrary, to Coke America now seemed wrapped in an impenetrable fog.[31]

The Trouble with Marriage

Coke had been right about one thing. Providing for married preachers remained a challenge, compounding the already critical shortage of competent itinerants, particularly in New England, the West, and the South. This wasn't a new problem, of course, but every year it seemed to get worse. Writing from the Virginia conference in February 1802, Asbury fretted that "Portsmouth, Bertie, Roanoke, Haw River, Guilford, and Salisbury [circuits] should each have an additional preacher, if we had them; yea, Petersburg, Hanover, Williamsburg, and Richmond also; but the Lord hath not sent them, and how can we make them?" Complaints like this appear regularly in his journal and letters from this period, the shortages magnified by the flood of new converts joining the church in the post-1799 revivals. "We have about forty traveling preachers in the South Conference; and we want fifty, we have about forty in the Virginia Conference, and we want sixty," Asbury wrote to the preacher Bennet Kendrick in January 1804.[32]

Earlier in his career, Asbury had preferred that his itinerants remain single, leading some to later conclude that he was a misogynist, jealous that his preachers not be contaminated by contact with women. The reality is less sinister and more complex. It wasn't women, but the cost of supporting married preachers that he feared. "Marriage is an holy and honorable station," Asbury wrote to the preacher Thomas Sargent in January 1804, but it usually required a preacher to locate. "Thus, when, for the time, we should have age and experience in the ministry, we have youth and inexperience; and such have charge—this, not of choice, but necessity," Asbury commented in 1803 to James Quinn, who was himself considering marriage.[33]

Since young men and women showed no inclination to quit marrying in these relatively prosperous times (Quinn married a few weeks after his conversation with Asbury), something had to change. The church had to find the means to support more married preachers. "Many will, and perhaps ought to marry, and to Continue in the work," Asbury advised the veteran preacher Thomas Morrell in February 1801. By the spring of 1802 Asbury estimated that there were fifty married preachers in the connection, "some with three others with five and some with Eight or Ten children." Unable to come up with enough money, the annual conferences were often "too much afraid of employing married preachers," Asbury wrote, "but it must, it will be done." There was no other choice. Finding adequate housing and support for married preachers increasingly occupied Asbury's time in the coming years.[34]

The problem of married itinerants went deeper than the issue of financial support alone, as Asbury knew. Except for a few who were stationed in cities, married itinerants had to "stretch their loves," as Asbury put it, leaving their families for weeks or months at a time to ride their circuits. Consider the case of Richard Sneath. After receiving his appointment to New Jersey's Bethel circuit at the Philadelphia conference meeting in June 1798, Sneath "set out for home but with forebodings of sorrow." His wife, he knew, would be furious that he had decided to preach another year. In this he "was not deceived." Arriving home, he discovered that she had already learned "that I intended traveling again" and "was in a fury." Sneath left a few days later for his circuit. Though his farm near Radnor, Pennsylvania, located about 12 miles northwest of Philadelphia, was only a day's ride from some parts of his circuit, he didn't return home again until September. When he did, he cut his foot with an ax while chopping wood with his sons, requiring eleven weeks of convalescence for the wound to heal. This period of "confinement was a very great trial to me," Sneath wrote. "The circuit lay heavy on my mind." He left for his circuit in late November 1798, not returning home again until the following April and then again in June. He never really enjoyed farming, and when home he spent much of his time thinking about his circuit appointments. "This [farming] is not my eliment," Sneath reflected while home haying on one occasion. "My mind is not so well satisfied in anything as the work of the ministry." In the meantime, his wife and sons kept the farm running well enough to survive.[35]

Whether or not his wife was a Methodist isn't clear, but she certainly didn't like Sneath's long absences, and his family suffered from his neglect. When home in June 1799, he recounted that his "soul" was "very much distress[ed] by the turbulance and ill humor of my wife." Still, the couple got along well enough to conceive a son when Sneath next returned for eleven days in late October and early November 1799. More difficult times soon followed. Hearing that his family "was sick and out of order," he returned home in February 1800, and was "alarmed at seeing my daughter laid to bed with a son in her arms[;] what a distress to parents to see there children take bad ways." Apparently Sneath hadn't even known that his daughter was pregnant. Though "in much trouble of mind," he returned to his circuit less than two weeks later. When he returned home four months later, he was "surprised" to learn that his daughter had agreed to marry the father of her child, the doings of his children largely a mystery to him. Sneath stayed home for only three days following the birth of his son on July 24, 1800, writing that "I find that it is best for me to have little to do with the world[,] for it draws my attention too much." When he moved to Philadelphia to take Lawrence McCombs's place that year, there is no indication that his wife joined him in the city, which isn't surprising considering the temporary nature of the appointment, the expense of city living, and the demands of maintaining their family and farm back home, let alone their own shaky relationship.[36]

The problem for Asbury was what to do with preachers like Sneath. Asbury probably wasn't specifically aware of the degree of Sneath's detachment from his family and his conflicts with his wife, but he was aware of the tremendous strain that the itinerant system placed on married preachers in general. It wasn't an easy problem to solve, and for now Asbury attempted to make only small modifications to the circuit system.

On top of all this, Asbury wasn't infallible when it came to making circuit appointments, and his decisions could sometimes seem arbitrary and uncaring to even the most dedicated preachers. Consider the case of William Colbert, who began riding circuits in 1790. In 1802 Colbert became a presiding elder in the Philadelphia conference, first for the Albany and Genesee districts, and then in 1804 for the Chesapeake district. Though his father, a widower who lived in Baltimore, was struggling with his health, Colbert worked tirelessly to fulfill what he saw as "an important charge!" Shortly after attending a quarterly meeting in Bucks County, Pennsylvania, thirty-nine-year old Colbert met twenty-one-year old Elizabeth "Betsey" Stroud, daughter of Colonel Jacob Stroud, founder of Stroudsburg, Pennsylvania. Jacob Stroud's family had lived in Northampton County for more than two decades, and by 1799, he owned more than 10,000 acres of land. His had been a life of hard work and steady advancement in the rough and tumble of frontier settlement. Though most of her family remained Quakers, Betsey Stroud had joined the Methodists.[37]

William later remembered that when he first met Betsey at a quarterly meeting on the Bristol circuit, she was wearing "an olive coloured silk gown" and appeared "genteel, plain, and well dressed," all that a Methodist preacher could hope for. Following the meeting, another preacher suggested that since William and Betsey were headed to the same destination, some 30 miles away, they should ride together. They left before sunrise with William determined "to conduct myself while traveling with this young woman with the propriety that becomes one of my profession. And I was on my guard." It was no use. "Before the going down of the sun I found my heart united with her," he later remembered. "I now found she had got possesion of my heart, and could not help being glad." Two weeks later they saw each other again at a quarterly meeting on the Chester circuit and agreed to exchange letters while Colbert continued his rounds. For Colbert, "my life became a burden to me without her." Despite opposition from Stroud's family, the two were married on November 1, 1804.[38]

For a while it seemed that the couple could cope with balancing an itinerant ministry and marriage. At times Betsey traveled with William on his rounds. In between she stayed with family and friends, mostly in and around Stroudsburg. "I pray unto the Most High, that next to the Salvation of my soul, it may be my greatest study to render her life with me as agreable as our circumstances will admit," William wrote in January 1805, shortly after leaving Betsey in Soudersburg, Pennsylvania. It helped that Betsey was as committed to Methodism as William. "May we both love and serve in true humility, is the sincere desire of thy unworthy companion," Betsey wrote to William in March 1805 while he was away on his rounds. "Thou dost mention my bearing with thee," she wrote, referring to an earlier letter from William. "Be assured my love it will be pleasing to have thee with me, but I have a desire to discourage thee in missing any part of thy duty on my account, I am very sorry to be the cause of any persons neglecting any part of their duty, especially one so near and dear, but as it seems to be convenient for thee, I am much pleased to hear of thy coming soon, though I do not expect the time will be very short to either of us."[39]

At the May 1805 Philadelphia conference Asbury appointed Colbert to Philadelphia with Michael Coate and James Smith. Though he was no longer a presiding elder, Colbert believed that the Philadelphia station was "more important." Yet for several months Betsey remained in Stroudsburg, 100 miles to the north, because they were unable to arrange suitable housing in Philadelphia. Meanwhile William suffered "much dejection of spirit on account of my unsetled situation in Life." "I am some times affraid I shall get impatient to see thee. I cannot help being unhappy at times while absent from thee," he wrote to Betsey, "My dearest of all on earth," in June 1805. He spent an inordinate amount of time simply walking the city's streets. It didn't help that Philadelphia's Methodists seemed unconcerned with his plight and unwilling to provide assistance when he asked. The culture of Methodism didn't make room for a circuit rider's family, as Colbert now discovered. "I have felt myself much cast down," he wrote on June 27, 1805. "The prime of my days have been spent in the service of an ungrateful public, whose interest (I can say without boasting,) I have been instrumental in the hands of God of promoting; unto whom necessity compelled me to make my wants known, and in return have got my feelings wounded instead of my wants being relieved!"[40]

Colbert's dejection continued through the fall of 1805, culminating in a rift with Betsey, who was pregnant at the time and who took refuge among her Quaker relatives. "This has been a day of sore trial to me:—that one who ought to be above all one to encourage me in the blessed work, to which I believe I am called will walk no more with me. She turns her back on me and goes among the people who of all people, stand most in the way of our usefulness," William wrote on November 3, 1805. A month later Betsey was in Philadelphia, where, on December 4 she gave birth to a girl. The child died twelve hours later, "taken away by that God who does all things well," according to Colbert. He believed that the baby died because he wasn't worthy of her. Always a traumatic event, the death of a child can push a couple apart, and this was the case for Betsey and William. William preached the next day, and a week later sent to Asbury a generally favorable report on the Philadelphia churches, along with a brief comment on the passing of his daughter "to a better place."[41]

Over the next few months William quarreled with several of Betsey's relatives, including her sister Jemima and brother Daniel, "a rigid uncharitable quaker." The Strouds weren't used to deferring to newcomers. "Language cannot describe the trouble of my mind," William wrote that February. That month he also entered into a public debate with a well-known visiting English Quaker, who, according to Colbert, "aimed some deadly blows" at Methodism during a Quaker meeting he attended. Colbert continued to correspond with Asbury, whom he deeply admired, until the Philadelphia conference in April 1806. There Colbert expected to be reappointed to Philadelphia, but, much to his chagrin, was instead moved to the nearby Burlington circuit. "I do feel it a hardship, that I should be for ever so unnecessarily tost about, without any respect to my circumstances and situation in Life. I feel very seriously disposed to dissist from traveling and I do not know but I should if it was not for fear of a reproach on myself in its being said—that stationing me in a City had so lifted me up that I was too proud to go on a circuit," Colbert wrote the day he received his new appointment. Why Asbury didn't give Colbert a second year in Philadelphia isn't clear, though his family problems must have been obvious to all. "It is true I am by no means a great preacher, nor have I the loudest of voices,"

Colbert wrote to Asbury a few days after the Philadelphia conference. Yet his removal had "been what many did not expect," considering that passions over the recent schism in Philadelphia had subsided during the year and "not a few" were "converted to God." Besides, Colbert had spent so much money setting up house for himself and Betsey that he couldn't afford to buy a horse. It seemed a waste to so quickly overturn all his efforts to settle in the city. Here, then, was the crux of the matter: Colbert expected accommodation for his new status as a married preacher, of which Asbury took no notice.[42]

Though they had no horse, Betsey accompanied William part of the way on his first round of the Burlington circuit in May 1806. "Poor Betsey, what is it I do not suffer on thy account!" William wrote on May 24, shortly after the two parted. "Brought from a house of plenty to endure the hardships of the life of an Itinerant Methodist Preacher[']s wife, unnecessarily tost from place to place by an unfeeling Bishop." Colbert didn't think that he could "serve under" Asbury "longer than this year." "The present Form of our Church Government I am satisfied with, tho' it invest the Bishop with such power. But I am much dissatisfied with the Bishops partiality and disrespect to the most delicate circumstances and situations of men." Perhaps if Asbury had left Colbert in Philadelphia another year, it would have allowed him enough time to sort out his personal problems. Then again, maybe not. Colbert's predicament wasn't the sort that yielded to easy solutions, pitting as it did the demands of marriage and family against a career designed for single men. At most, Asbury could only have left him in Philadelphia another year, following the new two-year limit passed at the recent General Conference, and it seems apparent that Colbert's preaching wasn't entirely successful in Philadelphia. Besides, in recent years Asbury had bent the rules to keep George Roberts and Thomas Lyell in the connection, yet both had left anyway. "My very dear Billy," Asbury wrote to Colbert in July 1806. "I am pleased for your own sake that you are still in the work God hath called you to, and blessed you in. I am for myself fully determined never! never! to perswade any man to stay with us, for such men will go, in the end." That was the lesson that Asbury had learned from the departure of Roberts, Lyell, Williston, and others like them, and he now applied it to Colbert's situation. And yet there was a certain arbitrariness to Asbury's decisions, as Colbert knew. After all, Asbury had transferred Thomas Morrell from Baltimore to New York City to be near his ailing father, but had taken no notice of Colbert's father, indeed may not have even known that his father was in poor health. Asbury's partiality was unintentional, but it was partiality nonetheless. Still, if there was a better way to organize the church, Colbert couldn't see it.[43]

Colbert stayed, and his prospects gradually improved. In the past, he himself had been critical of preachers who had left the connection to marry, and he was determined not to appear like them. In 1804, while presiding over the Genesee district, Colbert had come to know a young preacher, Samuel Budd, who, though not yet twenty, appeared "very zealous and had been useful." But soon after the year's third quarterly meeting, Budd married a woman he had only recently met and "went off to the Jersey with his wife, and left his business unsettled." "I look upon such men to be a disgrace unto the ministry, and I should not wonder if the curse of God was to follow such men as would leave the work of God for the sake of a woman," Colbert wrote at the time. How could he now do the same? Unwilling to admit any fault in the matter or to impugn the church as a whole, Colbert instead directed his frustration at Asbury. Yet over time he must have realized that his troubles didn't all arise from his recent appointment. Betsey's father died in July 1806, leaving them a substantial house with land, where they now moved and where, on October 21, Betsey gave birth to a second daughter. Still, Colbert soon despaired of "all hope of doing any good in this country," since his efforts to preach in the area bore little fruit. His family needed a home, but a house and farm required extensive upkeep, leaving him little time to preach. "This day I have been married two years, and little beside trouble ever since," he recorded on November 1, 1806. Colbert was able to bring his ailing father from Baltimore to live with them, but then on January 12, 1807, their second daughter died in Betsey's arms after a sudden illness that left William only a few moments to baptize her. In 1807 Colbert was appointed to the Kent circuit on the peninsula, and in 1808 he was simply designated a missionary for Pennsylvania. Gradually his life settled into a pattern, with his time divided between home and traveling, accompanied at times by Betsey or his father. Unlike Richard Sneath, whom he saw now and then at conferences and on the road, Colbert was unwilling to ignore his family for long stretches of time. Consequently his ministry never had the same scope or intensity as before his marriage. Shortly after the death of their second daughter, Colbert longed to "leave all litterally, and follow Christ, Preaching that eternal Gospel of truth which I have preached for years and been powerfully blessed in," but that was no longer possible.[44]

This was the reality that Asbury had to deal with. Despite his misgivings about some of his preachers' marriages, he continued to push wealthier circuits to accommodate them. His methods for doing so were sometimes calculating and even sly. In November 1803 he arrived in Charleston, South Carolina, where the society had constructed a new parsonage that was as yet unfurnished. Asbury rode directly to the house, hitched his horse, put his saddlebags in one of the rooms, and sat down on the doorstep, waiting to be discovered. The first to recognize him was an elderly black man, who informed

Asbury that no one lived in the house. "I know that," he replied. The man offered to guide Asbury to some place more accommodating, but he insisted that he would spend the night in the parsonage. Word soon spread that the bishop was at the parsonage and intended to stay there. One by one locals arrived offering to put him up in their homes, but he refused. Uneasy with the idea of the bishop sleeping on the floor in a bare room, people began to bring items to make him comfortable; someone brought a bed, someone else a table and chairs, another kitchen utensils, until the house was pretty well furnished. What might have taken months was accomplished overnight. Asbury "continued a week in Charleston, lodging in our own house . . . receiving my visitors, ministers and people, white, black, and yellow; it was a paradise to me." After Asbury left, the city's preachers were able to begin using the parsonage without additional expense.[45]

Dealing with the needs of an increasing number of married preachers led Asbury to reflect at uncharacteristic length on his own choices. "If I should die in celibacy, which I think quite probable, I give the following reasons for what can scarcely be called my choice," he wrote in his journal on January 27, 1804. He had begun "public exercises" at age sixteen or seventeen and had joined Wesley's traveling connection at twenty-one. At twenty-six he had come to America, intending on "returning to Europe at thirty years of age." But the war intervened, and the resulting turmoil, Asbury now claimed, "was no time to marry or be given in marriage." At thirty-nine he became bishop of the new American church, requiring him to travel extensively and relentlessly. "I could hardly expect to find a woman with grace enough to enable her to live but one week out of the fifty-two with her husband," he observed. Besides, "what right has any man to take advantage of the affections of a woman, make her his wife, and by a voluntary absence subvert the whole order and economy of the marriage state, by separating those whom neither God, nature, nor the requirements of civil society permit long to be *put asunder*? it is neither just nor generous." And it was exactly what itinerants like Richard Sneath were doing. Who then could blame Asbury for preferring celibacy for himself and his preachers?[46]

There was, of course, more to it than that. The time Asbury spent with women as he traveled was almost always in group or family settings, surrounded by men, including husbands, sons and preachers. He maintained long-standing and genuine friendships with women like Sarah Dallam, Elizabeth Dickins, and Mary Withey, but in fact he saw these women only once or twice a year at most. Writing to Mary Tabb, he admitted, "My female correspondents are few except a few of the preachers' wives that write me with their husbands in the same letter." The church was his family, and he viewed its women as mothers, sisters, and near cousins, but not potential romantic partners. Beyond that, women remained largely a mystery to him. His parents' shaky marriage and his mother's possessiveness probably also served as a warning against anything more intimate. In further defense of his own celibacy, Asbury added that he "had little money," much of which had gone to "administer to the necessities of a beloved mother." Here was more truth than he probably realized. He had never been able to break sufficiently free of his mother's influence to consider forming a separate family of his own. Now that she was gone, it was simply too late.[47]

21

"I see, I feel what is wrong in preachers and people, but I cannot make it right"

Heat rolled in waves from parched soil as Asbury and Whatcoat made their way through Pennsylvania and Ohio in late summer 1805. "The earlier fruits and productions of the year have been very abundant; but without a rain, the latter fruits and grain must fail," Asbury observed. It might have been a metaphor for the church. At the moment, each of the church's thirty-two districts promised "great success." By the summer of 1806 membership exceeded 130,000. "I think we congregate 2 millions in a year; and I hope for 100,000 souls convicted, converted, restored, or sanctified," Asbury wrote to Henry Smith that July. All the same, Asbury's theology prepared him for the inevitability of human failure. Despite all its promise, the revival might easily dry up under the scorching sun of apathy.[1]

The bishops were headed to Kentucky for the Western conference, where Asbury "completed my plan for the coming year, and submitted it to the presiding elders, who suggested but two alterations." With these in hand, and after preaching to about three thousand on the conference's closing Sunday, he and Whatcoat continued south through Tennessee, the Carolinas and into Georgia. By late November, Asbury was back in Charleston for his customary winter hiatus.[2]

Taking advantage of the availability of books in Charleston, Asbury used some of his free time to read. This included a couple of Methodist standbys, but mostly popular new releases. He had recently read four hundred pages of John Marshall's immensely popular biography of George Washington, the first volume of which was published the year before, and now he reread Jonathan Edwards' biography of David Brainerd, the famous colonial New England missionary to the Indians. Finding that "my eyes fail," (by this time he used reading glasses) he resolved to "keep them for the Bible and the conferences," but nevertheless pressed on through Charles Atmore's lengthy *Methodist Memorial*, published in 1801 in Bristol, England, which contained sketches of Wesley's early preachers. After Atmore, Asbury pored over several hundred pages of Wesley's journal. "These books suit me best—I see there the rise and progress of Methodism," he concluded. But he continued to read non-devotional books as well. In January he reread "the Jewish Antiquities," William Whiston's much-read translation of the writings of Flavius Josephus, which Asbury had first encountered in 1778. He also read British explorer Mungo Park's *Travels in the Interior Districts of Africa* (1799), an account of his exploration of the Gambia and Niger rivers. Park's entertaining account was a best seller, with editions in French and German. While in Charleston, Asbury also read Thomas Haweis's massive *An Impartial and Succinct History of the Revival and Progress of the Church of Christ, From the Birth of Our Saviour to the Present Time*, first published in England in 1800, but not in America until 1807. Asbury had heard Haweis preach as a boy in West Bromwich, and the book later influenced his last major address to the church in 1813. As always, his reading, when he had the time, was eclectic and relatively up to date.[3]

As Asbury and Whatcoat traveled north during the spring of 1806, neither bishop was in particularly good health, though it was Whatcoat who fared the worst. In Dover, Delaware, he was "taken with a fit of the gravel," according to Asbury, who feared he would die. Asbury left Whatcoat in Dover, too sick to travel. As Asbury made his way to Philadelphia in April for the conference's annual meeting, he could only speculate that perhaps his friend was already dead.[4]

As Whatcoat's health deteriorated, Asbury came up with a plan to call a special general conference of seven delegates from each of the seven conferences in the summer of 1807 to elect an additional bishop and make provisions for delegated quadrennial conferences, rather than general conferences open to all itinerant preachers who had traveled four years (a limitation introduced in 1800). Having followed accounts of the Lewis and Clark expedition, he could see a point in the near future when the church would extend "to the Pacific Ocean." But it wouldn't get there resting "upon shoulders burdened with the weight of threescore years, and deeply read in cares," he wrote to Thornton Fleming, presiding elder of the Monongahela district, in November 1806. By June 1806 the Baltimore, New York, and New England conferences had agreed, and in the coming months the Western and South Carolina conferences also consented.[5]

But the plan unraveled at the Virginia conference in February 1807, under a withering attack from Jesse Lee, who opposed "an irregular Conference, to make improper Bishops," as he put it in a letter to Ezekiel Cooper in April. "The Virginia conference would not let it be debated at all, which greatly displeased F. A. [Francis Asbury]," Lee wrote to Cooper in May. It was a bitter pill for Asbury. The "great odium" with which the Virginians dealt with the matter seemed to him like "[O']Kelley over again." Once again, he found himself groping for a way to protect Methodism's larger connectional structure against forces that threatened to fragment the church.[6]

The rebuke of the Virginia conference was all the more troubling since by that time Whatcoat was already gone. After leaving New England in June 1806, Asbury had hoped to stop by Dover and check up on his friend. But when he reached Philadelphia on July 8, he learned that Whatcoat had died three days earlier. His passing was a loss but also a mercy, considering the state of his health. He had been a "faithful friend for forty years... who ever heard him speak an idle word? when was guile found in his mouth?" Asbury wrote. "A man so uniformly good I have not known in Europe or America." Whatcoat had died broke, without money enough to pay his last traveling expenses, had those caring for him required payment. But of course they didn't. Who asks such things of a saint?[7]

The Asburyan Episcopacy

Despite the opposition of the Virginia conference, by the spring of 1808 everyone knew that something had to be done to shore up the episcopacy and more clearly define the church's polity. The preachers realized that Asbury couldn't shoulder the burden of the episcopacy alone, and that should he die, the church would face a crisis. This became the central issue of the 1808 General Conference, which convened in Baltimore on May 6 with 129 preachers present. As it developed, the conference addressed three basic issues: what to do about Thomas Coke, how to replace Richard Whatcoat, and what the future role of the General Conference should be. Up to this point, the General Conference had the power to change any rule or doctrine and to appoint or recall bishops at its discretion, though it had never done the latter. This had seemed reasonable in the 1780s, when everything was up for grabs, but hadn't they reached a collective consensus on basic doctrine and practice over the last thirty years? Most agreed they had. With Coke absent in Britain, Asbury took a surprisingly prominent role in the proceedings, though he was still by no means the most vocal participant.

Coke's relationship to American Methodism had grown increasingly vague since the last general conference. He hadn't visited the country since 1804, knew next to nothing of the new western territories, and had never met most of the current itinerant preachers. His first visit to the United States, from November 1784 to June 1785, had been his longest and most important, but that was more than twenty years ago. What's more, his 1791 overtures to Bishop William White proposing a merger of the Methodist and Episcopal churches in America had, almost by accident, recently become generally known for the first time. White had kept the matter to himself (as had Asbury) for more than a decade until, in 1804, the Episcopal minister Simon Wilmer of Chestertown, Maryland and the Methodist preacher John McClaskey, then assigned to the Chestertown circuit, contacted him. White replied to Wilmer and McClaskey with a brief account of his correspondence and conversations with Coke more than a decade before.[8]

The thread of the story was then picked up by John Kewley, a Methodist turned Episcopalian who was engaged in a dispute with Maryland Methodists over the legitimacy of the Methodist episcopacy and the ordinations derived from it. Kewley had joined the Methodist connection as a preacher on trial in 1801 and was appointed to the Clarksburg circuit in the Pittsburgh district. In 1802 he was assigned to the Allegheny circuit, but the next year his name disappears from the annual minutes altogether. He was ordained a deacon in the Protestant Episcopal Church in June 1803. Somehow, Kewley had become deeply disaffected with Methodism, and he now intended to expose what he saw as the church's inconsistencies.[9]

As the controversy unfolded, White sent a letter to the Episcopal priest James Kemp, rector of Maryland's Great Choptank parish, in which he transcribed Coke's letter of April 24, 1791, calling for a reunion of the two churches. Kewley then published White's letter to Kemp, including the full text of Coke's 1791 letter, in a pamphlet entitled *An Enquiry Into the Validity of Methodist Episcopacy, With an Appendix, Containing Two Original Documents, Never Before Published*. Kewley used Coke's proposal to White to argue that Coke himself had doubted the legitimacy of his ordination at Wesley's hands. This, of course, wasn't really Coke's concern, and Kewley's argument isn't convincing on this point. It certainly wasn't likely to sway many Methodists, though Kewley seems to have believed otherwise. He addressed Asbury by name in the pamphlet's preface, with the hope that he would become "convinced of the errors of Methodism," and "renounce them as I have done; and use all your influence to put an end to the 'schism' and to lead your mistaken brethren back to the unity of the Church." That would be the day. Kewley's pamphlet would have quickly dropped from sight if it hadn't been for the light it shed on Coke's past conduct.[10]

The 1808 General Conference began debating Coke's status by publicly reading two letters from Coke. In the first, dated November 16, 1807, Coke reiterated his earlier offers to come to America as an equal of Asbury, but not "merely to preach." If the American preachers "agree that I shall have a full right to give my judgment in every thing, in the general and annual conferences, on the making of laws, the stationing of the preachers, sending out missionaries, and every thing else, which, as a bishop or superintendent, belongs to my office," then he would "come over to you for life." At this point Coke didn't know that his 1791 scheme had become public knowledge, or how much this had shaken the American preachers' confidence in him.[11]

Once he learned this, he wrote a second letter on January 29, 1808, attempting to justify the 1791 affair. Coke explained that the Methodist connection had been "like a rope of sand," and could only "be saved from convulsions by a union with the old Episcopal Church," or so he believed at the time. The controversy brewing in Virginia under O'Kelly had indeed shaken the church's foundation, but Coke, who had initially backed O'Kelly, was as much responsible for stirring this up as anyone. Coke argued that he hadn't consulted Asbury before contacting bishop White because "it was impossible. I was at and near Philadelphia, and he was somewhere in the South." This wasn't true, even if Coke remembered it that way. On the day that Coke wrote to White in April 1791, he and Asbury were traveling together in Virginia, probably sleeping in the same room.[12]

None of this won Coke any new friends. The conference chose to deal with Coke by continuing him at his present status with the provision that "he is not to exercise the office of superintendent or bishop among us in the United States until he be recalled by the General Conference, or by all the annual conferences respectively." Writing to Ezekiel Cooper after the conference, Coke confessed that this provision "affected me at first reading," but that he "fully approved of [it] on cool reflection." Approve or not, there was little he could do about it. For his part, Asbury remained on friendly terms with Coke, continuing to send him updates on the American connection.[13]

Having dispensed with Coke, the conference turned to the question of replacing Whatcoat. There were motions to elect one, two, and seven new bishops. The latter proposal, by Ezekiel Cooper, would have provided a bishop for each of the seven annual conferences, essentially a diocesan system, with Asbury functioning as something of an archbishop or an elder statesman among colleagues. This would have been a dramatic change, amounting to an admission that a bishop couldn't adequately govern more than one annual conference at a time. It also would have created a more democratic and decentralized polity, something that Cooper would continue to push for at this and future conferences.[14]

Cooper's diocesan proposal had been circulating among the preachers for several months, to the extent that its supporters were accused of "electioneering." Given several months to turn the idea over in his mind, Asbury concluded that it would corrupt the Methodist system by encouraging localism over connectional unity. "I shall never be an *Arch Superintendent* much less an *Arch Bishop*," he wrote to Nelson Reed, presiding elder of the Baltimore district, in December 1807. Despite the difficulty of attending all the annual conferences, like "Great George Washington," he would rather "lay my commission at the feet of the General Conference" and retire than agree to Cooper's plan. Instead, Asbury favored having two or three bishops who "should do their best to attend every conference and all that are or shall be in the union every year; and visit the seventeen states and territories as oft as possible and have their eyes and ears in every part of the Connection. This is the true Wesleyan Superintendency... formed in the constitution of 1784 and has been in operation ever since."[15]

The majority of the preachers agreed. Cooper's support was mostly limited to the Philadelphia and New York conferences, where he had directed the church's publishing business for the past decade. Asbury and the system he represented were a known quantity proven over time. Thousands upon thousands had received the word under his episcopacy. What could Cooper guarantee? When the issue finally came to a vote, the conference elected only one new bishop, choosing William McKendree, who received ninety-five votes against twenty-four for Cooper, four for Jesse Lee, three for Thomas Ware, and two for Daniel Hitt.[16]

McKendree was Asbury's choice, and the two complemented one another well. After returning to the church following the O'Kelly schism of 1792, McKendree had served as a presiding elder in the Virginia, Baltimore, and, most recently, Western conferences, where he supervised much of the explosive growth there between 1800 and 1808. Like Asbury, McKendree was known for traveling light and doing without. He had also developed a reputation as a careful and fair-minded administrator. Nathan Bangs described McKendree as "the life and soul" of the preachers in the West. Over the years Asbury had traveled with McKendree and appointed him to examine and station the preachers in the West. Following the Western conference in October 1802, as the two rode to North Carolina, Asbury became so sick that, in his own words, "My dear M'Kendree had to lift me up and down from my horse, like a helpless child." By 1808 the two knew one another well.[17]

McKendree was like Asbury in another way: he wasn't a great public speaker. Some who knew him from his younger days in Virginia remembered this and wondered if he was really cut out to be a bishop. To answer this question, Asbury arranged for McKendree to preach a Sunday sermon in front

William McKendree (1757–1835). (From Abel Stevens, *History of the Methodist Episcopal Church in the United States of America*, vol. 3 [New York: Carlton & Porter, 1867].)

of a packed congregation at Baltimore's Light Street Church a few days before the election. McKendree's initial appearance in the pulpit was less than reassuring. He was tall for the time, about 6 feet, and relatively good looking. But he was shabbily dressed in ill-fitting clothes made of coarse cloth. His vest was too short, and when he raised his hands, his red flannel undershirt showed. More than that, when he began, as Nathan Bangs later recalled, "he seemed to falter in his speech, clipping some of his words at the end, and occasionally hanging upon a syllable, as if it were difficult for him to pronounce the word. I looked at him not without some feeling of distrust—thinking to myself, 'I wonder what awkward backwoodsman they have put in the pulpit this morning, to disgrace us with his mawkish and uncouth phraseology?'" McKendree's sermon text included Jeremiah 8:22: "Is there no balm in Gilead; is there no physician there? why then is not the health of the daughter of my people recovered?" Though he started slowly, when he got to describing the blessings of God's balm for his people, "he seemed to enter fully into the element in which his soul delighted to move and have its being, and he soon carried the whole congregation away with him into the regions of experimental religion." As McKendree began to feel his subject, it was "like the sudden bursting of a cloud supercharged with water," according to Bangs. William Colbert, who was also there, found it "vain to resist" the current of McKendree's thought. People began to shriek, shout, groan, weep, and finally fall to the floor throughout the church. Bangs watched a "very large, athletic-looking preacher" sitting next to him suddenly collapse "as if pierced by a bullet." Bangs himself felt his "heart melting under emotions which I could not resist." Any doubts about McKendree's depth vanished. Asbury was heard to say that the sermon would make McKendree a bishop, and it did.[18]

With the election of McKendree settled, the conference took up the issue of restructuring the church's governing rules, particularly with regard to the role of the quadrennial general conferences. The problem, as Asbury saw it, was that the general conferences, which had always met in Baltimore, tended to be dominated by representatives from the Baltimore and Philadelphia conferences, along with a few influential Virginians. Indeed, at the present conference there were thirty-one members from Baltimore and thirty-two from Philadelphia, comprising almost half of the total. Only seven members came from New England, and only eleven each from the Western and South Carolina conferences. In response, the New York conference brought a memorial, endorsed by the New England, Western, and South Carolina conferences, calling for the creation of a delegated General Conference. The day after the New York memorial was read, Asbury made a motion to create a committee of "an equal number from each of the annual conferences," which shrewdly assured that the committee couldn't be dominated by the central conferences, to draft a response.[19]

At its first meeting, the committee elected a subcommittee consisting of Ezekiel Cooper, Joshua Soule, and Philip Bruce. Cooper and Soule produced competing plans, while Bruce was content simply to back Soule's proposal. The main difference between the two plans had to do with the episcopacy. Cooper's plan stipulated only that the conference couldn't "do away" with the episcopacy or "reduce our ministry to a presbyterial parity." Soule's went further, restricting the General Conference so as not to "destroy the plan of our itinerant general superintendency." In other words, it prohibited the General Conference from creating a diocesan system as Cooper favored. Soule's proposal prevailed in the larger committee of fourteen and then came before the entire conference.[20]

The committee's report also proposed that future general conferences be made up of seven delegates from each annual conference, chosen by ballot, plus an additional delegate for each ten members after the first fifty. So, if a conference had eighty preachers, it would get ten delegates (seven plus three). Second, it stipulated that "the General Conference shall not revoke, alter, or change our Articles of Religion, nor establish any new standards of doctrine." More specifically, it couldn't "change or alter any part or rule of our government, so as to do away [with the] episcopacy, or destroy the plan of our itinerant general superintendency," except "upon the joint recommendation of all the annual conferences, then a majority of two-thirds of the General Conference succeeding shall suffice to alter any of the above restrictions." At stake was whether or not reformers like Cooper could change the church's basic polity by a simple majority vote. Was the church's episcopal structure a matter of convenience, easily altered, or should it be protected against all but the most measured change?[21]

By this stage in its development, the Methodist church was as rife with competing agendas as any organization of its size. Jesse Lee led the initial opposition to the report, fearing that it would reduce the influence not only of the powerful central conferences, but also of the older preachers. On the floor, Lee argued that delegates to future general conferences ought to be chosen by seniority rather than by election.[22]

Ezekiel Cooper wasn't done either. After a day of intense debate over Lee's objection, Cooper once again tried to turn the discussion back to the issue of episcopal control. On Monday afternoon, May 16, he asked to postpone the present debate so as to introduce a "new resolution, as preparatory to the minds of the brethren...on the present subject." Cooper's motion called for the election of presiding elders "without debate" once a year at the annual conferences. This, in effect, would have accomplished much of what Cooper had wanted from a diocesan episcopacy, only at a different level. Bishops might still circulate through the whole connection, but presiding elders would be strictly local selections, not episcopal appointees, thus making them more answerable to their conferences than to the bishops. Debate on Cooper's motion occupied all of Tuesday and Wednesday morning, May 17 and 18, before losing seventy-three to fifty-two. This ended Cooper's efforts, at least for the present, to decentralize and democratize the church's polity in a fairly radical way. The church had prospered under the current episcopal plan, and the majority of the preachers couldn't be persuaded to abandon it.[23]

This didn't necessarily mean that they knew exactly what they wanted. They were groping for a way to adapt to new complexities without changing the general outcome. When the first resolution of the report—that "The General Conference shall be composed of delegates from the Annual Conferences"— was finally brought to a vote on Wednesday afternoon, it went down to defeat, sixty-four to fifty-seven. Now what? The conference had rejected quite a few proposals, but had yet to approve anything. All that was clear was that the majority of the preachers from the central conferences were as yet unwilling to give up their de facto control of the General Conference.[24]

Fed up with this impasse, all but one delegate from the New England conference and two from the Western decided to pull out and return home. But Asbury and McKendree were determined to hold things together. With the help of New England's Elijah Hedding, they arranged a meeting with the disgruntled preachers and convinced them to stay. For the next several days Asbury did what he did best in these situations, talking with small groups late into the night, patiently building a consensus. By this point in his career, he had developed a recognizable style in dealing with these situations. "If he could not carry a point, he did not force it against the wind and tide, but calmly sat down till the blast was gone by, and with a placid dignity made a virtue of necessity, or, with discriminating wisdom, brought the measure forward in a less exceptional shape, and at a more convenient time," one observer wrote. Debate on the committee of fourteen's report resumed the next Monday, May 23, with a motion that future general conferences "be composed of one member for every five members of each annual conference." This was essentially the same plan that had been rejected the week before, but this time it passed by "a very large majority."[25]

Now came the question of how the delegates would be chosen. At this point Joshua Soule cleverly proposed "that each annual conference shall have the power of sending their proportionate number of members to the General Conference, either by seniority or choice, as they shall think best." This "Yankee trick," as Lee later called it, neutralized much of Lee's opposition, since it upheld the right of individual conferences to manage their own affairs. Lee had used seniority as a wedge issue to oppose a delegated conference, but, as Soule knew, he was also a firm advocate for the autonomy of annual conferences. Soule worded his motion so as to force Lee to choose between the two. It was shrewd politics, and it worked. Lee was left speechless long enough for the motion to pass.

Once Soule's motion passed, opposition to the remaining provisions of the original committee report fell away. By midday Tuesday the conference had adopted the rest of the so-called Restrictive Rules that formed something akin to a new constitution for the church. In short, these rules provided for a delegated General Conference that was prohibited from revoking or changing "our articles of religion," or establishing "any new standards or rules of doctrine, contrary to our present existing and established standards of doctrine," unless approved by all the annual conferences and two-thirds of the General Conference. Future changes would have to have overwhelming support and pass through a drawn-out process of review. The new rules also protected, in disciplinary cases, the right to trial by committee for preachers, or before the society for members, and stipulated that proceeds from the Book Concern and Chartered Fund could only be used "for the benefit of the traveling, supernumerary, superannuated, and worn-out preachers, their wives, widows, and children." This, in combination with McKendree's election to the episcopacy, was as much as Asbury could have hoped for.[26]

The conference did one other thing with regard to Jesse Lee. It turned down his request to publish his recently completed history of American Methodism. Asbury didn't like the book, particularly Lee's (mostly accurate) description of Asbury's hiding out in Delaware during the revolution.[27] But there was more to it than that. While Lee's book is filled with first-hand observations that historians have mined again and again, it also contains errors that annoyed those who had lived through the events Lee described.[28] Most of Lee's mistakes concern districts he hadn't visited in years. The committee appointed to review the book, made up of one member from each of the seven conferences, concluded that Lee's history was "more like a simple and crude narrative of the proceedings of the Methodists than a history." Lee published the book anyway two years later, under the title A Short History of the Methodists.[29]

The Crest of the Wave

All of this was a relief to Asbury, alleviating some of the anxiety he had felt since Whatcoat's health failed. It meant that he could expect to finish his career under the system he had spent his adult life crafting, what historian Edward Drinkhouse later termed the "Asburyan Episcopacy." Characteristically, Asbury's response was to redouble his efforts, despite his sixty-two years. From February 1807 to February 1808, he had ridden 5,000 miles in his annual tour, and there would be no letting up now. Henry Boehm, Asbury's new traveling companion, arrived a day late for his scheduled meeting with Asbury at Perry Hall following the General Conference, only to find that the bishop had left without him. "He never waited for any man, and he wanted no man to wait for him," wrote Boehm, who caught up with Asbury the next day. Riding through Maryland, Asbury and Jane, his favorite horse, suffered from the unusually warm weather, what he called "Georgia heat," but he pressed on anyway.[30]

Asbury had invited Henry Boehm to travel with him specifically because he was fluent in German, in an effort to build bridges with German-speaking settlers.[31] Boehm, who had just turned 33, came from a family of Swiss and

German pietists who had settled in Lancaster County, Pennsylvania. He joined the church in 1798 at a quarterly meeting held at Boehm's Chapel, a Methodist meetinghouse built in 1791 on land donated by his brother, Jacob Boehm. The meeting offered an auspicious beginning to Boehm's career in the church, with "Sinners crying for mercy all over the house, below, and in the Galleries," according to the circuit preacher William Colbert. Joining the traveling connection in 1800, Boehm outlived just about everyone active in the church at the time (he died in 1875 at one hundred years of age).[32]

Boehm's manuscript journal confirms that he frequently preached in German or followed Asbury's sermons with an exhortation in German when the two were in areas dominated by German audiences. "Many of my German Brethren seemed so elivated as if they naver had heard the gospel in their mother tongue," Boehm recorded after preaching in German on July 12, 1810. "Great liberty in speaking to a people who had not heard the gospel in their mother tongue for ten or twelve years, at least some of them," he wrote a month later in Ohio. At Asbury's request, Boehm arranged for the *Discipline* to be translated and published in German in 1807. Asbury was so pleased with

Boehm's Chapel, Lancaster County, Pennsylvania. (Photo by the author.)

the results that the next year he had Boehm translate and publish a collection of tracts.[33]

Crossing into Ohio with Boehm in early August, Asbury vowed "never, in future, to cross the mountains before the first of September," because of the debilitating heat. One 70-mile stretch took thirty-nine hours to cover, riding twenty-three and resting sixteen, "by crooked paths," with "plenty of stones, rocks, hills, and springs of water," according to Boehm. It left Asbury "unable to stand, walk, or kneel," by his own account. From Ohio they made their way briefly into Indiana, where Asbury observed that "in this wild there may be twenty thousand souls already." As it happened, Methodist preachers had already crossed over the Mississippi River into Missouri, though Asbury had neither the time nor the stamina to follow them. That task he left to William McKendree, who crossed the Mississippi to attend a series of camp meetings in Missouri in July and August 1808. Meanwhile, Asbury traveled with a group that included Boehm, the preacher Benjamin Lakin, and his wife, the irrepressible Betsey Lakin. "I feel for the people of this territory; but we must suffer with them, if we expect to feel for them as we ought," Asbury wrote on September 9 after crossing into Kentucky. This was the crux of the problem with a "local episcopacy" in Asbury's mind: "it cannot be interested for its charge as it should be, because it sees not, suffers not with, and therefore feels not for, the people." He took comfort in knowing that he was so familiar a sight in many places that "people call me by my name as they pass me on the road."[34]

Asbury's episcopal tours of 1809 and 1810 were much the same. He never let up, presiding at all seven annual conferences for 1809 and eight for 1810, including the new Genesee conference, located in upstate New York and the northern reaches of Pennsylvania. Asbury and McKendree created the Genesee conference in 1810 to insure that present and future bishops would have to at least visit the region, which was remote from either New York City or Philadelphia, before making decisions about it. In all, Boehm estimated that he and Asbury rode 4,778 miles from December 1809 to December 1810.[35]

The pace of growth remained steady, even if the fervor of the revival had begun to fade, with the greatest increases in the Western, New York, and New England conferences. Membership increased by 7,405 in 1808, 11,043 in 1809, and 11,527 in 1810. At that point it stood at 163,033. "I feel as if this would be the greatest year that hath ever been known in Europe, or America for the power of God," Asbury wrote to Ezekiel Cooper in March 1810.[36] Camp meetings had become "as common now, as quarter meetings were 20 years back," Asbury wrote to Elijah Hedding. He expected the church to hold six hundred camp meetings in 1810.[37]

All of this stretched resources to the breaking point, particularly with regard to the traveling preachers. Asbury heard from one circuit preacher, Allen Green, who rode the Monongahela circuit in western Virginia, that by summer 1810 his circuit included "twenty-eight [preaching] appointments to fill in twenty-five days, besides meeting one thousand seven hundred in classes." This was, of course, in addition to the demands of traveling in the backcountry across a circuit that encompassed some 2,500 square miles. It is little wonder, then, that so many circuit riders quit after only a few years.[38]

The size and complexity of the traveling connection was both a blessing and a curse. The church needed more preachers than it had and constantly needed to find replacements for those who quit. Without a continual supply of new recruits the whole thing would grind to a halt. Of the approximately 1,250 preachers who joined the traveling connection between 1769 and 1806, only 334, or 27 percent, were still riding circuits in 1809. Of these, only 115, or about one-third, had more than five years experience. Only ten of the preachers who held conference appointments in 1809 had begun circuit preaching before 1785. The majority of those who left the itinerancy, 762 out of 916, served as unpaid local preachers. They quit traveling not because they had lost faith in the church, but because circuit riding was simply too demanding. Only fifty-seven of the 1,250 preachers who had joined since 1769 left the church or were expelled, a testament to Asbury's administrative skill (see table 21.1). The fluidity of it all was nonetheless overwhelming. Asbury was like a swimmer straining against a tide, moving neither forward nor backward. At some point his strength would fail, but he was determined to put that moment off as long as possible.

TABLE 21.1   Status in 1809 of itinerant preachers who joined the traveling connection 1769–1806

Division	Total number of itinerants	Died in the work	Located or stopped traveling	Left the church	Expelled from the church	Still held a conference appointment in 1809
Joined 1769–1784	126	25	78	6	7	10
Joined 1785–1792	288	35	198	13	4	38
Joined 1793–1800	261	20	161	9	4	67
Joined 1801–1806	325	6	90	3	7	219
Never moved beyond probation	250	11	235	1	3	0
Totals	1250	97	762	32	25	334

Sources: Jesse Lee, A Short History of the Methodists (Baltimore: Magill and Clime, 1810), 319–44; Minutes of the Annual Conferences of the Methodist Episcopal Church for the Years 1773–1828, 2 vols. (New York: T. Mason and G. Lane, 1840), 1:5–175.

"A Revolution in the Church"

Apart from the pressure of growth, success itself seemed to be eating away at the church's foundation. This wasn't a new issue, of course, but it now seemed to take on increased significance. Asbury had always believed that poverty and suffering were allies of true spirituality. Taking note of the termination of Thomas Jefferson's unpopular embargo on trade with Europe in April 1809, he couldn't help but "fear much that these expected *good times* will injure us:—the prosperity of fools will destroy; therefore affliction may be best, and God may send it, for this is a favoured land: Lord save us from ruin as a people!" He tended to use a lot of exclamation points when reflecting on the dangers of creeping affluence. "Respectable! Ah! there is death in that word," he wrote from New York a week later. "O Lord, save thy now despised Methodist children from the praises of the people of this world!"[39]

Despite all of the church's success, Asbury sensed a crisis looming on the horizon. "As to building houses, taking new places, extending to the extremities of our Borders, to the most distant settlements, and forming, and enlarging congregations, we excel," he wrote to Thomas Coke in June 1810. Could there be anything wrong with this kind of success? Well, yes. In the church's oldest strongholds "preachers and people, in Towns, Cities are too much on the Lees.... Now is the time of danger, many Rich people have Joyned us, we monopol[ize] religion in some places, all together; as if the offence of the cross was ceasing." Earlier preachers had been tested by fire, but it all came too easily now. "What was Methodism 40 years ago? There was everything to be done, things were not made ready for our hands," he wrote to Zachary Myles of Baltimore in August 1810. "We are losing the spirit of missionaries and martyrs, we are slothful, we can only tell how fields were won, but by our brethren and sisters, not by us," he added in a letter to Lewis Myers, a presiding elder in the South Carolina conference, later that month.[40]

The proof of this could be seen in an increase in conspicuous consumption. While in Rhode Island in May 1809, Asbury lamented that New England Methodists seemed intent on building "grand" houses with steeples and pews, even if it meant stooping to hold lotteries to raise the money. "Our *ease in Zion* makes me feel awful," he wrote in July 1810 while in upstate New York. "Ah, poor dead Methodists! I have seen preachers' children wearing gold—brought up in pride. Ah, mercy, mercy!" What hope was there if even the preachers didn't know better? "How shall preachers who are well provided for maintain the spirit of religion!" Asbury wondered in March 1811.[41]

Evidence of the same could be seen in every region, not just in the cities of the East. Ohio, which was quickly becoming one of the church's strongholds, was a good example. Asbury had first set foot in Ohio in June 1786, though it was another decade before he spent much time there. Once he did, he quickly realized the region's potential. While traveling across southern Ohio for the first time in the fall of 1803, he was struck by the fertility of the land, "as fine lands as any in America." By 1809 the price of such abundance had become evident. "Here are folks from most of the eastern States, and of all professions," he wrote from Milford on the Little Miami River. "They have good land, and this rarely makes people any better."[42]

The upshot of all this was predictable. Writing to Jacob Gruber, presiding elder of the Greenbrier district in the Baltimore conference, in August 1809, Asbury lamented an increase in "backsliding" among members of long stand-ing and a rash of "sudden conversions" that were "not sound nor . . . lasting." How could it be otherwise, when Methodists now had it so easy, with so much to distract them? "It is a wonder we are not worse; and our shame, we are not better," he wrote to an old friend in England.[43]

Asbury's response was to set himself apart as an example of deliberate sacrifice, shunning the easy way. He had previously acquired a two-wheeled sulky and installed a stiffer shaft in the spring of 1809 to take the pounding of backcountry roads. It broke anyway that July in Pennsylvania, and again in Ohio in August. He finally sold the sulky in November 1810. Without it he could "better turn aside to visit the poor; I can get along more difficult and intricate roads; I shall save money to give away to the needy; and, lastly, I can be more tender to my poor, faithful beast." He also continued his practice of staying with ordinary members, rather than seeking out the homes of the rich. After spending the night at the estate of a wealthy South Carolina planter in December 1810, he felt obliged to comment in his journal that "it seldom happens that I seek such a shelter." His piety, lived out for all to see, had always been a pillar of his authority, and it was no different now.[44]

If it was martyrdom he wanted, his colleagues were ready to oblige. He had little rest, either on the road or at conferences and camp meetings. "I slept about five hours last night," he reported on one such occasion in Ohio, typical of many. "A crowd of company, and hogs, dogs, and other annoyances to weary me." Locals, eager to hear their bishop, often scheduled more appointments for him than he could handle. "I might murmur at this, and perhaps I do . . . I can truly say my life is like a daily death," he wrote while in western Virginia in August 1809, after learning that locals had published speaking engagements for him without asking. Apart from preaching, there were always people who wanted to see him. "We seldom lodge at a house without the company of preachers: we are pleased to see them; but would be better pleased to know they were on their circuits, faithfully at work," Asbury groused in February 1809, while on his way to the Virginia conference. In New York the next summer, the wife of a preacher complained that she had tried to see him earlier at Trenton, New Jersey, but he was constantly "crowded" around. He could only tell her that it was even worse "in the back settlements—a cabin has not always two rooms."[45]

The worst were the letters, which piled up for him everywhere. "I have at least twenty letters to answer, and but one day" to do it, he wrote near Carlisle, Pennsylvania, in July 1809. Complaints like this are routine in his journal. Letters arrived by the dozens in packets that awaited him at cities and towns along his annual route. He often rose at 4:00 a.m., in part to pray, as he always had, but now also to write letters before hitting the road. "I have at least near a thousand letters and papers put into my hands a year, all calling for some responsibility," he wrote to Nathan Bangs in 1810. No wonder many of his letters from this period have a stream-of-consciousness feel to them.[46]

Among his correspondents, Asbury increasingly heard from preachers unhappy with their appointments and societies unhappy with their preachers. One layman, writing to Ezekiel Cooper in March 1808, characterized this increasing contentiousness as "a new Era and what some call a Revolution in the Church." Much of this wrangling revolved around two related issues: the reluctance of circuits to support married preachers and the demands of married preachers for appointments that were convenient for their families. Societies had always been reluctant to take on the extra financial burden of a preacher's family, but the issue took on new importance as more preachers tried to remain in the itinerancy after they married. "The time has nearly arrived, that we may expect a change of Preacher's for this place," the leaders of the Asbury Methodist Church in Wilmington, Delaware, wrote to the bishop for whom their church was named on March 15, 1808, in anticipation of the Philadelphia conference meeting the next week. The church didn't expect the present minister, John McClaskey, to be reappointed to Wilmington, "neither do we wish it." The members had nothing against McClaskey as a preacher— he had "faithfully declar[ed] to us the counsels of God"—but they claimed they couldn't afford him. McClaskey was married, and the cost of his and his wife's allowance plus their room and board came to $350 a year. "This sum, tho. small for him, we find large for us, and very difficult to raise," the church leaders wrote. They asked Asbury to send "a single Preacher the ensuing year, as we cannot provide for a man with a family." Asbury complied, sending William Bishop to Wilmington. Of course that meant finding somewhere else for McClaskey, who Asbury shuffled off to the Kent circuit in Delaware.[47]

On the other side were the preachers. Asa Shinn wrote to Asbury on February 7, 1808, just before the Baltimore conference, apologizing for having been "hindered" in meeting his obligations the past year on the Monongahela circuit because of his wife's poor health. The coming year would probably be no better. "I may spend the remnant of my days more in *suffering* than *doing*," Shinn informed Asbury. Nevertheless, he asked Asbury to reappoint him to the same circuit, since it was "doubtful whether it will be prudent or practical" for his wife to move. Asbury compromised, appointing Shinn to the adjacent Greenfield circuit. A week after Shinn's letter, William Page wrote to Asbury requesting "a Circuit Convenient to my family." Page had in mind that he might serve "as a Missionary within the bounds of this [the Monongahela] District," preaching in the "many Large & populous Settlements," that had sprung up outside the boundaries of the present circuits. Asbury couldn't do this, but he did assign Page to the Ohio circuit, not far from the Redstone circuit that Page had ridden the year before.[48]

In much the same fashion, James Coleman wrote to Asbury on May 11, 1810, a week before the New York conference, that though he was blessed with health, "my Famely is feble and Sickley." Finding it difficult to move his family in their distressed state, Coleman planned to build them a house in Ridgefield, Connecticut, on land provided by his father-in-law. He therefore asked Asbury to appoint him to the nearby Redding or Croton circuits. In this case, Asbury didn't comply, perhaps because he realized that Coleman was likely to neglect his circuit too much, traveling back and forth between his family and his appointments. Coleman was instead granted supernumerary status. He returned to circuit preaching on the Litchfield circuit in 1811.[49]

These examples represent the increasingly delicate balancing act that Asbury had to perform between frugal churches and married preachers. On the whole, Asbury blamed the preachers more than the people when things didn't work out. The concerns raised by Shinn, Page and Coleman were legitimate, but they nonetheless represented a trend that he found worrisome. With Methodism's newfound respectability, the "rich" were now joining the church, including their daughters, who then married Methodist preachers. The expectation of these couples was for the kind of relative prosperity that one or both of them had grown up in, not the privation and uncertainty that had always been a part of the itinerant life. More important, married preachers who didn't eat and sleep in the homes of the people had a different kind of relationship with their congregations. "Our preachers get wives and a home, and run to their *dears* almost every night: how can they, by personal observation, know the state of the families it is part of their duty to watch over for good," Asbury complained while in Rhode Island in June 1810. By that time, he had seventy married preachers to accommodate, estimating that they lost one quarter to one half of their time visiting their families. Managing the appointments of all the circuit preachers "may possibly be my martyrdom," he wrote to Coke in May 1809. "I see, I feel what is wrong in preachers and people, but I cannot make it right," he wrote in September 1808 as he slogged his way through the Kentucky backcountry.[50]

He had to wonder how much of real substance was left for him to do. Was he already a quaint relic of the past in his own church? It wasn't yet clear, but he had a suspicion which way things were headed.

22

What God Allows

Either way, Asbury didn't intend to go easy. By 1811 he had to be the toughest sixty-six-year-old alive.

Outwardly, he looked much as he had forty years ago when he stepped ashore in Philadelphia, the inevitable effects of age notwithstanding. Henry Boehm, who knew him best at this time, describes him as 5 feet 9 inches tall and 151 pounds, "erect in person, and of a very commanding appearance." He had "rugged" features, though "time and care" had left deep wrinkles (perhaps another sign of his failing heart). His blue eyes were still "so keen that it seemed as if he could look right through a person." When Jacob Young first met Asbury in 1803, he remembered that the bishop "fixed his eye upon me as if he would look me through." "There was as much native dignity about him as any man I ever knew," Boehm wrote. "He seemed born to sway others. There was an austerity about his looks that was forbidding to those who were unacquainted with him." Asbury dressed plainly but neatly, holding "in utter abhorrence all approaches to external pomp," according to one observer. He now favored black clothes, though in the past he had worn gray and even light blue. He wore a "low crowned, broad-brimmed hat, a frock coat, which was generally buttoned up to the neck, with straight collar," Boehm remembered. Another preacher remembered Asbury as being "spare and tall, but remarkably clean, with a plain frock coat, drab or mixed waistcoat, and small clothes of the same kind." He wore knee breeches with leggings and shoe buckles, perhaps similar to ones he had made back in Birmingham as a metalworker's apprentice. This had been the fashion for many years, though now the younger preachers were beginning to wear the new style pantaloons, or long trousers, a practice Asbury "heartily disapproved," according to Boehm. When only one preacher, Seth Mattison, arrived at the Genesee conference in 1813 wearing "knee-buckles and gaiters; which was the bishop's manner of dress," Asbury "manifested his approbation by embracing him most cordially," according to Abner Chase, who was himself wearing long pants.[1]

The years after the General Conference of 1808 were, in some measure, a period of retrenchment for Asbury. In part this was necessitated by failing health. He was beset by another round of ailments beginning in January 1811, first by pain in his feet and then by the flu. As in the past, for treatment he resorted to an emetic, cream of tartar. In July 1811 he applied a poultice to his right foot in hopes of easing the swelling and "severe" pain, to little avail. That month he again suffered a series of intermittent fevers.[2]

By late October he had recovered somewhat, only to be "stricken with acute rheumatic pain" in his knee in mid-November. Describing himself as "a prisoner

Francis Asbury (c. 1812). (From Abel Stevens, *History of the Methodist Episcopal Church in the United States of America*, vol. 1 [New York: Carlton & Porter, 1867].)

with pain," he applied a blister, which didn't help. The pain forced him to once again ride in a sulky, despite the trouble of maneuvering it over backcountry roads. He continued in this condition through the end of 1812. "I cannot easily describe the pain under which I shrink and writhe," he wrote that December.[3] Near the end of January he wrote to Jacob Gruber that he had lost "the use of both *feet*" three weeks earlier, and had to be "handed [carried] from place to place." By February he was back on crutches. The fevers and swelling in his feet and knee continued, for which he applied blisters and took emetics. In September his face became swollen, and the following month he first complained of "pleuritic pains in the breast." Entries in his journal became more sporadic toward the end of the year, and a friend gave him "an old gig worth forty-five dollars" to ease his way.[4]

And yet he managed to attend every annual conference: eight meetings in 1811 and nine in 1812 and 1813, after the Western conference was split into the Ohio and Tennessee conferences. He rode 4,000 to 6,000 miles each year, over sometimes treacherous roads and through all kinds of weather. During one stretch in the summer of 1811, he rode 1,600 miles in sixty days, preaching as he went. He visited Canada for the first and only time in July 1811 and wanted to go to Mississippi, but the preachers at the 1813 Tennessee conference wouldn't let him. Each year the conferences gave him $200 total for traveling expenses, barely enough to cover basic necessities. "If we were disposed to stop at taverns (which we are not), our funds would not allow it," he wrote in July 1813 while in New York. Three weeks later he ran out of cash and had to borrow $5 to continue on. Bad weather was harder on him now. Asbury's journal for these years contains increasing numbers of references to riding in the rain, probably because he was more mindful of how dangerous a fall on slippery roads could be for someone in his condition.[5]

The impending end of his life pushed Asbury back to first things. He "revived" his practice of fasting on Fridays and promoted it among the preachers, along with two general fasts annually for the entire church. He also took renewed interest in the doctrine of sanctification, believing that the church had let it slip from view. "I fear a great failure in the doctrine of sanctification," he wrote to John Sale, presiding elder of the Kentucky district, on September 24, 1812. That same day he wrote to James Quinn, presiding elder of the Muskingum district, urging him to "See *sanctification, feel it, preach it, live it . . . Let us be as one soul.*"[6]

Asbury also adopted the "custom" of visiting the graves of departed friends. He found solace in their memories and in the belief that they had completed their life's work, had gone on to a better place. Following their path was increasingly on his mind. "How my friends remove or waste away! yet I live," he wrote in December 1813. Among the graves he frequented was Henry Willis's, which he first "wept at" in June 1808, according to Henry Boehm.

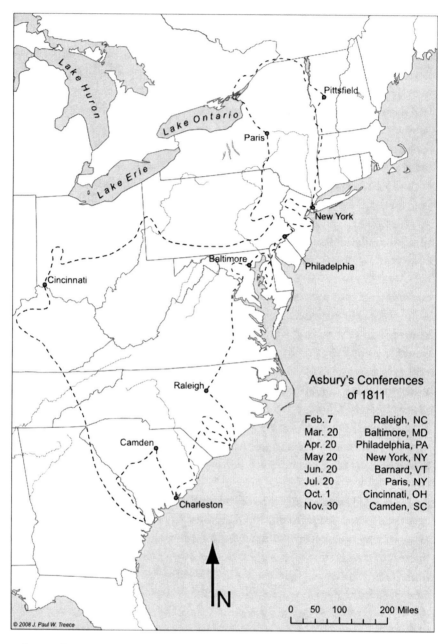

Asbury's Conferences of 1811

Feb. 7	Raleigh, NC
Mar. 20	Baltimore, MD
Apr. 20	Philadelphia, PA
May 20	New York, NY
Jun. 20	Barnard, VT
Jul. 20	Paris, NY
Oct. 1	Cincinnati, OH
Nov. 30	Camden, SC

0 50 100 200 Miles

© 2008 J. Paul W. Treece

Asbury's 1811 tour covered more than 3900 miles, beginning and ending near Charleston, South Carolina. (Map by J. Paul W. Treece, University of Missouri Geography, 2008.)

Willis, one of Asbury's former traveling companions, had died earlier that year, after a circuit preaching career from 1779 to 1790 and then a period of prolonged poor health. Asbury stopped by Willis's grave near Pipe Creek, Maryland, whenever he could, recording visits in March 1811 and August 1813.[7]

Old friends yet living, especially widows, also occupied more of his thoughts. Asbury not only stopped to see Henry Willis's grave, but also to visit his widow, Ann Willis, who had been left with six young children. At the Willis's, in Boehm's words, "the bishop kissed and encircled in his arms the six orphaned children of his departed friend, and blessed them in the name of the Lord, and prayed with them." He also corresponded with Willis, giving her news of his work and asking her to "help me sister by your prayers. . . . be Frank's *sister* and *his mother* and prompter, to all good." There are more than thirty references to visiting widows in Asbury's journal for the years 1811 to 1813.[8]

Asbury's Notebook

If he was thinking more about the past, his habits of discipline wouldn't let him forgo his responsibilities in the present. Asbury devoted much of his time on each annual tour to planning the appointments for the coming year. Boehm observed that "the bishop always planned his work far ahead, and when he came to a conference he had but to carry out his plan." As they rode together, Asbury "freely" discussed possible appointments with Boehm, sometimes asking his advice about where to assign various preachers. As a result, "the preachers tormented me to know where they were going," but Boehm kept the bishop's confidence, which of course was why Asbury trusted him. Asbury also discussed his plans with the presiding elders and listened to the examinations of the preachers at their respective annual conferences before finalizing his plans. "I have heard him in open conference request the preachers to give him a representation of their cases before making out their stations, that he might understand their peculiar circumstances, and act accordingly," observed Nathan Bangs, who knew Asbury during this period. "He would get all the information he could from circuits, preachers, letters, and presiding elders, etc., then make the appointments," another preacher remembered.[9]

To organize his thoughts, Asbury "used to keep a private memorandum of all the preachers throughout the whole connection, wherein he noted down their various talents and qualifications for the work of the ministry," according to Abner Chase, who was admitted on trial at the New York conference in May 1810. At least some of these notes survive in a volume made up of individual sheets of paper, 104 pages in all, that were evidently collected and bound at some later date, probably after Asbury's death. Though it isn't signed, most of the notebook is in Asbury's handwriting. It contains more than 2,040 evaluations of individual preachers at twenty-eight annual conference meetings from 1810 to 1813. Some preachers appear more than once in the notebook, indicating that Asbury updated his evaluations when necessary. Most of the entries occupy only one line, which makes sense given the constraints on Asbury's time and on what he could carry.[10]

The notebook reveals Asbury's priorities and the care he took in his evaluations. His appointments weren't spur-of-the-moment decisions. It also indicates just how short of preachers the church really was. Asbury's entries generally address four concerns: a preacher's piety, his ability to preach, other strengths he might possess, and limitations that held him back. In general, more attention is given to the question of piety than to any other. Asbury used words like "pious," "zealous," and "faithful" to describe preachers meeting a certain standard, the absence of these terms reflecting a negative evaluation. A sincere devotion to prayer, Bible reading, and meditation were important to Asbury and always had been. His conception of what constituted a vibrant spiritual life was one of the constants of his career. "Pious[,] useful[,] sensible" was how he described John Wesley Bond, who later served as his last traveling companion, at the 1811 Baltimore conference. At the 1813 Ohio conference Asbury wrote of Jacob Young, who had been riding circuits for about a decade, "his heart is in the work[,] seeks warmly perfect Love[,] God has blest him." This was about as good as he could hope for; Asbury appointed Young presiding elder of the Ohio district for 1813.[11]

Piety alone wasn't enough, of course. The ability to deliver the word mattered too. What Asbury was looking for here was a combination of "gifts"—the ability to speak clearly and persuasively—and diligence. At the 1810 Baltimore conference he described Robert R. Roberts as a "good preacher blest of God" who left the "people pleased," which seems accurate given the course of Roberts's career. At the same conference Asbury described Enoch George as a "Laborious, excellent man," who was a "diligent[,] gifted preacher." Two years later he still felt the same about George, describing him as a "fire kindled preacher" who was "deeply devoted after holiness." As a result, Asbury sent George to the important Baltimore circuit in 1810 and then made him presiding elder of the Potomac district in 1811. Roberts and George were later elected to the episcopacy to replace Asbury after his death in 1816.[12]

Others received less glowing evaluations. At the 1811 South Carolina conference Asbury noted that Richmond Nolley "cannot preach" and was therefore only "useful in hospitals[,] gaol [and the] poor house." A year later Asbury gave Nolley a similar evaluation, noting that he was "pious" and "prudent" and good at visiting "house to house," but not, presumably, at preaching. With this in mind, Asbury sent Nolley on a mission to the remote Tombigbee region of Alabama for two years. There he traveled from settlement to settlement, ministering to people in their homes, but rarely having to speak before large assemblies. In one famous encounter, Nolley followed fresh wagon tracks to the camp of a family newly arrived on the upper reaches of the Tombigbee River. "What!" exclaimed the man when he discovered Nolley's identity. "Have you found me already? Another Methodist preacher!" Having already left Virginia and Georgia in hopes of breaking his wife's and daughter's attachment to the church, he was dismayed to find a circuit rider "before my wagon is unloaded." In 1814 Nolley moved to the Attakapas circuit in Louisiana, where he died the following winter from exposure after falling off his horse in a stream, several miles from the nearest house. His death was widely celebrated as an example of dedication to the church, though none of the accounts mention the limitations that led Asbury to send him to the frontier in the first place.[13]

Apart from preaching ability, Asbury occasionally noted other strengths a preacher might possess. He described some as "studious" and "given to reading," and others as good "disciplinarians." At the 1811 Baltimore conference he noted that John Swartzwelder was not only "upright" and "useful," but also that he "speaks German," a talent that Asbury took into consideration in appointing Swartzwelder to districts with lots of German speakers.[14]

More numerous are comments on various limitations that held preachers back. For some these involved health problems. At the 1811 Virginia conference Asbury noted that Thomas Neely was "Bleeding in [his] Lungs," but might be able to resume preaching in six months. Neely was granted supernumerary status, a sort of injured reserve list, but never recovered sufficiently to take a circuit, locating in 1813. Others, whose conditions were less severe, soldiered on, much as Asbury had always done. At the 1810 Baltimore conference Asbury noted that Gerard Morgan had "good abilities," but couldn't "endure hardship." Likewise, Job Guest was an "acceptable preacher," but "weak in [the] breast [and] throat." Appointed to ride circuits nonetheless, both survived the year to be reappointed in 1811. Greenleaf Norris wasn't so fortunate. At the 1810 New England conference Asbury noted that Norris was "diligent" and "well received as a preacher," but that he was also "sick." In fact, Norris died the following year of consumption in Boston while appointed to the Lynn circuit.[15]

Chronic debt was another concern. Falling into debt had always been viewed as a moral failing by Methodists, and Asbury expected the preachers to set an example in this regard. Elijah Willard came before the 1810 New England conference seeking to be admitted on trial, but when Asbury and the preachers discovered that Willard was $100 in debt and married with a child, they turned him away. Levi Shinn met a similar fate that same year at the Baltimore conference. Asbury noted that Shinn was "pious" and "useful," but also that he was married with three children and had "slender property" to support them. John Newman was likewise "Totally Rejected" at the Baltimore conference in 1812 even though he was "pious" and had a "great mind," because he was $80 in debt.[16]

For some, it was a combination of factors that made them unsuitable for the itinerancy. Joseph Piggot was admitted on trial at the Western conference in 1811 with a reputation as a "gifted exhorter" and assigned to the Letart Falls circuit in Ohio. By the 1812 conference, Asbury had heard enough about Piggot to conclude that he was, in reality, a "small man" with a "Little mind," who had recently married to boot. Asbury dropped Piggot from the connection with the simple notation, "Done."[17]

And then there were the preachers who failed to consistently travel and preach, often because of family obligations. Peter Cartwright is a good example. Born in Virginia in 1785, Cartwright moved with his family to Kentucky about 1790. There he was converted and joined the Methodist church under John Page in 1801. Cartwright began circuit preaching in 1803 and married in August 1808 at the age of twenty-two. Sometime during the winter of 1808–1809 his father died, requiring Cartwright to leave his circuit for several months to settle the estate. In his autobiography, Cartwright claims that he never again missed this much time away from his circuit and never more than six months total for his entire career. In fact, the probate dragged on for about a year, requiring a good deal of Cartwright's attention. In an effort to accommodate Cartwright, Asbury and McKendree appointed him to the Livingston circuit in Kentucky for the 1810 conference year, which is where his father's farm was located. Nonetheless, at the Western conference in November 1810, Asbury noted that Cartwright had "lost half [the] year" and was "once absent 10 months." More than that, he described Cartwright as "too light" and "Airy," leading to "complaints" about him, certainly not the impression one gets from Cartwright's memoir. Asbury returned Cartwright to the Livingston circuit for 1811, but the results were much the same. At the Western conference meeting in the fall of 1811, he noted that Cartwright had been "9 months in the year upon his own account." Eventually Cartwright straightened out his family issues enough to focus more directly on his preaching. By the fall of 1812 Asbury had gained a new measure of confidence in Cartwright, describing him as "blessed" and possessing "good sense," and appointed him presiding elder of the Wabash district in Indiana.[18]

Asbury's patience with Cartwright becomes more understandable when he is compared with his colleagues, many of whom were less than stellar. In 1811

Asbury described Joshua Lawrence as "not studious[,] travelled some, to me Doubtful," William Compton as "imprudent with the [opposite] sex," James Bateman as "pious[,] gifted but Languid," and James Quail as "not Great, never will be great." Yet he gave each a circuit appointment for the year. In 1813 Asbury noted that Charles Dickinson "Blunders but improves" and could only muster enough enthusiasm for Abraham Trail to say that he was "better than he used to be." Both were reappointed. The church had some truly brilliant preachers and a lot of capable ones, yet such was his need that Asbury was obliged to employ just about every reasonably pious candidate who wasn't too sick, broke, or hopelessly muddled. The wonder is that he made it work at all. Writing to Jacob Gruber, presiding elder of the Monongahela district in September 1811, Asbury complained that the connection was bogged down with "weights, cyphers, drones . . . whilst some are chained like slaves to the gallies of labor." If Asbury was a tyrant, he ruled a motley crew.[19]

Once the appointments were made, Asbury had neither the time nor the inclination to listen to complaints from preachers unhappy with their assignments. He developed the practice of having Boehm bring his horse to a side door while he read the appointments on the last day of conference, so that he could make a quick getaway as soon as he had finished. Imagine Asbury reading the appointments slowly and carefully, folding his paper, uttering a closing prayer, and then striding, as quickly as his sore feet would allow, to his horse at the door, as the room erupted into a dozen conversations. "He thus avoided importunity, and no one could have his appointment changed if he desired to, for no one knew where to find the bishop," Boehm recalled.[20] The incredible disappearing bishop—now you see him, now you don't.

Pulling Back

Even Asbury, stubborn as he was, realized that neither he nor the church could go on like this for long. So he began to turn more of the decision making over to William McKendree. Asbury and McKendree both attended the 1810 Virginia and Genesee conferences, but only McKendree signed the conference minutes, indicating that only he officially presided. Writing to the itinerant preacher Martin Ruter in March 1810, Asbury noted that he had "given" McKendree "the chair of every Conference. It is time in the thirty-nine years of my labors to wind up."[21]

Yet if he was willing to let McKendree preside at conferences, he was still reluctant to yield control over the annual appointments, that jewel in Asbury's episcopal crown. He was particularly uncomfortable with McKendree's efforts to formalize the presiding elders' advisory role when it came to stationing the preachers. What Asbury had always done informally, as witnessed by his notebook, McKendree now attempted to make an official part of conference proceedings. The issue came to a head in 1811. "I am fully convinced of the utility and necessity of the council of Presiding Elders in stationing the preachers," McKendree wrote to Asbury that October, in response to Asbury's continued objections. McKendree proposed a kind of compromise by which Asbury would form a plan to station the preachers as he had always done, and then McKendree would review this plan with the "assistance" of the presiding elders. "But I still refuse to take the *whole* responsibility upon myself," McKendree wrote. By 1812 McKendree seems to have won over his senior colleague. That September Asbury wrote to John Sale that he had become "a kind of Vice President" to McKendree. "I am unspeakably happy in the presidency of Bishop McKendree in the conferences, and the stationing. I retire with prudence," he wrote to Christopher Frye that November. Shortly after this, he quit keeping his notebook.[22]

The transition from Asbury's personal, almost apostolic, control over the appointment process to McKendree's committee-oriented style was subtle but momentous. Asbury hadn't only made the circuit appointments, he had embodied the commitment to Christ and the church that each preacher was expected to carry to his circuit. Sensing that no one could now fill this role, McKendree pulled back from setting himself up as Asbury's sole successor. Much as John Wesley had had no single successor in Britain, Asbury would have none in America. McKendree's system was more democratic and in principle less prone to favoritism, but it required the presiding elders as a group to step up and join him in collectively filling Asbury's shoes. Conferences and committees often lack an identity and are liable to sink to the lowest common denominator. In this case, that denominator turned out to be not all that low. One of Asbury's strengths was his willingness to tolerate strong personalities in leadership positions, even when they cut across his views, and the church now reaped the benefits of this. Methodism wasn't a personality cult; it was more of a culture. Wesley's theology and practice (his method) had been flexible enough for Asbury to adapt to the American context. Now Asbury's method was modified by McKendree and others. Asbury wasn't entirely comfortable with this process (Wesley hadn't been either), but his theology prepared him for just such an eventuality. All men fail; ultimately the church is in God's hands. And yet somewhere in the recesses of his mind Asbury couldn't escape the fear that there was something fundamentally wrong.

By the spring of 1812, Asbury had relinquished enough administrative responsibilities to consider a trip to Britain. He dropped hints to this effect in some of his letters to British Methodists, including Thomas Coke and Thomas Roberts. The idea so alarmed the delegates to the General Conference of 1812, meeting that May in New York, that they formed a committee in response. The committee concluded "that it is our sincere request and desire that Bishop Asbury would relinquish his thoughts of visiting Europe, and confine his labours to the American connexion so long as God preserves him." Asbury refused to give the idea up. Writing to Christopher Frye in August 1812, he suggested that by the time of the 1816 General Conference he might be in "Europe" or "heaven" (it was the latter). The British conference responded with an invitation that Asbury received in March 1813. "We have news from the English Conference. It has given me an invitation to my native land, engaging to pay the expenses of the visit," he wrote on March 7. Asbury wrote back thanking the British conference and suggesting that two "younger" preachers might accompany him once the War of 1812 had subsided. Alas, by the time the fighting ended he was no longer fit for the journey.[23]

As for the war itself, Asbury says little, which isn't surprising considering his general misgivings about politics. He does refer to the war as a conflict "between our people and the English people," but otherwise refused to take sides. "Calamity and suffering are coming upon them both: I shall make but few remarks on this unhappy subject; it is one on which the prudent will be silent," he wrote on August 8, 1812. When asked to preach a sermon to a group of Pennsylvania volunteers a few weeks later, he chose as his text Jeremiah 2:13, "For my people have committed two evils; they have forsaken me the fountain of living waters, and hewed them out cisterns, broken cisterns, that can hold no water." This could hardly have been the kind of rousing martial sermon that the officers were hoping for, especially considering Asbury's often laconic delivery. One can imagine the new recruits scratching their heads, wondering exactly what they were being encouraged to do, while the officers fidgeted in the back. Asbury did make a point of shaking hands with each soldier as they left, but he wasn't asked to preach any more sermons of this sort. By 1814 he was complaining that people had become "so greatly agitated" by the war that "Bibles are laid aside for the news papers."[24]

General Conference of 1812

As ninety delegates representing eight annual conferences convened in New York City the first week in May for the General Conference of 1812, they could take satisfaction knowing that membership stood at two hundred thousand, an increase of forty thousand since the last general conference. They could also reflect, as Asbury had written to Thomas Coke the previous September, that the church held four hundred to five hundred camp meetings annually and could claim to "congregate, possibly, three millions."[25]

Electing delegates succeeded in smoothing out inequities in regional representation, but it also eliminated much of the democratic ferment seen in 1808. Asbury mostly left McKendree to frame the conference's agenda (Thomas Coke didn't attend), limiting his own role to that of a senior consultant. Still, when McKendree read an address to the conference on the state of the church as a way to frame an agenda, Asbury was taken aback, rising to ask, "I never did business in this way; and why is this new thing introduced?" McKendree shrewdly replied, "You are our father; we are your sons. You never had need of it. I am only a brother, and have need of it." Asbury merely sat down, realizing that in some measure the church had passed him by.[26]

Seven years earlier, Asbury had written that his authority rested on, "1. Divine authority, 2. Seniority in America. 3. The election of the General Conference. 4. My ordination by Thomas Coke, William Philip Otterbein . . . Richard Whatcoat, and Thomas Vesey. 5. Because signs of an apostle have been seen in me." McKendree could have made a similar argument—he had served since 1788, been elected and ordained in much the same manner, and presumably could claim a divine mandate—but he chose a more bureaucratic turn. In so doing, he attempted to remove at least a measure of the apostolic component from the equation, replacing it with a greater emphasis on facilitating discussion. Yet when McKendree "invited a committee of the most respectable and influential members" to serve as his "council," they responded with "a distant and reserved carriage." Religion is about more than a smooth-running bureaucracy. The preachers realized that if there was something to be gained under McKendree, there was also something to be lost. Could a committee replace a prophet?[27]

The conference revisited four old issues—the selection of General Conference delegates based on seniority, slavery, the sale of "spirituous or malt liquors" by preachers, and the election of presiding elders—ultimately to little effect. Jesse Lee raised the issue of seniority, as he had in 1808, only to lose again. The issue of slavery wasn't brought up until the last day of the conference, with a bland motion "requesting the conference to inquire into the nature and moral tendency of slavery," which was tabled and never pursued. A motion early in the conference by James Axley of Tennessee "that no stationed or local preacher shall retail spirituous or malt liquors without forfeiting his ministerial character among us" was tabled several times before going down to defeat.[28]

The lack of attention to slavery must have stirred mixed emotions in Asbury. He remained convinced of the moral evil of slavery, but he was also aware that positions on both sides had hardened in recent years. At the Western conference in October 1808, some of the preachers had even "hissed" at Asbury as he tried to mediate "a long, weary, and warm debate" over slavery, as one preacher described it.[29]

After that, Asbury's journal is relatively silent on the topic, as are his letters, though he does record often preaching to and worshipping with African Americans. He also continued to ordain black preachers and encourage separate black meetings. "We have a great change and a gracious prospect here in Charleston, and in the neighborhood among both descriptions of people," he wrote in November 1808, while in the city where racial issues were the most prominent. "By our coloured missionaries the Lord is doing wonders among the Africans."[30]

Beyond that, accommodation seemed to be the only solution in the South. "We are defrauded of great numbers by the pains that are taken to keep the blacks from us; their masters are afraid of the influence of our principles," Asbury had complained in February 1809, while in North Carolina.

> Would not an *amelioration* in the condition and treatment of slaves have produced more practical good to the poor Africans, than any attempt at their *emancipation?* The state of society, unhappily, does not admit of this: besides, the blacks are deprived of the means of instruction; who will take the pains to lead them into the way of salvation, and watch over them that they may not stray, but the Methodists? Well; now their masters will not let them come to hear us. What is the personal liberty of the African which he may abuse, to the salvation of his soul; how may it be compared?

This represented the culmination of a shift in Asbury's thinking on slavery, and the present General Conference seemed to agree, if only by its silence. The antislavery heyday of the 1780s must have seemed a lifetime away.[31]

Asbury's reaction to the defeat of the motion prohibiting preachers from selling liquor was presumably less ambiguous. He had long used wine for his health and had never been a teetotaler, though he had always disapproved of distilled liquor and abhorred drunkenness. Now he increasingly came to see "vile whisky" as "the prime curse of the United States," particularly in the South and, to a lesser extent, the West. After preaching in Georgetown, South Carolina, in January 1813, he reflected that of the church's one hundred white members, most were women: "the men kill themselves with strong drink before we can get at them." "What a land is this of widows; and men sick, dying, and drunken!" he wrote that February, while still in South Carolina.[32]

The consumption of distilled spirits in the United States had been on the rise for several decades. According to one estimate, by 1810 the per capita consumption of distilled spirits by those fifteen and older was about 8.7 gallons each year, more than triple today's rate and much higher than in colonial America. This national binge eventually gave rise to the temperance movement, the broadest social reform effort of the nineteenth century. Methodists slowly came to see rising consumption as a crisis, but it took time. The General Conference of 1796 had urged shopkeepers not to serve customers enough liquor to get them drunk, but went no further. The year before, the itinerant James Jenkins spent a quarter on the Seleuda circuit in South Carolina, where he "deemed it my duty plainly to reprove the practice of distilling." Local Methodists were so offended that they gave him only $8 for his services that quarter. Methodists ultimately took up the cause of temperance in a big way, but in 1812 partaking of a convivial dram, or selling it to someone else, seemed too ingrained in even the ministry to legislate it out. Asbury was ahead of the curve, yet long experience with issues like slavery had taught him just how difficult it was to press an unpopular position.[33]

The question of electing presiding elders concerned Asbury more keenly, as it had at previous conferences, bearing directly as it did on the appointive powers of the bishops. "It is said the wise men in New York conference have discovered that it will be far better to elect the presiding elders in conference, and give them the power of stationing the preachers. I suppose we shall hear more of this," he had predicted while in New York in July 1811. He was right. At the 1812 General Conference Laban Clark, then stationed in New York City, made a motion calling for the election of the presiding elders by their annual conferences.

Troubled by this proposal, Asbury wrote to Clark on May 16, 1812, several days before the conference voted on his motion. "I fear you have shewed the appearance of severity in conference," he began. Asbury challenged Clark's proposal on two levels. First, he argued that it addressed a problem that didn't exist. "Is not your motion in conference, directly Levelled at our chartered privilege, for 40 years, [which has] never [been] designedly abused[?]" Second, he attempted to play on Clark's loyalty to him. "Am I not your father?" Asbury asked. "If Thy Father has sinned against thee tell him as a son, to a Father, with great pla[i]nness; yet tenderness because he is an old man among men, now weak in Body and mind. I am thy Father; and the greatest Friend thou hast in the world, *a spiritual Friend*; if not I wish to be so. I hope our trials . . . will end in Greater confidence Love and union, so wishes, so prays, yours to serve, F. Asbury." There is something almost sycophantic in this plea, or at least a degree of petulance that seems uncharacteristic of Asbury's earlier career. He was losing touch with the younger preachers, and it frustrated him. At this point in his career, he saw himself primarily as an apostle, a spiritual father, not a constitutional bureaucrat. Couldn't Clark see that the church needed more of the former and less of the latter?[34]

Clark's response two days later is a study in gentle firmness, in many respects more impressive than Asbury's outburst. "I am pleased that you open your mind to me with freedom. But I am extreemly pained that your feelings have been wounded!" Clark wrote. "Nothing can be more distant from me than designedly to injure the feelings of . . . the man whom I esteem and reverance above all other. . . . You sir have an interest in our connection, and an influence over it, that no other man can have." At the same time, once Asbury was no longer "with us," it would be impossible to put off the calls for change. Clark saw his proposal to elect presiding elders as a way to preserve the office against those who would eliminate it entirely. "Presiding Elders have not always had the confidence of the preachers in their charge—it was not your fault that they had not," Clark wrote. "Would it not be a means of conciliating the affections of the preachers, if they could have a choice in their rulers? I candidly confess it is my serious belief it would." Clark intended his motion as a compromise that "would be the preservation of our connexion and the peace & glory . . . of your last days."[35]

Debate on Clark's motion began on Monday, May 18, and continued through Tuesday afternoon. Those in favor of election argued that it squared better with American democracy and provided a fairer system of checks and balances for the circuit preachers. Asbury wasn't really the target here. Like Clark, most of the preachers were already focused on what would come next. Hence, they were careful to argue, according to Nathan Bangs, "That however safely this prerogative might be exercised by Bishop Asbury, especially in the infancy of the Church, when the number of preachers was few, it had now become impossible, on the increase of preachers and people, for a bishop to exercise such a tremendous power intelligibly and safely to all concerned."[36]

Those opposed to the motion argued that the church wasn't a civil government, and that in any event most governmental positions were filled by appointment rather than election, which was certainly more the case in the early nineteenth century than today. They further contended that elections would lead to "an electioneering spirit" and might make a presiding elder "fear to do his duty," lest he lose votes. Besides, whatever the bishops lost by not residing in a particular conference they more than made up for with their "knowledge of the *whole* work." The problem was so vexing because, as Nathan Bangs observed, "there must, in the nature of things, be an umpire somewhere." The church had prospered to date, but once Asbury was gone, who would that umpire be? In the end, Clark's motion lost by a vote of forty-five to forty-two.[37]

Debate on this issue continued at successive general conferences for another sixteen years, eventually leading to the formation of the Methodist

Protestant Church in 1830, which abolished the episcopacy and presiding eldership and even allowed for the election of class leaders by their classes. Asbury was long gone by then, but he could feel the ground shifting under his feet in 1812.[38]

The 1812 General Conference did two other things that closely concerned Asbury. First, it appointed a committee to see what could be done about writing a history of American Methodism. For years Asbury had been badgering the presiding elders to send him accounts from their districts that could be compiled into a history. He made another push for this in the year leading up to the 1812 General Conference. "I have stricken out a plan for a complete letter-history of Methodism, by our presiding elders," he wrote to Thomas Douglass, presiding elder of the James River district in the Virginia conference, in February 1811. Under Asbury's plan, the presiding elders were supposed to interview the circuit preachers and "aged" members in their district, and then submit a "complete historical letter neatly [and] correctly done" to their annual conference. "It will make a grand history in about fifty letters," Asbury wrote. "The plan is plain and possible." Maybe so, but most of the presiding elders either didn't comply or did so in a slipshod manner. The committee appointed to read the letters at the General Conference concluded that they "contain some valuable information," but were otherwise "not sufficiently full on different points." The General Conference then authorized the New York conference to "engage a historian to digest and arrange the materials thus furnished, and prepare them for the press," but nothing ever came of it, much to Asbury's dismay.[39]

Second, the conference passed a resolution requesting the bishop to "sit to a good painter," whose work would then be turned into an engraving, with enough copies printed to "supply the connexion." Asbury proved less than cooperative. After the conference adjourned, Daniel Hitt, the conference secretary, wrote to Benjamin Tanner, who was to arrange for the portrait to be painted in Philadelphia, that Asbury had "taken his departure," on his "No[r]thern, Western & Southern tour." "If he lives & retains health sufficient to travel," he was scheduled to stop in Philadelphia in April 1813, but even then it was "uncertain, whether or no he will consent to sit for his likeness to be taken."[40]

The Valedictory Address

Knowing that his time on this earth might indeed be short, Asbury sat down in August 1813 to compose a valedictory address to William McKendree and the church as a whole. In it, he championed two themes: the necessity of maintaining an itinerant ministry and the apostolic authority of the episcopacy. The first had been central to his conception of Methodism since his first days in America. The second had been growing on his mind for the past several years.[41]

Asbury began by advising that there should only be three bishops, traveling continually through the nation and meeting together at each annual conference. This was to guard against the "growing evil of locality in bishops, elders, preachers, or Conferences," a threat that he had battled from Pilmore in the 1770s through O'Kelly in the 1790s to the present. Asbury admitted that "locality is essential to cities and towns," but since America was overwhelmingly rural, the itinerant nature of the connection needn't be abandoned. "Guard particularly against two orders of preachers: the one for the country, the other for the cities," he warned. Why was "locality" such a threat? Because it inevitably led to corruption. Settled ministers too often sold their services to the highest bidder. Indeed, there were already "too many" young preachers "whom we can view in no other light . . . than as men going into the ministry by their learning, sent by their parents or moved by pride, the love of ease, money or honor." It needn't be so. "You know, my brother, that the present ministerial cant is that we cannot now, as in former apostolic days, have such doctrines, such discipline, such convictions, such conversions, such witnesses of sanctification, and such holy men. But I say that we can; I say we must." The issue here wasn't youth but commitment. "Never be afraid to trust young men; they are able, and you will find enough willing to endure the toils and go through the greatest labors; neither are they so likely to fail as old men are," Asbury wrote.[42]

Related to this discussion were issues of education and politics. Too often it was the case "that schools, colleges, and universities undertake to make men ministers that the Lord Jesus Christ never commanded to be made." Experience taught that "a plowman, a tailor, a carpenter, or a shoemaker!" could preach as well as "a college-taught man." "We may rationally conclude that learning is not an essential qualification to preach the gospel," Asbury asserted. "It may be said no man but a fool will speak against learning. I have not spoken against learning. I have only said that it cannot be said to be an essential qualification to preach the gospel." Hadn't he been a metalworker's apprentice?[43]

If education was to be approached warily, politics was to be avoided completely. "As to temporal power, what have we to do with that in this country?" Asbury asked. "We are not senators, congressmen, or chaplains; neither do we hold any civil offices." In fact, Jesse Lee currently served as chaplain to the U.S. House of Representatives, an appointment that Asbury viewed with suspicion rather than pride. "We neither have, nor wish to have, anything to do with the government of the States, nor, as I conceive, do the States fear us. Our kingdom is not of this world. For near half a century we have never grasped at power," Asbury wrote.[44]

The second major argument of the valedictory address had to do with the apostolic nature of the episcopacy. Asbury argued that "the apostolic order of things was lost in the first century," when itinerant ministry was abandoned. "There were no local bishops until the second century," he claimed. "Those who were ordained in the second century mistook their calling when they became local and should have followed those bright examples in the apostolic age," among them Paul, Barnabas, and Timothy. The Reformation "only beat off a part of the rubbish, which put a stop to the rapid increase of absurdities at that time; but how they have increased since!" Until the Methodists showed up, that is. "In 1784, an apostolic form of Church government was formed in the United States of America at the first General Conference of the Methodist Episcopal Church." What was at stake now was no less than the future of Christianity. He had come to America believing that he was part of a cosmic drama of vast significance. As lofty as his goals had been then, American Methodism's success now led him to conclude that his office was even more important than he had first realized. Little of value stood between him and the apostle Paul, whose ministry Asbury now believed he had fought for four decades to restore.

These were Asbury's main points, but his own words account for only about half of the valedictory address. The remainder is made up of extended quotations from Thomas Haweis's *An Impartial and Succinct History of the Rise, Declension and Revival of the Church of Christ From the Birth of Our Saviour to the Present Time*, first published in London in 1800, though Asbury quoted from the second American edition, published in Baltimore in 1807. How typical for Asbury to thrust a shield between himself and critics, to rely on an outside authority to support his argument. While his thesis could hardly have been bolder, he chose to rely on an obscure English cleric to make much of his case for him.[45]

Neither impartial nor succinct (it runs more than one thousand pages), Haweis's history, according to his biographer, set out to "trace the faithful remnant of God's people which had persisted through even the darkest ages." The parts of Haweis that interested Asbury most argued that the first-century apostles were primarily, in Haweis's words, "itinerant evangelists," and that "it was a great and serious evil introduced, when philosophy and human learning were taught as a preparation for a Gospel ministry," as Asbury put it when he first read Haweis in 1805. Asbury took Haweis's book as independent confirmation that Methodist patterns had always been the practice of sincere Christians in every age. Would this kind of vital piety continue among American Methodists? Asbury wouldn't have written the valedictory address if he hadn't had his doubts.[46]

23

End of the Road

As 1813 drew to a close, Asbury was still determined to remain
a factor in the church, particularly at the annual conferences. He
hoped his presence alone would be a bulwark against complacency
and that his death would be as much an example as his life had
been. "Mr. Wesley had requested that he might not live to be idle,"
Asbury remarked to a friend during this period. "But I feel no
liberty to make such a request: I must leave it to God; it may be his
will that, as the people have seen my strength, to let them see my
weakness also."[1]

Henry Boehm quit traveling with Asbury following the Philadelphia
conference in April 1813. At the General Conference of 1812, where it
had been generally known that Boehm and Asbury would soon part
ways, Lewis Myers made a motion that the conference express its
"gratitude" to Boehm and offer him "some compensation" for collecting
overdue accounts related to the Book Concern as he traveled with
Asbury. The conference did vote its thanks, but no compensation.
"Thanks are cheap," Boehm wryly concluded.[2]

John Wesley Bond replaced Boehm as Asbury's traveling companion.
Bond's parents were converted under the preaching of Robert
Strawbridge, and Asbury had known them since the 1770s. Bond had
only joined the itinerancy in 1810, but he quickly gained Asbury's trust.
"John W Bond without exception is the best aid I every had," Asbury wrote
to Nelson Reed in February 1815.[3]

Coke's End

Asbury and the church faced another transition in 1814, though one that proved far less dramatic than it might have a decade before. Thomas Coke abruptly died at sea while sailing for India and Sri Lanka with a band of missionaries. Coke had steadily drifted away from American Methodism in recent years, busy with missionary endeavors to Africa, Asia, and the West Indies. He was instrumental in sending ten missionaries to Sierra Leone in 1796, though that effort failed because the missionaries, unprepared for the rigors of life in Africa, set to bickering among themselves and soon returned home. For the next decade the West Indies occupied most of Coke's attention with regard to missions, until about 1805 when he began to seriously consider a mission to India. By 1809 he had narrowed his focus to Sri Lanka, then known as Ceylon.[4]

The death of his wife, Penelope, in January 1811 plunged Coke into near despair. Asbury sent his condolences when he learned of Penelope's passing, though he could not resist suggesting that perhaps she had died because Coke "loved her more than God." This was harsh, even by the standards of early nineteenth-century Methodists, who often saw death as just one more way that God disciplined his children. It could hardly have given Coke much comfort, whatever Asbury's intention. Shortly after returning from his family home in Brecon, South Wales, where he had gone to bury Penelope, Coke confessed to friends that he was "very much distressed in mind." Only the prospect of foreign missions kept him from longing "to drop my Body, & be with my dear, dear, dear Penelope."[5]

Even so, Coke didn't remain single for long. That December he married Anne Loxdale, fifty-five, less than a year after Penelope's death. Writing to Mary Bosanquet Fletcher, wife of the Methodist minister and theologian John Fletcher, Coke suggested that it was Penelope who directed him to Loxdale from beyond the grave. "I bless God, he has given me the very counterpart of my late dear Wife in my present," Coke wrote in July 1812. "I cannot possibly tell which of them is most excellent. But my present dear Wife is probably more extensively useful in the Church. In large Societies she can meet one or two Classes of a day." Alas, the couple was married less than a year. Anne died on December 5, 1812.[6]

Grief-stricken once again, Coke threw himself into planning the mission to Sri Lanka and began an intensive study of Portuguese. The British conference, concerned about the cost, limited his party to seven. "I am now dead to Europe, and alive for India. God himself has said to me, 'Go to Ceylon,'" Coke wrote to Samuel Drew in June 1813. "I had rather be set naked on the coast of Ceylon, without clothes, and without a friend, than not go there." Yet, after losing two wives in close succession, Coke craved a companion. In late 1813 he proposed to, and very nearly married, a young woman he barely knew who evidently had designs on his money. Only the timely intervention of friends who knew the woman's family prevented a union that would have set her creditors on Coke, and perhaps led to his arrest.[7]

Coke's band of missionaries sailed for India on December 30, 1813, erasing all doubt about his relationship to American Methodism. "I hope Dr. Coke will devote the last of his days nobly, not in making many books, but in his apostolic mission in those two vast quarters of the globe, Asia and Africa," Asbury wrote to Zachary Myles when he learned of Coke's departure. Coke's party sailed in two ships that were parts of a fleet headed south from Europe around Africa. They had a stormy and difficult passage, though, as a seasoned traveler, Coke's calmness was a source of comfort to the others. He made it as far as the Indian Ocean, where he died suddenly in the night on May 3, only three weeks from India.[8]

It was some time before Asbury learned of Coke's death, given the logistics of communication from India to England and then on to the United States. "Doctor Coke died near the coast of Asia, was found Dead upon the cabin floor! Buried at Sea!" Asbury wrote to Jacob Gruber in July 1815. As was typical of Asbury, in death he chose only to remember the good in Coke. "He was in his temper, quick.—It was like a spark; touch it and it would fly; and was soon off . . . But jealousy, malice, or envy; dwelt not in a soul so noble as that of Coke," Asbury declared in a funeral sermon for Coke. This was accurate of Coke at his best and more than fair. Coke was "a gentleman, a scholar, and a bishop, to us— and as a minister of Christ, in zeal, in labours, and in services, the greatest man in the last century," Asbury wrote in his journal. Coke had had his differences with the American preachers, Asbury included, yet he had stood by the American church for thirty years, and for this Asbury honored him.[9]

"A living death"

As he made his way through the Carolinas in early 1814, Asbury tried to settle into his familiar travel routine, but it didn't last. He met the South Carolina conference at Fayetteville, North Carolina, on January 12, after which he had, in his words, "a serious attack of pleuritic fever, with little intermission of pain" for fifteen days. He nevertheless made it to Norfolk for the Virginia conference on February 20, and then on to the Baltimore conference, beginning March 16. Following the Baltimore meeting, he took ill at Perry Hall for three days, treating himself with an emetic. He and Bond then rode to Philadelphia for the conference's annual meeting, April 6 through 14.[10]

From there they crossed the Delaware River to New Jersey in a steamboat. During the crossing "it came on to rain very hard, and as there was no shelter to the boat . . . the Bishop was taken very sick, and had a severe spell of vomiting on board," according to Bond. They pressed on until Asbury "was taken worse on the road, and vomited much." They tried to find "a little Beer or Wine" to soothe Asbury's stomach, "but there was none to be had" among their friends. Bond prepared "a dose of medicine" by taking a tablespoon of "rhubarb, one of Peruvian Bark and two (there ought to have been three) nutmegs grated," adding them to a pint of water and boiling the mixture down to half a pint. After straining the brew, Asbury took a "wineglassful" every two hours. His condition deteriorated until he collapsed at the home of a friend in New Jersey, about seventeen miles from Philadelphia, on April 24. There he was seized with "a violent ague" followed by a high fever.[11]

It was in this condition that Henry Boehm found him, having heard of Asbury's distress. Boehm arrived on May 3, observing that Asbury was "so very low he was scarcely able to breathe." For two weeks he seemed to hover between life and death, with Bond and Boehm attending him around the clock. "His lungs were much affected; the discharge of mucus exceedingly great: his cough was very distressing, and his old astmatical complaint being agravated thereby, he at some times appeared near strangling," according to Bond. For treatment, Asbury, by his own recollection, was blistered sixteen times (Bond says seventeen) and bled three times. At one point, when his "flesh was nearly cold" and "his pulse could scarcely be perceived," a "warming pan with live coles was passed slowly over the bed for some time," and he was given "spiced wine and columbo," according to Bond.[12]

Slowly Asbury began to mend, but the toll on his system was immense. He was "so exceedingly reduced in the flesh, the bones appeared in danger of cutting through the skin," Bond observed. "I am now a walking skeleton," Asbury wrote to Christopher Frye on July 23. "He never fully recovered from that sickness, and he was physically unfit to go round his diocese again," Boehm later wrote. "It was a living death, a perpetual martyrdom." Yet he insisted on pushing on. "I would not be loved to death, and so came down from my sick room and took to the road, weak enough," Asbury wrote on July 19 in one of his first journal entries since April.[13]

Asbury professed not to fear death, and the cheerfulness with which he bore up under his illness seemed to bear this out. He later told Bond that it was "the severest, and sweetest affliction" he had ever felt. At one point during his illness, Asbury asked for a mirror. "Observing how his flesh had wasted away, and how exceedingly ghastly his appearance was; he smiled," remembering the General Conference's request that he sit for a portrait. Turning to Bond, he remarked, "If they want my likeness *now* they may have it." Bond records that even at his weakest Asbury continued to pray and sing with as much breath as he could spare.[14]

Others prayed as well. Early nineteenth-century Methodists generally didn't believe in divine healing in the way that would become popular in the later nineteenth and twentieth centuries. Sickness could be a judgment or a mercy; either way enduring it was a duty, an expression of one's faith. But on this occasion Bond and others prayed directly for Asbury's healing. A preacher from Philadelphia told Bond that in the city prayers for the bishop "were not prefaced as usual with 'If it be thy will.'—'If consistent with the wisdom of thy providence' etc. But it seemed that their faith would take no denial. Their cry was, 'Lord spare him.'" In part, this was a response to Asbury's holiness, which seemed to merit a miracle, something beyond what ordinary believers could expect. It was also a reflection of how much Methodists still looked to him to define the church. They weren't sure what they would be without him.[15]

To ease his way, the Philadelphia conference gave Asbury a small four-wheeled carriage, and he and Bond set out for the West, reaching Pittsburgh on July 23. There Asbury wrote to Christopher Frye, presiding elder of the Monongahela district, that his cough was so "incessant," with such "powerful expectoration!" that he could get only three hours sleep per night. "I am now a walking skeleton," he added. By the time they reached Cincinnati for the Ohio conference the first week in September, Asbury was coughing up blood and too sick to preside. Writing to the presiding elder, Nelson Reed, he confessed that "a Boy 6 years of age would excel me in strength...I cannot even Eat without difficulty." Yet he continued anyway, attending the Tennessee conference in Logan County, Kentucky, in late September and the South Carolina conference in Milledgeville, Georgia, at the end of December. There he "preached at the ordinations, but with so feeble a voice that many did not hear: I had coughed much and expectorated blood."[16]

Who would have blamed him if he had hunkered down in Charleston or some other retreat to regain his strength? Wouldn't a year off have been understandable? No, he had come too far for that. He wouldn't be caught idle at the end, wouldn't lose the chance to demonstrate the meaning of faithfulness. He knew that his condition was a topic of conversation among the preachers.

With this in mind, he headed north in January 1815 determined to do three things: preach, collect money for the poor, and visit old friends. Each was, in its own way, an expression of his faith. Preaching was the basic way that Methodists communicated their ideas to the broader populace and a duty (by definition) of all preachers. Asbury was determined that no one should think himself above preaching as often as possible. "Such was the shattered state of his lungs in the latter part of his life, that it afflicted him very much to preach; especially to large congregations. His cough was always greatly irritated by it," Bond wrote, reflecting on this period. "Ah!, I may always calculate on losing half the nights sleep at least, after preaching in the day. But I will freely give that, to have an opportunity of inviting poor sinners to my blessed Saviour," Asbury told Bond. Nothing, nothing should take precedence over preaching salvation to the lost. "Preach as if you had seen heaven and its celestial inhabitants and had hovered over the bottomless pit and beheld the tortures and heard the groans of the damned," Asbury advised his preachers that July.[17]

Of course, Asbury's preaching had never been all that good, particularly after 1807 when he left off regularly recording sermon outlines in his journal, and now it got even worse. The press of administrative duties and the decline of his health conspired to prevent him from any systematic preparation. Most of his sermons were given off the top of his head. "It seemed impossible for him to give that attention to reading and study which is essential for" good preaching, wrote Nathan Bangs, who knew Asbury during this period. "In his latter days his manner of preaching changed—he was often quite unmethodical in his arrangement—sometimes abruptly jumping . . . from one subject to another, intermingling anecdotes of an instructive character, and suddenly breaking forth in most tremendous rebukes of some prevalent vice, and concluding with an admonition full of point and pathos," Bangs noted. Regardless, just the act of preaching was its own testimony. His speaking could still strike "the beholder with an awe which may be better felt than described," the result of "an unearthly appearance, full of dignity . . . yet softened with . . . patience," Bangs wrote.[18]

This was exactly the reaction of Mary Pocahontas Cabell, who heard "old Bishop Asbury" preach at Lynchburg, Virginia, in February 1815. "His venerable appearance struck me with awe" as she watched "him ascend the Pulpit with his cane in one hand" and a preacher at the other. But the sermon itself was a disappointment. His "ideas" were so "unconnected that it was impossible to retain the thread of the discourse. This he continued far beyond my expectation, for I thought in a little time he would be so much exhausted . . . he frequently paused as if for the purpose of recovering breath." Cabell concluded that "old age rendered him incapable of performing his office to the satisfaction of his audience." But by now what he said was almost beside the point.[19]

As he traveled with Bond, Asbury collected small contributions from whomever was willing for what he called his "mite subscription," after the story of the widow's mite (Mark 12:42–44). Bond says that Asbury started this fund after hearing "an account of the great deficiency in the preacher's quarterage in the New-England Conference. The bishop thought it most likely that the same deficiency would prevail in Ohio and Tennessee conferences, and that many of the preachers, especially those with families, would suffer, or have to locate; in order to seek support by their own industry in some secular imployment." If the plan generated a surplus, Asbury hoped to use it to fund German-, French- and Spanish-speaking missionaries. No one was supposed to give more than a dollar, reflecting the grassroots nature of Asbury's plan. The money itself was important to Asbury, but he was also aware of the symbolic value of what he was doing. Here was the church's senior bishop, emaciated, poor, and suffering, begging for those in need. Poverty was nothing to be ashamed of, just the opposite. Social pretension was the enemy of true religion, of this Asbury remained sure. Why else limit contributions to a dollar?[20]

Connecting with old friends was another expression of Asbury's understanding of what Methodism was. He had always put people before ideas, had always been more concerned with maintaining the church's connectional nature than with formulating a systematic theology. His great gift to the church had been in working tirelessly to put the right people in the right places. Now, at the end, these links seemed as important as ever. As he passed through Virginia in February 1815, he preached in the home of Edward Dromgoole, who had joined the traveling connection in 1774. A month later in Baltimore, he visited Elizabeth Dickins, widow of John Dickins, the long-time book steward and one of Asbury's staunchest supporters (he also left Elizabeth Dickins $80 a year in his will of June 1813). On his way through Maryland and Delaware that April, he stopped to see Richard Bassett, former governor of Delaware and a friend for nearly forty years. A week later he saw Edward White, nephew of Judge Thomas White, at whose home Asbury had sheltered during the Revolutionary War. In New Jersey he called on Thomas Morrell, whom he had ordained in 1788. In June he stopped by the estate of Freeborn and Catherine Garrettson at Rhinebeck, New York, on his way south from New England. "On our route we called upon many of our old friends, Buck, Sale, Bonner, Smith, Butler," Asbury recorded as he passed through Ohio in September. "I have visited the families of Butler, Owens, Beale, Heath, Wright, Fowler, and Davis," he wrote a week later. And so it went everywhere. More than anything, Methodism was a connection of people.[21]

Yet for all his peaceful intentions, Asbury couldn't escape controversy. He hadn't forgotten the debates over episcopal authority at the General Conference of 1812. Though he and his supporters had won, it was clear that there were factions in the church separated by deepening divides. "Ah! have I lost the confidence of the American People and preachers? or of only a few overgrown members that have been disappointed; and the *city lords* who wish to be Bishops, Presiding Elders, Deacons, and to reign without us—over us?" Asbury wrote to the presiding elder, Thomas Douglass, shortly after the General Conference meeting. Having spent his career holding the church together, it would be a bitter end to see it all unravel.[22]

Now Jesse Lee brought new accusations against his use of episcopal authority. At the Virginia conference in February 1815, Asbury hadn't given Lee a circuit appointment, instead announcing that Lee would receive his appointment at the Baltimore conference in March. This was unusual, and Lee immediately concluded that Asbury was trying to prevent his election as a delegate to the 1816 General Conference. Once transferred, Lee would be ineligible to serve as a Virginia conference delegate, and it was unlikely that the Baltimore conference preachers would elect a newcomer. At the Baltimore meeting Asbury appointed Lee to the Fredericksburg circuit, located in the Baltimore conference, but Lee flatly refused to go. "It appears as if you were determined to be my enemy till you die," he wrote to Asbury on April 10. "It is high time for you to lay aside all anger, wrath and malice. After you have degraded me for years in my appointments, and cannot make a tool of me, or induce me to fall in with all your whims; you at last have trampled Methodism under your feet, and usurped a power that never belonged to you . . . thinking thereby to sink me," Lee wrote. If he didn't get an appointment in the Virginia conference, Lee threatened to "declare open war against you."[23]

Whether or not Lee's appointment had anything to do with the upcoming General Conference, it must have seemed a bitter irony to Asbury that he was still fighting the same battle that had occupied much of his career: the tendency for preachers to get comfortable in a circuit or district and refuse to leave. In one of his last letters, an address to the General Conference of 1816, Asbury warned the preachers against following the examples of James O'Kelly and William Hammet. After all these years, these episodes still burned brightly in his mind.[24]

Death, Asbury knew, was not far off. During 1815 he pushed himself to attend eight annual conferences before arriving back in South Carolina in December. From there, he and Bond set off after the first of the year, determined to make it to the General Conference in Baltimore that May. His letters from these final months have a hurried, at times almost incoherent, quality to them. When James Jenkins saw Asbury in early 1816, he was "overwhelmed with grief, and my heart sickened within me," at his physical condition. Jenkins was so overcome that he couldn't even pray with Asbury. On March

24, 1816, Asbury preached his last sermon in Richmond, Virginia. He was so weak that he had to be carried into the church, where he sat on a table to speak. A few days later he made it as far as the home of George Arnold in Spotsylvania County, where he died peacefully on March 31 "without a groan or complaint," as Bond sat by his side. It was a fitting place to breathe his last. Even today it is a rural, out-of-the-way place. A highway marker indicates that spot, but there is nothing else to see. Asbury died as he lived, unencumbered by this world's things, traveling a back road on his way to preach the gospel to lost souls.[25]

He was already a legend by the time of his death, as Asbury himself knew. "We must attend to our appointments, though we should speak but little, for the people wish to see us: we have lived and laboured so long, that we have become *a spectacle to men*," he had written the previous March. Death did nothing to tarnish his image. On May 1 the General Conference, then meeting in Baltimore, passed a resolution to remove Asbury's remains from the Arnolds' farm, where he had been buried, and bring them to Baltimore. On May 10 twenty thousand to thirty thousand people followed the coffin from the Light Street Chapel, where the General Conference was meeting, to the Eutaw Street Church where Asbury was buried. "It was the largest procession I ever saw," remembered Jacob Young, a delegate to the General Conference from Ohio.[26]

In his will, Asbury left his horse, books, and manuscripts to William McKendree. Following the General Conference, Jacob Young was assigned to

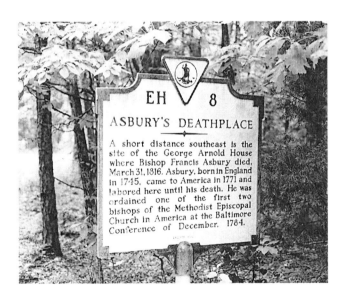

Marker identifying where Asbury died in Spotsylvania County, Virginia. (Photo by the author.)

collect these, along with some of Asbury's clothes, and take them across the Allegheny Mountains to McKendree in Wheeling, Virginia. The books, clothes, and papers were packed in valises, laid across Asbury's horse and covered by a large bearskin. Altogether, the horses and cargo "resembled those horses and packages which carried silver from one part of the country to the other," Young realized too late. As he headed into the mountains on his way to Uniontown, Pennsylvania, he passed an isolated settlement where a group of men eyed him at a tavern. "The thought struck me that there might be danger ahead." There was. Four or five miles down the road, on an isolated stretch, two of the men caught up with Young and asked him where he had come from. When he told them Baltimore, they asked if money was plentiful there. No, said Young, to which one of the men replied, "You appear to have plenty of it here." "No, sir; there is no money there. This horse and package belonged to Bishop Asbury, before his death," Young replied. "Is Bishop Asbury dead?" asked one of the men. "I have seen and heard him preach in my father's house." The men paused a few moments and then galloped off. Who would risk stealing the last earthly possessions of a saint?[27]

Epilogue

Bending Frank

There is a scene in *The Damnation of Theron Ware* that captures a
fundamental shift in nineteenth-century Methodism. Harold
Frederic begins his 1896 novel about the fall of a young Methodist
minister with a description of an annual conference meeting at
which the preachers are just about to receive their appointments for
the coming year. Seated in the church is a collection of "bent and
decrepit veterans" who could remember Asbury. They lean "forward
with trembling and misshapen hands behind their hairy ears,
waiting to hear their names read out on the superannuated list, it
might be for the last time." Surrounding these old men is a group
of middle-aged preachers, "generally of a robust type, with burly
shoulders, and bushing beards framing shaven upper lips, and who
looked for the most part like honest and prosperous farmers attired
in their Sunday clothes." Mixed in with these are "specimens of a
more urban class, worthies with neatly trimmed whiskers, white
neckcloths, and even indications of hair-oil,—all eloquent of citified
charges." There are even a few young seminary professors. Frederic
is quite clear as to how these groups relate to one another. "The
impress of zeal and moral worth seemed to diminish by regular
gradations as one passed to younger faces; and among the very
beginners, who had been ordained only within the past day or two,
this decline was peculiarly marked," Frederic writes. "It was almost
a relief to note the relative smallness of their number, so plainly
was it to be seen that they were not the men their forbears had

been."[1] The church wasn't what it used to be. What it had gained in refinement, it had lost in zeal.

The idea that Methodist zeal had declined was widely held by the late nineteenth century, even as the church continued to grow in size and respectability. Membership increased to more than 250,000 by 1820 and nearly half a million by 1830. By 1876 all branches of Methodism in the United States could count more than fifty-three thousand itinerant and local preachers, more than 2.9 million members, and more than 2.2 million children enrolled in Sunday schools. Growth in numbers brought new wealth. By 1860 American Methodists owned nearly twenty thousand buildings, almost 38 percent of all churches in the United States. These were valued at more than $33 million, nearly 20 percent of the value of all American churches. Following Asbury's death, Methodists launched a sustained campaign to build colleges and universities, opening more than two hundred schools and colleges between 1830 and 1860. This included Indiana Asbury (later DePauw) University in Greencastle, Indiana, named, ironically, for someone who by the end of his life doubted the value of colleges. Methodists were also leaders in popular publishing. By 1831 the *Christian Advocate and Journal*, published in New York City, had the largest circulation of any weekly paper in the nation. All of this brought political clout, particularly in new western states like Ohio, and a comfortable sense of middle-class security.[2]

Success is hard to argue with, yet many discerned a darker side to Methodism's rising social status. Many of these so-called "croakers" had known Asbury personally. Most of the dozens of circuit rider autobiographies written in the nineteenth century were, to some degree, jeremiads against the church's complacent prosperity. They decried a general decline in holiness and discipline but were particularly troubled by the erosion of the itinerancy. "I fear there is a tendency to locality," James Quinn wrote in 1851. He acknowledged that many believed the itinerancy "has had its day, and must go down." "Learned clergy, who study and write their sermons," couldn't be expected to "submit to the toils and privations of an itinerant life." When Methodists "have pews, and organs, and pay the choir to do their singing," when "the itinerant is snugly fixed in the village station, and the local preachers do[es] what little itinerant work is done," then "my fears come on," Quinn lamented. Writing in 1857, Jacob Young worried that "though the Church is not going down yet, there are strong indications that she is in extreme danger; and in that very day that itinerant preachers begin to love pleasure, ease and idleness, the Church will sink in their hands; and I am sorry to say there is a strong tendency in that direction."[3]

Asbury's long-time traveling companion, Henry Boehm, perhaps best summed up these misgivings. Boehm claimed that he "never belonged to the family of croakers," yet in his 1866 memoir he concluded that "there was a power among the fathers, both in the ministry and laity" that the church had lost. "In some matters I cannot but think that, as a Church, we have retrograded," Boehm wrote. "The people and preachers in that day were patterns of plainness; we conform more to the world, and have lost much of the spirit of self-denial they possessed. Our fathers paid great attention to Church discipline, and their preaching was more direct; they aimed at the heart, and looked for more immediate results than we of the present day."[4]

One thing was certain: There were no more Asburys. Almost no one of his generation was left by 1816. Richard Whatcoat and Thomas Coke were dead, as was John Wesley. Joseph Pilmore was still preaching in Philadelphia (he died in 1825), but his connection to Methodism had long since been severed. Of the preachers who joined the traveling connection before the Christmas Conference of 1784, only six still held conference appointments at the time of Asbury's death: Philip Bruce, Freeborn Garrettson, Jesse Lee, William Phoebus, Nelson Reed, and Thomas Ware. Lee died in September 1816, and Bruce and

Henry Boehm (1775–1875) late in life. (From Abel Stevens, *History of the Methodist Episcopal Church in the United States of America*, vol. 3 [New York: Carlton & Porter, 1867].)

Garrettson effectively retired the next year. Garrettson was perhaps the most respected of these preachers, but he had never been willing to leave his family and home overlooking the Hudson River, though he felt guilty for his relative idleness in retirement. He died in 1827. None of the rest came close to Asbury's stature in the church. Ezekiel Cooper might be added to the list of founding preachers who survived Asbury (he joined the traveling connection in 1785), but Cooper's most vigorous days were behind him, though he lived till 1847. Asbury had simply outlasted his peers.[5]

Saints are tough acts to follow. "When will the world, or the church, be favoured and blessed with such another *servant of God*, as that which we have lost? I never expect to see one come up to his standard," Ezekiel Cooper wrote shortly after Asbury's death. Of the two preachers elected to replace Asbury as bishops, Robert R. Roberts was married and Enoch George was a widower with young children. Roberts maintained a farm in western Pennsylvania after his election, and later one in Indiana, to support his family. They resembled Harold Frederic's solid, respectable middle-aged preachers more than Asbury. Put together, they couldn't match Asbury's single-minded devotion, nor were they any better at managing the preachers.[6]

Asbury was as Christ-like a figure as most Methodists could imagine. Tributes pointed to his intense spirituality and perseverance, his ability to connect with people, and his administrative finesse as the defining qualities of his career. "Nothing short of deep and uniform piety could so long have secured to him the love and confidence of a people who knew how to distinguish between the form and power of godliness," noted an obituary in the 1816 conference minutes. "He was always of a slender constitution, and yet never spared himself, but ventured through the greatest difficulties and dangers, in order to preach to the people and attend to the Preachers," Jesse Lee wrote shortly after Asbury's passing. Lee continued: "He was deeply pious, remarkably fervent and constant in prayer. His peculiar talent was for governing the Preachers . . . He was generally known throughout the United States, much esteemed, and greatly beloved . . . his advice requested, and his directions attended to," although not always by Lee, who had railed at Asbury about his annual appointment only the year before. Yet now that it was all over, Lee realized that a great divide had been crossed and not necessarily for the better.[7]

For many who had known Asbury, the passage of time did little to diminish their respect for him. "He was often afflicted, especially when far advanced in life, and frequently travelled and laboured, when he could scarcely put one foot before the other. A more indefatigable preacher I never knew," Freeborn Garrettson wrote in 1827. "Few men have a greater knowledge of human nature than he had. My intimacy with him was of about forty years standing...he was, I believe, perfectly free from the love of the world," Garrettson added. Writing in 1848, the New York preacher Abner Chase, who had joined the traveling connection in 1810, remembered that Asbury had "commanded a respect and veneration which no superintendent of our church at the present day can reasonably expect to receive." "He was the most unselfish being I was ever acquainted with," Henry Boehm concluded in his 1866 memoir. "Bishop Whatcoat I loved, Bishop M'Kendree I admired, Bishop Asbury I venerated." Jacob Gruber, who knew Asbury for more than a decade, but never traveled with him for an extended period, nevertheless described him as "the best friend I had in the world." The Genesee conference preacher Benjamin Paddock remembered sitting, at age twenty-six, by Asbury's side in April 1815 as the bishop recovered from a fever in Philadelphia. "The hours spent in his society I then felt to be the most precious of my whole life; nor have the many years I have lived since in the least changed my estimate of them. His words have been treasured up as if they were the utterances of inspiration itself," Paddock later recalled. "We have had other great and good men in the Episcopacy, but we have had but one Francis Asbury," wrote Paddock, who named his son after the bishop.[8]

Yet it didn't take long for contemporaries to begin bending Asbury's legacy. One of the first and most discerning analyses of Asbury's life was written by Ezekiel Cooper in the form of a funeral sermon, which Cooper preached at St. George's church in Philadelphia in April 1816 and published in 1819. The published version, at 230 pages, is more of a short biography than a sermon (one can only hope that the actual sermon was a good deal shorter). Cooper had known Asbury for more than thirty years and was aware of how closely the bishop's life had been watched. "Few, very few, have been so generally known...we have known him to be critically inspected, carefully watched, closely examined, thoroughly tested," Cooper wrote. He saw two primary strengths in Asbury's ministry: his deep piety, reflected in his legendary life of prayer and charity, and his ability to influence others, demonstrated by his administration of the preachers. "In almost every circle, where he moved, he gained a kind of irresistible ascendency, influence, and authority," Cooper observed. "What could he do, that he did not do? For he exhausted all his strength, broke down his constitution, spent his talents and his all, and wore out his life, for the good of man, and for the glory of God."[9]

Even so, Cooper saw in Asbury failings that extended to the church as a whole. If Asbury's life could serve as an example of all that was good in the church, it could also serve as a metaphor for what was wrong. To this end, Cooper freely admitted that Asbury wasn't a scholar or a consistently good preacher. But what concerned Cooper most was Asbury's reluctance to encourage more democracy in the church. "It has also been objected, 'That he was too fond of power, and too tenacious of maintaining his authority, and of supporting his power,'" Cooper wrote. "I have no difficulty in admitting, honestly and candidly, that the objections, when considered on general principles, are too well founded." Cooper believed that this reflected mostly a lack of patience. "In candour, we ought to admit, that, apparently, he was more deficient, in the exercise of *patience*, than in any one of the christian graces." This created a serious problem for the church. Asbury's piety had given him the humility to avoid abusing his extensive power, but would that be the case with future leaders? Cooper doubted it. He had been a leading advocate for greater democracy and decentralization in the church's polity for more than a decade, and he took this occasion to bend Asbury's legacy in that direction.[10]

Joseph Travis had a different concern. Travis's parents became Methodists under the preaching of Freeborn Garrettson, and Joseph himself was called to preach under Lorenzo Dow, joining the South Carolina conference in 1806. A confirmed southerner, Travis was "aware that there was some prejudice against Bishop Asbury in the South, arising from the introduction of that unfortunate clause in our General Rules concerning slavery." Writing on the eve of the Civil War in 1855, Travis set out to dispel any misgivings about Asbury's orthodoxy on the slave question. "In all the conversational and epistolary intercourse that I have had with Bishop Asbury, not one item was ever even hinted to me in favor of Abolition from the good old man," Travis wrote. This, of course, was a decidedly one-sided reading of Asbury, who became increasingly conflicted over slavery, especially after 1800. "He frequently spake of it with deep concern," remembered John Wesley Bond, who traveled with Asbury during the last two years of his life. Yet for all of his equivocation, Asbury never came to see slavery as anything but a moral evil. As sectional tensions increased, "he did not see what we as a ministry could do better than to try to get both masters and servants to get all the religion they could, and get ready to leave a troublesome world," Bond wrote. Still, Asbury considered anyone who continued to hold slaves out of "avarice . . . to be a slave-holder in *soul* . . . he could not see how a person who had a slave-holding soul in them could ever get to the Kingdom of Heaven," Bond wrote. This doesn't sound much like Travis's proslavery "good old man."[11]

Historians of the broader church had their own uses for Asbury. Nathan Bangs (1778–1862), who wrote one of the first comprehensive histories of American Methodism in 1839, celebrated Asbury's legendary piety and perseverance, his ability to judge human motivations and manage the conferences, his charity, and his ability to connect with people "in whatever company he appeared, whether religious or irreligious, whether high or low, learned or unlearned." No one, apart from perhaps Wesley himself, had ever led a life of greater diligence or integrity.[12]

Yet Bangs, like Cooper, saw faults in Asbury that spoke to larger concerns. After his appointment to New York City in 1810, Bangs became increasingly concerned with promoting the church's refinement. Reflecting the domesticated trajectory of Methodism in the mid-nineteenth century, Bangs noted that Asbury "sometimes manifested sternness bordering upon a hardheartedness." This, Bangs concluded, was because Asbury had never been a husband or father. Hence he "did not always make sufficient allowance for human frailties and for the unavoidable ills which accompany a married traveling preacher." Nor did he push "the people sufficiently in making provision for their ministers, particularly for men of families." Asbury "seemed to fear that if they were too well off as it respects this world's goods, they would lose their zeal and spirituality." Asbury's second mistake was not following up the disappointment of Cokesbury with another college, a mistake "which will require years of bitter

Nathan Bangs (1778–1862) in his later years. (From Abel Stevens, *History of the Methodist Episcopal Church in the United States of America*, vol. 3 [New York: Carlton & Porter, 1867].)

repentance and assiduous amendment to atone for, as it has thrown us behind the age in scientific and mental improvement," Bangs wrote.[13]

In his massive four-volume history of Methodism published in 1867, Abel Stevens mostly followed Cooper and Bangs in praising Asbury's perseverance and administrative skill. "His discrimination of character was marvelous; his administrative talents . . . placed him unquestionably at the head of the leading characters of American ecclesiastical history. No one man has done more for Christianity in the western hemisphere," Stevens wrote. Yet Stevens also shaped Asbury's legacy to reflect his own concerns. Stevens defended Asbury's isolation in Delaware during the American Revolution, arguing that it reflected a patriotic commitment to America when Wesley's other missionaries were fleeing to England. At the same time, Stevens was less sympathetic than Bangs toward Asbury's handling of the sacramental crisis in 1779 and 1780 because, in Stevens's view, Asbury didn't adequately respect the democratic process embodied in the regular conference schedule. Where Bangs was more concerned with protecting the episcopacy, Stevens, like Cooper, was more concerned with promoting democracy.[14]

For all of their differences, Cooper, Bangs, and Stevens agreed that Asbury had been an overwhelmingly positive force in American society. Not so Edward Drinkhouse. After forty years of obsessive study, Drinkhouse set out to write a history of the Methodist Protestant Church in 1892. When they broke with the main Methodist body in 1830, the Methodist Protestants rejected the episcopacy and the presiding eldership and gave laymen equal representation with the clergy in their general conferences. Drinkhouse's history is, more than anything else, a long argument against "the Paternal system of Asbury and the hierarchic features embodied by his pliant followers." After the formation of the American church in 1784, "with the fatality attending autocratic minds, finding himself sole master in America," it occurred to Asbury, "as is always the case with such typical characters, that the safe way to meet . . . incipient demands for a more liberal administration, was to tighten the fetters of personal authority." If Wesley's "autocratic instinct" was bad, Asbury's was worse, amounting to a "form of lunacy." In "the exercise of his rule-loving propensities—a dominating passion which knew no subordination . . . Paternalism found its personification," Drinkhouse tells us.[15]

Yet for all of the abuse that Drinkhouse heaps on Asbury, he largely agrees with Cooper, Bangs, and Stevens that the foundation of Asbury's authority was his piety and administrative skill. Asbury "ruled . . . by large consent . . . there being no one his equal in practical wisdom, in strategic ability, in arduous labors and single-eyed devotion." Though a few brave preachers "chafed under the Asburyan rule," most were simply overawed. "It was utterly incongruous with the free air all about them, but they saw in their leader such an example of unfeigned piety and self-sacrifice that they submitted for the gospel's sake."

Even to Drinkhouse, Asbury's career is regrettable only to the extent that it poisoned the well of democracy.[16]

Among nineteenth-century authors, Drinkhouse is perhaps alone in the depth of sarcasm he leveled against Asbury, but others developed similar lines of criticism. Nicholas Snethen, who traveled with Asbury for several years beginning in 1800, later became one of the leading advocates for more democracy in the church and helped to found the Methodist Protestant Church. Like nearly every analyst of Asbury's life, Snethen concluded that much of Asbury's influence rested on his reputation for piety and holiness. "He was morally good . . . He was temperate in all things . . . in meat, in drink, and apparel; not greedy of filthy lucre; not a lover of money, not a lover of this world; not proud. In regard to his passions, neither his friends nor his enemies had cause for pity or reproach. There is reason to believe, that at an early period, like a man of God, he submitted to the admonition, 'Flee also youthful lusts,'" Snethen declared in an 1816 funeral sermon for Asbury. Unfortunately, in Snethen's view, this same single-mindedness produced a degree of ambition that blinded Asbury to the concerns of others. "It cannot be concealed, that he was not incapable of the exercise of that awful attribute of power, hard-heartedness to those individual personal feelings and interests, which seem to oppose that execution of public plans. Constantly in the habit of making the greatest personal sacrifices to the public good, his mind could not balance betwixt the obligation of duty, and the accommodation, or conveniency of others." Snethen further argued that Asbury's judgment was impaired by his practice of pushing himself "beyond his strength. Nature cannot long be overdone with impunity. Had he known the art of doing less, he could have done better." The crux of Snethen's criticism was that Asbury didn't trust the judgment of others enough and used his moral authority to hold back dissent.[17]

Like Snethen, Alexander M'Caine traveled with Asbury as a young preacher but later rejected the legitimacy of episcopal Methodism and joined the Methodist Protestant Church. In his most polemical book, *Letters on the Organization and Early History of the Methodist Episcopal Church* (1850), M'Caine repeatedly asserted that the Methodist episcopacy was a "fraud" and that Asbury was *"bad at heart."* With regard to Wesley and Asbury, M'Caine writes that "Mr. Wesley resembles the countryman in the fable, who found the adder stiff and frozen in his field, who brought it to his house, placed it near the fire, did everything in his power to restore it to life. Mr. Asbury is like the adder, who, as soon as he was warmed and invigorated, began to *hiss*, and *strike* at all who stood in his way, until at last, he stuck his fangs in his benefactor to whom he owed his existence, and stung him to death." Even before Drinkhouse, M'Caine and Snethen fashioned an image of Asbury as autocrat that has continued to dominate current scholarship.[18]

The nineteenth-century biographies of Asbury published by Methodist presses took a more favorable view of their subject, as one might expect. They add detail but break little new analytical ground. Frederick Briggs, writing in 1874, asserted that the key to Asbury's influence was his single-minded devotion to proclaiming the gospel. "To what is his prodigious influence to be attributed?" asks Briggs. "To his extraordinary intellectual endowments, his great scholastic attainments, or his elevated and commanding social position?" Obviously not. "The explanation of the whole is that Francis Asbury ... lived for a purpose and aim." Early twentieth-century biographers agreed. For Ezra Squier Tipple, Asbury was defined by his piety and self-sacrifice. "No man ever lived who more steadfastly yearned after holiness than Francis Asbury," Tipple wrote. This gave Asbury the internal strength to put the good of the church before his own well-being. Self-sacrifice was the lesson that Tipple hoped his readers would learn from Asbury's life.[19]

What neither Asbury's admirers (Cooper, Bangs, Stevens, Emory, Briggs, and Tipple) or critics (Drinkhouse, M'Caine, and Snethen) doubted was that he was important. Drinkhouse in particular was obsessed with what he saw as Asbury's pervasive and pernicious legacy. Yet as the nineteenth century progressed, Asbury began to lose his salience in popular culture. "There is a man, not even named in our leading histories, who yet has wrought more deeply into American life in its social, moral, and religious facts than any other who lived and acted his part in our more formative period," began an 1866 article in *Harper's New Monthly Magazine*. What follows is a brief laudatory biography of Asbury that assumes, clearly enough, that readers know little about him. In the fifty years following his death, Asbury failed to become an American hero. "The names of Ethan Allen and Anthony Wayne have been more familiar to the popular ear of America than that of Asbury; yet how trivial their influence compared to his!" the anonymous author in *Harper's* concluded.[20]

Methodists themselves were largely responsible for Asbury's fall from popular grace. What the croakers decried, others celebrated. Upwardly mobile Methodists were glad to be rid of ministers "who preached dreary out-of-date sermons, and who lacked even the most rudimentary sense of social distinctions," as Harold Frederic put it in *Theron Ware*. Most were happy to see the church's general rise in wealth and social status. They agreed with a writer who scoffed at "good old Methodism" and "a certain class of deplorable croakers," in the *Christian Advocate and Journal* of 1841. "And is good old Methodism susceptible of no improvement? If our noble fathers, in the days of their poverty, *walked*, is that any sufficient reason why we, their sons, now that we can afford it, should not *ride*? What, sir, shall we be so wedded to old prejudices, that we must travel in an old Pennsylvania wagon, at the rate of two miles an hour, when all the world is flying by steam? . . . I trust, sir, that Methodism will repudiate all such prejudices, and keep pace with the spirit of the age." Under this kind of pressure, mandatory attendance at class meetings and other forms of communal discipline began to fall out of favor. In 1834 one minister even suggested that "wealthy members purchase immunity from discipline (especially concerning class meeting) by providing generous financial support for the church." Asbury couldn't have meant much to this kind of Methodist.[21]

By the twentieth century most Methodists saw themselves as part of the Protestant mainstream. From this vantage point Asbury looked different than he had in the nineteenth century. Much of this new historical perspective was shaped by William Warren Sweet (1881–1959), the dean of Methodist studies in the first half of the twentieth century. Sweet grew up in Baldwin City, Kansas, before attending college at Ohio Wesleyan University and seminary at Drew University, followed by a doctorate at the University of Pennsylvania. He then taught at Ohio Wesleyan and Depauw University before becoming professor of American Christianity at the University of Chicago. He was, according to his biographer, "the first trained, professional, American historian who specialized in religion."[22]

Sweet was shaped by his background in the church (he had planned to become a minister before his doctorate) and the academy. As was typical of historians of the early twentieth century, he believed that history could be pursued as an objective science, free of personal bias, in which the facts spoke for themselves. He was also deeply influenced by Frederick Jackson Turner's frontier thesis, which hypothesized that the availability of "free" frontier land had made possible the development of American democracy and individualism. Sweet's contribution was to find a role for the church (by which he mostly meant the Methodists, Baptists, Presbyterians, and Congregationalists) in this scheme, arguing that organized religion's greatest contribution to American life was in bringing civilization to the frontier. "On every American frontier life was crude, and ignorance and lawlessness were everywhere in evidence. The great majority of the people were indifferent to the prevailing conditions and accepted them as a matter of course," Sweet writes in one of his later books. Fortunately, all was not lost. In "every considerable community," there was "a little company of people, the majority of them constituting the membership and the ministry of the frontier churches, who believed that conditions could be changed; that life on every frontier could be raised to a higher level, and thus through them the seeds of culture were planted in the west." It was religion that refined "manners and taste," that created "new and higher interests," that inspired "men with loftier ambitions and sacrificial purpose."[23]

Within this framework Asbury is presented as a "benevolent despot," and an agent of order and control. In regard to the "religious frenzy" often associated with frontier revivals, Sweet assures his readers that it is "an entire misconception" that Asbury and his preachers did anything to promote such "extravagances." "Asbury, like Wesley, believed that everything should be done decently and in order. Indeed, order was his passion and this he communicated to his

Asbury monument, located at the intersection of Mt. Pleasant Street and 16th Street, Washington, D.C. (Photo by the author.)

preachers." Sweet's scholarship was voluminous (he published some twenty-five books, beginning in 1912) and he did more than anyone to make primary sources readily available. Nonetheless his interpretation of Asbury has done as much to obscure as illuminate. In Sweet's hands Asbury became the patron saint of decency and decorum.[24]

These views were reflected in what remained of Asbury's image in the broader culture. As the U. S. Army Band played "The Star-Spangled Banner" on a "perfect" October day in 1924, with "not a fleck of cloud in the sky," an imposing bronze statue of Asbury on horseback was unveiled in Washington, D.C., at the intersection of Sixteenth and Mount Pleasant streets. Celebrated amidst much fanfare in front of a distinguished audience—President Calvin Coolidge gave the keynote address—the unveiling marked a high-water mark for Methodist influence in American society, and perhaps for all of mainstream Protestantism. The Scopes monkey trial took place the next summer in Dayton, Tennessee. It is significant that the church selected Asbury to represent them, though it was a carefully crafted image of Asbury that the clergy and politicians chose to remember. To them Asbury was first and foremost a patriotic American. "On the foundation of a religious civilization which he sought to build our country has enjoyed greater blessings of liberty and prosperity than were ever before the lot of man," Coolidge declared amid cries of "Hear! Hear!" and vigorous applause. "Asbury must be called great, because he laid the foundation of the great Christian empire, of the increase of whose ministry and peace there shall be no end," Methodist Bishop J. W. Hamilton added.[25]

Granted, public celebrations of this nature are generally not the place to raise a controversy, but even the statue itself seems to reduce Asbury to a supporter of American progress and empire. The left side of the statue's pedestal reads: "IF YOU SEEK FOR THE RESULTS OF HIS LABORS YOU WILL FIND THEM IN OUR CHRISTIAN CIVILIZATION." On the right: "HIS CONTINUOUS JOURNEYING THROUGH CITIES, VILLAGES AND SETTLEMENTS FROM 1771 TO 1816, GREATLY PROMOTED PATRIOTISM, EDUCATION, MORALITY AND RELIGION IN THE AMERICAN REPUBLIC." Not very elegant and not very accurate. The effect is to obscure Asbury behind a haze of patriotic consensus, to make him seem no different from any of the generals memorialized in bronze throughout the city, only perhaps less well armed.[26]

But the monument builders had their own battles to fight. They were all too familiar with the growth of unbelief and agnosticism, which had been accelerating since the Civil War and seemed to threaten the intellectual foundations of religious faith as never before. This seemed particularly true among

The dedication of the Francis Asbury monument in Washington, D.C., October 15, 1924. (National Photo Company Collection, Prints & Photographs Division, Library of Congress, LC-DIG-npcc-26317.)

intellectual leaders. "As for God, sin, grace, salvation—the introduction of these ghosts from the dead past we regard as inexcusable, so completely do their unfamiliar presences put us out of countenance, so effectively do they, even under the most favorable circumstances, cramp our style," historian Carl Becker wrote in his influential book, *The Heavenly City of the Eighteenth-Century Philosophers* (1932). The ministers who dedicated the Asbury monument knew that Becker wasn't alone in his views. In fact, Becker was raised in a strict Methodist home in Iowa, which he later regarded as "the heart of the Methodist menace." In response, Methodist leaders crafted an Asbury who would appeal to people inclined to listen to Becker. Despite their praise for Asbury on that perfect October day, none of the monument builders wanted to live as he did. Consequently, they chose to preserve only a shadow of Asbury's life. By the 1920s the leadership of mainstream Methodism had crossed a great chasm, leaving Asbury, frozen in bronze, on the other side.[27]

The most sensational biography of Asbury is Herbert Asbury's *A Methodist Saint: The Life of Bishop Asbury*, published by Alfred A. Knopf in 1927. Having turned his back on his strict religious upbringing in a small town in south-eastern Missouri, Herbert intended to expose Francis as the demagogue of a fanatical religion that promised "spiritual loot" to gullible rubes. In an earlier book, *Up From Methodism* (he later wrote *Gangs of New York*), Asbury described growing up among Methodists on his father's side (he claims that Francis Asbury was the half-brother of his great-great-grandfather, but this is unlikely) and Baptists on his mother's side. The more devout the relative, the more repressive and sadistic their religion. "Among all my relatives I do not recall one whose home was not oppressed, and whose life was not made miserable and fretful, by the terrible fear of a relentless God whose principal occupation seemed to be snooping about searching for someone to punish," Asbury writes. There is a salacious quality to much of *Up From Methodism*. "It seemed impossible for Preachers or devout Brothers to say 'virgin' as casually as they did other words; they gloated over it, toyed with it, rolled it about their tongues and tasted the full flavor of it before it slid drippingly from their lips with amazing clarity of pronunciation. Usually they accompanied it with a doleful sigh," Asbury tells us. "I find myself full of contempt for the Church, and disgust for the forms of religion. To me such things are silly; I cannot under-stand how grown people can believe in them, or how they can repress their giggles as they listen to the ministerial platitudes and perform such mumm-eries as are the rule in all churches," Asbury concludes. No unbiased observer, this Herbert Asbury.[28]

Asbury begins *Methodist Saint* by informing his readers that while Elizabeth Asbury "was pregnant God appeared to her in a vision and told her that her child would be a boy and that the lad was destined to become a great religious leader and spread the Gospel among the heathen, although He did not specify the Americans." We are also told that Elizabeth was "ambitious" for Francis "to become Archbishop of Canterbury," and that her "favourite scriptural readings were the bloody horrors of the Old Testament, and those portions of the gospels which describe the agonies of Christ bleeding on the cross," which she dinned into Francis even during his infancy. And this is all on the first page! Later, Herbert tells us that at the time Francis came to America, "the people generally were not only weary of wresting a living from the wilderness, but had become alarmed and frightened by the clamours and excitements of the impending Revolution, and had reached that pitch of emotional insanity and instability which has always been essential to the success of Methodism."[29]

In a chapter entitled "The Father of Prohibition," Herbert tells us that Francis was "the real father of prohibition in the United States," who did more than anyone else to frighten good folk away from the enjoyment of a refreshing beverage. With evident glee Herbert describes the "jerking, barking, jumping, hopping, dancing, prancing, screeching, howling, writhing in fits and convulsions, falling in cataleptic trances" and other "holy antics" that attended camp meetings. "One child was considered especially blessed because she barked hoarsely, like a mastiff, while the best the others could do was to imitate spaniels or other small dogs," he informs us, though without citing a source. "Francis Asbury regarded camp-meetings with great favour; to him the spectacle of thousands of men and women and little children writhing in torment was a glorious visitation of the Lord, and he loved to hear a score of howling prophets belabouring the wicked." One has to admire the audacity of an author who, when faced with a lull in his narrative, simply makes something up, the more outrageous the better. In the end, Herbert's main complaint against Francis was that he didn't drink, smoke, or chase women enough. Instead, Francis's "whole life is a record of fearful grovelling before the Almighty." *Methodist Saint* is a fun read, but only if one doesn't take it too seriously.[30]

But many did. It is a testimony to just how little the reading public knew about Francis Asbury or early Methodism that Herbert Asbury could publish *Methodist Saint* with a leading commercial press to generally favorable reviews. The *New York Times* touted the book as "impressively documented" and "damaging to Methodism" in the way that it exposed the church's early fanaticism and "grotesque personalities."[31] This kind of reception helps explain why William Warren Sweet and the Asbury monument backers were anxious to make their founding figure seem so rational and respectable. They can perhaps be forgiven for only seeing in Asbury what they needed. They were willing to admit that he could be heavy-handed, but they insisted that he was also a calmly rational man who would have felt perfectly at home in modern America.

More recent biographers of Asbury have either largely accepted the Sweet synthesis or failed to capture the attention of historians or the broader public with an alternative interpretation. L.C. Rudolph's short but lively 1966 biography presents Asbury as well-meaning and self-sacrificing, but an autocrat nonetheless. He was the "kingpin" at conferences, who "ruled ... with an iron hand." Like Sweet, Rudolph roots Asbury's life in a "hyperdemocratic" frontier experience that, by its very nature, no longer connects to modern American life. This has the tendency to relegate Asbury to a bygone era, to make him seem quaint and not terribly relevant or even likeable. "No biographer should try to make him lovable, for this he would never allow himself to be," Rudolph writes. Yet Asbury loved and was loved, despite his flaws. His life was rich with human drama and spiritual commitments that still connect to our world.[32]

Driven by their own agendas, most commentators have missed the extent to which Asbury redefined the religious landscape of America. There was no blueprint for what he did, for building a large, strictly voluntary religious movement led by non-elites in a pluralistic society. Yet his understanding of what it meant to be pious, connected, culturally responsive, and effectively organized has worked its way deep into the fabric of American religious life. If ever there was an American saint, it was Francis Asbury.

What accounts for Asbury's legendary drive and single-minded persever-ance? Like all of us, he was the product of inherent traits and the sum of his experiences and the way he interpreted them. Had he not experienced an evangelical conversion and joined the Methodists, he probably would have married, had children, and become a fairly typical Birmingham-area artisan. Methodism gave Asbury's life a razor-sharp focus, a mission of unwavering certainty into which he could channel all his energies. The call to preach the gospel and warn sinners of the wrath to come justified distancing himself from an overly protective mother and a flawed father, crossing the ocean to a new land, and forgoing a more conventional lifestyle for the career of an itinerant preacher. It also gave him the confidence to grasp for leadership and defy senior colleagues, even John Wesley. Many preachers of his day believed that preaching the gospel and building up a community of believers were the most important things they could do in life. What made Asbury unique was his willingness to follow this reasoning to its logical conclusion. While others hedged their bets by combining ministry with marriage, family, and other pursuits, Asbury devoted all his energies to a single goal. He simply believed in a God who transcended this world.

He was not a demagogue. The image of Asbury as iron-fisted autocrat has obscured his ability to connect with people and understand them, especially as he matured and became more sure of himself. He was so successful as a leader in part because he allowed for a variety of opinions and approaches within the broad scope of the Methodist system. Asbury tried to find a place for just about everyone who was seeking God's grace. He was "unwilling, to cut off any member, whether in, or out of conference, until every prudential, and christian means, to reclaim, recover, and save them, had been used," as Ezekiel Cooper put it. That there were so few schisms in the church during his career is testimony to his success in this regard. Spiritual discipline was essential, he believed, but not rigid consensus, except on the most basic of doctrines.

His ability to understand others was also reflected in his cultural sensitivi-ty, which was as nuanced as that of any of his contemporaries. From the beginning of his career in America, Asbury had a better feel for the tension between faith and culture than most of the religious leaders around him.

No sooner had he arrived in America in 1771 than he concluded that Joseph Pilmore and Richard Boardman were making a mistake by staying in Philadelphia and New York and catering to elite sensibilities. This same feel for the direction of popular sentiment led Asbury to stay in America through the revolution and to endorse the enthusiastic style of southern Methodism. It generally helped him to choose wisely in deciding where to appoint individual preachers and who to elevate to positions of leadership. It also allowed him to appreciate the deep sincerity of religious commitment among African American converts, but prevented him from pushing for an unequivocal end to slavery. Asbury was too enmeshed in popular white culture to see the full extent of his own racism, though he was hardly unique in this regard. Engaging competing cultural agendas was bound to be a messy affair, and it was. It would have been easier to limit the number of cultural settings the church engaged, but this would have undermined the Methodist mission as Asbury saw it.

The Damnation of Theron Ware is about the fall of a young Methodist minister into unbelief and disgrace, driven by his vanity and ambition to rise in the world, an ambition made all the more apparent by the miserly intolerance of his congregation. The book portrays a church largely devoid of honesty, generosity, or sincere spiritual devotion, the opposite of everything Asbury spent his career trying to create. Toward the end, as Ware is in the process of jettisoning the last flimsy remains of his faith, Frederic writes that "His thoughts were absorbed ... by the contemplation of vast, abstract schemes of creation and the government of the universe, and it only diverted and embarrassed his mind to try to fasten it upon the details of personal salvation."[33] At this point the divide between Frederic's character and Asbury could hardly have been greater. In the decades after Asbury's death, Methodism came to embody something of both. Though he had hoped for better, Asbury wouldn't have been surprised.

Abbreviations

Bangs, *History*	Nathan Bangs, *A History of the Methodist Episcopal Church*, 3rd ed., 4 vols. (New York: T. Mason and G. Lane, 1839–1840)
BC	Barratt's Chapel, Frederica, Del.
BPL	City Archives and Local History Department, Birmingham Public Library, Birmingham, England
Briggs, *Asbury*,	Frederick W. Briggs, *Bishop Asbury: A Biographical Study for Christian Workers*, 3rd ed. (London: Wesleyan Conference Office, c. 1880s; first published in 1874)
Coke, *Extracts* (1793)	Thomas Coke, *Extracts of the Journals of the Rev. Dr. Coke's Five Visits to America.* (London: G. Paramore, 1793)
Coke, *Extracts* (1816)	Thomas Coke, *Extracts of the Journals of the Late Rev. Thomas Coke, L.L.D.; Comprising Several Visits to North-America and the West-Indies; His Tour Through a Part of Ireland, and His Nearly Finished Voyage to Bombay in the East-Indies: To Which is Prefixed a Life of the Doctor.* By Joseph Sutcliffe. (Dublin: R. Napper, 1816)

Dorland's	*Dorland's Illustrated Medical Dictionary*, 29th ed.
DUL	Rare Book, Manuscript and Special Collections Library, Duke University, Durham, N.C.
Garrettson, *Journal*	Freeborn Garrettson, *American Methodist Pioneer: The Life and Journals of the Rev. Freeborn Garrettson, 1752–1827*, ed. Robert Drew Simpson (Rutland, Vt.: Academy Books, 1984)
GTS	Garrett Evangelical Theological Seminary, Evanston, Ill.
HSP	Historical Society of Pennsylvania, Philadelphia, Pa.
JLFA	*The Journal and Letters of Francis Asbury*, ed. Elmer T. Clark, J. Manning Potts, and Jacob S. Payton, 3 vols. (London: Epworth Press; Nashville: Abingdon Press, 1958)
JRL	Methodist Archives and Research Centre, John Rylands University Library, Manchester, England
Lednum, *Rise*	John Lednum, *A History of the Rise of Methodism in America. Containing Sketches of Methodist Itinerant Preachers, from 1736 to 1785, Numbering One Hundred and Sixty or Seventy. Also a Short Account of Many Hundreds of the First Race of Lay Members, Male and Female, From New York to South Carolina. Together With an Account of Many of the First Societies and Chapels* (Philadelphia: published by the author, 1862)
Lee, *Short History*	Jesse Lee, *A Short History of the Methodists, in the United States of America; Beginning in 1766, and Continued till 1809. To Which is Prefixed a Brief Account of Their Rise in England, in the Year 1729, &c.* (Baltimore: Magill and Clime, 1810)
Lewis, *Asbury*	James Lewis, *Francis Asbury: Bishop of the Methodist Episcopal Church* (London: Epworth Press, c. 1927)
Lives (Jackson)	*The Lives of Early Methodist Preachers*, ed. Thomas Jackson, 6 vols. (London: Wesleyan Conference Office, 1866)
LLM	United Methodist Historical Society, Lovely Lane Museum, Baltimore, Md.

MAHC	Methodist Archives and History Center, which includes the collections of the Methodist Church General Commission on Archives and History and the Wesley and Methodist Collections of Drew University, Madison, N.J.
MDA	Maryland Diocesan Archives, Protestant Episcopal Church, Baltimore, Md.
MEC	Methodist Episcopal Church
MH	*Methodist History*
Minutes (1794)	*Minutes of the Methodist Conferences 1773 to 1794, Under the Superintendence of John Wesley, Bishops Asbury and Coke* (Botetourt, [Va]: n.p., 1794)
Minutes (1840)	*Minutes of the Annual Conferences of the Methodist Episcopal Church for the Years 1773–1828*, vol. 1 (New York: T. Mason and G. Lane, 1840)
Minutes (British)	*Minutes of the Methodist Conferences, From the First, Held in London, By the Rev. John Wesley, A. M. In the year 1744*, vols. 1–2 (London: Conference Office, 1812, 1813)
ODNB	*Oxford Dictionary of National Biography*, Oxford University Press, www.oxforddnb.com.
PWHS	*Proceedings of the Wesley Historical Society*
RMC	McGraw-Page Library, Randolph-Macon College, Ashland, Va.
SCL	Stockport Central Library, Stockport, England
SHC	Southern Historical Collection, University of North Carolina, Chapel Hill, N.C.
Simpson, *Cyclopedia*	Matthew Simpson, ed., *Cyclopedia of Methodism. Embracing Sketches of Its Rise, Progress, and Present Condition, With Biographical Notices and Numerous Illustrations*, rev. ed. (Philadelphia: Louis H. Everts, 1880)
SRO	Staffordshire Record Office, Stafford, England
Stevens, *History*	Abel Stevens, *History of the Methodist Episcopal Church in the United States of America*, 4 vols. (New York: Carlton & Porter, 1867)
Tipple, *Asbury*	Ezra Squier Tipple, *Francis Asbury: The Prophet of the Long Road* (New York: Methodist Book Concern, 1916)
VHS	Virginia Historical Society, Richmond, Va.

Wesley Letters (Telford)	*The Letters of the Rev. John Wesley, A. M., Sometime Fellow of Lincoln College, Oxford*, ed. John Telford, 8 vols. (London: Epworth Press, 1931)
Wesley Works	*The Works of John Wesley*, 15 volumes to date (Oxford: Clarendon Press, 1975–1983; Nashville: Abingdon Press, 1984–)
Wesley Works (1872)	*The Works of John Wesley*, ed. Thomas Jackson, 3rd ed., 14 vols. (London: Wesleyan Methodist Book Room, 1872; reprint, Grand Rapids: Baker Book House, 1991)
Wigger, *Taking Heaven*	John H. Wigger, *Taking Heaven by Storm: Methodism and the Rise of Popular Christianity in America* (New York: Oxford University Press, 1998; paperback, University of Illinois Press, 2001)

Notes

1. Lee, *Short History*, 64; Leroy M. Lee, *The Life and Times of the Rev. Jesse Lee* (Louisville, Ky.: John Early, 1848), 33.

2. James O'kelly, *The Author's Apology for Protesting Against the Methodist Episcopal Government* (Richmond: Printed by John Dixon for the author, 1798), 5. On Dickins, see M. H. Moore, *Sketches of the Pioneers of Methodism in North Carolina and Virginia* (Nashville: Southern Methodist Publishing House, 1884), 106–17; James Penn Pilkington, *The Methodist Publishing House: A History*, 2 vols. (Nashville: Abingdon Press, 1968), 1:46–52. On Dickins's letter to Wesley seeking his advice, see Garrettson, *Journal*, 391.

3. *JLFA*, 1:358–59. Asbury may have also visited Dickins's mother-in-law on June 17, 1780. See *JLFA*, 1:357. Edward Drinkhouse refers to Dickins as a "pervert to the views he held in 1778–79" after Manakintown. See Edward J. Drinkhouse, *History of Methodist Reform, Synoptical of General Methodism, 1702–1898; With Special and Comprehensive Reference to Its Most Salient Exhibition in the History of the Methodist Protestant Church*, 2 vols. (Norwood, Mass.: Norwood Press, 1899), 1:216. Ezekiel Cooper knew Asbury and Dickins perhaps better than anyone else. In a 1799 funeral sermon for Dickins, Cooper wrote of Asbury and Dickins: "in their acquaintance and confidential love, they were like unto *Jonathan* and *David* of old. They were as one in heart, in mind and mutual affection." Ezekiel Cooper, *A Funeral Discourse, on the Death of That Eminent Man the Late Reverend John Dickins*, 2nd ed. (Philadelphia: Asbury Dickins, 1799), 4.

4. Henry Boehm, *Reminiscences, Historical and Biographical, of Sixty-Four Years in the Ministry* (New York: Carlton & Porter, 1866), 435, 453; *JLFA*, 2:753. Many accounts of Asbury's life accept Nathan Bangs's exaggerated claim that

Asbury traveled 6,000 miles a year for forty-five years, or 270,000 miles in America, preached "not less than sixteen thousand four hundred and twenty-five sermons," and ordained four thousand preachers. During the height of his career, Asbury did travel this much, but early and late in his career his annual mileage was often considerably less. For estimates ranging from 4,000 to 6,000 miles a year, see *JLFA*, 1:402; 2:541, 556, 566, 708; 3:197, 198. In 1814 Asbury wrote to a friend that he had "travelled annually a circuit of 3000 miles, for forty-two years and four months." See *JLFA*, 3:499; Bangs, *History*, 2:399–400; Darius L. Salter, *America's Bishop: The Life of Francis Asbury* (Nappanee, In.: Evangel Publishing House, 2003), 114–15.

5. Many people remembered Asbury's habit of rising early to pray. "He was strictly attentive to the Economy of time, & rose frequently a 4 [and] hardly ever laid in Bed beyond 5 in the Morning when he was well," Lewis Myers, a Methodist preacher, wrote in 1820. See Lewis Myers to Samuel K. Jennings, July 20, 1820, MAHC.

6. On Joseph Smith as an autocrat, see, for example, Charles Sellers, *The Market Revolution: Jacksonian America, 1815–1846* (New York: Oxford University Press, 1991), 217–25. The most complete treatment of Smith is Richard Bushman's fascinating biography, *Joseph Smith: Rough Stone Rolling* (New York: Alfred A. Knopf, 2005).

7. *JLFA*, 1:126, 2:515, 531.

8. Drinkhouse, *Methodist Reform*, 1:305, 500; Jon Butler, *Awash in a Sea of Faith: Christianizing the American People* (Cambridge, Mass.: Harvard University Press, 1990), 272, 273. Drinkhouse's criticisms of Asbury largely follow the earlier criticisms of Alexander M'Caine, who argued that Asbury spent his career "constantly studying and plotting how he could enlarge his own powers." See Alexander M'caine, *Letters on the Organization and Early History of the Methodist Episcopal Church* (Boston: Thomas F. Norris, 1850), 119.

9. Ezekiel Cooper, *The Substance of a Funeral Discourse, Delivered at the Request of the Annual Conference, on Tuesday, the 23d of April, 1816, in St. George's Church, Philadelphia: on the Death of the Rev. Francis Asbury, Superintendent, or Senior Bishop, of the Methodist Episcopal Church* (Philadelphia: Jonathan Pounder, 1819), 21. The scripture passage is from Matthew 22:37 and 39.

10. Bangs, *History*, 2:364, 401; Cooper, *Substance*, 25–26; James O'kelly, *Vindication of the Author's Apology, With Reflections on the Reply and a Few Remarks on Bishop Asbury's Annotations on His Book of Discipline* (Raleigh: Printed for the Author by Joseph Gates, 1801), 61. I am grateful to Dr. Marilyn James-Kracke for helping me to work out the connection between Asbury's sore throats, fevers, and heart problems, and to Dr. Louise Thai for helping me to understand the specific connection between streptococcal pharyngitis and rheumatic fever.

11. Boehm, *Reminiscences*, 443, 447; John Wesley Bond, "Anecdotes of Bishop Asbury, No. 2," MAHC; Robert J. Bull, "John Wesley Bond's Reminiscences of Francis Asbury," *MH*, 4 (1965): 15; Nicholas Snethen, *A Discourse on the Death of the Reverend Francis Asbury, Late Bishop of the Methodist Episcopal Church in the United States* (Baltimore: John J. Harrod, 1816), 9; Harlan L. Feeman, *Francis Asbury's Silver Trumpet: Nicholas Snethen: Non-Partisan Church Statesman and Preacher of the Gospel, 1769–1845* (Nashville: Parthenon Press, 1950), 134; Roberts, untitled manuscript. Asbury once told

the Ohio preacher James Quinn, "If I were not sometimes to be gay with my friends, I should have died in gloom long ago." Quinn also remembered that in frontier cabins, "the good Bishop always made himself pleasant and cheerful with the families, so that they soon forgot all embarrassment." See John F. Wright, *Sketches of the Life and Labors of James Quinn, Who Was Nearly Half a Century a Minister of the Gospel, in the Methodist Episcopal Church* (Cincinnati: Methodist Book Concern, 1851), 164, 245. "Though at times subject to depression of spirits, and to temporary gloom, yet generally he was of a lively and cheerful disposition; sometimes in conversation with his friends, humorous and playful, yet always directing his anecdotes, of which he had a fund, to some good end," writes Nathan Bangs, remembering Asbury. See Bangs, *History*, 2:407–8.

12. George Peck, *Early Methodism Within the Bounds of the Old Genesee Conference from 1788 to 1828; Or, the First Forty Years of Wesleyan Evangelism in Northern Pennsylvania, Central and Western New York, and Canada* (New York: Carlton & Porter, 1860), 425. Bidlack rode circuits in the Genesee District from 1799 to 1810. See *Minutes* (1840) for these years.

13. Jeremiah Minter, *Scripture Proofs of Sorcery, and Warning Against Sorcerers* (Richmond, Va.: Ritchie & Trueheart, 1814), 7, 10, 11; O'Kelly, *Vindication*, 61; Snethen, *Discourse on Asbury*, 4. I am indebted to Lester Ruth for bringing the Minter passage to my attention. Nathan Bangs, who knew Asbury relatively late in his career, observed that "In whatever company he appeared, whether religious or irreligious, whether high or low, learned or unlearned, he generally had such ascendancy over the minds of others, that he could easily lead the conversation." Bangs, *History*, 2:411.

14. Henry Rack, *Reasonable Enthusiast: John Wesley and the Rise of Methodism* (London: Epworth Press, 1989), 352.

15. Peter Cartwright, *Autobiography of Peter Cartwright: The Backwoods Preacher*, ed. W. P. Strickland (Cincinnati: Cranston and Curts, 1856), 155; Francis Asbury to Daniel Hitt, Jan. 30, 1801, "The Letters Written to Daniel Hitt, Methodist Preacher 1788 to 1806," trans. by Annie Winstead, Upper Room, Nashville, 1967; Wigger, *Taking Heaven*, 191–92.

16. *JLFA*, 3:164; Lee, *Short History*, 382.

17. After largely completing this study, I was surprised to find how closely Asbury resembled the effective leaders described in Jim Collins's *Good To Great: Why Some Companies Make the Leap . . . and Others Don't* (New York: HarperCollins, 2001), 17–40, 120–43.

18. Snethen, *Discourse on Asbury*, 6, 8, 9. On Snethen, see Simpson, *Cyclopedia*, 812–13; Boehm, *Reminiscences*, 451; Bond, "Anecdotes No. 5."

19. Snethen, *Discourse on Asbury*, 6.

20. Boehm, *Reminiscences*, 446.

21. Boehm, *Reminiscences*, 448; Bond, "Anecdotes" nos. 3 and 6.

22. Boehm, *Reminiscences*, 445, 454–55; Bond, "Anecdotes No. 4;" Thomas Smith, *Experience and Ministerial Labors of Rev. Thomas Smith, Late an Itinerant Preacher of the Gospel in the Methodist Episcopal Church. Compiled Chiefly From His Journal*, ed. David Dailey (New York: Lane & Tippett, 1848), 34. George Roberts remembered that

whenever Asbury was given a new suit of clothes, he immediately gave the old suit away. See Roberts, untitled manuscript. Nathan Bangs also points to Asbury's charity as one of the keys to understanding his character and influence. See Bangs, *History*, 2:405–6.

23. George Roberts, untitled manuscript, [c. 1820], MAHC; Robert J. Bull, "George Roberts' Reminiscences of Francis Asbury," *MH*, 5 (April 1967): 25–35.

CHAPTER I

1. Thomas Coke And Henry Moore, *The Life of the Rev. John Wesley* (London: G. Paramore, 1792).

2. *JLFA*, 1:720; Wilbur Fisk, *Travels in Europe: Viz., In England, Ireland, Scotland, France, Italy, Switzerland, Germany, and the Netherlands*, 6th ed. (New York: Harper & Brothers, 1843), 607; Henry Herbert Prince, *The Romance of Early Methodism in and around West Bromwich and Wednesbury* (West Bromwich, England: Published by the author, c. 1925), 39; David J. A. Hallam, *Eliza Asbury: Her Cottage and Her Son* (Studley, England: Brewin Books, 2003), 1–3, 12; W. B. Stephens, *A History of the County Warwick: Volume VII: The City of Birmingham* in *The Victoria History of the Counties of England*, ed. R. B. Pugh (London: Oxford University Press, 1964), 87 (hereafter *V. C. H. Warwick*); Frederick W. Hackwood, *Handsworth: Old & New, A History of Birmingham's Staffordshire Suburb*, ed. Alan A. Vernon (1908; reprint, Studley, England: Brewin Books, n.d.), 38–40. Asbury made shorter autobiographical entries in his journal and letters. See *JLFA*, 1:123–25, 301; 2:43, 423, 489, 794; 3:278, 392, 417. On John Wyrley Birch, see: W. C. Sheldon, "The Birmingham Magistrate Who Suppressed the Rioters," *PWHS*, 4 (1904): 61–64.

3. *JLFA*, 1:720; Asbury to his parents, Oct. 30, 1795, MAHC; Prince, *West Bromwich*, 40; Hallam, *Eliza Asbury*, 3–7, 14–15; Harry C. Asbury, "Asbury Genealogy: Bishop Francis Asbury (1745–1816)," Tms, LLM; Parish Register and Bishops Transcript for St. Mary Parish, Handsworth, 1743–1745, BPL. Birmingham was a part of Staffordshire at the time of Asbury's birth. Some accounts claim that Joseph Asbury's marriage to Eliza was his second, suggesting he married Susan Whipple, the daughter of a Wednesbury farmer, in 1729 or 1730. She supposedly died after giving birth to a son, Thomas, who was raised by relatives before going to sea at age fifteen. See Harry Asbury, "Asbury Genealogy," and Herbert Asbury, *A Methodist Saint: The Life of Bishop Asbury* (New York: Alfred A. Knopf, 1927), 2–3. But David Hallam has done extensive research in the parish registers for the south Staffordshire area, 1700–1750, and uncovered no evidence of a Susan Whipple or indeed of a Whipple family.

4. *JLFA*, 1:720; Hallam, *Eliza Asbury*, 3–7; Prince, *West Bromwich*, 40; W. C. Sheldon, "The Landmarks of Bishop Asbury's Childhood and Youth," *PWHS*, 12 (1920): 97–103; Briggs, *Asbury*, 9–10; J. M. Day, *Asbury Cottage, Newton Road, Great Barr, Restored, re-opened and dedicated on Friday, 27th November, 1959* (Printed and published by the Metropolitan Borough of Sandwell, n.d.), 6–7. The first edition of Briggs's biography was published in 1874.

5. Asbury to his parents, June 7, 1784, MAHC; *JLFA*, 1:720; 3:36; Jeremiah Minter, *A Brief Account of the Religious Experience, Travels, Preaching, Persecutions From Evil Men, and God's Special Helps in the Faith and Life, &c. of Jerem. Minter, Minister of the Gospel of Christ* (Washington City; Printed for the Author, 1817), 26; Victor Skipp, *A History of Greater Birmingham-Down to 1830* (Birmingham, England: Published by the Author, 1980), 89–93. Birmingham's first historian, William Hutton, probably had people like Joseph Asbury in mind when in 1781 he wrote that "the people of Birmingham are more apt to get than to *keep.*" William Hutton, *An History of Birmingham to the End of the Year 1780* (Birmingham, England: Pearson and Rollason, 1781), ix, 10.

6. Thomas Rankin to Lord Darmouth, March 30, Dec. 29, 1774, Dec. 28, 1775, Jan. 15, 1776; Thomas Webb to Dartmouth, July 5, 1773, March 1, 1775, March 3, 1778, SRO. Rankin's letters were written from New York and Philadelphia, while Webb's were written from Philadelphia and Burlington, N.J. John Fletcher and John Wesley also corresponded with Dartmouth without mentioning Asbury. See Wesley to Dartmouth, Aug. 23, 1775; Fletcher to Dartmouth, Sept. 19, 1774, Dec. 15, 1779, SRO. Also see Peter Marshall, "Legge, William," *ODNB*, Jan. 21, 2005.

7. *JLFA*, 1:720–21; Fisk, *Travels*, 607; Hallam, *Eliza Asbury*, 21; John Money, "The Schoolmasters of Birmingham and the West Midlands, 1750–1790: Private Education and Cultural Change in the English Provinces During the Early Industrial Revolution," *Histoire Sociale-Social History* 9 (May 1976): 129–53; J. H. Plumb, "The New World of Children in Eighteenth-Century England," in *The Birth of a Consumer Society: The Commercialization of Eighteenth-Century England*, ed. Neil McKendrick, John Brewer, and J. H. Plumb (Bloomington: Indiana University Press, 1982), 286–315. James Lewis claims that Asbury's parents paid a shilling a week for his schooling, which would have been a considerable outlay. But Sneal's Green was a free school, established to "instruct 13 poor children to read English well, and to write," at no cost to their families. See Lewis, *Asbury*, 17; George Griffith, *The Free Schools and Endowments of Staffordshire* (London: Whittaker and Co., 1860), 429–31; William White, *History, Gazetteer, and Directory, of Staffordshire* (Sheffield, England: Printed for the Author, 1834), 298–99.

8. *JLFA*, 1:720–21; John Wesley Bond, "Anecdotes of Bishop Asbury No. 6," MAHC; Prince, *West Bromwich*, 40–41; Harry Asbury, "Asbury Genealogy"; Lewis, *Asbury*, 17; Briggs, *Asbury*, 11; Money, "Schoolmasters of Birmingham"; Hugh Cunningham, "The Employment and Unemployment of Children in England c. 1680–1851," *Past and Present*, 126 (February 1990): 115–50; Wilfrid Prest, *Albion Ascendant: English History, 1660–1815* (Oxford: Oxford University Press, 1998), 174–78. On the Bond manuscript, also see Robert J. Bull, "John Wesley Bond's Reminiscences of Francis Asbury," *MH* 4 (1965): 3–32. Also see: Lawrence Stone, *The Family, Sex and Marriage in England, 1500–1800* (New York: Harper & Row, 1977), 163–67; Robert W. Malcolmson, *Life and Labour in England, 1700–1780* (New York: St. Martin's, 1981), 64–65.

9. R. A. Houston, *Literacy in Early Modern Europe: Culture and Education, 1500–1800* (London: Longman, 1988), 16–25, 48–73, 130–54; W. B. Stephens, *Education in Britain, 1750–1914* (Basingstoke, U.K.: Macmillan, 1998), 1–39; Malcolmson, *Life and Labour*, 62.

10. *JLFA*, 1:123 and 1:720; George Shadford, "The Life of Mr. George Shadford. Written by Himself," in *Lives* (Jackson), 138, 140.

11. Fisk, *Travels*, 608; Day, *Asbury Cottage*, 7; Cooper, *Substance*, 64; Asbury, "Asbury Genealogy"; Eric Hopkins, *Birmingham: The First Manufacturing Town in the World 1760–1840* (London: Weidenfeld & Nicolson, 1989), 58–60; "The Early Years of Francis Asbury," *Wesley Historical Society, West Midlands Branch*, Vol. 1, Bulletin No. 2 (1965?): 11; Asbury, *Methodist Saint*, 8; Prince, *West Bromwich*, 42; Briggs, *Asbury*, 12–13; Lewis, *Asbury*, 17–18; Tipple, *Asbury*, 47–48;W. H. B. Court, *The Rise of the Midland Industries 1600–1838* (London: Oxford University Press, 1938; reprinted, 1965), 100–103, 108–9; *V.C.H. Warwick*, 87. Frederick Briggs collected local stories about the Asburys while serving as a minister in the Great Barr area in the mid-nineteenth century. In August 1802 Asbury wrote to John Rodgers of Walsall, Staffordshire, asking "Is she that was the Widow Griffin now living? in what Circumstances? and in what Station? be pleased to write me if she has religion." Asbury to Rodgers, Aug. 1, 1802, MAHC. One of forty water-powered mills located on the Tame River and its tributaries in Staffordshire, Old Forge had been in operation for more than a century, functioning as a slitting mill in Asbury's time. Sometime during 1766 and 1767 it passed into the hands of John Wright and Richard Jesson. Foxall family records indicate that Thomas Foxall worked for Jesson at Old Forge, but since Asbury left metalworking to begin circuit preaching in 1766, their time at Old Forge couldn't have overlapped by more than a few months. Thomas Foxall's son later wrote that his father "lived" with Richard Jesson for about twenty-five years before his death in 1789. This would put the beginning of their association at 1764. Perhaps Foxall worked for Jesson somewhere before Old Forge, and Asbury worked there too. D. Dilworth, *The Tame Mills of Staffordshire* (London: Phillimore, 1976), 40–52; Hallam, *Eliza Asbury*, 40–41.

12. *JLFA*, 1:125, 721. According to Jane Donovan, Foxall family tradition claims that Asbury was originally apprenticed to a master who treated him badly and that Asbury's father broke the apprenticeship in a scandalous manner. Thomas Foxall may have then taken Francis in as a favor. Unfortunately, there is no documentary evidence to support this story. Jane Donovan to John Wigger, e-mail correspondence, Dec. 19-24, 2005. The Foxall connection remains intriguing. Thomas and Mary Foxall had a son, Henry, who moved to America in 1795 and made a fortune producing cannons and shot for the United States Army and Navy. Asbury saw him regularly, both in Philadelphia and Georgetown, D.C. Eliza Asbury was close to the Foxalls in England and conveyed Foxall family news to Francis, presumably because he shared an interest in them. Yet Asbury never mentions any apprenticeship to the elder Foxall. Henry Boehm, Asbury's traveling companion from 1808 to 1813, wrote, "I was well acquainted with Mr. Foxall, and the bishop and he were like two brothers." It is odd that neither Asbury nor Henry Foxall mentioned this link if it existed. Briggs and Lewis had the advantage of being relatively close in time to the oral traditions they relied on, but their Methodist sympathies may have led them to favor an account of Asbury working for a fellow Methodist. *JLFA*, 2:195, 331, 630n., 664n.; Boehm, *Reminiscences*, 412–13; Jane Donovan, "Henry Foxall and the Arigna Iron Works," *MH*, 41:4 (July 2003): 179–91; John A. Vickers, "Asbury and the Foxalls," *MH*, 42:3 (April 2004): 178–79; Donovan, "Response to 'Asbury and the

Foxalls,' by John Vickers, *Methodist History*, 42:3 (April 2004), 178–79," *MH*, 43:1 (October 2004): 68; Homer L. Calkin, "Henry Foxall: Foundryman and Friend of Asbury," *MH*, 6:1 (October 1967): 36–49; Joseph Entwisle, "Memoir of the Late Rev. Henry Foxall," *Methodist Magazine*, vol. 7 (October 1824): 367–71.

13. Richard Brown, *Society and Economy in Modern Britain 1700–1850* (London: Routledge, 1991), 73, 75, 249, 258, 264, 402; John Money, *Experience and Identity: Birmingham and the West Midlands 1760–1800* (Montreal: McGill-Queen's University Press, 1977), 1–50; Steven King And Geoffrey Timmins, *Making Sense of the Industrial Revolution* (Manchester, England: Manchester University Press, 2001), 10–66, 208–22, 234–35, 244, 285–327; Jan De Vries, "The Industrial Revolution and the Industrious Revolution," *Journal of Economic History* 54:2 (June 1994): 249–70. Ann Kussmaul, "The pattern of work as the eighteenth century began," in *The Economic History of Britain Since 1700*, 2nd ed., ed. Roderick Floud and Donald McCloskey (Cambridge: Cambridge University Press, 1994), 1–11; Joel Mokyr, "Technological change, 1700–1830," in Floud and McCloskey, *Economic History*, 12–43; Nick Crafts, "The industrial revolution," in Floud and McCloskey, *Economic History*, 44–59; Maxine Berg, "Factories, workshops and industrial organisation," in Floud and McCloskey, *Economic History*, 123–50; Roger Schofield, "British population change, 1700–1871," in Floud and McCloskey, *Economic History*, 60–97. On the historiography of the Industrial Revolution, see Pat Hudson, *The Industrial Revolution* (London: Arnold, 1992), 1–36, 101–65; C. Knickharley, "Reassessing the Industrial Revolution: A Macro View," in *The British Industrial Revolution: An Economic Perspective*, ed. Joel Mokyr (Boulder, Colo.: Westview Press, 1993), 171–226; R. V. Jackson, "Rates of Industrial Growth During the Industrial Revolution," *Economic History Review* 45 (1992): 1–23; Maxine Berg And Pat Hudson, "Rehabilitating the Industrial Revolution," *Economic History Review* 45 (1992): 24–50. On the development of Birmingham and the West Midlands, see Skipp, *History of Birmingham*, 22–43; *V. C. H. Warwick*, 75–104; Marie B. Rowlands, "Continuity and Change in an Industrializing Society: The Case of the West Midlands Industries," in *Regions and Industries: A Perspective on the Industrial Revolution in Britain*, ed. Pat Hudson (Cambridge: Cambridge University Press, 1989), 103–31; Pat Hudson, "The Regional Perspective," in Hudson, *Regions and Industries*, 5–38; Conrad Gill, *History of Birmingham, Volume 1: Manor and Borough to 1865* (London: Oxford University Press, 1952), 120, 126; Robert K. Dent, *The Making of Birmingham: Being a History of the Rise and Growth of the Midland Metropolis* (Birmingham, England: J. L. Allday, 1894), 141–47; William Hawkes Smith, *Birmingham and Its Vicinity, As a Manufacturing & Commercial District* (London: Charles Tilt, 1836), part 2, 17–21; Maxine Berg, *The Age of Manufactures: Industry, Innovation and Work in Britain, 1700–1820* (Oxford: Basil Blackwell, 1985), 287–314; Maxine Berg, Pat Hudson And Michael Sonenscher, "Manufacture in Town and Country Before the Factory," in *Manufacture in Town and Country Before the Factory*, ed. Berg, Hudson, and Sonenscher (Cambridge: Cambridge University Press, 1983), 1–32. On the consumer revolution of this period, see: Neil McKendrick, "The Consumer Revolution of Eighteenth-Century England," in *Consumer Society*, 9–33; Maxine Berg, "New Commodities, Luxuries and Their Consumers in Eighteenth-Century England," in *Consumers and Luxury: Consumer Culture in Europe 1650–1850*, ed. Maxine Berg and

Helen Clifford (Manchester, England: Manchester University Press, 1999); 63–85; Lorna Weatherill, *Consumer Behaviour and Material Culture in Britain 1660–1760* (London: Routledge, 1988); Joel Mokyr, "Demand vs. Supply in the Industrial Revolution," in *The Economics of the Industrial Revolution*, ed. Joel Mokyr (Totowa, N.J.: Rowman & Allanheld, 1985), 97–118. On Birmingham's "open" political structure and diversity, see Hutton, *Birmingham*, 86–87; Money, *Experience and Identity*, 11–12. On open and closed communities, see Dennis R. Mills, *Lord and Peasant in Nineteenth Century Britain* (London: Croom Helm, 1980), 23–24, 60–61, 64–94; Brown, *Society and Economy in Modern Britain*, 375–79.

14. Percy Hartill, *The Story of All Saints' Parish Church West Bromwich* (Gloucester, England: Crypt House Press, n.d.), 19; Michael W. Flinn, *The History of the British Coal Industry*, vol. 2, *1700–1830: The Industrial Revolution* (Oxford: Clarendon Press, 1984), 15–28; Marie B. Rowlands, *Masters and Men in the West Midlands Metalware Trades Before the Industrial Revolution* (Manchester, England: Manchester University Press, 1975), 1–28, 78–109, 125–28; Richard B. Prosser, *Birmingham Inventors and Inventions: Being a Contribution to the Industrial History of Birmingham* (Birmingham, England: Published for Private Circulation, 1881; reprint, East Ardsley, England: S.R. Publishers, 1970), 48–77; *V. C. H. Warwick*, 91; Court, *Midland Industries*, 136–39, 143–48, 191–216; Hopkins, *Birmingham*, chaps. 1–4; Skipp, *History of Birmingham*, 44–54; Charles Wilson, *England's Apprenticeship 1603–1763*, 2nd ed. (London: Longman, 1984), 300–4. On overseas trade and the demand for British goods in North America, see Timothy Breen, "An Empire of Goods: the Anglicization of Colonial America 1690–1776," *Journal of British Studies* 25 (1986): 467–99; T. H. Breen, *The Marketplace of Revolution: How Consumer Politics Shaped American Independence* (New York: Oxford University Press, 2004), part one; Hudson, *Industrial Revolution*, 181–90. Hudson argues that the "consumer revolution" had less impact than most others suggest. See Hudson, *Industrial Revolution*, 173–80; Brown, *Society and Economy*, 163–82; Stanley L. Engerman, "Mercantilism and overseas trade, 1700–1800," in Floud and McCloskey, *Economic History*, 182–204. On trade and the rise of consumer markets in eighteenth-century Briton, see Linda Colley, *Britons: Forging the Nation 1707–1837* (New Haven: Yale University Press, 1992), 55–100; John J. Mccusker, *Essays in the Economic History of the Atlantic World* (London: Routledge, 1997), 43–75, 222–44.

15. Adam Smith, *An Inquiry into the Nature and Causes of the Wealth of Nations* (first edition published in 1776; reprint, New York: The Modern Library, 1937), 114–15; Rowlands, *Masters and Men*, 125–66; Julian Hoppit, *Risk and Failure in English Business 1700–1800* (Cambridge: Cambridge University Press, 1987), 8, 57–58, 62, 72. The phrase "dark satanic mills" is from the preface to William Blake's *Milton a Poem*. See William Blake, *Milton a Poem*, ed. Robert N. Essick and Joseph Viscomi (London: William Blake Trust/Tate Gallery Publications, 1993), 94.

16. *V. C. H. Warwick*, 7:98–104; Samuel Timmins, "The Industrial History of Birmingham," in *Birmingham and the Midland Hardware District*, ed. Samuel Timmins (London: Robert Hardwicke, 1866), 207–24; John Alfred Langford, *A Century of Birmingham Life: Or, A Chronicle of Local Events, from 1741 to 1841*, 2 vols. (Birmingham: E. C. Osborne, 1868), xx–xxiii; Court, *Midland Industries*, 140. There were as many as 8000 buckle makers and 2500 iron chape makers in the Birmingham region by the

middle of the eighteenth century. Other trades in eighteenth-century Birmingham were also subdivided to a remarkable degree. In 1770 there were nearly 50 trades with five or more businesses located in the city, including 83 button makers, 45 platers, 44 buckle makers, 38 gun and pistol makers, 33 brass founders and 23 jewelers. This tally would have varied from year to year as small producers moved from one specialty to another to take advantage of shifting demand. The same kind of specialization took place in other manufacturing centers in the West Midlands. By 1770 there were 118 lock makers producing 26 kinds of locks in Wolverhampton and 138 locksmiths making 19 kinds of locks in Willenhall. See *V. C. H. Warwick*, 7:99; Rowlands, *Masters and Men*, 131–32.

17. Hallam, *Eliza Asbury*, 18; Dilworth, *Tame Mills*; Skipp, *Birmingham*, 65–66; Frederick W. Hackwood, *The History of West Bromwich* (Birmingham, England: Birmingham News & Printing, 1895), 84. Great Barr and West Bromwich were characterized by mixed farming and industry, particularly nail making. They were less industrialized than Wednesbury, which contained few farmers by this time. On coal mining and iron production in south Staffordshire, see Smith, *Birmingham and Its Vicinity*, 22–66. On coal transportation, see Flinn, *British Coal*, 146–52, 180–89.

18. Wigger, *Taking Heaven*, 49.

19. *JLFA*, 2:333; 3:243. The debate over what impact the industrial revolution had on workers' quality of life is one of the thorniest in the scholarship on the Industrial Revolution. Though real wages seem to have increased in the industrializing West Midlands in the second half of the eighteenth century, they fell or remained stagnate elsewhere in England as the price of consumer goods rose. The overall quality of life for West Midlands metalworkers was probably as good as that of nearby agricultural laborers or those who worked in more traditional domestic economies, but for many earning a living remained precarious. M. J. Daunton, *Progress and Poverty: An Economic and Social History of Britain 1700–1850* (Oxford: Oxford University Press, 1995), 420–41; Roderick Floud, Kenneth Wachter, and Annabel Gregory, *Height, Health and History: Nutritional Status in the United Kingdom, 1750–1980* (Cambridge: Cambridge University Press, 1990), 275–305, 325–27; N. F. R. Crafts, "Real Wages, Inequality and Economic Growth in Britain, 1750–1850: A Review of Recent Research," in Peter Scholliers, ed., *Real Wages in 19th and 20th Century Europe* (New York: Berg, 1989), 75–95; Stephen Nicholas and Richard H. Steckel, "Heights and Living Standards of English Workers During the Early Years of Industrialization, 1770–1815," *Journal of Economic History* 51:4 (1991): 937–57; F. W. Botham and E. H. Hunt, "Wages in Britain During the Industrial Revolution," *Economic History Review*, 40:3 (1987): 380–99; Brown, *Society and Economy*, 314–26; E.H. Hunt, "Wages," in *Atlas of Industrializing Britain 1780–1914*, ed. John Langton and R. J. Morris (London: Methuen, 1986), 60–68; Steven King, *Poverty and Welfare in England 1700–1850: A Regional Perspective* (Manchester, England: Manchester University Press, 2000), chaps. 4–7; Deborah Valenze, *The First Industrial Woman* (New York: Oxford University Press, 1995), 13–28; Prest, *Albion Ascendant*, 267–70; David Hackett Fischer, *The Great Wave: Price Revolutions and the Rhythm of History* (New York: Oxford University Press, 1996), 132–33. Also see Hopkins, *Birmingham*, 102–34. On child labor during this period, see Cunningham, "Employment and Unemployment of Children." On the debate over whether the integrity of the family increased or declined

during the industrial revolution, see King and Timmins, *Industrial Revolution*, 244–84. On the historiography of women and the Industrial Revolution, see Hudson, *Industrial Revolution*, 225–36.

20. Hallam, *Eliza Asbury*, 17–18; William Hutton, *An History of Birmingham* 2nd ed. (Pearson and Rollason, 1783; reprint, East Ardsley, England: E. P. Publishing, 1976), 84; William Hutton, *The Life of William Hutton, F.A.S.S., Including a Particular Account of the Riots at Birmingham in 1791, and the History of His Family, Written by Himself, and Published by His Daughter, Catherine Hutton* (London: Baldwin, Cradock and Joy, 1817), 110; Alfred Camden Pratt, *Black Country Methodism* (London: Charles H. Kelly, 1891), 92–94; Langford, *Birmingham Life*, 42–44, 86; Frederick W. Hackwood, *Old English Sports* (London: T. Fisher Unwin, 1907), 227–88.

21. *JLFA*, 1:720; Parish Register, St. Mary's, Handsworth, May 28, 1749, BPL; George Roberts, untitled manuscript c. 1820, MAHC. Joseph and Eliza's first parish church was St. Mary's, Handsworth. When they moved to the cottage on Newton Road they moved into St. Margaret's parish. Why did they then choose to bury Sarah at St. Mary's, their former parish church? Distance-wise, All Saints', where Edward Stilling-fleet preached, was closer than St. Margaret's. On St. Mary's, see: J. C. H. Tompkins, *The Parish Church of St. Mary, Handsworth* (no publication information). On Great Barr and St. Margaret's, see Richard A. Woodall, *The Barr Story: Milestones in the Development of Great Barr, Pheasey, Streetly, Sutton, Kingstanding, Newton, Hamstead, Perry Barr and Aldridge* (N. A. Tector, 1951), 17.

22. Bond, "Anecdotes," 3.

23. *Wesley Works*, 19:343–49; Hackwood, *West Bromwich*, 85–88; Prince, *West Bromwich*, 14–34; Pratt, *Black Country Methodism*, 142–52.

24. "Modern Christianity: Exemplified at Wednesbury," in *Wesley Works*, 9:132–58. Also see Richard P. Heitzenrater, *Wesley and the People Called Methodists* (Nashville: Abingdon Press, 1995), 132–33; Hackwood, *West Bromwich*, 85–88; Charles H. Goodwin, "Vile or Reviled? The Causes of the Anti-Methodist Riots at Wednesbury Between May, 1743, and April 1744 in the Light of New England Revivalism," *MH*, 35:1 (October 1996): 14–27; Rowlands, *Masters and Men*, 158–61; Elizabeth W. Gilboy, *Wages in Eighteenth Century England* (Cambridge: Harvard University Press, 1934), 80–134; Hopkins, *Birmingham*, 152; Hunt, "Wages," 63. Rowlands and Gilboy indicate that skilled workers probably earned from ten to fifteen shillings per week at this time. Steven King suggests that most agricultural workers would have earned six to seven shillings per week. There were twenty shillings to the pound, twelve *d* (pennies or pence) to the shilling and twenty-one shillings to the guinea during this period. See King, *Poverty and Welfare*, 48, 123. John Wesley continued visiting the Birmingham area for more than forty years, generally in March on his way from Bristol. On Methodism in Birmingham, see W. C. Sheldon, *Early Methodism in Birmingham: A Historical Sketch* (Birmingham: Buckler & Webb, 1903), 5–27.

25. Prince, *West Bromwich*, 42; Briggs, *Asbury*, 12–13; *JLFA*, 1:123, 1:720.

26. *JLFA*, 1:123–24, 1:721, and 2:168; Bond, "Anecdotes," 24; Hallam, *Eliza Asbury*, 22. During this time the church at Great Barr was a chapel-of-ease to Aldridge. On All Saints' Parish Church, see Hartill, *Story of All Saints'*, 19–23. On Venn, see Leonard W.

Cowie, "Venn, Henry," *ODNB*, Jan. 21, 2005. On Haweis, see Edwin Welch, "Haweis, Thomas," *ODNB*, Jan. 21, 2005. Asbury was also moved by the preaching of "Bagnel" or "Bagnall," evidently Gibbons Bagnall (1719–1800) a Church of England minister with connections to the countess of Huntingdon. See Thompson Cooper, rev. Robert Brown, "Bagnall, Gibbons," *ODNB*, Jan. 21, 2005.

27. *JLFA*, 1:124 and 1:721; Barrie Trinder, *The Industrial Revolution in Shropshire* (London: Phillimore, 1973), 267–83; Patrick Ph. Streiff, "Fletcher, John William," and C. J. Podmore, "Ingham, Benjamin," *ODNB*, Jan. 21, 2005.

28. Shadford, "Life," 142–43.

29. *JLFA*, 1:124–25 and 1:721; Joseph Benson, *The Substance of a Sermon Preached on the Occasion of the Death of Mr. Alexander Mather; On Sunday the 31st of August, 1800, At the Chapel in Queen-Street, and at the New-Chapel, City Road, London* (London: Printed at the Conference-Office, 1800), 23–29; Atmore, *Memorial*, 256–66; Simon Ross Valentine, "Mather, Alexander," *ODNB*, Jan. 21, 2005. Born in Brechin, Scotland, Mather was converted under Wesley's preaching while working as a baker in London in 1754, joining the itinerant connection in 1757.

30. On Wesley's conversion, see Rack, *Reasonable Enthusiast*, 103, 144–57.

31. *JLFA*, 1:125; Wigger, *Taking Heaven*, 15–16. On Wesley's doctrine of salvation, see Kenneth J. Collins, *The Scripture Way of Salvation: The Heart of John Wesley's Theology* (Nashville: Abingdon Press, 1997); Randy L. Maddox, *Responsible Grace: John Wesley's Practical Theology* (Nashville: Kingswood Books, 1994); Thomas Langford, *Practical Divinity: Theology in the Wesleyan Tradition* (Nashville: Abingdon Press, 1983), especially chapters 1 and 2. Also see Robert E. Cushman, *John Wesley's Experimental Divinity: Studies in Methodist Doctrinal Standards* (Nashville: Kingswood Books, 1989). On Methodist piety in European religion, see Ted A. Campbell, *The Religion of the Heart: A Study of European Religious Life in the Seventeenth and Eighteenth Centuries* (Columbia: University of South Carolina Press, 1991), especially 115–24.

32. John Wesley, "Christian Perfection: A Sermon Preached by John Wesley," in *Wesley Works*, 2: 104, 105, 120; John Wesley, *A Plain Account of Christian Perfection. Minutes* (British), 1:7–8, 1:24–25, 1:35–38, and 1:80–81. Wesley gives a succinct explanation of the nature and importance of Christian Perfection in answer to Question 57 of the *Minutes of Several Conversations Between the Reverend Mr. John and Charles Wesley, and Others. From the Year 1744, to the Year 1780*, in John J. Tigert, *A Constitutional History of American Episcopal Methodism*, 2nd ed. (Nashville: Methodist Episcopal Church, South, 1904), 585–86. On Wesley and sanctification also, see Collins, *Scripture Way*, 153–90; Maddox, *Responsible Grace*, 176–90; Langford, *Practical Divinity*, 39–43; Rack, *Reasonable Enthusiast*, 395–401; Dee Andrews, *The Methodists and Revolutionary America, 1760–1800: The Shaping of an Evangelical Culture* (Princeton: Princeton University Press, 2000), 20–21. John Fletcher, the vicar of Madeley and a close ally of Wesley's, understood perfection in much the same way. "The light that I now see the thing in, is this: As the body is not capable of perfection on this side [of] the grave, all those powers of the soul whose exertion depends, in part, on the frame, and well being of the body, or the happy flow of the animal spirits, will not, cannot be perfected here. Of this sort are, I apprehend, I. The understanding. 2. The memory, & 3ly the passionate affections-Or

the affections as they work by means of the animal spirits on the animal frame,"
Fletcher wrote to Wesley in February 1766. "The one power then that I see can be
perfected here because it is altogether independent from the body, is *the will*, and of
course the *affections so far* as they work in the will." Madeley was not far from Asbury's
home, and Fletcher's concern for holiness and perfection probably influenced Asbury's
understanding. See John Fletcher to John Wesley, Feb. 17, 1766, Fletcher Tooth Collection, Box 36, JRL.

33. *JLFA*, 1:125, 722. Even relatively late in life John Wesley himself had doubts
about his own spiritual condition. See Rack, *Reasonable Enthusiast*, 545–47.

34. Fisk, *Travels*, 608; Prince, *West Bromwich*, 43, 55–56; Briggs, *Asbury*, 18; Lewis,
Asbury, 18; Hackwood, *West Bromwich*, 89, 91; Hallam, *Eliza Asbury*, 32. Besides Ault,
Asbury's companions included James Mayo, James Bayley, and Thomas Russell. Mayo
and Ault succeeded Asbury as class leader at Bromwich Heath. Mayo later moved to
Birmingham, Bayley became a park-keeper on Dartmouth's Sandwell estate, and Rus-
sell became a carpenter.

35. Wigger, *Taking Heaven*, 13–15; David Hempton, *The Religion of the People: Methodism and Popular Religion c. 1750–1900* (Routledge: London, 1996), 1–72; David Hemp-
ton, *Methodism and Politics in British Society 1750–1850* (Stanford: Stanford University
Press, 1984), 14–16; David Hempton, *Religion and Political Culture in Britain and Ireland: From the Glorious Revolution to the Decline of Empire* (Cambridge: Cambridge
University Press, 1996), 25–48; John Walsh, "'Methodism' and the Origins of
English-Speaking Evangelicalism," in *Evangelicalism: Comparative Studies of Popular
Protestantism in North America, the British Isles, and Beyond, 1700–1990*, ed. Mark A. Noll,
David W. Bebbington, and George A. Rawlyk (New York: Oxford University Press,
1994), 19–37; John Walsh, "Methodism and the Common People," in *People's History
and Socialist Theory*, ed. Raphael Samuel (London: Routledge & Kegan Paul, 1981),
354–62; Alan D. Gilbert, *Religion and Society in Industrial England: Church, Chapel
and Social Change 1740–1914* (London: Longman, 1976), 39, 62, 67; Alan D. Gilbert,
"Methodism, Dissent and Political Stability in Early Industrial England," *Journal of
Religious History*, 10 (June 1978): 381–99; David Hempton And Myrtle Hill, *Evangelical
Protestantism in Ulster Society 1740–1890* (London: Routledge, 1992), 3–142; Bernard
Semmel, *The Methodist Revolution* (New York: Basic Books, 1973); Robert Currie, "A
Micro-Theory of Methodist Growth," *PWHS*, 36 (October 1967): 65–73; Andrews, *The
Methodists*, 22. For a more cynical view of Methodist expansion in England, see Paul
Langford, *A Polite and Commercial People: England 1727–1783* (Oxford: Clarendon Press,
1989), 243–57, 264–76. The social and political impact of English Methodism has
produced an enormous literature, beginning with Elie Halevy's famous thesis and
dominated, until relatively recently, by the work of E.P. Thompson. See E. P. Thompson,
The Making of the English Working Class (New York: Pantheon Books, 1964), 350–75 and
417–19; Hempton, *Religion of the People*, 3–6; Elie Halevy, *England in 1815*, trans. E. I.
Watkin and D. A. Baker (First published in French in 1913; reprint, New York: Barnes
and Noble, 1968); Anthony Armstrong, *The Church of England, the Methodists and
Society, 1700–1850* (London: University of London Press, 1973), 83–102; Robert F.
Wearmouth, *Methodism and the Common People in the Eighteenth Century* (London:

Epworth Press, 1945), 202, 216–68; Wellman J. Warner, *The Wesleyan Movement in the Industrial Revolution* (London: Longmans, Green and Co., 1930), 3–12, 271–82.

CHAPTER 2

1. *JLFA*, 1:721–722, 2:43, 3:392.

2. *JLFA*, 1:722; John Wesley, "A Plain Account of the People Called Methodists," and "Thoughts Upon Methodism," in *Wesley Works*, 9:260–64, 528–29; Fisk, *Travels*, 608; David Lowes Watson, *The Early Methodist Class Meeting* (Nashville: Discipleship Resources, 1985), 67–94; David Francis Holsclaw, "The Demise of Disciplined Christian Fellowship: The Methodist Class Meeting in Nineteenth-Century America" (PhD diss., University of California Davis, 1979), 18–39; Charles C. Keys, *The Class-Leader's Manual* (Cincinnati: Cranston and Stowe, 1851), 11–20, 219–28; Wigger, *Taking Heaven*, 80–81. Also see *Wesley Works* (1872), 8:248–68 and 13:258–61. Foy hasn't been identified apart from Wesley's account. See "Who was Captain Foy?" *PWHS* 3 (1901), 3:64–65.

3. *Wesley Works*, 9:262, 528–29.

4. *Wesley Works*, 9:78, 262–67; Watson, *Class Meeting*, 93–119; Collins, *Scripture Way*, 160; Wigger, *Taking Heaven*, 17, 81–85; Joseph Nightingale, *A Portraiture of Methodism: Being an Impartial View of the Rise, Progress, Doctrines, Discipline, and Manners of the Wesleyan Methodists* (London: Longman, Hurst, Rees, and Orme, 1807), 190–200. The proportion of Methodists joining a band was always relatively low, never more than 25 percent in Britain. See Philip F. Hardt, *The Soul of Methodism: The Class Meeting in Early New York City Methodism* (Lanham, Md.: University Press of America, 2000), 11–13.

5. Hackwood, *Old English Sports*, 159–66, 186–87, 224–88, 296–325; Robert W. Malcolmson, *Popular Recreations in English Society 1700–1850* (Cambridge: Cambridge University Press, 1973), 15–171, 106; J. H. Plumb, "The Commercialization of Leisure," in *Birth of a Consumer Society*, 265–85; Barry Reay, *Popular Cultures in England, 1550–1750* (London: Longman, 1998), 4–35, 132–67; *Wesley Works*, 4:326, 327, 9:70–72; *Wesley Works* (1872), 7:506, 8:270; *Minutes* (British), 1:173.

6. Prince, *West Bromwich*, 47; Lewis, *Asbury*, 18; Tipple, *Asbury*, 51.

7. *Wesley Works*, 9:262; Hardt, *Soul of Methodism*, 14–15; Nightingale, *Portraiture*, 181–83; Wigger, *Taking Heaven*, 84.

8. Watson, *Class Meetings*, 110–16.

9. *Wesley Works*, 3: 270, 276; John Walsh, "John Wesley and the Community of Goods," in *Protestant Evangelicalism: Britain, Ireland, Germany, and America c.1750–c.1950: Essays in Honour of W.R. Ward*, Studies in Church History, Subsidia 7 (Oxford: Basil Blackwell, 1990), 25–50. The quotations from Wesley are from the sermon "The More Excellent Way." Also see Wesley's sermon "The Danger of Increasing Riches," *Wesley Works*, 4:178–86. The works by William Law that most impressed Wesley in this regard were *A Practical Treatise Upon Christian Perfection* and *A Serious Call to a Holy Life*.

10. *Wesley Works*, 2:560–61; *Minutes* (British), 1:50. Also see *Wesley Works*, 2:268–80.

11. *JLFA*, 1:722; Bond, "Anecdotes," 25; *JLFA*, 1:722.

12. *JLFA*, 1:125, 170, 301, 721; Wigger, *Taking Heaven*, 27; *Minutes*, Q. 26, in Tigert, *Constitutional History*, 551–52. These are the so-called Large Minutes that formed the basis of the early American Disciplines.

13. W. Orp to Francis Asbury, May 23, 1766, MAHC; John Lenton, "William Orpe's letter of May 23, 1766, to Francis Asbury," *MH*, 44:1 (October 2005): 56–59. Orp is sometimes spelled Orpe in Methodist records. According to Lenton, Orpe was born in 1743 in Staffordshire, joined the traveling ministry in 1764, and left it in 1767.

14. Jonathan Rodell, "Francis Asbury's First Circuit: Bedfordshire, 1767," *MH* 42:2 (January 2004): 110–21; *Minutes* (British), 69, 70; *Wesley Works*, 22:99; John Walsh, "The Cambridge Methodists," in *Christian Spirituality: Essays in Honour of Gordon Rupp*, ed. Peter Brooks (London: SCM Press, 1975), 249–83; Joan Anderson, *Early Methodism in Bedford* (Bedford, England: Rush & Warwick, 1953), 7–16; Joyce Godber, *History of Bedfordshire, 1066–1888* (Luton, England: Bedfordshire County Council, 1969), 339, 354–55. The senior preacher on the Bedfordshire Circuit was James Glassbrook. He later became a Presbyterian minister in New York, where Asbury saw him again in May 1787, calling him "my old friend." *JLFA*, 1:540; Frank Baker, *From Wesley to Asbury: Studies in Early American Methodism* (Durham, N.C.: Duke University Press, 1976), 112.

15. Rodell, "Asbury's First Circuit" (quotations from p. 118); *Wesley Works*, 22:67–68, 107; *Minutes* (British), 71, 76; Anderson, *Methodism in Bedford*, 11–16; Nigel R. Pibworth, *The Gospel Pedlar: The Story of John Berridge and the Eighteenth Century Revival* (Welwyn, England: Evangelical Press, 1987), 31–110. From 1758 through the early 1760s local Methodists had enjoyed the support of John Berridge, the evangelical vicar at Everton. John Wesley and John Fletcher preached in Berridge's church, and he occasionally substituted for Whitefield in London. By Asbury's time, Berridge had fallen out with Wesley over the latter's perfectionism.

16. *JLFA*, 2:43; *Minutes* (British), 1:15, 16, 17. Also see: 1:18–21, 67–71, 95.

17. *Minutes* (British), 1:13, 18, 21, 44, 51, 52, 79, 80.

18. *Minutes* (British), 1:16, 17, 52, 67, 68, 95.

19. *Minutes* (British), 1:15, 16, 64.

20. *Minutes* (British), 1:15, 20, 62–69, 79, 96.

21. *Minutes* (British), 1:69–75; Asbury to his parents, Oct. 26, 1768, MAHC.

22. Asbury to his parents, Oct. 26, 1768.

23. Asbury to his parents, Oct. 26, 1768, and Jan. 7, 1784, MAHC; Tipple, *Asbury*, 316.

24. Asbury to his parents, Oct. 26, 1768.

25. Francis Asbury to Elizabeth Asbury, Nov. 6, 1769, MAHC; *JLFA*, 1:125; *Minutes* (British), 1:83; Asbury to his parents, July 20, 1770, MAHC.

26. *Minutes* (British), 1:89, 90; John A. Vickers, "Francis Asbury in the Wiltshire Circuit," *MH* 16 (April 1978): 185–89. Much of Vickers's information comes from a "History of Methodism in Hampshire," written by John Sundius Stamp around 1826.

27. *Minutes* (British), 1:89–99, 108. King and Williams appear in the 1770 British minutes, were dropped from the 1771 minutes, and reinstated in 1773. Barbara Heck's name is spelled Hick in some accounts. On the origins of Methodism in New York and Maryland, see Andrews, *The Methodists*, 31–34; Samuel A. Seaman, *Annals of New York Methodism, Being a History of the Methodist Episcopal Church in the City of New York from*

A.D. 1766 to A.D. 1890 (New York: Hunt & Eaton, Cincinnati: Crantson & Stowe, 1892), 6–9, 14–25, 34, 48–51; Ruthella Mory Bibbins, *How Methodism Came: The Beginnings of Methodism in England and America* (Baltimore: American Methodist Historical Society of the Baltimore Annual Conference, 1945), 25–44, 85–109; Edwin Schell, "Beginnings in Maryland and America," in *Those Incredible Methodists: A History of the Baltimore Conference of the United Methodist Church*, ed. Gordon Pratt Baker (Baltimore: Commission on Archives and History, The Baltimore Conference, 1972), 2–17; Baker, *Wesley to Asbury*, 33–44, 72–79, 113; Frank Baker, "Early American Methodism: A Key Document," *MH* 3:2 (1965): 3–15; Samuel J. Fanning, "Philip Embury, Founder of Methodism in New York," *MH* 3:2 (1965): 16–25; William Crook, *Ireland and the Centenary of American Methodism* (London: Hamilton, Adams, and Co., 1866), 87–116, 147–69; J. B. Wakeley, *Lost Chapters Recovered from the Early History of American Methodism* (New York: Printed for the Author, 1858), 34–218; Frederick E. Maser, *Robert Strawbridge: First American Methodist Circuit Rider* (Rutland, Vt.: Academy Books, 1983), 11–25; Bangs, *History*, 1:47–61; Stevens, *History*, 1:51–91. Marvin Ellis Harvey, "The Wesleyan Movement and the American Revolution" (PhD diss., University of Washington, 1962), 65–80.

28. *JLFA*, 1:4; 2:162; Briggs, *Asbury*, 24; Lewis, *Asbury*, 21; Prince, *West Bromwich*, 48; Asbury, "Asbury Genealogy." In November 1812 Asbury wrote to the American Methodist local preacher Samuel Mitchel that when he departed England for America, "My thought was to serve a mission of five or six years and return, but the revolution kept me on the continent." See "More Asbury Letters," *World Parish*, vol. 3 (August 1959): 65.

29. S. Faithorn, Mary Farmer, M. Butler, and Eliza Web to Mrs. Asbury, Aug. 27, 1771, MAHC; John Allen to Elizabeth Asbury, Jan. 20, 1772, MAHC.

30. *JLFA*, 1:4; Baker, *Wesley to Asbury*, 105.

31. *JLFA*, 1:4–5.

CHAPTER 3

1. Bernard Bailyn, *The Peopling of British North America* (New York: Random, 1986), 9, 100–1, 111–31; Robert V. Wells, *The Population of the British Colonies in America Before 1776: A Survey of Census Data* (Princeton, N.J.: Princeton University Press, 1975), 284; J. Potter, "The Growth of Population in America, 1700–1860," in *Population in History: Essays in Historical Demography*, ed. D. V. Glass and D. E. C. Eversley (Chicago: Aldine, 1965), 631–63; Darrett B. and Anita H. Rutman, "'Now-Wives and Sons-in-Law': Parental Death in a Seventeenth-Century Virginia Colony," in *The Chesapeake in the Seventeenth Century: Essays on Anglo-American Society*, ed. Thad W. Tate and David L. Ammerman (New York: W.W. Norton, 1979), 153–82; Carville V. Earle, "Environment, Disease, and Mortality in Early Virginia," in Tate and Ammerman, *Chesapeake in the Seventeenth Century*, 96–125; Darrett B. Rutman and Anita H. Rutman, "Of Agues and Fevers: Malaria in the Early Chesapeake," *William and Mary Quarterly*, 3rd Ser., Vol. 33 (1976), 31–60; Jon Butler, *Becoming America: The Revolution Before 1776* (Cambridge: Harvard University Press, 2000), 32–36; Alan Taylor, *American Colonies* (New York:

Viking, 2001), 314–37. According to Bailyn, the American population increased 37 percent in the 1760s alone. See Bailyn, "1776," 447.

2. T. H. Breen, "An Empire of Goods: The Anglicization of Colonial America, 1690–1776," *Journal of British Studies* 25 (1986): 467–99. Bernard Bailyn, "1776: A Year of Challenge-a World Transformed," *Journal of Law and Economics* 19 (1976): 437–66; Butler, *Becoming America*, chap. 4; Taylor, *American Colonies*, 302–14; John Carswell, *From Revolution to Revolution: England 1688–1776* (New York: Charles Scribner's Sons, 1973), 187; John J. Mccusker and Russell R. Menard, *The Economy of British America, 1607–1789* (Chapel Hill: University of North Carolina Press, 1985), 51–70, 211–35, 277–94; T. H. Breen, *The Marketplace of Revolution: How Consumer Politics Shaped American Independence* (New York: Oxford University Press, 2004), especially part 1. Richard Bushman dates the beginning of "the refinement of America" at about 1690. See Richard L. Bushman, *The Refinement of America: Persons, Houses, Cities* (New York: Alfred A. Knopf, 1992), xii, 3–203.

3. David Hackett Fischer, *The Great Wave: Price Revolutions and the Rhythm of History* (New York: Oxford University Press, 1996), 120–42.

4. On the early history of St. George's Church, see Francis H. Tees, *The Story of Old St. George's: American Methodism's Oldest and Most Historic Church* (n.p., 1941), 8–65; Joseph Pilmore, *The Journal of Joseph Pilmore, Methodist Itinerant*, ed. Frederick E. Maser and Howard T. Maag (Philadelphia: Message Publishing for the Historical Society of the Philadelphia Annual Conference of the United Methodist Church, 1969), 27–28. Philadelphia Methodists purchased the uncompleted St. George's in 1769 for the bargain price of £650 from a German Reformed congregation that couldn't afford to finish it.

5. *JLFA*, 1:10. Pilmore was also spelled Pilmoor or Pillmoor in some records. Pilmore himself seems to have mostly used Pilmoor in England and Pilmore in America, and his name is spelled Pilmore in the register recording his baptism. See John Lenton, "Joseph Pilmore's Origins," *MH*, 44:4 (July 2006): 262–65. On Pilmore's and Boardman's careers in America, see Baker, *Wesley to Asbury*, 86–93; Stevens, *History*, 1:93–109. On Boardman, see John Lenton, "More Information on Richard Boardman," *MH*, 44:2 (January 2006): 125–28.

6. *JLFA*, 1:16. Robert Williams had been an itinerant preacher in Ireland from 1766 to 1768, but he didn't come to America as such. According to Jesse Lee, before leaving Ireland Williams sold his horse to pay his debts, arriving at the quay carrying only his saddlebags, a bottle of milk, and a loaf of bread. Williams apparently planned to finance his preaching in America by reprinting copies of Wesley's books, a scheme that later irritated both Wesley and the other preachers in America. See Lee, *Short History*, 19; Baker, *Wesley to Asbury*, 44–46. One of the reasons Wesley may not have completely trusted Williams was that he was an outspoken critic of the Anglican clergy. See Crook, *Ireland*, 137–38.

7. *JLFA*, 1:10–24; Briggs, *Asbury*, 51–70.

8. When Pilmore first organized the Philadelphia society in December 1769, he only stipulated that, after a period of probation, "those who walk according to the

Oracles of God, and thereby give proof (of) their sincerity, will readily be admitted into full connexion with the Methodists." Pilmore, *Journal*, 29, 56, 59, 73, 109.

9. Pilmore, *Journal*, 85, 142; Frank Bateman Stanger, "The Rev. Joseph Pilmore, D. D.: A Biographical Sketch," in Pilmore, *Journal*, 235–49; Jos. Smith to John Lockwood, June 29, 1869, Sept. 6, 1875, Oct. 13, 1875, and March 30, 1876, W.D. Johnson to John Lockwood, Feb. 24, 1877, Lockwood Papers, JRL; Lenton, "Pilmore's Origins." Lockwood apparently intended to write a biography of Pilmore, corresponding with a number of people in England and America concerning Pilmore and Richard Boardman.

10. Pilmore, *Journal*, 83, 109, 111, 112, 113.

11. Pilmore, *Journal*, 39–128.

12. *JLFA*, 1:25.

13. Pilmore, *Journal*, 202.

14. "Extract of a Letter from Norfolk, July 28," *Virginia Gazette*, Number 1096, July 30, 1772.

15. Pilmore, *Journal*, 163, 179. Also see 184, 185. In Norfolk, Va., Pilmore invited a Baptist preacher to preach in his place at a Methodist service (p. 192). A former carpenter from Philadelphia, Hart had been preaching in Charleston for twenty years by the time of Pilmore's visit and was South Carolina's leading Baptist. Hart did more than anyone to build connections between South Carolina's Baptist churches, but, like Pilmore, he never really felt comfortable in the backcountry, preferring life in Charleston. See Rachel N. Klein, *Unification of a Slave State: The Rise of the Planter Class in the South Carolina Backcountry, 1760–1808* (Chapel Hill: University of North Carolina Press, 1990), 83–89, 277–81; Loulie Latimer Owens, *Saints of Clay: The Shaping of South Carolina Baptists* (Columbia, S.C.: R. L. Bryan, 1971), 32–38; Leah Townsend, *South Carolina Baptists 1670–1805* (Baltimore: Genealogical Publishing, 1978), 20–25, 111–13.

16. Pilmore, *Journal*, 137, 188, 191.

17. *JLFA*, 1:28, 29, 30, 32, 35, 48.

18. *JLFA*, 1:28.

19. *JLFA*, 1: 28, 33–34, 35. Pilmore, *Journal*, 134.

20. *JLFA*, 1:37. On the early history of New York City Methodism, see Andrews, *The Methodists*, 32, 34–38; Wakeley, *Lost Chapters*, 42–73.

21. Wigger, *Taking Heaven*, 87; Richard O. Johnson, "The Development of the Love Feast in Early American Methodism," *MH* 19 (January 1981): 67–83; Clarke Garrett, *Spirit Possession and Popular Religion: From the Camisards to the Shakers* (Baltimore: Johns Hopkins University Press, 1987), 78–79. Robert Williams issued love feast tickets in New York City as early as 1769. See Seaman, *Annals*, 482–83; Simpson, *Cyclopedia*, 550–51; Wakeley, *Lost Chapters*, 195; Christophers, *Class-Meetings*, 120–23. The itinerant Thomas Ware wrote that the "nature and design" of love feasts was "to take a little bread and water, not as a sacrament, but in token of our Christian love, in imitation of a primitive usage, and then humbly and briefly to declare the great things the Lord had done for them in having mercy on them." See Ware, *Sketches*, 63. An 1807 account by a nonMethodist noted that those who spoke in love feast expressed "the same routine of striving, resistance, yielding, conviction, conversion, trials, temptations, present feelings, and future resolutions . . . varying only in those circumstances which the

accidental differences of condition in life may have occasioned." See Nightingale, *Portraiture*, 206. On the necessity of keeping closed love feasts, see Giles, *Pioneer*, 176, 250. For accounts of often dramatic love feasts, see William Watters, *A Short Account of the Christian Experience, and Ministerial Labours, of William Watters. Drawn up by Himself* (Alexandria, Va.: S. Snowden, 1806), 76; Chase, *Recollections*, 28; Paddock, *Memoir*, 48; Brunson, *Western Pioneer*, 87–88.

22. *JLFA*, 1:39; 3:14.

23. On the early history of New York City Methodism and the John Street Church, see Seaman, *Annals*, 27–42; Wakeley, *Lost Chapters*, 50–103; Baker, "Early American Methodism." Since only the Reformed and Anglican churches enjoyed full recognition in New York, Wesley Chapel was constructed with a fireplace and chimney so that it technically qualified as a dwelling house. See Fanning, "Philip Embury."

24. *JLFA*, 1:41–42. On Lupton and Newton, see *JLFA*, 1:41, n. 148, 1:46, n. 171, n. 172; Seaman, *Annals*, 30–33, 61, 64, 69, 422–24, 429–30; Wakeley, *Lost Chapters*, 75–79, 80–83.

25. *JLFA*, 1:45, 46, 131.

26. *JLFA*, 1:46.

27. *JLFA*, 1:49.

28. Watters, *Short Account*, 108–9; *Minutes* (1794), 97; Schell, "Beginnings," 4–8, 17–20; Stevens, *History*, 1:73–80, 83–91, 131–40; Maser, *Robert Strawbridge*, 3–42; Bibbins, *How Methodism Came*, 29–44; John Bowen, *Robert Strawbridge and the Rise and Progress of Methodism on Sam's and Pipe Creeks, Md.* (Westminster, Md., 1856; reprinted by the Strawbridge Shrine Association, n.d.), 6–16; Crook, *Ireland*, 149–69; Cooper, *Substance*, 69. According to Schell, Maser, and Bibbins, Strawbridge purchased the 50-acre farm near Sam's and Pipe creeks for £50 in 1773. Strawbridge was part of a large migration of Irish to America that had yet to reach its peak in 1760. Bernard Bailyn writes that between 1764 and 1776, fifty-five thousand Protestant Irish immigrated to America, representing 2 percent of the total population of Ireland in 1760. See Bailyn, "1776," 449. According to Dee Andrews, an inventory after Strawbridge's death lists only the possessions of a small farmer and no slaves. His two sons were apprenticed as orphans. See Andrews, *Methodists*, 286, n. 145.

29. Other Strawbridge converts included Richard, Josias, and Sarah Dallam, at whose home Asbury recovered from malaria in 1773, Thomas and Phoebe Bond, whose son John Wesley Bond sat by Asbury's side as he lay dying in 1816, and several members of the Watters family. Bibbins, *How Methodism Came*, 45–49, 51–52; Garrettson, *Journal*, 388; Henry Smith, *Recollections and Reflections of an Old Itinerant. A Series of Letters* (New York: Lane & Tippett, 1848), 204–5; *JLFA*, 1:55, 66, 70, 193, 201; Lednum, *Rise*, 19.

30. James B. Bell, "Anglican Clergy in Colonial America Ordained by Bishops of London," *Proceedings of the American Antiquarian Society* 83 (1973): 103–60; William Stevens Perry, ed., *Historical Collections Relating to the American Colonial Church*, vol. 4, *Maryland* (New York: AMS Press, 1969), 337, 346; Sandra Ryan Dresbeck, "The Episcopalian Clergy in Maryland and Virginia, 1765–1805" (PhD diss., University of California Los Angeles, 1976), 62, 69; Frederick L. Weis, *The Colonial Clergy of Maryland, Delaware and Georgia* (Baltimore: Genealogical Publishing, 1978), 61; John K. Nelson, *A Blessed Company: Parishes, Parsons,*

and Parishioners in Anglican Virginia, 1690–1776 (Chapel Hill: University of North Carolina Press, 2001), 317; Thomas Rightmyer to John Wigger, e-mail, May 12, 2006. Reade (Read or Preade) was ordained a deacon by the Bishop of Rochester at the request of the Bishop of London. Born in Virginia, Reade was one of an increasing number of American-born Anglican clerics in the colonies. He remained at St. Paul's Parish from 1775 to 1778.

31. *JLFA*, 1:57–58. Also see *JLFA*, 1:95 for a similar incident that occurred the following year. On the rise of more egalitarian communication styles in this period, see Harry S. Stout, "Religion, Communications, and the Ideological Origins of the American Revolution," *William and Mary Quarterly*, 3rd Ser., 34:4 (October 1977): 519–41.

32. John Wesley to John King, July 28, 1775, *Wesley Works* (1872), 12:331. Pilmore, *Journal*, 25, 58, 163, 164; Maser, *Robert Strawbridge*, 35; Stevens, *History*, 1:87–91; John Atkinson, *Memorials of Methodism in New Jersey, From the Foundation of the First Society in the State in 1770, to the Completion of the First Twenty Years of Its History* (Philadelphia: Perkinpine & Higgins, 1860), 68–72. In Wesley's mind, King's shouting was a symptom of an unruly spirit. "Pray for an advisable and teachable temper!" he wrote to King in the same letter. "By nature you are very far from it: You are stubborn and headstrong." In all fairness to Pilmore, he had some good things to say about the preaching of King and Williams in his journal, even when they were in Philadelphia and New York. But overall, his judgment of the two was harsh. See Pilmore's *Journal*, 61, 85, 96.

33. *JLFA*, 1:155.

34. Lester Ruth, *A Little Heaven Below: Worship at Early Methodist Quarterly Meetings* (Nashville: Kingswood Books, 2000), 17–43; Wigger, *Taking Heaven*, 89.

35. *JLFA*, 1:54.

36. Carol Van Voorst, *The Anglican Clergy in Maryland, 1692–1776* (New York: Garland Publishing, 1989), 121–22, 156–57, 206, 210, 248; Dresbeck, "Episcopalian Clergy," 11, 29, 35, 36, 42, 59, 74, 75; Perry, *Historical Collections*, vol. 4, 336–37; Joan R. Gundersen, "The Search For Good Men: Recruiting Ministers in Colonial Virginia," *Historical Magazine of the Protestant Episcopal Church* 48:4 (December 1979): 453–64. One in six Maryland clergy of this period prompted public complaints, most commonly for drunkenness.

37. Pilmore, *Journal*, 169; Charles Woodmason, *The Carolina Backcountry on the Eve of the Revolution*, ed. Richard J. Hooker (Chapel Hill: University of North Carolina Press, 1953), 13, 44; Gary Freeze, "Like A House Built Upon Sand: The Anglican Church and Establishment in North Carolina, 1765–1776," *Historical Magazine of the Protestant Episcopal Church* 48:4 (December 1979): 405–432. After traveling from Baltimore to Norfolk, Va., with Robert Williams in 1772, William Watters wrote, "We found very few in the course of three hundred miles who knew, experimentally, any thing of the Lord Jesus Christ, or the power of his grace." Watters, *Short Account*, 27.

38. *JLFA*, 1:60.

39. *JLFA*, 1:82, 85–86; Pilmore, *Journal*, 210; *Minutes* (1794), 5–7; Stevens, *History*, 1:160–66. Also present at the general conference were Shadford, Boardman, Pilmore, Richard Wright, Thomas Webb, John King, Abraham Whitworth, and Joseph Yearby. William Watters, who was only twenty-two at the time, attended the conference as an

unofficial member. His name doesn't appear in the printed minutes. See Watters, *Short Account*, 30–31.

40. *JLFA*, 1:88.

41. *JLFA*, 1:54. On June 24, 1774, while in New York City, Asbury received a letter informing him that "Mr. Strawbridge was very officious in administering the ordinances." "What strange infatuation attends that man! Why will he run before Providence?" mused Asbury, indicating that at some point providence might allow for Methodist preachers to administer the sacraments. See *JLFA*, 1:120.

42. *Lives* (Jackson), 6:23, 57. Shadford claimed that his mission to America was the fulfillment of a prophetic dream given to him six years before his final decision to leave England. Also see Stevens, *History*, 1:148–56.

43. Rankin, untitled manuscript journal, GTS, 1–42. The quotations are from 5, 29. An edited version of the manuscript journal is given in *Lives* (Jackson) 5:136–75. Rankin's journal has been edited and published in several forms. To complicate matters, a number of pages are now apparently missing from the manuscript journal.

44. *Wesley Letters* (Telford), 6:57; *Lives* (Jackson), 5:175–85 (quotation from 177). Also see "A Short Account of Mr. Thomas Rankin: in a Letter to the Rev. Mr. John Wesley [Nov. 16, 1778], *Arminian Magazine* (London), 2 (1779): 182–98; Stevens, *History*, 1:142–48; Harvey, "Wesleyan Movement," 119–24. On Rankin's career in America, also see Baker, *Wesley to Asbury*, 95–98.

45. Pilmore, *Journal*, 206. Shadford notes his arrival in Philadelphia but not the sermon in his autobiographical account. See *Lives* (Jackson), 6:163.

46. *JLFA*, 1:85; Rankin, manuscript journal, 27; *Lives* (Jackson), 5:193–95. Pilmore and Boardman spent five months after the conference preaching in New York City and Philadelphia, though not under a regular appointment. On Boardman's post-American career and death, see "A Short Account of the death of Mr. Richard Boardman," *Arminian Magazine* (London), 6 (January 1783): 22–23; Crook, *Ireland*, 178–85; Stevens, *History*, 1:167–69; Lenton, "Richard Boardman."

47. *JLFA*, 1:109; Joan Rezner Gundersen, "A Petition of Early Norfolk County, Virginia, Methodists to the Bishop of London, Urging the Ordination of Joseph Pilmoor," *Virginia Magazine of History and Biography* 83:4 (1975): 412–21; Lee to William Prince Gibb, July 16, 1775, William Lee Letterbook, VHS, Richmond, Virginia; Pilmore to Thomas Tatham, March 21, 1784, record PLP 83.60.4, JRL. Lee didn't think highly of the Methodists. In two letters to Samuel Thorp from Brussels in 1782, Lee complained about a Mr. Brailsford, who "proves himself to be no unapt Disciple of his Tutor John Wesley" and a "Disciple of Jnᵒ Wesleys." See William Lee to Samuel Thorp, Oct. 18, 1782, and Nov. 29, 1782, William Lee Letterbook, VHS. On Lee, see Louis W. Potts, "Lee, William," *American National Biography*, ed. John A. Garraty and Mark C. Carnes (New York: Oxford University Press, 1999), 406–7.

CHAPTER 4

1. Asbury to his parents, Sept. 5, 1773, MAHC; *JLFA*, 1:91, 92. On earlier meetings with exhorters, see *JLFA*, 1:51, 61, 69.

2. Philip Gatch, *Sketch of Rev. Philip Gatch,* ed. John McLean (Cincinnati: Swormstedt & Poe, 1854), 6–13. On Gatch, also see Elizabeth Connor, *Methodist Trail Blazer Philip Gatch 1751–1834: His Life in Maryland, Virginia and Ohio* (Rutland, Vt.: Academy Books, 1970).

3. Gatch, *Sketch,* 16–20.

4. Gatch, *Sketch,* 20–26.

5. *JLFA,* 1:94–97; *Dorland's,* s.v. "malaria"; Mary J. Dobson, *Contours of Death and Disease in Early Modern England* (Cambridge: Cambridge University Press, 1997), 287–367; Darrett B. Rutman and Anita H. Rutman, "Of Agues and Fevers: Malaria in the Early Chesapeake," *William and Mary Quarterly,* vol. 33 (1976): 31–60; Jon Kukla, "Kentish Agues and American Distempers: The Transmission of Malaria from England to Virginia in the Seventeenth Century," *Southern Studies,* 25 (1986): 135–47; R.S. Bray, *Armies of Pestilence: The Impact of Disease on History* (New York: Barnes & Noble, 1996), 89–92, 100; Ernest Carroll Faust, "Malaria Incidence in North America," in *Malariology: A Comprehensive Survey of All Aspects of this Group of Diseases from a Global Standpoint,* ed. Mark F. Boyd (Philadelphia: W.B. Saunders, 1949), 749–63. I would also like to thank Mark F. Wiser of the Department of Tropical Medicine at Tulane University; Ross Coppel of the Department of Microbiology at Monash University, Australia, and Ted Nye of the Dunedin School of Medicine in New Zealand for helping me understand malaria. Asbury recorded subsequent fever attacks on Nov. 29, Dec. 7, and Dec. 18, 1773. Locals warned him to expect another fever on Jan. 14, but it didn't happen. *JLFA,* 1:98, 99, 103. Mal aria, a term introduced by Horace Walpole from Italy in 1740, literally means "bad air" and was often called "marsh fever" in southeast England. It was endemic to the marshlands of southeast England, particularly in Kent and Essex, since the sixteenth and seventeenth centuries.

6. *JLFA,* 1:112, 103, 120; Marilyn James-Kracke to John Wigger, e-mail, May 25, 2006; *Dorland's,* s.v. "ammonium carbonate"; Oscar Reiss, *Medicine in Colonial America* (Lanham, Md.: University Press of America, 2000), 183–211, 267–80; John Duffy, *From Humors to Medical Science: A History of American Medicine,* 2nd ed. (Urbana: University of Illinois Press, 1993), 64–71. Asbury apparently didn't have access to cinchona bark, which contains quinine and is effective against malaria, though he later used the bark in the 1790s for an unrelated fever.

7. Buckley, *Constitutional and Parliamentary History,* 51; Wigger, *Taking Heaven,* 151, 157–64.

8. *JLFA,* 1:26, 30–31, 32, 51, 55, 56, 61, 69, 71, 89, 99, 141, 182, 187, 204, 228, 229, 735, 2:636; Lednum, *Rise,* 42–44, 90; Andrews, *The Methodists,* 100–1. In October 1795 Asbury dined with Withey at Chester, noting that she had "lived a widow in this house thirty-one years, and hath kept one of the most complete houses of entertainment in America." *JLFA,* 2:64. Thomas Coke was also impressed with Withey's hospitality in 1784, writing that he was "sumptuously entertained." But Coke was more critical of Withey's lack of obvious spirituality than Asbury, noting "the landlady has certainly some love for the people of God; but alas! she neglects her own vineyard!" Coke, *Extracts* (1793), 15, 25. Among the many preachers who record boarding with Withey were Richard Whatcoat and Ezekiel Cooper. See Cooper, manuscript journal, MSS 1, GTS

(Sept. 22, 1788), 5:3, (Sept. 14, 1795), vol. 12. Asbury visited Withey's children and grandchildren as late as April 1814. *JLFA*, 2:754.

9. On March 24, 1775, Asbury notes that he "had a full house at Captain Ridgely's, whose wife is brought by grace to the knowledge of God in Christ Jesus." A month later, Asbury once again returned to the Ridgelys' home near Baltimore, this time dining and spending the night. Charles Ridgely's sister was Prudence Gough, wife of Henry Dorsey Gough, both Methodists. Rebecca Ridgely, who regularly corresponded with Asbury and at times gave him money, was another "mother in Israel, and both a friend and mother to me," according to Asbury. *JLFA*, 1:152, 154, 240; Henry Smith, *Recollections and Reflections of an Old Itinerant*, ed. George Peck (New York: Lane and Tippett, 1848), 189. On the Goughs and Ridgelys, see Edith Rossiter Bevan, "Perry Hall: Country Seat of the Gough and Carroll Families," *Maryland Historical Magazine* 45 (1950): 33–46; Charles G. Steffen, *The Mechanics of Baltimore: Workers and Politics in the Age of Revolution 1763–1812* (Urbana: University of Illinois Press, 1984), 270–72; Paul Otis Evans, "The Ideology of Inequality: Asbury, Methodism, and Slavery" (PhD diss.: Rutgers, 1981), 148–52.

10. *JLFA*, 1:96; 2:192, 232, 295, 302, 498, 667; Littlejohn, "Journal," July 5, 1777; Wigger, *Taking Heaven*, 161–64. When Asbury again stopped by the Dallams' in February 1775, he wrote "Sister Dallam has treated me with all the tenderness of a mother towards a son: and may He that will not forget a cup of water given in his name, abundantly reward her!" *JLFA*, 1:150.

11. *JLFA*, 1:104, 113.

12. *Minutes* (1794), 6–11; Watters, *Short Account*, 35–37; Lednum, *Rise*, 115. On Samuel Keene (also spelled Cain and Kain), see Perry, *Historical Collections*, 4:337, 347; Frederick Lewis Weis, *The Colonial Clergy of Maryland, Delaware and Georgia* (Baltimore: Genealogical Publishing Co., 1978), 51; Stevens, *History*, 1:245–49; William B. Sprague, *Annals of the American Pulpit*, vol. 5 (New York: Robert Carter & Brothers, 1861; reprint, New York: Arno Press and The New York Times, 1969), 311; Rightmyer to Wigger, e-mail, May 12, 2006. Keene was ordained a priest in London on Sept. 29, 1760. Though William Watters had been appointed to New Jersey by the 1773 conference, he actually spent much of the year on the Kent circuit, demonstrating the flexibility of the itinerant system (it was Philip Gatch who instead went to New Jersey). Kent County is located on Maryland's eastern shore, part of the Delmarva Peninsula. For another account of a preacher being moved between conferences, this time by Asbury, see Asbury's letter to William Duke, March 4, 1774, MAHC.

13. Watters, *Short Account*, 37.

14. Watters, *Short Account*, 38–39; Lednum, *Rise*, 128–29.

15. Watters, *Short Account*, 38–39. Philip Gatch had a similar exchange with Keene while stationed on the Kent circuit in 1775. Gatch, *Sketch*, 33–35; *JLFA*, 1:95. Thomas Rankin and Captain Webb got on much better with Keene, probably because of their loyalty to England in the run up to the Revolution. On July 1, 1775, Keene asked Rankin to preach for him, and afterwards the two had "some free & friendly conversation," according to Rankin. Rankin, mss. journal (July 1, 1775), 69. Also see Benjamin Abbott's exchange with a Presbyterian minister in Benjamin Abbott, *Experience and Gospel*

Labours of the Rev. Benjamin Abbott, ed. John Ffirth (New York: J. Emory and B. Waugh, 1839), 33–34.

16. *JLFA*, 1:116, 127, 128, 132.

17. Rankin, mss. journal (Oct. 28, Dec. 5, 1773, Feb. 13, 1774), 31, 35, 38; *Lives* (Jackson), 5:191, 192, 193.

18. Watters, *Short Account*, 41–42; Thomas Ware, *Sketches of the Life and Travels of Rev. Thomas Ware, Who Has Been an Itinerant Methodist Preacher for More Than Fifty Years* (New York: T. Mason and G. Lane, 1840), 252; Gatch, *Sketch*, 30.

19. *JLFA*, 1:117.

20. *JLFA*, 1:38, 111, 115, 122, 136, 138, 145, 148, 151. Among the treatments Asbury took for his fevers were emetics, designed to cause vomiting. See *JLFA*, 1:120.

21. *JLFA*, 1:118–19. While in New York in July 1774, Asbury wrote the first of the two autobiographical accounts in his journal. See *JLFA*, 1:123–25. Methodist preachers often recorded these kinds of self evaluations in their journals. On his twenty-eighth birthday, John Kobler lamented how much of his life "has been spent in the follies of youth, how much in the vanaties of childhood, how much have I slept away, & spent in trifleing Conversation, how much in dull Inactivity. In which time (as to the profit I was of to myself or others) I might as well not have been in existence." John Kobler, manuscript journal, LLM, Aug. 29, 1796.

22. *JLFA*, 1:127, 131.

23. Rankin to Dartmouth, Dec. 29, 1774, SRO. Asbury didn't even like Baltimore, which only had a population of sixty-seven hundred in 1776. See *JLFA*, 1:99–100, 107, 114.

24. *JLFA*, 1:140, 146–47; Rankin, mss. journal (Dec. 4, 1774), 59. On Asbury's dispute with Rankin, also see *JLFA*, 1:127, 128, 130, 132, 145.

25. William Duke, "Journal," 16 (Nov. 4, 1775); Feeman, *Silver Trumpet*, 76.

26. Asbury to Dromgoole, Jan. 9, 1775, Edward Dromgoole Papers, SHC; Briggs, *Bishop Asbury*, 88–89. Benjamin Abbott, who was converted under Whitworth's preaching, claims to have dreamed of Whitworth's fall into drunkenness three weeks before he actually heard of it. Abbott, *Experience*, 19; *JLFA*, 1:76, n. 33, 123; Gatch, *Sketch*, 31. Whitworth may have died in battle while fighting the British during the revolution. See Lednum, *Rise*, 129; Stevens, *History*, 1:202–3.

27. *JLFA*, 1:146–47. *Dorland's*, s.v. "sage" and "alum." Mallow refers to any plant of the genus Malva, the flowers and leaves of which are demulcent and emollient. Mustard can have counterirritant, stimulant and emetic properties. See *Dorland's*, s.v. "mallow," "Malva," and "mustard"; Reiss *Medicine in Colonial America*, 185–86.

28. *JLFA*, 1:151; Rankin, mss. journal (Feb. 22, 1775), 62.

29. *JLFA*, 1:114–15, 153, 156.

30. On the more interactive nature of this revival, see Ann Taves, *Fits, Trances, & Visions: Experiencing Religion and Explaining Experience from Wesley to James* (Princeton, N.J.: Princeton University Press, 1999), 78–90.

31. Devereux Jarratt, *The Life of the Reverend Devereux Jarratt*, ed. David L. Holmes (Cleveland: Pilgrim Press, 1995), vii–xx, 5–10; Nelson, *Blessed Company*, 136–38; Rightmyer to Wigger, e-mail, May 12, 2006.

32. Jarratt, *Life*, 8–46 (the quotation is from 31); Frederick Lewis Weis, *The Colonial Clergy of Virginia, North Carolina and South Carolina* (Boston: Society of the Descendants of the Colonial Clergy, 1955), 27; Gerald Fothergill, *A List of Emigrant Ministers to America, 1690–1811* (London: Elliot Stock, 1904), 36; Edward Lewis Goodwin, *The Colonial Church in Virginia* (Milwaukee: Morehouse Publishing, 1927), 281–82; Nelson, *Blessed Company*, 111, 117, 129, 312.

33. Jarratt, *Life*, 49, 55, 56; *JLFA*, 1:414. Jarratt could be abrasive and arrogant. He claims that on the voyage to England he twice saved the ship from disaster, once by thinking up a plan that hadn't occurred to the captain or crew, even though he knew little about ships or the ocean. He also claims that at his ordination examinations in London he excelled above all of the candidates from Oxford and Cambridge. See Jarratt, *Life*, 37–41. On Jarratt's role in the Virginia revival, also see Wesley M. Gewehr, *The Great Awakening in Virginia, 1740–1790* (Gloucester, Mass.: Peter Smith, 1965), 138–57; William Warren Sweet, *Virginia Methodism: A History* (Richmond: Whittet & Shepperson, 1955), 62–71.

34. *JLFA*, 1:209; *Minutes* (1794), 10, 14, 18; Jarratt, *Life*, 61–62; Nelson, *Blessed Company*, 199.

35. *JLFA*, 1:219–20; Jarratt, *Life*, 63.

36. Watters, *Short Account*, 27, 28, 29.

37. *JLFA*, 1:156, 157, 159, 161, 165, 175. While in Delaware in 1778, Asbury reflected on the necessity of expelling several "disorderly members-which always are a weight and a curse to any religious community." "And who can tell how often the Lord is displeased with his Church for the wickedness of some of its members?" Asbury asked on this occasion. "No doubt but this frequently checks the spiritual progress of the righteous; especially if ungodly members are known and not dealt with according to the Gospel." *JLFA*, 1:283.

38. *JLFA*, 1:166, 167, 168, 178.

39. *JLFA*, 1:210, 213, 214. Also see Bangs, *History*, 1:90–115.

40. *JLFA*, 1:214–16, 220. John Young Sr. was typical of converts for whom their class meeting was central to their religious experience. Young, who lived near the James River, was awakened after hearing John King preach in 1777. He joined the Methodists the next January and soon became a class leader. He was licensed to preach sometime between 1786 and 1788, but continued as a class leader even after moving from the Roanoke circuit to the Tar River circuit in 1788. See John Young, "A brief & very imperfect History of my past life drew up for my own satisfaction," (ca. 1819), DUL, 1–19.

41. *JLFA*, 1:211, 212.

42. *JLFA*, 1:213.

43. *JLFA*, 1:213–14, 217.

44. *JLFA*, 1:221; Rankin, mss. journal (June 30, 1776), 99–100; Rankin "Life," in *Lives* (Jackson), 5:206–8.

45. *JLFA*, 1:215–16, 221–22; Rankin, mss. journal (July 7, 1776), 101–2.

46. Lee, *Short History*, 51–52. Rankin says little about this meeting in his diary, except that "it fell far short of what we enjoyed the first Sunday I preached there." Rankin, mss. journal (July 14, 1776), 104.

47. Ware, *Sketches*, 252–53; Thomas Ware, "The Christmas Conference of 1784," *Methodist Magazine and Quarterly Review*, 14:1 (January 1832): 96–104. This exchange between Rankin and Asbury probably took place at the May 1777 conference at Deer Creek, in Harford County, Md. See *JLFA*, 1:238–39; Rankin, mss. journal (May 18, 1777), 136–37.

48. Ware, "Christmas Conference," 103.

49. Ware, *Sketches*, 170.

50. Asbury to Duke, Mar. 4, 1774, MAHC; Duke, "The Journal of William Duke, 1774–1776," TMs, ed. Edwin Schell, LLM. Duke was ordained in the Protestant Episcopal Church in 1785.

51. *JLFA*, 1:163, 164, 170, 182. Robert Williams appointed Asbury and Rankin executors over his will. Rankin, mss. journal (July 24, 1776), 107; *JLFA*, 1:178.

52. *JLFA*, 1:162, 166; Rankin, mss. journal (May 21, 1776), 96.

CHAPTER 5

1. *JLFA*, 1:164, 178, 180, 181.

2. Wesley to Rankin, March 1, 1775, and Wesley to Dartmouth, June 14, 1775; *Wesley Letters* (Telford), 6:142, 156. In the same letter to Dartmouth, Wesley admitted that "all my prejudices are against the Americans. For I am an High Churchman, the son of an High Churchman," taught from childhood to honor the king.

3. Wesley to Dartmouth, Aug. 23, 1775, SRO. "Need anyone ask for what motive this was wrote? Let him look around: England is in a flame! A flame of malice and rage against the king and almost all that are in authority under him," Wesley wrote on Nov. 11, 1775, referring to his pamphlet *A Calm Address to Our American Colonies*. "I labour to put out this flame. Ought not every true patriot to do the same?" *Wesley Works*, 5:471.

4. *Wesley Works* (1872), 11:80–90; Frank Baker, "The Shaping of Wesley's *Calm Address*," *MH* 14:1 (October 1975): 3–12; Allan Raymond, "'I fear God and honour the King': John Wesley and the American Revolution," *Church History* 45:3 (September 1976): 316–28; Andrews, *The Methodists*, 49–50; Stevens, *History*, 1:282–85; Harvey, "Wesleyan Movement," 228–34.

5. John Wesley, *A Calm Address to the Inhabitants of England*, 2nd ed. (London: R. Hawes, 1777); *Wesley Works* (1872), 129–40; *Wesley Letters* (Telford), 6:182; Donald H. Kirkham, "John Wesley's *Calm Address*: The Response of the Critics," *MH* 14:1 (October 1975): 13–23; Harvey, "Wesleyan Movement," 234–46, 254–57; Rack, *Reasonable Enthusiast*, 376–77; Hempton, *Religion of the People*, 77–90; Mark A. Noll, *America's God: From Jonathan Edwards to Abraham Lincoln* (New York: Oxford University Press, 2002), 69. Also see Owen H. Alderfer, "British Evangelical Response to the American Revolution: The Wesleyans," *Fides et Historia*, 8:2 (1976): 7–34.

6. Charles Wesley, *The Unpublished Poetry of Charles Wesley*, 3 vols., ed. S.T. Kimbrough Jr. and Oliver A. Beckerlegge (Nashville: Kingswood Books, 1988), 1:72, 96, 104, 109; Donald S. Baker, "Charles Wesley and the American War of Independence," *PWHS*, 34 (1964): 159–64; Donald S. Baker, "Charles Wesley and the American Loyalists," *PWHS*, 35 (1965): 5–9; Harvey, "Wesleyan Movement," 257–61.

7. *JLFA*, 1:181; Duke, "Journal," 17.

8. *JLFA*, 1:149; Simpson, *Cyclopedia*, 412; Sylvia R. Frey and Betty Wood, *Come Shouting to Zion: African American Protestantism in the American South and British Caribbean to 1830* (Chapel Hill: University of North Carolina Press, 1998), 104. Also see the exchange between Robert Glen, Sylvia Frey, and Betty Wood in the following: Robert Glen, "The History of Early Methodism in Antigua: A Critique of Sylvia R. Frey and Betty Wood's *Come Shouting to Zion*," *Journal of Caribbean History*, 35:2 (2001): 253–84; Sylvia Frey and Betty Wood, "A Rebuttal of 'The History of Early Methodism in Antigua: A Critique of Sylvia R. Frey and Betty Wood's *Come Shouting to Zion*,'" *Journal of Caribbean History* 36:1 (2002): 156–70; Robert Glen, "'The History of Early Methodism in Antigua': A Response to Frey and Wood," *Journal of Caribbean History*, 36:1 (2002): 171–78.

9. *Wesley Letters* (Telford), 6:142, 148, 150, Bangs, *History*, 115–16.

10. *Wesley Letters* (Telford), 6:173; *JLFA*, 1:161.

11. *JLFA*, 1:192; 2:246; Coke, *Extracts* (1793), 22; Simpson, *Cyclopedia*, 415; Lednum, *Rise*, 154–56; Thomas Lyell, "Autobiography," Aldert Smedes papers, SHC; Bevan, "Perry Hall," 33–46; Steffen, *Mechanics of Baltimore*, 270–72; Evans, "Ideology of Inequality," 148–52; Stevens, *History*, 1:235–40. It seems almost too much of a coincidence for the Goughs of Perry Hall in England, for whom Asbury's father probably worked, not to be related to the Goughs of Perry Hall in Maryland. But I know of no confirmed relationship between the two. Several accounts point to a connection between the Maryland Goughs and a wealthy merchant from Bristol, England. When Henry Gough died in 1808, Asbury wrote that "Mr. Gough had inherited a large estate from a relation in England . . ." *JLFA*, 2:569. Also see Lednum, *Rise*, 153; Bevan, "Perry Hall," 34; Henry Ridgely Evans, *Founders of the Colonial Families of Ridgely, Dorsey, and Greenberry, of Maryland* (Washington, D. C.: W. H. Lowdermilk, 1935), 37. When the itinerant Henry Smith first visited Perry Hall in 1806, he was awestruck, describing it as "the largest dwelling house I had ever seen." Smith, *Recollections*, 189. Thomas Coke believed that Henry Gough's wealth had, by December 1784, "robbed him I am afraid of a considerable part of his religion. . . . He intends to go to England next spring, to buy furniture for his house, which, I fear, will only still lower him in grace." Coke, *Extracts* (1793), 22.

12. Rack, *Reasonable Enthusiast*, 45–49, 105.

13. *JLFA*, 1:192–93, 490; Lednum, *Rise*, 169; Charlene M. Boyer Lewis, *Ladies and Gentlemen on Display: Planter Society at the Virginia Springs 1790–1860* (Charlottesville: University Press of Virginia, 2001), 17, 18, 48, 70 80, 114, 193–96; Thomas A. Chambers, *Drinking the Waters: Creating an American Leisure Class at Nineteenth-Century Mineral Springs* (Washington, D. C.: Smithsonian Institution Press, 2002); Carl-Bridenbaugh, "Baths and Watering Places of Colonial America," *William and Mary Quarterly*, 3rd Ser., Vol. 3, No. 2 (April 1946), 160–64; Ferdinand M. Bayard, *Travels of a Frenchman in Maryland and Virginia with a Description of Philadelphia and Baltimore in 1791*, trans. Ben C. McCary (Ann Arbor: Edwards Brothers, 1950), 39–52. Bayard describes the Methodists he met at Bath as pious hypocrites who "exhorted us not to eat to satisfy our appetite, but in order to preserve the strength needed for the service of the Lord," but who nevertheless ate greedily (43).

14. *JLFA*, 1:187, 191, 192, 193, 194, 195, 197, 198. The phrase *"noisy children"* is italicized in the 1792 edition of his journals, but not the editions published in 1821 and 1958. See "Discovery," ed. Frederick E. Maser, *MH*, 8 (October 1970): 56. On a visit to Berkeley Springs in September 1775, Presbyterian minister Philip Fithian recorded hearing "a Methodist Preacher . . . haranguing the People." Philip Fithian, *Philip Vickers Fithian: Journal, 1775–1776*, ed. Robert Greenhalgh Albion and Leonidas Dodson (Princeton, N.J.: Princeton University Press, 1934), 126.

15. *JLFA*, 1:492, 517–18, 548, 578, 606. On Virginia's warm springs, see Marshall S. Berdan, "The Spa Life: Taking the Cure in Antebellum Bath County," *Virginia Cavalcade*, 40 (Winter 1991): 110–19; Harry Evans Woodward, "They Called Them Watering Places," *Virginia Cavalcade*, 13:1 (1963): 21–27; John Edwards Caldwell, *A Tour Through Part of Virginia in the Summer of 1808*, ed. William M. E. Rachal (Belfast: Smyth and Lyons, 1810; reprint, Richmond: Dietz Press, 1951), 24–32.

16. *JLFA*, 1:228; *Minutes* (1794), 21, 25.

17. Littlejohn, "Journal," 3–27; Lednum, *Rise*, 198–99. Also see John Littlejohn, "Journal of John Littlejohn," Tms, trans. Annie Winstead, The Upper Room, Nashville, Tenn.; Richard Weiss, *Preecher and Patriot: The Journal and Memorandums of the Rev. John Littlejohn, A Pioneer Preacher in American Methodism* (Utica, Ky.: McDowell Publications, 2005). I am indebted to Richard Weiss, archivist at Kentucky Wesleyan College, for providing me with a copy of portions of Littlejohn's manuscript journal. All subsequent Littlejohn quotations are from his manuscript journal.

18. Littlejohn, "Journal," Dec. 25, 1777, May 5, 1777, July 4, 1777, July 8, 1777, Aug. 30, 1777. Also see March 28, 1777, Sept. 15 and 17, 1777.

19. *JLFA*, 1:190; Littlejohn, "Journal," March 15, 1778; Richard A. Overfield, "A Patriot Dilemma: The Treatment of Passive Loyalists and Neutrals in Revolutionary Maryland," *Maryland Historical Magazine*, 68:2 (1973): 147. Next to the Methodists, Anglicans and Quakers were the most suspect churches in the eyes of patriots. Anglican priests were in a difficult position, since the oaths they swore at their ordinations required them to pray for the king. Though the majority of Anglican laity sided with the American cause, many priests in Maryland and Delaware didn't. David L. Holmes, "The Episcopal Church and the American Revolution," *Historical Magazine of the Protestant Episcopal Church*, 48 (1978): 261–91. According to one estimate, nineteen of forty-six Anglican clergymen in Maryland were loyalists at the beginning of the war. See Anne Alden Allan, "Patriots and Loyalists: The Choice of Political Allegiances by the Members of Maryland's Proprietary Elite," *Journal of Southern History*, 38:2 (May 1972): 283–92. Also see Richard W. Pointer, "Religious Life in New York During the Revolutionary War," *New York History*, 66 (1985): 357–73; and Diana Hochstedt Butler, *Standing Against the Whirlwind: Evangelical Episcopalians in Nineteenth-Century America* (New York: Oxford University Press, 1995), 4–8.

20. *JLFA*, 1:161, 163; Wesley, *Letters* (Telford), 6:56–57; Harvey, "Wesleyan Movement," 181–201; Baker *Wesley to Asbury*, 51–63; Wakeley, *Lost Chapters*, 42–44, 141–55; Simpson, *Cyclopedia*, 906; Seaman, *Annals*, 23–24, 62, 487; John Atkinson, *Memorials of Methodism in New Jersey, From the Foundation of the First Society in the State in 1770, to the Completion of the First Twenty Years of Its History* (Philadelphia: Perkinpine &

Higgins, 1860), 28–35. Born in 1725, Captain Webb, as he was known in America, enlisted in the British army as a young man. In 1764 he became a barrack master in Albany, N.Y. (a civilian position), on half a lieutenant's pay. He was known by the courtesy title of captain even though he turned down a promotion to that rank to retire.

21. *JLFA*, 1:237; Harvey, "Wesleyan Movement," 202–27, 265–68; Baker, *Wesley to Asbury*, 65–66; David Hackett Fischer, *Washington's Crossing* (New York: Oxford University Press, 2004), 198. Fischer doesn't specifically identify Webb and Rankin as British informants, but Harvey does.

22. *JLFA*, 1:161, 164; Littlejohn, "Journal," Sept. 7, 1777; Bevan, "Perry Hall," 42; Evans, "Colonial Families," 21–24; Harvey, "Wesleyan Movement," 175–77.

23. Littlejohn, "Journal," Sept. 24, 1777; *JLFA*, 1:148; Cooper, *Substance*, 81; Lednum, *Rise*, 193; Harvey, "Wesleyan Movement," 291–92. The preacher Robert Lindsay left an account of sailing from America with Rankin in 1778. See Robert Lindsay to Edward Dromgoole, March 4, 1783, Edward Dromgoole Papers, SHC. Even George Shadford aroused patriot suspicions. See E. C. Branchi, trans., "Memoirs of Philip Mazzei," *William and Mary Quarterly*, 2nd series, 9:4 (October 1929): 249; Harvey, "Wesleyan Movement," 273–86, 317–27; Sweet, *Virginia Methodism*, 88–92.

24. Rankin to Matthew Mayer, March 16, 1773, and July 7, 1778, Mayer family papers, SCL. Rankin wrote, and Wesley published, a less candid assessment of Rankin's tenure in America in the *Arminian Magazine*. See "A Short Extract of Mr. Thomas Rankin: in a Letter to the Rev. Mr. John Wesley [Nov. 16, 1778]," *Arminian Magazine* (London), 2 (1779): 197–98. Rankin and Mayer carried on a lengthy correspondence from at least 1765 to 1778. Mayer was an influential and relatively wealthy local preacher in Stockport, England. Also see Robert Glen, "Methodism and the American Revolution: Insights from a neglected Thomas Rankin letter," *PWHS*, 52:2 (May 1999): 34–38. I am indebted to Professor Glen for leading me to this collection at Stockport. Americans saw Rankin's actions differently than he himself depicted them, of course. Thomas Ware later wrote that Rankin "was an elder brother, a chief man, and a high-toned loyalist. After independence was declared, he deemed it to be his duty, and the duty of all the preachers sent to America by Mr. Wesley, to return home. Not being able to prevail with Mr. Asbury to accompany him, he forsook his charge, and went within the British lines, they having possession of Philadelphia, and there declared from the pulpit, that it was his belief that God would not revive his work in America, until they submitted to their rightful sovereign, George the Third." Ware, "Christmas Conference," 102.

25. *JLFA*, 3:21–22; Andrews, *The Methodists*, 54–55. Between December 1774 and January 1776, Rankin wrote a series of letters to the Earl of Dartmouth, secretary of state for the colonies, which dealt almost as much with political issues as religious. Asbury sent no similar political assessments to Dartmouth, his former neighbor in England, or to anyone else. See Thomas Rankin to Lord Dartmouth, March 30, 1774, Dec. 29, 1774, Dec. 28, 1775, and Jan. 15, 1776, SRO. The last two letters are remarkably sympathetic to the American position given Rankin's later sentiments.

26. *JLFA*, 1:130, 138, 236; Littlejohn, "Journal," Sept. 9, 1778. Asbury's determination to stay in America grew during 1777. See *JLFA*, 1:228, 235, 249;

Tipple, *Asbury*, 124–26. James Dempster remained in America but became a Presbyterian. See Wakeley, *Lost Chapters*, 250–54.

27. *JLFA*, 1:300, 303, 325.

28. *JLFA*, 1:262–64; May, "Francis Asbury and Thomas White"; Harold B. Hancock, *The Loyalists of Revolutionary Delaware* (Newark: University of Delaware Press, 1977), 60–70; Keith Mason, "Localism, Evangelicalism, and Loyalism: The Sources of Oppression in the Revolutionary Chesapeake," *Journal of Southern History*, 56:1 (February 1990); Lednum, *Rise*, 204–6.

29. *JLFA*, 2:642; Ware, *Sketches*, 80; May, "Francis Asbury and Thomas White;" Boehm, *Reminiscences*, 474–75; Williams, *Garden of Methodism*, 46–47; Henry C. Conrad, "Samuel White and His Father Judge Thomas White," *Papers of the Historical Society of Delaware*, 40 (1903), 1–13; Lednum, *Rise*, 267–72; Stevens, *History*, 1:314–15; Benjamin Abbott, *The Experience and Gospel Labours of the Rev. Benjamin Abbott* (Philadelphia: Solomon W. Conrad for Ezekiel Cooper, 1801), 95–96.

30. Overfield, "A Patriot Dilemma," 140–59; Mason, "Localism, Evangelicalism, and Loyalism," 23–54; Hancock, *The Loyalists of Revolutionary Delaware*, 60–88; Ronald Hoffman, *A Spirit of Dissension: Economics, Politics, and the Revolution in Maryland* (Baltimore: Johns Hopkins University Press, 1973), 197–236.

31. *JLFA*, 1:265–67; May, "Francis Asbury and Thomas White;" Watters, *Short Account*, 36; Lednum, *Rise*, 115, 162; E. C. Hallman, *The Garden of Methodism* (n.p.: Peninsula Annual Conference of the Methodist Church, n.d.), 12.

32. *JLFA*, 1:268, 269, 282, 284, 311; Lednum, *Rise*, 206–7.

33. Ware, *Sketches*, 250–52.

34. *JLFA*, 1:231, 236, 264, 266, 275, 313, 316, 325; Lednum, *Rise*, 206, 232–37; Garrettson, *Journal*, 170, 391; Lee, *Short History*, 58–59; Stevens, *History*, 1:280–81; Williams, *Garden of Methodism*, 35–36, 41; Andrews, *The Methodists*, 57; Harvey, "Wesleyan Movement," 308–14; Overfield, "A Patriot Dilemma," 140–59; Mason, "Localism, Evangelicalism, and Loyalism," 23–54; Hoffman, *A Spirit of Dissension*, 196–241. On Benjamin Abbott's experiences during the war, see Abbott, *Experience*, 27–28, 34–35; John Fea, "Rural Religion: Protestant Community and the Moral Improvement of the South Jersey Countryside, 1676–1800" (PhD diss., State University of New York at Stony Brook, 1999), 415–17. Even in Virginia William Watters heard a parson declare that Methodist preachers were "a set of Tories, under a cloak of religion," whose "nasty stinking carcasses" should be made to "pay for our pretended scruples of conscience." Watters signed an oath of allegiance in Virginia while riding the Brunswick circuit in 1777, though some of his colleagues refused to do so. See Watters, *Short Account*, 49–50, 60–61.

35. *JLFA*, 1:338, 339; Garrettson, *Journal*, 69, 74, 82–83, 85, 91, 96, 98–100, 391; Lee, *Short History*, 59–60; Lednum, *Rise*, 207, 214–15, 250–53; William, *Garden of Methodism*, 30–38. Thomas White and Thomas Hill Airey wrote letters on Garrettson's behalf. Airey also co-signed a bond for Garrettson, and Caesar Rodney issued certificates testifying to Garrettson's character. See Garrettson, *Journal*, 404–5. Caleb Pedicord followed Garrettson into Dorchester County in 1780. There he was attacked on a road and beaten "until the blood ran down his face." Lednum, *Rise*, 264; Stevens, *History*, 2:30–34; Cooper, *Substance*, 85–89, 95. Thomas Coke later described Cambridge, Md.,

as "this town, which has been remarkable above any other on the Continent for persecution." Coke, *Extracts* (1793), 19. Born in England, Clow came to the Delmarva Peninsula at a young age with his parents. According to Garrettson, Clow "laid aside his religion, and began to raise a [Tory] company," intending "to make his way through the country to the Chesapeake to join the British, whose fleet at that time lay in the Chesapeake Bay." Years later, Freeborn Garrettson claimed that an investigation by Gov. Caesar Rodney determined that Clow's party included only two Methodists. Garrettson, *Journal*, 68, 74, 150, 208; Bangs, *Garrettson*, 64; Lednum, *Rise*, 214; May, "Francis Asbury and Thomas White;" Hancock, *Loyalists of Delaware*, 80–81; Hoffman, *Spirit of Dissension*, 234–36; Mason, "Localism, Evangelicalism, and Loyalism;" Cooper, *Substance*, 91; quoted in May, "Francis Asbury and Thomas White," 152; Hallman, *Garden of Methodism*, 11–12.

36. Littlejohn, "Journal," July 31, 1777, June 12, 1778. Also see entries for June 24, 1777, Aug. 11, 1777, March 9, 1778. Asbury doesn't mention the meeting with Littlejohn in his journal.

37. *JLFA*, 3:298, 2:642. Also see Lee, *Short History*, 58.

38. Joseph Everett, "An Account of the Most Remarkable Occurrences of the Life of Joseph Everett," *The Arminian Magazine* (Philadelphia), 2 (1790): 559–60, 604–5; Lednum, *Rise*, 272–78; Conrad, "Samuel White," 7; Robert E. Pattison, "The Life and Character of Richard Bassett," *Papers of the Historical Society of Delaware*, 29 (1900): 3–19.

39. For two opposing nineteenth-century interpretations of Asbury's retirement at the Whites', see Lednum, *Rise*, 210–11, and Boehm, *Reminiscences*, 291–93. Also see Briggs, *Asbury*, 120–29; Lewis, *Asbury*, 66–71; Tipple, *Asbury*, 129–30; Rudolph, *Francis Asbury*, 35–38. Even Freeborn Garrettson, who had nothing against Asbury, wrote in 1827, "Mr. Asbury had a quiet retreat at Judge White's, in the state of Delaware, and that, during the hotest time of our conflict." Garrettson, *Journal*, 392. Ezekiel Cooper largely defended Asbury's seclusion in Delaware as necessary in a funeral sermon for Asbury in 1816. Cooper, *Substance*, 90–93.

40. *JLFA*, 1:236, 239, 242, 243, 245, 247, 248, 250, 252. Newton's book was quite popular in America. Advertisements for subscriptions to print Newton's *Dissertations on the Prophecies* appear in the Aug. 31 and Sept. 7 and 11, 1786, issues of the *New-York Packet*. Editions of the books Asbury read include: Thomas Newton, *Dissertation on the Prophecies, Which Have Remarkably Been Fulfilled, and At This Time Are Fulfilling in the World*, 5th ed., 3 vols. (London: John, Frances, and Charles Rivington, 1777); Isaac Watts, *Death and Heaven; Or the Last Enemy Conquer'd, and Separate Spirits Made Perfect* (London: John Clark, Eman. Matthews, and Richard Ford, 1722); Richard Baxter, *A Call to the Unconverted to Turn and Live and Accept of Mercy While Mercy May be Had as Ever They Would Find Mercy in the Day of Their Extremity From the Living God* (London: Nevil Simmons . . . and Nathaniel Ekins, 1658); Richard Baxter, *Gildas Salvianus, the Reformed Pastor* (London: Printed by Robert White, 1656); Richard Baxter, *The Saints Everlasting Rest* (London: Printed by Robert White, 1650); George Sale and Others, *An Universal History, From the Earliest Account of Time*, 65 vols. (London: Printed for T. Osborne, 1747–1768); Samuel Walker, *Fifty Two Sermons, on the Baptismal Covenant, the Creed, the Ten Commandments, and Other Important Subjects*, 2 vols. (London: Printed by J. and

W. Oliver, 1763); William Law, *A Serious Call to a Devout and Holy Life* (London: Printed for G. Robinson, 1772). Asbury may have been reading an earlier collection of sermons by Samuel Walker, *The Christian. Being a Course of Practical Sermons* (London: Printed by J. Oliver, 1755). It is possible that Asbury was reading Robert Walker's *Sermons on Practical Subjects* (Edinburgh: Printed by A. Murray & J. Cochran, 1777). But this seems unlikely since Robert Walker was a staunch Calvinist and Asbury reports reading the sermons "with much pleasure." On Robert Walker, see Stewart J. Brown, "Walker, Robert," *ODNB*, Jan. 20, 2005. On Baxter's *Reformed Pastor*, also see *JLFA*, 3:436.

41. The books of Isaac Watts, Richard Baxter, and William Law were widely read and some had been in print for decades. Watts (1674–1748) was an Independent minister and writer, especially of hymns. Richard Baxter (1615–1691) was a Puritan minister who published some 135 books, including the three classics that Asbury read in 1777. William Law (1686–1761) was educated at Cambridge but refused to sign an oath of allegiance to the new king of England in 1716. Samuel Walker was a Church of England clergyman, educated at Oxford, who had some sympathy for the Wesleys. See Isabel Rivers, "Watts, Isaac," N. H. Keeble, "Baxter, Richard," Isabel Rivers, "Law, William," and J. S. Reynolds, "Walker, Samuel," *ODNB*, Jan. 20, 2005.

42. *JLFA*, 1:260; Stephen D. Snobelen, "Whiston, William," *ODNB*, Dec. 21, 2004; F. l. Cross and E. A. Livingstone, eds. *The Oxford Dictionary of the Christian Church*, 2nd ed. (Oxford: Oxford University Press, 1974), s.v. "Whiston, William." A Cambridge-educated clergyman, Whiston followed Isaac Newton as Lucasian professor of mathematics at Cambridge in 1702. Whiston was expelled from Cambridge in 1710 for heresy and later attended Baptist meetings. He published more than 120 books and pamphlets on a wide range of topics, including Newtonian natural philosophy and biblical prophecy, but his most enduring publication was the translation of Josephus that Asbury read. Several editions of Whiston's translation of Josephus were published in London and Edinburgh between 1737 and 1777.

43. *JLFA*, 1:261, 263; James William Kelly, "Flavell, John," Alexander Gordon and Jon Mae, "Hartley, Thomas," Richard C. Allen, "Hartley, David," *ODNB*, Dec. 21, 2004; *Dictionary of National Biography*, 1938 ed., s.v. "Flavel, John." Among Flavell's more popular books were: *Husbandry Spiritualized: Or, The Heavenly Use of Earthly Things, Navigation Spiritualized: Or, A New Compass for Seamen*, and *Sacramental Meditations Upon Divers Selected Places of Scripture*. Editions of the books Asbury read include: John Flavel, *The Whole Works of the Reverend Mr. John Flavel, . . . in Two Volumes. . . .* (London: printed by R.J. for Tho. Parkhurst; Hugh Newman; Andrew Bell; and Tho. Cockerill, 1701); Thomas Hartley, *Sermons on Various Subjects: With a Prefatory Discourse on Mistakes Concerning Religion, Enthusiasm, Experience, &c.* (London: Printed for the Author, 1754); David Hartley, *Observations on Man, His Frame, His Duty, and His Expectations* (London: Printed by S. Richardson, 1749). Thomas Hartley was a Cambridge-educated minister who later became a follower of Emanuel Swedenborg. David Hartley was a Cambridge-educated physician whose writings on human nature often took a religious turn.

44. *JLFA*, 1:266; Brian W. Kirk, "Alleine, Joseph," *ODNB*, Dec. 21, 2004.; Timothy Larson, ed. *Biographical Dictionary of Evangelicals* (Leicester: Inter-Varsity Press, 2003),

s.v. "Alleine, Joseph." Wesley published an edition of Alleine's *Christian Letters* in 1778. Alleine, the son of an artisan, attended Oxford and was then ordained as a Presbyterian. He was expelled from his living in 1662 under the Act of Uniformity, and later jailed for continuing to secretly preach.

45. *JLFA*, 1:268; Isabel Rivers, "Doddridge, Philip," *ODNB*, Dec. 21, 2004; Cross and Livingstone, *Oxford Dictionary of the Christian Church*, s.v. "Doddridge, Philip." The quotation from Doddridge is from Isabel Rivers's article. At least ten editions of *Rise and Progress* had been published by 1771, including a tenth edition printed that year in Boston by D. Kneeland for Thomas Leverett. Doddridge (1702–1751) was an independent minister and writer who also ran an academy in Northampton, England. During one year he preached 140 sermons, once writing that good preaching ought to be "evangelical," "experimental," "plain," and "affectionate," opinions that Asbury could easily endorse.

46. *JLFA*, 1:268–73; Gordon DesBrisay, "Barclay, Robert," *ODNB*, Dec. 21, 2004. Recent editions of Bunyan's and Barclay's books include: John Bunyan, *The Holy War, Made by Shaddai Upon Diabolus, For the Regaining of the Metropolis of the World, Or, The Losing and Taking Again of the Town of Mansoul* (Glasgow: J. And J. Robertson, 1777); Robert Barclay, *An apology for the True Christian Divinity* (Philadelphia: Joseph Cruk-shank, 1775). Barclay (1648–1690) was a Quaker who had a prolific, if brief, career writing books in defense of Quaker beliefs. The most famous of these was the *Apology*, reprinted many times in several languages. Asbury may have been reading an edition published in Philadelphia in 1775 and advertised as the ninth edition in English.

47. *JLFA*, 1:284–87; Isabel Rivers, "Hervey, James," *ODNB*, Dec. 21, 2004; *Dictionary of National Biography*, 1938 ed., s.v. "Hervey, James." Editions of the relevant works by Doddridge, Orton and Hervey include: Philip Doddridge, *The Family Expositor: Or, A Paraphrase of the New Testament. With Critical Notes*, 6 vols. (London: John Wilson, 1739–1756); Job Orton, *Memoirs of the Life, Character and Writings of the Late Reverend Philip Doddridge, D.D.* (Salop: J. Cotton and J. Eddowes, 1766); James Hervey, *Theron and Aspasio: Or, A Series of Dialogues and Letters, Upon the Most Important and Interesting Subjects. . . . ,* 3 vols. (London: John and James Rivington, 1755), 1–2, *Eighteenth Century Collections Online*, Jan. 19, 2005, http://galenet.galegroup.com/. Wesley's critique of *Theron and Aspasio* is included in *A Preservative Against Unsettled Notions in Religion. By John Wesley, M.A.* (Bristol: E. Farley, 1758), 211–36, *Eighteenth Century Collections Online*, Jan. 19, 2005, http://galenet.galegroup.com/.

48. *JLFA*, 1:291–93; Hugh de Quehen, "Prideaux, Humphrey," *ODNB*, Dec. 21, 2004; Cross and Livingstone, *Oxford Dictionary of the Christian Church*, s.v. "Prideaux, Humphrey." Prideaux's *Old and New Testament Connected* was first published in two volumes and later in four volumes. See, for example, Humphrey Prideaux, *The Old and New Testament Connected in the History of the Jews and Neighbouring Nations*, 11th ed., 4 vols. (London: J. And R. Tonson and S. Draper, and H. Lintot, 1749). Prideaux (1648–1724) was an Oxford-educated clergyman who became the dean of Norwich.

49. *JLFA*, 1:293–94. What bothered Asbury most about Calvinism was his belief that it encouraged antinomianism. See *JLFA*, 1:428, 449; 3:33.

50. Hervey, *Theron and Aspasio*, 2:300; Wesley, *Preservative Against Unsettled Notions*, 224; Wesley, *Letters* (Telford), 4:295. Hervey prepared a response to Wesley that was published in 1765, after Hervey's death. See James Hervey, *Eleven Letters From the Late Rev. Mr. Hervey, To the Rev. Mr. John Wesley; Containing An Answer to That Gentleman's Remarks on Theron and Aspasio* (London: Charles Rivington, 1765), *Eighteenth Century Collections Online*, Jan. 19, 2005, http://galenet.galegroup.com/.

51. The term "mere Christianity" was of course later borrowed by C. S. Lewis. On Lewis and Baxter, see Alan Jacobs, *The Narnian: The Life and Imagination of C. S. Lewis* (New York: HarperCollins, 2005), 212–13. On Asbury's reading and theology, also see Edward M. Lang, *Francis Asbury's Reading of Theology: A Bibliographic Study* (Evanston, Ill.: Garrett Theological Seminary Library, 1972).

52. *JLFA*, 1:264. On Edwards, see George M. Marsden, *Jonathan Edwards: A Life* (New Haven: Yale University Press, 2003). On the development of theology in America during this period, see E. Brooks Holifield, *Theology in America: Christian Thought from the Age of the Puritans to the Civil War* (New Haven: Yale University Press, 2003); Mark A. Noll, *America's God: From Jonathan Edwards to Abraham Lincoln* (New York: Oxford University Press, 2002).

53. *JLFA*, 1:296–97; Ann Hughes, "Clarke, Samuel," and Barry Till, "Watson, Thomas," *ODNB*, Dec. 21, 2004. Editions of Clarke's and Watson's books include: Samuel Clarke, *A General Martyrology, Containing a Collection of All the Greatest Persecutions Which Have Befallen the Church of Christ, From the Creation, to Our Present Times: Wherein is Given an Exact Account of the Protestant Sufferings in Queen Mary's Reign* (Glasgow: J. Galbraith, 1770); Thomas Watson, *A Body of Practical Divinity, Consisting of Above One Hundred and Seventy Six Sermons on the Lesser Catechism Composed by the Reverend Assembly of Divines at Westminster*, 5th ed. (Glasgow: Printed by John Hall for James Tweedie, 1759). Clarke (1599–1682) was a Cambridge-educated clergyman who, because of his Presbyterian beliefs, was expelled from the Church of England in 1662 after the restoration of the monarchy. Watson (d. 1686), like Clarke, was a Cambridge-educated clergyman put out of the church under the Act of Uniformity.

54. *JLFA*, 1:297–301; Steve Hindle, "Bruen, John," S. J. Guscott, "Hinde, William," and Nigel Aston, "Newton, Thomas," *ODNB*, Dec. 21, 2004. Editions of Newton's book include: Thomas Newton, *Dissertation on the Prophecies, Which Have Remarkably Been Fulfilled, and At This Time Are Fulfilling in the World*, 5th ed., 3 vols. (London: John, Frances, and Charles Rivington, 1777). Even Edward Drinkhouse admitted that Asbury's "reading was almost omnivorous." See Drinkhouse, *Methodist Reform*, 209–10. By 1777 at least five editions of *Dissertation on the Prophecies* had been printed; by 1835 there were twenty editions.

55. The books Asbury was reading were among the most popular items available in American bookshops. A search of an early American newspapers digital database indicates that the books of Doddridge, Flavell, and Hervey were popular during the 1760s and 1770s, as were books by Bunyan, Barclay, Edwards, Orton, Prideaux, and Watson. I counted fifty-four advertisements for books by these authors between August 1762 and February 1775 in *The Boston Gazette, and Country Journal, Rivington's New-York Gazetteer, The New Hampshire Gazette, and Historical Chronicle, The New-London*

Gazette, The Boston News-Letter and New-England Chronicle, The Providence Gazette; and Country Journal, and *The Boston Weekly News-Letter.* Accessed at: *Early American Newspapers Digital,* Nov. 3, 2004, http://infoweb.newsbank.com/.

56. Hatch, *Democratization*; Gordon Wood, *The Radicalism of the American Revolution* (New York: Alfred A. Knopf, 1992); Leonard W. Levy, *The Establishment Clause: Religion and the First Amendment,* 2nd rev. ed. (Chapel Hill: University of North Carolina Press, 1994), 27–78.

57. Roger Finke and Rodney Stark, "How the Upstart Sects Won America: 1776–1850," *Journal for the Scientific Study of Religion,* 28 (1989), 27–44. Also see Roger Finke and Rodney Stark, *The Church of America 1776–1990: Winners and Losers in Our Religious Economy* (New Brunswick: Rutgers University Press, 1992).

CHAPTER 6

1. *JLFA,* 1:238–239; "The Leesburg Minutes of the Methodist Connection, 1775–1783," *Virginia United Methodist Heritage, the Bulletin of the Virginia Conference Historical Society,* 5 (fall 1977), 15; Lee, *Life of Jesse Lee,* 78; Gatch, *Sketch,* 76; Watters, *Short Account,* 57; Garrettson, *Journal,* 390; James W. May, "From Revival Movement to Denomination: A Re-examination of the Beginnings of American Methodism" (PhD diss., Columbia University, 1962), 105–6; Sweet, *Virginia Methodism,* 79–85. Gatch's account differs slightly from the Leesburg minutes.

2. *JLFA,* 1:234, 235, 239; Watters, *Short Account,* 56–57; Garrettson, *Journal,* 390; Lednum, *Rise,* 190; "Leesburg Minutes," 14; *Minutes* (1794), 20–21; John J. Tigert, *A Constitutional History of American Episcopal Methodism* (Nashville: Methodist Episcopal Church, South, 1904), 85–91. On Daniel Ruff, see Stevens, *History,* 2:17–18; Atkinson, *Methodism in New Jersey,* 99–103.

3. Watters, *Short Account,* 68–69; Garrettson, *Journal,* 390; "Leesburg Minutes," 17; Lee, *Life of Jesse Lee,* 78–79. The printed minutes are again silent on this debate. But the manuscript minutes include the question: "Shall anything be done at present with respect to administering the ordinances?" The answer: "Resolved unanimously to put it off till next conference."

4. Asbury may have also been encouraged to act by "agreeable news" he heard on March 30, 1779. Apparently, he only now learned that American officers had intercepted a letter he wrote to Thomas Rankin in 1777 stating that "he was so strongly knit in affection to many of the Americans that he could not tear himself away from them; that he knew the Americans, and was well satisfied they would not rest until they had achieved their independence." See *JLFA,* 1:299; Ware, *Sketches,* 251–52; Lednum, *Rise,* 226. May, "Francis Asbury and Thomas White." Ware claimed that he heard this account from someone who later became governor of Delaware, most likely Richard Bassett.

5. *JLFA,* 1:300; *Minutes* (1794), 29; Watters, *Short Account,* 72–73; Jarratt, *Life,* 64–65; "Leesburg Minutes," 19–22; Tigert, *Constitutional History,* 97–104; Stevens, *History,* 2:56–58. It isn't clear exactly who was invited to the conference at Thomas White's, but even William Watters says that he "had no notice sent me." Watters

somehow found out about the conference and attended, though sick. See Watters, *Short Account*, 72.

6. Watters, *Short Account*, 73.

7. Watters, *Short Account*, 72–73; Gatch, *Sketch*, 68–73; Lee, *Short History*, 63–64; Lee, *Life of Jesse Lee*, 79–83; Connor, *Methodist Trail Blazer*, 103–12; Tigert, *Constitutional History*, 104–9; Stevens, *History*, 2:59–62; *Minutes* (1794), 31–33; "Minutes of Conference from the year 1774 to the year 1779 [from minutes kept by Philip Gatch]," *Western Christian Advocate* 4/5 (May 26, 1837): 18–19, in *The Methodist Experience in America: A Sourcebook*, vol. II, ed. Russell E. Richey, Kenneth E. Rowe, And Jean Miller Schmidt (Nashville: Abingdon Press, 2000), 63–65. On Ellis and Cole, see Stevens, *History*, 2:39–41.

8. *JLFA*, 1:5, 48n., 145, 183, 195, 287, 300, 432, 682n., 2:154, 486; May, "Revival Movement," 65. Asbury probably read Wesley's abridgements of Edwards's *A Narrative of the late Work of God, at and near Northhampton* and *Some Thoughts Concerning the Present Revival of Religion in New England*. Edwards published *An Account of the Life of David Brainerd* in 1749. See Marsden, *Jonathan Edwards*, 150–69, 284–90, 323–33. Other Methodists, including John Wesley, Thomas Coke, and Jesse Lee, avidly read the *Life of Brainerd*. See Coke, *Extracts* (1793), 9; Lee, *Life of Jesse Lee*, 63; Wesley, *Letters* (Telford), 6:57.

9. *JLFA*, 1:721; Rankin, mss. journal, 12–13; *Lives* (Jackson), 5:144, 183; Lee, *Short History*, 31; Abbott, *Experience*, 66; May, "Revival Movement," 66–70; Harry S. Stout, *The Divine Dramatist: George Whitefield and the Rise of Modern Evangelicalism* (Grand Rapids, Mich.: Eerdmans, 1991), 87–112.

10. Gatch, *Sketch*, 50–51; Gewehr, *Great Awakening*, 106; May, "Revival Movement," 72; Jewel L. Spangler, "Becoming Baptists: Conversion in Colonial and Early National Virginia," *Journal of Southern History*, 67:2 (May 2001): 243–86; Sweet, *Virginia Methodism*, 38–43; Rhys Isaac, *The Transformation of Virginia 1740–1790* (Chapel Hill: University of North Carolina Press, 1982; reprint, New York: W.W. Norton, 1988), 143–205, 243–322; Philip N. Mulder, *A Controversial Spirit: Evangelical Awakenings in the South* (New York: Oxford University Press, 2002), 37–65; Sandra Rennie, "The Role of the Preacher: Index to the Consolidation of the Baptist Movement in Virginia from 1760 to 1790," *Virginia Magazine of History and Biography*, 88 (1980): 430–41; Deborah Vansau Mccauley, *Appalachian Mountain Religion: A History* (Urbana: University of Illinois Press, 1995), 201–37; Thomas E. Buckley, *Church and State in Revolutionary Virginia, 1776–1787* (Charlottesville: University Press of Virginia, 1977), 8–70; Gregory Wills, *Democratic Religion: Freedom, Authority, and Church Discipline in the Baptist South, 1785–1900* (New York: Oxford University Press, 1997), 7–8.

11. Gatch, *Sketch*, 69. James Meacham, who spent his preaching career in the South, offered a typical opinion while riding the Bertie circuit in North Carolina in 1788. "O the Devil and the Anabaptists-how they spoil the sweet work of Methodism. I have ever observ'd to my sorrow, where e'r we, (under God) begin a good work among the people, they follow us with the cry of water, and Quench . . . the fire of love." Meacham, mss. journal, Dec. 10, 1788, Jul.13, 1790, May 28, 1792, Aug. 19, 1794, June 18, July 14, Sept. 20, 1795, Dec. 10, 1796. Asbury enjoyed some early hospitality from Baptists in New England,

but later relations were much the same there as in the South. According to Connecticut-born Methodist itinerant Billy Hibbard, "It became a proverb, 'The Methodists shake the bush, and the Presbyterians and Baptists catch the birds.'" *JLFA*, 1:680–82; Billy Hibbard, *Memoirs of the Life and Travels of B. Hibbard, Minister of the Gospel, Containing an Account of His Experience of Religion; and of His Call to and Labours in the Ministry for Nearly Thirty Years* (New York: Printed for the Author, 1825), 175.

12. *JLFA*, 1:176, 305. Also see 1:306, 344, 379.

13. *Minutes* (1794), 6; Pilmore to Miss Bosanquet, n.d., record PLP 83.60.3, JRL. It would be wrong, as Russell Richey argues, to characterize the sacramental crisis as strictly a North/South division. Though contemporaries used the terms "north" and "south" to describe the two factions, it was really a division between the upper South and the lower South. See Russell E. Richey, "The Formation of American Methodism: The Chesapeake Refraction of Wesleyanism," *Methodism and the Shaping of American Culture*, ed. Nathan O. Hatch and John H. Wigger (Nashville: Kingswood Books, 2001), 197–221; Russell E. Richey, *Early American Methodism* (Bloomington: Indiana University Press, 1991), 47–64.

14. *Minutes* (1794), 10, 33; Lee, *Short History*, 64; *JLFA*, 1:149, 304.

15. *JLFA*, 1:295, 300, 308, 319, 333, 344, 345. Peninsula Methodists continued to have a checkered relationship with Anglican ministers, but there were a few bright spots. Asbury enjoyed a supportive relationship with "my very dear friend," Samuel Magaw, the Anglican rector of Christ Church in Dover, Del., whose preaching Asbury admired. On Magaw, see *JLFA*, 1:135, 299, 300, 302, 303, 304, 308, 310, 314, 321, 324, 338, 341, 342, 344, 345, 355; 2:468; Nelson Waite Rightmyer, *The Anglican Church in Delaware* (Philadelphia: Church Historical Society, 1947), 62–65; Lednum, *Rise*, 233, 254. Magaw (d. 1812) was ordained in England in 1767.

16. *JLFA*, 1:314; Garrettson, *Journal*, 72–73, 77, 84, 92, 96, 101, 102, 108, 113, 117.

17. *JLFA*, 1:322, 346.

18. Gatch, *Sketch*, 44–55; Watters, *Short Account*, 79; Atkinson, *Methodism in New Jersey*, 91–94; Connor, *Methodist Trail Blazer*, 46–53; M. H. Moore, *Sketches of the Pioneers of Methodism in North Carolina and Virginia* (Nashville: Southern Methodist Publishing House, 1884), 196–204.

19. *JLFA*, 1:347; Tigert, *Constitutional History*, 109–16; Watters, *Short Account*, 79–80.

20. "Leesburg Minutes," 24–30; *Minutes* (1794), 35–40; *JLFA*, 1:347; Lee, *Short History*, 66–67; Lee, *Life of Jesse Lee*, 83–84; Stevens, *History*, 2:76–78. There are minor discrepancies between the manuscript and printed minutes. The former lists only Asbury and Garrettson as delegated to attend the southern conference. Watters was added later.

21. *JLFA*, 1:349; Watters, *Short Account*, 80.

22. *JLFA*, 1:349–50.

23. "Leesburg Minutes," 26; *Minutes* (1794), 37; *JLFA*, 1:350; Watters, *Short Account*, 80–81; Leroy Lee, *Life of Jesse Lee*, 84–86; Lee, *Short History*, 67–68; Tigert, *Constitutional History*, 116–20; Stevens, *History*, 79–82; Cooper, *Substance*, 100–1; MacClenny, *James O'Kelly*, 40–41.

24. James O'Kelly claims that it was his and John Dickins's idea to suspend the ordinances for a year and refer the matter to John Wesley. Nicholas Snethen says it was Asbury's. See: "Leesburg Minutes," 30; 1795 *Minutes*, 39; Watters, *Short Account*, 80–81; O'Kelly, *Author's Apology*, 5; Nicholas Snethen, *A Reply to an Apology for Protesting Against the Methodist Episcopal Government* (Philadelphia, 1800), 8; Charles Franklin Kilgore, *The James O'Kelly Schism in the Methodist Episcopal Church* (Mexico 1, D. F.: Casa Unida De Publicaciones, 1963), 6; W. E. Macclenny, *The Life of Rev. James O'Kelly, and the Early History of the Christian Church in the South* (Indianapolis: Religious Book Service, 1950), 40–41; Wigger, *Taking Heaven*, 24.

25. Bangs, *History*, 1:128. Briggs, Tipple and Lewis generally agree with Bangs. See Briggs, *Asbury*, 130–38; Tipple, *Asbury*, 131–32; Lewis, *Asbury*, 78.

26. Drinkhouse, *Methodist Reform*, 1:213, 219, 223, 225, 229. Abel Stevens takes a position between Bangs and Drinkhouse. He agrees with Drinkhouse that Fluvanna was the legally appointed conference, but is far more sympathetic to Asbury. Stevens, *History*, 2:62–66. Also see Russell E. Richey, *The Methodist Conference in America: A History* (Nashville: Kingswood Books, 1996), 27–30.

27. *JLFA*, 1:351; Lee, *Short History*, 68.

28. *JLFA*, 1:353, 369, 387.

29. Asbury, *Extract*, 135; *JLFA*, 1:354, 356, 359, 360, 362, 364, 365, 366, 368, 370, 379, 383, 384; [Edwin Schell], "Discovery," ed. Frederick E. Maser, *MH*, 9 (Jan. 1971): 43. The 1821 and 1958 editions of Asbury's journal give the Aug. 26, 1780, entry as: "O, how good did that feel!" See *JLFA*, 1:376.

30. *JLFA*, 1:190. Also see 43, 50, 51, 56, 57, 89.

31. *JLFA*, 1:273–74; *Wesley Works* (1872), 11:74 and 79; Rankin, mss. journal (July 20, Aug. 29, 1775), 72, 77; Wigger, *Taking Heaven*, 134; Evans, "Ideology of Inequality," 1; Winthrop D. Jordan, *White Over Black: American Attitudes Toward the Negro, 1550–1812* (Chapel Hill: University of North Carolina Press, 1968), 269–311. Wesley's *Thoughts Upon Slavery* draws from the writings of Anthony Benezet, with whom he corresponded, and encouraged by the British abolitionist Granville Sharp. See Roger Anstey, *The Atlantic Slave Trade and British Abolition 1760–1810* (Atlantic Highlands, N.J.: Humanities Press, 1975), 239–42.

32. Asbury, *Extract*, 18, 21, 24. Edwin Schell first noticed the discrepancies between the 1792 and 1802 editions of Asbury's journal and the 1821 and 1958 editions. See "Discovery," ed. Frederick E. Maser, *MH*, 8 (October 1970): 53–57; Edwin Schell, "Discovery," ed. Frederick E. Maser, *MH*, 9 (January 1971): 34–43. The latter incorrectly dates the April 28, 1779, entry as April 23, 1779. Also see Edwin Schell, "Asbury's Journal: A Textual Comparison of the Lovely Lane Copy of Vol. 2 (1779–1780) with the Annotated Edition," LLM.

33. *Minutes* (1794), 38; "Leesburg Minutes," 27–28; Watters, *Short Account*, 40.

34. *JLFA*, 1:222; 298; Watters, *Short Account*, 90.

35. Asbury, *Extract*, 103, 104, 108, 114–15; *JLFA*, 1:355, 362, 363; Schell, "Discovery," *MH*, 9 (January 1971): 41.

36. The reference is to 1 Kings 18.44.

CHAPTER 7

1. *JLFA*, 1:402, 427, 433, 456, 461, 462, 463; 3:33.

2. *JLFA*, 1:407, 422, 440, 447, 456–457; 3:29. Also see 3:34.

3. *Minutes* (1794), 17, 20, 69; Wakeley, *Lost Chapters*, 260–98, 459; Stevens, *History*, 1:421– 22; *JLFA*, 1:440; *Wesley Letters* (Telford), 6:249; Seaman, *Annals*, 72–81; Pilkington, *Methodist Publishing*, 1:57, 66; George Burgess, *List of Persons Admitted to the Order of Deacons in the Protestant Episcopal Church, in the United States of America, From A. D. 1785, to A. D. 1857* (Boston: A. Williams, 1875), 3; Edwin G. Burrows and Mike Wallace, *Gotham: A History of New York City to 1898* (New York: Oxford University Press, 1999), 240–61. Methodists were only allowed to use the building on Sunday evenings, since Hessian troops used it Sunday mornings. In January 1777 Wesley wrote to a friend that he had received news from New York "that all the Methodists there were firm for the Government, and on that account persecuted by the rebels." Spraggs was paid a total of £557 for his services from May 1778 to June 1783, a substantial salary by Methodist standards. After the war Mann immigrated to Nova Scotia, where Freeborn Garrettson found him in 1787, mentioning him favorably in a letter to Wesley. Mann died in Nova Scotia in 1816. See Seaman, *Annals*, 76–77; Garrettson, *Journal*, 248, 250, 392; Wakeley, *Lost Chapters*, 205, 260–66. Spraggs joined the itinerancy in 1774. After the war he became rector of the Old Protestant Episcopal Church in Elizabeth, N.J.. See *Minutes* (1794), 9–10; Seaman, *Annals*, 77; Wakeley, *Lost Chapters*, 279–90; *JLFA*, 1:188, 263.

4. *Minutes* (1794), 19, 21, 24, 92; Seaman, *Annals*, 79–81; Wakeley, *Lost Chapters*, 293–301; Pilkington, *Methodist Publishing*, 1:55–58, 66–68; Lednum, *Rise*, 173; Dickins to Dromgoole, July 4, 1783, Edward Dromgoole Papers, SHC; John B. Matthias, "The Journal of John B. Matthias," Ms, MAHC, 6, 12–57. Born in 1767 in Germantown, Pa., Matthias was a ship's joiner who married in 1790 and became a local preacher in 1793. See Sprague, *Annals*, 7:244ff; Seaman, *Annals*, 248. After the war Asbury reconciled with many of the lay leaders of New York Methodism who had opposed his disciplinary measures in the 1770s, including William Lupton, Henry Newton, and John Chave. *JLFA*, 1:121–22, 467.

5. Sweet, *Virginia Methodism*, 96; *JLFA*, 1:427; 3:29–32; *Minutes* (1794), 55; Lee, *Short History*, 73–76; Stevens, *History*, 2:102–6; Bangs, *History*, 1:143–44.

6. *JLFA*, 1:450; 3:31–32; Wesley to Dromgoole, Sept. 17, 1783, Edward Dromgoole Papers, SHC; Drinkhouse, *Methodist Reform*, 241. Luke Tyerman gives transcripts of Asbury's Sept. 20, 1783, letter and Wesley's Oct. 3, 1783, letter that are slightly different than the printed versions cited here. See Tyerman, "A Collection of Manuscript Biographies of Early Methodists," MAB, B, vol. 1, JRL.

7. *JLFA*, 1:460; Ware, *Sketches*, 83–84.

8. Ware, *Sketches*, 56–57, 73–79.

9. *JLFA*, 1:402, 411, 412, 420, 426, 429, 444, 446.

10. Asbury to his parents, June 7, 1784, MAHC; Lednum, *Rise*, 37; Seamen, *Annals*, 23, 69, 78, 426; Wakeley, *Lost Chapters*, 85–86, 202. Sause was treasurer of the New York society.

11. Asbury to his parents, June 7, 1784; Rack, *Reasonable Enthusiast*, 257–69; Stout, *Divine Dramatist*, 156–73.

12. Bond, "Anecdotes," MAHC; Robert J. Bull, "John Wesley Bond's Reminiscences of Francis Asbury," *MH*, 4 (1965): 24.

13. William Ormond, "William Ormond Jr's Journal," 5 vols., DUL, vol. 2, entries for Jan. 1 and 22, April 18, May 17 and 28, 1796. Also see M. H. Moore, *Sketches of the Pioneers of Methodism in North Carolina and Virginia* (Nashville: Southern Methodist Publishing House, 1884), 248–53.

14. Ormond, "Journal," vols. 2 and 3, quotations from entries for July 29, Oct. 12, 1796, March 18, 1797, Dec. 18, 1798, March 8 and 9, 1800. Also see entries for Aug. 5, 26, Dec. 7 and 31, 1796; Jan. 11, Feb. 19, 24, Dec. 11, 1797; March 30, April 27, July 9, Aug. 8, 1798; May 22, June 9, 1799; Feb. 17, June 3, July 17, 30, Aug. 13, 1800.

15. *Minutes* (1840), 1:116; Ormond, "Journal," vol. 4, quotations from entries for Dec. 10 and 22, 1800, July 23, 1801. Also see entries for Sept. 29, Oct. 10, 13, Dec. 6, 9, 15, 20, 1800; Jan. 14, Feb. 1, 10, March 1, 30, April 1, May 2, 13, June 1, 19, Aug. 1, 12, 16, Nov. 29, 1801; Jan. 29, 1802; Feb. 9, May 2, June 29, 1803.

16. Minter, *Brief Account*, 1–13; Sarah Jones, *Devout Letters: Or, Letters Spiritual and Friendly. Written by Sarah Jones, Corrected and Published by Jeremiah Minter, Minister of the Gospel* (Alexandria: Samuel Snowden, 1804), 11, 17. Jones's letters to local preacher Edward Dromgoole are full of the same kind of language. See Jones to Dromgoole, Sept. 4, 1788, and two undated letters, "A Copy of Letters to E. Dromgoole," Edward Dromgoole Papers, SHC.

17. Jones, *Devout Letters*, 33, 37, 147.

18. Minter, *Brief Account*, 13–14; JLFA, 2:671.

19. JLFA, 2:672; Coke, *Extracts* (1793), 152; Minter, *Brief Account*, 15–19; Minter, *Scripture Proofs of Sorcery*, 10; Jones, *Devout Letters*, 48; *Minutes* (1794), 149–64. James O'Kelly questioned Jones at length and was convinced that she and Minter had committed adultery. See Cynthia Lynn Lyerly, "A Tale of Two Patriarchs; Or, How a Eunuch and a Wife Created a Family in the Church," *Journal of Family History*, 28:4 (October 2003): 490–509.

20. Minter, *Brief Account*, 20–23, Jones, *Devout Letters*, 48; 140–50. On Minter and Jones, also see Christine Leigh Heyrman, *Southern Cross: The Beginnings of the Bible Belt* (Knopf, 1997; reprint, Chapel Hill: University of North Carolina Press, 1997), 132, 152; Cynthia Lynn Lyerly, *Methodism and the Southern Mind, 1770–1810* (New York: Oxford University Press, 1998), 40–41, 109–10; Lester Ruth, ed., *The Spirituality and Life of Early Methodists: A Reader* (Nashville: Abingdon Press, 2005).

21. JLFA, 2:34; Minter, *Brief Account*, 21.

22. JLFA, 1:471; Coke, *Extract*, (1793), 13–14, 16; Cooper, *Substance*, 104–5.

CHAPTER 8

1. *Minutes* (1794), 40, 144–45.

2. Frank Baker, *John Wesley and the Church of England* (Nashville: Abingdon Press, 1970), 218–82; Rack, *Reasonable Enthusiast*, 471–534. According to Coke, in 1783 Asbury

wrote to Wesley informing him "of the extreme uneasiness of people's minds" in America "for want of the sacraments: that thousands of their children were unbaptized, and the members of the society in general had not partaken of the Lord's Supper for many years." Coke and Moore, *Life of Wesley*, 351.

3. Thomas S. Chew to Edward Dromgoole, Aug. 20, 1784, Edward Dromgoole Papers, SHC; Burgess, *List of Deacons*, 3; Baker, *John Wesley*, 218–33; Rack, *Reasonable Enthusiast*, 495–505; Gareth Lloyd, *Charles Wesley and the Struggle for Methodist Identity* (Oxford: Oxford University Press, 2007), 193–96; John S. Simon, "Elections to the Legal Hundred," *PWHS*, 13 (1922), 15. More pertinent to America, or so Wesley hoped, was his revision of the prayer book, published as *The Sunday Service of the Methodists in North America*. It was little used in America. According to Jesse Lee, most American preachers were "fully satisfied that they could pray better, and with more devotion while their eyes were shut, than they could with their eyes open," and preferred extemporaneous prayer to reading from the prayer book. The result, according to Lee, was that "after a few years the prayer book was laid aside." Lee notes that after the Christmas Conference, "The Superintendents, and some of the Elders, introduced the custom of wearing gowns and bands, but it was opposed by many of the preachers, as well as private members, who looked upon it as needless and *superfluous*." Hence, "after a few years it was given up, and has never been introduced among us since." Lee, *Short History*, 102–3; Baker, *John Wesley*, 234–55; Rack, *Reasonable Enthusiast*, 509–10; Drinkhouse, *Methodist Reform*, 307.

4. Word that Joseph Pilmore was anxious for ordination, even if it meant leaving the Church of England, may have been one of the reasons Wesley replaced him with Asbury and Rankin. In late 1770 or early 1771, Pilmore wrote to a friend in England that the "chief difficulty" American Methodists "labour under is want of Ordination & I believe we shall be Obliged to procure it by some means or other." See Frederick E. Maser, "A Revealing Letter from Joseph Pilmore," *MH* 10:3 (April 1972): 54–58.

5. Baker, *John Wesley*, 257–58.

6. *Wesley Letters* (Telford), 7:30–31, 238–39; *JLFA*, 3:38; Baker, *John Wesley*, 256–82; Rack, *Reasonable Enthusiast*, 510–20; John Vickers, *Thomas Coke: Apostle of Methodism* (London: Epworth Press, 1969), 68–79; Briggs, *Asbury*, 151–57; Stevens, *History*, 2:155–57, 165–68; Drinkhouse, *Methodist Reform*, 67–75, 252–62. For Whatcoat's brief account of Wesley's ordinations, see Richard Whatcoat, *Memoirs of the Rev. Richard Whatcoat. Late Bishop of the Methodist Episcopal Church*, ed. William Phoebus (New York: Joseph Allen, 1828), 17–18.

7. Vickers, *Coke*, 53–67; Stevens, *History*, 2:151–55; Drinkhouse, *Methodist Reform*, 51–53, 101–2.

8. Ware, "Christmas Conference," 104. On Coke's preaching, Ware wrote: "His voice was too weak to command with ease a very large audience. He could nevertheless sometimes do it; and at those times his preaching was very impressive. Some of the best scholars in America have been heard to say, that Dr. Coke spoke the purest English they ever heard."

9. *JLFA*, 1:471–72; Coke, *Extracts* (1793), 13; Wakeley, *Lost Chapters*, 302–3.

10. *JLFA*, 1:471–72, 745; Coke, *Extracts* (1793), 16. Phillip Barratt was converted under the preaching of Freeborn Garrettson. He was sheriff of Kent County from 1775 to

1779 when he was elected to the Delaware General Assembly. Barratt owned some 800 acres of land. He died on Oct. 28, 1784, two weeks before Asbury and Coke's first meeting. See Allen B. Clark And Jane Herson, *New Light on Old Barratt's: A History of Barratt's Chapel* (n.p.: Commission on Archives and History, Peninsula Conference, United Methodist Church, 1986), 1–4, 14–21. In a portion of his journal published in 1789, Coke wrote: "After dining in company with eleven of the preachers at our sister Barret's . . . I privately opened our plan to Mr. Asbury. He expressed considerable doubts concerning it, which I rather applaud than otherwise; but informed me that he had received some intimations of my arrival on the continent; and as he thought it probable I might meet him on that day, and might have something of importance to communicate to him from Mr. Wesley, he had therefore called together a considerable number of the preachers to form a council." See Thomas Coke, "The Journal of Thomas Coke, Bishop of the Methodist-Episcopal Church," *Arminian Magazine* (Philadelphia), vol. 1 (1789), 243.

11. When Garrettson first met Coke (the day before Coke's first meeting with Asbury) he was "somewhat surprised" to hear "Mr. Wesley's new plan opened (respecting ordination). I thought I would sit in silence." Garrettson soon took to the new plan, writing that Wesley's ordinations "gratified the desires of thousands of his friends in America." Garrettson, *Journal*, 122, 243; *JLFA*, 1:472; Coke, *Extracts* (1793), 16; Lee, *Short History*, 89.

12. *JLFA*, 1:472–73; Coke, *Extracts* (1793), 23; Coke, "Journal," *Arminian Magazine* (Philadelphia), 1:291–92; Whatcoat, *Memoirs*, 21; Warren Thomas Smith, "The Christmas Conference," *MH* 6 (July 1968): 3–27; Drinkhouse, *Methodist Reform*, 279. Coke says "near sixty" attended the conference. Alexander M'Caine gives the number of preachers at the Christmas Conference as sixty-five. See Alexander M'caine, *Letters of the Organization and Early History of the Methodist Episcopal Church* (Boston: Thomas F. Norris, 1850), 77–78.

13. *JLFA*, 1:474; Watters, *Short Account*, 102; Ware, *Sketches*, 106; Ware, "Christmas Conference," 98–101; Garrettson, *Journal*, 122; Whatcoat, *Memoirs*, 21–23; Wakeley, *Lost Chapters*, 304–5; Wigger, *Taking Heaven*, 42. According to Thomas Ware, John Dickins proposed the name Methodist Episcopal Church. It isn't clear how many itinerant preachers there were at the time of the Christmas conference. The minutes from the May 28, 1784, conference list eighty-three itinerants appointed to circuits, not counting Asbury. Edwin Schell has compiled a list of 115 preachers related to the Christmas Conference, including Coke, Whatcoat, Vasey, and thirty-two preachers received on trial during the conference year 1784–85. The discrepancy is largely the result of these thirty-two preachers who joined during the 1784–85 conference year, some of whom were never received into full connection. See *Minutes* (1794), 65–69; Edwin Schell, "Fate of Methodist Preachers Related to Conference at Christmas 1784 (to 1799)," unpublished mss, LLM. William Philip Otterbein, a German minister and Asbury's friend, joined Coke, Whatcoat, and Vasey in consecrating Asbury a superintendent. For a more complete discussion of Coke's role in establishing the Methodist Episcopal Church in America, see Vickers, *Coke*, 79–99. James O'Kelly later claimed that Asbury wasn't elected by the conference, but only appointed by Wesley. Nicholas Snethen collected

evidence to answer O'Kelly. See O'Kelly, *Author's Apology*, 9; Kilgore, *O'Kelly Schism*, 8; Snethen, *Reply*, 9–10; O'Kelly, *Vindication*, 7–8; Nicholas Snethen, *An Answer to James O'Kelly's Vindication of His Apology* (Philadelphia: S. W. Conrad, 1802), 9–10.

14. Thomas Coke, *Substance of a Sermon Preached at Baltimore, in the State of Maryland, Before the General Conference of the Methodist Episcopal Church, December 27, 1784. At the Ordination of the Rev. Francis Asbury to the Office of Superintendent* (New York: T. Mason and G. Lane, 1840), 5–15; Coke, "Journal," *Arminian Magazine* (Philadelphia), 1:291.

15. MEC, *Minutes of Several Conversations Between The Rev. Thomas Coke, LL. D., The Rev. Francis Asbury and Others, At a Conference, Begun in Baltimore, in the State of Maryland, on Monday, the 27th of December, in the Year 1784. Composing a Form of Discipline for the Ministers, Preachers and Other Members of the Methodist Episcopal Church in America* (Philadelphia: Charles Cist, 1785), as given in Tigert, *Constitutional History*, 549 (hereafter 1785 *Discipline* (Tigert)).

16. Jesse Lee, William Watters, Thomas Haskins, and Ezekiel Cooper wrote that the vote to form the new church was unanimous, as was, according to Cooper, Lee, and others, the vote to elect Coke and Asbury superintendents. A decade later, James O'Kelly remembered that the vote to establish the new church was unanimous, but that Coke and Asbury were never actually elected by the conference. O'Kelly's claim notwithstanding, the bulk of evidence suggests that both measures, in fact, carried without dissent. Lee, *Short History*, 89; Watters, *Short Account*, 102; Atkinson, *Methodism in New Jersey*, 324–25; O'Kelly, *Author's Apology*, 9; Smith, "Christmas Conference," 22; Andrews, *The Methodists*, 69–70; Drinkhouse, *Methodist Reform*, 286–304; M'Caine, *Letters*, 70–105; Stevens, *History*, 186–88.

17. William Smith, *Life and Correspondence of the Rev. William Smith*, ed. Horace Wemyss Smith, 2 vols. (Philadelphia: Ferguson Bros., 1880), 2:243–46; Emora T. Brannan, "Episcopal Overtures to Coke and Asbury during the Christmas Conference, 1784," *MH*, 14:3 (April 1976): 203–12; Sprague, *Annals*, 5:158–63, 208–11, 246–50. John Andrews earned BA (1765) and MA (1767) degrees from the College of Philadelphia and was ordained a deacon and priest in London in 1767. William West attended William and Mary and was ordained a deacon and priest in 1761. Rightmyer to Wigger, e-mail, May 16, 2006.

18. Coke may have been using Wesley for cover. Andrews and West probably told Coke and Asbury that they were acting under the direction of Smith, who had recently been elected a bishop of the Protestant Episcopal Church in Maryland. The Methodists probably also knew that Smith had a drinking problem, which in part eventually prevented his consecration. Smith, *Life and Correspondence*, 245–46; Brannan, "Overtures," Drinkhouse, *Methodist Reform*, 267–68; Smith, "Christmas Conference," 22–23; Andrews, *The Methodists*, 69–70; William Wilson Manross, *A History of the American Episcopal Church* (New York: Morehouse Publishing Co., 1935), 205–6; Charles C. Tiffany, *A History of the Protestant Episcopal Church in the United States of America* (New York: Christian Literature Co., 1895), 405; Clara O. Loveland, *The Critical Years: The Reconstitution of the Anglican Church in the United States of America, 1780–1789* (Greenwich, Conn.: Seabury Press, 1956), 32.

19. Frank Baker, *Representative Verse of Charles Wesley* (London: Epworth Press, 1962), xi, liii, 370; Charles Wesley, *The Unpublished Poetry of Charles Wesley*, ed. S. T. Kimbrough Jr. and Oliver A. Beckerlegge, 3 vols. (Nashville: Kingswood Books, 1992), 3:81; A Methodist of the Church Of England, *Strictures on the Substance of a Sermon Preached at Baltimore in the State of Maryland, Before the General Conference of the Methodist Episcopal Church, on the 27th of December 1784: At the Ordination of the Rev. Francis Asbury, to the Office of Superintendent. By Thomas Coke, L.L.D. Superintendent of the said Church* (London: G. Herdsfield, 1785), 4; Vickers, *Coke*, 41, 69, 100–3; Lloyd, *Charles Wesley*, 95, 207–8; Richard P. Heitzenrater, *Wesley and the People Called Methodists* (Nashville: Abingdon Press, 1995), 37, 38, 79, 172, 192–312. Though Charles was in Bristol at the time of the 1784 ordinations, he didn't learn about them for two months. John kept him in the dark as long as possible, knowing what his brother's response would be. Coke and Charles Wesley had been at odds with one another since at least 1779, when Coke wrote to John Wesley that he viewed Charles as "an *enemy* to Methodism." Writing to John Wesley in April 1784, Coke only suggested that he make a fact finding trip to America. Not until August 1784 did he apparently agree to the ordination plan. Charles distrusted the American Methodists and their "fanatical spirit," as he wrote to John Fletcher in June 1785. In August 1785 Charles wrote to his wife that he had preached a sermon at Bristol urging the society "to continue in the ship [i.e., to remain in the Church of England] when the Dr. [Coke] comes to turn them all dissenters." Charles Wesley to Mary Fletcher and John Fletcher, June 21, 1785, Charles Wesley to Sarah Wesley, Aug. 15, 1785, Charles Wesley Papers, JRL. Coke to John Wesley, Dec. 15, 1779, April 17, 1784, Aug. 9, 1784, Tms copies, Thomas Coke Papers, JRL.

20. Charles Wesley, notebook containing undated notes, c. 1751, directed to John Wesley, item DDCW 8/5, Charles Wesley Papers, JRL.

21. Charles Wesley to John Horton, June 26, 1772, Charles Wesley Papers, JRL. In this letter Charles writes that "my Br[other's] first object was the M[ethodists] & then the Church: my first for Church & then the M[ethodists]." On Charles Wesley's opposition to a separation from the Church of England and his declining influence on his brother John, see Charles's letters to Walter Sellon of Feb. 4, 1755, Dec. 14, 1754, and a letter dated only 1754, items DDCW 6/92A, 6/92B, and 6/92C, and letters to Mark Davis of Dec. 10, 1772, and May 22, 1773, items DDCW 7/60 and 1/62, Charles Wesley Papers, JRL. Also see Heitzenrater, *Wesley*, 115–16, 176, 184, 206, 237, 270; Lloyd, *Charles Wesley*, 110–79.

22. Asbury to his parents, June 7, 1784, MAHC. I am indebted to David Hallam, biographer of Eliza Asbury, for pointing out how unusual it was for a Briton to use fall rather than autumn.

23. In March 1784 Pilmore wrote to a friend in Nottingham that "how Providence will dispose of me in future is quite uncertain. If I should stay in Europe, Nott[ingha]m would be more agreable than many other Places, but it is most likely I shall go over the Atlantic." In 1794 Pilmore became rector of Christ Church in New York City, where, by 1804, his salary was £600 a year. Thomas Lyell, another Methodist preacher turned Episcopalian who succeeded Pilmore as rector of Christ Church, recalled that "Rev. Mr. Pilmore was a man of fine, commanding personal appearance and address, good natural endowments, and a very ready and powerful eloquence." His "literary

attainments" were "limited," but "his labours in the ministry were crowned with very extensive success" among New York Episcopalians. In 1804 Pilmore became rector of St. Paul's Church in Philadelphia. There he married the "rich and beautiful" niece of Quaker reformer Anthony Benezet. Pilmore remained friendly to Methodism (he died in 1825), but he and Asbury rarely saw each other after 1773. See Pilmore to Thomas Tatham, March 21, 1784, record PLP 83.60.4, JRL; *Minutes* (1794), 5–7; Stanger, "Joseph Pilmore," in Pilmore, *Journal*, 235–254; B. Schofield to John Lockwood, Oct. 30, 1875, Lockwood Papers; Thomas Lyell, untitled autobiography, Aldert Smedes Papers, SHC, vol. C, 9–10; Frank Baker, *John Wesley*, 228, 231; Sprague, *Annals*, 5:268–69.

24. Frederick E. Maser, "More Light on Joseph Pilmore," *MH*, 16:1 (October 1977): 54–55; Pilmore to Charles Wesley, April 10, 1786, and September 27, 1786, Early Preachers Collection, JRL. Also see Pilmore to John Atlay, Early Preachers Collection, JRL. A number of other English preachers and clergy wrote to Charles Wesley to express their dismay over his brother's ordinations. See for example William Pine to Charles Wesley, Nov. 25, 1784, and Richard Dillion to Charles Wesley, Aug. 26, 1786, Charles Wesley Papers, JRL.

25. Jarratt to Dromgoole, May 31, 1785, and March 22, 1788, Edward Dromgoole Papers, SHC; *JLFA*, 3:83; Smith, "Christmas Conference," 23. In July 1780 the Anglican priest Archibald McRobert wrote to Jarratt ridiculing the Methodists as "a designing people, void of the generous and catholic spirit of the gospel," who "countenance so many illiterate creatures void of all prudence and discretion that I have no expectation of any good and lasting effects from their misguided zeal." McRobert was convinced that the Methodists' "professed adherence to the church is amazingly preposterous and disingenuous." At the time Jarratt disagreed, but he later concluded that "Mr. McRobert's judgment of them [the Methodists] was more accurate than mine." See Jarratt, *Life*, 7, 85–92. Born in 1737 and educated at King's College, Aberdeen, McRobert was ordained in London in 1761 and later became a Presbyterian. Weis, *Colonial Clergy*, 34; Fothergill, *Emigrant Ministers*, 43; Goodwin, *Colonial Church*, 290; Nelson, *Blessed Company*, 193, 202, 314, 335, n. 8; Rightmyer to Wigger, e-mail, May 12, 2006. After Jarratt's death in 1801, Asbury preached a funeral sermon for him and later visited his widow. Asbury noted that Jarratt "was the first who received our despised preachers-when strangers and unfriended, he took them to his house, and had societies formed in his parish." *JLFA*, 2:289, 291–92, 293, 328, 329. Also see Sweet, *Virginia Methodism*, 108–17.

26. Alexander M'caine, *The History and Mystery of Methodist Episcopacy, Or, A Glance at "The Institutions of the Church, As We Received Them From Our Fathers"* (Baltimore: Richard J. Matchett, 1827); John Emory *A Defence of "Our Fathers," and of the Original Organization of the Methodist Episcopal Church, Against the Rev. Alexander M'Caine and Others* (New York: Phillips & Hunt, 1827), 32–59. M'Caine responded the next year with *A Defence of the Truth, As Set Forth in the History and Mystery of Methodist Episcopacy, Being a Reply to John Emory's "Defence of Our Fathers."* (1828; reprint, Baltimore: Sherwood & Co., 1850). On Emory, M'Caine, and the Methodist Protestant Church, see Simpson, *Cyclopedia*, 340–41, 572, 602–7. Also see Thomas E. Bond, *The Economy of Methodism Illustrated and Defended: In a Series of Papers* (New York: Lane & Scott, 1852). Emory was elected a bishop of the MEC in 1832.

27. Bangs, *History*, 1:158–66; Stevens, *History*, 2:189–94; Drinkhouse, *Methodist Reform*, 252, 285–304. Early biographers of Asbury generally follow Emory, Bangs, Stevens' line of argument, though they predictably emphasize Asbury's role in the American church's founding. See Briggs, *Asbury*, 158–70; Tipple, *Asbury*, 134–57; Lewis, *Asbury*, 96–99.

28. 1785 *Discipline* (Tigert), 554–56; *Minutes* (1794), 83; Donald Mathews, *Slavery and Methodism: A Chapter in American Morality, 1780–1845* (Princeton, N.J.: Princeton University Press, 1965), 3–19, 296–98; Wigger, *Taking Heaven*, 140. Asbury and Coke's 1785 *Minutes* were adapted from John Wesley's so-called Large Minutes of 1780. The 1785 *Minutes* represented the first edition of the *Discipline* published in America.

29. *Minutes* (1794), 91–92, 103, 117, 131, 145, 161, 178, 195, 213; *Minutes* (1840), 1:52, 69, 74, 81, 87, 93; Williams, *Garden of Methodism*, 111.

30. *JLFA*, 1:362, 403, 413, 494n., 539n., 681n., 682n.; *New-York Packet*, Sept. 11, 1786; Lednum, *Rise*, 281–82; Boehm, *Reminiscences*, 88–92; Warren Thomas Smith, *Harry Hosier: Circuit Rider* (Nashville: Upper Room, 1981); William Henry Williams, *The Garden of American Methodism: The Delmarva Peninsula, 1769–1820* (Wilmington: Scholarly Resources, 1984), 143, 145, 153.

31. Coke, *Extracts* (1793), 16, 18; Freeborn Garrettson also developed a very favorable opinion of Hosier's preaching beginning in 1784 and continuing in 1790 as the two toured New England together. See Garrettson, *Journal*, 237, 238, 251, 266, 267, 268, 269, 270. Hosier's later career was clouded with difficulties. At some point in the 1790s Hosier apparently became an alcoholic, drinking heavily for years before eventually reclaiming his preaching ministry. William Colbert, who knew Hosier in Philadelphia from 1804 to 1806, reports that by then Hosier was once again an effective preacher. He died in Philadelphia in May 1806. See Colbert, "Journal," entries for Sept. 15, 1804; Jan. 12 and 27, Feb. 6, Feb. 19, March 26, June 6, July 24, Sept. 20, 1805; March 22, April 30, May 18, 1806.

32. *JLFA*, 1:442. Asbury had been a frequent guest in the Worthington home prior to this. See *JLFA*, 1:106, 110, 230n., 231, 237, 241, 348, 385, 441.

33. Coke, *Extracts* (1793), 35–39. Coke was apparently indicted in at least two Virginia counties for preaching against slavery, and also was followed by a man with a gun intent on shooting him. Coke, *Extracts* (1793), 69; Gewehr, *Great Awakening*, 247; L. C. Matlack, *The Antislavery Struggle and Triumph in the Methodist Episcopal Church* (Phillips & Hunt, 1881; reprint, New York: Negro University Press, 1969), 51–52.

34. Coke, *Extracts* (1793), 36–39; MacMaster, "Liberty or Property," 48–50.

35. Coke, *Extracts* (1793), 45; *JLFA*, 1:488, 489; Henry Wiencek, *An Imperfect God: George Washington, His Slaves, and the Creation of America* (New York: Farrar, Straus and Giroux, 2003), 5, 275. Writing to the Marquis de Lafayette in May 1786, Washington noted that "to set them [the slaves] afloat at once would, I really believe, be productive of much inconvenience and mischief; but by degrees it certainly might, and assuredly ought to be effectual." George Washington to Marquis de Lafayette, May 10, 1786, *The Writings of George Washington: From the Original Manuscript Sources 1745–1799*, vol. 28, Dec. 5, 1784–Aug. 30, 1786, ed. John C. Fitzpatrick (Washington: United States Government Printing Office, 1938), 424. Washington's views were similar to Jesse Lee's,

whose father was a slaveholder. See Jesse Lee, *Memoir of the Rev. Jesse Lee: With Extracts from His Journals*, ed. Minton Thrift (New York: N. Bangs and T. Mason, 1823; reprint, New York: Arno Press, 1969), 78–79; Lee, *Life of Jesse Lee*, 160, 168–71, 343–45. Later, after the repeal of the 1784 conference anti-slavery rules and the failure of the petition to the Virginia Assembly, Asbury had dinner at Roberdeau's to discuss "the difficulties attending emancipation, and the resentment some of the members of the Virginia legislature expressed against those who favoured a general abolition." *JLFA*, 1:498.

36. Fredrika Teute Schmidt And Barbara Ripel Wilhelm, "Early Proslavery Petitions in Virginia," *William and Mary Quarterly* 30:1 (January 1973): 133–46; George Washington to Marquis de Lafayette, May 10, 1786, *Writings of Washington*, 424. On the Methodist emancipation petition and the proslavery counter petitions, see Lyerly, *Methodism and the Southern Mind*, 125–27; Robert M. Calhoun, *Evangelicals & Conservatives in the early South, 1740–1861* (Columbia: University of South Carolina Press, 1988), 125–27; Merton L. Dillon, *Slavery Attacked: Southern Slaves and Their Allies 1619–1865* (Baton Rouge: Louisiana State University Press, 1990), 97–105.

37. Petitions from Amelia County (Nov. 10, 1785), Brunswick County (Nov. 10, 1785), Halifax County (Nov. 10, 1785), Hanover County (two petitions, Nov. 16, 1784), Henrico County (Nov. 16, 1784; also see petition dated June 8, 1782), Lunenburg County (Nov. 29, 1785), Mecklenburg County (Nov. 8, 1785), and Pittsylvania County (Nov. 10, 1785) that are located in the Legislative Petitions at the Library of Virginia, Richmond, Va.

38. Undated speech in Green Hill Papers, SHC; *JLFA*, 1:487; Coke, *Extracts*, 36–37; Lee, *Short History*, 116; Richard K. Macmaster, "Liberty or Property? The Methodists Petition for Emancipation in Virginia, 1785," *MH*, 10:1 (October 1971): 44–55; Robert Alexander Armour, "The Opposition to the Methodist Church in Eighteenth-Century Virginia" (PhD diss., University of Georgia, 1968), 86–88; 1798 Brunswick County Sheriff's assessment, and 1803 fire insurance policy from the Assurance Society, Financial and Legal Papers, Edward Dromgoole Papers, SHC. Coke claimed that Asbury visited the governor of North Carolina and "gained him over" to the Methodist position on emancipation. See Coke, *Extracts* (1793), 37. Asbury doesn't mention this visit in his journal.

39. Coke, *Extracts* (1793), 32–33, 39; Jarratt, *Life*, xviii–xix; Devereux Jarratt to John Coleman, April 15, 1790, in Devereux Jarratt, *Thoughts on Some Important Subjects in Divinity: In a Series of Letters to a Friend* (Baltimore: Warner & Hanna, 1806), 81–84; Jarratt to Edward Dromgoole, May 31, 1785, and March 22, 1788, Edward Dromgoole Papers, SHC; Robert Mccolley, *Slavery and Jeffersonian Virginia* (Champaign: University of Illinois Press, 1964), 148–53; Nelson, *Blessed Company*, 392, n. 18. Jarratt remembered his March conversation with Coke differently. Writing in 1790, Jarratt claimed that he had only sought to give Coke some friendly advice, "without any suspicion it would offend the gentleman." In 1791 Jarratt was taxed on 717 acres and seventeen slaves. Rightmyer to Wigger, e-mail, May 12, 2006. For a more sympathetic description of Jarratt by a Presbyterian minister, see William Hill, *Autobiographical Sketches of Dr. William Hill: Together With His Account of the Revival of Religion in Prince Edward County* (Richmond: Union Theological Seminary in Virginia, 1968), 57.

40. *Virginia Gazette*, Jan. 1, 1767, 1, 2; Jan. 22, 1767, 2; June 11, 1767, 1; Armour, "Opposition," 12–43.

41. 1785 *Discipline* (Tigert), 554–56; *Minutes* (1794), 83; Coke, *Extracts* (1793), 46. On Methodism and the Coming of the Civil War, see Richard Carwardine, *Evangelicals and Politics in Antebellum America* (New Haven: Yale University Press, 1993; reprint, University of Tennessee Press, 1997); and Richard J. Carwardine, "Methodists, Politics, and the Coming of the American Civil War," in *Methodism and the Shaping of American Culture*, ed. Nathan O. Hatch and John H. Wigger (Nashville: Kingswood Books, 2001), 309–42. According to Jesse Lee, the antislavery rules adopted at the Christmas Conference "were but short lived, and were offensive to most of our southern friends; and were so much opposed by many of our private members, local preachers, and some of the travelling preachers, that the execution of them was suspended at the conference held in June following, about six months after they were formed; and they were never afterwards carried into full force." Lee, *Short History*, 97.

42. Jarratt, *Thoughts on Divinity*, 84; *JLFA*, 3:82.

43. *JLFA*, 1:299 n. 14, 324, 358; "Leesburg Minutes," 26; Thomas Haskins, Mss. Journal, Nov. 11, 1782, Library of Congress; quoted in John Abernathy Smith, "Cokesbury College: Kingswood in America," *MH*, 28:4 (July 1990), 220; Pilkington, *Methodist Publishing*, 1:51; Stevens, *History*, 2:41. On Asbury and Magaw, see Rightmyer, *Anglican Church in Delaware*, 120, 162; Lyman P. Powell, *The History of Education in Delaware* (Washington: Government Printing Office, 1893), 54–55. Born in 1735, Magaw earned a degree from the College of Philadelphia in 1757 and was ordained in London in 1767. He served as a Society for the Propagation of the Gospel missionary at Dover, Del., and Kent County, Del., from 1767 to 1781. He was rector of St. Paul's Church in Philadelphia from 1781 to 1804. Frederick V. Mills Sr., *Bishops by Ballot; An Eighteenth-Century Ecclesiastical Revolution* (New York: Oxford University Press, 1978), 20; Rightmyer to Wigger, e-mail, May 12, 2006.

44. Coke, *Extracts* (1793), 16; Smith, "Cokesbury College," 221; Heitzenrater, *Wesley*, 105–6, 125–27, 168–69; Anson W. Cummings, *The Early Schools of Methodism* (New York: Phillips & Hunt, 1886), 21; William Hamilton, "Some Acount of Cokesbury College," *Methodist Quarterly Review*, XLI (April 1859): 175–78. Also see Bangs, *History*, 1:229–40.

45. Coke, *Extracts* (1793), 22, 24, 46; *JLFA*, 1:490; Lee, *Short History*, 112–13; Bangs, *History*, 1:229–40; Smith, "Cokesbury College," 222–23; George W. Archer (a.k.a. Hesper Bendbow), *An Authentic History of Cokesbury College* (n.p.: N. N. Nock; reprint, Bel Air, Md.: Bel Air Times, 1924), 6–8; Bernard C. Steiner, "The History of University Education in Maryland," in *Johns Hopkins University Studies in Historical and Political Science*, vol. 9, ed. Herbert B. Adams (Baltimore: Johns Hopkins Press, 1891), 22–24; Bernard C. Steiner, *History of Education in Maryland* (Washington: Government Printing Office, 1894), 230–31. On the naming of Cokesbury, see John Emory, *Defence of "Our Fathers,"* 93–94; Drinkhouse, *Methodist Reform*, 292.

46. Coke, *Extracts*, 14–45.

CHAPTER 9

1. Ware, *Sketches*, 245–46.

2. *JLFA*, 1:481. Thomas Coke likewise "baptized a great many children, and administered the sacrament to a great many communicants" during his 1784–1785 visit to the United States. Coke, *Extracts* (1793), 18.

3. *JLFA*, 1:480, 490–94.

4. *JLFA*, 1:495, 497, 506. I am indebted to Connie Greiff for the description of a Jersey wagon, taken for a 1783 account by Johann David Schoepf. On wagon travel in New Jersey during this period, see Wheaton J. Lane, *From Indian Trail To Iron Horse: Travel and Transportation in New Jersey 1620–1860* (Princeton, N.J.: Princeton University Press, 1939), 115–69.

5. *JLFA*, 1:509, 511, 536, 537, 538; Coke, *Extracts* (1793), 49–67. For a more thorough discussion of Coke's second visit to the United States, see Vickers, *Coke*, 114–23.

6. *JLFA*, 2:512; 3:49; Whatcoat, *Memoirs*, 9–19; Richard Whatcoat, "The Journal of Richard Whatcoat," ed. George H. Bost, Tms dated December 1939, GTS, 1–2; Briggs, *Asbury*, 20–21. On Whatcoat and Asbury attending class meetings together in England, see Boehm, *Reminiscences*, 127; Cooper, *Substance*, 66; Wright, *James Quinn*, 303; Young, *Autobiography of a Pioneer*, 175. Young says that Whatcoat had been Asbury's class leader in England.

7. Coke, *Extracts* (1793), 67; *JLFA*, 3:65; *Wesley Letters* (Telford), 8:91.

8. *JLFA*, 1:594; 3:13.

9. *JLFA*, 2:164. Methodists continued to informally use "Rev." and "Mr." anyway. Nicholas Snethen repeated Asbury's defense of the title bishop against attacks from James O'Kelly. See Snethen, *Reply*, 11; O'Kelly, *Vindication*, 10; Snethen, *Answer*, 13–14. Jesse Lee was troubled that the new title had been adopted without a vote of all the preachers. In 1788 it was finally voted on, with the majority of preachers agreeing to the change from superintendent to bishop. Lee, *Short History*, 125–26; Bangs, *History*, 259–61; Drinkhouse, *Methodist Reform*, 343, 349–65.

10. James O'kelly, *Essay on Negro-Slavery* (Philadelphia: Prichard & Hall, 1789), 19; O'Kelly, *Author's Apology*, 65; Durward T. Stokes and William T. Scott, *A History of the Christian Church in the South* (n.p., 1973), 1–2; W.E. Macclenny, *The Life of Rev. James O'Kelly and the Early History of the Christian Church in the South* (Indianapolis: Religious Book Service, 1950), 11–16; James E. Atkins, "Early Methodism in Surry County, VA. and Carsley United Methodist Church," unpublished mss., VHS, 6. O'Kelly married Elizabeth Meeks of Surry County, Va., in 1759.

11. James O'Kelly to an unknown correspondent, April 1787, *JLFA*, 3:51–53; O'Kelly, *Author's Apology*, 11. Also see Charles Franklin Kilgore, *The James O'Kelly Schism in the Methodist Episcopal Church* (Mexico City: Casa Unida De Publicaciones, 1963); *JLFA*, 3:60–64.

12. JLFA 3:547; Lee, *Life of Jesse Lee*, 280–81; Ware, *Sketches*, 129–31; William Hammet, *Rejoindre: Being a Defence of the Truths Contained in An Appeal to Truth and*

Circumstances, In Seven Letters, Addressed to the Reverend Mr. Morrell (Charleston: Silliman, 1792), 22. The letter from Eliza Asbury isn't extant.

13. Lee, *Short History*, 122–24; Vickers, *Coke*, 119; Sprague, *Annals*, 7:70; Drinkhouse, *Methodist Reform*, 244–45. Sprague and Drinkhouse date the exchange between Coke and Reed in 1796.

14. Asbury says relatively little about these events in his journal, and James O'Kelly acknowledges that Asbury stayed in the background throughout the 1787 affair. Whatcoat, *Memoirs*, 24; Lee, *Short History*, 122; Coke, *Extracts* (1793), 71–73; O'Kelly, *Author's Apology*, 11; Bangs, *History*, 1:256–58; Drinkhouse, *Methodist Reform*, 327–30. Following the Baltimore conference, John Hagerty, a Baltimore conference preacher, wrote to Edward Dromgoole that "we have concluded to have no more Superintendents than we now have & the Doct [Coke] Exercises no Authority when out of the States & when in them 1. ordains. 2 presides in Conference as Moderator & 3 Travels at large, Mr Asbury acts as our Chief Ruler at all times." Hagerty to Dromgoole, May 14, 1787, Edward Dromgoole Papers, SHC.

15. *Minutes* (1794), 119; Coke, *Extracts* (1793), 104–17; *JLFA*, 3:50–51. Asbury says remarkably little about Coke's 1789 tour of America in his journal. See *JLFA*, 1:592, 595, 598. But he wrote to Thomas Morrell in November 1789 that the 1789 Baltimore conference "warmly urged, that he [Coke] should visit us as Doctor Coke, and not as our bishop; but this was like death to him." Apparently as a concession to Coke, his title as bishop remained unchanged. See Asbury to Thomas Morrell, [November 1789], *World Parish* (April 1960): 22–23. Nicholas Snethen later defended Asbury against James O'Kelly, writing that Asbury didn't make or advocate the motion to drop Wesley's name. See O'Kelly, *Author's Apology*, 12–13; Snethen, *Reply*, 10, 12–13; O'Kelly, *Vindication*, 9, 11–14; Snethen, *Answer*, 11, 14, 16–18; Kilgore, *O'Kelly Schism*, 11–12.

16. Wesley to Whatcoat, July 17, 1788, John Davies Collection, GTS; Asbury to Morrell, Sept. 9, 1789, Thomas Morrell Collection, GTS; *JLFA*, 3:75; Drinkhouse, *Methodist Reform*, 336. Asbury largely blamed Thomas Rankin for distorting Wesley's view. See *JLFA*, 3:63.

17. Coke to Asbury, Aug. 10, 1787, Methodist Research Collection, MAHC. Earlier Asbury had written to his parents, "I comfort myself that while the Doctor [Coke] lives, and remains in England, I shall insure you a friend." *JLFA*, 3:46–47.

18. Lee, *Short History*, 126–27, 131; *Minutes* (1794), 87–92, 110–17.

19. *JLFA*, 1:560, 606; Cox to Coke, July 1787, *Arminian Magazine* (Philadelphia), 2 (1790), 91–95. Jesse Lee reported that in 1787 alone eighteen hundred were converted on the Brunswick circuit, sixteen hundred on the Sussex circuit, and eight hundred on the Amelia circuit. Lee, *Short History*, 131. Edward Dromgoole agreed with Lee's estimate of eighteen hundred converted on the Brunswick circuit in 1787. See *JLFA*, 1:560, n. 4. On revivals also see *JLFA*, 1:531, 533, 567, 579, 608, 609; Sweet, *Virginia Methodism*, 121–25.

20. Lee, *Short History*, 126–31.

21. Garrettson, *Journal*, 134; Whatcoat, *Memoirs*, 24. John Hagerty also describes "a very great outpouring of Spirit" on the Talbot circuit on the peninsula, with five hundred to six hundred joining the church. See Hagerty to Edward Dromgoole, March 3, 1787, Edward Dromgoole Papers, SHC.

22. Lee, *Short History*, 126–27; Coke, *Extracts* (1793), 105–13; Coke to Cooper, July 7, 1789, Cooper MSS 17, GTS.

23. *JLFA*, 1:574, 578, 581, 625; Asbury to Winscom, May 27, 1789, Tms, MAHC; Ellis to Edward Dromgoole, Feb. 23, 1790, Edward Dromgoole Papers, SHC.

24. Asbury to Cooper, Dec. 24, 1788, GTS. Asbury added that "Sermons ought to be short and pointed . . . briefly explanatory and then to press the people to conviction, repentance, faith and holiness." In 1799 there were thirty white classes in Baltimore with 531 members and twelve black classes with 290 members. See Baltimore City Station, Methodist Episcopal Records, Microfilm reel 408, Maryland Hall of Records, Annapolis.

25. Ezekiel Cooper, "A Short Account of the Life and Experience of Ezekiel Cooper, written by himself at the desire of, and presented to Francis Asbury[,] Bishop of the Methodist Episcopal Church in North America," [c. 1791] MS, Cooper MSS 3, GTS, 1, 8, 9, 17, 29, 31; Garrettson, *Journal*, 54, 148. By his own account, Cooper was born on Feb. 22, 1763, and baptized in the Church of England. See Ezekiel Cooper, manuscript journal, Cooper MSS 1, GTS, 1:1. The part of Caroline County that Cooper was born in was then part of Queen Anne's County.

26. Cooper, "Short Account," 31–49; *Minutes* (1794), 68, 79, 92, 103, 117. Asbury ordained Cooper a deacon on June 3, 1787, while in New York, and an elder on Dec. 14, 1788, while in Baltimore. See the original ordination certificates, signed by Asbury, BC. A similar account of Cooper's early life, conversion, and call to the ministry can be found in the first volume of his manuscript journal, Cooper MSS 1, GTS, 1:1–43. According to this account, Cooper briefly trained as a joiner in 1783 (31).

27. Asbury wasn't alone in believing that Baltimore Methodists needed more discipline. When Thomas Chew was stationed in Baltimore in 1784, he wrote, "I believe its high time to purge the Classes in general, for unless the rubbish is remov'd out of the way we shall travel slowly, and those who would willingly join with us are deter'd by the disorderly walk of many professors." Chew to Edward Dromgoole, Aug. 20, 1784, Edward Dromgoole Papers, SHC.

28. Cooper to Asbury, "A Brief Account of the Work of God in Baltimore: Written by E. C. in an Epistle to Bishop Asbury," [c. December 1790], TMS, BC; Cooper, "Short Account," 47–48. Also see Cooper's manuscript journal for 1789, Cooper MSS 1, GTS, 5:19–101; George A. Phoebus, *Beams of Light on Early Methodism in America. Chiefly Drawn From the Diary, Letters, Manuscripts, Documents, and Original Tracts of the Rev. Ezekiel Cooper* (New York: Phillips & Hunt, 1887), 85–101. "Religion is a common topic of conversation now in this town.& you can scarce go in a shop, walk the street or market but you hear one and another upon the subject of religion," Cooper wrote to Coke. See Cooper to Coke, Aug. 28, 1789, Cooper MSS 16, GTS. Hagerty had similar success in Annapolis and Baltimore (including Fell's Point) 1788–1790. See Sweet, *Methodists*, 138, 142–43.

29. Cooper, "Brief Account;" *JLFA*, 1:608. Cooper provides a similar defense of the revival against accusations that it was mostly "madness, disorder & confusion," or "a work of the devil," in a letter to an unknown correspondent, Aug. 11, 1789, Cooper MSS 16, GTS. Cooper's role in the Baltimore revival also demonstrates the flexibility (some would say arbitrary prerogative) that characterized Asbury's appointments of the

preachers. At the Baltimore conference in September 1789, Asbury appointed Cooper to Annapolis, but then instructed him to remain in Baltimore until November, presumably to continue the revival. See Cooper, "Brief Account." When Cooper finally got to Annapolis, he found it slow going. "We have had a sifting time in this Town. I have turned out about as many as I've received," he wrote to Asbury. Cooper to Asbury, Aug. 14, 1790, Cooper MSS 16, GTS.

30. Cooper, manuscript journal (Sept. 15 and 16, 1789), 5:62, 63. Asbury describes the first of these meetings only as follows: "I had but few hearers at Hunt's chapel, but the Lord was present, and I am persuaded there was not an unfeeling soul in the house." *JLFA*, 1:608.

31. *JLFA*, 1:534, 555, 561, 577; *Minutes* (1840), 1:10, 28. The six annual conferences were in South Carolina, Georgia, Virginia, Baltimore, Philadelphia, and New York City. See *JLFA*, 1:564, 567, 572, 579, 580. On the revivals from 1785 to 1789, also see *JLFA*, 1:531, 533, 567, 579, 608, 609.

32. *JLFA*, 1:534, 577.

33. Coke, *Extracts* (1793), 105–6.

34. *JLFA*, 1:533. On the hardships of travel that Asbury faced during this period, also see *JLFA*, 1:500, 505, 507, 508, 510, 516, 517, 518, 519, 521, 534, 536, 562, 573, 576, 591, 594, 595, 596. On the Great Dismal Swamp, see Charles Royster, *The Fabulous History of the Dismal Swamp Company* (New York: Vintage Books, 1999); *The Great Dismal Swamp*, ed. Paul W. Kirk Jr. (Charlottesville: University Press of Virginia, 1979); Bland Simpson, *The Great Dismal: A Carolinian's Swamp Memoir* (Chapel Hill: University of North Carolina Press, 1990), 1–21; Alexander Crosby Brown, *The Dismal Swamp Canal* (Chesapeake, Va.: Norfolk County Historical Society, 1971), 17–43.

CHAPTER 10

1. *JLFA*, 1:490, 499, 512, 519, 546, 555, 578; Stevens, *History*, 253–56; Gerald O. Mcculloh, "Cokesbury College, an 18th Century Experimental Model," *MH*, 7:4 (July 1969): 3–8.

2. Francis Asbury, "To the Friends and Benefactors of Cokesbury College," Baltimore: William Goddard, Sept. 15, 1787; Smith, "Cokesbury College," 224–27; Frank Baker, "John Wesley and Cokesbury College's First President," *MH*, 11:2 (January 1973): 54–59; Steiner, *Education in Maryland*, 234–38; Hamilton, "Account of Cokesbury," 179–81; Cummings, *Early Schools of Methodism*, 30; Archer, *Authentic History of Cokesbury*, 9–10; Burgess, *List of Deacons*, 4. After meeting with the Cokesbury trustees on Dec. 23, 1786, Asbury reported, "We find we have expended upwards of £2000; we agreed to finish two rooms, and to send for Mr. Heath for our president." *JLFA*, 1:527. In March 1787, shortly before Heath came to America, Wesley described him as "a middle-aged Clergyman, who is going over to Cokesbury-College, and is, I believe, thoroughly qualified to preside there. *Wesley Works* (1872), 4:364 (March 23, 1787). Also see journal entry for Aug. 6, 1787. On Wesley's financial support of Heath during the spring and summer of 1787, see Wesley to Peard Dickinson, June 5, 1787, *Wesley Works* (1872), 12:459; and Wesley to Samuel Bradburn, July 10, 1787, *Wesley Works* (1872),

13:125. Heath died about 1805 or 1806 while serving as rector of Norborne Parish, Berkeley County, Va. See Rightmyer, *Anglican Church in Delaware*, 121. On Truman Marsh, see Burgess; Rightmyer to Wigger, e-mail, May 12, 2006.

3. *JLFA*, 1:578, 581, 583, 584, 612; Smith, "Cokesbury College," 227–31; Hamilton, "Account of Cokesbury," 181–83; Steiner, *Education in Maryland*, 239–41; Cummings, *Early Schools of Methodism*, 30–31; J. Hall Pleasants, "Jacob Hall, Surgeon and Educator, 1747–1812," *Maryland Historical Magazine*, 8:3 (Sept. 1913): 217–35.

4. Coke, *Extracts* (1793), 106, 107, 110–112; *JLFA*, 1:597; Thomas Coke And Francis Asbury "To the Friends of Cokesbury College," May 29, 1789, *JLFA*, 3:72–73. Coke and Asbury had also previously published subscription letters for Cokesbury. See Thomas Coke And Francis Asbury, "An Address to the Annual Subscribers for the Support of Cokesbury College," May 18, 1787, *JLFA*, 3:54–60. In September Asbury published his own appeal. See Francis Asbury, "To the Friends and Benefactors of Cokesbury College," Sept. 15, 1787, MAHC. John Hagerty's assessment of Cokesbury fell somewhere between Asbury's and Coke's. Hagerty wrote to Edward Dromgoole, "I expect there has some unfavourable reports spread thro your country about the College, but it may be relied on that things are not so bad there. I came from visiting it with Brother Reed on Friday last. Mr. Otterbein heard the boys examined by Doct[or] Hall and they improve in their learning. We inquired into their Morrels also and can hear no evil at present except they are not so deeply engaged about their souls as could [be] wished." See William Warren Sweet, *The Methodists: A Collection of Source Materials*, Religion on the American Frontier, 1783–1840 Series, vol. 4 (Chicago: University of Chicago Press, 1946), 139.

5. Asbury to Edward Dromgoole, Dec. 24, 1791, Edward Dromgoole Papers, SHC; *JLFA*, 1:612; Wigger, *Taking Heaven*, 176; Sylvanus Milne Duval, *The Methodist Episcopal Church and Education Up to 1869* (New York: Teachers College, Columbia University, 1928), 65–66; William Warren Sweet, *Indiana Asbury-DePauw University 1837–1937: A Hundred Years of Higher Education in the Middle West* (New York: Abingdon Press, 1937), 22–24; David B. Potts, *Wesleyan University 1831–1910: Collegiate Enterprise in New England* (New Haven: Yale University Press, 1992); Simpson, *Cyclopedia*, 235–36, 330.

6. *JLFA*, 1:440, 445, 601, 607.

7. Watters, *Short Account*, 100–1, 117, 133–39; *Minutes* (1840), 1:99, 105, 112, 120, 132, 136. Watters died in 1827.

8. Asbury to Winscom, Aug. 15, 1788. For a somewhat different perspective, see Andrews, *The Methodists*, 159–60; Williams, *Garden of Methodism*, 74; Michael G. Nickerson, "Historical Relationships of Itinerancy and Salary," *MH*, 21 (1982), 43–59.

9. *JLFA*, 1:603 Thomas Coke also commented on the discouraging prospects in Pennsylvania and New Jersey in 1789. See Coke, *Extracts* (1793), 112–13. Also see John Fea, "Rural Religion: Protestant Community and the Moral Improvement of the South Jersey Countryside, 1676–1800" (PhD diss., State University of New York at Stony Brook, 1999), 401.

10. Garrettson, *Journal*, 11.

11. Lee, *Short History*, 123; Garrettson, *Journal*, 9, 133, 254–55, 393; Drinkhouse, *Methodist Reform*, 313–17; J. H. Wigger, "Freeborn Garrettson," *Biographical Dictionary of Evangelicals*, ed. Timothy Larsen (Leicester, England: Inter-Varsity Press, 2003), 250–51.

Christine Heyrman presents Garrettson's appointment to New York as a form of exile Asbury imposed to punish Garrettson for his supernaturalism. See Heyrman, *Southern Cross*, 71. With Asbury's approval, Garrettson had originally set out for Boston in May 1788. But when he got to New York and perceived how extensive the needs and opportunities were there, he decided to postpone his excursion to New England and concentrate on New York for the time being. Garrettson did make it to Connecticut the following year, 1789. See Garrettson, *Journal*, 135, 260, 393.

12. Diane Lobody, "Lost in the Ocean of Love: The Mystical Writings of Catherine Livingston Garrettson" (PhD diss., Drew University, 1990), 34–41; Clare Brandt, *An American Aristocracy: The Livingstons* (Garden City, N.Y.: Doubleday & Company, 1986), 3, 82, 92, 117, 134, 146; Wigger, *Taking Heaven*, 166–67. Also on the Livingstons, see Cynthia A. Kiener, *Traders and Gentlefolk: The Livingstons of New York, 1675–1790* (Ithaca: Cornell University Press, 1992). On the Beekmans, see Philip L. White, *The Beekmans of New York in Politics and Commerce, 1647–1877* (New York: New-York Historical Society, 1956). Hagiographies of Catherine Garrettson include Charles Wesley Buoy, *Representative Women of Methodism* (New York: Hunt & Eaton, 1893), 243–333.

13. Catherine Livingston Garrettson, untitled autobiography, Tms, MAHC, 3–9.

14. *Minutes* (1794), 114, 117, 128, 131; *Minutes* (1840), 1:201, 214, 232, 249; Garrettson, *Journal*, 11–13, 135–36; *JLFA*, 1:598; Coke, *Extracts* (1793), 113.

15. Asbury waited more than a decade after the war to add an entry for April 24, 1780, to his journal: "I became a citizen of Delaware." Small as this claim to political participation is, it isn't in the earliest printing of this portion of his journal (the 1802 edition). It only appears in the 1821 and 1858 editions. See *JLFA*, 1:346; [Francis Asbury], *An Extract From the Journal of Francis Asbury, One of the Bishops of the Methodist Episcopal Church: From January 1ˢᵗ, 1779, to September 3d, 1780* (Philadelphia: Ezekiel Cooper, 1802), 95; [Edwin Schell], "Discover," ed. Frederick E. Maser, *MH*, 9 (January 1971), 41.

16. Francis Asbury to George Washington, April 24, 1786, Dreer collection, HSP; *JLFA*, 3:70–72; Morrell to Ezekiel Cooper, Aug. 26, 1827, BC; *Arminian Magazine* (Philadelphia), 1 (1789), 284–286; *Daily Advertiser* (New York), June 3, 1789; Bangs, *History*, 1:279–86.

17. Asbury to Morrell, Sept. 9, 1789, Thomas Morrell Collection, GTS; Morrell to Cooper, Aug. 26, 1827, BC; Vickers, *Coke*, 126–30; Drinkhouse, *Methodist Reform*, 382–85.

18. On Methodists and politics in the early republic, see Nathan O. Hatch, "The Democratization of Christianity and the Character of American Politics," in *Religion and American Politics: From the Colonial Period to the 1980s*, ed. Mark A. Noll (New York: Oxford University Press, 1990), 92–120; John M. Murrin, "Religion and Politics in America from the First Settlements to the Civil War," in Noll, *Religion and American Politics*, 19–43.

19. Bangs, *History*, 1:244–45.

20. [MEC], *Proceedings of the Bishop and Presiding Elders of the Methodist-Episcopal Church, in Council Assembled, at Baltimore on the First Day of December, 1789* (Baltimore: William Goddard and James Angell, 1789), 3–7; *JLFA*, 1:614–15; Garrettson, *Journal*, 265; Lee, *Short History*, 146–53.

21. Lee, *Short History*, 148–53; Bangs, *History*, 302–6.

22. O'Kelly also later claimed that Asbury refused two "worthy" elders places at the council meeting. Nicholas Snethen answered that the two weren't presiding elders and therefore not entitled to seats. O'Kelly also claimed that Edward Morris, the elder who represented North Carolina at the council meeting, married and located soon after the meeting because "he would not travel under such a government." O'Kelly, *Author's Apology*, 13, 15–17, 18; Snethen, *Reply*, 15–18; O'Kelly, *Vindication*, 15–18; MacClenny, *James O'Kelly*, 61–73. On the incorporation issue, see Asbury to Ezekiel Cooper, Nov. 16, 1789, Cooper MSS 18, GTS. The transcript of this letter given in *JLFA*, 3:76–77 is incomplete. Asbury wasn't, of course, the only one to believe that the millennium was near, or that the Methodist church would play an important role in bringing it about. In identical letters to Ezekiel Cooper and Thomas Morrell written on Oct. 30, 1789, Thomas Coke wrote that God "I believe, will make the Methodist Connection the grand Instrument of bringing on the much to be wished for, the most ardently to be prayed for, Millennium." See Coke to Cooper, Oct. 30, 1789, Bishops' Autographs, and Coke to Morrell, Thomas Morrell Collection, GTS.

CHAPTER 11

1. Thomas Morrell, *Truth Discovered, or An Answer to the Reverend William Hammet's Appeal to Truth and Circumstances* (Charleston: I Silliman, 1792), 19–20; Ware, *Sketches*, 196–97. The 1791 minutes contain a Sept. 16, 1791, letter from Asbury warning Methodists "to be more cautious how they receive strange preachers." William Hammet later claimed that this warning was aimed specifically at him, but this seems unlikely, and Asbury denied it. *Minutes* (1794), 164; *JLFA*, 1:717.

2. *JLFA*, 3:122. The membership figures are from Wigger, *Taking Heaven*, 198–99.

3. *JLFA*, 1:620; 3:81.

4. *JLFA*, 1:625; Richey, *Methodist Conference*, 31, 37–44. On the 1790 district conferences, see *JLFA* 1:625, 628, 638–639, 641, 642, 647, 648–49, 650, 651; on the 1791 conferences, see 1:668, 670, 671, 672, 673, 674, 675, 698; on the 1792 conferences, see 1:704, 706, 708, 712, 713, 714, 716, 724, 726, 729, 730, 733, 735, 737.

5. *JLFA*, 1:627, 629. On early Methodism in Kentucky, see Bangs, *History*, 1:251–54.

6. *JLFA*, 1:498, 512, 513, 514, 525, 550, 573, 593, 596, 611, 629–632. Also see 1:492, 509, 510, 515, 517, 519, 533, 575, 592, 607, 608, 612, 613.

7. *JLFA*,1:632; *Minutes* (1794), 124; Gregory Evans Dowd, *A Spirited Resistance: The North American Indian Struggle for Unity, 1745–1815* (Baltimore: Johns Hopkins University Press, 1992), 95–115; John R. Finger, "Witness to Expansion: Bishop Francis Asbury on the Trans-Appalachian Frontier," *The Register of the Kentucky Historical Society*, 82:4 (1984): 334–57.

8. *JLFA*, 1:632–635; Whatcoat, manuscript journal, Aug. 1, 1789–May 25, 1791 (May 3, 1790), GTS. Asbury was at prayer when Peter Massie and John Clark approached him while the other men waited below. Also see Whatcoat, *Memoirs*, 26. A transcript of Whatcoat's journal, Aug. 1, 1789–Dec. 31, 1790, is given in Sweet,

Methodists, 74–122. Whatcoat and Asbury traveled together for much of this time, and Whatcoat's account parallels Asbury's journal.

9. *JLFA*, 1:635–40; A. H. Redford, *The History of Methodism in Kentucky*, vol. 1 (Nashville: Southern Methodist Publishing House), 67–70, 85–88.

10. *JLFA*, 1:641–42.

11. James Meacham, mss. journal, microfilm, DUL, entries for Feb. 26, March 11, 12, April. 4, 11, 17, 23, 1790; James O'kelly, *Essay on Negro Slavery* (Philadelphia: Prichard & Hall, 1789).

12. *JLFA*, 1:642; O'Kelly, *Apology*, 20, 21; O'Kelly, *Vindication*, 3–4.

13. *Discipline* (1785) in Tigert, *Constitutional History*, 549; David Sherman, *History of the Revisions of the Discipline of the Methodist Episcopal Church* (New York: Nelson & Phillips, 1874), 25–26, 164–65. Wesley admitted that his power might seem "arbitrary," but maintained that it wasn't "*unjust, unreasonable*, or *tyrannical.*" *Minutes* (British), 1:58–61; John Wesley to John Mason, Jan. 13, 1790, in Wesley, *Letters* (Telford), 8:196.

14. *JLFA*, 1:642, 644; O'Kelly, *Apology*, 22–24; Snethen, *Reply*, 19–20; O'Kelly, *Vindication*, 19–22; Snethen, *Answer*, 20–21; *Minutes* (1794), 140; MacClenny, *Life of O'Kelly*, 67–69; Kilgore, *O'Kelly Schism*, 15–16.

15. Whatcoat, mss. journal (June 20–Aug. 11, 1790); Meacham, mss. journal, Sept. 1, 5, 1790.

16. *JLFA*, 1:643–50.

17. *JLFA*, 1:650–51; Asbury to Ezekiel Cooper, Nov. 12, 1790, Cooper MSS 18, GTS; *Minutes* (1794), 131, 145.

18. *JLFA*, 1:644, 655–56. Much of James Meacham's and John Kobler's manuscript journals, to name only two, are devoted to similar examinations of core spirituality.

19. *JLFA*, 3:90–92. This letter is undated but probably written about this time. Ezekiel Cooper asked a similar set of questions in letter to a New York Methodist. See Cooper to Lancaster S. Burling, Nov. 23, 1807, Cooper MSS 16, GTS.

20. *JLFA*, 1:657, 659, 666; O'Kelly, *Apology*, 24–26, 28, 29; [MEC], *Minutes Taken at a Council of the Bishops and Delegated Elders of the Methodist-Episcopal Church: Held at Baltimore, in the State of Maryland, December 1, 1790* (Baltimore: W.Goddard and J. Angell, 1790); Kilgore, *O'Kelly Schism*, 16–17. Snethen later defended Asbury with regard to Cokesbury's finances. See Snethen, *Reply*, 21; O'Kelly, *Vindication*, 22–23; Snethen, *Answer*, 21–22.

21. *JLFA* 1:667–68, 3:93; O'Kelly, *Apology*, 29.

22. *JLFA*, 1:668–71; Coke, *Extracts* (1793), 148–51; O'Kelly, *Apology*, 29–30.

23. O'Kelly, *Apology*, 30; *JLFA*, 2:672; 3:94–95, 99; Coke, *Extracts* (1793), 152–53; M'Caine, *Letters*, 118; Drinkhouse, *Methodist Reform*, 295; John A. Vickers, "The Churchmanship of Thomas Coke," *MH*, 7:4 (July 1969): 15–28; William White to James Kemp, Oct. 30. 1806, MDA. White's letter to Kemp gives a full transcript of Coke's letter to White, April 24, 1791.

24. The quotations are from White's transcript of Coke's letter. See White to Kemp, Oct. 30, 1806. Also see Drinkhouse, *Methodist Reform*, 398–99; *Minutes* (1794), 161; Thomas Wallcut to James Freeman, Oct. 31, 1789, Thomas Wallcut papers, box 2, folder 1, American Antiquarian Society, Worcester, Mass.;William Capers, "Autobiography," in

Life of William Capers, D.D., One of the Bishops of the Methodist Episcopal Church, South, ed. William M. Wightman (Nashville: Southern Methodist Publishing House, 1859), 140. Coke's desire for a reunion with the Episcopal Church in America fits with his growing attachment to the Church of England in this period. In August 1790 he wrote to William Wilberforce assuring him that rumors that he favored a separation from the Church were false. "I not only wish for no such thing but would oppose a separation from the establishment with my utmost influence, even if that, or a division in the connection, was the unavoidable alternative." Coke to Wilberforce, Aug. 24, 1790, transcript, Thomas Coke Papers, JRL.

25. The quotations are from White to Kemp, Oct. 30, 1806. Also see *JLFA*, 3:96; Vickers, *Coke*, 176–90; Drinkhouse, *Methodist Reform*, 399–414. Vickers gives a fuller and more sympathetic account of Coke's reunification efforts than I have presented here. According to Drinkhouse, White kept Coke's letter secret until 1806, when a public debate in Maryland over the letter's existence forced him to make it public. In the letter, Coke also blamed Asbury for publishing portions of his (Coke's) journal in the *Arminian Magazine* that contained criticisms of Devereux Jarratt, and which, Coke now claimed, he had written in haste and never intended for publication.

26. *JLFA*, 1:673, 3:99; Coke, *Extracts* (1793), 154–57; Coke to Seabury, May 14, 1791, transcript, Thomas Coke papers, JRL; Drinkhouse, *Methodist Reform*, 407; Vickers, *Coke*, 175–76; 192–95; Tiffany, *Protestant Episcopal Church*, 406–8; Stokes and Scott, *Christian Church*, 9–10; M'Caine, *History and Mystery*, 27.

27. Coke to Morrell, May 17, 1791, Thomas Morrell Collection, GTS; *JLFA* 3:383; Drinkhouse, *Methodist Reform*, 406–7, 505–6; Vickers, *Coke*, 184,186–87; Bangs, *History*, 1:327–34. In another letter written before he left America, Coke asserted that from the time Wesley learned of his "excommunication" from the American minutes in 1787, "he began to hold down his head and to think he had lived long enough." Drinkhouse, *Methodist Reform*, 406–7; M'Caine, *Letters*, 112. Drinkhouse argues that Asbury learned of Coke's reunification scheme by opening a letter from White to Coke that was given to Asbury in Baltimore in a few days after Coke left in early May 1791. See Drinkhouse, *Methodist Reform*, 409–14. A copy of this letter is printed, without date, in William White, *Memoirs of the Protestant Episcopal Church in the United States of America* (Philadelphia: S. Potter & Co., 1820), 430–31; and in Bangs, *History*, 2:204–5. White wrote to Coke that he could see difficulties in Coke's plan, but that "I do not think them insuperable, provided there be a conciliatory disposition on both sides.-So far as I am concerned, I think that such a disposition exists."

28. J. G. J. Bend, "Over righteousness," mss sermon dated Aug. 29, 1791, and Bend to Duke, Nov. 3, 1798, MDA; Sprague, *Annals*, 5:353–55. Duke was a former Methodist preacher who was ordained a deacon in the Protestant Episcopal Church by Bishop Samuel Seabury in November 1785. Bend was ordained a deacon in the Protestant Episcopal Church by Bishop Provoost in July 1787. Burgess, *List of Deacons*, 3; Sprague, *Annals*, 5:309–14. The cover of Bend's sermon, "Over righteousness," lists four dates on which he preached it: Sept. 4, 1791; March 8, 1795; Aug. 15, 1802; and Feb. 24, 1811.

29. Coke to Benson, July 15, 1791, transcript, Thomas Coke Papers, JRL; Cooper to Coke, Aug. 11, 1791, Cooper MSS 16, GTS.

30. *JLFA*, 1:674, 3:101–2; Coke to Cooper, Nov. 22, 1791, Bishop's Autographs collection, GTS; Asbury to Edward Dromgoole, Dec. 24, 1791, Edward Dromgoole Papers, SHC; Vickers, *Coke*, 186–91; Drinkhouse, *Methodist Reform*, 406–14. On Nov. 6, 1791, Asbury wrote to Freeborn Garrettson, "Dr. Coke has made uncommon acknowledgments to me. And wishes to come to be anything under me here." *MH* 39:3 (April 2001): 205. With Coke now repentant, Asbury attempted to bridge some of the gap with O'Kelly. "Let all past conduct between thee and me, be buried, and never come before the Conference, or elsewhere,-send me the dove," Asbury wrote to O'Kelly in September 1791. Asbury admitted that when "thy face was not towards me" in the dispute over the council, "[I] did not treat thee with that respect due to one who had suffered so much for the cause of truth and liberty." If this letter led to any sort of temporary reconciliation, O'Kelly doesn't acknowledge it in his memoirs. *JLFA*, 3:104–5; O'Kelly, *Apology*, 31; Drinkhouse, *Methodist Reform*, 407.

31. *JLFA*, 1:673–77, 681, 684; 3:98.

32. S. G. Goodrich, *Recollections of a Lifetime, or Men and Things I Have Seen: In a Series of Familiar Letters to a Friend, Historical, Biographical, Anecdotal, and Descriptive,* 2 vols. (New York: Miller, Orton and Mulligan, 1856), 1:216–18; Richard D. Shiels, "The Methodist Invasion of Congregational New England," in *Methodism and the Shaping of American Culture,* ed. Nathan O. Hatch and John H. Wigger (Nashville: Kingswood Books, 2001), 257–80; Lee, *Short History*, 161–65; Bangs, *History*, 1:290–95. On the resurgence of New England Congregationalism in the 1790s, see David W. Kling, *A Field of Divine Wonders: The New Divinity and Village Revivals in Northwestern Connecticut, 1792–1822* (University Park, Pa.: Pennsylvania State University Press, 1993), 12–34, 234–37; and James R. Rohrer, *Keepers of the Covenant: Frontier Missions and the Decline of Congregationalism, 1774–1818* (New York: Oxford University Press, 1995).

33. *JLFA*, 1:678–79. Jonathan Edwards the younger was the minister of the White Haven Church in New Haven.

34. *JLFA*, 1:679, 684–85.

35. *JLFA*, 1:686–91, 725.

CHAPTER 12

1. William Glendinning, *The Life of William Glendinning, Preacher of the Gospel. Written by Himself* (Philadelphia: Printed for the Author, at the office of W.W. Woodward, 1795), 10–32. Quotations from pp. 11, 12, 15, 17, 19, 29–30. Also see Bangs, *History*, 2:255; Lednum, *Rise*, 152. Benjamin Rush met Glendinning in Philadelphia on June 2, 1792, recording the essence of his story much as it is given in Glendinning's memoir. See Benjamin Rush, *The Autobiography of Benjamin Rush: His "Travels Through Life" Together With His Commonplace Book for 1789–1813,* ed. George W. Corner (Princeton, N.J.: Princeton University Press, 1948), 220–21.

2. Glendinning, *Life*, 2–11; *Minutes* (1794), 14, 18, 20, 24, 28, 32, 36, 44, 52, 60, 67. Glendinning, spelled Glendenning in some records, joined the itinerancy on trial in 1775, the first year that his name appears in the minutes. In 1777 he was one of five American preachers appointed to take over the leadership of American Methodism

should all of Wesley's preachers return to Europe. See Watters, *Short Account*, 56–57; Lednum, *Rise*, 190.

3. Meacham, mss. journal, April 19, 24, 1790. Meacham records accounts of two other people who lost their mental balance. The first, Caleb Cole, the brother of the itinerant Leroy Cole, was a former circuit rider who by June 1795 had become "a poor Insane, distracted man." Meacham reports that "He appears in his reason, but quite restless, travels about to an fro, through the county & some days eats not any thing at all." The second was a woman Meacham encountered in January 1796. Meacham raises the possibility that the woman's condition might be physiological in nature: "I saw a Woman, who once was happy in God, & as I am told was one of the most sensible Women of her age but now is quite out of her reason, who can account for these things? Is it possible that Satan can have power to chane [chain] the right reason of a Human Soul, up in the dark caverns of distraction? Or is [it] a constitutional disorder?" Meacham, mss. journal, June 4, 1795, Jan. 15, 1796.

4. Glendinning, *Life*, 32–66 (quotations from pp. 38, 39–40, 41 and 53); *JLFA*, 1:658–59. Coke doesn't mention his exchange with Glendinning at the Petersburg conference in his journal, nor does Asbury. In September 1792 Glendinning wrote to the General Conference meeting in Baltimore, with the conference responding by letter in November 1792. Glendinnning subsequently wrote letters to Asbury in June 1793 and December 1794, and a letter to the traveling preachers as a body in December 1794. All essentially repeat Glendinning's criticisms of the church and his desire to return to the itinerancy, but only on his terms. See *JLFA*, 3:105– 06, 111–12; Glendinning, *Life*, 65–66, 68–70, 71–72, 73–76, 83–87, 88–92.

5. Glendinning, *Life*, 55–64; Garrettson, *Journal*, 96, 170; Philip Bruce to Daniel Hitt, Dec. 6, 1791, "Letters to Hitt"; *JLFA*, 1:659. For the excerpts from Garrettson's journal, see the *Arminian Magazine* (London), vol. 17 (January-October, 1794), pp. 3–9, 57–62, 113–19, 169–75, 225–31, 281–87, 337–43, 392–98, 449–55, 505–11. For examples of sensational supernatural stories from the *Arminian Magazine* (London), see vol. 8 (1785), 32–33, 93–96, 318–21, 375–78; vol. 9 (1786), 332–33, 384–86; vol. 10 (1787), 37–38, 427–29, 439–41. Asbury was even harsher in his assessment of Glendinning in a December 1791 letter to Edward Dromgoole, writing, "As to Glendinning, I believe Satan is in him and will never come out." Asbury to Dromgoole, Dec. 24, 1791, Edward Dromgoole Papers, SHC. For a different interpretation of Glendinning and Asbury, see Hyerman, *Southern Cross*, 28–33, 58–61, 63–66 (quotation from 59).

6. Abbott's autobiography is filled with descriptions of visions, prophetic dreams and raucous meetings. It was perhaps the most widely read Methodist memoir of the nineteenth and early twentieth centuries. At least 18 editions were published in the antebellum period. George Peck remembered that, about 1813, shortly after his conversion as a young man, his family gathered in the evening to read Abbott, one of the few books they had. "What a glorious time we had reading the Life of Benjamin Abbott! . . . What exclamations of wonder and pleasure there were! I remember well how sorry I was that the book is so small." Frank Bartleman, chronicler of the early Pentecostal movement, recalled receiving "great help" from Abbott's memoir about 1903. See George Peck, *The Life and Times of Rev. George Peck, D. D.* (New York: Nelson & Phillips, 1874), 51–52; Frank

Bartleman, *From Plow to Pulpit, From Maine to California* (n.p.: Frank Bartleman, 1924, 95–96; reprinted in *Witness to Pentecost: The Life of Frank Bartleman* (New York: Garland Publishing, 1985). On Abbott's dreams and broader influence, see Mechal Sobel, *Teach Me Dreams: The Search for Self in the Revolutionary Era* (Princeton, N.J.: Princeton University Press, 2000), 13; Taves, *Fits, Trances, & Visions*, 92–95.

7. Glendinning, *Life*, 79, 80. Glendinning also accused the Methodists of passing a "secret minute" in their annual conference recommending "to their people not to buy any books of me," and doing everything they could to keep him from preaching anywhere. With regard to Asbury, Glendinning wrote: "I think too much power and authority are lodged in the hands of one man, while the people are mere cyphers,-not only excluded from all share in government, but deprived even of a right to complain of any measure whatever. *Passive submission*, or *actual exclusion*, is your only alternative." He also accused southern Methodists of hypocrisy regarding their stance on slavery. Glendinning, *Life*, 67, 77, 94, 99, 101–2.

8. Glendinning and Asbury had something of a reconciliation in January 1814. Writes Asbury: "William Glendenning and I met, and embraced each other in peace." *JLFA*, 2:752. On Glendinning's later endeavors, see P. J. Kernodle, *Lives of Christian Ministers* (Richmond, Va.: Central Publishing Company, 1909), 44–46.

9. *Minutes* (British), 186; Coke, *Extracts* (1793), 49–66, especially 55. Coke was onboard the same ship with Hammet.

10. Coke reported that when he found Hammet, he "lay dangerously ill of a fever and ague, and a violent inflammation in one of his eyes, and was worn almost to a skeleton with . . . fatigue." Coke, *Extracts* (1793), 137, 142–46; William Hammet, *An Impartial Statement of the Known Inconsistencies of the Reverend Dr. Coke, in His Official Station, as Superintendent of the Methodist Missionaries in the West-Indies* (Charleston: W. P. Young, 1792), 5; D.A. Reily, "William Hammett: Missionary and Founder of the Primitive Methodist Connection," *MH*, 10:1 (October 1971): 30–43; Frederick E. Maser and George A. Singleton, "Further Branches of Methodism Are Founded," in *The History of American Methodism*, ed. Emory S. Bucke, 3 vols. (New York: Abingdon Press, 1964), 1:617–22; Vickers, *Coke*, 173–74. Hammet spelled his name with one "t," as did most of his contemporaries, thus I have adopted this spelling of the name.

11. *JLFA*, 1:668, 674; Lee, *Short History*, 206; Drinkhouse, *Methodist Reform*, 388; Reily, "William Hammett;" Hammet, *Rejoindre: Being a Defense of the Truths Contained in An Appeal to Truth and Circumstances, In Seven Letters Addressed to the Reverend Mr. Morrell* (Charleston: Printed for the Author by I. Silliman, 1792), 11–12, 27–28; John Dickins, *Friendly Remarks on the Late Proceedings of the Rev. Mr. Hammet* (Philadelphia: Printed by Parry Hall, 1792), 12; Thomas Morrell, *Truth Discovered*, 6–10, 16–43. Asbury heard Hammet preach in New York in late May 1791, noting that Hammet's first sermon was "not well received" and that his second was "still more exceptional." *JLFA*, 1:675; Taves, *Fits, Trances & Visions*, 93–94.

12. *JLFA*, 1:705, 706; Hammet, *Rejoindre*, 29, appendix, 1–4; Reily, "William Hammett."

13. Dickins, *Friendly Remarks*, 6, 7, 9–10, 35. Also see Thomas Morrell, *Truth Discovered*, 16–43. The pamphlets associated with this dispute reached a fairly wide audience. While

riding the Pamunkey circuit in Virginia in October 1792, James Meacham reports reading "three pieces of Controversy[,] two of which wrote by Mr. Hammet of Charlestown lately left the Methodist connection[;] he was an elder. The other wrote by the Rev.[d] T. Morrell of our order of the same place." Meacham, mss. journal, Oct. 25, 1792.

14. Reily, "William Hammet;" Drinkhouse, *Methodist Reform*, 389; John Phillips, *A Narrative Shewing Why the Rev. J. Phillips is Not in Connexion With the Episcopalian Methodists . . . Together With a Summary Account of His Connexion With, &c. The Rev. W. Hammet* (Charleston: Printed for the Author, 1796), 33. In a 1793 pamphlet, Coke wrote that the leaders of Hammet's home society had urged Coke not to admit Hammet as a preacher "on account of his excessive self-sufficiency," and that Wesley also voiced concerns. Coke also claimed that Hammet's Charleston church welcomed "men that keep Mulatto-mistresses, and others who are Polygamists, who have left their wives in the Northern States, and are now married in the Southern." Thomas Coke, *An Address to the Preachers Lately in Connexion with the Rev. John Wesley: Containing Strictures on a Pamphlet Published by Mr. William Hammet; Intitled, "An Impartial Statement of the Known Inconsistencies of the Rev. Dr. Coke, &c."* (London, 1793), 5–6, 14–19. Coke had evidently been hard on William Brazier prior to his split with Hammet. "I am sorry to say that it is not only my opinion but many others, that Brother Brazier has not received that good treatment from the Doctor, which he was entitled to. Sister Brazier & the Sick Baby are truly to be pitied, in being thus hurried backwards and forwards at the very great Expence & Risque of the Lives." Wm. Tead to William Hammet, Kingston, Jamaica, June 23, 1792, Hammet Papers, DUL. In 1794 Hammet's followers collected enough money to build a meetinghouse on Nassau Island in the Bahamas. See James Johnstone to William Hammet, April 5, 1794, Hammet Papers, DUL. Adam Cloud built a meetinghouse in Savannah after joining Hammet and still controlled the property in 1807. See Jesse Lee to Ezekiel Cooper, April 16, 1807, Cooper MSS 15, GTS.

15. Hammet, *Impartial Statement*, 13–16; Coke, *Address to the Preachers*, 16–19; Vickers, *Coke*, 149–72; Reily, "William Hammet." Baxter was a storekeeper on Antigua before Coke arrived in December 1786. A former class leader, he gave up storekeeping to become a missionary. See Joseph Sutcliffe's short biography of Coke in Coke, *Extracts* (1816), 19.

16. Coke, *Extracts* (1816), 247. Asbury wrote to Daniel Hitt in January 1804 from Rembert's Chapel, South Carolina, "Here Mr. Brazer, only surviving minister of Mr. Hammett's Fraternity, has had conversation with me and Bishop Coke, about giving up the whole concern to us." Asbury to Hitt, Jan. 21, 1804, "Letters to Hitt." Phillips, *Narrative*, iii–iv, 32–36; *JLFA*, 2:42; *Minutes* (1840), 1:48; Morrell, *Truth Discovered*, 31; Hammet, *Rejoindre*, 20; Reily, "William Hammett." Asbury was in Charleston in February 1795 and met Phillips soon after his split with Hammet. Phillips was "in want of money. Our friends opened their hearts and gave him twenty or thirty dollars. He is not clear on Original Sin; so that we cannot, and dare not employ him; yet . . . I hope he is a good man; but, good or bad, he ought not to starve." *JLFA*, 2:42. Dow repeated the charge that Hammet died drunk in *Cosmopolite* in 1815, leading Hammet's son to sue Dow for libel. Dow lost the case and was sentenced to twenty-four hours in jail and a fine of $1.00 plus costs, but the governor apparently pardoned him.

17. William Capers joined the itinerancy in 1808. He later came into possession of "a parcel of letters between Mr. Hammett and Mr. Wesley," given to him by one of Hammet's sons. The letters, according to Capers, indicate that Hammet "had the confidence of Mr. Wesley & to the last of his life." William Capers, "Autobiography," in William M. Wightman, *Life of William Capers, D. D., One of the Bishops of the Methodist Episcopal Church, South; Including an Autobiography* (Nashville: Southern Methodist Publishing House, 1859), 24, 88–90, Boehm, *Reminiscences*, 214–15.

18. JLFA, 3:110. Within a decade of Hammet's death, nearly all of his churches had joined the MEC.

19. JLFA, 1:711, 712, 733; Nathan Bangs, *The Life of the Rev. Freeborn Garrettson: Compiled From His Printed and Manuscript Journals* (New York: G. Lane & C. B. Tippett, 1845), 205.

20. John Kobler reported that there were 114 preachers present, while Thomas Morrell and Richard Whatcoat put the number at 116. John Kobler, "Journal, 1789–1799," entry for Nov. 1, 1792, LLM; Richard Whatcoat, "Journal," Nov. 1, 1792; Thomas Morrell, "Journal of Thomas Morrell," TMS, MAHC, entry for Nov. 2, 1792; *Minutes* (1794), 170–76.

21. M'Caine, *Letters*, 119; Stokes and Scott, *Christian Church*, 9–10; MacClenny, *O'Kelly*, 78. Also see Snethen, *Reply*, 22–23. Hammet also complained that the General Conference "is only to be an aristocratic one." See Morrell, *Truth Discovered*, 31.

22. Lewis Curts, *The General Conferences of the Methodist Episcopal Church, From 1792 to 1896* (Cincinnati: Curts & Jennings, New York: Eaton & Mains, 1900), 1–2; Drink-house, *Methodist Reform*, 408; O'Kelly, *Apology*, 31. On the O'Kelly schism also see Lee, *Life of Jesse Lee*, 273–87. As early as August 1791, Ezekiel Cooper warned Coke against further support of O'Kelly: "I fear our brother in the lower part of Virginia is too much prejudiced against Mr. A. and I candidly believe his ambition carries him to measures unbecoming a servant of Jesus in filling others minds, with his own prejudices to strengthen his party." Cooper to Coke, Aug. 11, 1791, Cooper MSS 16, GTS.

23. Curts, *General Conferences*, 2–3; Ware, *Sketches*, 181–82, 220–21; O'Kelly, *Apology*, 35; O'Kelly, *Vindication*, 5. William Colbert noted in his journal that O'Kelly's motion was "abley defended by O'Kelley, Ivey, Hull, Garrettson, and Swift-and oppos'd by Reed, Willis, Morell, Everett and others." Colbert, "Journal," 1:85 (Nov. 2, 1792).

24. JLFA, 1:734. It isn't clear exactly when Asbury sent this letter to the conference. It is dated Nov. 8, 1792, in his published journal, but by then the debate and final vote on O'Kelly's motion was over. O'Kelly later wrote that "after leaving conference in the height of the dispute," Asbury "sent letters back, and in them did he plead against the appeal." O'Kelly, *Vindication*, 26.

25. Ware, *Sketches*, 220–21; Kobler, "Journal," Nov. 1, 1792; O'Kelly, *Apology*, 38; Snethen, *Reply*, 27–32; JLFA, 3:114; MacClenny, *James O'Kelly*, 87–95. On Hull, see Chreitzberg, *Methodism in the Carolinas*, 86–87. Methodism, O'Kelly later wrote, ought to consist of "districts . . . formed in a kind of confederacy." See O'Kelly, *Apology*, 12.

26. Watters, *Short Account*, 96–98, 106; Watters located in 1783. He reentered the traveling connection in 1786, but only for two quarters. Watters, *Short Account*, 99, 108.

27. Kobler, "Journal," Nov. 1, 1792; Bangs, *Life of Garrettson*, 206. "It was surely a very fatal hour of papal darkness in which a law passed, that an injured brother and

minister in the church of Christ, should have no redress!" O'Kelly later lamented. See O'Kelly, *Apology*, 39.

28. O'Kelly, *Apology*, 40–43; Kilgore, *O'Kelly Schism*, 25–27; Stokes and Scott, *Christian Church*, 11–15. Nicholas Snethen and others later concluded that O'Kelly left the church for three reasons: (1) he was frustrated at not being elected a bishop; (2) he was bitter at having a manuscript rejected for publication; and (3) he feared being expelled for holding Unitarian beliefs. See Snethen, *Reply*, 32–33, 43; O'Kelly, *Vindication*, 27–28; Snethen, *Answer*, 24–46.

29. O'Kelly, *Vindication*, 29, 30, 59. Asbury later concluded that "to make himself independent," O'Kelly had "dragged in the little Doctor, whom, a little before, he would have banished from the continent." See Asbury to Thomas Morrell, June 6, 1793, *World Parish* (April 1960): 31.

30. Meacham, mss. journal, Sept. 9, 1795; Watters, *Short Account*, 107.

31. *JLFA*, 1:736; O'Kelly, *Apology*, 43–44; Snethen, *Reply*, 34–36; O'Kelly, *Vindication*, 28–29; Kilgore, *O'Kelly Schism*, 27–28.

32. O'Kelly, *Apology*, 45–51; Lee, *Short History*, 202–203; Kilgore, *O'Kelly Schism*, 30–33; Stokes and Scott, *Christian Church*, 22, 25–27; Leroy Lee, *Jesse Lee*, 284–285; MacClenny, *James O'Kelly*, 4, 110–22; *JLFA*, 1:775, 3:124. O'Kelly's followers met for an earlier conference at Piney Grove, Va., on the Amelia circuit on Aug. 2, 1793. Following the conference, they sent Asbury a petition to call a special conference, which Asbury rejected.

33. Meacham, mss. journal, Nov. 27, Dec. 25–30, 1792, Jan. 5, 9, 11, 13, 31, Feb. 3, 11, 15, 16, 17, 22. The quotation is from March 22, 1793. William Spencer was another young preacher who might have followed O'Kelly but didn't. "I love my dear Brother O'Kelly as I do my own soul," Spencer wrote while riding the Surry circuit in 1792. William Spencer, "Diary," typescript for June 9–July 31, 1790, RMC, pp. 20–22; *Minutes* (1794), 140, 170. Spencer rode the Cumberland circuit in O'Kelly's district in 1792.

34. Meacham, mss. journal, July. 22, Aug. 13, 16, 17, 25, Sept. 2, Oct. 8, 10, 12, 1794, Feb. 16, April 6, July 29, 31, 1795 (quotations are from Aug. 25, 1794, and July 31, 1795). Olive is mentioned in MacClenny, *James O'Kelly*, 131, 150.

35. *JLFA*, 3:138.

36. C. J. Taylor, a Methodist living on the Limestone circuit in Kentucky, wrote to a friend in January 1796 that "the work of God" seemed to be "at a stand" throughout the district. "O Kelly's party is in some circuits; the devil is in all of them." The Methodist preachers Henry Smith and John Watson also remarked on the rise of the "Republicans" in Kentucky in 1796. See Taylor to Daniel Hitt, Jan. 22, 1796; Smith to Hitt, March 23, 1796, and April 25, 1796, and Watson to Hitt, July 15, 1796, "Letters to Hitt"; Kilgore, *O'Kelly Schism*, 33–34, 37; Sweet, *Virginia Methodism*, 134; Lee, *Short History*, 205; Stokes and Scott, *Christian Church*, 37–51; MacClenny, *James O'Kelly*, 121–68. MacClenny says that the name Christian Church was adopted in August 1794. But Nicholas Snethen still called O'Kelly's followers Republican Methodists in 1800. See Snethen, *Reply*, 60. In 1926, before its merger with the Congregational Church, the Christian Church numbered only about 112,000 members. O'Kelly died in 1826. Also see James E. Atkins, "Early Methodism in Surry County, VA. and Carsley United Methodist Church," unpublished mss, VHS; Bangs, *History*, 345–46, 351–56.

37. Robert Paine, *Life and Times of William McKendree, Bishop of the Methodist Episcopal Church* (Nashville: M. E. Church, South, 1893), 17–125 (quotation from 56); E. E. Hoss, *William McKendree: A Biographical Study* (Nashville: M. E. Church, South, 1914), 9–61; Gorrie, *Eminent Methodist Ministers*, 271–72; Simpson, *Cyclopedia*, 577–78.

38. *JLFA*, 1:736; MEC, *Minutes Taken at the Several Conferences of the Methodist-Episcopal Church, in America, For the Year 1793* (Philadelphia: Printed by Parry Hall for John Dickins, 1793), 9; *Minutes* (1794), 208; Paine, *William McKendree*, 123–29; Hoss, *William McKendree*, 61–65.

CHAPTER 13

1. Asbury to his parents, Sept. 1, 1793, [1794], Sept. 22, 1794, Oct. 30, 1795, MAHC; *JLFA*, 3:137.

2. *JLFA*, 1:743–761. The quotation is from 746.

3. *JLFA*, 1:357, 751, 762, 764; Asbury to Morrell, Feb. 17, 1791, *World Parish* (April 1960): 30; Marilyn James-Kracke to John Wigger, e-mails, May 15 and 26, 2006.

4. *JLFA*, 767. In the South, the most prolonged debate over whether religion should be generally established or left to private conscience occurred in Virginia, where Jefferson's bill for religious freedom was finally passed in 1785 after several years of debate. Massachusetts maintained some form of establishment until 1833, Connecticut until 1819, and New Hampshire until 1818. See Leonard W. Levy, *The Establishment Clause: Religion and the First Amendment*, 2nd ed. (Chapel Hill: University of North Carolina Press, 1994), 27–68; Sidney E. Mead, *The Lively Experiment: The Shaping of Christianity in America* (New York: Harper & Row, 1963), 103–33; Thomas E. Buckley, *Church and State in Revolutionary Virginia 1776–1787* (Charlottesville: University Press of Virginia, 1977).

5. Ezekiel Cooper, untitled manuscript journal, GTS (Oct. 18, 1793), vol. 10; George A. Phoebus, *Beams of Light on Early Methodism in America: Chiefly Drawn From the Diary, Letters, Manuscripts, Documents, and Original Tracts of the Rev. Ezekiel Cooper* (New York: Phillips & Hunt, 1887), 175.

6. Lee to Cooper, Aug. 11, 1789, Cooper MSS 15, GTS.

7. Lee, *Life of Jesse Lee*, 215–49; Phoebus, *Beams of Light*, 159–61. On Lee's appointments from 1790 to 1793, see *Minutes* (1794), 144, 159, 176, 191.

8. Cooper, mss. journal (Feb. 9, March 23, 1793), vol. 9, (June 6, 1793), vol. 10; Phoebus, *Beams of Light*, 159–61, 164, 165; Asbury to Morrell, June 6, 1793, July 13, 1793, *World Parish* (April 1960): 31, 32–33. James Mudge, *History of the New England Conference of the Methodist Episcopal Church, 1796–1910* (Boston: Published by the Conference, 1910), 47.

9. Cooper, mss. journal (July 31, Aug. 1, 1793), vol. 10.

10. Cooper, mss. journal (Aug. 1, 1793), vol. 10; Phoebus, *Beams of Light*, 167–70.

11. *JLFA*, 1:767; Cooper, mss. journal (Aug. 1, Dec. 20, 1793), vol. 10; Phoebus, *Beams of Light*, 168, 172; Asbury to Thomas Morrell, Jan. 22, 1794, *World Parish* (April 1960): 34; Jesse Lee gives only a single line to the 1793 Lynn conference in his history of early American Methodism. See Lee, *Short History*, 193. Leroy Lee also avoids discussing the 1793 Lynn conference in his biography of Jesse Lee, noting only that "It is often wise

'to conceal a matter,' especially when its publication does not tend to edification." Lee, *Life of Jesse Lee*, 292–93.

12. Cooper, manuscript journal (Oct. 2, 1794), vol. 11; Phoebus, *Beams of Light*, 190. Lee and Cooper remained friends and carried on an active correspondence for many years. For example, see Lee's letters to Cooper, April 16 and May 27, 1807, Cooper MSS 15, GTS.

13. *JLFA*, 1:769; *Minutes* (1794), 179.

14. *Dorland's*, s.v. "Fever, yellow"; Michael B.A. Oldstone, *Viruses, Plagues, and History* (New York: Oxford University Press, 1998), 45–72; Dorothy H. Crawford, *The Invisible Enemy: A Natural History of Viruses* (Oxford: Oxford University Press, 2000), 23–27; R.S. Bray, *Armies of Pestilence: The Impact of Disease on History* (New York: Barnes & Noble, 1996), 107–13; Bob Arnebeck, *Destroying Angel: Yellow Fever, Benjamin Rush and the Birth of Modern Medicine*, http://members.aol.com/Fever1793.

15. For Rush's account of the epidemic, see Benjamin Rush to Julia Rush, letters dated Aug. 21 to Nov. 11, 1793, in Benjamin Rush, *Letters of Benjamin Rush*, ed. L.H. Butterfield, 2 vols. (Princeton, N.J.: Princeton University Press, 1951), 2:637–745. Rush gives a detailed description of the methods he used to treat yellow fever in an Oct. 3, 1793, letter to John R. B. Rodgers. See Rush, *Letters*, 2:694–700. On the man from whom Rush took 144 ounces of blood, see Rush to John Redman Coxe, Sept. 19, 1794, Rush, *Letters*, 2:750. On Rush and his use of calomel and jalap, see John Duffy, *From Humors to Medical Science: A History of American Medicine*, 2nd ed. (Urbana: University of Illinois Press, 1993), 62–68; J.H. Powell, *Bring Out Your Dead: The Great Plague of Yellow Fever in Philadelphia in 1793* (Philadelphia: University of Pennsylvania Press, 1949), 69–89, 114–39, 202–15.

16. *JLFA*, 1:770 (also see 3:122); Catherine Garrettson, "Journal," June 30, 1793, Garrettson papers, MAHC; Arnebeck, *Destroying Angel*.

17. *JLFA*, 1:770–777, Asbury to Ezekiel Cooper, Nov. 23, 2793, Cooper MSS 18, GTS.

18. *JLFA*, 1:778; 2:3–6; James-Kracke to Wigger, e-mail, May 26, 2006. On Asbury's and Bruce's illnesses, also see Asbury to Thomas Morrell, Jan. 22, 1794, *World Parish* (April 1960): 34.

19. Asbury's reading included four hundred pages of Thomas Prince's magazine, *Christian History* (the pro-Great Awakening periodical favored by Jonathan Edwards and published 1743–1745 in Boston), William Gordon's history of the American Revolution (published in 1788), and a five-hundred-page collection of sermons delivered in 1733 by Isaac Watts and five other ministers. As always, Asbury's reading was fairly eclectic when he had the time for it. Thomas Prince, ed., *The Christian History, Containing Accounts of the Revival and Propagation of Religion in Great-Britain, America, etc.* (Boston: S. Kneeland and T. Green for T. Prince, No. 1–104, March 5, 1743–Feb. 23, 1745); William Gordon, *The History of the Rise, Progress, and Establishment of the Independence of the United States of America*, 4 vols. (London: Printed for the Author, 1788; reprinted in New York in 1789 and 1794); Isaac Watts, Daniel Neal, and John Guyse, eds., *Faith and Practice Represented in Fifty-Four Sermons on the Principal Heads of the Christian Religion: Preached at Berry Street, 1733, by Six Ministers*, 2 vols. (London, 1735; reprinted in 1739, 1757, and 1792). On Edwards and *Christian History*, see Marsden, *Jonathan Edwards*, 279–80.

20. Asbury to Kobler, Jan. 22, 1794, MAHC. Kobler acknowledged receiving "directory letters" from Asbury and meeting "our dear Bishop" at Botetourt County, Va., in May 1794. Barnabas McHenry served as president of the Kentucky conference. See Kobler, "Journal" for April 1 and May 24, 1794.

21. Kobler, "Journal," Oct. 6, 1797; Simpson, *Cyclopedia*, 520–21; *Minutes* (1794), 140, 150, 156, 167, 173, 189; James. B. Finley, *Sketches of Western Methodism: Biographical, Historical and Miscellaneous* (Cincinnati: Methodist Book Concern, 1854), 163–64. Kobler apparently became a deacon and elder almost simultaneously. Kobler, "Journal," May 25, 1793, and May 24, 1794.

22. M. H. Moore, *Sketches of the Pioneers of Methodism in North Carolina and Virginia* (Nashville: Southern Methodist Publishing House, 1884; reprint Greenwood, S.C.: Attic Press, 1977), 83–92; *JLFA*, 2:650–51; Boehm, *Reminiscences*, 323–25. Poythress died in 1818. He may have started losing his mental grip about 1794 or 1795. See Finley, *Sketches*, 138–41; Redford, *Methodism in Kentucky*, 1:37–43, 97–99.

23. *JLFA*, 2:3–111 (quotation from 84). The 2,300 mile figure for early 1796 is Asbury's own estimate; see *JLFA*, 2:90.

24. Asbury to Morrell, June 6, 1793, *World Parish* (April 1960): 31. Asbury estimated that he was writing a thousand letters a year in January 1796. See *JLFA*, 2:76. I calculated the percentage of Methodists in Maryland, Virginia, and North Carolina in 1796 from the *Minutes* (1840), 1:68–69.

25. MEC, *The Doctrines and Discipline of the Methodist Episcopal Church, in America, Revised and Approved at the General Conference, Held at Baltimore, in the State of Maryland, in November, 1792: in Which Thomas Coke and Francis Asbury presided*, 8th ed. (Philadelphia: John Dickins, 1792), 32. The ninth edition of the *Discipline*, published in Philadelphia in 1797, contains this same passage.

26. Asbury to Cooper, Jan. 2, 1795, Cooper MSS 18, GTS; *JLFA*, 1:747–748; 2:51, 55, 79, 92, 94, 95; *Discipline* (1784), in Tigert, *Constitutional History*, 538–39.

27. Cooper, mss. journal (July 14–19, 1794), vol. 11; Phoebus, *Beams of Light*, 186–87.

28. Asbury to Cooper, Nov. 23, 1793, Cooper MSS 18, GTS; Cooper, mss. journal (Feb. 10, April 8, 9, 1794), vol. 11; Asbury to Morrell, Jan. 22, 1794, *World Parish* (April 1960): 33; Dickins to Cooper, April 10, 1794, Cooper MSS 15, GTS; Scherer, *Ezekiel Cooper*, 85–87; Phoebus, *Beams of Light*, 191; Simpson, *Cyclopedia*, 257. Cooper frequently uses the initials "P.B." to refer to Polly Bemis in his journal, but he also mentions a "sister Maria Bemis" in a Sept. 15, 1794, journal entry.

29. Cooper, mss. journal (June 13, 20, July 11, Aug. 7, 1794), vol. 11.

30. Cooper, mss. journal (Sept. 12, 15, 18, 26, Oct. 1, 17, 19, 1794), vol. 11.

31. Cooper, mss. journal (Oct. 25, Nov. 24, 1794), vol. 11.

32. *JLFA* 2:48, 66. On Reuben Ellis, see Moore, *Pioneers of Methodism*, 196–204; *Minutes* (1840), 67.

33. Asbury to Cooper, Jan. 2, 1795, Cooper MSS 18, GTS; Francis Asbury to Martha Haskins, Feb. 17, 1796, Methodist Bishops collection, HSP.

34. *JLFA*, 2:84.

CHAPTER 14

1. *JLFA*, 1:747; 2:6, 39, 77, 110. Asbury's remarks on black and white membership in Georgetown are from his Dec. 27, 1796, journal entry. The annual conference minutes give Georgetown's membership as six whites and 70 African Americans in 1796 and eight whites and 115 African Americans in 1797. *Minutes* (1840), 1: 69, 74. Writing to John Kobler in March 1795, Asbury observed that "I have not spent my time altogether in vain in Charleston[,] poor Joseph[']s Brethren [the African Americans] are coming to Jesus." Asbury to Kobler, March 27, 1795, MAHC. Audience size apparently varied quite a bit in Charleston. In February 1796, Asbury noted that he had "a thousand or twelve hundred hearers, and two or three hundred of these change with the day." *JLFA*, 2:78. Also see Will Gravely, "'. . . many of the poor Affricans are obedient to the faith,' Reassessing the African American Presence in Early Methodism in the United States, 1769–1809," in *Methodism and the Shaping of American Culture*, ed. Nathan Hatch and John Wigger (Nashville: Kingswood Books, 2001), 175–95.

2. *JLFA*, 2:6, 8, 40, 41, 78.

3. *JLFA*, 2:7, 109.

4. *JLFA*, 1:105, 2:144, 151; 1798 Brunswick County Sheriff's assessment, Financial and Legal Papers, Edward Dromgoole Papers, SHC; Sweet, *The Methodists*, 123–24.

5. *JLFA*, 2:62; Kenneth L. Carroll, "Religious Influences on the Manumission of Slaves in Caroline, Dorchester, and Talbot Counties," *Maryland Historical Magazine* 56 (June 1961): 176–97; Henry C. Conrad, "Samuel White and His Father Judge Thomas White," *Papers of the Historical Society of Delaware* 40 (1903): 1–13; William H. Williams, *Slavery and Freedom in Delaware, 1639–1865* (Wilmington, Del.: Scholarly Resources, 1996), 69–70, 122–27, 152–53, 158–59; Wigger, *Taking Heaven*, 137–138. Thomas White's will was probated March 7, 1795, in Dover, Del. On religion, slaveholding, and manumission in Philadelphia during this period, see Gary B. Nash And Jean R. Soderlund, *Freedom By Degrees: Emancipation in Pennsylvania and Its Aftermath* (New York: Oxford University Press, 1991), 153–60. I calculated the percentage of free African Americans in Caroline, Dorchester, and Talbot counties in 1790 and 1810 from a table given in Carroll (p. 177). Disciplinary cases involving members buying and selling slaves dominated many quarterly meetings in the upper South. See Wigger, *Taking Heaven*, 141–42.

6. *JLFA*, 2:44, 46, 77, 78. On March 26, 1795, while riding through rural South Carolina, Asbury recorded: "Last night I spent an hour with the blacks in their quarters, and it was well received by them. It will never do to meet them with the whites. By this means our preachers lose all their fruit." *JLFA*, 2:46.

7. Richard Allen, *The Life Experience and Gospel Labors of the Rt. Rev. Richard Allen, To Which is Annexed the Rise and Progress of the African Methodist Episcopal Church in the United States of America* (1793; reprint, New York: Abingdon Press, 1960), 15–16; Gary B. Nash, "New Light on Richard Allen: The Early Years of Freedom," *William and Mary Quarterly*, ser. 3, vol. 46 (1989): 332–340; Burton Alva Konkle, *Benjamin Chew, 1722–1810* (Philadelphia: University of Pennsylvania Press, 1932), 57–124; Gary B. Nash And Jean R. Soderlund, *Freedom by Degrees: Emancipation in Pennsylvania and its Aftermath* (New York: Oxford

University Press, 1991), 146–47; Harry V. Richardson, *Dark Salvation: The Story of Methodism as It Developed Among Blacks in America* (Garden City, N.Y.: Anchor-Press/Doubleday, 1976), 65–75; Andrews, *The Methodists*, 88. Allen's memoir was discovered by Daniel Payne in a trunk in the possession of Allen's youngest daughter in 1850. See Daniel A. Payne, *History of the African Methodist Episcopal Church* (Nashville: Publishing House of the A.M.E. Sunday-School Union, 1891; reprint, New York: Johnson Reprint Corporation, 1968), iv-v.

8. A similar set of emancipation papers were apparently drawn up for Richard's brother John. Allen, *Experience*, 15–17; *JLFA*, 1:310; Andrews, *The Methodists*, 140–41; Nash, "Richard Allen." In 1805 Garrettson wrote, "Many years ago, I preached a sermon, in the state of Delaware, on, *Thou art weighed in the balance, and found wanting* & Richard Allen, a colored man, told me some time ago, it was a means of his spiritual, and bodily freedom." See Freeborn Garrettson, *Dialogue Between Do-Justice and Professing-Christian. Dedicated to the Respective and Collective Abolition Societies, and To All Other Benevolent, Humane Philanthropists, in America* (Wilmington, Del.: Peter Brynberg, 1805), 35–36.

9. Allen, *Experience*, 18–19; Nash, "Richard Allen"; Andrews, *The Methodists*, 141; George, *Segregated Sabbaths*, 28–30; William H. Williams, *Slavery and Freedom in Delaware, 1639–1865* (Wilmington, Del.: Scholarly Resources 1996), 220. Once free, Allen, like most former Delaware slaves, took a surname. Why he chose Allen isn't known, though most former slaves took a familiar white name, so long as it wasn't their former owner's. See Gary B. Nash, *Forging Freedom: The Formation of Philadelphia's Black Community, 1720–1840* (Cambridge: Harvard University Press, 1988), 80–88.

10. Allen, *Experience*, 19–23; Andrews, *The Methodists*, 141–42; George, *Segregated Sabbaths*, 30–32. According to a testimonial written in October 1785, Allen also traveled to New York, Virginia, and the Carolinas, and spent two months visiting an unnamed Indian tribe between gaining his freedom and the date of the testimonial. Nash, "Richard Allen," 339. Lorenzo Dow later claimed that Asbury had forced Allen to stop itinerating and locate (Allen chose Philadelphia) because he was "jealous" of Allen's "power." See Lorenzo Dow, *History of Cosmopolite: Or the Writings of Rev. Lorenzo Dow: Containing His Experience and Travels, in Europe and America* (Cincinnati: Anderson, Gates & Wright, 1859), 545 (in the section entitled "Strictures on Church Government").

11. Allen, *Experience*, 24; Charles H. Wesley, *Richard Allen: Apostle of Freedom* (Washington, D.C.: Associated Publishers, 1935), 269–71; Andrews, *The Methodists*, 144; Nash, *Forging Freedom*, 98–99; Williams, *Slavery and Freedom*, 230; Gary B. Nash, *Race, Class, and Politics: Essays on American Colonial and Revolutionary Society* (Urbana: University of Illinois Press, 1986), 324–31; Julie Winch, *Philadelphia's Black Elite: Activism, Accommodation, and the Struggle for Autonomy, 1787–1848* (Philadelphia: Temple University Press, 1988), 5–7. On the Free African Society and Absalom Jones, see William Douglass, *Annals of the First African Church, in the United States of America, Now Styled the African Episcopal Church of St. Thomas* (Philadelphia: King & Baird, 1862), 16–19, 118–22. On the decline of slavery and the rise of a free African American community in the 1780s and 1790s, see Nash and Soderlund, *Freedom by Degrees*, chaps. 4-6. Allen identifies the elder who used "degrading and insulting language" only as "Mr. W——," and two other preachers who opposed a separate African American church at about the

same time as "Rev. C—— B——," and "Rev. L—— G——." Caleb Boyer served Philadelphia's district elder in 1786, but the district's elders in 1787 were John Haggerty and William Gill, and there were no preachers with the initials C.B. or L.G. assigned to the city in 1787. Allen is probably combining a number of incidents here in his memory. In 1788 Richard Whatcoat was the district's presiding elder, while Lemuel Green was assigned to Philadelphia as an elder. In 1789 Henry Willis and Lemuel Green were the district elders, and in 1790 Whatcoat was again elder and assigned to Philadelphia. In 1791 Lemuel Green was the district's presiding elder and Henry Willis was listed as supernumerary in Philadelphia. See *Minutes* (1794), 90, 109, 113, 114, 127, 142, 143, 157, 158. Caleb Boyer left the traveling connection in 1788, locating in Dover, Del. See Lednum, *Rise*, 304–5. It seems unlikely that the offending elder was Whatcoat. In 1785 Allen and Whatcoat ministered together in Baltimore. Allen later wrote that he "found great strength" in traveling with Whatcoat, adding of Whatcoat that "in his advice he was fatherly and friendly. He was of a mild and serene disposition." It was probably Henry Willis who vigorously opposed the plan for an African church, along with Caleb Boyer and Lemuel Green. Allen, *Experience*, 22.

12. Allen, *Experience*, 25–27. Several of Allen's biographers claim that the dramatic withdrawal from St. George's occurred in November 1787. This couldn't have been the case, since the galleries weren't constructed until 1792, and McClaskey didn't become presiding elder until that year as well. Much of the confusion arises from the fact that Allen gives few dates for this and related events in his autobiography. Carol George, Harry V. Richardson, Charles H. Wesley, Daniel Payne, Howard Gregg, Leon Litwack, and E. Franklin Frazier place the withdrawal from St. George's in 1787. See George, *Segregated Sabbaths*, 55; Richardson, *Dark Salvation*, 65; Wesley, *Richard Allen*, 52–53; Payne, *History of the African Methodist Episcopal Church*, 4; Howard D. Gregg, *History of the African Methodist Episcopal Church* (Nashville: Henry A. Belin, 1980), 12–13, 16; Leon F. Litwack in *North of Slavery: The Negro in the Free States, 1790–1860* (Chicago: University of Chicago Press, 1961), 191–92; and E. Franklin Frazier in *The Negro Church in America* (New York: Schocken Books, 1974), 33. Francis Tees notes that the galleries at St. George's weren't constructed until 1792, at a total cost of "£476.16.0 ½." See Tees, *Old St. George's*, 41. Writing in 1862, John Lednum noted, "About 1791, the galleries were put in it [St. George's], after the Methodists had owned it more than twenty years." See Lednum, *Rise*, 47. Milton C. Sernett correctly dates the gallery incident in *Black Religion and American Evangelicalism: White Protestants, Plantation Missions, and the Flowering of Negro Christianity, 1787–1865* (Metuchen, N.J.: Scarecrow Press, 1975), 117, n. 24–26, pp. 218–220.

13. Allen, *Experience*, 28; Benjamin Rush to Julia Rush, Sept. 18 and 25, 1793, Rush, *Letters*, 2:669, 684; Nash, *Race, Class, and Politics*, 338–41; Nash, *Forging Freedom*, 121–25; Absalom Jones And Richard Allen, *A Narrative of the Proceedings of the Colored People During the Awful Calamity in Philadelphia, in the Year 1793; and a Refutation of Some Censures Thrown Upon Them in Some Publications* (Philadelphia, 1794; reprinted in Allen, *Life Experience*), 48–49. On Allen and Jones rallying the Philadelphia African American community to aid the sick during the yellow fever epidemic, see Powell, *Bring Out Your Dead*, 94–101.

14. Allen, *Experience*, 29–30; Andrews, *The Methodists*, 147; Nash, *Race, Class, and Politics*, 341–42; Benjamin Rush to Julia Rush, Sept. 25, 1793, Rush, *Letters*, 2:683.

15. Allen, *Experience*, 29–30. After Allen declined, the leaders of the new church turned to Absalom Jones, who was well respected, but not an inspiring preacher. Exempt for the usual Greek and Latin tests, Jones was ordained a deacon in 1795 and a priest in 1804, but St. Thomas wasn't admitted to the yearly Episcopal convention until 1862. Douglass, *Annals*, 85–106; 140–71; Will B. Gravely, "The Rise of African Churches in America (1786–1822): Re-examining the Contexts," *Journal of Religious Thought*, 41 (1984): 61; Burgess, *List of Deacons*, 5; Nash, *Race, Class, and Politics*, 342–43; Andrews, *The Methodists*, 147; Winch, *Black Elite*, 11–12.

16. *Minutes* (1794), 192–93; Garrettson, *Journal*, 15; Bangs, *Freeborn Garrettson*, 209. On McClaskey, see Atkinson, *Methodism in New Jersey*, 352–56. Caleb Boyer and Lemuel Green were also gone from Philadelphia by 1792. Boyer located in Dover, Del., in 1788, and Green was stationed in New York in 1792. During the yellow fever epidemic, Catherine and Freeborn Garrettson left the city, spending part of their time in Maryland. See Catherine Garrettson, "Journal," June 1793–September 1794.

17. Allen, *Experience*, 31; *JLFA*, 2:18; B. T. Tanner, *An Outline of Our History and Government for African Methodist Churchmen, Ministerial and Lay* (Philadelphia: Grant, Faires & Rodgers, 1884), 17, 146; Wesley, *Richard Allen*, 77–78. Francis Tees writes that Allen purchased the blacksmith's shop in 1787 and hauled it to the lot at Sixth and Lombard streets. But it seems unlikely that this occurred at such an early date. See Tees, *Old St. George's*, 114.

18. *JLFA*, 2:18; Tanner, *Outline*, 145–49; African Methodist Episcopal Church, *Articles of Association of the African Methodist Episcopal Church of the City of Philadelphia in the Commonwealth of Pennsylvania* (Philadelphia: John Ormond, 1799), 4, 8; Andrews, *The Methodists*, 148; Wesley, *Richard Allen*, 79–81.

CHAPTER 15

1. *JLFA*, 2:75, 161; Lee, *Short History*, 114; Steiner, "University Education in Maryland," 28; Simpson, *Cyclopedia*, 235–36; Smith, "Cokesbury College," 234. Smith says that the college burned on December 7, 1795. When Coke heard the news that Cokesbury had burned, he wrote, "I doubt not but it was done on purpose." Coke, *Extracts* (1816), 233.

2. John Dickins, "The State and Description of Cokesbury College, situated at Abingdon, in the State of Maryland," *Arminian Magazine*, 1 (1789), 589–90; Jarratt, *Life*, 108; Lee, *Short History*, 112–13; Bangs, *History*, 1:240; Simpson, *Cyclopedia*, 235–36; Smith, "Cokesbury College," 224; Dewey M. Beegle, "Cokesbury College Excavation," *MH*, 7.4 (July 1969): 9–14. In November 1789 Asbury wrote to Thomas Morrell concerning Cokesbury, "I am in good hope that two stories out of three will be nearly finished." In January 1791 he was still looking forward to when "our house is finished." See Asbury to Morrell, Nov. 1789, *World Parish* (April 1960), 23; Asbury to Morrell, Jan. 20, 1791, Thomas Morrell Collection, GTS. In October 1795, Asbury calculated the value of "all the property belonging to Cokesbury College," at £7,104. *JLFA*, 2:65.

3. Coke, *Extracts* (1816), 111; *JLFA*, 1:597; William Colbert, "A Journal of the Travels of William Colbert, Methodist Preachers Thro' Parts of Maryland, Pennsylvania, New York, Delaware and Virginia" original manuscript, GTS, (Nov. 29, 1791), 1:115 (hereafter Colbert, "Journal" MS); Stevens, *History*, 258–59; Steiner, *Education in Maryland*, 232–41; Cummings, *Early Schools of Methodism*, 21–31; Hamilton, "Account of Cokesbury College," 181–84; Archer, *Authentic History of Cokesbury*, 10–16; J. Hall Pleasants, "Jacob Hall, Surgeon and Educator, 1747–1812," *Maryland Historical Magazine*, 8:3 (September 1913): 217–35. The Sheridan chapters were evidently from *A Course of Lectures on Elocution* (London, 1762). Colbert was stationed on the Harford Circuit in Maryland in 1791. *Minutes* (1794), 157. The typescript of Colbert's journal (hereafter Colbert, "Journal" TMS), also at GTS, is faithful to the original.

4. Thomas Dromgoole to Edward Dromgoole, Oct. 27, 1793, Edward Dromgoole Papers, SHC; Smith, "Cokesbury College," 227–33; Lee, *Short History*, 113; Steiner, "University Education in Maryland," 24–27; Steiner, *Education in Maryland*, 241–42; Hamilton, "Cokesbury College," 184.

5. *JLFA*, 2:29, 30, 31; Asbury to Ezekiel Cooper, Jan. 2, 1795, Cooper MSS 18, GTS; Smith, "Cokesbury College," 233–34; Steiner, "University Education in Maryland," 28; Hamilton, "Account of Cokesbury College," 184; Pleasants, "Jacob Hall," 229–30. By late 1795 Asbury was convinced that Cokesbury's curriculum had become too secular. In November 1795, he wrote to Nelson Reed, presiding elder over the district encompassing Cokesbury, "I wish you to be particularly cautioned against corrupt Latin authors being taught in the College & [which] filleth the minds of youth with infidelity, and Lust." Asbury to Reed, Nov. 13, 1795, MAHC.

6. *JLFA*, 2:90, 111; Smith, "Cokesbury College," 234–35; Bangs, *History*, 1:241–42; Steiner, "University Education in Maryland," 28–29; Steiner, *Education in Maryland*, 243–44; Cummings, *Early Schools of Methodism*, 32–33; J. Thomas Scharf, *History of Baltimore City and County* (Philadelphia: Louis H. Everts, 1881; reprint, Baltimore: Regional Publishing Company, 1971), vol. 1, 225, 238. On the burning of the academy, see J. Thomas Scharf, *The Chronicles of Baltimore* (n.p., 1874; reprint, Port Washington, N.Y.: Kennikat Press, 1972), 279.

7. Jarratt, *Life*, 108; *JLFA*, 2:75, 3:171; Asbury to Thomas Haskins, Jan. 11, 1796, St. George's MEC, Philadelphia. On Jan. 30, 1796, Asbury wrote to John Hagerty in Baltimore, "Oh! had I have spent as much thought and care about the Church as about that altar of bassok [Cokesbury] which is burnt down how happy I might have been." Asbury to Hagerty, Jan. 30, 1796, MAHC. Adding insult to injury, in 1806 Thomas Rankin demanded that Asbury repay £100 he had invested in Cokesbury from the estate of Robert Williams, of which Asbury and Rankin were executors. *JLFA*, 3:355.

8. *JLFA*, 2:102–3; Colbert, "Journal" MS (Oct. 8, 1796), 2:144; Coke, *Extracts* (1816), 218–32.

9. *JLFA*, 2:103; [MEC], *Journals of the General Conference of the Methodist Episcopal Church, Volume 1, 1796–1836* (New York: Carlton & Phillips, 1855), 11–12 (hereafter *General Conference Journal*). No manuscript minutes survive from the 1796 general conference.

10. *JLFA*, 1:760, 2:9, 10–11, 76, 92; Ware, *Sketches*, 222–24. Philip Sands was appointed to the Roanoke circuit in 1793, but apparently moved to Guilford by the time

Asbury met with him in April 1794. See *Minutes* (1794), 188, 207. Swannanoa is also spelled Swanino in conference records, and Asbury spells it Swannanoah. Membership on Yadkin and Swannanoa circuits combined was 714 in 1794, while in 1795 membership on Yadkin was 519 and membership on Swannanoa was 236. See *Minutes* (1840), 57, 60.

11. *JLFA*, 2: 92; *General Conference Journal*, 20–22; Lee, *Short History*, 234–45; MEC, *Articles of Association of the Trustees of the Fund for the Relief and Support of the Itinerant, Superanuated, and Worn-Out Ministers and Preachers of the Methodist Episcopal Church, in the United States of America, Their Wives and Children, Widows and Orphans* (Philadelphia: John Dickins, 1797). Asbury and Coke wrote to Pennsylvania lawyer and politician John Dickinson that the fund was intended "for the support of our Travelling Preachers among the Mountains and in the Western Territories, and to supply the wants of our Superannuated Preachers, and the Widows and Orphans of Preachers. . . . The Principal of all Subscriptions, Grants, Legacies, &c is never to be touched." See Thomas Coke and Francis Asbury to John Dickinson, Nov. 17, 1796, Logan Papers, HSP. The first trustees of the fund were John Dickins, Thomas Haskins, Jacob Baker, Henry Manly, Burton Wallace, Josiah Lusby, Hugh Smith, Caleb North, and Cornelius Comegys. On Sept. 4, 1796, Ezekiel Cooper wrote, "Last week brothers Haskins, Dickins, McClaskey & myself fully considered and agreed upon the principles of incorporation for a chartered fund for the better support of our itinerant ministry. And brother Haskins has accordingly drawn up an instrument for the charter, and if approved of by the General Conference, it is to be established as an Incorporated Fund for the uses & purposes therein mentioned." Cooper, mss. journal (Oct. 7, 1796), vol. 12; Phoebus, *Beams of Light*, 223. In 1839 Nathan Bangs complained that the fund was still inadequate. Bangs, *History*, 2:44–51.

12. *JLFA*, 3:122.

13. Coke to Cooper, Dec. 6, 1797, and Dec. 18, 1798, Cooper MSS 17, GTS; Coke, *Extract* (1816), 246. Coke continued to press this theme. "I continually bemoan that great deficiency among you—*the want of support for a married Ministry*," he wrote to Cooper the next year. See Coke to Cooper, Jan. 12, 1799, GTS.

14. *JLFA*, 2:103; Lee, *Short History*, 248–49; Phoebus, *Memoirs of Richard Whatcoat*, 81–84; Colbert, "Journal" MS (Oct. 28, 1796), 2:148; Ormond, Journal, Oct. 26–28, 1796; Kobler, "Journal," Oct. 27, 1796; Coke, *Extracts* (1816), 232; Vickers, *Coke*, 233–34; Warren A. Candler, *Thomas Coke* (Nashville: M.E. Church, South, 1923), 172–76.

15. Coke to the Baltimore Annual Conference, Jan. 6, 1807, Cooper MSS 17, GTS. Also see a nearly identical letter from Coke to the New York Annual Conference, Jan. 6, 1806, quoted in Vickers, *Coke*, 234–35.

16. *JLFA*, 2:104, 115; Coke, *Extracts* (1816), 233–45; Vickers, *Coke*, 234–35. Quotation from Coke to the Baltimore Annual Conference, Jan. 6, 1806.

17. Baker, *Wesley to Asbury*, 162–82; Tigert, *Constitutional History*, 463–74, 533–602; Sherman, *History of the Discipline*, 30. Meanwhile a 1797 edition of the *Discipline* appeared that made only minor changes from the 1792 edition.

18. MEC, *The Doctrines and Discipline of the Methodist Episcopal Church in America. With Explanatory Notes, by Thomas Coke and Francis Asbury*, 10th ed. (Philadelphia: Henry

Tuckniss, 1798). Quotations from 36 and 138–39; also see 40–46, 47–53, 169–71. Also see Tigert, *Constitutional History*, 554–56; Sherman, *History of the Discipline*, 115–20.

19. *JLFA*, 2:117, 121; Coke, *Extracts* (1816), 249; Francis Asbury to Ezekiel Cooper, Oct. 24, 1797, Cooper MSS 18, GTS; Baker, *Wesley to Asbury*, 158.

CHAPTER 16

1. *JLFA*, 2:116, 117, 119, 3:159; Lester S. King, *The Medical World of the Eighteenth Century* (Chicago: University of Chicago Press, 1958), 123–55.

2. *JLFA*, 2:121–131, 3:162; Kobler, "Journal," March 31, 1797. There are significant gaps in Asbury's journal for 1797: from April 9 to June 10 (except for an entry on May 27), from June 10 to July 3 (except for entries on June 18 and 25) and from July 31 to Sept. 10.

3. *JLFA*, 2:131, 132; John Duffy, *From Humors to Medical Science: A History of American Medicine*, 2nd ed. (Urbana: University of Illinois Press, 1993), 66–74. Burdock was used to treat arthritis, rheumatism, and skin disorders. The root is more potent than the leaves, and burdock is usually taken internally as a dried powder or as a tea. Applying it to the skin would have given minimal relief. C. W. Fetrow and Juan R. Avila, *Professionals Handbook of Complementary & Alternative Medicines*, 2nd ed. (Sprinhouse, Penn.: Sprinhouse, 2001), 132–35; Marilyn James-Kracke to John Wigger, e-mail, June 2, 2006; King, *Medical World*, 128; Saul Jarcho, *Quinine's Predecessor: Francesco Torti and the Early History of Cinchona* (Baltimore: Johns Hopkins University Press, 1993), 1–11, 192–204, 259–61; Reiss, *Medicine in Colonial America*, 188, 195, 200, 211–12; *Dorland's*, s.v. "cinchona"; Juliet Burba, "Cinchona Bark," www.bell.lib.umn.edu/Products/cinch.html.

4. John Wesley, *Primitive Physic: or An Easy and Natural Method of Curing Most Diseases*, 21st ed. (Philadelphia: John Dickins, 1789), 88; John Wesley *Primitive Physic: John Wesley's Book of Old Fashioned Cures and Remedies*, ed. William H. Paynter (Plymouth, England: Parade Printing, 1958), 5; Alfred Wesley Hill, *John Wesley Among the Physicians: A Study of Eighteenth-Century Medicine* (London: Epworth Press, 1958), 111–31.

5. *JLFA*, 3:157–58.

6. *JLFA*, 2:133, 3:164, 165.

7. *JLFA*, 135, 136; Lee, *Short History*, 252; Colbert, "Journal" MS (Oct. 10–15, 1797), 2:214–15; Phoebus, *Beams of Light*, 233–34.

8. *JLFA*, 2:139–40; Coke to Thos. Williams, April 5, 1797, Tms, Thomas Coke Papers, JRL.

9. The English Conference to "Mr. Francis Asbury, and all the Conferences of the People Called Methodists in America," Aug. 10, 1797; *Minutes* (British), 1:383–85; Vickers, *Coke*, 237–39.

10. *JLFA*, 2:141–50, 3:167–68; Lee, *Short History*, 252–53. Jackson joined the traveling connection in 1789 in South Carolina and located in 1815. *JLFA*, 2:178.

11. Coke to the Baltimore Annual Conference, Jan. 6, 1806; Vickers, *Coke*, 240–41; Candler, *Life of Coke*, 233–34.

12. *JLFA*, 2:142, 145, 149, 151, 152, 153, 155, 160, 163; Fetrow and Avila, *Alternative Medicines*, 92–95, 294–96, 815–18; James-Kracke to Wigger, e-mail, June 7, 2006; Oscar

Reiss, *Medicine in Colonial America* (Lanham, Md.: University Press of America, 2000), 185, 188. According to Reiss, Virginia snakeroot was known as a "stimulating aromatic tonic" (190). John Dickins wrote in July 1798, "A few days ago, I had a letter from Mr. Asbury who was then at New York & much mended by the means of abstaining from all flesh of every kind." Dickins to Edward Dromgoole, July 12, 1798, Edward Dromgoole Papers, SHC.

13. Ormond, "Journals," vol. 1, entries for Dec. 20, 1791, March 31, July 10, 23, 27, Aug. 2, 12, 18, 23, 1792; *Dorland's*, s.v. "laudanum," "opium," "potassium nitrate" and "saltpeter"; Reiss, *Medicine in Colonial America*, 197–198, 201, 203, 207–11; Duffy, *Humors*, 180–81; Cassedy, *Medicine in America*, 29. Camphor comes from the wood of *Cinnamomum camphora*; applied topically to the skin it can relieve itching and act as an anti-infective. See *Dorland's* s.v. "camphor."

14. Ormond, "Journals," vol. 1, entries for Aug. 26 and 30, Sept. 15 and 19, 1792; *Dorland's*, s.v. "pokeroot" and "pokeweed"; Fetrow and Avila, *Alternative Medicines*, 615–17.

15. Ormond, "Journals," vol. 4, quotations from March 9 and 14, 1801; Duffy, *Humors*, 70; *Dorland's*, s.v. "sulfur."

16. *JLFA*, 2:141, 152, 153, 160.

17. After reading Wesley's journal in February 1795, Asbury concluded: "I am now convinced of the great difficulty of journalizing. Mr. Wesley was, doubtless, a man of very general knowledge, learning, and reading, to which we may add a lively wit and humour; yet, I think I see too much credulity, long, flat narrations, and coarse letters taken from others, in his Journal: but when I come to his own thoughts, they are lively, sentimental, interesting, and instructing." See *JLFA*, 2:42. Asbury recorded only two sermon outlines during 1808–1810. See *JLFA*, 2:595, 639. Good examples of sermon notebooks are Ezekiel Cooper's sermon books begun in 1785 and 1792, Ezekiel Cooper Papers, MAHC.

18. "I move in a little carriage, being unable to ride upon horseback," Asbury wrote to his mother in June 1798. See Asbury to Elizabeth Asbury, June 3, 1798, MAHC. On Asbury's use of a carriage from June 1797 through 1800, see *JLFA*, 2:128, 130, 164, 171, 176, 188, 190, 194, 200, 209, 210, 211, 213, 216, 217, 249. Also see Richard Whatcoat, manuscript journal, Aug. 13, 1797–May 30, 1800, GTS (entries for March and April, 1798).

19. *JLFA*, 2:160, 161, 163; Francis Asbury to Elizabeth Asbury, June 3, 1798, and June 28, 1799, MAHC.

20. *JLFA*, 2:648. This was in September 1810.

21. *JLFA*, 2:164–65; O'Kelly, *Apology*, 46, 58, 88. Just as O'Kelly's resentment hadn't abated, Coke didn't temper his criticism of O'Kelly. Before sailing from Charleston for Ireland in February 1797, Coke wrote that he had his "doubts, whether religion has gained ground or not on this Continent, since my last visit." But of one thing he had "no doubt—that *O'Kelly* and his schismatic party have done unspeakable injury to the cause of God!" Coke, *Extracts* (1816), 249. Asbury and O'Kelly "met in peace," almost by accident in Winchester, Va., in August 1802. *JLFA*, 2:359, 3:253.

22. *General Conference Journal*, 44; Feeman, *Silver Trumpet*, 19–23; Simpson, *Cyclopedia*, 812–13. For Asbury's assessment of O'Kelly in September 1799, see *JLFA*, 2:204–5.

23. *JLFA*, 2:166, 167.

24. *JLFA*, 2:170; Lee, *Short History*, 253; Stephen Allen and W. H. Pilsbury, *History of Methodism in Maine, 1793–1886* (Augusta, Me.: Charles E. Nash, 1887), 28, 29.

25. *JLFA*, 2:169, 171, 173. Also see Lisa Wilson, *Life After Death: Widows in Pennsylvania, 1750–1850* (Philadelphia: Temple University Press, 1992), 1–19.

26. *JLFA*, 2:173–174; Asbury to Cooper, Oct. 4, 1798, Cooper MSS 18, GTS; Pilkington, *Methodist Publishing*, 1:114–15.

27. Pilkington, *Methodist Publishing*, 1:92–101; Phoebus, *Beams of Light*, 259–60; Bangs, *History*, 2:67–71. The debt the Book Concern owed to the Chartered Fund after 1796 isn't clear. Financial records were destroyed in a fire at the Book Concern in 1836.

28. Thompson to Hitt, Nov. 21, 1792, Dickins to Hitt, Jan. 21, 1794, and May 9, 1794, "Letters to Hitt"; Cooper, *Funeral Discourse on John Dickins*, 3. Jesse Lee wrote that Dickins's "skill and fidelity as editor, inspector, and corrector of the press, were exceedingly great. He conducted the whole of his business with punctuality and integrity. . . . His death was more sensibly felt by the Methodist connection in general, than we had ever known or felt in the death of any other preacher that died among us." Lee, *Short History*, 255.

29. Cooper, mss. journal (Dec. 16, 1797), vol. 12; Phoebus, *Beams of Light*, 243–44; Wigger, *Taking Heaven*, 163, 177.

30. Cooper, mss. journal (Nov. 22, 1796, April 16, 1797), vol. 12; Phoebus, *Beams of Light*, 224, 229.

31. Cooper, mss. journal (Dec. 2, 1798), vol. 13; Asbury to Cooper, Jan. 8, 1799, Cooper MSS 18, GTS; Phoebus, *Beams of Light*, 264–66; Pilkington, *Methodist Publishing*, 1:118–22; Scherer, "Ezekiel Cooper," 103–4. Asbury had hoped that Asbury Dickins, son of John and namesake of Francis, who had attended Cokesbury College, would assist Cooper in running the Book Concern. But the younger Dickins didn't share his parents' religious convictions to the same degree. He published Cooper's funeral sermon for his father in 1799, but then began publishing more secular books. His shop became a gathering place for Philadelphia's literary circle. Charles Brockden Brown was a regular, and Dickins promoted his novels *Arthur Mervyn, or Memoirs of the Year 1793* (1799 and 1800) and *Edgar Huntley, Memoirs of a Sleepwalker* (1799). In late 1800 Dickins began publishing the Federalist weekly, the *Port Folio*, edited by Joseph Dennie. See Pilkington, *Methodist Publishing*, 1:52, 92, 123, 128–31; Steven Watts, *The Romance of Real Life: Charles Brockden Brown and the Origins of American Culture* (Baltimore: Johns Hopkins University Press, 1994), 101–30; Harold Milton Ellis, "Joseph Dennie and His Circle: A Study in American Literature From 1792 to 1812," *Bulletin of the University of Texas* 40 (July 1915; reprint, New York: AMS Press, 1971), 129–78.

32. *JLFA*, 2:195; Cooper, mss. journal (May 5, June 6, 1799), vol. 13; Phoebus, *Beams of Light*, 267–68; Pilkington, *Methodist Publishing*, 1:125.

33. MEC, *Minutes Taken at the Several Conferences of the Methodist-Episcopal-Church in America for the Year 1799* (Philadelphia: Ezekiel Cooper, 1799), 22–24.

34. Asbury to Cooper, Jan. 7, 1801, from Camden, S.C. (also includes a note from Richard Whatcoat to Cooper), GTS; Phoebus, *Beams of Light*, 270–72; Pilkington, *Methodist Publishing*, 1:127; Scherer, *Ezekiel Cooper*, 105–17.

35. Lee, *Short History*, 255; *JLFA*, 2:179–91 (quotations from 184 and 191); 3:162; James-Kracke to Wigger, e-mail, June 6, 2006.

36. *JLFA*, 2:192–94, 195.

37. Asbury to Cooper, June 10, 1799, GTS; Francis Asbury to Elizabeth Asbury, June 28, 1799, MAHC; *Dorland's*, s.v. "consumption," "dropsy," "hydrothorax," "pleurisy."

38. *JLFA*, 2:196; Asbury to Morrell, Aug. 9, 1799, Thomas Morrell Collection, GTS.

39. *JFLA*, 2:196–217. The quotations are from 203, 204, 207, 209, 210. For Lee's summary of 1799, see *Short History*, 256–61.

CHAPTER 17

1. These figures were derived by comparing the data from Edwin A. Schell's article, "Methodist Traveling Preachers in America, 1773–1799," *MH* 2:2 (January 1964), 53–67, with the annual conference minutes for 1799.

2. I also greatly benefited from Mr. Schell's updates to his earlier article, which he shared with me during a visit to the Lovely Lane Museum in Baltimore, in May 1998. The fate of the unaccounted-for preacher is unknown.

3. Lyell, untitled autobiography, 1–7.

4. *JLFA*, 2:222–223, 3:183; Shipp, *Methodism in South Carolina*, 324–33; Moore, *Pioneers of Methodism*, 271–80; Albert Deems Betts, *History of South Carolina Methodism*, (Columbia, S.C.: Advocate Press, 1952), 170; F. A. Mood, *Methodism in Charleston: A Narrative of the Chief Events Relating to the Rise and Progress of the Methodist Episcopal Church in Charleston, S. C.* (Nashville: Methodist Episcopal Church, South, 1856), 86. Shipp concludes that Dougherty's "supremacy as a preacher in his day was never disputed by any competent witness" (p. 327), and Moore writes that "as an earnest, forcible, eloquent minister of the gospel of Christ, he was equaled by few in any Church in his day" (p. 272). This is high praise considering that neither Shipp nor Moore had any sympathy for Dougherty's abolitionism.

5. *JLFA*, 2:222–23, 3:183. In a similar manner, Asbury wrote to Alexander M'Caine trying to convince him to take the Norfolk, Va., circuit for 1799, arguing "you will not need to preach above 4 or 5 times in 7 Days. 2dly your accomodations will be good. 3dly There is a small revival of religion; and the face of things is pleasing. 4thly you will be able to keep out of the weather when it is changable. 5thly you can write to any part of the world, or most parts of the Continent and kingdom." It worked; M'Caine took the Norfolk station for 1799 conference year. See Asbury to M'Caine, March 29, 1799, Gratz collection, HSP.

6. *JLFA*, 2:252, 3:192; Price, *Holston Methodism*, 1:285–91, 307–10, 331–36; Smith, *Recollections*, 49, 51; *Minutes* (1840), 47, 93; Redford, *Methodism in Kentucky*, 1:249–64; Ellen Eslinger, *Citizens of Zion: The Social Origins of Camp Meeting Revivalism* (Knoxville: University of Tennessee Press, 1999), 183. William Lambeth (or Lambuth) was the preacher initially assigned to the Cumberland circuit in Page's place for 1800. Born in Virginia in 1865, Lambeth entered the itinerancy in 1795. After his year on the Cumberland circuit (1800–01), he married and located in Smith County, Tenn., where he earned a living making combs. See Price, *Holston Methodism*, 1:306. Living within the bounds of the Cumberland circuit was the former Methodist preacher James Haw, who had joined O'Kelly's church and persuaded a number of other local and traveling

preachers to do the same. On Haw and Page, see Redford, *Methodism in Kentucky*, 1:54–62, 135–41.

7. *JLFA*, 3:192; Price, *Holston Methodism*, 1:291–292; Smith, *Recollections*, 89.

8. Kobler, "Journal," July 29, 1798; *Minutes* (1840), 81; Henry Smith, *Recollections*, 64, 350; William Burke, "Autobiography of William Burke," in James B. Finley, *Sketches of Western Methodism: Biographical, Historical, and Miscellaneous* (Cincinnati: Printed for the Author, 1854), 56; *Minutes* (1840), 1:94, 99. Even with Smith on the Scioto circuit, the Miami circuit in Ohio was left without a circuit preacher in 1800. In 1806 Smith once again turned Asbury down when the bishop tried to transfer him from Baltimore to Charleston, S.C. Smith later regretted this decision, writing that the preacher who accepted Asbury's request "was more righteous than I; for he obeyed the call like an obedient son in the gospel, but I was disobedient." See Smith, *Recollections*, 214–17, 337–38; *JLFA*, 3:353–54.

9. Henry Smith, *Recollections*, 31. On Henry Smith, see Price, *Holston Methodism*, 1:303–5.

10. Smith, *Recollections*, 290; Gatch, *Sketch*, 189.

11. Boehm, *Reminiscences*, 190, 440–441; Bond, "Anecdotes;" Boehm, mss. journal, especially Aug. 14, 1808, Jan. 30, 1809.

12. Boehm, *Reminiscences*, 440–41; Bond, "Anecdotes."

13. Dickins, *Friendly Remarks*, 6–7.

14. Cooper, *Funeral Discourse*, 120, 121; Snethen, *Discourse on Asbury*, 5.

15. Abel Stevens, *Life and Times of Nathan Bangs, D.D.* (New York: Carlton & Porter, 1863), 128; Tipple, *Asbury*, 304. For a similar assessment of Asbury's preaching, see Wakeley, *Heroes of Methodism*, 23–26.

16. *Discipline* (1798), 86.

17. These tabulations are drawn from Ormond's "Journals," vols. 1–5. Also see Moore, *Pioneers of Methodism*, 248–53; John Wigger, "Fighting Bees: Methodist Itinerants and the Dynamics of Methodist Growth, 1770–1820," in *Methodism and the Shaping of American Culture*, ed. Nathan O. Hatch and John H. Wigger (Nashville: Abingdon Press, 2001), 127–28. I am indebted to T. J. Tomlin for the pointing out the "people under siege" theme.

18. *JLFA*, 2:818–24.

19. *JLFA*, 2:221; Paul F. Boller, *George Washington and Religion* (Dallas: Southern Methodist University Press, 1963), 24–44; David L. Holmes, *The Faiths of the Founding Fathers* (New York: Oxford University Press, 2006), 59–71; Peter Lillback, *George Washington's Sacred Fire* (Bryn Mawr, Pa.: Providence Forum Press, 2006); Michael Novak and Jana Novak, *Washington's God: Religion, Liberty, and the Father of Our Country* (New York: Basic Books, 2006), 211–27.

20. *JLFA*, 2:223–31.

21. *JLFA*, 2:231, 3:186–87; "Journal of the General Conference," 1, 4, 6, 7; *Minutes* (British), 2:31; Vickers, *Coke*, 222–27, 241–45. I have compared the manuscript minutes of the 1800 General Conference, located at Drew University, with the printed minutes and noted discrepancies where they exist. Jesse Lee reports 119 preachers at the conference, Thomas Morrell, 116. See Lee, *Short History*, 266; Morrell, "Journal," May

1800. On April 21, 1798, Coke wrote almost identical letters to Ezekiel Cooper and Richard Whatcoat informing them that, "Unless I am particularly wanted in America, I believe I shall spend the next Winter in England, God willing, which will enable me to settle all my little affairs in this country in the completest manner, so as to be ready to devote myself to the service of my American Brethren." See Coke to Whatcoat, April 21, 1798, photocopy, MAHC; Coke to Cooper, April 21, 1798, Cooper mss. 17, GTS. In December 1798 and on January 12, 1799, Coke wrote to Cooper about his efforts on behalf of the Irish preachers and Methodists of the Channel Islands. Coke to Cooper, Dec. 18, 1798, Cooper mss. 17, GTS; Coke to Cooper, Jan. 12, 1799, GTS, Tms copy in Thomas Coke Papers, JRL. Also see Thomas Coke to Henry Moore & Mr. Palmer, Dec. 8, 1798, Coke to Henry Dundas, Dec. 12, 1798, Coke to unnamed American correspondent [Ezekiel Cooper?], Dec. 18, 1798, Tms, Thomas Coke Papers, JRL, and Coke to Henry Dundas, Jan. 9, 1799, PLP 28.10.1, JRL.

22. "Journal of the General Conference," 4–5.

23. "Journal of the General Conference," 5–10; Simpson, *Cyclopedia*, 535. On Poythress, see Price, *Holston Methodism*, 1:311–17.

24. Simpson, *Cyclopedia*, 934–36; Whatcoat, *Memoirs*, 9–30; Gorrie, *Eminent Ministers*, 212–23.

25. "Journal of the General Conference," 11; Whatcoat, *Memoirs*, 29; Whatcoat, mss. journal, May 12, 1800; Thrift, *Jesse Lee*, 268–69; Lee, *Short History*, 267–68. Asbury and Coke signed Whatcoat's ordination certificate on May 18, 1800. Original at GTS.

26. "Journal of the General Conference," 9; Jenkins, *Experience*, 94; Lee, *Short History*, 278; *Extracts of Letters*, 8. Tolleson is misspelled as Folleson in the printed minutes.

27. "Journal of the General Conference," 17–18; Wigger, *Taking Heaven*, 141–42. Lattomus is spelled Lathomus in the minutes. On Lattomus, see Hedges, *Crowned Victors*, 42–43.

28. "Journal of the General Conference," 18–19. A motion by William McKendree that the annual conferences appoint committees "to draw up proper addresses to the state legislatures, from year to year, for a gradual abolition of slavery" also passed.

29. MEC, *The Address of the General Conference of the Methodist Episcopal Church, to all their Brethren and Friends in the United States* (n.p., May 23, 1800).

30. "Journal of the General Conference," 17, 25; Sherman, *Discipline*, 115–19.

31. Lee, *Short History*, 271–72; JLFA, 2:195, 506, 568, 596, 694; George, *Segregated Sabbaths*, 70; Reginald F. Hildebrand, "Methodist Episcopal Policy on the Ordination of Black Ministers, 1784–1864," *MH* 20 (April 1982): 124–27.

32. JLFA, 2:264–65; Chreitzberg, *Methodism in the Carolinas*, 89. The 1801 minutes show Blanton locating that year.

33. JLFA, 2:266; John Harper to Ezekiel Cooper, November 1800, Cooper MSS 15, GTS; Mood, *Methodism in Charleston*, 87–89.

34. JLFA, 2:266; Harper to Cooper, November 1800; Moore, *Pioneers of Methodism*, 277–78; Shipp, *Methodism in South Carolina*, 329–30; Betts, *South Carolina Methodism*, 91–92, 169; Mood, *Methodism in Charleston*, 89–90; Chreitzberg, *Methodism in the Carolinas*, 78, 85; Lyerly, *Methodism and the Southern Mind*, 117. The file containing the Harper letter also has clippings of published letters by Cooper and Harper. Kugley is

also spelled Coogley in some accounts. Harper ended up staying in Charleston through 1801. In 1803 he located, settling in Columbia, S.C., as a local preacher. On Harper, see *JLFA* 2:56, 160, 413.

35. Moore, *Pioneers of Methodism*, 277–78; *Extracts of Letter*, 18–19.

36. Harper to Cooper, November 1800; *JLFA*, 2:272; Dillon, *Slavery Attacked*, 107; Thomas D. Morris, *Southern Slavery and the Law, 1619–1860* (Chapel Hill: University of North Carolina Press, 1996), 347; L.C. Matlack, *The Antislavery Struggle and Triumph in the Methodist Episcopal Church* (Phillips & Hunt, 1881; reprint, New York: Negro Universities Press, 1969), 66–67. Mood says that Asbury preached one sermon in Charleston in early 1802. Mood, *Methodism in Charleston*, 91. An 1803 law modified the 1800 statute by prohibiting breaking up meetings where "members of any religious society are assembled, before 9 o'clock at night, provided a majority are white people." See Morris, *Slavery and the Law*, 347.

37. *JLFA*, 2:281, 283; Francis Asbury and Richard Whatcoat to Thomas Morrell, Feb. 6, 1801, MAHC.

38. *JLFA*, 2:41, 283; Jenkins, *Experience*, 96–97, 102, 103; Moore, *Pioneers of Methodism*, 278.

39. *JLFA*, 2:283, 286, 355, 371; Alexander M'Caine to George Roberts, Sept. 30, 1802, Cooper MSS 15, GTS.

40. Mood, *Methodism in Charleston*, 65; Moore, *Pioneers of Methodism*, 277; Matlack, *Antislavery Struggle*, 67–68; Bennett, *Memorials of Methodism in Virginia*, 129–30. Moore's account is largely drawn from Shipp, *Methodism in South Carolina*, 329. Cynthia Lynn Lyerly makes a similar point in *Methodism and the Southern Mind*, 5. This myth has been perpetuated by some Methodist historians. See, for example, Charles W. Ferguson, *Methodists and the Making of America: Organizing to Beat the Devil* (Austin, Tex.: Eakin Press, 1983), 205–08.

CHAPTER 18

1. Smith, *Experience*, 38, 45, 55–60, 76–79.

2. *JLFA*, 2:398, 340, 351, 557; 3:268; Francis Asbury to John Rodgers, Aug. 1, 1802, MAHC.

3. *JLFA*, 2:229, 234–35; Richard Whatcoat to Elizabeth Asbury, June 1800, MAHC; *Extracts of Letters, Containing Some Account of the Work of God Since the Year 1800. Written by the Preachers and Members of the Methodist Episcopal Church, to Their Bishops* (New York: Ezekiel Cooper and John Wilson, 1805), 3, 14–15; Lee, *Short History*, 273–74. Internal evidence suggests Whatcoat wrote to Eliza Asbury shortly after the New York conference in June 1800. Lee concluded that 150 were converted during the conference; Whatcoat says 109.

4. *JLFA*, 2:235–40; Whatcoat to Elizabeth Asbury, June 1800.

5. *JLFA*, 2:240–54. Asbury was particularly disappointed with the condition of Bethel School, which was languishing. "Perhaps brother Poythress and myself were as much overseen with this place as Dr. Coke was with . . . Cokesbury." *JLFA*, 2:253.

6. *JLFA*, 2:256–57, 260.

7. *JLFA*, 2:247, 248; George Roberts to Paul Hick, Nov. 10, 1800, MAHC; Moore, *Pioneers*, 304; Lee, *Short History*, 275–77; *Extracts of Letters*, 14–15. George Roberts speculated that some turned to the Methodists because they were the only church to remain open through a yellow fever epidemic in Baltimore. See *Extracts of Letters*, 7–8. According to Thomas Morrell, who was stationed with Roberts in Baltimore in 1800, membership in Baltimore and nearby Fell's Point increased from 985 in 1799 to 1,315 in 1801. Morrell, "Journal," January 1800 to May 1801.

8. *JLFA*, 2:249; *Extracts of Letters*, 4, 6, 8–10, 15–18.

9. *JLFA*, 2:260; Wigger, *Taking Heaven*, 198–200.

10. Whatcoat to Elizabeth Asbury, June 1800, MAHC; Whatcoat, *Memoirs*, 32–33. On the story of David and Jonathan, see 1 Samuel 18–20. For examples of letters from Asbury and Whatcoat, see Asbury and Whatcoat to Stith Mead, Jan. 6, 1801; Asbury and Whatcoat to Stith Mead, Jan. 20, 1801; Asbury and Whatcoat to Thomas Morrell, Feb. 6, 1801, MAHC. For examples of Asbury arranging his itinerary in advance, see *JLFA*, 3:202–4, and Asbury to Ezekiel Cooper, March 27, 1801, Cooper MSS 18, GTS.

11. *JLFA*, 2:296–97; Whatcoat, *Memoirs*, 34.

12. *JLFA*, 2:291, 295, 296, 297, 298, 300. In 1805 the University of Pennsylvania appointed Physick to a chair of surgery, the first of its kind in America. Duffy, *Humors*, 97.

13. Cooper, mss. journal (undated entry following the entry for July 1, 1800), vol. 13; Phoebus, *Beams of Light*, 285–87; *Minutes* (1840), 1:86, 88, 92, 94, 98; Andrews *The Methodists*, 175. Cooper had married Thomas Haskins and Eliza Richards on April 4, 1799, near Philadelphia. See Cooper, mss. journal (April 4, 1799), vol. 13. Lemuel Green and Charles Cavender, who had been stationed in Philadelphia in 1799, located in 1800.

14. Cooper, mss. journal (undated entry following July 1, 1800), vol. 13; Phoebus, *Beams of Light*, 288; Andrews, *The Methodists*, 174; Richard Sneath, "diary," in Mrs. Walter Aborn Simpson, *The History of Bethel Methodist Episcopal Church, Gloucester County, New Jersey* (n.p., 1945), 92, 98.

15. Sneath, "diary," 35, 79–107; *Minutes* (1840), 1:82, 88, 94; Hedges, *Crowned Victors*, 209. Born in Ireland in 1751, Sneath came to America in 1774, joined the Methodists in 1782, and entered the itinerancy in 1796. In 1798 he rode the Bethel circuit and in 1799 the Burlington circuit, both in New Jersey, and in 1800 Pennsylvania's Chester and Strasburg circuit near Philadelphia. On the Chester circuit (which was divided from Strasburg in 1804), encompassing Chester County, Pa., see Edwin Gardner, "History of Chester-Bethel M.E. Church" Tms, 6–27, BC.

16. See the thirteen letters exchanged between Ezekiel Cooper and Lawrence McCombs, Feb. 21 to March 5, 1801, MAHC. Cooper and McCombs had an earlier run-in when they were stationed in New York City together. See McCombs to Cooper, March 2, 1795, Cooper MSS 15, GTS.

17. Cooper, mss. journal (undated entry following July 1, 1800), vol. 13; Phoebus, *Beams of Light*, 287, 289. In January 1801 Asbury wrote to Cooper from South Carolina thanking him for occupying "the middle ground" between the two factions. Asbury to Cooper, Jan. 7, 1801, GTS.

18. *JLFA*, 2:272, 273; Sneath, "diary," 91, 99–107. Asbury doesn't mention meeting Sneath in his journal, but Sneath records the occasion in his. On the messengers who brought tidings of woe to Job, see Job 1:14–19. Asbury stayed at Manley's home when he passed through Philadelphia in July 1802, August 1805, and July 1806. See *JLFA*, 2:356, 476, 512.

19. Cooper, mss. journal (undated entry following July 1, 1800), vol. 13; Phoebus, *Beams of Light*, 290; *JLFA*, 3:207–10.

20. Cooper, mss. journal (undated entry following July 1, 1800), vol. 13; Phoebus, *Beams of Light*, 290; *JLFA*, 1:30; Lednum, *Rise*, 41–44; Andrews, *The Methodists*, 175–76; "Historical Sketch of the Methodist Episcopal Union Church, Philadelphia, PA.," *The Epworth Gleaner*, 5:7 (March 1896): 4–6; "M. E. Union Church: A Resume," *The Epworth Gleaner*, 10 (1901): 4. Cooper moved in with Budd when Elizabeth Dickins moved to a new home in January 1800. He moved out in July 1800. See Cooper's journal, Jan. 1 and July 1, 1800.

21. United Societies of the People Called Methodists, "Constitution," 1–34, scrapbook entitled "A Book of Antiquities Collected and Arranged by Francis H. Tees," St. George's Methodist Church, Philadelphia; MEC, *The Doctrines and Discipline of the Methodist Episcopal Church*, 8th ed. (Philadelphia: John Dickins, 1792), 6–14, 45–48, 228–57; MEC, *The Doctrines and Discipline of the Methodist Episcopal Church*, 9th ed. (Philadelphia: John Dickins, 1797), 6–14, 45–48, 172–201; MEC, *The Doctrines and Discipline of the Methodist Episcopal Church*, 10th ed. (Philadelphia: John Dickins, 1798), 9–30, 132–35; Sherman, *Discipline*, 101–15, 300–32. The members of the first conference of the United Societies were: Charles Cavender, Thomas Haskins, John Hewson Jr., John Gouge, John Hood, Lambert Wilmer, Thomas Ballinger, Samuel Harvey, Jacob Baker, Caleb North, James Doughty, John Hewson Sr., James Swain, and William Budd.

22. Asbury to Thomas Haskins, June 26, 1801, MAHC; Asbury to Haskins, July 11, 1801, MAHC; Asbury to Cooper, Dec. 31, 1801, Cooper MSS 18, GTS; *JLFA*, 3:218, 223, 242, 248, 283. Also see Asbury to Haskins, June 11, July 10, 1801, MAHC; Asbury to Cooper, Dec. 31, 1801, Cooper MSS 18, GTS. Asbury's journal was published as *An Extract From the Journal of Francis Asbury, One of the Bishops of the Methodist Episcopal Church: From January 1st, 1779, to September 3d., 1780* (Philadelphia: Printed for Ezekiel Cooper, 1802).

23. *JLFA*, 3:197, 198, 202, 219, 251, 256, 325; Asbury to Thomas Haskins, June 26, 1801, MAHC; Asbury to Thornton Fleming, Aug. 21, 1802, MAHC.

24. *JLFA*, 2:304, 451; 3:206, 213–214, 219, 228, 268; Whatcoat, *Memoirs*, 34–35. Asbury outlined this new division of labor with Whatcoat in a letter to Coke, Aug. 20, 1801. See *JLFA*, 3:222.

25. *JLFA*, 2:304–10; 3:226, 228.

26. *JLFA*, 2:311, 313, 314; 3:230; Whatcoat, *Memoirs*, 35–36. On Hutchinson, see Atkinson, *New Jersey*, 425–32.

27. *JLFA*, 2:315; 3:228.

28. Cooper, mss. journal (undated entry following July 1, 1800), vol. 13; Asbury to Cooper, Dec. 31, 1801, Cooper MSS 18, GTS; *JLFA*, 3:237; Phoebus, *Beams of Light*, 290–91.

CHAPTER 19

1. *JLFA*, 2:333–34, 354.

2. Asbury to Morrell, Feb. 6, 1801, MAHC; Morrell, "Journal," July 30, 1796, May 1801. On Morrell, also see Atkinson, *Methodism in New Jersey*, 381–86.

3. Asbury to Morrell, Feb. 6, 1801, MAHC; Morrell, "Journal," May 1801 to July 1802 and September 1805.

4. *JLFA*, 2:353–54; 3:257; Asbury to John Rodgers, Aug. 1, 1802, MAHC; David Hallam to John Wigger, e-mail, Oct. 8, 2001; Briggs, *Bishop Asbury*, 352. I am especially indebted to David Hallam for the information on Emery.

5. *JLFA*, 2:334–36, 3:239; Whatcoat, *Memoirs*, 37–38; Asbury to Stith Mead, May 31, 1802, MAHC; Learner Blackman, "Journal, 1800–1804," Tms, MAHC, 2; *Minutes* (1840): 1:92, 98.

6. *JLFA*, 2:336–37; 3:240, 241.

7. Sargent to Morrell, June 8, 1803, Thomas Morrell Collection, GTS.

8. *JLFA*, 2:340, 342; Asbury to Mead, May 31, 1802; Whatcoat, *Memoirs*, 38.

9. *JLFA*, 2:342–44, 345, 351; Asbury to Mead, May 31, 1802; Whatcoat, *Memoirs*, 38.

10. *JLFA*, 2:360, 362; 3:249–50; Asbury to Whatcoat, Aug. 10, 1802, GTS; Asbury to Thornton Fleming, Aug. 21, 1802, MAHC.

11. Asbury to Roberts, December 1802, Tms, LLM; *JLFA*, 3:251, 253, 255; *Minutes* (1840), 1:104, 111.

12. Robert B. Semple, *A History of the Rise and Progress of the Baptists in Virginia* (Richmond, Va.: Pitt and Dickinson, 1810), 41–42; Paul K. Conkin, *Cane Ridge: America's Pentecost* (Madison: University of Wisconsin Press, 1990), 26–63; Leigh Eric Schmidt, *Holy Fairs: Scotland and the Making of American Revivalism* (Princeton, N.J.: Princeton University Press, 1989), 50–68; Eslinger, *Citizens of Zion*, 187–212; Richard C. Traylor, "Born of Water and the Spirit: Popular Religion and Early American Baptists in Kentucky, 1776–1860," (PhD diss., University of Missouri, 2003), 121–76.

13. Ruth, *Heaven Below*, 17–35; Tucker, *Methodist Worship*, 71–75; Coke, *Extracts* (1793), 34–35; Samuel W. Williams, *Pictures of Early Methodism in Ohio* (Cincinnati: Jennings and Graham; New York: Eaton and Mains, 1909), 56; Russell E. Richey, "From Quarterly to Camp Meeting: A Reconsideration of Early American Methodism," *MH* 23 (July 1985), 199–213; Richey, *Methodist Conference*, 59–61; Kenneth O. Brown, "Finding America's Oldest Camp Meeting," *MH*, 28:4 (July 1990): 252–54. Brown argues that the oldest Methodist camp meetings date from the 1790s.

14. Ware, *Sketches*, 234, 235; Gatch, *Sketch*, 108, 127; Smith, *Recollections*, 83; Wigger, *Taking Heaven*, 93–94; Williams, *Pictures*, 54–55; Abner Chase, *Recollections of the Past* (New York: Published for the Author, 1848), 27, 29; Connor, *Gatch*, 185–95.

15. Lee, *Short History*, 280; Charles A. Johnson, *The Frontier Camp Meeting: Religion's Harvest Time* (Southern Methodist University Press, 1955, 1985), 30. Albert Shipp argues that the first camp meeting was held in 1794 in Lincoln County, western North Carolina. Shipp, *Methodism in South Carolina*, 271–72; Price, *Holston Methodism*, 1:355–57. I benefited from reading an unpublished manuscript article by

Lester Ruth, "Reconsidering the Emergence of the Second Great Awakening and Camp Meetings Among Early Methodists."

16. *JLFA*, 2:402, 403, 3:300. Describing a camp meeting near Pittsburgh in August 1803, Asbury claimed that a Catholic "brought whiskey to give away, but some of the guards seized his bottle." *JLFA*, 3:270.

17. Asbury to Mead, May 31, 1802.

18. *JLFA*, 2:388, 402, 409; 3:269; Williams, *Garden of Methodism*, 87.

19. James B. Finley, *Autobiography of Rev. James B. Finley, Or Pioneer Life in the West*, ed. W.P. Strickland (Cincinnati: Jennings & Pye; New York: Eaton & Mains, 1853), 367; Cartwright, *Autobiography*, 51–52. James Ward, presiding elder for the Greenbrier district in 1803, reported "one woman struck down & lay 14 hours, other fell but did not lye so long" at a quarterly meeting. See Ward to Daniel Hitt, Nov. 1803, "Letters to Hitt."

20. Francois Andre Michaux, *Travels to the West of the Allegheny Mountains* (London: B. Crosby, 1805; reprinted in *Early Western Travels 1748–1846*, ed. Reuben Gold Thwaites, 3 vols., Cleveland: Arthur H. Clark, 1904), 3:249; John Melish, *Travels Through the United States of America, in the Years 1806 & 1807, and 1809, 1810, & 1811* (Philadelphia: Printed for the Author; Belfast: Reprinted by J. Smyth, 1818), 43.

21. Cartwright, *Autobiography*, 48; Dow, *Cosmopolite*, 181–84.

22. *JLFA*, 2:524, 551; 3:326 (also see 3:322, 369, 373); William Chandler to Daniel Hitt, July 6, 1806, "Letters to Hitt"; Joseph Everett to Ezekiel Cooper, July 7, 1807, Cooper MSS 15, GTS. On July 30, 1807, Asbury wrote to Stith Mead, "We have 2500 Dollars to pay, on the Eastern Shore of Virginia, no Law, or Justice for Methodists." Asbury to Mead, July 30, 1807, MAHC.

23. *JLFA*, 2:546, 3:327; Asbury to Stith Mead, July 30, 1807, MAHC; Finley, *Autobiography*, 366; Lee, *Short History*, 315. Preachers in the West remained generally suspicious of the jerks and other ecstatic phenomena. "I think we should humble ourselves and pray that God would deliver his church from such exercises," Learner Blackman wrote. Blackman, "Journal," 13. Peter Cartwright writes, "There were many other strange and wild exercises into which the subjects of this revival fell; such, for instance, as what was called the running, jumping, barking exercise. The Methodist preachers generally preached against this extravagant wildness. I did it uniformly in my little ministrations, and sometimes gave great offense." Cartwright, *Autobiography*, 51–52. In December 1804, Enoch George, presiding elder for the Baltimore district, wrote, "I find in most places, our Jumping is changed to tears & prayers, groanings & supplications: when this revolution is accomplished, I shall begin to look out for times of genuine power from the presence of the Lord: but while the present system of Jumping lasts; we cannot expect anything of magnitude." A year earlier George wrote that "the singing those whirling tunes, common among us, has destroyed that Solemnity which belongs to the Religion of the Gospel." See Enoch George to Daniel Hitt, May 26, 1803, and Dec. 19, 1804, "Letters to Hitt."

24. Daniel Drake, *Pioneer Life in Kentucky, 1785 to 1800*, ed. Emmet Field Horine (New York: Henry Schuman, 1948), 194.

25. William G. Mcloughlin, *Revivals, Awakenings, and Reform: An Essay on Religion and Social Change in America, 1607–1977* (Chicago: University of Chicago Press, 1978),

1–23, 98–140 (quotation from 107). McLoughlin largely locates the Second Great
Awakening in post-1812 New England, and his analysis of the Methodists is limited to a
discussion of their role in "southern camp meetings." On the Second Great Awakening
as social control, see Paul E. Johnson, *A Shopkeeper's Millennium: Society and Revivals in
Rochester, New York, 1815–1837* (New York: Hill and Wang, 1978); Curtis D. Johnson,
Islands of Holiness: Rural Religion in Upstate New York, 1790–1860 (Ithaca, N.Y.: Cornell
University Press, 1989), 77–86. On the awakening and the market revolution, see
Charles Sellers, *The Market Revolution: Jacksonian America, 1815–1846* (New York: Oxford
University Press, 1991), 202–68; Richard Carwardine, "'Antinomians' and 'Arminians':
Methodists and the Market Revolution," in *The Market Revolution in America: Social,
Political, and Religious Expressions, 1800–1880,* ed. Melvyn Stokes and Stephen Conway
(Charlottesville: University Press of Virginia, 1996), 282–307. On the "isomorphic"
relationship between nineteenth-century revivalism and the broader culture, see George
M. Thomas, *Revivalism and Cultural Change: Christianity, Nation Building, and the
Market in the Nineteenth-Century United States* (Chicago: University of Chicago Press,
1989).

26. Johnson, *Frontier Camp Meeting,* xix, 8; Bernard A. Weisberger, *They Gathered at
the River: The Story of the Great Revivalists and Their Impact Upon Religion in America*
(Little Brown, 1958; reprint, Chicago: Quadrangle Books, 1966), 11; Catharine
Cleveland, *The Great Revival in the West, 1797–1805* (Chicago: University of Chicago
Press, 1916); Walter Brownlow Posey, *The Development of Methodism in the Old
Southwest, 1783–1824* (Tuscaloosa, Ala.: Weatherford Printing, 1933); T. Scott Miyakawa,
Protestants and Pioneers: Individualism and Conformity on the American Frontier (Chicago:
University of Chicago Press, 1964); John B. Boles, *The Great Revival, 1785–1805*
(Lexington: University Press of Kentucky, 1972); Dickson D. Bruce Jr., *And They All
Sang Hallelujah: Plain-Folk Camp-Meeting Religion, 1800–1845* (Knoxville: University
of Tennessee Press, 1974). On Sweet, see the epilogue and James L. Ash, *Protestantism
and the American University: An Intellectual Biography of William Warren Sweet* (Dallas:
Southern Methodist University Press, 1982).

27. Williams, *Garden of Methodism,* 77; Kobler, "Journal," April 2, 1797; Eslinger,
Citizens, 213.

28. Eslinger, *Citizens,* 162–241. Apart from the long shadow of Turner's frontier
thesis, the revival has perhaps been linked to the frontier because of the visibility of
Presbyterians, for whom it was mostly a western phenomenon. It also deviated from
more typical Presbyterian patterns of respectability, systematic education and calm,
rational analysis. Presbyterian accounts dwelt on people falling during meetings because for Presbyterians it was so novel. Despite the visibility of Cane Ridge and a few
other large sacramental meetings, many Presbyterians were skeptical of the revival from
the start, and their participation quickly became more peripheral than that of the
Methodists and Baptists. While Methodist membership in Kentucky more than tripled
between 1800 and 1810, and jumped tenfold between 1800 and 1820, Presbyterian
membership in the state remained essentially flat from the start of the revival to 1820.
Wigger, *Taking Heaven,* 199–200; Conkin, *Cane Ridge,* 118; Eslinger, *Citizens,* 187–241;
Boles, *Great Revival,* 87–88. The Lutheran pastor Paul Henkel (1754–1825) describes

several attempts by Presbyterians to extend the revival into the North Carolina piedmont in 1801 and 1802. See William J. Finck, trans., *A Chronological Life of Paul Henkel, From Journals, Letters, Minutes of Synod, etc.* (New Market, Va.: privately printed, 1937; reprinted 1957), 29–32, 36–38, 45; Homer M. Keever, "A Lutheran Preacher's Account of the 1801–1802 Revival in North Carolina," *MH*, 7 (October 1968): 38–55.

29. Asbury to Stith Mead, May 31, 1802, MAHC.

30. Asbury to Morrell, Feb. 6, 1801, MAHC; Asbury to John Rodgers, Aug. 1, 1802, MAHC; *JLFA*, 2:257, 310, 314, 364, 412; 3:197, 199, 230, 249, 256.

31. *JLFA*, 2:316, 380; 3:261.

32. *JLFA*, 2:319; 3:256; Asbury to Roberts, December 1802, Tms, LLM. Also see *JLFA*, 2:305, 363, 368, 378, 401; 3:226.

33. *JLFA*, 2:483, 515, 523, 609; Finley, *Autobiography*, 363, 365, 370–73; Cartwright, *Autobiography*, 45–48.

34. *JLFA*, 2:313; 3:256; Asbury to Roberts, December 1802. Also see *JLFA*, 2:279, 306, 369, 378, 382, 423–24, 427, 428; Asbury to John Rodgers, Aug. 1, 1802, MAHC. On the Baptist impulse, see Traylor, "Water and Spirit," 1–63.

35. Asbury to Cooper, July 26, 1805, Cooper MSS 18, GTS; *JLFA*, 3:326.

CHAPTER 20

1. *JLFA*, 2:364; 3:252; *Minutes* (1840), 1:35, 111; Wigger, *Taking Heaven*, 198–200; Smith, *Recollections*, 84; *Dorland's*, s.v. "lead acetate."

2. *JLFA*, 2:4, 365; James-Kracke to Wigger, e-mail, June 7 and 9, 2006. Asbury mentions taking laudanum as early as January 1794.

3. *JLFA*, 2:375, 382, 385, 393, 397, 400, 404, 409; 3:268, 271; Whatcoat to Daniel Hitt, "Letters to Hitt." On Asbury's health during 1803, see *JLFA*, 2:378, 381, 389, 391, 396; 3:261, 263.

4. Whatcoat, *Memoirs*, 40–41; *JLFA*, 2:397, 399; 3:262, 268; *Dorland's*, s.v. "Gravel."

5. Coke to Cooper, Aug. 29, 1803, Tms; Coke to Whatcoat, Nov. 2, 1803, Tms; Coke to the New York Conference, Jan. 6, 1806, Tms; Thomas Coke Papers, JRL; Coke to the Baltimore Annual Conference, Jan. 6, 1807, Cooper MSS 17, GTS; *JLFA*, 3:336; Vickers, *Coke*, 243–47. "I am yours. In America only I conceive myself at home.& it would be my supreme earthly delight if I know my own heart, to hide myself in your woods, & labor, & dwell among you," Coke wrote to Daniel Hitt in February 1801. "I am yours to command," he added in March 1802. See Coke to Hitt, Feb. 28, 1801, and Mar. 1, 1802, "Letters to Hitt." He repeated this same phrase in an 1802 letter to Ezekiel Cooper. See Coke to Cooper, March 6, 1802, GTS.

6. Coke to Sturgeon, September 1803, Tms; Coke to Mr. Wrigley, September 1803, Thomas Coke Papers, JRL.

7. *JLFA*, 2:418; 3:272, 337; Coke to Whatcoat, Nov. 2, 1803; Coke to the Baltimore Annual Conference, Jan. 6, 1807.

8. Coke to the Baltimore Annual Conference, Jan. 6, 1807; *JLFA*, 3:337.

9. *JLFA*, 3:274, 277; Asbury to Hitt, Jan. 21, 1804, "Letters to Hitt."

10. *JLFA*, 2:421; 3:277, 282; Asbury to Hitt, Jan. 21, 1804; Robbins to Hitt, March 1, 1804, "Letters to Hitt." Before leaving Charleston in January, Coke wrote to Ezekiel Cooper in Philadelphia, "I am not coming to heal breaches, because I have no hopes." See Coke to Cooper, Jan. 21, 1804, GTS.

11. "Journal of the General Conference," 35; Drinkhouse, *Methodist Reform*, 498–503; Curts, *General Conferences*, 65–69; Lee, *Short History*, 299–303. The 1800 General Conference stipulated that only preachers who had traveled as regular itinerants for four years could attend the General Conference as members. See "Journal of the General Conference," 16. Whatcoat attended the first ten days of the 1804 conference and then withdrew because of a "violent" "inflammation in my eyes." Whatcoat, *Memoirs*, 41.

12. "Journal of the General Conference," 33–50; Methodist Book Concern, 1807 statement, MAHC; Asbury to Cooper, Dec. 31, 1801, Cooper MSS 18, GTS; *JLFA*, 3:287–289; Sherman, *History of the Discipline*, 32–33. The conference asked Coke to revise the hymn book, which he left unfinished but Asbury completed. See *JLFA* 2:554, 556, 558, 559; Francis Asbury, *A Selection of Hymns from Various Authors* (New York: Daniel Hitt, 1808).

13. "Journal of the General Conference," 42–46; *JLFA*, 3:300, 301.

14. *JLFA*, 2:432, 681–82; 3:221, 297, 299, 369; Ormond, "Journal," vol. 5, March 12, 1803. After leaving the itinerancy, Thomas Lyell wrote that "there is scarcely anything, of all that he possesses of this world's goods, that a Methodist preacher prefers to his horse, and in general they have very fine ones-and *ought to have*, for they owe much at times to their fleetness." Lyell, untitled autobiography, vol. B, p. 6–7.

15. *JLFA*, 2:242, 243, 3:293, 294, 326; Asbury to Wilkins and Charles Ridgley, June 22, 1799, MAHC; George Roberts to Paul Hick, Nov. 18, 1799, MAHC; Simpson, *Cyclopedia*, 758–59; Colbert, "Journal" MS, (Oct. 20 and 28, 1796), 2:146, 148; Thomas Morrell, "Journal," Tms, File 1646–6–3:18; MAHC, entry for May 1801; Thomas Sargent to Ezekiel Cooper, July 27, 1804, Cooper MSS 15, GTS; Asbury to Daniel Hitt, July 28, 1805, "Letters to Hitt." For Roberts's appointments from 1790 to 1806, see *Minutes* (1840).

16. *JLFA*, 2:433, 439; 3:296, 316, 317, 326, 373; Asbury to Morrell, July 21, GTS; Asbury to Cooper, July 26, 1805, Cooper MSS 18, GTS; Lee, *Short History*, 298; Wakeley, *Lost Chapters*, 386–87. Strebeck was ordained into the Episcopal ministry in July 1804; Williston wasn't ordained until March 1810. Burgess, *List of Deacons*, 7, 8; Rightmyer to Wigger, e-mail, May 12 and 16, 2006. Lyell admitted, after he left the church, that the effectiveness of the itinerant system rested on the commitment of the preachers to take their stations without dissent. "Had it been otherwise, had an appeal from Mr. Asbury's decision in the arrangement been admitted the itinerant system would have been instantly impeded if not altogether jeopardized," Lyell later wrote. Lyell, untitled autobiography, vol. B, 20. The Episcopal priest Joseph G. J. Bend, rector of St. Paul's Church in Baltimore, wrote to another former Methodist, William Duke, that Williston had left because he could no long countenance "that indecorous conduct & which is so generally considered among the Methodists, as proof of great zeal & piety." "It is much to be lamented," Bend concluded, that the Methodists "cannot think it compatible with Christian duty to give up the ranting, noise, and other follies, which disgrace their profession, & to promote the cause of the gospel in the same rational and dignified way, in which the Clergy of almost all other churches proceed." Bend to Duke, Jan. 14, 1805, MDA.

17. Enoch George to Daniel Hitt, Aug. 15, 1805, "Letters to Hitt"; Coate to Cooper, March 5, 1805, Cooper MSS 15, GTS.

18. *JLFA*, 2:442–44; 3:302; Whatcoat, *Memoirs*, 41; Asbury to Hitt, Aug. 22, 1804, Henthorn to Hitt, Sept. 23, 1804, "Letters to Hitt."

19. *JLFA*, 2:444; *Dorland's*, s.v. "Ipecac"; Whatcoat, *Memoirs*, 41–42; James-Kracke to Wigger, e-mail, June 7, 2006.

20. *JLFA*, 2:446; 3:303; Asbury to Hitt, Nov. 7, 1804, "Letters to Hitt." The passage given in *JLFA*, 3:303 is only part of a longer letter to Hitt begun on Nov. 7. In fact, Asbury and Whatcoat made it to the 1805 Baltimore conference. See Asbury to Thomas Morrell, April 1, 1805, GTS; *JLFA*, 2:465.

21. *JLFA*, 2:463; 3:306–7; Virginia Annual Conference Minutes, 1805, RMC. Asbury wrote a motivational address on behalf of the Virginia conference at its request. See "An affectionate Address from the Virginia Conference of the Methodist Episcopal Church to all their official Brethren, Local Preachers, Class Leaders, and Stewards, in the Quarterly Meeting Conferences, in the Districts and Circuits of their Charge," in a letter from Asbury to Stith Mead, presiding elder, March 8, 1805, MAHC.

22. Baltimore Annual Conference minutes for 1805, TMS, LLM.

23. Virginia Annual Conference Minutes, 1802 and 1803; Whatcoat, *Memoirs*, 37; *JLFA*, 2:329, 382. At the 1802 Virginia Conference, Asbury records that "There was great strictness observed in the examination of the preachers' characters: some were reproved before the conference for their lightness and other follies," evidently a reference to Jeremiah King's case.

24. *JLFA*, 2:463; Virginia Annual Conference Minutes, 1805. The same pattern can be seen in the Baltimore Annual Conference Minutes.

25. *JLFA*, 2:474; 3:322. Coke also wrote to Richard Whatcoat announcing his marriage, and his intention to "make you no more *transitory* visits. If I come at all, it will be for my life." Coke to Whatcoat, May 1, 1805, GTS.

26. Coke to Bradburn, April 5, 1805, Thomas Coke Papers, JRL; Coke to Whatcoat, May 1, 1805, John Davies Collection, GTS; Vickers, *Coke*, 248–54.

27. Coke sent his circular letter to a number of American preachers. For example, see Coke to Ezekiel Cooper, June 1, 1805, Cooper MSS 17, GTS; Coke to William Colbert, June 1, 1805, William Colbert Collection, GTS; Coke to Daniel Hitt, June 1, 1805, "Letters to Hitt"; *JLFA*, 3:318–21.

28. *JLFA*, 2:498, 501, 506, 514, 517, 535; 3:333–339; 1806 Baltimore Annual Conference minutes, TMS, LLM.

29. 1806 Baltimore Annual Conference minutes, TMS, LLM. The conference further instructed Coke to address his replies to the conference in its "Officical capacity," and not to individual preachers.

30. Coke to Ezekiel Cooper, Jan. 6, 1807, Cooper MSS 17, GTS (same as letters sent to the Philadelphia and Baltimore conferences); Quinn to Daniel Hitt, May 20, 1806, "Letters to Hitt"; Vickers, *Coke*, 255–56.

31. *JLFA*, 3:341–345, 347; Asbury to Daniel Hitt, April 28, 1806, "Letters to Hitt."

32. *JLFA*, 2:329; 3:280. "We have a considerable supply of preachers, but not more than we have work for, but many have families that we cannot support," Asbury wrote to Stith Mead. See Asbury to Mead, June 27, 1803, mss copy, DUL. Also see *JLFA*, 3:263, 273.

33. *JLFA*, 3:275; Quinn, *Sketches*, 78.

34. Asbury to Morrell, Feb. 6, 1801, MAHC; Asbury to Stith Mead, May 31, 1802, MAHC; *JLFA*, 3:279–280; *Minutes* (1840), 1:95. Also see *JLFA*, 3:263.

35. *JLFA*, 3:240; Sneath, "diary," 38, 44, 54, 60, 87.

36. Sneath, "diary," 60, 71, 80, 87, 90. Internal evidence in Sneath's diary suggests that his family moved from near Radnor to the vicinity of Soudersburg and Strasburg, Lancaster County, Pa., sometime between February and May, 1800. See Sneath, "diary," 80, 87. Sneath remained in the itinerancy until his death in October 1824. After his first wife, died he married Tamzon Williams Bates. Bates and her former husband, Daniel, were Methodists, and Sneath had frequently stayed at their home while stationed on the Bethel, Burlington, and Strasburg and Chester circuits. Hedges, *Crowned Victors*, 209; Sneath, "diary," 35.

37. *Minutes* (1840), 1:105, 112, 120; Francis S. Fox, *Sweet Land of Liberty: The Ordeal of the American Revolution in Northampton County, Pennsylvania* (University Park, Pa.: The Pennsylvania State University Press, 2000), 113–119. Asbury ordained Colbert a deacon on Nov. 1, 1792, and an elder on Nov. 14, 1792. See Colbert's ordination certificates, signed by Asbury, GTS.

38. Colbert, "Journal" MS (July 17, 1804, Oct. 17–22, 1804, Nov. 1, 1804, April 20, 1805), 5:1664, 1701–3, 1706–7, 1775; William Colbert, untitled manuscript, nineteen pages, GTS. According to this account, Colbert was born on April 20, 1765, his parents were from England, his mother, who could read and write well, died on Oct. 7, 1782; he was converted in 1785 and began exhorting in public in 1789.

39. Colbert, "Journal" MS, Jan. 3, 1805, 5:1729; Elizabeth Colbert to William Colbert, March 20, 1805, William Colbert Collection, GTS.

40. Colbert, "Journal" MS (May 22, June 14, 27, 1805), 5:1784, 1792, 1798; William Colbert to Elizabeth Colbert, June 4, 1805, William Colbert Collection, GTS; *Minutes* (1840), 1:133.

41. Colbert, "Journal" MS (Sept. 16, Nov. 3, Dec. 4, 5, 1805), 5:1825–27, 1845–46, 1863–64; William Colbert to Asbury, Dec. 13, 1805, William Colbert Collection, GTS.

42. Colbert, "Journal" MS (Jan. 15 and 29, Feb. 11 and 17, April 21, 1806), 6:1887–88, 1895, 1903, 1906–14, 1940–41; Colbert to Asbury, April 26, 1806, William Colbert Collection, GTS.

43. Colbert, "Journal" MS (May 24, 1806), 6:1952–53; Asbury to Colbert, July 8, 1806, William Colbert Collection, GTS.

44. Colbert, "Journal" MS (Feb. 25, 1804, Aug. 9, Sept. 6, Oct. 21, 26, and 29, Nov. 1, 1806, Jan. 12, 1807), 5:1610–13; 6:1983–84, 1991, 2002, 2003, 2005, 2025–26; *Minutes* (1840), 1:150, 163.

45. *JLFA*, 2:414; Mood, *Methodism in Charleston*, 92–94; Chreitzberg, *Methodism in the Carolinas*, 82–85.

46. *JLFA*, 2:423.

47. *JLFA*, 2:423, 3:371.

CHAPTER 21

1. *JLFA*, 2:463, 475–76, 509–10, 522; 3:332, 345, 351; "An Affectionate Address from the Virginia Conference of the Methodist Episcopal Church to all their Official Brethren, Local Preachers, Class Leaders, and Stewards, in their Quarterly Meeting Conferences, in the Districts and Circuits of their Charge," May 8, 1805, signed by Francis Asbury and sent to Stith Mead, presiding elder, MAHC. "It is our priveledge to Lend but not to Borrow of other Denominations," Asbury wrote to Rebekah Ridgley on Aug. 16, 1804. "Great Meetings by Encampments by thousands I hope will be Frequent and Conversions by hundreds." See Asbury to Ridgley, Aug. 16, 1804, MAHC. Asbury repeated the hope that one hundred thousand would be converted in the coming year in March 1807. See Francis Asbury to unknown correspondent at Perry Hall, March 10, 1807, LLM.

2. *JLFA*, 2:476–86.

3. *JLFA*, 1:721; 2:484, 486–87, 494; John Marshall, *The Life of George Washington*, 5 vols. (Philadelphia: C.P. Wayne, 1804–07); Mungo Park, *Travels in the Interior Districts of Africa, Performed Under the Direction and Patronage of the African Association in the Years 1795, 1796, and 1797* (London: W. Bulmer, 1799); Charles Atmore, *The Methodist Memorial* (Bristol, England: Richard Edwards, 1801); Atmore, *An Appendix to the Methodist Memorial: Containing a Concise History of the Introduction of Methodism on the Continent of America* (Manchester, England: W. Shelmerdine, 1802). It is unclear whether Asbury read Jonathan Edwards's original publication of Brainerd or Wesley's abridged edition. See Jonathan Edwards, *An Account of the Life of the Late Reverend Mr. David Brainerd* (Boston: D. Henchman, 1749); John Wesley, *An Extract of the Life of the Late Rev. Mr. David Brainerd: Missionary to the Indians* (Bristol, England: William Pine, 1768). The son of a ship's captain, Atmore was converted under Joseph Pilmore's preaching in 1779, after Pilmore had returned to England. An appendix to his *Methodist Memorial*, published in 1802, contains a summary of American Methodism's remarkable growth. On Asbury's first reading of Whiston's *Works of Flavius Josephus*, see chapter 5. On Atmore and Park, see John A. Vickers, "Atmore, Charles," and Christopher Fyfe, "Park, Mungo," *ODNB*, Feb. 1, 2005.

4. *JLFA*, 2:501; Francis Asbury to Daniel Hitt, April 28, 1806, "Letters to Hitt."

5. *JLFA*, 2:498, 501, 506, 508, 517, 525; 3:356, 357; "Journal of the General Conference," 16.

6. *JLFA*, 2:530; Jesse Lee to Ezekiel Cooper, April 16 and May 27, 1807, GTS; Francis Asbury to Edward Dromgoole, Feb. 11, 1807, Edward Dromgoole Papers, SHC; "Minutes of the Annual Virginia Conference of the Methodist Episcopal Church begun and held in the Town of Newbern, North Carolina February 2nd 1807," MSS, RMC; William W. Bennett, *Memorials of Methodism in Virginia, From Its Introduction Into the State in the Year 1772, to the Year 1829* (Richmond: Published by the Author, 1871), 505–9; Stevens, *History*, 4:440. Lee later wrote that the special general conference "would have overset and destroyed the rules and regulation of the Methodists, respecting the election and ordination of Bishops.& The bishop laboured hard to carry the point, but he laboured in vain." Lee, *Short History*, 348–49. Nathan Bangs notes Jesse Lee's role in

"warmly" opposing the plan, and Asbury's "great grief" at the outcome. Bangs says that the special conference was to meet in May 1807, but more contemporary accounts place the proposed meeting in July. See Bangs, *History*, 2:177–78.

7. *JLFA*, 2:512; 3:346–47, 349, 358. For Nicholas Snethen's tribute to Whatcoat, see Feeman, *Silver Trumpet*, 77–78. William Chandler was in the room as "Bishop Whatcoat change worlds, with all the marks of victory in Christ." William Chandler to Daniel Hitt, July 6, 1806. Obituaries for Whatcoat uniformly praised his humility and piety. The *Boston Gazette* described him as a "truly pious, worthy man." A much longer obituary appeared in Philadelphia's *Poulson's American Daily Advertiser*, on July 24, with shorter notices appearing in other New England papers. "He professed purity of heart, and no one that knew him doubted his being in possession of it," wrote Henry Boehm, who knew Whatcoat for sixteen years. "A holier man has not lived since the days of the seraphic [John] Fletcher, whom in some respects he strikingly resembled." "May I die his death and my last end by like his," the preacher Thornton Fleming wrote. Boehm, *Reminiscences*, 138–43; Thornton Fleming to Daniel Hitt, Aug. 24, 1806, "Letters to Hitt"; *Boston Gazette*, July 17, 1806, vol. 20, no. 40, 2; *Poulson's American Daily Advertiser*, July 24, 1806, vol. 35, 3; *The Providence Gazette*, July 19, 1806, vol. 43, 3; *The New Hampshire Gazette*, vol. 51, no. 33, 3, *Early American Newspapers Digital*, Nov. 2, 2004, <http://infoweb.newsbank.com/>.

8. William White to Simon Wilmer, July 30, 1804, MDA; [MEC], *Minutes Taken at the Several Annual Conferences of the Methodist Episcopal Church in America for the Year 1804* (New York: E. Cooper and J. Wilson, 1804), 20; Bangs, *History*, 2:196–206; Stevens, *History*, 4:442–43; Sweet, *Virginia Methodism*, 159. Coke made a similar proposal to the bishop of London in 1799 to reunite British Methodism with the Church of England. See Vickers, *Coke*, 202–3.

9. MEC, *Minutes Taken at the Several Annual Conferences of the Methodist-Episcopal Church, in America, For the Year 1801* (Philadelphia: Ezekiel Cooper, n.d.), 3, 18; MEC, *Minutes Taken at the Several Annual Conferences of the Methodist Episcopal Church, in America, For the Year 1802* (Philadelphia: Ezekiel Cooper, n.d.), 4, 17; MEC, *Minutes Taken at the Several Annual Conferences of the Methodist Episcopal Church, in America, For the Year 1803* (Philadelphia: Ezekiel Cooper, n.d.). Bishop Thomas Claggett ordained Kewley a deacon in the Protestant Episcopal Church on June 3, 1803. See Burgess, *List of Deacons*, 6. Since Kewley never entered into full connection, it is not surprising that the 1803 minutes do not list him as having located or withdrawn.

10. William White to James Kemp, Oct. 30, 1806, MDA; John Kewley, *An Enquiry Into the Validity of Methodist Episcopacy; With an Appendix, Containing Two Original Documents, Never Before Published* (Wilmington, Del.: Joseph Jones, 1807); Sprague, *Annals*, vol. 5, 374–77; Bangs, *History*, 2:205–6, 220–25; Drinkhouse, *Methodist Reform*, 1:405. Bishop William White ordained Kemp a deacon in the Protestant Episcopal Church on Dec. 26, 1789. See Burgess, *List of Deacons*, 4. For a reply to Kewley that avoids discussing Coke, see George Bourne, *Remarks Upon a Pamphlet Entitled "An Inquiry Into the Validity of Methodist Episcopacy." Dedicated to the "Right Reverend Fathers in God," to Mr. Kewley, &c.*, 2nd ed. (Baltimore: Geo. Dobbin and Murphy, for John Hagerty, 1807). Also see John Kewley to Joseph Jackson, Sept. 19, 1806, MDA. This

letter discusses correspondence between Simon Wilmer and William White relating to Coke that Kewley had recently seen. The debate over the nature of Coke's ordination was picked up again in the 1820s by Alexander M'Caine and John Emory. See M'Caine, *History and Mystery*, 24–27; Emory, *Defence of "Our Fathers"*, 46–59; M'Caine, *Defence of the Truth*, 22–28, 57–70.

11. "Journal of the General Conference," 53; *JLFA*, 3:375; Colbert, "Journal," 7:17 (May 6–7, 1808).

12. *JLFA*, 1:672; 3:383; Vickers, *Coke*, 187–91; Bangs, *History*, 2:206–10. Coke repeated many of the arguments from his January 29 letter, including the phrase "rope of sand," in a letter to Ezekiel Cooper. See Coke to Cooper, March 1, 1808, GTS.

13. "Journal of the General Conference," 56; Thomas Coke to Ezekiel Cooper, Sept. 8, 1808, Cooper MSS 17, GTS; Bangs, *History*, 2:211–20; Drinkhouse, *Methodist Reform*, 1:505–6; Leroy Lee, *Jesse Lee*, 432–35; Tigert, *Constitutional History*, 316–22.

14. "Journal of the General Conference," 59–60.

15. Francis Asbury to Nelson Reed, Dec. 10, 1807, and Daniel Hitt to Nelson Reed, Dec. 10, 1807, MAHC. Asbury and Hitt were traveling together, and their letters to Reed were sent together. On Dec. 14, 1807, Asbury wrote to Elijah Hedding of New England that "The men that feel and see as they ought, say no partial superintendency over an Annual Conference! No arch superintendency of one over the whole! No abolition of the general apostolical Wesleyan superintendency! No abolition of what was practiced by the General Assistants till the year 1784, and ever since, in well qualified order &" *JLFA*, 3:380.

16. "Journal of the General Conference," 59–60; Colbert, "Journal," 7:18–19 (May 11–12, 1808); Joseph Mitchell, "The Election of Bishop McKendree Reconsidered," *MH*, 12:2 (January 1974): 19–31; Frederick Norwood, "The Church Takes Shape," in *The History of American Methodism*, ed. Emory S. Bucke, 3 vols. (New York: Abingdon Press, 1964), 477. The motion for seven bishops was made by John McClaskey and seconded by Ezekiel Cooper. See Bangs, *History*, 2:235; Leroy Lee, *Jesse Lee*, 435–36. Asbury wrote to Coke in May 1809 that "the General Conference was certainly directed of God" in its choice of McKendree. *JLFA*, 3:410. Thomas Coke wrote to Cooper that he preferred McKendree "before all the Preachers in the United States" except one, presumably Cooper. Coke to Cooper, Sept. 8, 1808.

17. *JLFA*, 2:364–67; Smith, *Recollections*, 50, 59–60; Bangs, *History*, 2:111; Paine, *William McKendree*, 129–64; Albea Godbold, "Bishop William McKendree and His Contribution to Methodism," *MH*, 8:3 (April 1970): 3–12.

18. Colbert, "Journal," 7:17 (May 8, 1808); Boehm, *Reminiscences*, 181–82; Paine, *William McKendree*, 175–79; Hoss, *William McKendree*, 106–9; Wakeley, *Heroes*, 109–11; Stevens, *History*, 4:440–41. Bangs's account of McKendree's sermon was recorded in his unpublished journal, and then apparently rewritten in the 1820s. See Mitchell, "Election of McKendree Reconsidered."

19. "Journal of the General Conference," 16, 51–58; Tigert, *Constitutional History*, 297–301; Bangs, *History*, 2:226–28; Drinkhouse, *Methodist Reform*, 1:507. One of the reasons Asbury supported a delegated general conference was his belief that too much time and energy was lost by the preachers attending conference. Writing to Jacob Gruber in August 1809, Asbury reported that membership had increased by 11,000 the

past conference year. "It might have been 20,000 had not General Conference taken the attention of 130 chief men, some 2, others 3, others 6 months from the work," he added. *JLFA*, 3:411.

20. Tigert, *Constitutional History*, 302–4; Drinkhouse, *Methodist Reform*, 1:507–8.

21. "Journal of the General Conference," 61–62; Tigert, *Constitutional History*, 304–5.

22. Tigert, *Constitutional History*, 305–6; Paine, *William McKendree*, 169; Leroy Lee, *Jesse Lee*, 439–42. Jesse Lee had earlier been a proponent of a delegated general conference. On July 7, 1791, Asbury records in his journal that "This day brother Jesse Lee put a paper into my hand, proposing the election of not less than two, nor more than four preachers from each conference, to form a general conference in Baltimore, in December, 1792, to be continued annually." *JLFA*, 1:687.

23. "Journal of the General Conference," 62–63; Colbert, "Journal," 7:19–20 (May 16–17, 1808); Tigert, *Constitutional History*, 306–8; Norwood, "The Church Takes Shape," 476; Bangs, *History*, 2:231, 332; Drinkhouse, *Methodist Reform*, 1:510; Charles Elliott, *The Life of the Rev. Robert R. Roberts, One of the Bishops of the Methodist Episcopal Church* (New York: G. Lane & C. B. Tippett, 1846), 156–57. Unfortunately, several pages are missing from Colbert's journal after May 17.

24. "Journal of the General Conference," 63; Tigert, *Constitutional History*, 309.

25. "Journal of the General Conference," 67; Tigert, *Constitutional History*, 309–10; Paine, *William McKendree*, 170; Drinkhouse, *Methodist Reform*, 511–12, 535; Stevens, *History*, 4:440–41; Elliott, *Robert R. Roberts*, 157–59; D. W. Clark, *Life and Times of Rev. Elijah Hedding* (New York: Carlton & Phillips, 1855), 172–73.

26. "Journal of the General Conference," 67–68; Tigert, *Constitutional History*, 311–14; Drinkhouse, *Methodist Reform*, 1:506; Leroy Lee, *Jesse Lee*, 442–443; Norwood, "The Church Takes Shape," 477–79; Richey, *Methodist Conference*, 64–68. Henry Boehm compares the church before and after the general conference to the nation under the Articles of Confederation and then the Constitution. See Boehm, *Reminiscences*, 181.

27. On Lee's description of Asbury's seclusion in Delaware, and Asbury's reaction to it, see Lee, *Short History*, 58; *JLFA*, 2:640–42.

28. Lee, *Short History*, 319–44; MEC, *Minutes* (1840), 1:5–175. Toward the end of the book (as it finally appeared in 1810), Lee gives a twenty-five-page summary, broken down into five lists, of all the preachers who joined the itinerancy from 1769 to 1806, and it contains numerous mistakes. It indicates that seventeen senior preachers had left the connection by 1809 who, in fact, still held conference appointments, several of them as presiding elders. Ten of the seventeen were actually at the General Conference. Among these was Nelson Reed, one of the members of the committee that reviewed Lee's manuscript, whom Lee incorrectly listed as having left the connection in 1800. The preachers Lee incorrectly lists as having located by 1809 are: Daniel Asbury, John Crawford, Thomas Daughaday, Robert Dillion, William Gassaway, Enoch George, Morris Howe, Aaron Hunt, Benjamin Lakin, William Phoebus, John Pitts, Nelson Reed, Joseph Rowen, Elijah R. Sabin, Robert Sparks, Nathan Swain, and Elijah Woolsey. The nine at the conference were: Asbury, Dillion, George, Lakin, Phoebus, Pitts, Reed, Sabin, Sparks, and Swain. Lee apparently failed to take notice of the fact that these

preachers had located earlier in their careers and then returned to service. Lee's list also indicates that another eleven senior preachers had located by 1806 who still had conference appointments at the time. These preachers, with the dates they located, were: George Armstrong (1808), William Atwood (1807), Samuel Cowles (1807), William Early (1807), Aaron Humphrey (1809), Caleb Kendall (1807), Thomas Nelson (1807), William Page (1809), Josias Randle (1809), John Ruth (1807), and Samuel Steward (1808). Three other preachers are listed with conference appointments in 1806 who died during the year: Peter Jayne, James Lattomus, and Richard Whatcoat. Lee's list further omits the names of at least eight preachers who joined the itinerancy and held a conference appointment for more than one year, and indicates that four preachers never moved beyond probationary status who did. The omitted preachers, with the dates they entered the traveling connection, were: Richard Webster (1774), David Bartine (1793), William Jones (1801), Thomas Madden (1802), Eleazar Wells (1806), Jonas Weston (1806), Thomas Whitehead (1806), and John Wilkinson (1806). The preachers who moved beyond probation and were received into full connection, with the year they entered the itinerancy, were: Benjamin Hill (1804), Samuel Howe (1802), Henry Redstone (1804), and Asa Smith (1800). Lee says that he included all the itinerant preachers except "a few who never went to their circuits." See Lee, *Short History*, 339. These preachers, with the year they first appear in the minutes, apparently include: Hollis Hanson (1777), Joseph Reese (1777), Richard Ogborn (1778), Stith Parham (1779), Newman Spain (1786), Thomas Carroll (1789), Gregory Johnson (1790), Daniel Hall (1790), William Dyer (1792), John Halliday (1792), Thomas Everard (1796), Bela Willis (1806), and John Wooster (1806).

29. "Journal of the General Conference," 53, 63, 66. Lee may have revised the manuscript between the General Conference and its publication in 1810. When Asbury first saw the book in June 1810, he wrote that "it is better than I expected." See *JLFA*, 2:640.

30. *JLFA*, 2:566, 573; Boehm, *Reminiscences*, 187–88.

31. Methodists had long had connections with German-speaking pietists. Philip William Otterbein, ordained in the German Reformed Church, was one of the ministers who assisted at Asbury's ordination in 1784. Henry Boehm's father, Martin Boehm, had been a Mennonite preacher until he was expelled for welcoming the Methodists into his home. Asbury could be harsh in his criticisms of German-speaking evangelicals, particularly what he perceived as their lack of effective discipline and organization, but he also realized that they were an important constituency in Pennsylvania, Ohio, and surrounding states. On Asbury and Germans, see *JLFA*, 2:613, 646; 3:425; F. Hollingsworth, "Notices of the Life and Labours of Martin Boehm and William Otterbein; and Other Ministers of the Gospel Among the United German Brethren," *Methodist Magazine*, vol. 6 (June 1823): 210–14; Kenneth E. Rowe, "Martin Boehm and the Methodists," *MH*, 8:4 (July 1970): 49–53; Paul F. Blankenship, "Bishop Asbury and the Germans," *MH*, 4:3 (April 1966): 5–13; J. Manning Potts, "Attempts at Union 150 Years Ago," *MH*, 1:4 (July 1963): 31–36; Jeffrey P. Mickle, "A Comparison of the Doctrines of Ministry of Francis Asbury and Philip William Otterbein," *MH*, 19:4 (July 1981): 187–205; Donald K. Gorrell, "Ohio Origins of the United Brethren in Christ and Evangelical Association," *Methodist History*, 15:2 (January 1977): 95–106. Also see

A. W. Drury, *The Life of Rev. Philip William Otterbein: Founder of the Church of the United Brethren in Christ* (Dayton, Ohio: United Brethren Publishing House, 1902); William J. Hinke, *Ministers of the German Reformed Congregations in Pennsylvania and Other Colonies in the Eighteenth Century* (Lancaster, Pa.: Historical Commission of the Evangelical and Reformed Church, 1951), 71–79; Bangs, *History*, 2:365–76. Also see MEC Philadelphia Conference to the United German Brethren, April 25, 1812, MAHC.

32. Colbert, mss. journal, Mar. 10–11, 1798; Boehm, *Reminiscences*, 32; Ware, *Sketches*, 234. Martin Boehm, Henry's father, preached in German at this meeting.

33. Boehm, mss. "Journal," July 12, 1810, Sept. 10, 1810; *JLFA*, 2:612, 615, 643, 645, 646, 648, 649; 3:403; Boehm, *Reminiscences*, 12–13, 57, 174, 185; Simpson, *Cyclopedia*, 114–15; "Bishop Francis Asbury and the Reverend Henry Boehm," *Journal of the Lancaster County Historical Society*, 70:3 (1966): 129–61. Boehm writes that in 1808 "Bishop Asbury was anxious I should travel with him, especially on account of the Germans" (Boehm, *Reminiscences*, 185). Boehm records numerous instances of preaching in German while he and Asbury traveled together. On Asbury's efforts at union with the United Brethren, see *JLFA*, 3:403–4. On the history of the United Brethren, see A. W. Drury, *History of the Church of the United Brethren in Christ* (Dayton, Ohio: Otterbein Press, 1924), 27–250; Samuel S. Hough, ed., *Christian Newcomer: His Life, Journal and Achievements* (Dayton, Ohio: Church of the United Brethren in Christ, 1941); John W. Schildt, *In the Fullness of Time: A Brief Overview of the Beginnings of the United Brethren in Christ Church Written in Celebration of the 200th Birthday of the Church, September 25, 2000* (no publication information), 1–39.

34. *JLFA*, 2:577, 578, 580, 646; Asbury to Elijah Hedding, Dec. 28, 1808, Methodist Bishops collection, HSP; Boehm, "Journal," June 30–July 1, 1808, 726–27; Paine, *William McKendree*, 185–91; Boehm, *Reminiscences*, 191–205. On Benjamin and Betsey Lakin, see Wigger, *Taking Heaven*, 67.

35. Boehm, "Journal," Dec. 22, 1810, 56. For an example of how Boehm's descriptions of difficult traveling conditions could be more dramatic than Asbury's, compare their accounts of crossing the Cataloochee Creek on Nov. 30, 1810 in Boehm, "Journal," Nov. 30, 1810, 49–50; *JLFA*, 2:654. Boehm, *Reminiscences*, 299–302; George Peck, *Early Methodism Within the Bounds of the Old Genesee Conference From 1788 to 1828* (New York: Carlton & Porter, 1860), 168–69; F. W. Conable, *History of the Genesee Annual Conference of the Methodist Episcopal Church, From Its Organization by Bishops Asbury and McKendree in 1810, to the Year 1872* (New York: Nelson and Phillips, 1876), 21–24. Boehm says that objections to the creation of the Genesee conference were raised at the 1810 meeting of the Virginia conference. But the Virginia conference minutes for 1810, which run twenty-one pages long in Thomas Douglass's neat hand, make no mention of this debate. A note that "Some time was spent in cursory conversation respecting the duties of the several orders of the Ministry," might be an oblique reference to this debate. See "Virginia Conference Minutes," vol. 1, RMC.

36. Asbury to Cooper, March 6, 1808, Cooper MS 18, GTS; *JLFA*, 3:430; *Minutes* (1840), 160, 171, 183–84, 211. Both Asbury and Boehm frequently noted increases in each conference. See Asbury to Cooper, March 6, 1808, Cooper MSS 18, GTS; Asbury to unknown correspondent, Dec. 6, 1808, MAHC; Asbury to Coke, June 2, 1810, GTS;

JLFA, 2:563, 580, 582, 585, 601, 608, 631, 633, 651, 652, 3:381, 391, 395, 399, 402, 407, 425, 432, 434, 435; Boehm, "Journal," for these years.

37. *JLFA*, 3: 380–381, 418. On camp meetings that Asbury attended or heard about from 1808 to 1810, see *JLFA*, 2:576, 580, 583, 584, 586, 594, 611, 612, 614, 620, 635, 643, 646, 647, 648, 649; and Henry Boehm's manuscript journal for 1808 to 1810.

38. *JLFA*, 2:645. On the development of the Monongahela and surrounding circuits, see Wallace Guy Smeltzer, *Methodism on the Headwaters of the Ohio: The History of the Pittsburgh Conference of the Methodist Church* (Nashville: Parthenon Press, 1951), 90–91; Raymond Martin Bell, "Methodism on the Upper Ohio Before 1812," Tms, Washington and Jefferson College, Washington, Pa., 1963.

39. *JLFA*, 2:600, 602. Politics were always a particularly corrupting influence in Asbury's mind. He made it clear in his journal that he concerned himself as little as possible with the politics of this world. After briefly speculating on the nature of cotton smuggling relative to America's relationship with England and France while in Charleston, S.C., in December 1809, he quickly added, "I am mainly ignorant of these things, and have no wish to be wiser." "Methodist preachers politicians! what a curse!" he wrote in April 1810 while in Maryland. *JLFA*, 2:622, 634.

40. Francis Asbury to Thomas Coke, June 2, 1810, GTS; *JLFA*, 3:432, 433.

41. *JLFA*, 2:603, 643, 666.

42. *JLFA*, 405, 615. On Methodism in Ohio, see John Wigger, "Ohio Gospel: Methodism in Early Ohio," in *The Center of a Great Empire: The Ohio Country in the Early American Republic*, ed. Andrew R. L. Cayton and Stuart D. Hobbs (Athens: Ohio University Press, 2005), 62–80.

43. *JLFA*, 3:391, 411. At one stop in western Pennsylvania, Asbury "took occasion to be very plain, giving my hearers to understand that frames and feelings would not supply the neglect of family and closet worship, and the duties we owe to each other in society." *JLFA*, 2:612.

44. *JLFA*, 2:610, 612, 614, 652, 656, 3:406–8. "Since I am on horseback my fetters are gone," Asbury wrote on Nov. 19, 1810, after selling the sulky. *JLFA*, 2:653. Asbury's austerity sometimes led to misunderstandings. In rural Maryland in March 1810 he apparently offended locals by refusing a ride in a coach. "Will my character never be understood? But gossips will talk. If we want plenty of good eating and new suits of clothes, let us come to Baltimore; but we want souls." *JLFA*, 2:632.

45. *JLFA*, 2:593, 613, 615, 643.

46. *JLFA*, 2:611, 3:439. Also see *JLFA*, 2:623, 627, 629, 633, 638, 639, 645, 3:411, 425, 432, 435, 436.

47. Isaac Davis to Ezekiel Cooper, March 18, 1808, Cooper MSS 15, GTS; Asbury MEC, Wilmington, Del., to Asbury, March 15, 1808, BC; *Minutes* (1840), 1:162–63. Churches sometimes used presiding elders as lobbyists to get at Asbury. In March 1806 Joseph Smith wrote to Daniel Hitt, presiding elder of the Baltimore district, asking for John Pitts to be reappointed to the Alexandria circuit. "My Dear Brother, if you can find liberty and have any influence with our Rev. Father, let your friendly hand try to help us." Nevertheless, Asbury moved Pitts to the Baltimore city station. See Smith to Hitt, March

8, 1806, "Letters to Hitt"; Minutes (1840), 132, 140. For Asbury's reaction to these sorts of problems, also see *JLFA*, 2:599, 640.

48. Shinn to Asbury, Feb. 7, 1808, Tms, LLM; Page to Asbury, Feb. 16, 1808, Tms, LLM.

49. Coleman to Asbury, May 11, 1810, MAHC; *Minutes* (1840), 1:178, 201.

50. *JLFA*, 2:578, 639, 3:410, 425, 438. Writing in his journal in January 1810, Asbury complained, "Erasmus Hill may possibly sell the Gospel for a rich wife, as three or four others have done. Should I say here, And thou, Francis, take heed? Not of this sin." *JLFA*, 2:628. The Virginia conference was known as the bachelor conference because it had only three married preachers in 1809. "The high taste of these southern folks will not permit their families to be degraded by an alliance with a Methodist travelling preacher; and thus, involuntary celibacy is imposed upon us: all the better; anxiety about worldly possessions does not stop our course, and we are saved from pollution of Negro slavery and oppression," Asbury wrote while presiding at the Virginia Annual Conference in January 1809.

CHAPTER 22

1. Boehm, *Reminiscences*, 438–39; George Roberts, untitled manuscript, c. 1820, MAHC; Abner Chase, *Recollections of the Past* (New York: Published for the Author by Joseph Longking, 1848), 83; Young, *Autobiography*, 107; Bangs, *History*, 2:401, 406; Tipple, *Asbury*, 303; Drinkhouse, *Methodist Reform*, 185. For a similar assessment of Asbury's bearing, see Wakeley, *Heroes of Methodism*, 22. Young notes that by 1803 Asbury wore glasses to read. Asbury was in part reacting to changes in fashion and the way clothing was made, from mostly custom made in the eighteenth century to ready-made in the nineteenth century. See Claudia B. Kidwell and Margaret C. Christman, *Suiting Everyone: The Democratization of Clothing in America* (Washington, D.C.: Smithsonian Institution Press, 1974), 19–64; Michael Zakim, *Ready-Made Democracy: A History of Men's Dress in the American Republic, 1760–1860* (Chicago: University of Chicago Press, 2003), 1–36; Diane Crane, *Fashion and Its Social Agendas: Class, Gender, and Identity in Clothing* (Chicago: University of Chicago Press, 2000), 27–28.

2. *JLFA*, 2:662, 663, 667, 678, 679, 680, 681, 682–83.

3. *JLFA*, 2:687, 691, 697, 699, 700, 709, 713, 715; Asbury to Solomon Sias, Dec. 15, 1811, TMS, LLM.

4. *JLFA*, 2:721, 722, 723, 724, 726, 730, 732, 738, 742, 744, 745, 746; 3:469, 470.

5. *JLFA*, 2:677, 680, 682, 692, 708, 712, 713, 737, 739, 744; 3:453–54, 455. On taverns, see Sharon V. Salinger, *Taverns and Drinking in Early America* (Baltimore: Johns Hopkins University Press, 2002), 54–71, 211–16.

6. *JLFA*, 2:692, 704, 731, 733, 734; 3:453, 457, 458, 466; Asbury to Sale, Sept. 24, 1812, *World Parish*, 3 (February 1959): 41.

7. *JLFA*, 2:571, 666, 694, 740, 747; Boehm, *Reminiscences*, 189–90. On Henry Willis, see MEC, *Minutes Taken at the Several Annual Conferences of the Methodist Episcopal Church, in the United States of America, For the Year 1808* (Baltimore: Ezekiel Cooper and J. Wilson, 1808), 16–18.

8. Boehm, *Reminiscences*, 189; Asbury to Ann Willis, Sept. 7, 1812, and Aug. 29, 1813, MAHC. For other references to visiting widows 1811–1813, see *JLFA*, 2:661, 662, 664, 665, 669, 673, 687, 691, 693, 700, 702, 706, 710, 711, 712, 715, 722, 723, 725, 731, 738, 746.

9. Boehm, *Reminiscences*, 192, 439, Bangs, *History*, 2:403; Tipple, *Asbury*, 305. "Even after the conference adjourned, have I known him to make alterations to accommodate a brother who thought himself aggrieved, or to meet a case not before known," added Bangs.

10. Francis Asbury, untitled notebook, MAHC (hereafter referred to as the "Asbury notebook"); Chase, *Recollections*, 49. The notebook is cataloged under the title, "Examination of ministers in the six original annual conferences, 1810–1813." Some entries are out of chronological order. I am indebted to Dale Patterson of the MAHC for identifying that the notebook was originally a collection on loose sheets that were later stitched together. Some pages don't indicate at which conference they were made, however they can be identified by comparing them to the annual minutes. Also included in the notebook are lists of letters answered and other miscellaneous notes.

11. Asbury notebook, notes from 1811 Baltimore and 1813 Ohio conferences; Jacob Young, *Autobiography*, 305–7.

12. Asbury notebook, notes from 1810 and 1812 Baltimore conferences.

13. Asbury notebook, notes from South Carolina conferences of 1811, 1812; *Minutes* (1840), 1:275–276; Wigger, *Taking Heaven*, 56; S. R. Beggs, *Pages from the Early History of the West and North-West* (Cincinnati: Methodist Book Concern, 1868), 298; Bangs, *History*, 388–90. This story appears in a number of nineteenth-century Methodist histories. Tombigbee is sometimes spelled "Tombeckbee" in Methodist records.

14. Asbury notebook, notes from 1811 Baltimore conference.

15. Asbury notebook, notes from 1810 New England and Baltimore conferences, and 1811 Virginia conference; *Minutes* (1840): 1:191, 200, 206, 208–9, 219.

16. Asbury notebook, notes from 1810 New England conference, and 1810 and 1812 Baltimore conferences.

17. Asbury notebook, notes from 1811 and 1812 Western conferences; *Minutes* (1840), 1:188, 198.

18. Asbury notebook, notes from 1811 and 1812 Western conferences, and 1813 Tennessee conference; *Minutes*, (1840), 1:184, 198, 230; Robert Bray, *Peter Cartwright: Legendary Frontier Preacher* (Urbana: University of Illinois Press, 2005), 1–61, 268. On Cartwright, also see James Leaton, *History of Methodism in Illinois, from 1793 to 1832* (Cincinnati: Walden and Stowe, 1883), 99–100, 218–27. The Western, Ohio, and Tennessee conferences were usually held in the fall preceding the conference year. Cartwright attended the 1809, 1810, and 1811 Western conference meetings, but his case receives no special attention in the otherwise extensive minutes. Sweet, *Rise of Methodism*, 153–207.

19. Asbury notebook, notes from 1811 Virginia and Philadelphia conferences and 1813 Virginia and South Carolina conferences; *Minutes* (1840), 1:199–201, 230–31; *JLFA*, 3:453.

20. Boehm, *Reminiscences*, 303.

21. Virginia Annual Conference Minutes, Feb. 8, 1810, RMC; Sweet, *Rise of Methodism*, 153–207; Asbury to Ruter, March 11, 1810, *World Parish*, 3 (August 1959): 61; Conable, *Genesee Conference*, 21.

22. Asbury to Frye, Nov. 27, 1812, *World Parish*, 3 (August 1959): 64; Francis Asbury to John Sale, Sept. 24, 1812, *World Parish*, 3 (February 1959): 40; Paine, *McKendree*, 223–24.

23. *JLFA*, 2:724, 727; 3:469–70, 471; "Journal of the General Conference," 82, 94; Asbury to Frye, Aug. 20, 1812, *World Parish*, 3 (August 1959): 63.

24. *JLFA*, 2:701, 705, 707; Asbury to Solomon Sias, Jan. 25, 1814, TMS, LLM. Jacob Young witnessed Asbury's sermon to the soldiers near Uniontown, Pa. Young recalled that Asbury's text was Luke 3:14 and that "On the whole, I will say it was an admirable sermon." See Young, *Autobiography*, 292–94. On the war, also see *JLFA*, 2:709, 710, 728, 730. Daniel Hitt wrote to Asbury and Boehm in November 1812 expressing his relief that to that point none of the preachers had been captured or killed. The only loss that Hitt could think of was a shipment of books that sank in the Ohio River. See Hitt to Asbury and Boehm, Nov. 10, 1812, MAHC. On Methodists and the War of 1812, see Bangs, *History*, 2:347–49, 351–53, 383–84, 455–59.

25. *JLFA*, 3:455, 466.

26. "Journal of the General Conference," 78; *General Conferences from 1792 to 1896*, 75–76; Paine, *William McKendree*, 226–27. The account of the exchange between Asbury and McKendree comes from a letter written in 1855 by the preacher Henry Smith, who attended the conference as a delegate from the Baltimore conference.

27. *JLFA*, 2:470; Bangs, *History*, 2:309; Paine, *McKendree*, 233; Tigert, *Constitutional History*, 328–29.

28. "Journal of the General Conference," 83–101.

29. Young, *Autobiography*, 249–50; Sweet, *Rise of Methodism*, 147; Robert Paine, *Life and Times of William M'Kendree*, 2 vols. (Nashville: Methodist Episcopal Church, South, 1870), 1:215–16. On a motion from Asbury himself, the 1808 General Conference had authorized the printing of one thousand *Disciplines* for use in the South Carolina conference with the entire section on slavery left out. "Journal of the General Conference," 72; Curts, *General Conferences 1792 to 1896*, 74; Tigert, *Constitutional History*, 322–23; MEC, *the Doctrines and Discipline of the Methodist Episcopal Church*, 12th ed. (New York: E. Cooper and J. Wilson, 1804), 215–16; MEC, *the Doctrines and Discipline of the Methodist Episcopal Church*, 14th ed. (New York: John Wilson and Daniel Hitt, 1808), 210–11.

30. *JLFA* 2: 568, 584, 596, 694; Reginald F. Hildebrand, "Methodist Episcopal Policy on the Ordination of Black Ministers," *MH*, 20 (April 1982): 126–27. On Asbury's persistent contact with African American believers, see *JLFA*, 2:567, 569, 621, 622, 628, 629, 633, 634, 635, 636, 637, 662, 668, 673, 688, 691, 692, 693, 696, 699, 716, 721, 723, 726, 739, 741; 3:409–10.

31. *JLFA*, 2:591.

32. *JLFA*, 2:704, 721, 722. Asbury's concern about the problem of drink had been growing for some time. *JLFA*, 1:626, 627, 632, 633, 747; 2:45, 46, 81, 82, 402, 413; 3:256. In March 1805 he wrote: "it is lawful to eat, but not to gluttony; it is lawful to drink, but not to drunkenness." *JLFA*, 2:465.

33. *Journals of the General Conferences*, 28–29; Jenkins, *Experience*, 74; W. J. Rorabaugh, *The Alcoholic Republic: An American Tradition* (Oxford: Oxford University Press, 1979), 7–8, 232–33; Robert H. Abzug, *Cosmos Crumbling: American Reform and the Religious Imagination* (New York: Oxford University Press, 1994), 81–104; Ronald G. Walters, *American Reformers 1815–1860* (New York: Hill and Wang, 1978), 123–43; Eric Burns, *The Spirits of America: A Social History of Alcohol* (Philadelphia: Temple University Press, 2004), 7–45; Gary L. Abbott Sr., "Southern Comfort: Indulgence and Abstinence in the South," in *Religion and Alcohol: Sobering Thoughts*, ed. C. K. Robertson (New York: Peter Lang, 2004), 195–207.

34. Asbury began his letter to Clark by recalling that at the 1810 New York conference, which met at Pittsfield, Mass., Clark had apparently been unhappy with his appointment to the Litchfield circuit. "Since the conference in Pittsfield, or before[,] your countenance appears cloudy towards me, what have I done? What have I said?" Asbury now asked. *JLFA*, 2:680; Asbury to Clark, May 16, 1812, GTS.

35. Clark to Asbury, May 18, 1812, GTS.

36. "Journal of the General Conference," 92–93; Bangs, *History*, 2:338–39.

37. "Journal of the General Conference," 93; Bangs, *History*, 2:339–47.

38. Bangs, *History*, 2:333–37; Simpson, *Cyclopedia*, 572, 602–7, 798, 812–13, 814; Feeman, *Silver Trumpet*, 26–32; Richey, *Methodist Conference*, 89–94. A motion similar to Clark's was defeated in 1816 but passed in 1820, though the victory was short-lived. When Joshua Soule, who had been elected to the episcopacy at that conference, resigned in protest (he was reelected in 1824) and William McKendree also weighed in against the measure, it was suspended until 1824, when it was once again suspended, and finally rescinded in 1828.

39. *JLFA*, 3:446–48; "Journal of the General Conference," 96, 101; Bangs, *History*, 2:322–23.

40. "Journal of the General Conference," 92, 103. The letter from Hitt to Tanner is included in the manuscript conference minutes, but not in the printed minutes.

41. "I addressed a valedictory statement of my opinion to Bishop M'Kendree, on the primitive Church government and ordination; I shall leave it with my papers," Asbury recorded in his journal on Aug. 1, 1813, while in Lancaster, Pa. *JLFA*, 2:739.

42. *JLFA*, 3:475–76, 488.

43. *JLFA*, 3:476, 481.

44. *JLFA*, 3:480. Nicholas Snethen was appointed the first Methodist chaplain to the U.S. House of Representatives in 1811. "Great Snethen is chaplain to Congress!" Asbury wrote in October 1811 when he first heard the news. "So; we begin to partake of *the honour that cometh from man*: now is our time of danger." *JLFA*, 2:687.

45. Thomas Haweis, *An Impartial and Succinct History of the Rise, Declension and Revival of the Church of Christ; From the Birth of Our Saviour to the Present Time*, 2 vols. (Baltimore: Abner Neal, 1807). Born in Redruth, Cornwall, in 1734, Haweis experienced an evangelical, though not Methodist, conversion at about twenty. The next year he went up to Christ Church, Oxford, where he was ordained a deacon in the Church of England in 1757 and a priest the following year. After a stint in London, Haweis became Rector of All Saints in Aldwincle, Northamptonshire, in 1764. He was known for evangelical preaching and promotion of foreign missions, particularly to Tahiti and Africa. He also

became a chaplain to the countess of Huntingdon. See Arthur Skevington Wood, *Thomas Haweis, 1734–1820* (London: SPCK, 1957).

46. Wood, *Haweis*, 221; Haweis, *Impartial History*, 78, 87, 150; *JLFA*, 2:488; 3:479–89. There are slight differences in punctuation between the 1807 edition of *Impartial History* and how it is rendered in Asbury's published journal. I have followed Haweis. In 1805 Asbury evidently read the English edition of Haweis, published in London by J. Mawman in 1800.

CHAPTER 23

1. Bond, "Anecdotes of Bishop Asbury, No. 6."

2. Asbury appointed Boehm one of the executors of his will. Boehm, *Reminiscences*, 414–15; "Journal of the General Conference," 100.

3. Asbury to Reed, Aug. 26, 1814, MAHC; John Wesley Bond, "Journal of John Wesley Bond, 1814–1819," TMS, LLM, p. 1; *JLFA*, 2:761; *Minutes* (1840), 1:324–25.

4. Vickers, *Coke*, 287–98, 335–37.

5. *JLFA*, 3:448–49, 450; Coke to Mr. & Mrs. Brackenbury, Feb. 16, 1811, Thomas Coke Papers, JRL; Vickers, *Coke*, 337–38.

6. Coke to John Dutton, July 7, 1812, Thomas Coke Papers, JRL; Vickers, *Coke*, 338–40.

7. Thomas Coke to Samuel Drew, June 28, 1813, TMS, Thomas Coke Papers, JRL; Vickers, *Coke*, 341–53.

8. *JLFA*, 3:499; Vickers, *Coke*, 355–66; Drinkhouse, *Methodist Reform*, 143–49.

9. Asbury to Jacob Gruber, July 19, 1815, MAHC; *JLFA*, 2:780; Bond, "Anecdotes, No. 3." On Coke's death, also see Bangs, *History*, 376–80.

10. *JLFA*, 2:752, 753, 754, 755.

11. Bond, "Journal," 5–6; Bond, "Anecdotes, No. 1."

12. Boehm, *Reminiscences*, 420; Bond, "Anecdotes, Nos. 1 and 2;" *JLFA*, 3:506.

13. Bond, "Anecdotes, No. 2;" *JLFA*, 2:756; 3:506; Boehm, *Reminiscences*, 421. On Asbury's illness, see Bangs, *History*, 2:361–64.

14. Bond, "Anecdotes, No. 2." "My soul has been without a doubt, or a cloud in all my afflictions, though the greatest I have ever experienced, and the most difficult to recover from," Asbury informed Jacob Gruber on July 7, 1814. Asbury was too weak to write the letter and had to employ an amanuensis. Asbury to Gruber, July 7, 1814, MAHC.

15. Bond, "Anecdotes, No. 2." After praying for Fanny Newell to be healed from "spotted fever" in 1811, Asbury declared, "She will get well," and she did. See Fanny Newell, *Memoirs of Fanny Newell; Written by Herself*, 3rd ed. (Springfield: G. & C. Merriam, 1833), 97–99.

16. *JLFA*, 2: 756, 758, 759, 767; 3:506; Francis Asbury to Nelson Reed, Aug. 26, 1814, MAHC.

17. *JLFA*, 2:785; Bond, "Anecdotes, No. 6." During 1815 Asbury revived his practice of recording sermon outlines in his journal. *JLFA*, 2:786, 787–88, 788–89, 790, 791–92, 796.

18. Bangs, *History*, 2:364, 399.

19. Mary Pocahontas Cabell to Susan Hubbard, March 21, 1815, Hubbard Family Papers, SHC; *JLFA*, 2:774. Cabell also noted that Asbury's "articulation" was "very much injured from the loss of his teeth."

20. *JLFA*, 3:526–31; Bond, "Anecdotes, No. 2." Others also remembered Asbury promoting the mite subscription during his last year. See Lewis Myers to Samuel Jennings, July 20, 1820, MAHC; Cooper, *Substance*, 169; Bangs, *History*, 2:357, 382.

21. *JLFA*, 2:774, 776, 778, 779, 780, 782, 783, 790, 791, 3:473. Asbury respected Garrettson's family life, writing, "I do believe God dwells in this house," when he visited Rhinebeck in July 1802. But it always him pause to realize that his friend would likely never venture far from his beloved home. See *JLFA*, 2:243, 353. In January 1814, Asbury met and "embraced" William Glendinning in North Carolina. See *JLFA*, 2:752.

22. *JLFA*, 3:392; Bennett, *Methodism in Virginia*, 584. This letter is provisionally dated May 27, 1808, in *JLFA*, but the context given in Bennett indicates that the letter followed the General Conference of 1812.

23. *JLFA*, 3:513.

24. In transferring Lee to the Baltimore conference, Asbury may have been trying to move him closer to Washington, D.C., where Lee had served as chaplain to the House of Representatives since 1809 and the Senate since 1814, appointments that many Virginia preachers resented. Lee eventually went to Annapolis in 1816. *JLFA*, 3:514, 534–35; Leroy Lee, *Jesse Lee*, 461, 486, 488–92.

25. *JLFA*, 2:801–3; 3:556; Jenkins, *Experience*, 177; John Wesley Bond to William McKendree, April 1, 1816, given in Bull, "Bond's Reminiscences," 5–7. According to William Capers, in January 1816 Asbury told him, "I am a dying man . . . I shall never see another Conference in Carolina." See Capers, *Life*, 185. In an 1816 funeral sermon, Nicholas Snethen wrote that once Asbury reached the Arnolds', he experienced "swelling in the hands and feet," that "began to extend to body," possibly an edema associated with congestive heart failure. See Snethen, *Discourse on Asbury*, 13. For examples of fairly incoherent letters written by Asbury, see Asbury to Gruber, July 19, 1815, MAHC; *JLFA*, 3:524. On Asbury's death, also see Bangs, *History*, 2:391–96; Bennett, *Memorials*, 613–15.

26. *JLFA*, 2:777, 803–7; "Journal of the General Conference," 104, 106, 126; Bond, "Anecdotes, No. 7"; Young, *Autobiography*, 323; Chase, *Recollections*, 94; Leroy Lee, *Jesse Lee*, 495–97. Charles Giles remembered that the funeral procession was a mile in length. See Giles, *Pioneer*, 231. Asbury's body remained at the Eutaw Street Church in Baltimore until June 1854, when it was removed to the Mount Olivet Cemetery in Baltimore. Tipple, *Asbury*, 297–99.

27. *JLFA*, 2:732; 3:472–73; Young, *Autobiography*, 325–26.

EPILOGUE

1. Harold Frederic, *The Damnation of Theron Ware*, ed. Everett Carter (Cambridge, Mass.: Harvard University Press, 1960), 4–5.

2. Wigger, *Taking Heaven*, 175–80; John Wigger, "Methodismus/Methodisten: II. Kirchengeschichtlich, 3. Nordamerika," in *Religion in Geschichte und Gegenwart*, ed.

Hans Dieter Betz, Don S. Browning, Bernd Janowski, and Eberhard Jüngel, 4th ed. (Tübingen, Germany: J. C. B. Mohr [Paul Siebeck], 2001), vol. 5; Wigger, "Ohio Gospel."

3. Quinn, *Sketches*, 267; Jacob Young, *Autobiography*, 527; Wigger, *Taking Heaven*, 185.

4. Boehm, *Reminiscences*, 140, 492; Wigger, *Taking Heaven*, 188.

5. *Minutes* (1840), 1:284–86, 290–92. On Bruce, see Moore, *Pioneers*, 180–95. For short biographies of Cooper, Phoebus, Reed, and Ware, see Simpson, *Cyclopedia*, 256–57, 715, 746, 896–97. On Lee, see Bangs, *History*, 3:57–64. On Garrettson, see John Wigger, "Garrettson, Freeborn," *Biographical Dictionary of Evangelicals*, ed. Timothy Larsen (Leicester, England: Intervarsity Press, 2003), 250–51; John Wigger, "Garrettson, Freeborn," *Religion in Geschichte und Gegenwart*, ed. Hans Dieter Betz, Don S. Browning, Bernd Janowski, and Eberhard Jüngel, 4th ed. (Tübingen, Germany: J. C. B. Mohr [Paul Siebeck], 2000), vol. 3. Garrettson and Cooper kept up a correspondence until Garrettson's death. See letters from Garrettson to Cooper in the Cooper manuscript collection, GTS. George Shadford also died in March 1816. See Bangs, *History*, 3:64–72.

6. Cooper, *Substance*, 199; Simpson, *Cyclopedia*, 404–5, 760–61; P. Douglass Gorrie, *The Lives of Eminent Methodist Ministers; Containing Biographical Sketches, Incidents, Anecdotes, Records of Travel, Reflections, &c. &c.* (Auburn: Derby & Miller, 1853), 294–338; Charles Elliott, *The Life of the Rev. Robert R. Roberts, One of the Bishops of the Methodist Episcopal Church* (New York: Lane and C. B. Tippett, 1846); Bangs, *History*, 3:43, 53. Born in Virginia in 1767 or 1768 and awakened under the preaching of Devereux Jarratt, Enoch George began circuit preaching in 1789. George briefly located in 1799 and again in 1801 when he married. He rejoined the itinerancy in 1803. His wife apparently died in 1816, shortly before the General Conference at which he was elected a bishop. See Benjamin St. James Fry, *The Lives of Bishops Whatcoat, M'Kendree, and George* (New York: Carlton & Phillips, 1852), part 3, 7–78; Benjamin St. James Fry, *The Life of Enoch George: One of the Bishops of the Methodist Episcopal Church* (New York: Carlton & Porter, 1856), 7–78; *Minutes* (1840), 1:85, 97, 112. William McKendree was the last bachelor elected bishop until the 1960s. See Albea Godbold, "Bishop William McKendree and His Contribution to Methodism," *MH*, 8:3 (April 1970): 8.

7. *Minutes* (1840), 1:274; Leroy Lee, *Jesse Lee*, 497–98. For a similar assessment of Asbury, see Snethen, *Reply*, 51–52.

8. Garrettson, *Journal*, 400–1; Chase, *Recollections*, 95, Boehm, *Reminiscences*, 459; Tipple, *Francis Asbury*, 306; Z. Paddock, *Memoir of Rev. Benjamin G. Paddock* (New York: Nelson & Phillips, 1875), 137–38.

9. Cooper, *Substance*, 22, 25, 115, 171, 172. Also see 129, 130, 135, 166–67, 190.

10. Cooper, *Substance*, 124, 179. By 1820 Cooper largely agreed with Nicholas Snethen, a founder of the Methodist Protestant Church, on the need for more democracy in the church. See Cooper to Snethen, July 26, 1820, Cooper MSS 16, GTS. On Cooper's activities relative to democratic reform in the church from 1808 to 1824, see Lester B. Scherer, *Ezekiel Cooper, 1763–1847: An Early American Methodist Leader* (n.p.: Commission on Archives and History of the United Methodist Church, 1965), 136–63.

11. Joseph Travis, *Autobiography of the Rev. Joseph Travis, A. M.* (Nashville: E. Stevenson & F. A. Owen for the Methodist Episcopal Church, South, 1856), 14, 30, 31, 95; Bond, "Anecdotes of Bishop Asbury, No. 5"; Bull, "Bond's Reminiscences," 22. "We

thought," Asbury is said to have remarked in 1812, "we could ill the monster [slavery] at once, but *the laws and the people* were against us, and we had to compromise the matter, or lose the South." See Henry Bascom, *Methodism and Slavery* (Frankfurt, Ky.: Hodges, Todd, and Pruett, 1845), 6.

12. Bangs, *History*, 2:396–412 (quotation from 411).

13. Bangs, *History*, 2:402–3, 414–15, 416. Abel Stevens, *The Life and Times of Nathan Bangs, D.D.* (New York: Carlton & Porter, 1863), 47, 82, 87–91, 184–86, 219; Wigger, *Taking Heaven*, 189–90; Hatch, *Democratization*, 201–4.

14. Abel Stevens, *History of the Methodist Episcopal Church in the United States of America*, 4 vols. (New York: Carlton & Porter, 1867), 1:277, 322; 2:56–66; 4:508.

15. Drinkhouse, *Methodist Reform*, iii, v, 2, 243, 339; Simpson, *Cyclopedia*, 602–3. On Wesley's love of power, see *Methodist Reform*, 41, 45.

16. Drinkhouse, *Methodist Reform*, 3, 4. Drinkhouse's heroes when it came to standing up to Asbury were Strawbridge, O'Kelly, and Snethen. See *Methodist Reform*, 179.

17. Snethen, *Discourse on Asbury*, 4, 6, 9.

18. Alexander M'Caine, *Letters on the Organization and Early History of the Methodist Episcopal Church* (Boston: Thomas F. Norris, 1850), 60, 66, 114.

19. Briggs, *Asbury*, 392; Tipple *Asbury*, 309.

20. "Francis Asbury," *Harper's New Monthly Magazine*, vol. 33, no. 194 (July 1866): 210–21. Most of this article is drawn from Asbury's journal.

21. Frederic, *Theron Ware*, 7; David Holsclaw, "The Demise of Disciplined Christian Fellowship: The Methodist Class Meeting in Nineteenth-Century America," PhD diss., University of California, Davis, 1979), 121; Wigger, *Taking Heaven*, 186, 189; "Old Fashion Methodism," *Christian Advocate and Journal*, Oct. 27, 1841; quoted in Holsclaw, "Demise," 72.

22. Ash, *Protestantism and the University*, xiv.

23. William Warren Sweet, *Religion in the Development of American Culture, 1765–1840* (Gloucester, Mass.: Peter Smith, 1963), 161–62; Ash, *Protestantism and the University*, chaps. 2, 3, 4. On objectivity and Turner's frontier thesis, see Peter Novick, *That Noble Dream: The "Objectivity Question" and the American Historical Profession* (Cambridge: Cambridge University Press, 1988), 47–108; Georg G. Iggers, *Historiography in the Twentieth Century: From Scientific Objectivity to the Postmodern Challenge* (Middletown, Conn.: Wesleyan University Press, 1997, 2005), 34–47.

24. Sweet, *Religion in American Culture*, 115; William Warren Sweet, *Methodism in American History* (New York: Methodist Book Concern, 1933), 159.

25. H. K. Carroll, ed., *The Francis Asbury Monument in the National Capital* (n.p.: Francis Asbury Memorial Association Press of the Methodist Book Concern, 1925), 13, 31, 33.

26. Carroll, *Asbury Monument*, 66. Writing in 1916, Ezra S. Tipple also saw Asbury as a promoter of "human democracy" against "paternalism and aristocracy." See Tipple, *Asbury*, 181.

27. Carl Becker, *The Heavenly City of the Eighteenth-Century Philosophers*, 2nd ed. (New Haven: Yale Nota Bene, 1932, 2003), 48; Burleigh Taylor Wilkins, *Carl Becker: A Biographical Study in American Intellectual History* (Cambridge, Mass.: M.I.T. Press,

1961), 7–13, 149–50; William H. Mcneill, "Carl Becker, Historian," *The History Teacher*, 19:1 (November 1985): 89–100; James Turner, *Without God, Without Creed: The Origins of Unbelief in America* (Baltimore: Johns Hopkins University Press, 1985), 171–269; George M. Marsden, *The Soul of the American University: From Protestant Establishment to Established Nonbelief* (New York: Oxford University Press, 1994).

   28. Herbert Asbury, *A Methodist Saint: The Life of Bishop Asbury* (New York: Alfred A. Knopf, 1927), 53; Herbert Asbury, *Up From Methodism* (New York: Alfred A. Knopf, 1926), 3, 91, 98, 168.

   29. Asbury, *Methodist Saint*, 1, 51–52.

   30. Asbury, *Methodist Saint*, 137, 248, 249, 258, 264. Having exhausted his store of venom, Herbert Asbury covers the last twenty years of Francis Asbury's life in just twenty pages.

   31. "Bishop Asbury as the Devil's Foe: Methodism's Founder in America Sought to Build Up a 'Poor Man's Religion,'" *New York Times*, April 3, 1927, ProQuest Historical Newspapers (1851–2003).

   32. L. C. Rudolph, *Francis Asbury* (Nashville: Abingdon Press, 1966), 58, 60, 100, 109, 145. Rudolph's reliance on Herbert Asbury's *Methodist Saint* is disappointing, as is his reluctance to place Francis Asbury in a larger context. "When the reader wants Asbury in a broader context of Methodist history, let him go to the three-volume *History of American Methodism* published in 1964," writes Rudolph (p. 222). The best recent biography of Asbury is Darius Salter's *America's Bishop*, a close reading of sources that breaks from the Sweet synthesis, but in exchange assumes a decidedly Wesleyan perspective.

   33. Frederic, *Theron Ware*, 240.

Index

CPSIA information can be obtained at www.ICGtesting.com
Printed in the USA
BVOW061304060912

299629BV00003B/2/P